Please
return
materials
on time

HIGHLINE COLLEGE LIBRARY
P.O. BOX 98000
DES MOINES, WA 98198-9800

DEMCO

Ryoma

LIFE OF A RENAISSANCE SAMURAI

RYOMA

Life of a Renaissance Samurai

ROMULUS   HILLSBOROUGH

RIDGEBACK
PRESS

San Francisco

Book design by Yuki Rosen

For information contact:
Ridgeback Press
PO Box 27901-790
San Francisco, CA 94127 USA
(415) 841-0508
ridgebak@dnai.com

Publisher's Cataloging-in-Publication Data
Hillsborough, Romulus.
        Ryoma : life of a Renaissance samurai / Romulus
    Hillsborough. -- 1st ed.
        p. cm.
        Includes index.
        LCCN: 98-67919
        ISBN: 0-9667401-7-3

        1. Sakamoto, Ryoma, 1836-1867. 2. Japan--History--
    Restoration, 1853-1870. 3. Samurai--Japan--Biography.
    I. Title.

    DS881.5.S35H55 1999   952'.025'092 [B]
                                         QBI98-1523

This book is dedicated to the spirit of freedom in the soul of man.

Sakamoto Ryoma
Courtesy of Kochi Prefectural Museum of History

CONTENTS ❁

❀ LIST OF ILLUSTRATIONS ❀

MAP OF JAPAN

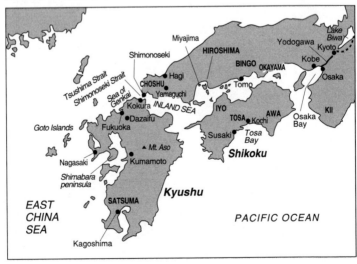

MAP OF KYOTO

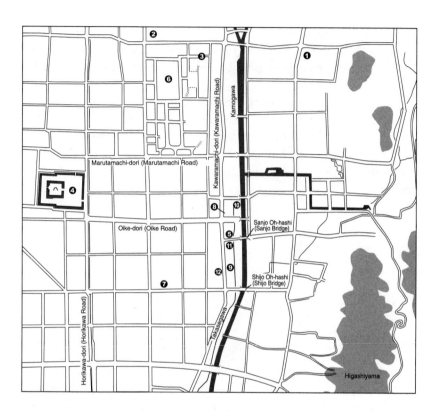

1 Land Auxiliary Force headquarters
2 Satsuma estate at district of the Two Pines
3 Site of assassination of Anenokoji Kintomo
4 Nijo Castle
5 Ikedaya
6 Imperial Palace
7 Satsuma headquarters
8 Choshu headquarters
9 Tosa headquarters
10 Ikumatsu's house
11 Vinegar Store
12 The Ohmiya (Ryoma's hideout above warehouse)

 ACKNOWLEDGMENTS

The author is deeply indebted to the following people and institutions for their invaluable inspiration, ideas, and support, without which this book would not have been possible. Names are listed alphabetically.

Yuko Caputo, Minako Cohen, Yoshimori Fumoto, Jeff Honick, Robert Howard, Christopher Hunt, InfoGate, Mamoru Matsuoka, Saichiro Miyaji, Modern Japanese Language School, Tae Moriyama, Mariko Nozaki, Tsutomu Ohshima, Yuki Rosen, Ryoma History Museum, Tosa Shidan-kai, David Stern, Norio Suzuki, Masao Tanaka, John Teramoto

 ILLUSTRATIONS

Sakamoto Ryoma (standing)
Courtesy of Kochi Prefectural Museum of History

Sakamoto Ryoma (seated)
Courtesy of Harutaka Miyoshi

Katsu Kaishu
Courtesy of Takaaki Ishiguro

Saigo Kichinosuke
Courtesy of Kagoshima Prefectural Museum of Culture Reimeikan

Katsura Kogoro
Courtesy of Takahiko Kido and Yamaguchi Museum

Nakaoka Shintaro
Courtesy of Urausucho Kyoikuiinkai

Takasugi Shinsaku
Courtesy of Togyo-an

NOTE ON JAPANESE PRONUNCIATION

The pronunciation of vowels and diphthongs are approximated as follows:

a   as in "car"
e   as in "pen"
i   as in "police"
o   as in "low"
u   as in "sue"
ai as in "sky"
ei as in "bay"
au as in "now"
ii There is no English approximation of this sound. There is a slight pause between the first "i" and the second "i".

Note that an "e" following a consonant is not a hard sound, but rather a soft one. For example, *sake* is pronounced "sa-kay," and *Kameyama* "kah-may-ya-ma."

There are no English approximations for the following sounds. They consist of only one syllable.

ryo
myo
hyo
kyo
ryu
kyu
tsu

❖ AUTHOR'S NOTE ❖

All Japanese surnames in this book appear before the given names, in keeping with Japanese tradition. I have used the Chinese calendar rather than the Gregorian one to ensure authenticity and to preserve the actual flavor of mid-19th-century Japan. The Roman alphabet rendering of Japanese terms has been employed when I felt that translation would be syntactically awkward or semantically inaccurate. Contrarily, I have translated proper nouns which I thought would lend themselves favorably to English. Romanized Japanese terms other than names are italicized, except for those words, such as "samurai" and "geisha," which are commonly used in modern American English. I have avoided pluralizing Japanese terms, but a plural or singular meaning should be clear from the context in which a term is used. For example, "a samurai" is singular, whereas "two samurai" is plural.

❂ PREFACE ❂

Sakamoto Ryoma has been the subject of a highly esteemed scholarly work in the English language*, the purpose of which I will take the liberty to surmise has been to instruct the student of Japanese history. Somerset Maugham once wrote that the most essential quality for a novel is that it be entertaining. "No one in his senses reads a novel for instruction or edification," wrote this master of English letters. "If he wants instruction or edification he is a fool if he does not go to the books written to instruct and edify." It has been my intention to go beyond the scope of the novel to both instruct and entertain, in the first biography of Sakamoto Ryoma ever to appear in the English language in story form.

It is a cultural loss that an historical figure of such magnificent stature has failed to gain the full attention of the Western world for nearly a century and a half. It is a tragedy that the general public's sources of information about the era of the samurai have, for the most part, been travesties of Japanese history and culture in the forms of popular fiction and movies. I hope this book rectifies the situation.

I began researching the life of Sakamoto Ryoma about thirteen years ago, while living in Tokyo. I had been in Japan for eight years, and was fluent in written and spoken Japanese. At first I read everything available on my subject. My research included over forty books about Ryoma's life, historical period, and prominent contemporaries, all of his extant letters, of which there were over 120 in publication, and numerous articles and other pieces from Japanese history journals, magazines and museum pamphlets. I traveled to those areas in Japan where Ryoma was most active, including the cities of Kyoto, Nagasaki, Kagoshima, Hagi, Kochi, and the picturesque fishing village of Tomo on the Inland Sea.

I sat in the room at a Japanese-style inn in Fushimi where Ryoma often slept, and where he was ambushed and nearly killed by government police agents. I visited the former brothel in Nagasaki, which is now a first-class Japanese-style hotel, where Ryoma was wont to carouse during the turbulent last years of his short, colorful life. I went to the same Japanese inn in Kyoto where one of Ryoma's comrades-in-arms employed his geisha-lover and future wife as a spy to divulge vital information from high-ranking government officials. I will never forget my visit to the home of Masao Tanaka, a direct descendent of a boyhood friend of Ryoma's, located in the mountains northwest of Kochi Castletown. The house was the same one that Ryoma often visited in his youth, and where he apparently stopped, in need of cash, on the outset of a subversive journey he made in 1861 as the envoy of a revolutionary party leader. "My family lent Ryoma money at that time," the elderly Mr. Tanaka told me, as we stood atop a giant rock behind the house, looking out at the Pacific Ocean far in the distance. Mr. Tanaka informed me that Ryoma liked to sit atop this same rock when he visited the Tanaka family, and where he would indulge in wild talk of one day sailing across the ocean to foreign lands. "Ryoma never repaid the money, so I guess he still owes us," Mr. Tanaka joked.

Here I have mentioned a few of the pleasures I encountered during the many years that I researched and wrote this historical biography. The hardships, however, were far more prevalent. The greatest hardship I faced was not the heavy responsibility of adhering to historical and cultural fact. Rather, it was fathoming the depths of the heart and soul of a genius who had lived and died in a culture completely foreign to my own, nearly a full century before my birth.

Romulus Hillsborough
San Francisco
September 1998

* *Sakamoto Ryoma and the Meiji Restoration*, by Marius B. Jansen (Stanford University Press)

"...any life which merits living lies in the effort to realize some dream, and the higher that dream is the harder it is to realize."

Eugene O'Neill

Prologue

The year was 1867 and Ryoma was beside himself with anxiety. The outlaw-samurai was waiting at his Kyoto hideout for an answer to the single most important question in Japan: Would the Shogun restore the Emperor to power, peacefully relinquishing his family's rule of two and a half centuries? Or would the great samurai clans of the southwest, Imperial edict in hand, declare war on the Shogun's military government at Edo, causing chaos throughout the nation, and possible attack from the foreign powers of the West?

Waiting with Ryoma were fellow ronin–outlaw-samurai who had abandoned their clans to fight for the Loyalist cause of overthrowing the Shogunate, restoring Imperial rule and fortifying the Japanese nation in the face of foreign subjugation. The atmosphere at Ryoma's hideout was tense. Should word arrive that the Shogun refused to relinquish power, Ryoma and his men were prepared to attack Nijo Castle, assassinate the Shogun, then cut open their bellies in defiance.

But why would the leader of a band of outlaws be among the first to hear of the Shogun's momentous decision? How could Sakamoto Ryoma, a petty samurai, command the respect of feudal lords throughout Japan?

Theirs was a bloody time of the arrival of "Black Ships" from the West, political intrigue, turbulence and assassination, in which Sakamoto Ryoma–outlaw-samurai, pistol-bearing swordsman, freedom-fighter, pioneering naval commander, entrepreneur and statesman, a youth ahead of his time with an imagination as boundless as the Pacific Ocean–was a leader in the revolution to overthrow the shogunate and form a unified democracy in Japan.

1

Sakamoto Ryoma (seated)
Courtesy of Harutaka Miyoshi

Part I

Forging the Dragon

Black Ships

The polished dark wooden floor of the Hineno Fencing Dojo reflected the late morning sunlight which filtered into the room through four small windows. The muscular youth wore a pair of wide trousers of dark blue cotton, a robe of the same material and color, and a quilted vest lined with pliant strips of bamboo. Protective gloves covered the backs of his hands, a shield protected his face. His long hair was disheveled after a hard practice session, his body covered with sweat.

At five feet, ten inches tall, the youth towered over the middle-aged sword master. Armed with a bamboo practice sword, he walked steadily to the center of the floor. The clean smell of sweat calmed him, and prepared him for a battle which he knew must end in death.

Master and pupil bowed to one another. The pupil slowly raised his sword to face-level, his dark brown eyes focused on his master's, his bare feet planted firmly on the wooden floor, his face devoid of expression. He broke the silence with a piercing guttural wail, as the master intercepted the attack a fraction of an inch above his right temple. Master Hineno countered with lightning speed, slashing downward across Ryoma's abdomen, then up the side of his chest to the base of his jaw. "That's all," the sword master firmly commanded, and the match was over.

Had Ryoma not been born into a samurai household, he might never have touched a sword, and certainly would not have been molded into an expert swordsman by age seventeen. Ryoma's family, in fact, derived from a prosperous *sake* brewer. In 1770 the *sake* brewer purchased the rank of merchant-samurai, which, although among the bottom rungs of the two-sworded class, was nevertheless included among the warrior caste. This distinction placed the Sakamoto family among the topmost of the four levels of feudal society: samurai, peasant, craftsman and merchant, in this respective order. The samurai Sakamoto Ryoma was born in the castletown of Kochi, capital of the great domain of Tosa, on the Japanese island of Shikoku, on the fifteenth day of the eleventh month of the sixth year of the Era of Heaven's Protection, or by Western reckoning, November 15, 1835.

According to one legend Ryoma's pregnant mother dreamt of a fire-breathing beast–half dragon, half horse–which came "flying into her womb." Another fantastic story tells that Ryoma was sired by his mother's pet tomcat, since the woman was accustomed to sleeping with the furry creature cuddled between her belly and thighs. A third story has it that Ryoma's father thus named the infant because he was born with a face full of moles, and hair covering his back. But as these accounts are mere legend, their validity remains an eternal mystery, while the name Ryoma, "Dragon-Steed," remains an eternal symbol of freedom.

Ryoma's closest companion during childhood was his elder sister, Otome. Though just three years older, Otome had raised Ryoma from his eleventh year, after the death of their mother. Otome was as large as her sizable younger brother, and skilled in the martial arts of fencing, wrestling, riding and swimming. She never despaired of Ryoma, who until the age of fourteen had the reputation among his peers as a "runny-nosed, bed-wetting crybaby." Ryoma's father and elder brother were embarrassed by his disposition, which was unbecoming of a samurai. When the family was informed by the local schoolmaster that Ryoma was not only constantly bullied by his classmates for his propensity to wet his pants and cry, but that he did not have the mental capacity for scholarship, both father and brother worried that Ryoma was mentally retarded.

Otome, however, decided that if Ryoma was not suited for scholarship, then he would take up the study of swordsmanship. She soon enrolled him at the Hineno Dojo, a local fencing academy. At first, Ryoma seemed no more inclined for *kendo* than he had been for intellectual pursuit. He was constantly getting hit with a practice sword on the backs of his hands and the side of his head, and thrown to the hard wooden floor, at which time he would inevitably cry. After a few months of training, however, a big change began to appear in Ryoma. He thrived on the rigorous practice. No matter how hard he was hit, he would not let loose his grip on his sword; no matter how hard he was thrown, he would not cry. Eventually Ryoma began developing muscles on parts of his body which had previously been covered with baby fat. By his third year of *kendo* training, Ryoma had become one of the toughest and most skilled swordsmen at the *dojo*.

*   *   *

The Japanese island of Shikoku, meaning "Four Provinces," consisted of just that, with Tosa being the largest of the four. Tosa was a fan-shaped mountainous province of temperate climate, which comprised the entire southern portion of the smallest of the four main Japanese islands. Kochi Castletown was situated in the vicinity of Kochi Castle, along the southern border of the domain, just inland from the Pacific.

Tosa was one of some 260 feudal domains, or *han*, into which Japan was divided. Each *han* was overseen by samurai, and ruled by a feudal lord, or *daimyo*. The Shogun, head of the Tokugawa family, was the mightiest *daimyo* of all. He dominated the Japanese nation from his military government at Edo, which was known throughout the land as the Tokugawa Bakufu.

In the spring of 1853, Ryoma left his native Kochi for Edo. The Shogun's distant capital was the home of the top fencing academies in Japan, and it was at Edo that the young samurai would further his study in the way of the sword. Beside his long and short swords which he wore thrust through his sash at his left hip, Ryoma carried with him his father's written words of admonition: "*Do not forget for an instant that loyalty and filial piety are the most important elements of your training. Do not become attached to material things and squander gold and silver for them. Do not give yourself up to sensuality, forget the importance of your country, or allow your heart to become corrupted.*"

Two weeks after leaving home, Ryoma reached the last stage of the Tokaido Road. The Tokaido was the main thoroughfare which stretched some 300 leagues along the east coast of the main Japanese island of Honshu, between the Imperial capital of Kyoto and the Shogun's capital of Edo. From here he got his first sight of the sprawling city, and the towering white keeps of Edo Castle, the stronghold of the Tokugawa Bakufu.

Ryoma was overwhelmed by the sheer energy of the city: the crowds, the two-storied merchants' shops of black tile roofs lining the streets, the outdoor tea shops, numerous food stalls, restaurants and taverns. Here a *daimyo* was being carried through the streets in a luxurious palanquin of lacquered wood and split bamboo; there a young woman emerged from a shop, elegantly dressed in brightly colored silk; a Buddhist priest, in a black clerical robe and conical basket hat, stood nearby begging for alms; a dignified samurai, perhaps a government official, walked down the street, his swords thrust through his sash, his topknot neatly tied and folded over his cleanly shaven pate. Here was a well-to-do merchant, swordless of course, but dressed in a fine silken kimono. A peddler pulled a two-wheeled cart loaded with myriad household items. Wicker brooms, straw baskets, wooden ladles, and small bamboo pails stuck out from the top and all sides of the cart, which passed by a musical quartet of three gaily costumed men and one woman. One of them, an old man wearing a long pointed cap, sang passionately to the music of a flutist, a *shamisen* player and a pounder of wooden blocks.

Protocol compelled Ryoma to report directly to the official Tosa headquarters, located at the center of the city near Edo Castle. Each of the 266 feudal lords maintained official headquarters in Edo to house official representatives at the Shogun's capital. The size, scale and number of these headquarters differed according to the wealth and rank of the individual *daimyo*. The larger *han*, including Tosa, maintained more than one official headquarters, each large enough to house hundreds, and in some cases thousands, of samurai. The maintenance of *han* headquarters was required by the Law of Alternate Attendance, whereby all feudal lords were obligated to reside in the capital in alternate years. During their absence from Edo, the lords were required to leave their wives and heirs at their Edo residences as virtual hostages, a protective measure used by the central government against possible insurrection in the provinces.

Due to Ryoma's low social standing in the Tosa hierarchy, he was little concerned with official matters. Accordingly, after reporting his arrival at Tosa headquarters, he went directly to the academy of the celebrated sword master Chiba Sadakichi, one of the top fencing schools in Edo.

Ryoma practiced fencing daily during his first several weeks in Edo. He soon earned a reputation as a promising young swordsman, and developed a close friendship with the sword master's son, Chiba Jutaro. Then an event occurred one sweltering afternoon in the sixth month of the sixth year of the Era of Long Happiness which was to change not only the life of Sakamoto Ryoma, but the fate of the entire Japanese nation.

On June 3, 1853, Commodore Matthew Perry of the United States Navy led a flotilla of four "Black Ships" into Sagami Bay, to the Port of Uraga, just south of Edo, sparking the greatest uproar in the two and a half centuries of Tokugawa rule. Perry carried a letter addressed to the Shogun from President Millard Fillmore, demanding a treaty between the United States and Japan. When a Bakufu official informed the Americans aboard ship that Japanese law required all foreign affairs to be handled at the port city of Nagasaki in Kyushu, he was told in no uncertain terms that the President of the United

States had ordered Perry to deliver his message directly to the Shogun in Edo. Perry had nothing more to say, but rather anchored his four heavily armed warships just off the coast, as if to prepare for an attack on the Japanese capital.

The Bakufu was perplexed. There had been several incidents in the past of foreign ships appearing off the Japanese coast, but this was the first time that a fleet of warships had threatened Edo. The Japanese capital, in fact, had never seen such magnificent ships. Two were steamers, which could move about freely, independent of sails or the winds. All four ships were mounted with great guns along both sides, totaling eighty in all–enough firepower to devastate the wooden city.

Until now, the Bakufu had been more concerned with preserving its rule than competing technologically with the rest of the world. As long as the government could keep the foreigners out, the rest of the nation would have to abide by the laws it dictated. To prevent would-be insurgents from secretly traveling overseas, the Bakufu had for centuries banned the building of large ships. As a result, Japan had become so technologically backward that it was now unable to defend itself from the Western powers that threatened to dominate Asia.

Perry's demands for a treaty presented the Bakufu with the greatest dilemma in its history. Acquiescence, it reasoned, would lead to subjugation by the West; rejection, it worried, might lead to a war which it could not hope to win. But the central government also realized that samurai throughout Japan would demand a war against the "evil barbarians who dared to invade the sacred land." Reports of the Opium War in China during the previous decade, by which the British now dominated the great Middle Kingdom, served as an omen of dire consequence to the Japanese.

The Shogun's Senior Council, to be sure, was scared out of its wits. From now on, it would gradually adopt an official stance of *Opening the Country*, while samurai throughout Japan would scream for *Expelling the Barbarians*. Ryoma, for his part, displayed his own contempt for the foreign intruders in a letter to his father. "*It looks like we're going to have a war soon,*" he wrote. "*If so, I'll be cutting off some foreign heads before returning to Tosa.*"

Before Ryoma could fulfill his vow, however, the Americans suddenly raised anchor and departed, just six days after their first appearance off the Edo coast, but not before Perry had received the Bakufu's promise to answer the demands for a treaty during the following year. A treaty between the United States and Japan was completed in March

1854, ending over two and a half centuries of Japanese isolation. Although the treaty made no provision for foreign trade, it entitled American ships to purchase food and other necessities from the Japanese, and assured them amicable treatment in case of shipwreck off the Japanese coast. Two Japanese ports were opened; one at Shimoda, just a short distance from Edo; the other at Hakodate, on the distant northern island of Ezo.

While marking a turning point in the history of Japan, the treaty also aroused in the heart of the eighteen-year-old Sakamoto Ryoma his first feeling of resentment toward the Bakufu, which had been humiliated by the Americans. Ryoma, like most samurai throughout Japan, resented the intrusion of the unwanted foreigners, and deplored the Shogun's government for having become too weak to keep the foreigners out. Until now, Ryoma's personal development had been focused solely on the forging of his draconic spirit through intense training in the way of the sword. Now, with the coming of the Black Ships, he was beginning to formulate his first political outlook on the world, albeit his was still one which needed a great deal of refinement.

*   *   *

Ryoma made great progress at the Chiba Dojo, receiving intermediate rank within a year. Rank in the Hokushin-Itto Style was divided into three levels: basic, intermediate and senior. The attainment of senior rank was tantamount to mastering the art, thus qualifying a swordsman to establish a fencing *dojo* of his own. But Ryoma's official permission to remain in Edo expired in the summer of 1854, when he returned home. At Kochi Castletown he could not keep his mind off the great American warships he had seen in the previous year. He fantasized that one day he might command his own Black Ship. Then one day, in hope of finding a sympathetic ear, he paid a visit to Kawada Shoryo, an artist and scholar of Western studies who lived in the castletown.

Aside from his many drawings in Chinese ink–dragons were his specialty–Shoryo, whose name meant "Little Dragon," was a prolific writer. Among his works was *An Account of an American Castaway*, about a young Tosa fisherman, Nakahama Manjiro, who had been shipwrecked off an uninhabited Japanese island in 1841. The fourteen-year-old boy was rescued by an American whaling ship, befriended by the captain, and taken to the United States for an education. Upon Manjiro's return to Japan in 1852, he was ordered by the Lord of Tosa to report his American experiences to Shoryo, who wrote a fascinating account of Western technology, society and culture, which, since the coming of Perry in the previous year, had become an object of extreme interest not only to the local Tosa government, but to the Edo Bakufu as well.

When Ryoma first appeared at the front gate of Shoryo's house, the sophisticated scholar showed no interest in the uneducated young swordsman. Ryoma was dressed sloppily in a pair of faded gray wide trousers, or *hakama*, and a wrinkled black jacket. Displayed in white on the front of the jacket was the Sakamoto family crest: a Chinese bellflower enclosed by overlapping squares which formed an eight-pointed star. Through his sash, at his left hip, hung his long and short swords. On his broad forehead, just above the left brow was an unsightly wart. His large tanned face was spotted with moles, and, as usual, his hair was unkempt. "My name is Sakamoto Ryoma. I've heard about your interest in Western culture," he said, in short, abrupt spurts, his right hand tucked into the breast of his kimono.

"What do you want?" Shoryo asked impatiently.

"I've just returned from Edo. I've seen the Black Ships with my own eyes."

"So what?"

"So..." Ryoma paused momentarily, before blurting, "I've come to ask what you think ought to be done about the barbarians."

"I'm just an artist. I have no opinion on the matter," Shoryo lied.

But Ryoma was persistent, and eventually convinced the scholar to invite him inside to discuss Western culture. Ryoma was a good listener, and Shoryo, once he began speaking, poured forth his knowledge of the West. He told of the leaps and bounds by which Western countries were progressing in the fields of science and industry, the practical use to which technology was being put, both militarily and industrially, and of the concept of the joint-stock company.

"As for all the recent talk of *Expelling the Barbarians*," Shoryo said, "we simply don't have the means by which to enforce it. You said you've seen the Black Ships. Well, those are only the beginning of what's to come in the near future. Narrow-minded men who nowadays are inclined to rant and rave about keeping the foreigners out are simply ignorant of the technological power of the West. But that doesn't mean that we should run blindly into a policy of *Opening the Country* either. Before opening the country—and that's what we must do if we expect to protect ourselves from foreign subjugation–we must first prepare ourselves militarily. To do so, we must import the advanced military methods and technologies of the West.

"Being an island nation, Japan is first going to have to develop a navy. But before we can do that, we must increase our knowledge of navigation. To do so, we will need to purchase foreign ships. The little junks we have now are like children's toys compared to the great warships of Europe and America.

"The Americans have built roads made of iron rails that span a distance much greater than the entire length of Japan. On these rails they run steam-powered locomotives to transport men and cargo."

"Locomotives?" Ryoma interrupted. "What's a locomotive?"

"A locomotive is a self-propelled vehicle made of iron, which runs on steel rails and pulls other cars behind it. But what we need more than locomotives are steamships, with which we could transport passengers and cargo along the coast of Japan. In the process we could raise funds to buy more steamships, until we had developed a small navy. All the while we could be improving our navigation skills. But unless we get started very soon, it's going to be too late." Shoryo paused to take a deep breath. "This is the only way to save our nation from foreign subjugation," he grimly concluded. "We don't have the luxury of time to argue among ourselves whether we must open Japan or keep the foreigners out."

Ryoma left Shoryo's house fascinated by what he had heard, but in his heart still felt that *Expelling the Barbarians* was the only policy that a man of integrity could support. Yielding to the foreign demands would be cowardly, he thought, unbecoming of a samurai. But Ryoma realized that Shoryo was right: Japan simply did not have the military means by which to defend itself from foreign invasion.

*   *   *

It was pouring rain when Takechi Hanpeita returned to Tosa Han headquarters in Edo. His *hakama* was drenched, but a wide conical basket hat kept his face and upper body dry. At six feet tall, Hanpeita carried his tightly knit frame with the dignity of a highly polished swordsman, as he proceeded calmly through the iron-studded oaken double outer gate of Tosa headquarters.

"Takechi-sensei," called a voice from the guardhouse at the gate. Inside were several young men who had been waiting for Hanpeita to

return. These lower-samurai of Tosa idolized the charismatic swordsman at whose fencing *dojo* in Kochi most of them had trained before
coming to Edo.

"What's the matter?" Hanpeita asked, sensing something wrong.

"A samurai named Sakamoto Ryoma has just arrived today," one of
the men said. "He's been assigned to your room, Sensei."

Hanpeita entered the guardhouse to get out of the pouring rain. "So,
Ryoma has finally arrived," Hanpeita said, removing his basket hat.
"I've been expecting him. His older brother wrote me that he'd be
coming."

"But Sensei, Sakamoto has referred to you in the most insulting
way. He's been calling you..." the man paused.

"Well, say it."

"'Fish chin.'" The man grimaced.

"We can't forgive the outrage," insisted another man angrily.

"Never mind," said Hanpeita, shrugging.

Takechi Hanpeita was a model of samurai temperance. He was
known throughout Tosa as a skilled swordsman and accomplished
Confucian scholar. He had been initiated in the Itto Style of fencing
three years ago at the age of twenty-four, when he had established his
own academy in Kochi Castletown. It wasn't long before this petty
samurai had attracted some eighty followers from among his social
peers, all of whom referred to him with the honorable title of "sensei."

Since coming to Edo in the previous summer, Hanpeita had been
practicing at one of the three greatest fencing academies in the capital. This was the *dojo* of the renowned sword master Momonoi
Shunzo. Likewise, Ryoma, who had returned to Edo in the fall of
1855, continued his practice at the Chiba Dojo throughout the first
half of 1857. One afternoon in late summer of that year Ryoma
returned to his barrack room to find Hanpeita waiting for him.
Despite the great contrast in their natures, the two had developed a
close friendship over the past year. Hanpeita wore a light cotton robe;
his hair was combed neatly, and tied into a topknot which was folded
over his shaven pate. He was sitting on the floor in the formal position, back straight, powdering the blade of his sword. "A samurai must
always be ready for battle," he told Ryoma. His pale face was expressionless, save his powerful dark eyes.

"Don't you ever relax?" Ryoma said, leaning back against the wall.

"Powder your sword," Hanpeita demanded, handing Ryoma a small
box of powder.

"Later," Ryoma muttered. "I'm too tired now."

"Ryoma, we must prepare for war. Haven't you heard that the barbarians in Shimoda are pressuring the Bakufu to sign another treaty?"

During the previous summer, the American envoy, Townsend Harris, had set up the first United States Consulate in Japan in the port village of Shimoda to negotiate a commercial treaty. However, before the Bakufu could sign such a treaty, protocol demanded that it obtain sanction from the Imperial Court in Kyoto. The Imperial Court, however, had been excluded from the business of government for two and a half centuries. The founders of the Bakufu had designed measures to prevent contacts, both politically and socially, between the feudal lords and the court. Through the years, however, Bakufu supervision of the Imperial Court had waned. Meanwhile, the principal "outside lords" (descendants of those *daimyo* who became retainers of the first Tokugawa Shogun only after he had defeated his enemies some two and a half centuries before)–namely Tosa, Choshu and Satsuma–had formed matrimonial alliances with families at court. These alliances would prove important during the revolutionary years of the 1860s, when the Bakufu would begin to crumble.

With internal trouble weighing heavily upon the nation, the fencing academies in Edo developed into centers of anti-foreign, and consequently anti-Bakufu, sentiment. The men training at these schools resented the Bakufu its weakness in dealing with the foreigners. As the commercial treaty with Harris began to materialize, samurai throughout Japan assumed an increasingly hostile attitude toward the Bakufu, their moral support now focused on the Imperial Court at Kyoto.

Emperor Komei himself harbored blind hatred for things foreign. When the Bakufu petitioned for Imperial sanction for a commercial treaty with the Americans, they were flatly refused. Although the Emperor held no political power, his prestige of ancient times had not diminished. The first Tokugawa Shogun, in fact, had only obtained his rank after being conferred by the Emperor with the official title of "Commander in Chief of the Expeditionary Forces Against the Barbarians."

"Alright, Fish Chin," Ryoma said, making fun of Hanpeita's protruding chin, "I'll powder my sword." Ryoma drew his sword from its black lacquered sheath, and began applying the lubricating powder.

"This is no laughing matter, Ryoma," Hanpeita admonished. "We must prepare for war."

In the autumn of 1857 Ryoma was appointed head of the Chiba Dojo. In the following January, five years after entering the *dojo*, he received the coveted senior rank in the Hokushin-Itto Style. He was still only twenty-two.

This was the fifth year of the Era of Peaceful Rule–1858 by Western reckoning–one of great difficulty for the Tokugawa Bakufu. The military government faced two critical problems: dealing with increased foreign demand to open the country to commercial trade, and deciding on an heir to the present Shogun. After signing the first treaty with the United States in 1854, Japan had been pressured into similar treaties with Great Britain, France, the Netherlands and Russia. None of these five nations, however, were satisfied with the initial treaties, which did not provide for trade with Japan.

Concerning the problem of shogunal succession, the Bakufu was in desperate need of a new leader in these extremely critical times. The present Shogun, Tokugawa Iesada, was mentally retarded. One of the favorite pastimes of the Commander in Chief of the Expeditionary Forces Against the Barbarians was stewing potatoes with women in the inner-palace of Edo Castle. And since Shogun Iesada had no interest in the opposite sex, he was childless at the age of thirty-five, presenting the Bakufu with the difficult problem of deciding on an heir to his rule.

Within the Bakufu arose two opposing positions concerning succession. On one side were the 145 hereditary lords, direct retainers of the Shogun, whose ancestors had supported the first Tokugawa Shogun during the great wars at the turn of the seventeenth century. These lords, who occupied all the important governmental posts, were most concerned with maintaining the existing order of things to protect themselves. They argued that shogunal succession must be decided according to tradition, and thus be given to the child-Lord of Kii, a close relative of the Shogun. Opposing the hereditary lords was a small group of practical *daimyo* who argued that succession be given to the more able Lord Yoshinobu, the son of the Lord of Mito.

The clans of Mito, Kii and Owari–the elite Three Tokugawa Branch Houses–descended from the three youngest sons of the first Tokugawa Shogun. In the event that a Shogun failed to produce an heir, succession came from one of these elite houses. Mito, however, had been traditionally excluded from succession. The Lord of Mito, Tokugawa Nariaki, was nevertheless determined that his son should succeed the Shogun.

The Mito faction argued that although the Lord of Kii was indeed a close relative of the Shogun, at age twelve he was simply too young to rule. After the death of the present Shogun, these lords hoped to modify the Bakufu through the selection of an able heir. They would unify the nation through the formation of a political coalition within the Bakufu, which would consist of the lords of the greatest domains in Japan. The conservative hereditary lords, who advocated maintaining the two-and-a-half-century-old Tokugawa hegemony, bitterly opposed them.

The Lord of Mito was a staunch exclusionist, who supported the policy of *Expelling the Barbarians*. Opposing him was a powerful man by the name of Ii Naosuke, Lord of Hikone, the largest of the hereditary *han*. Lord Ii advocated a period of trade with the West in order to allow Japan to strengthen itself financially and technologically. He argued that this was the only way that the nation would be able to perfect its defenses and avoid subjugation.

Amid this turmoil, Edo's fencing schools continued to attract samurai from all over Japan. The pending problems of shogunal succession and the Western threat were the topics of the day, with anti-foreign seclusionism being passionately embraced by these young swordsmen. At the center stage of political discourse were three of Edo's top fencing schools: the Chiba Dojo (Sakamoto Ryoma, head), the Momonoi Dojo (Takechi Hanpeita, head) and the Saito Dojo (Katsura Kogoro, head). Ryoma took little interest in the complicated affairs of state, but rather continued to dedicate himself to *kendo*. Having recently been officially initiated in the Hokushin-Itto Style, Ryoma now enjoyed a reputation as one of the leading young swordsmen in the capital.

One evening in late April 1858 Hanpeita was reading a book titled *A History of Japan*, and waiting for Ryoma to return to their barrack room. Upon Ryoma's return, Hanpeita closed the book, and placed it on his desk. Hanpeita's facial expression was typically void of expression. "Ryoma," he said, "have you heard what's happened today?"

"No."

"You haven't heard about the biggest disaster of our time?"

"No."

"The Lord of Hikone, Ii Naosuke, has been named Bakufu regent."

"So?"

"Is that all you can say?" Hanpeita was annoyed at Ryoma's lack of concern for political affairs. "Ryoma, you'd better start educating yourself. As head of the Chiba Dojo, you have a special duty to be aware of what's going on in our nation. The Bakufu is too weak to oppose foreign demands. Lord Nariaki of Mito is one of the few men in Edo with the nerve to stand up to the Bakufu. He calls for absolute refusal of the foreign demands to open our nation."

"Hanpeita," Ryoma interrupted, "I've been thinking about all this talk of *Expelling the Barbarians*. How does anyone expect to be able to do that with just a bunch of talk? I've seen the Black Ships. Those guns could do a lot of damage. We'll need a lot more than just philosophy to stop them."

"That's true. But with the Bakufu giving in to the demands of the filthy barbarians, Lord Nariaki has decided to seek support from the Imperial Court at Kyoto, which has been completely cut off from governing for centuries."

"The Imperial Court?" Ryoma repeated with a puzzled look.

"Yes, because the Imperial Court shares Lord Nariaki's views."

The Lord of Mito had become a natural leader of the samurai who were perfecting their skills in the traditional martial arts. Unfortunately, however, most of the proponents of exclusionism, though educated in Japanese history, literature and traditional Confucian philosophy, remained ignorant of the West, and so consequently had no idea what they would be up against in case of war. The same was true of the court nobles, and even Emperor Komei himself.

"But the Bakufu has also requested Imperial support," Hanpeita continued.

"Why?"

Hanpeita explained that the Bakufu had recently panicked upon hearing reports of continued Western advances into China. Edo was consequently persuaded by the United States to agree to a commercial treaty before Japan would meet a similar fate. "But," Hanpeita continued, "since it is required by law that the Bakufu secure Imperial sanction for foreign treaties, Edo has turned to Kyoto for support."

"Why does the Bakufu need Imperial sanction?" Ryoma asked.

"Because of the law requiring Imperial sanction. Without such sanction the Bakufu would have trouble getting support for treaties from the *daimyo* throughout Japan. "But," Hanpeita's eyes lit up, "this means that Kyoto is in the process of replacing Edo as the center of national politics."

The Mito faction now claimed that the Shogun was merely an

Imperial agent, who at the beginning of the seventeenth century had been commissioned by the Emperor to protect Japan from foreign invasion. The Imperialists insisted that true political authority still belonged to the Emperor in Kyoto. They argued that since the Shogun was no longer able to keep the foreigners out, the Emperor and his court must be restored to power to save the nation. As a result, the national government was gradually developing into a twofold structure: while the Bakufu continued to rule at Edo, the ancient Imperial Court was undergoing a political renaissance at Kyoto. With this came the political education of young court nobles in Kyoto, who throughout the entire reign of the Tokugawa had been completely excluded from national affairs. Even the Emperor himself was a political novice. He harbored no anti-Bakufu designs, and his chronic xenophobia was due to a fear of things Western brought on by ignorance of the outside world.

A look of disdain flashed in Hanpeita's eyes. "Word has it that His Imperial Majesty has been deeply grieved over the course of recent events."

Since its establishment, the Tokugawa Bakufu had justified its rule by claiming to ease and protect the Emperor, handling all governmental affairs for him. However, things had suddenly taken a drastic turn: the Imperialists now held the Shogun responsible for dishonoring and upsetting His Sacred Majesty, through failure to deal firmly with the foreigners.

"This is a crime that cannot be forgiven," Hanpeita said. He paused, took a long, thin wooden-stemmed pipe from his desk, filled its small brass bowl with tobacco. Reaching into the nearby brazier with a pair of wooden sticks, he picked up a burning coal, lit the pipe and resumed speaking. "At first, some of the senior officials at court were persuaded by conniving Bakufu officials to issue Imperial sanction to open the country to foreign trade. But then, some of the younger nobles organized a protest meeting, and the sanction was recalled. The court instructed the Bakufu to continue being faithful to the existing Tokugawa institutions. It argued that violation of the sound laws handed down by the first Shogun would disturb the people and make it impossible to preserve lasting tranquillity." Hanpeita paused again to smoke his pipe. "Being forced into further treaties with the barbarians would be a disgrace to our national honor," Hanpeita continued bookishly. "And thanks to the wisdom of His Sacred Majesty, Edo's devious request for Imperial sanction has been refused. But," Hanpeita pounded his fist on the desk, "just today Lord Ii was appointed regent, the most powerful post in the Bakufu."

Hanpeita tapped the ashes out of his pipe into a short wooden ashtray. "And so," he said, his dark, penetrating eyes seething, "although the Bakufu would like to open the country, the Imperial Court has courageously called for absolute refusal to the demands of the barbarians."

Ryoma reached over the desk, and grabbed Hanpeita's wrist. "Men like you and I must stick together," he said, the sudden passion in his voice surprising his friend. "We must seize some of the barbarian warships, and drive them out by force."

"Be serious!" Hanpeita shouted, apparently irritated by Ryoma's simplicity. "You must start educating yourself."

Ryoma spent the following months training at the Chiba Dojo, where he was living most of the time. He hadn't returned to his room at Tosa headquarters for nearly a month, partly in order to avoid Hanpeita. While he admired his friend, Hanpeita had lately become a nuisance by taking it upon himself to educate Ryoma. Then, one evening in the middle of July Ryoma returned to his barrack room, exhausted after a particularly strenuous practice.

"Ryoma," Hanpeita said, "I want you to come with me to meet a couple of men from Choshu. It will be an opportunity to exchange ideas."

"If this is another one of your schemes to educate me, Hanpeita, forget it. I've heard about Regent Ii, the treaty and the shogunal succession."

"So, you've heard about Ii's blasphemy," Hanpeita said, surprised at Ryoma's apparent knowledge of current events.

"Blasphemy?" Ryoma repeated with a puzzled look. "Why do you call it blasphemy?"

Unlike the studious Hanpeita, Ryoma was not interested in politics. Having been told since childhood that he was intellectually inept, he had avoided study. After all, the "runny-nosed, bed-wetting crybaby" had been obliged to leave school when the headmaster informed his father that he was not suited for scholarship. It had been then that he discovered *kendo* practice. This was an area in which he naturally excelled. It was through *kendo* that he acquired unwavering self-confidence. The way of the sword, he determined, was the road he would continue to follow.

"Ryoma, you must be more aware of what is going on in the nation," Hanpeita urged. Then in a low voice he added, "The Bakufu is no longer to be trusted."

Regent Ii had recently authorized a commercial treaty with the Americans without obtaining Imperial sanction. His action was considered nothing short of *lese majesty* by the proponents of *Imperial Reverence and Expelling the Barbarians*, a new battle cry among radical samurai. Ii was compelled to act quickly when American Consul Townsend Harris threatened that if the Bakufu did not have the authority to sign a treaty without Imperial consent, the United States would have no alternative but to stop negotiations with Edo, and deal with the ruler which could indeed authorize a treaty. In short, Harris seemed prepared to go to Kyoto to negotiate directly with the Imperial Court. The Bakufu panicked at the sudden ultimatum. If the United States went through with its threat, Edo would lose its authority, and every foreign country which sought a treaty with Japan would naturally follow the American example of dealing directly with the inept Imperial Court. This, reasoned the regent, would spell disaster for the entire nation.

"Then, less than one week after signing the commercial treaty which has laid our sacred nation bare to the wicked barbarians," Hanpeita continued in a seething tone, "and as if to add insult to injury, the Bakufu proclaimed the child-Lord of Kii heir to the Shogun. The treacherous regent has not only double-crossed His Imperial Majesty, but he has destroyed Lord Yoshinobu's chances for succession."

Shortly after the twelve-year-old Lord of Kii was selected to succeed his cousin as commander in chief of the Tokugawa regime, the imbecilic Shogun Iesada conveniently died, and was enshrined among his ancestors. The young *daimyo*, meanwhile, became the fourteenth Shogun, Tokugawa Iemochi.

"Ryoma, I'm asking you to come with me this evening as a personal favor. The Choshu men are expecting to see Sakamoto Ryoma, the head of the Chiba Dojo. One of them is Katsura Kogoro, head of the Saito Dojo."

"Katsura Kogoro will be there?" Ryoma, who had heard of Katsura's great skill with a sword, was suddenly more interested. "Alright, Hanpeita. I'll go."

Two samurai walked through the low wooden front gate of a restaurant near Tosa headquarters. Takechi Hanpeita was immaculately dressed in a black kimono, *hakama* of royal blue cotton, and a gray jacket displaying the Takechi family crest. His hair was oiled and combed, and his topknot folded neatly over his shaven pate. In contrast, Ryoma was sloppily clad in a faded black kimono, and a jacket so worn that his family crest was barely visible, and as usual, his long hair was uncombed. Both men wore their long and short swords thrust through the sash at their left hip.

The proprietress of the restaurant escorted the two men to a private room on the second story, where two other samurai sat on the floor, drinking at a low wooden table. "Takechi-sensei, thank you for coming," one of them said. This was Katsura Kogoro, suave of speech and gentle of manner. He was dressed formally in a dark blue jacket and black *hakama*; his hair was tied neatly into a topknot. His intelligent face was pale, his features almost effeminate; but his grand demeanor and dark, piercing eyes betrayed a great strength of character. The adopted son of an upper-samurai, Katsura, age twenty-five, had come to Edo five years before to practice *kendo* at the famed Saito Dojo. He was soon appointed head of the *dojo*, and with the coming of Perry began studying Western shipbuilding, artillery and infantry to prepare for war against the foreigners. His recent promotion to an official post in the Choshu government was due to his superior ability as both scholar and swordsman. "And this must be Sakamoto-san, whom I've heard so much about," Katsura said. Sitting next to Katsura was a sullen youth of just nineteen, his face badly pocked from the smallpox which had nearly killed him in his childhood. This was Takasugi Shinsaku, the future revolutionary commander of the Choshu Army. "Takechi-sensei, Sakamoto-sensei," Takasugi bowed to the two well-know Tosa swordsmen, "it's an honor to meet you." Takasugi's courtesy was pure protocol. Mere proficiency in the way of the sword was not sufficient to earn the true respect of such men as Katsura and Takasugi. Both were disciples of the celebrated revolutionary teacher Yoshida Shoin, from the great southwestern domain of Choshu, which, like Mito, held some extremely radical ideas concerning the Bakufu, the Imperial Court and the foreigners.

Ryoma and Hanpeita returned the formalities, then sat down at the table, placing their long swords at their right sides. The Choshu men had already been drinking before the Tosa men arrived, and they were anxious to discuss the issues which had come to possess their very souls. Katsura poured a round of drinks. "Sakamoto-san, what are your ideas concerning *Imperial Reverence and Expelling the Barbarians?*" he asked, feeling out the Tosa swordsman. By now the slogan had captured the heart and soul of samurai throughout Japan. Its mere utterance could heat the blood of almost every spirited man in the land. There were few men considered to be of any worth who were not willing to lay down their lives for the cause of *Imperial Reverence and Expelling the Barbarians*.

Takechi Hanpeita was gradually becoming the leader of the Tosa radicals; Katsura Kogoro and Takasugi Shinsaku were dedicated disciples of Yoshida Shoin, the leader of the Choshu radicals. These champions of things Japanese shared with the Confucian scholars of Mito a deep reverence for the Emperor of Japan. Ryoma, however, was different. His strange way of thinking had recently become an enigma to his comrades who trained in the way of the sword. Holding the rim of his *sake* cup against his mouth, Ryoma stared hard into Katsura's eyes.

"Revering His Imperial Majesty and expelling the wicked barbarians from the sacred soil of Japan is the only way to save our nation," Hanpeita answered for his friend, as Ryoma silently drained his cup.

"Takechi-sensei," Katsura said, "I'm sure we share the same ideas and feelings in our mutual dedication to the cause." Then refilling Ryoma's cup, Katsura repeated his question.

"Well," Ryoma said nonchalantly, replacing his cup on the table, "*Imperial Reverence and Expelling the Barbarians* is a good cause. But what are you going to do with it?"

"You don't seem to understand," said Takasugi. "The Son of Heaven is the only rightful ruler of Japan. His ancestors ruled from the dawn of the Japanese nation, until the House of Fujiwara gained control of the political power one thousand years ago," Takasugi explained bookishly. "The Fujiwara ruled on the Emperor's behalf for the next five hundred years, until the formation of the first Bakufu. After that the Emperor remained politically powerless in Kyoto, while the military regimes of four successive families ruled the empire. To assure that the Emperor would remain powerless, the first Tokugawa Shogun, the founder of the present Bakufu, drastically decreased the allowance granted to the Emperor by his predecessors, and made laws prohibiting the Emperor from leaving Kyoto, forbidding the feudal lords from visiting the Imperial capital for personal reasons, and declaring that the Emperor dedicate himself to scholarship and poetry. In order to see that his laws were obeyed, the Shogun sent one of his ministers to

Kyoto as his official representative to oversee the Imperial Court."

With the newfound peace under Tokugawa rule, came an unprecedented flourishing of scholarship among the samurai, including the study of national politics. To ensure that the samurai would learn how to serve their feudal lords and govern the commoners, the Bakufu and the individual lords encouraged the study of Confucianism. A school of thought eventually developed which professed that the true ruler whom all Japanese must serve was the Son of Heaven, in the Imperial capital at Kyoto. And ironically, the group most responsible for establishing this school of thought–the very foundation for *Imperial Reverence and Expelling the Barbarians*–was Mito, one of the elite Three Tokugawa Branch Houses.

Ryoma, who rarely read books, had trouble grasping what Takasugi had told him, but nevertheless declared in perfect calm, "Until we can devise a way to combat the cannon that are mounted on the foreign warships, I'm afraid that we aren't going to be able to keep the barbarians out."

"How do you propose fighting them?" Takasugi asked.

"By developing a fleet of warships of our own."

"I agree entirely," Katsura said. "But first things first. Before we can fight the barbarians, we are going to have to get rid of the poisonous elements in Japan." Lowering his voice, the Choshu radical added, "Ii and his lackeys must be dealt with." Katsura shared the outrage of samurai all over Japan toward the regent's recent completion of a commercial treaty without Imperial sanction. "If things are allowed to remain as they are in the Bakufu, the barbarians will subjugate Japan, as they have China."

"Let's make a pledge here tonight," Ryoma pounded his fist on the table, "that we never allow that to happen."

"Let's drink to that!" Katsura raised his cup.

"Down with the barbarians," Takasugi roared.

"To His Sacred Majesty," Hanpeita said, and the four men drank deeply.

An Awakening

The August heat was sweltering, and nearly two years had passed since the Dragon's return to Edo. Samurai throughout the capital and indeed Japan were enraged over the drastic measures that Regent Ii Naosuke had enforced during his first four months in power. The animosity mounting between the supporters of opening the country to free trade, and those who vowed to expel the barbarians had reached a point of no return.

In the fall of 1858 Ryoma's official permission to study in Edo had once again expired, and he was recalled to his native Kochi. Traveling on foot from Edo along the Tokaido Road, he reached Kyoto one week later. Under a crisp, blue October sky, Ryoma crossed the Sanjo Bridge, one of several arched wooden bridges spanning the Kamogawa which flowed southward through the eastern portion of the ancient city from the mountains to the north. Parallel to the Kamogawa, just a stone's throw to the west, was the Takasegawa, a canal and important trade route between Kyoto and the neighboring town of Fushimi to the south. The Takasegawa was lined with houses of local merchants and stately residences of feudal lords. Among these was the Kyoto headquarters of Tosa Han, Ryoma's immediate destination. Due to the political uproar in Kyoto caused by xenophobic samurai and court nobles who opposed Regent Ii's decision to open Japan to foreign trade, the Bakufu had recently made it mandatory for all samurai traveling through the city to report to the headquarters of their respective *han.*

The turbulence was sparked by the regent's punishment of the three great feudal lords who had opposed the sealing of the commercial treaty with the Americans without Imperial sanction. In June, five days after the treaty had been signed, the Lords of Mito and Owari, two of the Three Tokugawa Branch Houses, entered Edo Castle uninvited to rebuke the Bakufu's decision to sign the treaty, and to express their disapproval of the choice of the child-Lord of Kii as heir to the Shogun. They argued that the Imperial Court supported the candidacy of Lord Yoshinobu, the seventh son of the Lord of Mito. They maintained that although the commercial treaty had indeed been sealed without Imperial sanction, the court might be appeased if Yoshinobu were appointed shogunal heir.

Ignoring these pleas, the Bakufu officially announced on the following day that the Lord of Kii would succeed Shogun Iesada. In order to strengthen his absolute rule over the military government, the regent ordered the punishment of the Lords of Mito and Owari, as well as that of the Lord of Fukui, another high-ranking *daimyo* who had also expressed his displeasure with Bakufu policy. These three *daimyo* were forced to retire, and placed under house confinement, while Lord Yoshinobu was banned from entering Edo Castle. As Mito, Owari and Fukui were among the Tokugawa Bakufu's most important retainers, the regent's punitive measures not only shocked the entire nation, they also aroused the outrage of the samurai of these three *han*.

In August, the regent ordered the wholesale arrest of anti-foreign Imperialist samurai who had come to Kyoto to urge the court to issue an edict for the regent's abdication, the revocation of the punishments handed out to Mito, Owari and Fukui, and reconsideration of shogunal succession. As a result of this insurgency, an Imperial proclamation was secretly delivered to Mito rebuking the commercial treaty and the punishment of the three lords, and ordering the Lord of Mito to hold counsel with other feudal lords to find the most suitable way to assure national peace and avoid derision from foreign countries.

Adamant over what he considered treason by Mito, the regent took drastic measures. The "Great Purge of Ii Naosuke" began with the arrest of over one hundred supporters of *Imperial Reverence and Expelling the Barbarians*, including court nobles, Bakufu officials, feudal lords and samurai. Unprecedented in scope and severity, the punishment was harshest on those the regent mistakenly assumed had initiated the secret Imperial proclamation: the Lord of Mito and his retainers. The retired Mito *daimyo* was placed under house arrest; his son, who had recently succeeded him, was confined to his residence and prohibited from performing his official duties; another son, Lord Yoshinobu, was forced to retire from political life and placed under house confinement; four of the eight men arrested during the purge who would eventually die in prison were Mito samurai.

*   *   *

As the sun set over the ancient Imperial capital, Ryoma could see the towering five-storied pagoda of Toji Temple–black against a brilliant orange sky–two leagues southwest from where he stood on the western bank of the Kamogawa. He intended to visit a childhood friend, Hirai Kao, but had been warned that the Sanjo house, where she was staying, was under the surveillance of Bakufu spies. Kao was the younger sister of Hirai Shujiro, a mutual friend of Ryoma's and Hanpeita's from Kochi Castletown. Unlike most upper-samurai, Shujiro and Kao were devout proponents of *Imperial Reverence and Expelling the Barbarians*, and had many friends among the lower-samurai in Kochi. A younger sister of the Lord of Tosa had recently married a prince of the Sanjo, one of the most powerful families at court and avid supporters of *Imperial Reverence and Expelling the Barbarians*. Kao, the daughter of a well-connected upper-samurai of Tosa, had been appointed maid-in-waiting to the Tosa princess.

Ryoma walked slowly northward along the river until night came. He was anxious to hear from Kao of the drastic measures the regent had taken with the radicals at court, but perplexed as to how he could get into the house of a court noble without being noticed.

As Ryoma silently approached the Sanjo house, just east of the Imperial Palace, he cursed the revealing light of the full moon, and hid himself in the bushes. From here he could see the house, and the second-story window which he had been told belonged to the room in which Kao slept. Suddenly there was the sound of someone moving nearby, and Ryoma released the latch to the sheath of his sword. As the noise came gradually closer, he drew the blade. Whoever it was now seemed to be less than three paces away, but still Ryoma could not make out the figure. Sweat ran down his forehead and both sides of his face, but he remained perfectly still. Then moonlight glistened from two sparkling eyes, and Ryoma had to repress his laughter.

"A cat," he muttered to himself, then stood up quietly and scaled a long white earthen fence which surrounded the Sanjo house. Just below the window of Kao's room were black-tiled eaves, which Ryoma reached by climbing a big willow tree beside the house. He stepped onto the eaves, slid open the window, and entered the house.

"Kao," he whispered. "It's me, Sakamoto Ryoma."

"Ryoma?" Kao recognized his face in the moonlight shining through her chamber window.

"I need to talk to you."

"How did you get in here?"

"I snuck in."

"You must leave before someone sees you," the girl protested. "Go to Chifuku Temple tonight. It's at the top of Yoshida Hill." Kao wrote a short note of introduction to the priest of this Zen temple, handed it to Ryoma. "I'll meet you there tomorrow morning. I'm so glad to see you, Ryoma. I have many things to tell you. But one thing I must warn you of first: under no circumstances are you to tell anyone of our meeting."

Ryoma left the house, and silently stole through the surrounding neighborhood. After reaching the Sanjo Bridge, he walked eastward into the thickly wooded hills above the city. He spent the night at the Zen temple, in a simple one-room cottage, located in a wooded area just behind the main hall. When he awoke early next morning he was escorted by a monk to a small house on the temple grounds. The house stood in front of a pond surrounded by an immaculately kept garden. Lush bamboo grass grew beneath and around small pines. Plum, cherry and peach trees stood gray and bare with the coming of winter. Leafy camphor trees shaded the pond; camellia trees blossomed red, white and pink. Rocks of various shapes and sizes were neatly arranged along the water's edge, and a weathered wooden boat lay at the mossy shore.

Ryoma plucked a blade of bamboo grass near the entrance of the house, put it in his mouth, removed his sandals and entered. Inside the house Kao sat in the formal position on an immaculate *tatami* floor, greeting Ryoma with a bow, hands extended in front of her. She wore a kimono of pea-green silk, a small lacquered comb in her hair, and around her midriff a cream-colored sash.

Ryoma removed both swords from his hip and sat down cross-legged facing Kao, the blade of bamboo grass protruding from his mouth. Three of the walls were of a dark yellow earthen clay. Finely polished cedar logs were built into the threshold of the sliding screen doors. The ceiling was of woven cedar bark; a single log was built into an alcove to the right of the girl. A white camellia had been placed in a flower vase of light green ceramic, which was arranged at the center of the otherwise bare alcove. On the plain yellow wall behind the vase hung a scroll of calligraphy in black Chinese ink. The sliding door behind Kao was open wide, and Ryoma had a wonderful view of the garden and the dark green pond in the background.

Between Kao and Ryoma was a hearth, built into the floor. On the hearth was a steaming iron kettle, and next to this, on the bare *tatami*, a teacup of black porcelain. Within reach were other utensils of the tea ceremony: a small black lacquered container of powdered green tea, a slender bamboo spoon for the powder, and a bamboo whisk to stir the bitter, frothy tea. A small tray of sweet bean cakes had been placed in front of Ryoma. He removed the chewed blade of grass from his mouth, placed it on the tray, and took one of the cakes in his hand. As Kao poured hot water into the cup and made tea, Ryoma inserted the entire cake into his mouth, wiped his hand on the front of his jacket, then smiled. "Very good," he said, and, without ceremony, slurped some tea.

"You're the same as ever, Ryoma." Kao seemed more amused than disturbed by Ryoma's lack of manners. "You're lucky you weren't arrested last night. Bakufu spies have been watching the Sanjo house for weeks. We can't have any visitors. Regent Ii is convinced that anyone who has anything to do with the Sanjo is in cahoots with us against the Bakufu."

"What are you doing there?" Ryoma asked.

"I'm serving Lady Tomi, who recently married the son of the former Lord Keeper of the Imperial Seal."

As Kao explained, although she was officially in Kyoto as maid-in-waiting to the sister of the Lord of Tosa, she was secretly serving the radical Sanjo family of court nobles. She was aiding "Imperial Loyalists," as the Imperialist samurai now called themselves, who had come to Kyoto to urge the court to act against Ii's sealing of the commercial treaty without Imperial sanction.

"How long will you stay in Kyoto?" Ryoma asked.

"As long as I can be of use to the Imperial cause. I am dedicated to my Lady, the Sanjo family and the overthrow of the Bakufu for the sake of the Japanese nation," Kao whispered.

"The overthrow of the Bakufu?" Ryoma exclaimed.

Ryoma had reason to be startled. The dominance of the Bakufu over the entire nation was beyond question. Even the radicals of Mito did not harbor the slightest ambitions of toppling the Bakufu. Rather, they despised the Bakufu's regent, whom the Lord of Mito and his followers labeled "a traitor disgracing the divine Emperor and the sacred nation." But the stage of history had already been set. The *coup de theatre* which would transform the conglomerate of 260 feudal clans into a single, unified nation was under way; and although Sakamoto Ryoma was yet unaware, his was to be a leading role in the great drama ahead, which would be the revolution to overthrow the Tokugawa Bakufu.

Shortly after his return to Kochi, Ryoma received a letter from a Mito samurai by the name of Sumiya Toranosuke, whom he had never met. Sumiya was traveling through western Japan on a campaign to organize opposition against the "dictator" Ii Naosuke. He had heard of the well-known Tosa swordsman, Sakamoto Ryoma, from men at the Chiba Dojo in Edo. In his letter, Sumiya wrote that he would like to meet Ryoma, and that he would be waiting for him at the Tachikawa Border Station, which separated Tosa from the neighboring province of Iyo. Pleased by his recent notoriety, Ryoma immediately set out on the long trek through the mountains to Tachikawa, arriving on the following morning.

Sumiya was dressed all in black. His full head of hair was tied in a topknot, and his sideburns extended down to his earlobes. He was unshaven, but his refined features, clear eyes and manner of speech made it apparent that he was a man of culture.

"Sakamoto-san, I appreciate your coming," the radical Loyalist from Mito greeted the Tosa swordsman, then without hesitation got straight to the point. "What do you think about the blasphemy in the national government?"

"I'm not exactly sure what you mean," Ryoma said.

An educated man would surely have realized that Sumiya was referring to Ii's recent purge of his political enemies who had opposed the sealing of the commercial treaty without Imperial sanction. Ignoring Ryoma's remark, Sumiya continued in a bookish manner. "*Men of High Purpose* are now concentrating their collective energies to organize enough support to restructure the present regime in Edo, and in so doing avenge not only the unjust punishments inflicted upon our virtuous Lords Nariaki and Yoshinobu, but also the immoral irreverence Ii has displayed toward court nobles in Kyoto, and even toward the Son of Heaven Himself."

"I see," Ryoma said, scratching the back of his neck. Although he was genuinely concerned with Mito's plight, the content of Sumiya's words was beyond his present grasp. "To tell you the truth, I'm really not very familiar with what is happening in the Edo government or in the Imperial Court," he admitted.

As the swordsman's ignorance was apparent, Sumiya abandoned his discourse to get to more immediate concerns. "I'd like to ask for your help in gaining entrance into Tosa for a few days so that I can talk with some of your people about Ii's atrocities."

Notwithstanding Ryoma's sympathy for this champion of *Imperial Reverence and Expelling the Barbarians*, the former head of the Chiba Dojo was a mere lower-samurai; despite his efforts, he was unable to arrange permission for Sumiya to enter Tosa.

The Mito man was grieved. Not only had he wasted precious time waiting at the border station for Ryoma's response, but he was also disappointed at the ignorance of the reputable swordsman for whom he had harbored such high expectations.

The meeting, however, was by no means a wasted endeavor. In fact, Sakamoto Ryoma's short encounter with the Mito Loyalist at the Tachikawa Border Station that chilly afternoon in November 1858 would one day have a great effect on the history of Japan. Bothered and embarrassed at his lack of knowledge concerning national affairs, Ryoma decided to educate himself.

On the next day Ryoma visited the home of Takechi Hanpeita, the master of the Zuizan Dojo, recently returned from Edo. In addition to fencing, Zuizan (Hanpeita has recently taken this pseudonym) taught Japanese and Chinese history and philosophy, with an emphasis on Confucianism. This ancient Chinese doctrine, which taught a code of morals based on filial piety and submission to authority, was, in strictly ethical terms, the most prolific source of the code of the samurai.

"Hanpeita, I need your advice," Ryoma said, accepting a cupful of *sake* from Hanpeita's wife, Tomiko.

"About what?"

"Will you recommend some books that will give me a general understanding of the political situation in Japan?"

"Start by reading history," Hanpeita said.

"History? To understand current problems?"

"Yes. History teaches knowledge through example," declared the Confucian scholar. "History is the foundation of scholarship." Hanpeita stood up and walked over to a desk on the other side of the room. "Here," he said, "read these." He handed two handwritten volumes to Ryoma. One was titled *A History of Japan*, a celebrated Imperialist work popular among the supporters of *Imperial Reverence and Expelling the Barbarians*. The other was a Chinese history book.

Ryoma's scholastic endeavors during this period were by no means limited to these two studies of Oriental history. Shortly after reading them he visited Kawada Shoryo, to borrow a copy of *An Account of an American Castaway*. The book fascinated Ryoma. It told of a democratic system of government, whereby people elected their leaders. *"The people of the nation vote to elect a president every four years."* Ryoma repeated this sentence several times to understand the meaning. *"There is an official document called the 'Bill of Rights' which guarantees fundamental rights and privileges to the people. The Bill of Rights is a part of the Constitution, upon which all of the laws are based."* The concept which confused Ryoma most was that of a congress elected by the people, and which made the laws. *"This is a political system which has been created to protect the 'civil rights' of the people."* Ryoma read this sentence over and over again, because he could not understand the concept of "civil rights."

On the next day Ryoma visited Shoryo again. "Your book is fascinating," he said. "The Americans have some incredible ideas. To think that the people choose their Shogun."

"Not a Shogun," Shoryo laughed. "A president."

"What's a president?"

"The president of the United States is the leader of the people, who is chosen by the people every four years to represent them."

"Do you mean that even the peasants can choose their leader?" Ryoma was amazed.

"Ryoma," Shoryo spoke deliberately, "there are no peasants in the United States. But a farmer can become the president. Anyone can, regardless of lineage."

"That's fantastic!" Ryoma blurted, slapping his thigh. "But what are civil rights?"

"Civil rights are the personal liberties guaranteed to each individual citizen by the *Constitution of the United States of America.*"

"What's the *Constitution*?" Ryoma asked.

"The *Constitution* is the document which states the principles and laws of the United States that determine the powers and duties of the government, and which guarantees civil rights to the people."

During the following months Ryoma often visited Kawada Shoryo to learn the details of American government and democracy. The Western scholar also told Ryoma of everything he himself had learned about the joint-stock company and the booming industrialism of Europe and America, while they discussed a mutual dream of one day acquiring a Western-style steamer to operate their own shipping company.

In the Wake of the Storm

By spring of the sixth year of the Era of Peaceful Rule, 1859, Takechi Hanpeita had become the undisputed leader of the self-styled Men of High Purpose who lived in and around Kochi Castletown. Most of these men were of lower-samurai stock, some were peasants, others the sons of village headmen from the surrounding countryside. They talked among themselves of the dire necessity of fortifying the nation to protect it from the Western onslaught. They cursed Regent Ii Naosuke for sullying the sacred nation with foreign treaties. They pledged their alliance to Imperial Reverence and Expelling the Barbarians, vowing to die before they would allow the foreigners free rein in Japan.

Master Zuizan, age twenty-nine, was the champion in Tosa of the xenophobic Imperial cause, and Sakamoto Ryoma, twenty-three, was his right-hand man. The two, however, were an unlikely team. The reserved sword master was a rigid moralist who shunned everything Western, while the Dragon harbored preposterous dreams of one day commanding a Western-style warship.

The bright sun illuminated the crystal-blue sky above the castletown on the fifth day of March. It was the morning after the heads of upper-samurai households had been invited by the Lord of Tosa to drink *sake* at his castle, an honor from which Ryoma, Hanpeita and the other lower-samurai were excluded.

"Ryoma," Nakaoka Shintaro hollered as he stormed into the Sakamoto house amid a gathering of several young samurai. Shintaro was the first son of a powerful village headman from the mountainous district of Aki, whose family had long ago been awarded the privilege of having a surname and bearing the two swords of the samurai. One of Hanpeita's leading disciples, Shintaro began his formal education in his early childhood under a Buddhist priest, and afterwards studied under a doctor of Chinese medicine, at whose academy he became a teacher at just fourteen. Later Shintaro moved to the castletown, where he entered Hanpeita's fencing *dojo*, and now, at the age of twenty, studied literature, philosophy and fencing under Master Zuizan. "Zuizan-sensei has sent me here," Shintaro said, his fists clenched in anger, his eyes flashing. "Ikeda Toranoshin's younger brother, Chujiro, was murdered last night by an upper-samurai. Zuizan-sensei wants you to come to Toranoshin's house immediately."

Ikeda Toranoshin, also a lower-samurai, was Ryoma's junior at the Hineno Dojo in Kochi. "Where's Tora?" Ryoma asked, as he stood up and grabbed his two swords.

"He's held up in his house with Zuizan-sensei and about twenty others," Shintaro said, then relayed the events of the previous night as he had heard them.

The spring air was sullen in the neighborhood around Kochi Castle. It was the final night of the annual Peach Blossom Festival, when the heads of the upper-samurai households were invited by the Lord of Tosa to drink *sake* at his castle. The hour was growing late, and Yamada Koei, an upper-samurai with a reputation as a bad drunk, had just left the castle with his tea instructor. As they were about to pass the main gate of Eifuku Temple, just west of the castle, Yamada collided with a man who had been walking in the opposite direction. This was Chujiro, the younger brother of Ikeda Toranoshin. "Impertinence!" roared Yamada, grabbing Chujiro's sleeve. Although Chujiro tried to avoid trouble, the drunken man was adamant. "A lower-samurai," he thundered, identifying Chujiro's social rank by the clothes he wore. "Apologize immediately, or die!" he raged, ignoring the urging of his tea instructor to let the matter alone.

As Yamada continued his drunken tirade, a young boy who was an acquaintance of Chujiro happened by. Shrouded under the cover of the quarter-moon darkness, the frightened boy hid in the nearby bushes, where he witnessed the ensuing horror.

Chujiro refused to apologize, and Yamada became enraged at what he considered an insult to his social superiority. "Your name," he demanded, but Chujiro, overcome by resentment and fear, remained silent. Yamada drew his sword in a flash of deadly blue, and a split second later blood sprayed like a fountain from Chujiro's chest.

The young witness to the murder ran to the nearby house of Chujiro's older brother, who upon hearing what had happened, raced with the boy to the scene of the murder. Here Toranoshin found his brother's body lying in a pool of blood, and at a distance of about fifty paces from the temple gate, spotted Yamada washing his bloodied hands in a stream. Confirming with the boy that this was indeed his brother's murderer, Toranoshin drew his long sword, quietly crept through the bushes, and was upon his unsuspecting victim in a matter of seconds.

"I avenge my brother's murder," Toranoshin screamed, as his sword flashed into a crimson spray, and Yamada's head dropped to the ground. Not yet satisfied with his revenge, Toranoshin now went after the petrified tea instructor. "I revenge my brother's murder," he repeated, before thrusting his sword, still wet with Yamada's blood, into the heart of the genteel artist.

The living room of Toranoshin's house was filled with lower-samurai when Ryoma and the others arrived. Some wore *kendo* training uniforms, others armor. While some of them were busy lubricating the blades of their swords, others polished spears, and all were heatedly discussing the impending battle with the upper-samurai who demanded that Toranoshin be handed over to the authorities.

"I say we attack right away," one man said. "If they think we're going to turn over Toranoshin, they're crazy," hollered another. "They'll have to kill all of us first."

"Calm down!" demanded a stern voice at the center of the room. "Ryoma, I'm glad you've come." This was Master Zuizan, recently appointed by the Tosa government as inspector of all swordsmen in the domain.

"Where's Tora?" Ryoma asked.

"He's back there." Hanpeita gestured with his head toward the rear of house. "Turning him over to the authorities would be a crime which I could not easily condone," Hanpeita said calmly, stroking his long chin. "*Seppuku* would be much more honorable."

"What?" Ryoma shouted. "That's crazy! You want him to commit *seppuku* for avenging the cold-blooded murder of his brother! He's a hero, not a criminal."

"Toranoshin acted with complete honor," said a younger man who was sitting away from the others. This was Ike Kurata, who had grown up in the same neighborhood as Ryoma. "Ryoma," Kurata seethed, "first they kill Chujiro, then they have the gall to demand that Toranoshin die. I say, down with the upper-samurai and this rotten *han*."

For the past two and a half centuries the lower-samurai of Tosa Han had been suppressed by the upper-samurai. The lower-samurai had originally been the retainers of the House of Chosokabe, the former ruler of Tosa. When the first Tokugawa Shogun defeated his enemies at the decisive Battle of Sekigahara at the turn of the seventeenth century, he confiscated the lands of the Chosokabe, who had sided against him, and awarded them to a minor feudal lord, the head of the

House of Yamanouchi, who, although not a direct Tokugawa retainer, had not fought against the Shogun. When Yamanouchi occupied Tosa, he brought with him his own vassals, who became the upper-samurai of Tosa Han, direct Yamanouchi retainers. The vassals of the banished Chosokabe either fled to other domains where they became peasants, or remained in their native land as second-class samurai. Dress codes were established so that the two classes could be easily distinguished. The lower-samurai were forbidden to wear wooden clogs, a privilege which was reserved for direct Yamanouchi retainers. Nor were the lower-samurai allowed on certain occasions to wear silk, and no matter how hot the weather, it was against the law for any but upper-samurai to carry a parasol to screen the sunlight when in close vicinity to the castle.

"This is war," insisted another lower-samurai. "Let's attack now."

"We'll divide Tosa in half, and avenge the dishonor done our ancient lord," bellowed another.

"Quiet!" Ryoma demanded. "Let's get some order into this mess. Now first of all, everyone calm down."

Hanpeita broke the short silence that followed. "Toranoshin is a brave and honorable man. And in order to avoid war..." Hanpeita was suddenly interrupted by a scream from the rear of the house. Drawing his sword, Ryoma, followed by Kurata and Shintaro, raced through the long wooden corridor and into a small room. At the center of the *tatami* floor kneeled Toranoshin, sprawled forward. In his right hand he clenched a short sword drenched in blood, which he had plunged into his belly up to the hilt. His left arm was extended in front of him, his fingers contorted in agony.

"Tora!" Ryoma screamed, then kneeled down and took his friend in his arms.

"Kill me!" Toranoshin begged deliriously, blood trickling from his mouth. As the dying man entered a state of shock, his hands began twitching furiously, but his bulging eyes focused on Ryoma.

Hanpeita and the others rushed to the room. "Toranoshin, you don't deserve this," one of them screamed. Indeed, had this been any of the other 260 Japanese fiefdoms, Toranoshin may well have been rewarded for his valor and fraternal loyalty, and certainly he would not have been branded a criminal. But things in Tosa were cut and dry: it was a crime, under any circumstances, for a lower-samurai to strike a direct retainer of the House of Yamanouchi.

"Tosa Han is rotten," Ryoma muttered, still holding Toranoshin in his arms. Kurata, now kneeling on the floor next to Ryoma, looked up at the others and screamed, "Call for a doctor! We need a doctor to save his life!"

"Silence!" Hanpeita ordered. "Toranoshin, you will not have died in vain. You are a brave warrior," he solemnly declared. "Kurata, he's suffered enough. Perform the duties of a second."

Tears of rage filled Kurata's eyes. "Toranoshin, I swear that your brave death will be avenged. We'll tear this rotten *han* apart."

"Kura, show the compassion of a warrior!" Ryoma screamed, holding Toranoshin in an upright position. "He's suffered enough. Perform the duties of a second right away."

"Ikeda Toranoshin!" cried Kurata, beside himself with anger and grief, "you are the bravest of samurai." He drew his long sword, raised it high above the neck of his comrade.

"Thanks, Kurata," gasped Toranoshin.

"We'll meet in heaven," Kurata screamed, and an instant later Toranoshin's head lay in front of the corpse, blood pumping from the neck in gruesome, audible spurts. Kurata wiped the blood from his sword with his sleeve, resheathed the blade, and screamed, "Vengeance! We must get vengeance!"

"What are we waiting for?" yelled another man. "Let's go. We must avenge the death of the Ikeda brothers."

"Wait!" Hanpeita roared, commanding the attention of the some twenty men present. "Shintaro, take care of the body," he said. "Ryoma, you take everyone to my house and make sure that nobody does anything rash. I'm going to report this to the authorities."

"But Sensei," Kurata objected, tears of rage flowing down his face, "we can't forgive this. We must avenge Toranoshin's brave death."

"Down with the upper-samurai!" Shintaro shouted. "Down with Tosa Han!"

"Down with the Yamanouchi!" several others shouted.

"Calm down!" Hanpeita ordered, silencing the entire group. Glaring through steely eyes the sword master said, "Everyone go with Ryoma. We must act coolly, deliberately and most of all accurately. We will strike when the time is right," declared the undisputed leader of all young samurai of the lower classes in Tosa Han.

*   *   *

Around this time, a quite separate event of even greater consequences incited contempt throughout the population of upper-samurai in Kochi Castletown. The Lord of Tosa, Yamanouchi Yodo, had been forced into retirement by Ii Naosuke, and subsequently placed under house arrest at his villa in Edo.

Yamanouchi Yodo, who as an outside lord had no authority in the Edo government, was nevertheless considered one of the "Four Brilliant Lords" of his time. With the coming of Perry in 1853, the then twenty-seven-year-old Tosa *daimyo*, an accomplished poet and swordsman, took it upon himself to write a letter to the Bakufu, advising absolute refusal of the American demands to open the country. *"Since refusal will undoubtedly mean war with the barbarians,"* he wrote, *"it is of utter importance for Japan to prepare itself for war if we are to avoid becoming another China."* With only direct retainers of the Shogun invited to express opinions in national affairs, such a bold display by an outside lord was unprecedented.

Yodo's brazen personality even vexed his own government ministers, most of whom were far older than the self-styled "poet warrior" when he ascended to Tosa rule at age nineteen. During a ceremonial party in the Grand Hall of Kochi Castle, too much *sake* had led some of the more loquacious ministers to express disapproval for their young lord's display of bravado on the previous day, upon his return from his first official visit to Edo. When Yodo's entourage of some four hundred samurai reached the vicinity of Kochi Castle after weeks of travel, the *daimyo* was advised to remain seated in his palanquin, and allow himself to be carried along the road leading to the castle gates. This, after all, was considered the only proper manner for a *daimyo* to return to his realm. Not so for Yamanouchi Yodo, who preferred to portray the image of a powerful warlord of three centuries passed, during the age when respect from one's vassals could only be earned through sheer strength. Paying little regard to customs which had, in his mind, become effeminate through the comforts of two and a half centuries of peace, Lord Yodo called for his own horse, climbed out of his palanquin, mounted the steed and rode majestically past the throngs of samurai and townspeople who waited in kneeled reverence until the procession had passed safely through the castle gates.

Yodo, who had been drinking alone on the following night in a room in the inner-palace, overheard the disapproving talk among his ministers in the Grand Hall. He proceeded to storm through the door, startling all present, and immediately grabbing one of them by the sleeve. "So, you've been ridiculing me behind my back," Yodo hollered.

Releasing the man, Yodo removed his silken kimono. Naked but for his loincloth, the muscular young lord challenged the befuddled minister to a wrestling match right there in the Grand Hall. The previously festive mood was now as solemn as the main hall of a Buddhist temple, as Yodo ordered his retainer to accept. "If you don't fight your hardest," he roared, "I'll order you to cut your belly open." Infuriated at the younger man's audacity, the minister charged him, but was immediately knocked off his feet by a powerful blow to the jaw. "Next!" the *daimyo* ordered another minister to attack, also knocking him down, before proceeding to beat up all twelve ministers in similar fashion.

Having quite literally subjugated his vassals, the Lord of Tosa stood at the center of the Grand Hall, arms folded at his bare chest. "I guess there's nobody here who can beat me," he snickered, then calmly put on his kimono before leaving his twelve befuddled ministers to themselves.

The "poet warrior" was also in the habit of lambasting other *daimyo*, most of whom he openly considered his mental inferiors. As his reputation spread, many of the feudal lords who were in attendance in Edo refused invitations to drink with him, fearing that an evening with the "Drunken Lord of the Sea of Whales"–Lord Yodo's *nom de plume* was indicative of both his love of *sake* and the whales which abounded off the Tosa coast–might lead to political discussion concerning the difficult times, and an inevitable tongue-lashing by the eloquent *daimyo*.

Yodo's wrath even extended to the lords of the Three Tokugawa Branch Houses. In the event that any of the other some 260 *daimyo* should encounter one of these three elite lords while traveling through the streets of Edo, he was required to alight his palanquin and pay the proper respects. To avoid such humiliation, most lords were in the custom of ordering their palanquin bearers to steer clear of any palanquin displaying the crests of Owari, Kii or Mito. No so Lord Yodo. One rainy day the Tosa *daimyo*, upon spotting the crest of Owari, ordered his own vehicle be stopped right along side of the esteemed Tokugawa retainer. Ignoring the downpour, Yodo alighted his palanquin, calmly walked over to that of the Lord of Owari, and paid the proper respects. Upon such an occasion, however, protocol also demanded that the Owari *daimyo* lean out of his own palanquin in acknowledgment of the respects paid. Accordingly, the Lord of Owari was, like Yodo, thoroughly drenched. Yodo's strategy worked: from this time on whenever a lord of the Three Tokugawa Branch Houses spotted the palanquin displaying the Tosa crest, he would inevitably order his bearers to steer clear of "that crazy *daimyo* of Tosa."

Yodo's boldness seemed to know no limits. During his first meeting with the head of the Shogun's Senior Council, Yodo muttered something about the heavy responsibilities of the elite councilor's high position.

"Not at all," the councilor graciously dismissed the flattery.

Here, however, the conversation took a sarcastic turn. "What I actually think," said Yodo, "is that you must have a very easy time and enjoy yourself in dealing with so many stupid *daimyo*. But I guarantee things won't be quite so easy with me."

Yodo had cause for indignation. Among the feudal lords in Japan, whose rule was hereditary, were literal morons who could neither read nor write. Others, having been pampered since birth, hadn't the faintest idea of the great problems facing the nation. In contrast, Lord Yodo was a gifted poet, accomplished scholar, eloquent speaker, and polished swordsman. As Lord of Tosa, he ranked nineteenth in revenue among all the feudal lords, and held a Fourth Imperial Court ranking, entitling him to sit among his peers before the Shogun, in the Great Hall of Edo Castle. It was natural for a man of his caliber to resent the archaic system which prohibited him from taking part in national affairs simply because he was an outside lord, while other "stupid *daimyo*" were invited to voice their opinions merely because of birthright.

Moreover, Yodo's brazen personality clashed with that of Regent Ii Naosuke. Just as the self-respecting "poet warrior" had spoken his mind to the head of the Shogun's Senior Council, he had recently made known to the Edo government his views concerning the defense of Osaka from possible foreign invasion. Drinking alone one night, as was his custom, Yodo composed a letter to the Bakufu from his official residence in Edo, advising that the best way to protect Japan's mercantile center would be to first burn the entire city to the ground. Quite a bold suggestion, considering that Osaka was a domain of the Shogun himself. Despite the Japanese saying *"There is but a fine line between insanity and genius,"* the Drunken Lord of the Sea of Whales had substantial reason for his radical views. *"The city is inhabited entirely by merchants,"* Yodo wrote. *"And most of these merchants know how to do little else but make money. In fact, if an Osaka merchant should happen to cross paths with a lone samurai, he would inevitably start quivering like a scared rabbit at the sight of the two swords. What would happen if a fleet of Black Ships were to open fire from Osaka Bay, before actually landing to invade the city? Surely you can't suppose that such cowardly merchants would take up arms and fight. As I know that you will agree, the useless inhabitants of Osaka would surely choose to run with their money in the opposite direction, leaving the entire city in the hands of the barbarians."* Yodo suggested that if Osaka were leveled to the ground so that one could see for leagues in all directions, the samurai assigned to protect the city would stand a far greater chance of repelling an invasion.

Upon reading Yodo's letter, Regent Ii, who was by now the absolute ruler of the Tokugawa regime, flinched, then muttered a single phrase under his breath, telltale of the Tosa lord's imminent confinement: "That son of a bitch!"

Fortunately, Yodo had recently recalled his favorite vassal, Yoshida Toyo, from temporary retirement, and appointed him as regent of Tosa Han, the most powerful post in the domain. Although Toyo was of the lower echelons of Tosa's upper-samurai classes, he was one of the most educated men in the *han,* who had first come to Yodo's notice in 1853, the year that Perry's fleet appeared off the coast of Edo. The pressing times had compelled the Tosa *daimyo* to recruit a group of able officials to organize a list of major reforms within his fiefdom. As leader of this group, Toyo became the target of animosity by the ousted members of the old guard, the highest stratum of Tosa society, who, in their preoccupation with maintaining the status quo, had lost sight of the necessity for economic reform in the face of modernization.

One hot summer night in 1854, while Toyo was in attendance upon his lord in Edo, an incident occurred which would result in four years of temporary retirement for Yodo's able but perhaps overly self-esteeming, if not notoriously obstinate, retainer. Yodo was holding a small party at his official residence for a distant relative who was stationed in Edo in Bakufu service. When Yodo's special guest became drunk he verbally ridiculed Toyo, and even tapped him on the head with his fan.

"Watch your manners!" Toyo burst out angrily, punching the Bakufu functionary square in the face. Then jumping on top of him and pinning him down on the floor, Toyo said furiously: "Not only have I dedicated my life to Lord Yodo, but I am also a minister of his great domain. Was it your intention to slight my lord by laying a hand on his loyal vassal?" Despite the man's frantic apologies, Toyo punched him again, and could only be stopped when Yodo himself physically intervened. Insulted, the guest suggested to Yodo that *seppuku* would be a just and proper punishment for his errant vassal.

Feigning indignation, Yodo ordered Toyo into another room until riled spirits could be calmed. In order to avoid further trouble with the Bakufu official, Yodo returned his favorite retainer to Kochi, where he was forced to resign his post and live quietly in a small village on the outskirts of the castletown.

Yodo was bewildered over the temporary loss of such an able man, whom he had every intention of reinstating when the time was right. The chance finally came four years later, shortly before Ii Naosuke's sudden rise to power. Then, when Yodo was forced into retirement and confined to his villa in Edo, Toyo quite naturally became first minister to the new Lord of Tosa. But since Yodo's heir was only thirteen years old at the time, Yoshida Toyo, at forty-three, assumed control of the Tosa government in the spring of 1859. Although there was great concern in Kochi that Ii Naosuke may go to such extremes as to abolish the Yamanouchi lineage and confiscate the entire Tosa domain, it was largely due to Toyo's scrutiny and wise negotiation with Bakufu officials that Yodo's punishment was kept to the minimal forced retirement and house confinement in Edo.

*　　　　　　*　　　　　　*

"Ryoma!" Takechi Hanpeita called at the front door of the Sakamoto house late one morning in the second week of March. "Have you heard the news?" he said, entering.

"What is it?" Ryoma, lying on the living room floor, replied drowsily.

"Ii Naosuke has been assassinated."

"What?" Ryoma started in surprise. Ii Naosuke was not only the most powerful man in Japan, but as Lord of Hikone, was always accompanied by an entourage of armed bodyguards. Getting through such an escort to take the head of the regent was a nearly impossible task, even for eighteen expert swordsmen who were resigned to die on the spot.

The impossible was achieved on the snowy morning of March 3, 1860, when a band of samurai, dedicated to the perpetuation of things Japanese, cut down Ii Naosuke at one of the main gates of Edo Castle, putting an abrupt end to the regent's reign of terror, and unleashing a wave of assassination which would not cease until after the downfall of the Tokugawa Bakufu seven years later.

"Seventeen men from Satsuma and one from Mito did the job," Hanpeita told Ryoma. "First they cut the devil while he was still in his palanquin. Then, after pulling him out onto the freshly fallen snow, they cut him up. Finally, the Mito man took the devil's head and ran with it to the front gate of the house of a member of Ii's Senior Council, where he committed *seppuku*."

Ryoma sat up straight, gave Hanpeita a hard look. "If the regent of the Tokugawa Bakufu can be cut down in cold blood at the very gates of Edo Castle," he said, "then there's no telling who might be next. People in Edo are going to go crazy, cutting down Bakufu officials left and right."

"Yes," Hanpeita agreed through steely eyes. "We Tosa men can't let Mito and Satsuma outdo us. We too have to prove our single dedication to the Imperial cause."

During the following months, Ryoma's house served as a gathering place for the disciples of Master Zuizan, and for other so-called *Men of High Purpose* who came to the castletown from throughout the seven districts of Tosa. With the death of the Ikeda brothers having ignited two and a half centuries of smoldering resentment into raging flames of anger toward the privileged upper classes, these young men had adopted a defiant attitude toward the establishment in Tosa. Then, with the assassination of Regent Ii Naosuke, the collective scorn of Tosa's lower-samurai was now also aimed at the Tokugawa Bakufu in Edo.

Nor was the radical effect of Ii's assassination limited to the lower-samurai of Tosa. Samurai from Choshu and Satsuma, the two most powerful "outside *han*," were now burning with a mutual resentment for the Edo regime which had subjugated them for the past two and a half centuries. In short, the fear by which the Bakufu had controlled the island nation began evaporating into thin air at the very instant the regent's warm blood dyed the freshly fallen snow a deep shade of crimson at the gates of the Shogun's castle.

The Lord of Tosa, however, was not inclined to oppose the Bakufu. Unlike the Mori of Choshu and the Shimazu of Satsuma, whose ancestors had been subjugated for having fought against the first Shogun, the Yamanouchi of Tosa owed its rule to the goodwill of the founder of the Tokugawa regime. Accordingly, the upper-samurai of Tosa neither shared the contempt for the Bakufu that prevailed among the lower classes of their fief, nor would they ever collectively stand against the Tokugawa. Although Lord Yodo would continue his call for change within the shogunal system, he would support his ancestral benefactor in Edo to the bitter end.

*   *   *

In addition to the foreign treaties, another issue which the Imperial Loyalists adamantly opposed was the call for an alliance between the Imperial Court at Kyoto and the military regime at Edo. By means of a *"Union of Court and Camp,"* as the proposed alliance was called, the Bakufu hoped to subdue the Loyalists. Those who claimed loyalty to the Emperor would certainly not wage war against Edo, for doing so would be tantamount to taking sides against the Imperial Court. The Tokugawa also reasoned that by uniting with the court, it would be able to maintain its absolute political authority which had been under question since the coming of Perry in 1853, and more recently with the assassination of the regent. But the plan had one great flaw: although the court would indeed recognize Edo's absolute political authority, by seeking to borrow Imperial prestige, Edo was acknowledging the power which Kyoto had recently come to wield.

Nevertheless, to secure a union with the court, the Bakufu proposed that a marriage be arranged between Shogun Iemochi, only fourteen years old, and Princess Kazu, the thirteen-year-old sister of Emperor Komei. Once the Princess was married to the Shogun and living within the confines of Edo Castle, a Loyalist attack on the Bakufu would be nothing short of an assault on the Imperial Family. In short, the Bakufu reasoned that once this political marriage had actually been achieved, the radicals would no longer be able to use their claim of "loyal dedication to the Son of Heaven" as a war banner by which to act against the Shogun, who would be directly related to the Emperor.

In order to persuade Emperor Komei to sanction the marriage proposal, the Bakufu claimed that such a bond would serve to unite the hearts of the Japanese people, thus consolidate national strength so that Japan would be in a better position to expel the "barbarian devils." Then, in July 1860, the Bakufu pledged the impossible: to expel the foreigners from Japan if the Princess would marry the Shogun, an offer which the chronically xenophobic Emperor could not refuse.

The Tosa Loyalist Party

Despite Sakamoto Ryoma's position of leadership among Men of High Purpose in Tosa, he had recently come to embrace secret ambitions that he could not yet disclose to his more traditional-minded comrades. Although he sympathized with their xenophobic sentiment, he was captivated by the idea of one day commanding a Western-style warship. Kawada Shoryo had taught him the futility of trying to expel the technologically advanced foreigners without first importing warships, guns and the expertise to use them. To achieve this, Japan would have to open itself to foreign trade. In this sense, Ryoma's views did not much differ from those of Tosa Regent Yoshida Toyo, nor certain farsighted Bakufu officials, including Ii Naosuke himself. But unlike the Tosa regent, and needless to say men of the Tokugawa, Ryoma reasoned that those who really meant to save Japan from foreign subjugation must put Western technology to use to overthrow the decrepit Bakufu, and replace it with a new government centered around the Imperial Court. However, as even the slightest mention of support for Opening the Country would be considered traitorous among his comrades, Ryoma was compelled to maintain a strict code of silence until the time was right. Frustrated, the Dragon waited.

Takechi Hanpeita had been on a year-long subversive journey to gain support for the Loyalist cause in some of the more powerful clans in Japan. Soon after his return to Kochi in the fall of 1861, the leader of the Tosa Loyalists paid a visit to the home of his right-hand man.

"Ryoma," Hanpeita said, "I have some important matters to discuss with you." The two men sat on the living room floor at Ryoma's home, next to a short, dark wooden table, on which were placed a large ceramic flask of *sake*, and two small cups. "I have some things to show you before I get into the details of what I've accomplished over the past year." Hanpeita accepted a cup of *sake* from Ryoma, but replaced it on the table without drinking. "I got this in Edo," Hanpeita said, reaching for his sword which he had previously placed on the floor at his left side. The hilt was made of sharkskin and wrapped with fine silk, the guard of polished gold, and the gilt deep blue scabbard lined with silver on its bottom edge. Hanpeita slowly drew the razor-sharp blade from the scabbard. "Beautiful, isn't it," he said. "It was made by one of the finest sword smiths in Edo." Holding the blade above the table, he proclaimed in a low, deliberate voice: "With this

43

we will cut down the enemies of the Emperor." Hanpeita slammed the blade back into the scabbard with a loud clang.

"I'll drink to that," Ryoma said, and drained his cup. Hanpeita did not drink. Rather, the stoic swordsman, who had recently acquired a reputation among *Men of High Purpose* for his dedication to the Emperor, produced a document from the breast of his kimono. "This," he said proudly, "is the *Manifesto of the Tosa Loyalist Party*."

"The Tosa Loyalist Party?"

"Yes. And this is our manifesto," Hanpeita said, staring hard at Ryoma, "to be signed by any Tosa man who will fight to unite Tosa in the struggle to overthrow the Bakufu, expel the barbarians, and return the political power to His Imperial Majesty in Kyoto."

"Unite Tosa?" Ryoma said in disbelief.

"Precisely!" said the leader of the Tosa Loyalist Party, thoughtfully stroking his long chin.

"You can't think that the upper-samurai will ever agree to unite themselves with the lower-samurai," Ryoma snickered.

"Leave that to me, Ryoma. I've promised the Loyalists of Choshu and Satsuma that I would unite Tosa under the banner of *Imperial Loyalism*. We've pledged to form an alliance between our three great *han* as soon as we can demonstrate our collective strength and dedication to the Emperor. That is why we must unite Tosa behind *Toppling the Bakufu and Imperial Loyalism*," Hanpeita uttered the new Loyalist slogan which was rapidly replacing *Imperial Reverence and Expelling the Barbarians* as the battle cry of *Men of High Purpose*.

"You can't be serious," Ryoma groaned. "How can you really believe that the *daimyo* and his ministers would ever listen to you? You're just a lower-samurai. They'd only laugh in your face, if they didn't have you arrested first. You know that it's prohibited to form political parties. But even if it wasn't, the idea that the Yamanouchi would ever vow to overthrow the Bakufu," Ryoma sneered at the blind loyalty of the Lord of Tosa for his ancestral benefactors in Edo, "is just not realistic."

"I'm absolutely serious," Hanpeita calmly objected to Ryoma's lack of enthusiasm for his meticulously devised plans. "With the strength in these arms," he vowed, again drawing his blade and holding it before his face, "I'll see to it that Tosa stands for *Toppling the Bakufu and Imperial Loyalism*."

As Hanpeita continued to explain, he intended to convince the Tosa authorities of the necessity of expelling the foreigners from Japan, but of the futility of trying to do so under the leadership of the decrepit shogunal system. He hoped that Lord Yodo, whom he reasoned would be able to see the virtue of his plan, would agree to lead an army of Tosa Loyalists into Kyoto, guard the Imperial Palace and restore the political power to the "Divine Emperor." In short, the Loyalists were plotting to overthrow the Bakufu for having yielded to foreign demands without Imperial sanction, and in so doing restore Japan's damaged pride.

"While I intend to persuade the Tosa authorities to support us," Hanpeita said, "I am fully aware that this plan can only be realized through the support of all the lower-samurai in the seven districts of Tosa. Only through such massive support can our noble goal be realized." Hanpeita handed the manifesto to Ryoma. "We already have eight signatures from men who were in Edo at the time we drew up the manifesto. Now, I ask that you, Sakamoto Ryoma, be the first to sign your name to it in Tosa. I'm counting on your support. I need your leadership to recruit more men." Hanpeita had recently taken the *nom de guerre* "Shield of the Emperor" for his dedication to *Imperial Loyalism*. His party's manifesto began as follows:

"*It is a source of deepest grief to our Emperor that our magnificent and divine country has been humiliated by the barbarians and that the Spirit of Japan, which has been transmitted from antiquity, is on the brink of being extinguished.*"

The manifesto continued to state that too many samurai, grown lazy and weak from the long years of Tokugawa peace, had lost the Spirit of Japan. Those who were most lazy and weak were the Tokugawa retainers who had yielded to foreign demands. It disdained the unjust chastisement of such a "*noble heart*" as Lord Yodo, who had been "*accused and punished for the wise advice he had given those in power.*" It proclaimed that every member of the party must be willing to "*go through fire and water to ease the Emperor's mind, to carry out the will of our former daimyo (Yodo), and to purge this evil from our people.*" Should any signatory put personal considerations before the cause, it admonished, "*he shall incur the punishment of the angered gods.*" Any such man, it explicitly warned, "*shall be summoned before his comrades to commit seppuku.*"

Ryoma finished reading the manifesto, placed it on the table. "The language is so pompous," he said, "so rigid. Just like you, Hanpeita. But if it means that much to you, I'll sign it. I'll dedicate myself to overthrowing the Bakufu, and saving our nation. But I don't see any possibility of the Tosa *daimyo* supporting us. And I know you know that the upper-samurai will never cooperate with the lower-samurai. They think we're no better than animals. But in the United States of America," Ryoma suddenly changed his tone, "the president has to consider the good of all of the people. The Tokugawa Shogun, on the other hand, has for the past two and a half centuries been concerned solely with the welfare of the Tokugawa Bakufu, with the feudal lords caring only for their own fiefdoms. This alone is enough to warrant the overthrow of the rotten Bakufu and the entire feudal system." Ryoma stopped speaking, his face red with anger. "Yes, Hanpeita, I'll sign." Ryoma picked up a writing brush, dabbed it on a block of black Chinese ink, signed his name in four large, bold characters to the list of sworn followers of the Tosa Loyalist Party. "Let me borrow your sword," he said, thinking it more appropriate to use Hanpeita's symbolic blade than his own. Unsheathing the blade, Ryoma pressed the tip of his left small finger on the edge, and sealed his name in blood. "Hanpeita," he said, grabbing his friend's hand, "even if we should succeed in uniting Tosa behind *Toppling the Bakufu and Imperial Loyalism*, I want you to realize that my signing this manifesto is not a pledge that I will remain in this rotten *han* and fight side by side with the upper-samurai."

"What do you mean?" Hanpeita gave Ryoma a hard look.

"What I mean is that I can't promise to be limited."

"Limited to what? To *Imperial Loyalism*?"

"No. I can't promise to be limited to toppling the Bakufu within the confines of Tosa."

"I don't follow you. What do you mean?"

"I mean exactly what I said. I don't know when I might be leaving this rotten *han*. But I will make one thing clear, Hanpeita. As long as Sakamoto Ryoma is alive, as long as there is blood flowing through these veins, breath in these lungs, strength in these arms, I pledge to topple the Tokugawa Bakufu."

Ryoma tightened his grip on Hanpeita's hand, and laughed to hold back the tears that were welling up inside his head. "But," he quickly added, staring straight into Hanpeita's eyes, "I have to do it my own way."

"What way is that, Ryoma?" Hanpeita said grimly.

"I haven't discovered it yet." Ryoma released his grip on Hanpeita's hand.

"Then, until you do, will you help me recruit men for the party?"

"Yes." Ryoma took his own sword. "I swear on my sword," he uttered the ancient pledge of the warrior. Releasing the latch, he drew the blade slightly from its sheath, then immediately slammed it back into place, clanging the silver guard against the metallic rim.

"On our swords!" Hanpeita repeated the pledge, clanging the guard of his own weapon. "This body, this mind, this very spirit within me is the shield of our cause," he solemnly pledged, his eyes too filling with tears. "And you, Sakamoto Ryoma, are the sword, and the very pillar of our noble struggle. Together we will overthrow the Bakufu," he proclaimed, as a single teardrop escaped the corner of his eye.

As Hanpeita continued to explain, his recently devised plan had come into being as a result of his meeting with revolutionary samurai from other *han* of Loyalist sentiment, namely Choshu, Mito and Satsuma.

"We've agreed that the proper measures must be taken soon against the Bakufu, as it has been plotting to convince the Imperial Court to sanction a marriage proposal between the Shogun and the Emperor's sister," Hanpeita said disdainfully. "Once the Princess is living within Edo Castle, she'll be a veritable hostage, and the Imperial Court will thus be forced to bend to the Bakufu's will. If that happens, we'll have even greater difficulty overthrowing the Bakufu and protecting Japan from the barbarians." The self-styled Shield of the Emperor paused, cleared his throat, then continued. "I particularly spent a lot of time this summer with men from Choshu," he said.

Choshu had ample reason for harboring a special hatred for the Bakufu. After his victory in the Battle of Sekigahara, the first Tokugawa Shogun confiscated eighty percent of the land of the former Choshu domain, which until then had been the largest in all of Japan, to ensure that his vanquished enemy could never pose a threat to Tokugawa rule. Soon after, however, Choshu began to industrialize its economy. At a time when the economy of the Bakufu, and indeed the economies of most of the fiefdoms throughout Japan, were dependent primarily on the production of rice, Choshu was engaged in such light industrial projects as the manufacture of paper and wax, and was meanwhile developing arable land to increase its annual rice yield. By 1853, the beginning of the end of Tokugawa rule, while other fiefs were struggling to subsist on their decrepit agricultural economies, Choshu had an annual income of nearly three times that of its predecessors at the outset of Tokugawa rule.

Latent anti-Bakufu sentiments in Choshu, simmering for the past two and a half centuries, eventually manifested themselves as *Imperial Reverence and Expelling the Barbarians*, and more recently as *Toppling the Bakufu and Imperial Loyalism*. The man who had reignited the flame of these anti-Bakufu sentiments was the martyred Loyalist teacher Yoshida Shoin, a victim of Regent Ii's purge. Among Yoshida's top disciples were three Choshu samurai who would not hesitate to use the great wealth of their *han* to purchase modern warships and weapons to challenge the Tokugawa. Their names were Takasugi Shinsaku, Kusaka Genzui and Katsura Kogoro.

One hot afternoon in the previous August, Hanpeita had met with Takasugi and Kusaka at an Edo teahouse to discuss the formation of Loyalist Parties in Choshu and Tosa, and the necessity for war to "cleanse the nation of the Western stain."

"Zuizan-sensei, please have a drink," Takasugi said, raising a porcelain flask to pour *sake* for Hanpeita. The eldest son of an elite Choshu samurai family, Takasugi had the uncanny ability to vacillate his subtle personality between that of wolf and poet.

Going through the formality of holding up his cup to accept a some *sake* from Takasugi, Hanpeita returned it to the table without drinking. "It will be necessary to consolidate our power," he said, looking hard at both men, who returned his powerful stare with equal intensity. "That's why I strongly propose an alliance between Satsuma, Choshu and Tosa. I doubt the ability of any one of our *han* alone to challenge the Bakufu forces in all-out war. But I also doubt that even the Bakufu could stand up against a Choshu-Tosa-Satsuma alliance."

"Zuizan-sensei," Kusaka began speaking in an excited but low voice. "Princess Kazu is due to leave Kyoto for Edo in October. We can't allow her to enter Edo Castle, because once she does she'll be a hostage. We are therefore planning to intercept the entire Imperial procession and personally return the Princess to the Imperial Palace."

"Then, after she is safely back in Kyoto...." Takasugi intervened, his voice trembling with passion.

"We are going to cut down the Tokugawa councilor Ando Nobumasa, the villain behind the scheme to marry the Shogun to the Princess," interjected Kusaka.

"Your intentions are just," Hanpeita said calmly, his voice void of emotion. "But it would be unwise to act too rashly at the present. I can see nothing of permanent value being gained by sending the Princess back to Kyoto, or even by cutting down Ando. Such deeds would only be ruinously costly to our cause, a waste of valuable Loyalist life. And even if you were successful in returning the Princess to the Imperial Palace, she would most likely be sent out again under a much stronger guard. Although assassinating Ando might temporarily ease our indignation, it would be a warning to the Bakufu to take even greater precaution. Besides, Ando can always be replaced."

"Zuizan-sensei," Kusaka said, his eyes wide open, "we must act now, before it's too late. The only way to deal with these matters is through violence. We have to destroy our enemies if we are to save the Empire. We must wash away the foul stench of the barbarians with the blood of the Tokugawa and its henchmen."

"Yes," Takasugi said, "the only way to drive out the barbarians is through force."

"There is no denying that," Hanpeita agreed. "All samurai must be prepared to die when the time is right, when the necessity arises. But right now I strongly propose that we return to our domains to organize support. Assassinating Ando would prove nothing. But if both of our *han* stood strongly against the Tokugawa, I am sure that the other *han* would follow suit. Besides, as you well know, our allies in Satsuma have vowed to unite with us in a triple alliance. Once this happens, the Bakufu will have no choice but to change its cowardly foreign policy."

Hanpeita poured another drink for Ryoma. "If Katsura hadn't suddenly shown up at that particular time," he said, "I might not have been able to convince those two to abandon their radical plans and work more methodically to organize consensus in Choshu."

"Choshu is Choshu," Ryoma suddenly exploded, "but this is Tosa. The Mori of Choshu have no special relationship with the Tokugawa. Their ancestors were merely defeated and subjugated by the Tokugawa two and a half centuries ago. But the Yamanouchi..." Ryoma paused. "You know more about it than I do, Hanpeita."

"Ryoma, I know how you feel about Tosa. I know how you feel about the upper-samurai. But we can't do anything without organization. We are powerless when split into factions. But consolidated, we would definitely be a force to be reckoned with. Choshu and Satsuma men have promised to persuade their respective governments to unite behind *Toppling the Bakufu and Imperial Loyalism*, and I must convince Yoshida Toyo of the same thing."

"You don't actually believe that Yoshida will listen to you," Ryoma scoffed. "The Tosa regent is dedicated to the House of Yamanouchi, which is loyal to the Tokugawa. Yoshida supports a *Union of Court and Camp*, which the Bakufu has been struggling to achieve."

"I am confident I can persuade Yoshida,' Hanpeita said. "But before I approach Yoshida, I have to organize support among our own men," he said, carefully refolding the blood-sealed manifesto of the Tosa Loyalist Party. Then, taking firm hold of the hilt of his sword, Hanpeita added coldly, "But if the regent should refuse, I'll have to find other means to deal with him."

"When you meet the regent," Ryoma said, looking hard at Hanpeita, "you should try to find a way to kill him."

"I just might have to," Hanpeita acknowledged through steely eyes.

"Yes," Ryoma laughed, "because a man who is easy to kill is useless."

"What do you mean?" Hanpeita gave Ryoma a puzzled look.

"I mean that you should not even deal with a man who is easy to kill. You should just leave him alone. But a man who would be hard to kill, is a man of wisdom."

"And?"

"Ryoma laughed again. "That's the kind of man you should be quick to fool into becoming your ally."

*   *   *

By the beginning of October, 192 Tosa men had signed the manifesto, and a good many more had pledged their allegiance to the Tosa Loyalist Party without actually affixing their names to the document, thus giving Hanpeita ample confidence to visit the home of the powerful Tosa regent.

"Zuizan-sensei," Toyo addressed in mock respect the rebel leader who sat facing him in the regent's drawing room. "You are aware that the Yamanouchi of Tosa have a much different relationship with the Bakufu than do either the Shimazu of Satsuma or the Mori of Choshu?" The regent spoke in a condescending tone, his large, intelligent face betraying ill humor at what he considered the "impudence of a lower-samurai."

"I'm aware of that," Hanpeita nodded slowly. "However..."

"If so," Toyo sharply interrupted, grasping a porcelain tea cup, "you should also be aware that it is neither wise nor profitable to be deal-

ing with criminal, anti-Bakufu elements in either Satsuma or Choshu.'
Toyo's threatening expression did nothing to offset Hanpeita's icy
glare.

"Yoshida-sensei," Hanpeita cunningly referred to the regent with the
honorable suffix rather than his official title, "unless our *han* also
takes the appropriate measures, it will lose out to Choshu and
Satsuma, as they are sure to unite to embrace the Emperor with thousands of troops at the Imperial Palace in Kyoto, and topple the
Tokugawa Bakufu. Such a display of military strength and *Imperial
Loyalism* will certainly attract support among other *han*, first in
Western Japan and then throughout the entire Empire. We must not
permit Tosa to be branded a traitor to the Emperor for not having officially endorsed *Imperial Loyalism*."

"Zuizan-sensei," Toyo laughed derisively, finishing his tea and putting down the empty cup, "you speak rot. The Shimazu are related
through marriage to the Yamanouchi. If the Lord of Satsuma was actually planning to lead an army into Kyoto, don't you think he would
first inform Lord Yodo's regent before taking such a drastic measure?
You shouldn't take to heart everything you hear. You don't seem to
have read enough Japanese history. Throughout the ages each time the
Emperor and the court nobles have voiced their opinions, trouble has
always followed. Whenever the court has tried to seize political power,
there has always been a war. And now they are starting to make noise
again in Kyoto. Certainly you know that it was the founders of the
three military governments throughout Japanese history who were
successful in bringing peace to our nation. Use your head! Give up
your sophomoric ideas. A man of your intelligence and influence
should be of service to Tosa, not a negative force working against us."

Yoshida Toyo supported Edo's drive for a *Union of Court and Camp*.
He reasoned that bumbling court nobles, who refused to cooperate
with the necessary moves to meet the changing times, needed to be
controlled, and such a union offered a satisfactory means by which to
dominate what he considered to be "the renegade Loyalists in Kyoto,"
whom Hanpeita was representing.

Hanpeita suppressed his rage, collected his thoughts and began to
speak in a cool, deliberate manner. "Yoshida-sensei, it is my every
intention to be of service to Tosa. I therefore implore you to heed our
manifesto." He thrust the document at his nemesis as if it were a
weapon by which he might topple the conservative Tosa regime.

Toyo ran his eyes over the blood-sealed manifesto, and sardonically laughed aloud. "You don't really believe that we could expel the barbarians without first opening up the country," he said, his previously sarcastic tone replaced by one of gravity. "First we must conduct trade with the barbarians in order to enrich ourselves to a degree that we can deal with them on our own terms. Zuizan-sensei, how would you expect to defeat the barbarians when we don't even have one decent warship of our own?" Toyo paused, then began reading aloud from the manifesto, a derisive grin on his face. "*We now join our forces in brotherhood to reactivate the Spirit of Japan...*'" He stopped reading. "In other words," Toyo scoffed, "what you are actually saying here is that a band of lower-samurai have taken it upon themselves to join forces with the upper-samurai to reform Tosa policy. How could you," he roared violently, "have the impudence to assume that I would even consider such a preposterous idea? It seems you are asking me to grant the lower-samurai the right to participate in the administration of Tosa."

"That's precisely what I'm asking. I implore you, Yoshida-sensei, for the good of Tosa and for the Empire..."

"Over my dead body," Toyo roared.

Hanpeita's eyes flashed as a dark thought crossed his mind, and a momentary silence resounded throughout the regent's drawing room.

"It would seem to me, Hanpeita," Toyo now condescendingly referred to the sword master by his given name, "that you have disregarded Tosa policy altogether." He continued reading aloud from the manifesto, handling the document by the tips of his fingers as if it were something filthy with which he did not want to dirty his hands: "*We swear by our deities that if the Imperial Banner is once raised we will go through fire and water to ease the Emperor's mind, to carry out the will of our former daimyo, and to purge this evil from our people.*'"

Toyo stopped reading, then threw the document on the floor. "In other words, Hanpeita, you totally disregard the Shogun to whom the Yamanouchi owe their very existence as ruler of our great domain. And in the same breath you have the audacity to pledge to carry out the will of Lord Yodo. That's not only a lie and a blatant contradiction, but it's also a complete insult to our *daimyo*. If I showed this to him, he'd have you cut open your belly." Toyo paused, drew his forefinger slowly across his neck, and added with sardonic laughter, "If he didn't have your head first."

*   *   *

"He's our only obstacle," Hanpeita uncharacteristically sighed, after relaying to Ryoma and his favorite disciple, Nakaoka Shintaro, the contents of his conversation with Yoshida Toyo. The recollection of having been made a fool of by the arrogant regent left the proud sword master with a bitter taste in his mouth and an ache in his gut that longed for revenge. Equally troubling him was the prospect of losing face among his Choshu and Satsuma allies for his failure to fulfill his pledge to unite Tosa under the banner of *Toppling the Bakufu and Imperial Loyalism.*

"Hanpeita, I've received official permission to leave Tosa for a month,' Ryoma said. Although ostensibly Ryoma's impending tour was for the purpose of observing fencing academies around western Japan, his actual intent was to gather information for Hanpeita on the political atmosphere in Choshu, particularly the development of Loyalist activities there.

"When do you leave?" Hanpeita asked.

"Tomorrow."

"I want you to deliver this message to Kusaka Genzui when you get to Hagi Castletown." Hanpeita reached into his desk for a letter he had written to the leader of the Choshu rebels. The short message explained the futility of attempting to convince the Tosa administration to stand up against Edo for *Imperial Loyalism.* Hanpeita had finally come to the realization that trying to convince the stubborn Tosa regent would be impossible. Force, reasoned the rebel leader, was the only alternative.

Hanpeita continued speaking to Ryoma and Shintaro in an icy tone: "I have decided to deal with Toyo the only way I can."

"How's that?" Ryoma asked, glancing at Shintaro.

"With this," Hanpeita replied firmly, drawing his long blade from its scabbard.

"Zuizan-sensei," Shintaro blurted, "Let me cut him."

"No," Hanpeita said, then turning to Ryoma asked, "What do you think about my decision?"

Ryoma shrugged, then said, "If killing Yoshida Toyo would mean that Tosa would unite against the Bakufu, I'd do it for you. But I don't believe that he is the only one in this rotten *han* who is against us. Even with Toyo eliminated, you would still have one more player to contend with," Ryoma scoffed. "Are you also prepared to cut down Lord Yodo himself? Because uniting Tosa against the Tokugawa, would be nothing short of a *coup d'etat,* and that's exactly what you'd have to do."

"Ryoma, are you with me or against me?" Hanpeita asked, evading the question which was out of the question.

"You know I'm with you. I just can't condone killing Toyo, or anybody else for that matter, without proper reason."

"Ryoma," Hanpeita roared, "you don't seem to understand. With Lord Yodo under house arrest in Edo, Toyo is the only person standing in our way. He must be eliminated."

"Hanpeita, I think we should get out of this rotten *han*. But if you insist upon working within its bounds, do me one favor."

"What's that?"

"Wait until I get back from Choshu. Wait and hear what the Choshu men have to say before you do anything drastic."

Choshu Han

While Ryoma would travel to Choshu as an envoy of the Tosa Loyalist Party, his mind had already taken a turn toward a less defined but exceedingly more stimulating course of action. He had grown despondent of Tosa, and longed to be rid of the bonds of feudalism–so much so, in fact, that he had recently made up his mind to flee his han. Although he had not yet informed even his closest friends, the "Dragon-Steed" had chosen to bolt, to abandon his han, and in so doing, forfeit home, family and security. He would become a ronin, a lordless samurai, an outlaw. "A samurai receiving a stipend from his lord," Ryoma was apt to say, "is like a bird being kept in a cage. If I don't feel in my heart that something is right, I get rid of it like I would an old cage." The old cage, to Ryoma, was his native Tosa.

Ryoma's ideals notwithstanding, the crime of fleeing one's han was among the most serious a samurai could commit, as becoming a ronin was tantamount to forsaking one's feudal lord. But it was an integral part of the unwritten code of the samurai that once a man had decided upon a goal, he must be ready to sacrifice his life in order to fulfill that goal. For Ryoma the goal was clear: building a modern navy and overthrowing the Tokugawa Bakufu. Only the means remained an enigma.

On January 15, 1862, just one day after Ryoma had reached Hagi Castletown in Choshu, Tokugawa Councilor Ando Nobumasa was attacked as he was about to pass through Sakashita Gate, one of the main entryways into Edo Castle. Not only was Ando the mastermind behind the plan to marry the Emperor's sister to the Shogun, but it was rumored that he was also behind a scheme to dethrone the xenophobic Emperor Komei and replace him with a Tokugawa puppet. Such sacrilege was too much for the Loyalists to endure; and although Ando survived the attack, his wounds were sufficient to force him to retire from his post soon after.

On the afternoon of the same day that the Sakashita Gate Incident had sent shock waves throughout the Shogun's capital, a lone *ronin* called at Choshu headquarters in Edo, looking for Katsura Kogoro.

While there had been no Choshu men directly involved in the assassination attempt, the unexpected visitor, a Mito man by the name of Kawabe, was fully aware that Katsura had known in advance of the secret plot. Although Kawabe had been included in the assassination squad, he had arrived late on the scene, only to discover from a distance that the attempt had failed and his six comrades had been cut down on the spot. "I've come with an urgent message for Katsura-san," the nerve-shattered *ronin* told a group of Choshu samurai at the outer gate of the headquarters.

Although the cunning Katsura had instructed the guards to send away the unwelcome visitor, Kawabe was adamant in his insistence on speaking with the influential Choshu official. Katsura's reluctance to meet with the *ronin* from Mito was only natural: he wanted at all costs to avoid dangerous suspicion that he, or any other Choshu man, was in any way involved in the assassination attempt earlier in the day. "Why doesn't he just go away and send me his message if it's so damned important?" Katsura thought irritably to himself.

But Kawabe, who had introduced himself with an alias, refused to leave until he could speak with Katsura. Convinced that the desperate man would not leave without being granted a meeting, Katsura had him brought to an empty hall located in the headquarters compound. Katsura was seated cross-legged on the polished dark wooden floor of the high-ceilinged hall when Kawabe appeared at the doorway. There were no furniture or fixtures in this room, which was as cold as the icy air outside.

"You must be Katsura-san," Kawabe said nervously. Although this was the first time the two had met, Kawabe had heard of Katsura's great fencing skills, and more recently the influence he wielded among the Choshu Loyalists. "I've come here today with a request of the utmost importance."

"Please keep your voice down." Katsura spoke calmly, without bothering to stand up. "Come, sit down, Kawabe-san," he whispered. Although the Mito *ronin* had not yet given his real name, Katsura had seen the list of names of the six men who had been cut down. And having been well-informed of the assassination plot, he also knew that there was one man, by the name he had just uttered, whose body had not been among the dead.

Kawabe entered the hall and sat down on the cold wooden floor, facing Katsura. "What is it?" the Choshu man asked in a soft, calm voice, only his eyes betraying his contempt for the unwelcome visitor.

"Please allow me to cut open my belly right here in this hall," Kawabe said, his voice trembling.

More than being amazed at the awesome request, Katsura was angered at Kawabe's lack of concern for the welfare of Choshu Han.

If it was to become known to the Tokugawa authorities that Katsura Kogoro had anything at all to do with the abortive assassination plot, not only would his own life be in danger, but Choshu itself could very well be subject to severe punishment. In short, for a man who was known to be directly involved in the assassination plot to visit, in broad daylight, one of the leading disciples of Choshu's martyred revolutionary teacher, Yoshida Shoin, at Choshu's official headquarters in Edo, was nothing short of insanity. Furthermore, Kawabe's concern for the welfare of his own *han* was limitless. His reason for fleeing Mito and becoming an outlaw was, unlike Ryoma's decision, out of loyalty to his *han*; by defecting, Kawabe and other Mito extremists could be certain that the Lord of Mito and his family would not be subject to punishment in connection with the Ando attack and their other subversive activities.

"Doesn't this idiot realize that if he kills himself here after so blatantly insisting on seeing me, that Choshu heads could very well roll?" Katsura thought to himself, as he stared hard at the very troubled man before him.

"I arrived too late to Sakashita Gate this morning," Kawabe continued in the same trembling voice. Then, reaching into his kimono, he produced a folded document. "This is the written vindication of the assassination." Kawabe handed the document to Katsura.

Titled *The Vindication of Men of High Purpose*, it began by stating that the traitorous plotting of Ando was even more blasphemous than that of Ii Naosuke, who had already paid for his crimes with his life. It likened the proposed marriage between the Emperor's sister and the Shogun to kidnapping the Princess from the Imperial Household. It denounced the *"Bakufu's secret scheming to dethrone Emperor Komei in case his Sacred Presence should not concede to shogunal demands."* But as the Lord of Mito was directly related to the Shogun, the Mito men clearly stated that they harbored no anti-Bakufu sentiment, but rather that the blame for the recent crimes rested entirely on the shoulders of the *"evil Councilor Ando Nobumasa."*

It was with this last point that Katsura completely disagreed. Like their counterparts in Tosa, the Choshu Loyalists clearly opposed the Bakufu. As a preliminary step for strengthening Japan in order to expel the foreigners, the Choshu and Tosa extremists insisted that it would be necessary to topple the *"treacherous and decrepit Bakufu."*

"Each of the six men involved in the attack," Kawabe said, "was expected to be carrying a copy of the vindication. But the Bakufu police apparently confiscated the copies from the bodies of the six. This is why I've come here. For the sake of Japan, I implore you to get this last remaining copy into the public eye."

Katsura, knowing well that he could not refuse the request, simply nodded.

"Thank you," Kawabe said, obviously relieved. "Now that I've accomplished my purpose, I will be able to follow my brave comrades into death with peace of mind." The Mito man's voice was calm now. "Would you do me the honor of serving as my second?" he asked, untying his sash and exposing his belly.

"Wait!" Katsura hissed. If Kawabe should commit *seppuku* right in front of him, he reasoned, there was no telling what the consequences might be. "There's no reason to be in a hurry to die. There is still an endless amount of work that needs to be done, and we need all the support we can get, especially from such dedicated men as yourself."

But no matter how hard Katsura tried to stop him, Kawabe remained determined to cut open his belly right there on the spot.

"How about some *sake*?" Katsura suggested. "As a farewell salute to this world."

"*Sake*?" Kawabe's eyes lit up. "A farewell salute," he repeated in a crazed tone. "Yes, that would be fine."

Relieved, Katsura stood up immediately, and left Kawabe alone just long enough to order *sake* to be brought into the hall before the deranged man could do anything drastic. As Katsura hurried through the dark wooden corridor which surrounded the building, a voice called from behind. "Katsura-san, is something wrong?" This was Ito Shunsuke, who, despite his humble lineage as the son of a samurai's attendant, had risen to official rank due to his reputation as a leading disciple of the late Yoshida Shoin. During the years that Ito, Katsura, Kusaka and Takasugi had studied at Shoin's private academy in Hagi Castletown, the great revolutionary teacher had praised Ito's keen ability of persuasion, and expressed his expectations for Ito's future as a politician. Shoin's predictions would prove correct a quarter of a century later when Ito would become the first prime minister of Japan. Now, at age twenty-one, Ito had recently been appointed Katsura's assistant at Choshu's official headquarters in Edo.

"Ito!" Katsura said. "Am I glad to see you!" After explaining the problem awaiting him in the hall, but being careful not to incriminate his assistant by making him privy of his previous knowledge of the assassination plot, Katsura asked Ito to try to persuade the Mito *ronin* to abandon his resolve to die. "I can't seem to convince him not to do it here, but maybe you can," he said. This was Katsura's sole worry. Whether or not Kawabe disemboweled himself was not a matter of great concern to the crafty Loyalist leader, who thus far had been able to avoid any suspicion for his role in the assassination plot.

Without further delay, Ito brought a flask of *sake* and two drinking cups into the hall, where he found Kawabe waiting silently. The future orator began speaking in the same convincing manner that would one day win him the top post in the Japanese government, but he could not persuade Kawabe to abandon his resolve to commit *seppuku*. Finally, Ito excused himself to report back to Katsura, who was anxiously waiting in a room at the other end of the corridor. "I'm not sure what he'll do," Ito said, "but he seems to be content drinking for the time..." As Ito was speaking, a loud scream of crazed ecstasy came from the other end of the building. "Wonderful! Wonderful!" the voice cried out.

"He must be drunk," Katsura said. "Let's go take a look."

Katsura and Ito hurried to the hall, where they found the Mito man keeled over on the cold wooden floor, writhing in a pool of blood. The two Choshu men stood at the entranceway momentarily dumbfounded, as Kawabe released a final gasp, and ceased to be.

The ronin from Mito had taken his life in perfect samurai manner. Even after slicing open his belly below the navel horizontally with his short sword, he had the self-control to readjust his grip on the hilt and pierce the right side of his throat, slashing all the way across to the left side of his neck. And then, in true samurai spirit, he let his body fall forward as his life gushed forth in red spurts. The dead man's right hand still tightly gripped the bloody hilt, while his left hand, extended in front of him, was clenched in a fist of agony. Such was the position of the body when Katsura and Ito found it.

"I'll have to report this to the magistrate's office," Katsura groaned.

"Couldn't we just bury the body without reporting it?" Ito asked lamely.

"If Kawabe hadn't come here in broad daylight, that might be possible. But since he was undoubtedly seen coming here, we must report it."

"But, Katsura-san, if we report this to the magistrate there will be a lot of questioning, and there's no telling where that might lead. The magistrate might even suspect that you were involved in the attack on Ando." Although Ito was unaware of Katsura's involvement in the plot, he had ample reason to worry for his safety: their martyred teacher had been executed by the Bakufu for treason two years previously.

"I think it would be best to report it right away," Katsura said. "If we do that, they'll be less apt to suspect that Choshu men were involved in any way."

That afternoon, Katsura and Ito reported the suicide to the magistrate in Edo, explaining that they neither knew Kawabe, nor why he had killed himself at Choshu headquarters. "I was out when it happened," Katsura lied. "I returned just after the incident." As Ito was ignorant of Katsura's involvement in the assassination plot, it was easy for him to support his superior's alibi. And as it was true that Katsura had never met Kawabe before, the magistrate had no evidence whatsoever against the Choshu men.

But further problems awaited Katsura upon his return to the Choshu estate that evening. A high-ranking Choshu official, Nagai Uta, opposed the ideas of Katsura and the rest of the radical Choshu Loyalists. Nagai had recently persuaded the Lord of Choshu to endorse what he termed a *Farsighted Plan for Navigation*, which was no more than the advocation of a *Union of Court and Camp*. Nagai's plan was to strengthen the Choshu position among both the court and the Bakufu by acting as arbiter to realize a union. Nagai was the archenemy of the disciples of Yoshida Shoin, who, in accordance with their secret agreement with Takechi Hanpeita, had been struggling to unite their *han* behind *Toppling the Bakufu and Imperial Loyalism*. During the previous summer, while Kusaka Genzui was planning the assassination of Ando by his own hand, Takasugi Shinsaku had been raring to cut down Nagai. Although Nagai did not know, it had been Katsura who saved his life by convincing both of these extremists that the time had not yet come for such drastic measures.

"So, Katsura," Nagai said to his nemesis, "are you sure you didn't have anything to do with the nasty business of today?"

Katsura's eyes flashed. "I don't know what you're talking about," he said coldly. "It's already been determined by the office of the magistrate that I had nothing to do with the incident."

"Is that so?" Nagai scoffed, as if he were able to read Katsura's mind. "It's common knowledge that you were one of Yoshida Shoin's favorite students. But I'll tell you what, Katsura. Just to make sure that there are no bothersome follow-up procedures, why don't I just put in a word or two with..." he paused to let Katsura wriggle on these last words. Although Nagai was shrewd, Katsura, who was even shrewder, remained calm. "I could always put a word in with, you know," Nagai continued, a complacent smile challenging Katsura's uncanny ability to remain cool, "the magistrate himself." As Nagai was the Choshu representative in charge of arbitrating to unite the court with the Bakufu, he was confident of his ability to call off any subsequent investigation of the Kawabe incident.

Katsura quickly saw through Nagai's strategy. He understood the goals of his political enemy. Nagai, of course, knew that Katsura was one of the leaders of the Choshu radicals. With Katsura in his present dangerous position, Nagai reasoned that he could certainly be persuaded to alter his political stance. Surely, Nagai assumed, Katsura would be willing to compromise his ideals to save his own neck.

But Katsura was crafty. "Nagai-san," he said, "anything you can do to fix things would be appreciated."

"Then if I pay the magistrate a visit, I can expect some cooperation on your part?" Nagai confirmed.

"Cooperation?" Katsura smiled sardonically. "Of course! You're a minister to Lord Mori, and I'm prepared to do anything for our *daimyo* and for Choshu Han."

The magistrate's investigation ended with light reprimands concerning Kawabe's suicide being handed down to Katsura and Ito. This was, of course, due to the close attention that Nagai had given the proceedings, fully expecting Katsura to cooperate in the promotion of his *Farsighted Plan for Navigation.*

Nagai, however, had badly misjudged Katsura's true intentions. Once he was entirely free of the worry of Bakufu harassment, Katsura, with Ito's help, produced numerous copies of the assassins' letter of vindication, and dispersed them among xenophobic sympathizers in Edo. Katsura's plan worked, and it wasn't long before the attack on Ando stirred the spirits of townspeople and samurai alike. The would-be assassins' claim that the Bakufu had planned the dethronement of Emperor Komei was particularly effective in arousing anti-Bakufu sentiment. In fact, when word of this eventually reached the Emperor, it did much to shatter any hopes among the Edo regime of achieving a union with the court in Kyoto.

*   *   *

Ryoma walked nearly a day and a half along a winding road that followed a swollen river flowing to the Inland Sea through the green mountains of Choshu. He finally reached a valley covered with rice fields, brown in the dead of winter, and dotted with the thatched hous- es of peasants who tended the fields to feed the samurai who populat- ed the nearby castletown. From here, Ryoma continued his steady pace toward Hagi, despite his tired feet and the cold wind which burnt his parched face. Finally, he caught sight of the main keep of Hagi Castle towering in the distance, five black-tiled tiers sweeping out from white earthen walls. Ryoma squinted to get a clearer view of the imposing edifice, built atop a perfectly symmetrical stone foundation, and surrounded on three sides by a deep moat. To the immediate north of the castle was a great wooded rock, which was more of a hill than a mountain, but served as ideal protection from possible attack from the Sea of Japan just below.

Ryoma walked anxiously through the town, just south of the castle, the streets lined with samurai houses fronted by high white earthen walls topped with black tiles. He stopped at one such house, the home of Kusaka Genzui, and without hesitation passed through the high wooden front gate. The sides of the two-storied house were of dark wood and white clay, the roof of black tiles. A young woman, Kusaka's wife, greeted Ryoma at the doorway. "So, this is the sister of the famous Yoshida Shoin," Ryoma thought to himself, impressed with her intelligent face. As Kusaka was not home, but expected back shortly, the woman invited Ryoma inside to wait. Soon Kusaka returned to find Ryoma sitting in his living room, near a glowing bra- zier, sipping hot *sake*.

"Welcome," the Choshu man said with a bow. "I've heard a lot about you from Zuizan-sensei."

Ryoma did not bother to stand up. "Cold outside, isn't it," he said. Ryoma's nonchalance confused Kusaka. Was not this the former head of the Chiba Dojo, the man who had once defeated Katsura Kogoro in a fencing match, and the right-hand man of Master Zuizan? Ryoma grinned, and produced a folded document from the breast of his kimono. "I've brought a letter to you from Takechi Hanpeita," he said.

Kusaka sat down and read the letter, in which Hanpeita had explained his loss of hope of convincing the Tosa regent to unite Tosa behind *Toppling the Bakufu and Imperial Loyalism*. Kusaka threw the letter down in disgust. "We are having similar difficulties in Choshu," he began feverishly. "There is a filthy traitor among us by the name of Nagai Uta, who has wriggled his way into power and tricked our *daimyo* into supporting the drive for a *Union of Court and Camp*."

Unlike his colleague Katsura Kogoro, Kusaka was unaware of the Ando assassination planned for the following day in Edo. Had he known of the plot, he may have been more hopeful about achieving the goals he and the other Choshu Loyalists had been striving for since the previous summer. "If Choshu continues on its present course," Kusaka said bitterly, a fiery look in his eyes, "before we know it, our *han* will become another Tokugawa lackey. The Satsuma men are also having problems convincing their *daimyo* to support us. Lord Hisamitsu, who is the father of the Satsuma *daimyo*, has taken control of the Satsuma government. He has apparently been successful at suppressing the Satsuma Loyalists. Our original plan for a triple alliance between Tosa, Satsuma and Choshu no longer seems feasible." Kusaka's eyes flashed into Ryoma's, as he added: "Please tell Zuizan-sensei that I don't think his plan has a chance."

The plan to which Kusaka referred was Hanpeita's scheme to unite the three powerful southwestern fiefdoms of Tosa, Satsuma and Choshu, march with their combined armies into Kyoto, where they would embrace the Emperor. The Loyalist forces would then topple the Edo regime and set up a new Imperial government in the ancient capital.

"The scoundrel Nagai is ruining Choshu," Kusaka said. "He has steered Choshu policy toward supporting the Bakufu."

"There is a similar situation in Tosa, with Regent Yoshida Toyo," Ryoma said. "But I don't care anymore."

"You don't care?" Kusaka repeated in disbelief. "What do you mean?"

"I've given up on Tosa. *Men of High Purpose* throughout Japan are going to have to join forces if we are to overthrow the Bakufu and save the nation from foreign invasion," Ryoma said, pounding his fist on the floor. "We can't rely on the court nobles or the feudal lords. We have nothing but our own brains, blood and guts."

Kusaka's eyes opened wide as he leaned forward. "You speak my thoughts," he said, clapping his hands loudly. Then, in a whisper, "I should cut Nagai."

It was Nagai's intention to save the ailing Bakufu by keeping Japan open to foreign trade, and in so doing import Western technology and culture. In this way he hoped to build modern ships by which to strengthen the nation militarily and expand Japan's economy. Nagai reasoned that this was the only way to avoid the catastrophe of foreign subjugation which had brought China and India to their knees.

Nagai's ideas did not greatly differ from those secretly harbored by Sakamoto Ryoma, as he sat drinking *sake* with the xenophobic Choshu extremist. In fact, Ryoma differed with Nagai on only one basic point: Ryoma was staunchly anti-Tokugawa. He felt that the Bakufu itself represented the greatest obstacle to the democratization of Japan. He desired nothing less than to topple the 250-year-old hegemony, create a modern navy to reach out beyond the shores of the island nation to the rest of the world, and in so doing, steer Japan into the modern age of which Kawada Shoryo had often spoken.

"We must rid our sacred land of the foreign stench," Kusaka said, "and to do so, we must destroy the Bakufu." Like Takechi Hanpeita, Kusaka was chronic in his hatred of things Western, which personified evil in the minds of the Imperial Loyalists. But unlike Hanpeita, whose Imperial fanaticism was religious, Kusaka's ideas were based on logic: unless Japan could expel the foreigners, it would surely suffer a fate similar to China and India.

Ryoma, however, knew in his heart of hearts that exclusionism was no longer possible. This is not to say that he had abandoned his antiforeign sentiments, but rather, he had taken a giant leap forward, beyond his comrades. Ryoma's vision did not stop at simply overthrowing the Bakufu; he desired more than anything the abolishment of the entire feudal system which maintained the existence of hundreds of individual *han*. He was aware of the necessity of uniting Japan into one nation, with a centralized government in Kyoto which would represent all of the *han*. His views of the Emperor possessed nothing of the religious fervor of Hanpeita and other xenophobic Loyalists. To Ryoma, the Imperial Court was no more than a means to an end to be utilized for the good of the nation, for the benefit of the Japanese people. For the time being, however, he wisely chose to keep these views to himself.

Ryoma spent the night at an inn in the castletown. Early the next morning a young samurai came to escort the celebrated Tosa swordsman to the official martial arts training hall of Choshu. "Sakamotosensei, we've all been waiting to see a demonstration of your excellent swordsmanship," Kusaka's messenger said. Ryoma's reputation was still that of the distinguished former head of the Chiba Dojo. There was not a swordsman in all of Hagi Castletown who was not aware that Ryoma had defeated the esteemed Katsura Kogoro in a fencing match several years before.

When Ryoma arrived at the training hall, Kusaka was waiting for him with a group of some forty anxious young men, all sitting on the polished wooden floor. Rather than being flattered by the respect that the Choshu men showed for his swordsmanship, Ryoma was inwardly annoyed. He had not come to Choshu as a mere swordsman, but as the messenger of the leader of the Tosa Loyalist Party. Moreover, he had already made up his mind to abandon Tosa, and was dedicated to nothing less than saving the entire Japanese nation. "Kusaka-san, I'm afraid you expect too much," he said, scratching the back of his neck with his left hand, his right hand tucked into his kimono. Several bundles of straw, each about three feet high, had been lined up along one side of the training hall. Much to Ryoma's chagrin, he was invited to display his technique by cutting through a bundle of straw.

"I'll go first," shouted one of the younger Choshu men, who jumped up and walked over to one of the bundles. The younger man drew his sword and proceeded to hack through the bundle of straw, butchering it in the process. Another young man jumped up, drew his sword and sliced another bundle in half, though his blade left a gash on the wooden floor. A third man cut through another bundle, but in his lack of control sliced open his own foot.

While Ryoma had indeed become a *Man of High Purpose* in his own right, he was nevertheless an expert swordsman. Unable to stand by and watch these younger men perform their low-level techniques, he calmly walked up to one of the straw bundles and called the attention of all present. "This is how you cut an inanimate object," he announced. The next instant Ryoma drew his sword with his right hand, and with a silver-blue flash, returned the blade to its scabbard before the severed bundle of straw fell to the floor.

The entire hall was silent. "Sakamoto-sensei," Kusaka broke the quiet, "would you please do us the honor of sparring with a few of our men?"

Unable to refuse, and much to his own dismay, Ryoma again found himself yielding to the wishes of his host. Ryoma's first opponent was a boy of no more than sixteen, who charged the celebrated swordsman, and to his own surprise, not to mention the astonishment of all present, scored an easy "kill." With the two following matches ending much the same way, Ryoma's final opponent took it upon himself to complain. "Sakamoto-sensei, please don't make fun of us. You must fight seriously."

Ryoma laughed, tossed his bamboo sword across the room, and raised his hands above his head. "I lost because I'm weak," he declared indifferently. It was at this moment that Kusaka recognized Ryoma as not just another expert swordsman, but a *Man of High Purpose* of a truly unique character.

On the night before Ryoma was to leave Hagi Castletown, Kusaka delivered a letter to him. "This is for Zuizan-sensei," he said. "But I'd like you to read it."

"Ultimately," Kusaka's letter began, *"it isn't enough for us to rely on our lords, and it isn't enough for us to rely on the court nobles. It is our opinion that we have no alternative but to assemble our rank and file and rise up in a righteous revolt. Forgive me for saying this, but even if your han and our han should be destroyed, it would not matter so long as our cause is just."* Profane words! Throughout the past two and a half centuries the idea of a samurai allowing his *han* to perish was blasphemy, but Sakamoto Ryoma cherished the thought.

"Kusaka-san," Ryoma said, grabbing the Choshu man firmly by the wrist, "we must abandon our *han* and fight for Japan. The Japanese nation is the only thing worth fighting for." A single teardrop trickled down the twisted face of the Dragon, who was now more determined than ever to achieve his goal.

*　　　　　　*　　　　　　*

From Hagi Ryoma traveled east to Osaka, where he came across a particularly interesting piece of information which would not only have a profound effect on his own life, but also on the history of Japan. Word had it that Shimazu Hisamitsu, the father of the Satsuma *daimyo* and *de facto* lord of the second largest fiefdom in Japan, was planning to lead an army of over 1,000 troops into Kyoto to embrace the Emperor in an unprecedented display of military strength in order to "correct the Bakufu's renegade policies" concerning foreign demands. As Choshu and Satsuma had long been bitter rivals, however, the Choshu Loyalists were suspicious of Lord Hisamitsu's true intentions. Never before in two-and-a-half centuries of Tokugawa rule had a *daimyo* escorted an army into the Imperial capital. Satsuma, Choshu suspected, planned to embrace the Emperor at the exclusion of the rest of the feudal domains, and set up an Imperial government by which the Lord of Satsuma would become the Shogun of a new "Satsuma Bakufu" in Kyoto.

Upon returning to Kochi in late February, Ryoma reported directly to the home of Takechi Hanpeita.

"Ryoma!' Hanpeita exclaimed, standing up from his desk to greet him.

"I've brought you a letter from Kusaka Genzui. You should forget about your plans for an alliance. As Kusaka has written, the Choshu Loyalists have given up hope in their *han*. The conservative Bakufu sympathizers in Hagi have gotten a firm hold on the government, and the Loyalists can't do a thing in Choshu. Kusaka himself has told me that he is going to flee Choshu, and bring the fight for the national cause to Kyoto. Forget about this rotten *han*, Hanpeita. If we hope to ever accomplish anything, we must leave Tosa and join forces with other *Men of High Purpose* throughout Japan." Ryoma slammed his fist on Hanpeita's desk, as a cold draft penetrated the thin walls of the house. Ryoma collected his thoughts, then relayed to the Shield of the Emperor the report of the impending *coup d'etat* in Kyoto.

Hanpeita read Kusaka's letter, went to the opposite side of the room, and picked up his long sword from a wooden rack in the alcove. Drawing the blade, he solemnly proclaimed, "I am left with no choice but to cut him down."

"Cut who down?" Ryoma started.

"The regent. Time is running out, as Kusaka has indicated in his letter. We must eliminate Yoshida Toyo soon if we are to unite Tosa behind *Toppling the Bakufu and Imperial Loyalism*. Once that is accomplished, the *Men of High Purpose* in Choshu will realize that if we can succeed, so can they. But timing is of the essence. We must remain levelheaded and plan things carefully before we act."

"Hanpeita," Ryoma shouted, again slamming his fist on the desk. "You use the term *Men of High Purpose* too lightly. Don't you realize that we *Men of High Purpose* must band together on our own if we are to save the nation? Forget about Tosa, and give up your stubborn ideas about this rotten *han*. They're futile. Like I've told you before, even if you kill the regent, you're not going to be able to do a thing unless you're willing to cut down Lord Yodo as well. Because you know as well as I do that Yamanouchi Yodo will never take up arms against the Tokugawa."

"Ryoma, it's an outrage to talk of Lord Yodo disrespectfully," Hanpeita reprimanded, slamming his sword blade back into the scabbard.

"There are some things that we just can't agree on," Ryoma groaned. "Don't tell me that you actually care about the *daimyo*, because I don't think there is a lower-samurai in all of Tosa who considers him with any more reverence than they do a freshly laid fart."

"Ryoma," Hanpeita roared, "that's enough disrespect. Now, are you with me or against me?"

"If you're willing to cut down the *daimyo* first, I'll kill Toyo myself. Otherwise, forget it. I just can't condone killing a man for no reason at all. And if you cut down the regent without killing Lord Yodo, it will be meaningless bloodshed."

"Ryoma," Hanpeita roared again, "I'm not asking you to cut anyone. I already have my pawns carefully chosen," he said through steely eyes. "Now, I must know: are you with me or against me?"

"Hanpeita, I can't believe what you're saying. Not only are you planning to kill a man, but you're going to use your own men as pawns in the bloody business. I'm with you, Hanpeita, but I won't have anything to do with killing Toyo."

"Then you're against me," Hanpeita concluded bitterly.

"No, I'm not against you, Hanpeita. But I've decided to leave Tosa," Ryoma suddenly disclosed his long-kept secret.

"Leave? But you just returned."

"I mean I've decided to flee Tosa. I won't return until things have changed," Ryoma declared, then after a short pause, "if I ever return at all. Things are starting to take shape, Hanpeita. They say that Satsuma is beginning to move. If we don't start now, it will be too late. How can you insist on wasting your time in Tosa? There is absolutely nothing you can do here. The action is in Kyoto and Edo, and that's where we belong."

"Then that's all the more reason for us to get organized," Hanpeita insisted, stroking his long chin. "We can't let the Satsuma men get the edge on us. We Tosa men must work quickly if we are to play a leading role in the drama that is unfolding before us."

"Forget about Tosa," Ryoma hollered indignantly. "The Yamanouchi are different from the Mori and the Shimazu. The Yamanouchi will never agree to oppose the Tokugawa."

"What will you do after you leave Tosa?" Hanpeita asked. "Even if you go to Kyoto, what will you do there? When will you realize that working together as one great *han* is the only way to produce positive results? What are you going to do as a *ronin*, an outlaw, a fugitive? Even if you are able to organize an army of five hundred *ronin*, what could you do? But if we had a whole *han* dedicated to overthrowing the Bakufu, then things would start to materialize. Think about it. We must not act rashly. We must plan everything out, step by step. That's the only way." Unlike the fiery Kusaka, Hanpeita's idea of revolution was based on calm, deliberate action, free of dangerous risk which might result in sudden downfall.

"Like Kusaka says," Ryoma hollered in exasperation, "we have to get started before the battle starts. We have to get ready, and Tosa is just not the place to do it. The lower-samurai can't do a thing in this rotten *han*. We have to go to Kyoto if we are to be of any use at all."

"That's where you're wrong, Ryoma. I've been talking to a few of the most powerful men in Tosa, men who are bitterly opposed to the regent. I've gotten their support. Once Toyo is eliminated, we'll have a direct hand in the government, if not officially, then actually."

Shortly after resuming power as regent, Yoshida Toyo forced into retirement the conservatives who had thus far been in charge of Tosa affairs, replacing them with his own progressive band of young disciples. Needless to say, the fallen old guard despised the ruthless regent; in order to eliminate him they were even willing to cooperate with Hanpeita's illegal Loyalist Party, made up almost entirely of lower-samurai.

"Hanpeita," Ryoma said angrily, "how could you even consider joining forces with the upper-samurai?"

"It's just a means to an end," Hanpeita said coolly, then asked, "When will you leave?"

"Soon."

"Then you won't at least stay long enough to help us cut Toyo?"

"Hanpeita," Ryoma groaned, "there's just no getting through to you. You're just as rigid as ever, and I guess you'll never change."

"One way or another," Hanpeita said, "I swear to you I will succeed in uniting Tosa under the banner of *Imperial Loyalism*. But to do so, I must eliminate Yoshida Toyo."

Part II

Flight of the Dragon

FLIGHT OF THE DRAGON

The Clean Emptiness of Freedom

After seeing with his own eyes the situation in Choshu, after hearing with his own ears the report of an impending coup d'etat in Kyoto, after feeling with his own heart repugnance for Hanpeita's cold-blooded plans, and after the long years of waiting to act, the Dragon finally decided the only choice left him was to flee the confines of Tosa for the wide open arena of Japan, and join other Men of High Purpose in the struggle to overthrow the Bakufu. More than loyalty to family and friends, more than dedication to kendo practice, and more than his blood oath to the Tosa Loyalist Party, the destruction of the Bakufu had taken absolute precedence in the mind of the twenty-six-year-old samurai. Though his friends and family may consider his actions drastic, Ryoma reasoned abandoning Tosa was the only course he could take in his struggle to save the nation.

A few weeks later Ryoma received a message from a fellow Tosa Loyalist by the name of Sawamura Sonojo. Nine year's Ryoma's junior, Sonojo had already fled Tosa, but had returned undercover to report to Hanpeita of the impending *coup d'etat* in Kyoto. In his short note, Sonojo informed Ryoma that the plans were set for hundreds of Loyalists who had recently fled their respective *han* to await the Satsuma *daimyo* at Osaka, and join his army on its march into Kyoto. Here they would embrace the Emperor, and, by so doing, gain the support of *han* throughout Japan to topple the Edo regime. Sonojo concluded his message by indicating that he would wait for Ryoma on the following night under the cover of darkness at Asakura Village, outside the castletown. From here the two could flee Tosa together, to join their comrades in the impending coup in Kyoto.

"I'm going to flee Tosa," Ryoma suddenly informed his elder brother, Gombei, who was sitting in his study. Gombei had become head of the Sakamoto household upon the death of their father, several years before.

"Are you crazy, Ryoma?" Gombei hollered, lunging forward.

"I didn't expect you to be happy about it, but it's the only thing I can do. I have to flee Tosa for the sake of nation."

"The nation!" Gombei screamed. "What about your own family? Are you willing to sacrifice us with your irresponsible behavior?"

"No, but..."

"But what, damn it?" Gombei indignantly scolded. "If you flee

72

Tosa, not only will your immediate family suffer, but the rest of your relatives may very well have a hard time of it as well. You know that our sister Otome's husband is stationed in Edo as the private physician to the retired *daimyo*. If you become a *ronin*, he'll lose his position sooner than you can piss. And worse than that, he'll most likely be put under house arrest. What would Otome do then? Have you even thought about that?"

"No, " Ryoma despondently admitted, as he looked down at his own large feet and shook his head silently.

"Damn it, Ryoma! I won't let you do it," Gombei screamed, before storming out of the room. He raced up the ladder staircase which led to Ryoma's room, where he confiscated both of Ryoma's swords, and left the house with them. Gombei knew that Ryoma would not leave Tosa without his swords.

But Ryoma was determined, and left immediately for Otome's house, in the mountains west of the castletown. "I've come to talk to you," he exclaimed, as he rushed into his sister's house.

"What's happened?" asked Otome, startled.

"I've tried to talk to our brother, but it's useless." After divulging his plans to Otome, Ryoma groaned, "I can't get it through our brother's head that the nation is more important than the Sakamoto household. But I thought that you, of all people, would understand."

Ryoma's respect for Otome was boundless. This sister who had raised him like a mother could, in her childhood, out-ride, out-swim and out-wrestle most of the boys in the neighborhood. Her skill with a sword was known throughout the castletown, and in later years she would become proficient with a pistol.

"So, you're really determined," Otome said, nodding in both admiration and envy, as she filled two cups with hot tea.

"I'm determined, or at least I was determined until I heard from our older brother that your husband would probably lose his position and possibly be put under house arrest."

"Ryoma," Otome struggled to hold back tears, taking firm hold of her brother's hands, "let me worry about that. You've decided to do this great thing for the nation, and I envy you for it. I only wish that I could go with you to join in the fight. But since I was born a woman, I can't. But you're a man. If you truly believe that fleeing Tosa is the right thing to do, then you must do it. I support you entirely."

"But it wouldn't be fair to your husband. My own immediate family is one thing, but I just couldn't let someone else take the blame for me."

"Trust me," Otome implored, squeezing Ryoma's hand to hold back tears. "If you don't do this thing, who will? It's a great and noble cause you are fighting for." She paused momentarily to collect her thoughts. "What does Takechi-san have to say about it?"

"Hanpeita is determined to work within the confines of Tosa, and stake everything on the Loyalist Party."

"And you have to get out of the cramped confines of Tosa, right?"

"You know me better than anyone," Ryoma said, laughing to hide his tears.

"I only ask that you write me once in a while. I'll want to know how you're doing, and what is happening in your life."

"But, I don't think I can do it," Ryoma said glumly.

"You can't do what?"

"I can't let your husband be punished for me."

"Ryoma," Otome looked straight into her brother's eyes, "you don't have to worry about that, because by the time word gets out that you've gone, I won't be living in this house anymore. I'm leaving my husband soon, and returning to our home in the castletown. Once I'm gone, my husband will have nothing to do with it. If this is the least I can do for our nation, then as a samurai woman this is what I must do."

"You can't leave your husband," Ryoma insisted.

As a samurai woman Otome's pride was insurmountable. As a samurai woman she had always resented being married to a man who took no interest in the martial arts. Nor did it help matters that at five feet and nine inches tall, Otome towered over her husband.

"Ryoma," Otome said gently, releasing her grip on her brother's hands, "I've been planning to leave him anyway. And you've given me a reason to do it right away."

"Why?"

"You know me better than anyone, right."

Ryoma nodded silently, staring hard into his sister's eyes.

"Well, then, you know that there is no way I can bear living with a man who can't keep his hands off of other women."

Rid of his guilt concerning his brother-in-law, Ryoma said good-bye to Otome and returned home before nightfall. Although he had made up his mind to meet Sawamura Sonojo on the following night, not only was Ryoma without money, but the expert swordsman was swordless. As an outlaw, Ryoma could not travel without funds, much less a sword, which he may very well need for protection.

Ryoma supposed that he might be able to get a sword from his relatives, the Saitani family. Established as a *sake* brewer in Kochi Castletown in the mid-seventeenth century, the Saitani family, who were also in the business of pawnbroking and money exchange, had amassed a fortune by the time the seventh generational family head purchased samurai status in 1770, left the family business to a younger brother, assumed the surname Sakamoto and moved to the house next door where Ryoma would be born three generations later. As Ryoma had grown up with the Saitani family, he knew that there were a number of swords stored in the warehouse of their pawnbroking business. But when he visited his relatives on the next morning he was disappointed to find that Gombei had already been there the night before. Gombei had brought Ryoma's swords to his relatives' home, and asked that they keep them under lock and key.

"Under no circumstances are you to let Ryoma into the warehouse, give him a sword or lend him money," Gombei had instructed the head of the merchant household who had always treated Ryoma like a son. "He's just told me that he plans to flee Tosa. But without a sword or money, Ryoma isn't going anywhere," Gombei said, trying to ease his mind with forced laughter.

Distressed, distraught and bordering on anger, Ryoma discovered that his relatives next door were not about to become accomplices to his crime. The afternoon had turned into evening, and Ryoma was still without sword or money as he lay in his room, half asleep, watching the sunset through the window and wondering how he would be able to meet Sonojo that same night, when he suddenly heard the sound of light footsteps.

"Ryoma, it's me, Ei," his sister whispered, gently sliding open the door.

In his sullen mood, Ryoma could not help wondering why this sister with whom he rarely spoke would choose this particular moment to visit him. Ei, older than Otome and younger than their eldest sister Chizu, had recently returned to the Sakamoto household after divorcing her husband. Although she had never been close with Ryoma, she had sensed that something was amiss between her two brothers. Inquiring with her relatives next door, she heard about Ryoma's dangerous, but, in her mind, noble intentions. As her relatives informed her of every detail of Ryoma's plan, she was aware that he was without a sword.

"Ah, hello," Ryoma feigned pleasant surprise. "I was just taking a nap," he said with one eye open.

"I've heard about your plan to flee Tosa," Ei whispered, gently closing the sliding screen door behind her.

"You have?" Ryoma said despondently.

"Yes, and I'm proud of you. But, Ryoma," Ei knelt on the floor next to her brother, "are you sure this is what you want to do? Do you know that you can never come home once you flee?"

Sitting upright, Ryoma answered with a dispirited nod.

"And you're prepared to possibly die alone, without family or friends, or even a proper burial?"

Yes," Ryoma said, looking into his sister's eyes. "A man must be willing to sacrifice himself for his beliefs."

"In that case," Ei gently took her brother's hand, "I have a gift for you," she said, then left Ryoma alone and wondering.

Soon Ei returned to Ryoma's room, which was now dim in the evening dusk. "This is for you, my brother. I hope it serves you well, and may you in turn serve yourself and the nation well by it." She knelt next to Ryoma, holding a sword in her hands.

Ryoma accepted the gift, firmly grasped the hilt and slowly drew the polished steel blade from the sheath. The heavy blade glistened blue in the dim light, its edge sharp as a razor's. Two feet and two inches long, it was slightly short for a man of Ryoma's size, who could easily have handled a blade two or three inches longer.

"What a sword," Ryoma exclaimed under his breath, "the length is good," he added, slashing the air in front of him. Ryoma felt more comfortable with a shorter blade for reasons of facility.

"The blade was forged by the master sword smith Yoshiyuki," Ei said with an undertone of subtle, but nevertheless absolutely real, heartrending sadness.

"How did you get a hold of an authentic Yoshiyuki?" Ryoma asked.

"My ex-husband gave it to me as a memento of our marriage," Ei said with downcast eyes.

"Are you sure you want me to have it? It must be very important to you."

"It's much more valuable to you. If this sword can be of use to you and the nation, then I feel that there will be meaning to my life."

"I'm honored to have it," Ryoma said, firmly grabbing his sister by the shoulders. A cold draft blew through the second-story window, and a telltale chill pierced Ryoma's body, as if an omen of lurking tragedy in the heart of one distressed soul.

Wasting no time, Ryoma bid farewell to his sister, quietly descended the ladder staircase, and with his prize sword thrust securely through his sash, he calmly walked out of the front door of his brother's house, prepared never to return. He ran to the home of a relative on the outskirts of the castletown, where he borrowed ten gold coins, then hurried through the darkness to Asakura Village to meet his comrade Sawamura Sonojo.

Had Ryoma been aware of the impending tragedy at his brother's house, he would undoubtedly have denied himself the ecstasy of flight. It wasn't until the following morning that Gombei found Ei dead in her room. She had taken her own life to atone for her crime of aiding Ryoma in his flight. In so doing the unhappy woman had correctly reasoned that the rest of her family would be pardoned for the felony, while at the same time she took bitter pleasure in the knowledge of her small contribution in the struggle to save the nation.

Of Murder and Fratricide

The Dragon had fled, and the intense ecstasy he derived from the clean emptiness of freedom was worth the dread and the danger. Although he had not yet formulated a concrete plan of action, abandoning Tosa was Ryoma's giant leap across the border which had separated him from freedom. The young samurai had chosen to throw himself into a cauldron of political and social chaos, heated by the myriad of raging hostility lurking in the dark to slay the Dragon on his wonderful quest for freedom. Freedom was what Ryoma had longed for, and it was for freedom that he had sacrificed both country and home. The freedom to act, the freedom to think, the freedom to be: these were the ideals that drove him on the thorny road toward salvation, the salvation of Japan.

Okada Izo stormed into Takechi Hanpeita's house one afternoon in late March. At age twenty-four, Izo was one of the most skilled swordsmen at the Zuizan Dojo. He had studied with Hanpeita at the Momonoi Dojo in Edo, where, like his master, he had also achieved senior ranking. Despite his lack of education, Izo's fencing skills were such that Hanpeita had included him on his recent fencing tour through southwestern Japan. Izo, a lower-samurai from the northern outskirts of the castletown, wore a thick black beard which intensified his wild nature.

Hanpeita was now actively plotting the assassination of Yoshida Toyo. "Timing is of the essence," had become his motto, and *Heaven's Revenge*, his battle cry. When Izo arrived, Hanpeita was talking with Nasu Shingo, a student at the Zuizan Dojo and dedicated Tosa Loyalist whom he had chosen to lead a three-man assassination squad. Shingo was the model warrior. At age thirty, he had a muscular, solid build, fierce black eyes, lean face and heavy jawbone. He had a swarthy complexion, and wore his long hair tied in a topknot.

"Sensei," Izo shouted excitedly, "have you heard?"

"Calm down, Izo!" Hanpeita scolded.

"But Ryoma's fled," Izo said. "He's actually done it."

"I know," Hanpeita lied, feigning calmness. "Tosa is no longer big enough for Ryoma." Although Hanpeita was not surprised by the news, he could not help but feel betrayed. "I have faith in Ryoma," Hanpeita said. "He will never commit an act which will shame the name of the Dragon."

Izo and Shingo looked blankly at Hanpeita, whose rhetoric confused them.

"Shingo, we must act soon," Hanpeita said.

"I'm ready to cut Toyo tonight," Shingo said, his eyes open wide.

"If you're going to kill him, I want a hand in it," said Izo.

"Izo, have you ever cut a man before?" Hanpeita asked scathingly.

"No."

"Then how do you know you'd be able to cut Toyo?"

"Trust me, Sensei," Izo declared with an eeriness that was matched by the coldness in Hanpeita's dark eyes.

"Your time will come," Hanpeita assured. "Be patient, and I'll have you inflicting *Heaven's Revenge* on all of our enemies."

"*Heaven's Revenge?*" Izo repeated the phrase. "What do you mean?"

"*Heaven's Revenge*," Hanpeita said, "on all those who stand in the way of our divine cause to restore the rule of the Sacred Empire to the Emperor."

"*Heaven's Revenge*," Izo muttered. "I like the sound."

Hanpeita continued: "Not yet, Izo. Shingo is going to cut Toyo. I don't want you to participate just yet. But your time will come very soon. If all goes as planned, you'll have your chance to inflict *Heaven's Revenge* in the very near future."

*   *   *

A heavy rain fell on the night of April 8, as Nasu Shingo and two others hid in the bushes along the road leading to Kochi Castle. Yoshida Toyo, who had been at the castle giving a lecture on Japanese history to the young *daimyo*, exited through the main gate of the fortress and crossed the drawbridge of the surrounding moat. A lantern-bearer walked before him, a young samurai attendant followed close behind. The hour was late, and Toyo had been drinking. He held a cream-colored umbrella to shield himself from the pouring rain, which had just extinguished the lantern in front of him, when he suddenly found himself surrounded by three sword-wielding samurai and an eternal darkness.

"*Heaven's Revenge!*" Shingo screamed. "This, Toyo, is for your crimes against Tosa." Hanpeita's hit man emitted a bloodcurdling wail, and brought his blade slashing down.

Toyo, himself an accomplished swordsman, deflected the attack with the bamboo shaft of his umbrella, and being only slightly grazed on the left arm, immediately drew his sword. As Shingo and Toyo fought furiously, the other two assailants, who had made short work of the two attendants, returned to help Shingo deliver the deathblow to the regent.

"Scoundrels!" roared Toyo, as one of his assassins attacked from the rear, slicing open his upper body. Toyo fell, and the pelting rain mixed with the regent's warm blood, producing a watery red which covered the ground around him. By Toyo's side lay a crippled umbrella, the creamy-white paper now streaked with mud and covered with a spray of crimson. As Toyo lay dying in the red, wet darkness, Shingo lifted his sword high in the air, brought it crashing down toward the regent's head. At that instant, Toyo gasped and instinctively jerked his head in a spasmodic gesture to avoid the inevitable. Shingo missed his target, and instead struck Toyo on the jaw. Blood sprayed from the dying man's face before Shingo delivered the deathblow, completely severing the head from the mangled body.

With Yoshida Toyo eliminated, Takechi Hanpeita seemed to have finally achieved success in his long-planned coup in Tosa. Shortly after the assassination, all of Toyo's disciples were dismissed from their administrative posts, and replaced with the conservative old guard who had resented the progressive regent's having forced them from office. None of these upper-samurai were unhappy about the murder of their rival, and most were secretly elated. Among them were two powerful Loyalist sympathizers, over whom Hanpeita had come to wield great influence. When these two men were appointed Great Inspectors of Tosa Han, positions which put them in charge of the police force, Master Zuizan's will, though masked it remained, found its way deep into the nerve center of the Tosa government.

Hanpeita delighted in his success at gaining control of the reins of power. Despite his low social status, by manipulating the two Great Inspectors the Loyalist leader believed himself to be in a position to steer Tosa policy on a rapid course toward *Toppling the Bakufu and Imperial Loyalism*, without interference from Toyo's ousted faction. But as the shrewd Loyalist leader congratulated himself on a job well done, the retired *daimyo* was raging in his Edo villa, where he had been under house confinement for the past three years. Yamanouchi Yodo, likened to a tiger by even the most powerful of feudal lords, was not about to sit back passively while a band of lower-samurai renegades assumed control of his own domain.

*   *   *

Loyalists throughout western Japan, stirred by the report that the father of the Satsuma *daimyo* would declare war on the Bakufu, had gathered in and around the Imperial capital. Here they awaited the Satsuma Army, with whom they would join forces to overthrow the Bakufu and restore the Emperor to power. Ryoma, however, no longer thought it feasible that a group of *ronin* would be able to challenge the Bakufu. Nor did he believe that the Satsuma leadership would play into the hands of emotionally-driven radicals, seething for their first opportunity to strike out at the Tokugawa.

Indeed, Satsuma's ultimate goals were similar to those of the Choshu and Tosa conservatives. Rather than plotting to overthrow the Bakufu, the crafty Lord Hisamitsu, who as father of the young *daimyo* was the most powerful man in the second largest feudal domain in Japan, intended simply to enhance his own political standing in national affairs with a display of military power "to correct the renegade policies of the Edo regime," thus assuming the role of great mediator between court and camp.

Meanwhile, the hordes of rebel *ronin* who had been waiting for the arrival of the Satsuma host had no intention of "correcting the Bakufu." These xenophobic extremists, led by prominent Satsuma and Choshu Loyalists, were out for nothing short of Tokugawa blood. They were burning inside with the desire to topple the "traitorous Bakufu which had shamelessly yielded to the barbarians' demands."

Ryoma, however, had an uncanny sense of timing which enabled him to view things from a much wider perspective than most of his comrades. He reasoned that the time for full-fledged revolution had not yet come. The Bakufu had ruled the land for two and a half centuries, and as of yet not one of the 266 *daimyo* dared to even dream of toppling the powerful military government. In fact, about ninety percent of the feudal lords, concerned solely with the welfare of their own clans, were not even aware that revolutionary activities were taking place. Not even the Lords of Choshu, Satsuma and Tosa, from which three *han* the champions of *Toppling the Bakufu and Imperial Loyalism* had emerged, harbored intentions of overthrowing the Tokugawa. Ryoma, however, did. As a means of revolution, he would develop a modern navy, by which he would topple the Tokugawa and fortify Japan against the Western threat. It was for this goal, and this goal alone, that he had fled his native Tosa.

Shortly after fleeing Ryoma began to doubt the wisdom of his original plan to participate in the Loyalists' uprising in Kyoto. His insight was proven correct by a tragedy which was meanwhile unfolding just outside the Imperial Capital.

The radical Loyalists in Kyoto abandoned hope in Satsuma when they realized that Lord Hisamitsu's actual intentions amounted to nothing more than a renewed version of the detested policy of a *Union of Court and Camp*. Among them were twenty Loyalists from Satsuma itself, who were now determined to achieve their goal with or without their lord's support. On April 23 they quit their barracks at Satsuma headquarters in Osaka, packed four small riverboats with guns and ammunition, and traveled up the river northeast to their meeting place just south of Kyoto, the Teradaya inn in Fushimi. Waiting for the Satsuma men to arrive were ten renegade samurai of other clans, who had come to the Teradaya to make the final arrangements for their plans to march into Kyoto, invade the Imperial Palace and assassinate Bakufu supporters who had "infested the court."

Upon reaching his official residence in Kyoto, the *de facto* leader of Satsuma heard that a group of his own samurai planned to take part in the uprising. "Go get them!" Lord Hisamitsu ordered one of his most trusted vassals on the eve of the planned attack. "I don't care about the damned *ronin* who are with them, but I want you to tell all Satsuma men to report here immediately."

"What if they refuse?" asked the samurai.

"Then cut them down on the spot," Lord Hisamitsu roared indignantly. Not to be deceived by his own vassals, he sent nine expert swordsmen who were not only intimate with the rebels, but were themselves devout Loyalists. This was the only possible way, he reasoned, to convince them to abandon their plan, and return to Satsuma headquarters immediately. Hisamitsu, however, was also well aware that the rebels were steadfast in their decision to carry out what they considered "the highest of all duties for the Imperial cause." In short, the Lord of Satsuma knew that since the rebels would not abandon or put off their plans, his vigilantes would be left with no choice but to draw their swords on their comrades. And to make things worse, the commander of the vigilantes, a man by the name of Narahara, was on particularly intimate terms with the leader of the Satsuma rebels, whose name was Arima.

Narahara's vigilantes reached the Teradaya at around midnight. As they approached the inn, Arima's rebels were busy in a second-story room preparing their guns and ammunition for the impending pre-dawn attack. Both rebels and vigilantes shared the same Loyalist ideals, and all of them were prepared to die to achieve them. Nor was this all that Narahara's men were ready to die for, as they prepared for their own deaths before five of them entered the Teradaya, the remaining four waiting anxiously outside.

"I believe there is a Satsuma samurai named Arima upstairs," Narahara said to the innkeeper at the entranceway. "Tell them Narahara is..."

Before he could finish speaking, his friend and foe, Arima, followed by three other Satsuma samurai, came running down the dark wooden staircase from the second floor. "Narahara! What are you doing here? Leave us alone!"

Narahara dropped to his knees at the base of the stairway, and pleaded with his comrade to surrender. "Arima, you must listen to me," he cried. "It's an order from Lord Hisamitsu. Come with us to Satsuma headquarters in Kyoto. Please, Arima, I beg you."

"Narahara," Arima roared defiance, "we've come this far. As I am a samurai I cannot go back on my vow, regardless of our lord's orders. You know that as well as anyone."

"Even if we have orders to kill you if you don't come with us?" Narahara asked pleadingly.

"It makes no difference."

It was at this instant that Narahara knew that he must cut down his friend, or else die. Although there was not a trace of animosity in his heart for this brave warrior, as a Satsuma samurai, and so as a man, Narahara had to obey the orders of his lord. This is not to say that Narahara was not every bit as dedicated to *Imperial Loyalism* as was Arima. In fact, he had even taken his dedication one step further: he was prepared to die at the Teradaya rather than kill his comrades.

But the young samurai standing to his immediate right had grown impatient with deliberation. *Daimyo* orders were *daimyo* orders, he reasoned, and he unlatched the sheath of his sword. "Arima," he hollered, his eyes flashing, "do you absolutely refuse to listen?"

"Impudence!" roared one of Arima's men.

As Narahara and Arima stared coldly at one another, the younger man drew his sword. "*Daimyo* orders," he screamed, as lantern light glistened blue off polished steel, and blood sprayed from the neck of the first victim of the "Fratricide at the Teradaya."

Next, another rebel by the name of Shibayama took predictably unpredictable countermeasures. Unwilling to abandon his resolution to go through with the planned coup at dawn, but equally unable to disobey *daimyo* orders, Shibayama made up his mind to become the next victim of the massacre. Placing his sword directly in front of him, he sat down in the formal position on the polished wooden floor. "Kill me," he hollered, his head slightly bowed forward, both hands placed firmly on the floor.

"Shibayama, prepare yourself for Heaven," screamed one of the vigilantes, drawing his sword. The screech of cold steel slicing through human bone filled the room, but Arima still made no effort to call upstairs for help. Shibayama's right shoulder had been sliced open down to the chest, but he stubbornly remained in the formal sitting position, as his assailant, in a gesture filled with mercy and wrath, raised his sword high, and with one clean stroke, severed the head from the body.

Thirty seconds after the fighting had begun, Arima drew his sword, and brought the blade crashing down toward the head of one of his assailants. The vigilante, holding his weapon with both hands, blocked Arima's attack just above the left temple, as sparks flashed off the clashing blades. "Arima, prepare to die," he wailed, following with a vertical counterattack. Arima blocked the attack just above his head, but in the process his sword was severed at the hilt. Perceiving inevitable death, the Loyalist leader threw his broken weapon to the floor, and like a raging bull charged his comrade, pinning him against the wall with the brute force of his own body.

Narahara stared in horror as Arima held the Satsuma samurai flush against the wall, and three more rebels came racing downstairs. "Hashiguchi!" Arima called the name of one of them. Hashiguchi stood frozen at the base of the stairs, unable to draw his sword on a samurai from his own *han*. "Drive your sword through us," Arima ordered. "Hurry, Hashiguchi. Drive your sword through us."

"Forgive me!" Hashiguchi cried, drawing his sword. Then, filled with bitter resolution, he thrust his weapon through Arima's back, impaling both his leader and the other man against the wall.

Narahara and the three other vigilantes cut their way through the three rebels at the base of the stairway, slaying these comrades and regretting they had ever been born. Narahara, beside himself now with sorrow, threw down both of his swords, and ran upstairs. "This is Narahara here," he screamed through hot tears. "Most of us are Satsuma samurai, and all of us are *Men of High Purpose*. Now listen to what I say," he pleaded. "Lord Hisamitsu understands how all of you feel. But please, you must listen to me. The *daimyo* has ordered all of you to Kyoto headquarters."

Although each man on the second floor had drawn his sword, so intense was Narahara's plea, so sincere his eyes, not one of them attacked.

Narahara threw himself down on both knees before the rebels. "Please," he screamed, his head bowed to the floor, "you must obey Lord Hisamitsu's orders. Otherwise, kill me right here and now." As Narahara finished speaking, silence permeated the room, followed by the sound of the resheathing of swords.

This first attempt at a military uprising aimed directly against the Tokugawa Bakufu was crushed before it had begun, but the flame of *Toppling the Bakufu and Imperial Loyalism* burning in the hearts of the rebels at the Teradaya inn, and indeed in the very spirits of men throughout Japan, was not to be extinguished.

*   *   *

"A complete waste of human life!" Ryoma roared upon hearing the news of the bloodbath at the Teradaya. He was with Sonojo in the town of Shimonoseki, a seaport in western Choshu, from where he had originally intended to travel by sea to Osaka, to join his comrades in Kyoto. "The uprising has been crushed. I'm going to Satsuma."

"Satsuma?" Sonojo gasped. "Are you crazy? The Satsuma men kill men like us."

"I want to see the warships in Kagoshima," Ryoma said. Years ago Kawada Shoryo had told Ryoma of his visit to Kagoshima, the castle-town of Satsuma Han. The Tosa scholar had been part of a study expedition to inspect the great reverberatory furnaces used in the manufacture of cannon and other heavy artillery in Kagoshima. Ryoma had recently heard that Satsuma was now constructing Western-style schooners as well. "Will you come with me?" Ryoma asked his friend.

"No, Ryoma. I'm going to Kyoto to see what I can find out at Choshu headquarters there," Sonojo said with downcast eyes.

Ryoma left Shimonoseki on the following day. But when he was refused entry into Satsuma, which was traditionally suspicious of samurai of other clans, he journeyed to Osaka in search of Sonojo, arriving in the city in early June. Three months had passed since he had fled Tosa, and he was nearly destitute. His only possession of value was the sword his sister had given him; so desperate was he for funds that he went to a pawnshop at the center of the city. "How much for this?" he asked, drawing the blade, and startling the timid pawnbroker.

"Ah, well..." the pawnbroker struggled for words.

"It's an authentic Yoshiyuki," Ryoma said.

"Yes, I see," the pawnbroker replied. "I could give you fifty *ryo* for it."

"Fifty *ryo* for this?" Ryoma repeated in disbelief, pointing to the silver pommel at the base of the hilt.

"For the whole sword," the pawnbroker laughed nervously.

"The sword's not for sale. Just the pommel. It's pure silver."

"I see. I could give you ten *ryo* for the pommel alone. It certainly is beautiful," the merchant added as if to appease the samurai.

"How about ten *ryo* and a piece of cloth?" Ryoma said.

"A piece of cloth?" the pawnbroker gave Ryoma a puzzled look.

"You heard me. A piece of cloth. Do you have one?"

"Why, yes. Right here."

"Then give it to me," Ryoma said, and removed the silver knob which secured the hilt to the blade. In its place he wrapped the piece of cloth around the base, collected his money and left the shop.

That evening Ryoma took a riverboat to Kyoto, and, upon his arrival the next morning, went directly to Choshu headquarters there.

"Sakamoto-san, I'm glad to see you're safe," Kusaka Genzui greeted him. "We've been worried about you. There are Tosa agents patrolling the streets of Kyoto and Osaka, and, in case you haven't heard, you're on their list of most wanted men."

"I knew that I would be before I fled," Ryoma said with a shrug.

"For the murder of Yoshida Toyo," Kusaka informed. As the assassination closely coincided with Ryoma's having fled the *han*, the Tosa authorities naturally suspected Hanpeita's right-hand man of the murder.

"Murder? Of Yoshida Toyo? I'm wanted for Yoshida's murder? Of all the stupid things," Ryoma shouted, not trying to conceal his anger. "So," he said, "they've finally done it."

"Yes."

"What's the situation like in Kyoto now?" Ryoma asked.

"Since the fiasco at the Teradaya, we've been paralyzed for fear of arrest. Everyone's waiting for the right time to move again."

"I see."

"Sakamoto-san, I really think it would be wise for you to stay here for a while until things calm down."

"Do you know anything about a Tosa samurai named Sawamura Sonojo?" Ryoma asked.

"Yes, he's here with us right now."

Ryoma spent the following month in hiding at Choshu's Kyoto head-quarters, until he began to feel like an animal in a cage.

"Sonojo," Ryoma said to his friend early one morning, after a long, hot sleepless night. "I've had enough. I have to get out of here."

"Huh?" Sonojo started from his sleep. "You can't leave. There are still hordes of Tosa agents looking for us all over the city."

"I'm just not made to stay in one place like this, Sonojo." Ryoma got up and thrust his sword through his sash.

"Would you rather be captured and put in jail?"

"No, I couldn't stand that either."

"Then stay here, at least for the time being," Sonojo pleaded. "You have no other choice."

"You always have a choice, Sonojo. It's just a matter of acting on your commitments."

"I see," Sonojo said, taken aback by the weightiness of Ryoma's words.

"The purpose of life," Ryoma continued, "is to act, and through action achieve great results."

"Where will you go?"

"I'm not sure. Maybe to Edo. Or maybe I'll sail to America on a Black Ship."

"You're crazy, Ryoma!"

"Perhaps so, but I can't stay here any longer."

"If you really insist on leaving," Sonojo said, "at least wait until the cover of night. Discuss the matter with Kusaka. Maybe he'll have some advice for you."

"Perhaps you're right," Ryoma halfheartedly agreed.

"Why Edo?" Kusaka asked Ryoma later that morning. "Edo is the Tokugawa stronghold. All of the most traitorous, anti-Imperial elements are gathered in..." Kusaka paused. "Wait a minute! If you insist on going to Edo, I have an idea."

"What's that?"

"You could put your sword to use, Sakamoto-san. What better purpose could an expert swordsman like yourself serve than to cut down the enemies of the Emperor?"

"Like who?"

"Within the Bakufu are two scoundrels who have taken Ii's place as the top proponents of yielding to the barbarians."

"Who are they?" Ryoma asked.

"One is a direct Tokugawa retainer by the name of Katsu Kaishu. He's the commissioner of the Shogun's navy. The other is a scholar from Kumamoto by the name of Yokoi Shonan. He's the chief political advisor to the Lord of Fukui. The Lord of Fukui has recently been appointed political director of the Bakufu."

"What about them?" Ryoma asked without much interest.

"You could do Japan a great service by cutting the scoundrels down. Both Katsu and Yokoi are two of the biggest obstacles to our cause, and..."

"In what way are they obstacles to our cause?" Ryoma interrupted.

"Katsu and Yokoi advocate the complete opening of our country and free trade with the barbarians."

"Free trade?" Ryoma grinned, swatting a mosquito on the back of his sweaty neck.

"Yes," Kusaka confirmed, giving Ryoma a puzzled look. "Katsu is one of the most outward proponents of opening Japan. And with Yokoi's appointment as chief political advisor to the most powerful Bakufu minister, in essence he has also become the most influential advisor for our national policy. And so, as an initial step toward toppling the Tokugawa, it would be very useful to eliminate these two traitors."

"Katsu Kaishu and Yokoi Shonan?" Ryoma confirmed the names. "Never heard of either of them, but I'll see what I can do." Ryoma stood up and thrust his sword through the sash of a new *hakama* which the Choshu men had given him, along with a new kimono, several pieces of gold and a pommel for his sword.

That evening at dusk Ryoma passed through the guarded gate of Choshu headquarters and out into the dangerous streets of the Imperial capital. From here the outlaw-samurai walked eastward on a two-week trek along the Tokaido Road to Edo, and, though unbeknown to him, the beginning of a new life.

*   *   *

Takechi Hanpeita, having included himself among the five hundred samurai accompanying the sixteen-year-old Tosa *daimyo* on his mandatory trip to Edo, reached Kyoto in late August, only four months after masterminding the assassination of Regent Yoshida Toyo. Having succeeded over the summer in uniting Tosa behind *Toppling the Bakufu and Imperial Loyalism*, Master Zuizan had unofficially usurped the reins of power in Kochi, as the Golden Age of the Tosa Loyalist Party got under way.

Hanpeita and his men used their influence in the Imperial Court, mainly with a radical young noble by the name of Sanjo Sanetomi, to effect an Imperial decree for the Lord of Tosa to stop in Kyoto *en route* to Edo. As Satsuma and Choshu had already stationed troops in Kyoto, the leader of the now powerful Tosa Loyalist Party deemed that Tosa should not allow itself to be left behind these two *han* who were working to achieve a close relationship with the Imperial Court. To further strengthen his grip on Tosa policy, as soon as the Tosa retinue arrived in Kyoto, Hanpeita arranged for a second Imperial decree ordering the *daimyo* to remain there. The decree was issued under the pretense of defending the court from possible foreign attack, but was actually for the purpose of defying the Tokugawa Law of Alternate Attendance in Edo. And so, the leader of the Tosa rebels had successfully manipulated the young *daimyo* into supporting *Toppling the Bakufu and Imperial Loyalism*, thus entering Tosa as a leading player in national politics.

The Kyoto scene on which the Tosa Loyalists appeared in the late summer of the second year of the Era of Bunkyu, 1862, was one of great political turbulence. Among the great "outside fiefs," the most prominent being Choshu, Satsuma and Tosa, existed sharp debate as to which of the three leading policies would best serve their individual interests. The first policy, *Support for the Bakufu*, connoted traditional restraint in national affairs among the Outside Lords, leaving such matters to direct Tokugawa retainers. The second, a *Union of Court and Camp*, would allow the most powerful of the Outside Lords a say in national affairs. The third policy, *Toppling the Bakufu and Imperial Loyalism*, spoke for itself.

In Tosa, *Support for the Bakufu* was the policy of the upper-samurai, particularly the conservative old guard who had been ousted by Yoshida Toyo, then reinstated, if only nominally, by the recent coup. Yoshida's staunch support of a *Union of Court and Camp* had led to his assassination by Hanpeita's Loyalists, who were determined to overthrow the Edo regime and restore the rule to the divine Emperor in Kyoto.

Further complicating things was a long-standing rivalry between the two most powerful Outside Lords on the Kyoto scene: Shimazu Hisamitsu of Satsuma and Mori Takachika of Choshu. In order to usurp undisputed leadership from Choshu as chief mediator between court and camp, Lord Hisamitsu had led an army into Kyoto in June, the intentions of which had so tragically been misinterpreted by, among others, his own samurai whom he ordered slaughtered at the Teradaya. Having succeeded in winning Kyoto's approval of his own proposal for a *Union of Court and Camp*, and being appointed by the court to establish order in Kyoto, the calculating Lord Hisamitsu, not to be misled by his own insurgent vassals, was assigned to escort an Imperial messenger to Edo, to order the Shogun to Kyoto for consultations with the Emperor. In face of the none-too-subtle threat of Lord Hisamitsu's armed guard of 1,000 strong, the Shogun agreed to the Imperial demand, which actually consisted of Satsuma's proposal.

Nor was the Lord of Choshu idle while his arch-rival from Satsuma was in Edo. By the workings of Katsura Kogoro in Edo, and much to the pleasure of Kusaka Genzui's band of radicals at Choshu's Kyoto headquarters, this *han* abandoned its former support of a *Union of Court and Camp*, and replaced it with an official policy of *Toppling the Bakufu and Imperial Loyalism*. Choshu's ploy–skillfully timed during Lord Hisamitsu's absence from Kyoto, and following the detested slaughter of Loyalists by Satsuma men at the Teradaya–proved for the time being to position Choshu ahead of Satsuma at the forefront of anti-Tokugawa Loyalists gathered in the Imperial capital. While Hisamitsu had been commissioned as Imperial escort, his purpose was merely to "correct the Edo regime," whereas Choshu was now prepared to act under Imperial decree to topple the Tokugawa. And although Takechi Hanpeita and his Tosa Loyalists were no less radical than their Choshu allies, the mere fact that *Toppling the Bakufu and Imperial Loyalism* had become the official policy of Choshu gave that *han* the political edge in Kyoto.

*   *   *

In August of the same year, just before Ryoma reached Edo and Hanpeita arrived in Kyoto, an event occurred near the foreign settlement of Yokohama, in the small village of Namamugi, which added fuel to the common fire raging in the hearts of xenophobes throughout Japan.

Upon successfully completing his mission in Edo, Lord Hisamitsu set out early one morning in late August to return to Kyoto. The Satsuma entourage–mounted guards, foot soldiers, luggage handlers and palanquins bearing the *daimyo* and other high officials–numbered seven hundred strong and extended over a mile. At the rear of the entourage, as if to flaunt his newfound power, Hisamitsu had placed an intimidating cannon, mounted onto a horse-drawn cart for all the world to see. One year, or even several months earlier, the Satsuma *daimyo* would never have dared to so blatantly challenge the heretofore undisputed authority of the Tokugawa regime.

Not a cloud blemished the clear blue sky as the military procession moved west along the Tokaido Road on the outskirts of Edo. Crowds waited patiently along the roadside for a glimpse at the parade. When it would finally reach their own village, the awed spectators would humbly drop to their knees, and thus remain until it had completely passed. Such was the common respect which Japanese custom, and even law, demanded for the entourage of a *daimyo*.

It just so happened that it was a Sunday. Although the days of the week were of no significance to the Satsuma samurai, whose reputation for valor had been unmatched throughout Japan for centuries, the foreigners living in nearby Yokohama were apt to make a holiday of the Christian day of rest.

As Hisamitsu's palanquin approached the small fishing village of Namamugi, just fourteen leagues west of Edo, a group of four Britons–three men and a woman–traveled leisurely on horseback along the same road in the opposite direction. The scene could not have been better arranged if it had been the mischief of some ancient Japanese demon intent on deepening the social mire of the times with which the land was already covered.

In order to prevent dangerous confrontations, the Edo government had made it a point to inform the foreigners in advance of approaching *daimyo* entourages. Thus informed, the foreigners were expected to stay away. Whether these particular Britons had not been informed of the Satsuma schedule or whether they had unwisely chosen to ignore the warning remains a mystery, but when the ill-fated four approached the heavily guarded palanquin of the Lord of Satsuma, they were immediately ordered, in no uncertain terms, to dismount, lead their horses to the side of road and let the array pass by. Not understanding Japanese, all four Britons remained in their saddles, infuriating the Satsuma samurai who took this as a blatant display of disrespect for their lord. Had the Britons been familiar with Japanese custom, tragedy may have been avoided. But one of the four, a merchant by the name of C. L. Richardson, had just recently arrived in Japan from a long stay in Shanghai. Having become accustomed to getting his way with the Chinese by brute intimidation, Richardson very foolishly assumed that "all Orientals, certainly being of the same timid nature, could easily be controlled."

This was poor Richardson's last misconception, as his group attempted to cut off the procession directly in front of the approaching black lacquered palanquin of the Satsuma *daimyo*, emblazoned in gold with the Shimazu family crest of an encircled cross, the ominous significance of which the foreigners had no idea. As such an act was considered to be the ultimate in rudeness, samurai were permitted by law to cut down the offenders.

"Dismount! Dismount immediately!" a samurai repeated in vain, as the party of four tried to pass by the procession.

"What's all the commotion?" Lord Hisamitsu muttered from inside his palanquin.

"A group of barbarians are in our way, My Lord," answered one of Hisamitsu's bodyguards.

"Then kill the impudent bastards!" Hisamitsu is said to have ordered.

Whether or not Hisamitsu actually instructed his men to commit murder, a white light flashed inside the brain of one expert swordsman who had been assigned the honorable position of personal guard to his lord's palanquin. This was Narahara Kizaemon, the older brother of the man who had led the vigilante group in the Teradaya fratricide. Drawing his sword, Narahara charged the nearest foreigner, let loose an ear-piercing guttural wail, as blood sprayed from underneath Richardson's clean white cotton shirt. His torso sliced open from left shoulder to right hip, the unfortunate man went into a state of shock before dropping like a dead weight from the back of his bewildered horse. As if Richardson had not had enough, another Satsuma warrior, crying "mercy of the samurai," put the poor man out of his misery with a final deathblow to the throat. Meanwhile, the other two Englishmen, too startled at first to even move, received lesser wounds to the body, before grabbing their bloodied reins and racing back to Yokohama. Although the Satsuma men were quite willing to cut the "male barbarians," they did no more harm to the woman than to cut off her long hair before allowing her to flee.

*   *   *

When the Satsuma host finally reached the Imperial capital, Lord Hisamitsu found that things were not as he had left them just a few months before. The radicals whom he thought he had so skillfully thwarted with the Teradaya slaughter were again raging through Kyoto like wildfire. He was furious to discover that his arch-rival, the Lord of Choshu, had gained the Imperial grace which had belonged to Satsuma before he had left Kyoto. And backed by the Choshu extremists, the Imperial Court was no longer to be appeased by Satsuma's middle-of-the-road policy of a *Union of Court and Camp*. Rather, the battle cry of *Reverence to the Emperor and Down with the Bakufu* reflected the sentiments raging among the Choshu zealots who had gathered in the Imperial capital when the Shield of the Emperor, basking in the glory of his recent coup in Kochi, led his Tosa Loyalists into Kyoto in August 1862, less than one month after Sakamoto Ryoma had left for he knew not what in the Shogun's capital at Edo.

The Dragon Soars

As the young fugitive warrior journeyed from defeat the clouds above suddenly began to seethe, the ocean grew dark and the spray from the waves danced in the air as if magnetized by the heavens. Just as the battle-weary samurai thought that the torrential winds would finally subside, a downpour burst forth, encompassing him in a bamboo forest of silver rain, followed immediately by the deafening roar of thunder.

As the distraught young warrior neared the brink of disaster, and feared that the deluge would never relent, a great white dragon suddenly appeared, soaring through the clouds above, then riding the crest of a wave below, radiating light through its heavenly course. With the head of a horse, antlers of a stag, demon eyes and serpentine neck, the entire body of the great white dragon was covered with the gleaming scales of a fish. With claws as sharp as those of a hawk and powerful tiger-like paws, the mythical demigod was adorned with the ears of a bull.

Though legend has it that the dragon is a natural sage, in truth the beast-god knew well of worldly desire. It is for this very reason that in ancient times, by means of some mysterious technique long forgotten, man had been able to tame the dragon, and even partake of its divine flesh.

But this particular dragon which had suddenly appeared for the brave young warrior was of a unique breed. Indeed this great white dragon could see 250 leagues into the distance and, unlike others of its kind, was the embodiment of freedom.

The fugitive warrior gazed up at the divine entity which seemed to have inherited the clouds, the very source of its limitless energy. Then, just as suddenly as it had appeared, the dragon disappeared into the heavens from whence it came, the sea once again grew calm, the clouds gave way to a limitless and nearly transparent blue, the mountains in the distance shone in effervescent green off the blessed sunlight that warmed the bones of the weary young warrior, bringing a picture-perfect climax to the impetuous entry and exit of the great white dragon.

Ryoma opened his eyes to find himself in Edo, at the house of his sword master's son and heir, Chiba Jutaro. His bedding was strewn about, and an uncanny sweat covered his body, despite the chill in the air on this late morning in early October. "What a dream," he muttered to himself, rubbed his eyes, then sat up to massage the sides of his aching head.

"Jutaro!" Ryoma called through the closed paper screen door of the young sword master's room, adjacent his own. Jutaro, who had been writing at his desk, lay his brush down. "Come in," he said.

Ryoma sat down on the matted floor next to Jutaro. "My head aches," he said. The two had drank long into the previous night, rehashing old memories from nine years past when Ryoma had first appeared at the Chiba Dojo in the spring of 1853, just before the arrival of Perry's flotilla and the beginning of the end of two-and-a-half centuries of Tokugawa peace.

"Oyasu," Jutaro called his wife, "bring tea."

"What are you writing?" Ryoma asked.

"A letter."

"To who?"

"To the most important political mind in Japan."

"Who's that?"

"Yokoi Shonan, the chief political advisor to Lord Matsudaira Shungaku, the retired *daimyo* of Fukui Han, who is now the political director of the Bakufu."

"'Expelling the filthy barbarians from the sacred soil of Japan,'" Ryoma began reading aloud from Jutaro's letter, "'is the most important task that faces all samurai of true courage.'"

"I'm absolutely dedicated to *Imperial Reverence and Expelling the Barbarians,*" Jutaro said.

"How do you know Yokoi Shonan?" Ryoma asked.

"I don't actually know him. I'm just writing him a letter. Lord Ikeda has promised me to get it delivered." Lord Ikeda was a minor *daimyo*, to whose son Jutaro had recently become private fencing instructor.

"More than just expelling the barbarians," Ryoma said, "we must concentrate our efforts on overthrowing the Tokugawa."

"Excuse me," Oyasu said, opening the door. She held a dark brown lacquered tray, on which were two porcelain tea cups and a tea pot.

"Jutaro," Ryoma said after Oyasu served the tea, "how would you like to come with me today?"

"Where? To cut down the Shogun?" Jutaro snickered, albeit in an unintentional whisper.

"No. But maybe one of his chief retainers," Ryoma answered nonchalantly.

"What?" Jutaro started.

"I'm going to visit the commissioner of the Bakufu Navy. A man by the name of Katsu Kaishu." Although Ryoma would have Jutaro believe that he was considering killing this elite Bakufu official, he actually harbored quite different intentions. Having heard that Kaishu had commanded a ship to the United States, manned entirely by Japanese, Ryoma had become fascinated with the man. Although Kaishu was detested as a traitor among the Loyalists, in his deepest heart, Ryoma, who had an innate passion for things maritime, had already formulated his own thoughts about the navy commissioner.

Ryoma's admiration was not unfounded. He reasoned that any man who had the courage to brave such a dangerous voyage must have some redeeming qualities. And recently, since returning to Edo, Ryoma had heard another interesting story concerning the pluck of this so-called traitor. When American Consul Townsend Harris was informed of the Bakufu's plan to send an all-Japanese crew across the Pacific on a ship designed to sail in only coastal waters, he dismissed it as a crazy idea. Instead, Harris advised the Japanese to use a larger ship and man it with experienced American and British sailors. While the Bakufu was ready to heed Harris' advice, Kaishu refused to listen, and eventually set sail on his pioneering journey without foreign assistance.

Ryoma's admiration for Kaishu and his fascination for Western ships notwithstanding, he was by no means willing to sell out to the foreigners. And although he no longer shared the blind xenophobia of his comrades, he resented as much as anyone the insult of ultimatum that the foreigners had presented to Japan concerning the opening of its ports. He particularly detested the shameless way that the Bakufu had yielded to foreign demands. But Ryoma, like Kawada Shoryo and Katsu Kaishu, was wise enough to realize the futility of trying to resist the inevitability of the times.

"You're crazy, Ryoma," Jutaro exclaimed. "How do you plan to get close enough to Katsu to cut him?" Then after a brief pause, he added, "Although I can't say I blame you. I'd like to kill the traitor myself."

"With this," Ryoma said, drawing his sword. "Are you coming with me. I'm going straight to Katsu's house. If at first he refuses to see me, I'll cut my way inside, and if I have to, I'll cut..."

"Hold it," Jutaro interrupted. "Here, have some more tea," he said, refilling both cups. "You still haven't told me how you plan to get into Katsu's house."

"Well," Ryoma began speaking slowly, "I was actually hoping to ask for your help."

"My help?"

"Yes. Through the Chiba name, I thought that you might be able to get a letter of introduction to Katsu from somebody high up."

"Ryoma," Jutaro exclaimed, his eyes brightening, "you just might have a point there. I think I might be able to get the Lord of Tottori to arrange a meeting for us with the Lord of Fukui."

"Huh?" Ryoma pressed his tea cup against his lips. "I don't follow you."

"The Lord of Fukui is apparently close with Kaishu. So, if we were to ask him to..."

Ryoma gulped down the tea, and slammed the empty cup on the matted floor. "Fantastic idea!" he exploded. "Let's go!" Ryoma grabbed his sword, and stood up to leave.

"Wait," Jutaro said. "First I'll have to pay a visit to the Lord of Tottori. Hopefully he'll arrange for us to meet the Lord of Fukui, and if all goes well, we'll have our chance to meet Katsu Kaishu this very evening. Then, we either straighten out Katsu's traitorous ideas about opening Japan to the barbarians," Jutaro said bitterly, "or else we cut him down."

Ryoma, however, had different intentions in mind. Like the great white dragon in his vision, he was searching for his own chance to inherit the clouds, to soar through the heavens on the boundless energy of vapor. An outlaw-samurai, a meager *ronin*, visiting an elite government official? Unheard of? Farfetched? Preposterous? Such words of restraint were not included in the vocabulary of Sakamoto Ryoma.

*   *   *

Katsu Kaishu was born in Edo in 1823, the only son of a petty Tokugawa retainer. At age six he was invited by a distant relative employed in the Shogun's inner-palace to view the wonderful gardens in the compound of Edo Castle. Having caught the eye, and apparently the fancy, of Shogun Tokugawa Ienari, from this day the young boy became the official playmate of the Shogun's grandson, spending most of his time in the confines of the castle, where he would continue this role for the next five years.

One day, on his way to the castle, Kaishu was attacked by a stray dog, and bitten in that most vulnerable of places of the male anatomy.

Although the actual wound was sewn up and healed soon after, the tender aftermath prohibited him from beginning *kendo* training until his fifteenth year, when he took up residence at the *dojo* of Shimada Toranosuke, one of the most reputable sword masters in Edo. Here, Kaishu's training was of much greater severity, both mentally and physically, than most men of the time had been apt to endure. It was to this training, which he continued daily for the next four years, that later in life Kaishu attributed his great success as innovative shogunal official, and even his ability to survive several attacks on his life. At age twenty, Kaishu was initiated at Shimada's *dojo*, qualifying him to become a *kendo* instructor in his own right. Two years later, however, he discontinued his training with the sword and took up the study of the Dutch language.

Throughout the period of Tokugawa rule, most knowledge of the West was transmitted by the Dutch to native scholars of Western learning. Although most so-called "Dutch scholars" studied medicine (Perry's flotilla was not to appear off the Edo coast for several years), Kaishu's keen sense of the times led him to pursue Western military science. He continued his studies for five years until 1850, when, at age twenty-seven, the Western scholar opened up his own private academy in his shoddy home in Edo's Akasaka district. From this time, Kaishu's reputation as an expert in things Western began to spread.

Within two years, in 1852, Kaishu had received requests from various *han* around Japan for the manufacture of Western-style cannon, which, with the aid of a blacksmith, he constructed according to the instructions in his Dutch textbooks. Kaishu first attracted significant attention among the Bakufu elite at age thirty with a brilliant letter of advice he had submitted to a national survey conducted by Edo in response to Perry's demands. His letter, which displayed a greater awareness of the times than any of the hundreds which the government had received, proposed that the Bakufu break an age-old tradition, and go beyond social class to recruit men of ability for these very pressing times. It also advised that the Bakufu begin international trade, using the profits thereby to build a modern navy.

Although the ranks of the Bakufu were filled with men of mediocre ability who had attained their posts due to nothing more than birthright, such was not the case for the entire Edo elite. And fortunately for Kaishu–and indeed the future of Japan–the talents of the young scholar caught the attention of Okubo Ichio, one of the most progressive and enlightened Tokugawa officials in these very troubled times.

Over the following six years, Kaishu dedicated himself to government service, during which time he was sent to study under Dutch naval experts in the port city of Nagasaki. It was here that Kaishu obtained the knowledge and skills to enable him to command the *Kanrin Maru*, the first Japanese-manned ship ever to sail to the Western world. Kaishu returned to Japan in May 1860, two months after the assassination of Ii Naosuke. With national policy at a temporary standstill pending the emergence of new Bakufu leadership, a discouraged Kaishu, now thirty-seven, retired into temporary obscurity. In the following year, with the restoration to power of his political ally and close friend, the Lord of Fukui, Kaishu's return to the national scene was secured. The maritime expert was appointed commissioner of the Shogun's navy in August 1862, only two months before Ryoma and Jutaro appeared at the front gate of his home carrying a letter of introduction from the Lord of Fukui.

*   *   *

Two swordsmen, one shoddy, the other immaculately dressed, increased their pace as they walked up the sloped road leading to the home of the navy commissioner, just after sundown on a chilly, cloudless October night. Earlier that day, Jutaro had arranged for an audience for Ryoma and himself with Lord Matsudaira Shungaku, the retired Fukui *daimyo* and most powerful official in the Edo regime, to request a letter of introduction to Katsu Kaishu. In the light of the full moon the two swordsmen appeared hostile, even dangerous, as they rapidly approached the house of the celebrated proponent of *Opening the Country*. "Jutaro!" Ryoma broke the moonlit silence, then suddenly stopped in his tracks near a high moss-covered stone wall at the side of the road, beyond which stood an ancient Shinto shrine. "Before we jump to any conclusions about Katsu," he said in a low voice, his back against the stone wall, "I think we ought to hear what he has to say."

"What do you expect to gain out of listening to a traitor like Katsu Kaishu?"

"I'm not sure he is a traitor. But if he is," Ryoma wrapped his right hand around the hilt of his sword, "he'll get what he has coming to him. But if he isn't," Ryoma grinned slightly, "I think Katsu might be able to teach us how to operate a Western-style warship."

"What?" Jutaro gasped in disbelief.

"Give me two or three of those ships the Bakufu has docked in Edo Bay, and I'll topple the Tokugawa myself," Ryoma boasted.

"You're crazy, Ryoma," Jutaro scoffed. "We're about to cut down a cowardly traitor, and you're talking nonsense. Let's go," he said, and the two men resumed their rapid gait up the slope toward Kaishu's house.

Jutaro could hardly be blamed for his indignation. For all intents and purposes, Ryoma's talk of learning how to operate a warship was nonsense. Although the Bakufu had set up a naval training center in Edo, for the past two-and-a-half centuries only vassals of the Shogun (or upon special request, samurai from certain elite *han*) were permitted to participate in any kind of Bakufu-sponsored military training. And since Ryoma was a lower-samurai from Tosa, he had as little chance of receiving recommendation by the Lord of Tosa as did the sons of farmers and merchants of that strictly segregated domain. And even if lower-samurai had been eligible, Ryoma was now an outlaw.

As the two approached the front gate, Ryoma again stopped and turned to face Jutaro. "Before we go in there," he said, gesturing with his chin toward the house, "I want you to know one thing. I'm not sure that I want to kill Katsu. I only insinuated that I was to convince you to come with me."

"You did what?" Jutaro gasped indignantly.

"Relax! I wanted you to come for your own good. I have the feeling that there's a lot more to Katsu than what most of us realize. Anyway, before we kill the man, we owe it ourselves to hear him out. Maybe he has something worthwhile to say."

"Ryoma! I can't believe I'm actually hearing these things from you, of all people. Katsu's a traitor. He's leading the way for the Westernization of Japan."

"If he's a traitor, then I'll be the first to cut him," Ryoma said, placing his hand on the hilt of his sword. "But the Westernization of Japan?" he scoffed. "We have to defend ourselves some way. You don't really believe that Japan has a chance against the barbarians without Western-style warships and technology. We certainly aren't going to drive the barbarians out with our swords alone."

The two samurai passed through the front gate, its dark brown wood badly weathered. A mossy stone walkway led to the front door of the two-storied house, which in the moonlight appeared to be in as much need of repair as the front gate.

"Is anyone home?" Jutaro called from the front entranceway, which was lit by a single lantern.

Presently an attractive, middle-aged woman carrying a white paper lantern appeared. "Yes, what might you want at this hour?" she asked. Her teeth were blackened and her eyebrows shaved, indicating that this was the lady of the household.

"We've come to see Katsu-sensei," the sloppily dressed samurai said. As was his habit, Ryoma held his right hand tucked into his kimono. "We have a letter of introduction from Lord Matsudaira Shungaku," he said, producing the document.

Katsu's wife took the letter, told the two visitors to wait, then disappeared into the dark house. She returned a few minutes later to escort them down a dark corridor leading to a drawing room which was adjacent to a study. Sliding open the screen door of the drawing room, the woman told them to wait inside.

Enter Katsu Kaishu. Although Ryoma and Jutaro could see only his silhouette through the thin paper screen which separated the drawing room from the study, they perceived a small man, just under five feet tall, with a wiry build, who, if standing next to either of them, would barely reach their shoulders.

"Don't take off your swords," Kaishu suddenly called out. Although neither man had intended to leave his swords in the drawing room, Kaishu seemed amused to go through the formality of permitting them to retain their weapons. "It just wouldn't be fitting of samurai in these troubled times to be so careless," he gibed. "You may enter as you are."

Not knowing what to expect next, the two men entered the study. Books–in Dutch, English, Chinese and the native script–were piled in heaps along one wall. In one corner was a globe of the world. In the alcove was a model of a triple-masted steamer, and next to this were two swords set in a rack made of deer antlers. In the middle of the room, with arms folded at his chest, stood the commissioner of the Shogun's navy.

At age thirty-nine, Katsu Kaishu was of a light complexion, and his piercing dark eyes displayed an inner strength which immediately impressed both swordsmen. His slightly aquiline nose, thin lips and small jaw produced an aristocratic air. With a full head of hair tied in a topknot, he was plainly dressed in a light blue kimono, gray *haka-ma* and a black jacket on which was displayed the Katsu family crest of a four-petaled flower in a circle. But the navy commissioner's aristocratic air was instantly shattered when he began speaking in his slick downtown Edo accent.

"Don't just stand there," he said with an amused grin which annoyed Jutaro. "Sit down!"

"So, this is the man that people say is selling out to the barbarians," Ryoma thought to himself. "And the same man who commanded the ship across the Pacific." His mind raced as he eyed the model ship in the alcove. Ryoma now realized that the man standing before him was not a typical member of the Bakufu elite. He had been in Edo long enough to know that those pusillanimous products of Edo's easy living were no different than the pampered sons of upper-samurai from Tosa, whom he had learned to despise. "I'm Sakamoto Ryoma from Tosa," he said brusquely.

Kaishu sat down on the *tatami* floor next to a wooden brazier, on which rested a small steaming kettle. "Well, Sakamoto Ryoma-san," he said, "sit down!" Placing their swords on the floor at their right sides, the younger men sat opposite Kaishu in the formal position.

"So, you've come to cut me down," Kaishu stunned both swordsmen with the nonchalance in which he spoke. "Why are you so surprised?" he continued in a calm, gibing tone, as he warmed his hands over the brazier. "You both have revenge written all over your faces, so you can forget about trying to hide it."

Ryoma and Jutaro remained silent, quite outdone by the smaller man's display of pluck. Although neither knew it, Kaishu had previously been warned of their visit in a message from Lord Shungaku. "*You can expect a sudden visit at any time now from two young swordsmen,*" the note began, before giving their names. "*As I estimate Sakamoto to be a youth of great character and potential, I have taken it upon myself to introduce him to you. But please be careful with him, as he is still young and a bit naive, and seems to harbor some wild ideas in favor of expelling the barbarians.*"

"You aren't the first ones who have been here with the same purpose in mind," Kaishu continued speaking in the same vibrant downtown accent. "People who call themselves *Men of High Purpose* come here every day to cut me down. Can you believe it? Who'd have ever thought that I'd be this sought after? I'm flattered, I tell you, simply flattered. But," Kaishu said with an amused grin, "I don't hold a grudge against any of them. They're only doing what they think is best for Japan, even if many of them are lacking a bit up here," he chuckled, tapping his temple with his index finger. "So, what I usually do, is invite them in for a long talk. And up to now, not even one of them has killed me," he said, bursting out in laughter.

So as not to be made a fool of, Jutaro felt inclined to speak, but before he could get a word in his loquacious host beat him to the verbal draw. "You must be the young sword master of the Chiba Dojo." The smooth-talking expert of things maritime cast a hard gaze into the fiery eyes of Chiba Jutaro.

With this unexpected and abrupt turn of things, Jutaro had now lost whatever intentions he may have had of killing Katsu Kaishu.

"Well, it certainly is something, isn't it," Kaishu responded to Jutaro's reluctance to speak, "to have such a reputed sword master in my home." Although Jutaro could not resist taking the compliment at face value, something about the way the little man spoke rang of irony.

Since having introduced himself a few moments ago, Ryoma had also remained silent, in the formal sitting position, back straight, head upright, and hands resting on his thighs. "Katsu-sensei," he began speaking reverently.

"You needn't call me 'Sensei,'" Kaishu interrupted, waving his hand in a gesture to show the two younger men that he was willing to talk to them on an equal level. "Relax," he said, motioning for them to sit cross-legged like himself. "Let's forget the formalities and start talking about things that really matter," he said, then clapped his hands twice loudly, a signal for his wife to serve hot tea. "Then, if you don't like what I have to say," Kaishu continued to amaze, "you can kill me and be on your way." With a pair of iron sticks, he picked up a glowing cinder from the brazier and lit a short bamboo pipe of tobacco. Slowly exhaling the smoke through his nostrils, he added, "Although I've practiced *kendo* myself, I wouldn't stand a chance against two expert swordsmen like yourselves. Besides, I keep the hilt of my sword so tightly fastened to the scabbard that I'd have trouble just drawing the damn blade."

No, Ryoma thought again, this is not a typical Bakufu official. "You're right, Katsu-san," he said. "The reason we came tonight was to kill you."

"Now that it's out in the open, why don't you tell me why you'd want to do a thing like that?" Kaishu asked, reaching for a large, metal ashtray. Gently tapping the ashes from his pipe into the ashtray, the navy commissioner said, "Actually, I already know why. I represent a government which has disgraced itself by being forced to sign a treaty with the barbarians permitting free trade with foreign nations against the will of his Sacred Majesty in Kyoto. And so," Kaishu continued speaking the younger men's thoughts, "I'm a traitor who advocates the cowardly policy of *Opening the Country.*"

"Yes," Ryoma spoke up, "the Bakufu has deceived the people, and is only concerned with its own welfare. The Bakufu no longer has the power to govern Japan. If we allow things to continue as they are, Japan is going to face the same humiliation as China."

"So, what else do you have to say, Sakamoto-san?" Kaishu snickered. "Don't you see? That's exactly why we must open our country to free trade. The only way we can beat the barbarians is by first opening up to them. But I wouldn't want you to think that I intend to sit back and watch them come into Japan to do whatever they please." Kaishu suddenly stopped speaking, as his wife appeared at the doorway to serve tea. "I'd love to cut the bastards to pieces," the navy commissioner continued. "But do you really believe that it's possible to keep the barbarians away?" Kaishu paused, sipped his tea. "What do you suppose would happen, Sakamoto-san, if Tosa Han, for instance, were attacked by the barbarians?"

"Tosa wouldn't stand a chance against their warships and cannon," Ryoma snickered. "The fight would be over as soon as it started."

"So, you understand," Kaishu said consolingly. "For us to fight the barbarians at this point would be like beating our heads against an iron wall." He chuckled at the unfortunate metaphor. "And with the way things are in Japan nowadays, I don't think it's such a good idea for Japanese to be killing Japanese. We must combine our resources and work together."

Ryoma recalled in dismay the massacre at the Teradaya, and even the assassination of Yoshida Toyo.

"Internal fighting will only leave us the more vulnerable to foreign attack," Kaishu said, took a deep breath, then continued lecturing. "Instead, we must concentrate on positive ways to avoid foreign subjugation. But exclusionism is not one of them," he said firmly, pounding his fist on the floor. "It's simply not realistic."

"But opening the country to the barbarians is?" Jutaro asked bitterly.

"My reasons for wanting to open Japan are a little different than what you probably think," said Kaishu, slowly raising his teacup to his mouth.

"How's that?" Ryoma asked.

"How old are you, Sakamoto-san?" Kaishu asked.

"Twenty-seven."

"Ha, ha! You're still green," Kaishu taunted. "But you seem to have potential. Anyway, back to your question. You wanted to know how I justify my support of *Opening the Country*, right, Chiba-san?"

Jutaro only nodded.

"Take a look at that," Kaishu said, reaching over to the large globe next to the pile of books. "See this tiny nation surrounded by nothing but ocean. It's no bigger than Japan. But what it has that Japan doesn't have is the most powerful navy in the history of the world. England has literally thousands of steamships which can travel anywhere on the globe. How else do you suppose it has become the wealthiest nation on the face of the earth? Certainly not from its own natural resources. Look at China," he pointed to the massive Middle Kingdom. "One of the largest countries in the world, but as you know, England has just about conquered it. But, again, England has something that neither China nor Japan has."

"A powerful navy," Ryoma interrupted.

"Exactly! Both military and merchant. England has become the wealthiest nation in the history of the world because of one thing: free trade and plenty of it. And by trading all over the world, it has amassed such wealth that no one can challenge it." Then after a slight pause, Kaishu added, "Not yet, anyway. But if things continue as they are now, we are never going to be able to stand up against England or America, not to mention France, Holland, Russia and others. No matter how much we rant and rave about the virtues of keeping the barbarians out, we just don't have the means to do so."

"That's just an excuse for opening the country!" Jutaro angrily spewed, grabbing his sword.

"Relax, Jutaro!" Ryoma said, immediately grabbing his friend by the wrist.

"And so," Kaishu calmly resumed, "we are going to have to develop our navy, which compared to those of the Western powers is still in its infancy. The few ships we have are like children's toys compared to the great warships of England and America. And when I say 'we are going to have to develop our navy,' I mean all of us together. Not just the sons of elite samurai. Most of them are useless anyway."

"All of us?" Ryoma asked.

"Yes. That means the both of you, myself and any other man with the will, guts and brains to do so."

"Katsu-sensei," Ryoma suddenly blurted out, "I've been wanting to do just that for the past eight years."

"Well, then, rather than wasting our time and energy screaming to expel the barbarians like a bunch of idiots, we must start training talented men in the naval sciences. I've submitted my plan to the Bakufu, but most of the ministers on the Senior Council are too stupid to understand it." Kaishu stunned the two younger men with this comment. "All they can tell me is that we don't have the money."

Ryoma glanced over his shoulder at Jutaro, drawing a snicker from the navy commissioner. "I know what you're thinking now," Kaishu said. "You're wondering how a Bakufu official like myself can actually say such a thing. You think I'm two-faced. But never mind."

"That's why we must topple the Tokugawa," Ryoma said bitterly. "It's the Bakufu itself which is holding Japan down."

"So, Sakamoto-san," Kaishu again snickered, "you think it would be quite amusing to get a retainer of the Shogun to agree with you."

"I suppose you're right," Ryoma shrugged.

"And I don't blame you. You think that the Tokugawa is more concerned about its own welfare than that of the rest of the nation. And you're absolutely right."

Ryoma and Jutaro were now beside themselves with awe for this unique Bakufu official.

"In this way," Kaishu continued, "the Bakufu is no different than the hundreds of *han* throughout Japan. But from now on, we must combine our strength and resources, and regardless of *han* or birthright or rank, we must rely on men of talent to bring our nation up to the technological level of the Western powers, or we must perish," Kaishu concluded firmly.

"And use the profits we gain from trading with the West to modernize so we can purchase our own warships and guns to develop our navy," Ryoma said.

"Exactly! But rather than merely purchasing the technology, we must import the expertise so that we can produce our own ships. To get the money to build iron mills and the necessary machinery and factories to produce warships and guns, we must trade with the rest of the world. And, Chiba-san," Kaishu directed his attention at the young sword master, "this means opening up to the barbarians. Only then will Japan be able to raise its head proudly to the rest of the world."

Ryoma was mesmerized. Kaishu's talk of forming a navy and going beyond class to recruit men of ability was identical to the ideas of

Kawada Shoryo. But these were no longer merely ideas. This was the commissioner of the Bakufu Navy, speaking on equal terms to him, a *ronin*, a wanted man and self-styled enemy of the very regime which Kaishu represented. This little man who sat before him seemed to radiate the aura of a giant. In fact, Ryoma felt that he had just met the greatest man in all of Japan.

Ryoma sat in the formal position, placed his hands directly in front of him, then, much to the astonishment of both Jutaro and Kaishu, bowed his head to the floor. "Katsu-sensei," he said, resuming an upright posture, "it was my intention tonight to perhaps kill you, but now I am ashamed of my narrow-minded prejudice. I beg you to accept me as your disciple."

"Ryoma!" Jutaro protested.

Not only was the young sword master shocked at the seemingly sudden conversion of his trusted friend, but even Katsu Kaishu himself was taken aback. Indeed this *ronin* from Tosa seemed to understand his ideas better than any of the self-styled *Men of High Purpose* whom the navy commissioner had thus far encountered.

"In that case," Kaishu said, "you can sit back and relax. I'll be glad to have you working with me. As a matter of fact, this calls for a drink to celebrate the occasion."

"No, Katsu-sensei. Not tonight." Ryoma was firm.

"No need for reservation with me, Ryoma," Kaishu said, referring to his new disciple familiarly, by his given name.

"If I drink, I won't be of any use tonight," Ryoma said. "Like you've told us, there are men all over Edo who would like to cut you down."

"And?" Kaishu was amused.

"I've just assigned myself as your personal bodyguard." Ryoma grabbed his sword. "If anybody wants to harm Katsu Kaishu," he said, "they are going to have to kill Sakamoto Ryoma first."

Although Kaishu had perhaps exaggerated in his talk of so many would-be assassins showing up at his home, Ryoma was dead serious. He had heard about the recent bloodbath in Kyoto, where the murder of Bakufu supporters had become an everyday occurrence. He had even heard rumors that Takechi Hanpeita was the mastermind behind the bloodshed, and that Okada Izo was his leading hit man. And although Edo was not yet as dangerous as Kyoto, since the assassination of Regent Ii Naosuke two years before, proponents of *Opening the Country* were not safe even in the Shogun's capital.

"Jutaro," Ryoma said, turning to his friend, "are you with me?"

Jutaro was confused, as anyone would have been who had accompanied Ryoma on this historical night. "Don't you think you ought to consider this a little more before making such a big decision?" he said, looking Ryoma straight in the eye.

"There's nothing more to consider. You heard what Katsu-sensei said. What could possibly be more important than helping him to build a navy?"

Chiba Jutaro was overcome, and much for his own good, by the clear foresight of Sakamoto Ryoma. "Alright," he shrugged. "You win. Katsu-sensei," Jutaro looked hard at the man whom he had considered killing earlier that very night, "sleep well. Sakamoto Ryoma and Chiba Jutaro will be standing guard until morning."

Bloodlust

Although the flame of patriotism for a united Japan which burned in Ryoma's heart had initially been sparked several years before by Takechi Hanpeita, and later fueled by the fiery rhetoric of Kusaka Genzui, it was the cool wisdom of Katsu Kaishu which steered him on a more definite course toward more definite goals. The navy commissioner would change the life of the outlaw-samurai, who until now had been groping in the dark for what he had just found. Kaishu was to Ryoma an endless source of energy–as the clouds were to the great white dragon of his fantastic vision. The Dragon had begun to soar.

Ryoma's thinking had developed into an eclectic realism, based on his love of freedom, and laced with a combination of anti-Bakufu and xenophilous elements which, to most of his emotion-driven comrades, seemed not only contradictory, but even traitorous. His friends could not help but feel that he had overnight taken a complete turnabout by substituting his anti-foreign convictions for a call to open the nation. And as if to add fuel to the fiery spirits of his comrades, Ryoma had even gone so far as to enter into the service of a leading Bakufu official whom other Men of High Purpose had branded an enemy to their cause and traitor to Japan. Some of Ryoma's comrades, upon hearing the news of his conversion, even concluded that he had abandoned Imperial Loyalism in support of the Bakufu, an assumption which was totally mistaken. Most of these zealots not only failed to realize that Ryoma's newly formed synthesis of ideals coincided logically with the merchant blood that flowed in his veins, but what's more, they refused to acknowledge the bitter reality that dealing with the rest of the world was the only way to modernize Japan, and save the nation from foreign subjugation.

While Takechi Hanpeita was officially a lower-samurai, he was now the *de facto* leader of Tosa Han. His following was numerous, and the influence he had suddenly come to wield was, for the time being, not to be challenged by even the retired *daimyo* himself, fuming in anger at his Edo villa.

"Izo!" Hanpeita called from his room at an inn in Osaka. Although Okada Izo had not been invited to become an official member of the Tosa Loyalist Party, he was absolutely loyal to the party leader. Master Zuizan was kneeling on the *tatami* floor, brush in hand, hunched over a bamboo landscape done in Chinese ink, on fine ivory-colored Tosa paper in various shades of black and gray, lodged deeply in his psyche from the annals of ancient Chinese literature.

Dressed only in a black cotton kimono, open at his chest on this scorching afternoon of the last day of July, Izo jumped up from the wooden floor where he had been dozing, just outside the entrance of his master's room. "Yes, Sensei. What is it?" Izo now held his long sword in his right hand, the short one stuck through his sash at his left hip, as he waited anxiously for Hanpeita to invite him inside.

"I have an assignment for you of utmost importance, Izo." Hanpeita spoke calmly, his face an expressionless void, his eyes never once leaving the Chinese landscape before him. The Loyalist leader had been sure to arrange for Okada Izo and several other expert swordsmen to accompany him to nearby Kyoto for reasons he had not yet disclosed.

Izo bowed deeply from the threshold. "Yes, Sensei," he said obeisantly, still not entering the room. His complete awe for his fencing master had intensified over the years by Hanpeita's penchant for assuming majestic airs, a technique which was effective with many of the Tosa men, but never with Sakamoto Ryoma. Since the assassination of Yoshida Toyo, Hanpeita had been using his rhetorical skill, laced with the solemn silver of samurai ethics and *Imperial Loyalism*, to dupe his less intellectual followers into obeying his every command. *Toppling the Bakufu and Imperial Loyalism* was the maxim, *Heaven's Revenge* the battle cry of the self-styled "Shield of the Emperor."

"Sit, Izo," Hanpeita gently ordered, as he put down his ink brush, replacing it with a small white fan. "You're like a fierce animal with a sword in your hand." Hanpeita calmly fanned his face, staring hard into the eyes of his overwhelmed disciple. "You're the perfect weapon of the Emperor," he continued to flatter. "Having trained you myself, I know that better than anyone else," he said calmly, still fanning his face. "The *daimyo* will leave Osaka for Kyoto in a few days."

"Yes, Sensei." Izo was like a vicious dog that could be controlled only by its master.

"There is a certain person who must not be there when our lord arrives."

"Yes, Sensei." Izo's eyes lit up at this chance for his first "assignment."

"That certain person is Inoue Saichiro, of the Tosa police force," Hanpeita whispered, a sinister grin on his otherwise expressionless face. "He's staying with the entourage of our *daimyo* at Tosa head-quarters in Osaka. We can't have him prying." Hanpeita feared that prying by the Tosa police might arouse suspicion, linking his Loyalist Party to the murder of the regent, and even possibly diminishing his *de facto* rule over Tosa policy. "This is your first opportunity to inflict *Heaven's Revenge.*"

"*Heaven's Revenge!*" Izo repeated the now familiar phrase with religious fervor. "*Heaven's Revenge.* Yes, Sensei, I understand." After bowing his head to the floor, he stood up, drew his sword, and with an animal-like expression slammed the blade, over two and a half feet long, back into its dark blue lacquered sheath. "I'll get started right away."

Four Tosa samurai sat at a table in a crowded Osaka *sake* house late in the afternoon on the second day of August. On the table were several ceramic flasks, all empty but one, from which Izo was pouring himself the last drink. "You both know Inoue quite well," Izo said to two of his comrades-in-arms.

"We'll invite him for a drink tonight, and get him so drunk he won't be able to defend himself," whispered one of the men.

"Then we'll take over from there," Izo snickered, putting his arm around the shoulders of the fourth man.

All four of these men resented their fellow lower-samurai, Inoue Saichiro, for having sided with the Yoshida Toyo faction, while Hanpeita's arch-enemy was still very much alive and completely in control of Tosa. Inoue had sold his soul, they reasoned, to the upper-samurai in turn for a chance of improving his own personal lot. And even worse, he was now working with the Tosa police, tracking down Yoshida's assassins.

That evening two of Izo's comrades went to Tosa headquarters in Osaka to invite the unsuspecting police agent on a drinking binge. After getting him sufficiently drunk, they led him over a bridge, above the river which flowed through the city, where Izo and another man were waiting. "Murata," Izo called one of their names, feigning surprise. The streets were empty this late at night, and aside from Izo's gruff voice, the only sound was the clean murmur of the river below. Izo and the other man quickly approached the three. "Hello, Inoue," Izo said nonchalantly.

"Izo? When did you get here?" the Tosa police agent suspiciously slurred.

"Never mind," Izo said, putting his arm around Inoue's shoulders. "Come, let's get some women and drink."

Before Inoue could reply, Izo slipped his arm around his neck in a vise-like headlock. "*Heaven's Revenge*," he wailed, and one of his three accomplices responded with a kick to Inoue's groin. As Inoue keeled over in pain, Izo produced a piece of rope he had brought for the purpose, wrapped it around the drunken man's neck, and proceeded to strangle the life out of him.

"Here, take this too, traitor," another man snarled, drew his sword and drove it through Inoue's neck, before the others threw the body into the river below.

Having felt the blood-lust from his first victim, Okada Izo had transformed into a murderer whose notorious *nom de guerre*, "The Butcher," was soon to be equated with *Heaven's Revenge* throughout Osaka and Kyoto. Izo experienced for the first time a rush of pleasure at the pit of his gut from the feeling of power which accompanied the act of murder. He had never felt so important, as if he too was now playing an essential role in realizing the lofty political goals of which Hanpeita had often spoken, but he himself so little understood.

Hanpeita and Izo sat in the sword master's private quarters at the Toranote Inn, located near Tosa headquarters in Kyoto. Private lodgings away from official Tosa headquarters, reasoned the Tosa Loyalist Party leader, would be necessary as a command post from which to devise his bloody plans for *Heaven's Revenge* against Tokugawa supporters, former henchmen of Ii Naosuke, and other undesirable elements whom Master Zuizan deemed best eliminated. "You did a good job on Inoue." Hanpeita praised his hit man as he would a dog, handing him a small pouch of gold coins as a reward.

Izo's eyes lit up. "Thank you, Sensei," he said, bowing his head to the floor. This was more gold than he had ever seen at once in all the twenty-five years of his heretofore impoverished life.

"And you can use this in your next assignment," Hanpeita said, handing Izo his own sword. Master Zuizan, the planner of murders, spoke these words with a sinister tinge of pleasure derived from the very power he felt in dictating the fate of his enemies.

"Who this time?" Izo asked eagerly.

"Honma Seiichiro," Hanpeita whispered.

"Honma!" Izo exclaimed in disbelief. "But I thought he was on our side."

"It is not for you to question my orders, Izo," Hanpeita calmly scolded, subduing his "wild dog" with an icy stare.

Izo could not understand why Hanpeita would want to murder this champion of *Toppling the Bakufu and Imperial Loyalism*. Honma, one of the pioneers of *Imperial Loyalism*, had visited the Tosa Loyalists in Kochi during the previous spring to urge their support in the planned uprising, which was later crushed by the slaughter at the Teradaya. After the fiasco, Honma negotiated the aid of radical court nobles, the success of which earned him the jealousy of the Tosa Loyalist Party leader, who now wanted this rival eliminated from the Kyoto scene.

It was a rainy night in Kyoto in late August when Honma, escorting a pretty young courtesan clad in a bright flowery kimono, stepped out from the gay realm of a bacchanalian pleasure palace and into a bloody hell of razor-sharp steel and eternal blackness. The courtesan screamed under a white paper lantern flickering in the dark rainy night, as nine swordsmen rushed out from nowhere to surround Honma.

"*Heaven's Revenge,*" wailed Izo, holding his drawn sword high above his head.

"Izo!" screamed Honma. "Is this another murder for Takechi Hanpeita?"

"*Heaven's Revenge!*" Izo screamed again. Honma drew his sword, but he was no challenge to Izo's overwhelming skill, as "The Butcher" emitted an ear-piercing guttural wail, diagonally slicing Honma from his left shoulder down to his right hip. Blood spurted like a fountain, spraying the white lantern above, and covering the shock-stricken courtesan who continued to scream bloody murder. "*Heaven's Revenge!*" wailed another swordsman, drawing his blade and impaling the chest of the frenzied woman, who slowly choked on her own blood. The assassins took Honma's head and ran with it to the grassy banks of the Kamogawa, where they mounted it on a bamboo spike stuck firmly in the soft mud.

Three days later Izo led another attack on vassals of a pro-Bakufu family of court nobles, who had been instrumental in both Ii Naosuke's purge and the marriage between the Emperor's sister and the Shogun. "*Heaven's Revenge!*" screamed Izo, delivering the death-blow to his fourth victim, the head of whom was also publicly displayed in the now bloody city of the Emperor. One week later Izo was accredited with the gruesome murder of another former supporter of

Ii. Before strangling this victim, "The Butcher" and his band of hit men first drove bamboo spikes through his penis and up his anus, as he screamed in agony. Not long after this, the head of three more Bakufu agents who had also been involved in Ii's purge were found on public display on the riverbank near Hanpeita's command post.

Having thus far succeeded in his plan to eliminate his enemies, the Shield of the Emperor, high on the glory of his sudden rise to power, continued to whisper his terrible command of *"Heaven's Revenge"* into the ear of his obedient hit man for the remainder of 1862 and into the following year. Before Hanpeita's reign of terror would end, the victims of the notorious "Butcher" would number twenty, earning Okada Izo the most feared reputation of all the radicals who had gathered in the ancient capital during the bloodbath of the 1860s.

*   *   *

A few weeks after Ryoma had entered the service of Katsu Kaishu, Takechi Hanpeita's elaborate palanquin appeared in front of the house of the navy commissioner, on a moonless night in October. The Shield of the Emperor, recently promoted to Imperial samurai status, had been serving as personal bodyguard to two Imperial messengers dispatched by the court to Edo to demand that the Bakufu renounce its foreign treaties and resume its policy of seclusionism, to, in Hanpeita's own words, "expel the filthy barbarians from the sacred soil of Japan."

Hanpeita, accompanied by two attendants, was dressed in silk, his topknot neatly tied and looped over his cleanly shaven pate. Instead of the long blade for which the sword master was known, he now wore the dainty ornamental sword of a court noble. Ordering his two attendants to remain with the palanquin, Hanpeita alighted, and approached the house. "Ryoma!" he called, staring hard at his friend in the dim light of a single lantern. Ryoma was sitting alone under the eaves of the front gate, his sword on his lap.

"Hanpeita," Ryoma returned the greeting. He had heard of the recent assassinations in Kyoto, and did not doubt rumors that Hanpeita was behind them. Nor did Ryoma doubt the hearsay that Hanpeita's key hit man was his old friend Okada Izo. Almost as much as the actual killing, Ryoma despised Hanpeita's uncanny ability to use people around him as pawns to realize his own personal glory. But despite these ugly thoughts that raced through his mind at his first sight of Hanpeita in over six months, Ryoma was glad to see him.

Hanpeita, for his part, felt a fast feeling of disgust. Not only had Ryoma abandoned Tosa and the Loyalist Party, but it now seemed that his friend, whom he had always greatly respected, had become a traitor to the very cause for which brave men from all over Japan had pledged, and indeed even laid down their lives. "Ryoma, what are you doing here?" Hanpeita said indignantly. "I couldn't believe that you'd actually be here, but now I see it's true."

Ryoma jumped to his feet. "You don't understand, Hanpeita. I know exactly what you're thinking, but you're completely mistaken. I'm working for the greatest man in Japan. And to answer you're question, I'm guarding him from crazy maniacs like you." Ryoma shook his head slowly. "What's become of you? What do you expect to gain by slaughtering people?"

"Why are you guarding a traitorous Bakufu official?"

"You just don't understand," Ryoma said.

"Then, you've turned against us?"

"No, I haven't turned against you."

"Then tell me," Hanpeita whispered, "do you still support *Toppling the Bakufu and Imperial Loyalism*? Are you still ready to give your life to protect Japan from the wicked barbarians, overthrow the Tokugawa and restore the power to the sacred Emperor? Or have you really sold out to those who want to open the country to foreign subjugation?"

"What do you think?" Ryoma retorted harshly, looking directly into Hanpeita's eyes, then lowering his voice to a whisper. "I'm still determined to topple the Bakufu. I'm still determined to restore the Emperor to power, and drive the barbarians out of Japan. But I have my own way of accomplishing these things."

Since meeting Katsu Kaishu, Ryoma had completely risen above the simplistic view that expelling the foreigners was inseparable from *Imperial Loyalism*, and that the open-door doctrine was tantamount to supporting the Bakufu. Unlike Hanpeita, and indeed almost every Loyalist in Japan, Ryoma realized that under the present circumstances Japan could not win a war against the Western powers. Unfortunately, the misinformed Imperial Court, and indeed the chronically xenophobic Emperor himself, were under the dangerous impression that Japan could never be subjugated. And capitalizing on Imperial ignorance, the Choshu and Tosa rebels, led by Kusaka Genzui on the one hand and Takechi Hanpeita on the other, had convinced the court in Kyoto to demand that the Edo regime renounce the foreign treaties.

Thus, the Bakufu found itself faced with a difficult dilemma. Neither bold enough to refuse the Imperial demands, which were supported by the Satsuma, Choshu and Tosa rebels, nor able to violate the foreign treaties for fear of triggering a war which it could not hope to win, the Bakufu had no choice but to appease the court with the vague promise to "eventually close the country to all barbarians." Encouraged by the Choshu and Tosa Loyalists, the court, in turn, insisted on a deadline for expelling the foreigners. If the Bakufu could not meet that deadline, it was insinuated that Imperial forces would attack Edo.

And so, despite Ryoma's realization that Japan was not yet militarily prepared to defend itself from foreign invasion, Hanpeita and his allies remained adamant in equating *Opening the Country* with a pro-Bakufu policy. Ryoma could not convince his comrades it was only by means of Kaishu's policy of openness that Japan could ever hope to stand up to the foreign demands.

"Then, tell me this," Hanpeita said, "are you still a Loyalist?"

"I'm Japanese," Ryoma answered bluntly.

Hanpeita gave Ryoma a hard look. The concept of simply "being Japanese" was contrary to the mind-set of the people who populated the conglomerate of feudal domains in this particular time in Japanese history. A samurai's country was his *han*. Accordingly, a Choshu samurai was of Choshu, while a Satsuma samurai was a man entirely of that *han*. Takechi Hanpeita was of Tosa, as were his followers in the Tosa Loyalist Party as well as his adversaries from the faction of Yoshida Toyo. Similarly, men of the court were Imperial nobles, while the Shogun's retainers, and samurai from the Tokugawa-related *han*, were men of the Bakufu. Things were cut-and-dry; one's social lot was predetermined by birth. Like Ryoma, however, Katsu Kaishu was an exception. Although as a shogunal retainer he had been born into the Tokugawa camp, his modern and farsighted outlook enabled him to see beyond the narrow scope of *han* and Bakufu, and to consider himself as one organic part of the whole of Japanese society.

"Of course you're Japanese?" Hanpeita said. "As I am. But you're also from Tosa."

"I'm Japanese," Ryoma repeated firmly. "I don't give a damn about Tosa or any of the other *han*. They're concerned only for themselves. If we are to save Japan from foreign subjugation, and I believe that's

what everyone is ranting and raving about, then we must work together as one unified nation. To hell with birthright, to hell with class, to
hell with the *han* and to hell with the *daimyo*," Ryoma hollered, as if
he were oblivious to the fact that he was standing in front of the home
of a high-ranking Bakufu official. Then, regaining his composure,
Ryoma looked straight into Hanpeita's eyes. "I'm still determined to
accomplish one thing," he whispered. "And that's to topple the
Tokugawa Bakufu. But I have my own way of doing it."

"By working for a traitorous Bakufu official?" Hanpeita seethed. "I
don't understand you at all."

"Like I told you before," Ryoma said, "the worst thing we can do is
to be killing each other."

"I can call off my dogs," Hanpeita said, "the men from Tosa, but I
can't guarantee that there won't be men from other *han* after you."

Although Ryoma shared the goal of Hanpeita and the Choshu and
Satsuma radicals, he differed greatly with them not only in his reasons
for wanting to topple the Bakufu, but also in the means by which he
would bring about the revolution. The Loyalists were striving to unite
the most powerful domains in western Japan (Tosa, Choshu and
Satsuma) into one Imperial faction, which would rally around the
Emperor, and topple the Bakufu with its combined military and political might. Unlike Ryoma, they refused to throw off their chains of
feudalism in their actions and ideals. Just as Hanpeita had insisted on
working within the feudal structure of Tosa Han, so too were the
Choshu and Satsuma men absolutely dedicated to their own respective
clans. As Ryoma well knew, however, even if the Loyalists were successful in overthrowing the Bakufu, they would again break up into
individual *han* to compete with one another for the political authority
which had been held by the Tokugawa for the past two-and-a-half centuries. Ryoma, on the other hand, viewed things from a scope that
exceeded the individual *han*. He now realized that the only way to
save Japan from foreign subjugation would be to get rid of the feudal
system entirely, which meant abolishing the clans altogether. Rather
than a conglomerate of individual *han*, each most concerned with its
own self-interest, Ryoma realized the absolute need to combine the
resources of all the clans, and form a unified nation to compete with
the rest of the world. But in his insight, he also realized that proposing such a concept would only further alienate his comrades. "Timing
is of the essence," he told himself, as he patiently awaited his chance
to act under the wing of Katsu Kaishu, and so prove to his comrades

the wisdom behind his newfound ideas. Not only did Ryoma understand the need for national unity, but his recent exposure to Kaishu's ideas had convinced him that the only realistic way to topple the Bakufu would be by first fortifying the nation against foreign subjugation, thus his perfect dedication to his mentor's school of thought which called for "knowing the enemy through importation of Western military and industrial technology."

"Hanpeita," Ryoma said as the two stood in front of Kaishu's house on this moonless night, "if you think I'm afraid for myself..."

"No. I know you too well for that," Hanpeita said. "But what are you doing?" he repeated, this time in a tone of genuine anguish, as if speaking to a younger brother.

"I just told you. I'm working for the greatest man in Japan. We're getting ready to build a navy. And with our navy, and this," Ryoma held up his sword, "and this," he tapped his temple, "I'll topple the Bakufu."

"By working with a Bakufu official?"

"This isn't the place to discuss the matter," Ryoma hesitated, glancing over his shoulder at the house. "By the way, when did you start traveling around in a palanquin? I didn't know you were so important," he snickered. "And what happened to your sword?" he gibed, pointing at the dainty weapon in Hanpeita's sash.

"I'm here on an Imperial mission," Hanpeita said.

"And I'm here recruiting men for our navy," Ryoma retorted. "Do you know anyone who would like to join?"

Hanpeita's pride in his recent elevation in social status lacked the cockiness that compelled Ryoma to brag about his newfound occupation of recruiting trainees for a naval academy which Kaishu was planning to establish. Lately, in fact, when Ryoma wasn't guarding Kaishu's house, the outlaw had been recruiting men to join him in his grand escapades.

"Ryoma, I could really use you with me, especially now," Hanpeita pleaded. Then in a whisper he added, "Tosa, Satsuma and Choshu have united in Kyoto, and we have the backing of the Imperial Court."

Much to the chagrin of the Lord of Satsuma, he had recently been bamboozled into lending his own name to the radical elements behind the Imperial messengers whom Hanpeita was escorting in Edo to demand that the Bakufu expel the foreigners. The conservative Lord of Satsuma, however, who had himself just returned from Edo after persuading the Bakufu of the importance of uniting with the court, was by no means an anti-Bakufu fanatic. But because during his absence from Kyoto the radicals at court had joined hands with the Choshu and Tosa Loyalists, he had no alternative, for the time being, but to endorse the alliance.

"It's only a matter of time," Hanpeita said with conviction, "before we topple the Bakufu."

"Damn it, Hanpeita," Ryoma turned his head to spit. "What are you thinking? Do you want to destroy our nation?"

"What do you mean?"

"If you don't know by now, I guess you never will," Ryoma said in disgust. "You'll never change, Hanpeita. You're just as rigid as ever. You can't rush things. The time just hasn't come. Like you've always said yourself: 'Timing is of the essence!' It's the same in *kendo*, and you should know that as well as anyone."

"You don't understand, Ryoma. Here you are guarding the enemy, when you should be working with us in Kyoto. We're ready to move, and nothing is going to stop us."

"What do you propose to do after the Bakufu is toppled? Who's going to rule then?"

"The Imperial Court, of course," Hanpeita answered without hesitation.

"The Imperial Court?" Ryoma said derisively. "That's fine, but who's going to keep the barbarians from attacking? That's where this man comes in," Ryoma said, pointing over his shoulder at Kaishu's house. "He's the most important man in Japan." Ryoma paused, folded his arms at his chest, and continued. "You might even say he's our last hope," he added with complete conviction. Then, placing his hand on the hilt of his sword, he said, "Just as the great sword masters have taught through the ages, and just as you yourself have always said, the surest way to defeat an enemy is to first understand him entirely." Ryoma paused again to take a deep breath. "And that's exactly what Katsu Kaishu is doing. The man has not only dedicated his life to understanding the West, but he's doing it for different reasons than you seem to understand."

"Which are?"

"Certainly not for his own glory, nor for the sake of any one individual *han*."

"Yes, but for the sake of the Tokugawa Bakufu," Hanpeita retorted.

"No, Hanpeita. You're wrong. Both Katsu-sensei and I are working for one thing."

"Which is?"

"I just told you," Ryoma said bluntly. "Japan. And I'll tell you this, too," he suddenly raised his voice, his face stone-serious. "If anything should happen to Katsu Kaishu, I'll personally see to it that those involved pay with their lives."

"Ryoma, let's talk again soon, at a more appropriate place."

"I don't know what more there is to say," Ryoma said sadly, realizing once and for all that the distance between himself and this close friend of his past had grown too great for the two to ever see eye-to-eye again.

"I'll be in Edo for a while longer," Hanpeita said.

"And I suppose you expect me to come to Tosa headquarters so I can be arrested," Ryoma snickered.

"No. I'm staying at the Imperial lodgings in the Ryunokuchi district. You can find me there," said the Shield of the Emperor, then turned around and, without looking back, returned to his palanquin.

Persuasion

A lone ronin strode through the false tranquillity of the darkness guided by the light of a full December moon. Snowflakes floated through the biting cold air, and clung to the eyebrows and tangled hair of the sword-bearing outlaw who kept a steady pace up the narrow road winding toward Chifuku Temple, in the maple-studded hills overlooking the Imperial capital from the northeast.

Silence permeated the night. The only sounds were the wind blowing through the trees, the man's steady breathing, a soft and constant pounding inside his head and his firm footsteps on the freshly fallen snow. Suddenly, as he was about to pass through the main gate of the Zen temple, he heard the thrashing of someone approaching at a dead run.

"Heaven's Revenge!" shrieked the assailant. The ronin drew his sword with lightning speed, intercepting flashing steel just above his left shoulder, as sparks flew in the air.

"Izo!" Ryoma roared, staring straight into his friend's eyes. Izo's eyes had changed since the last time the two had met. The change was overwhelming, and Ryoma felt an awful coldness in them, as the snow continued to fall softly. Ryoma could see in Izo's eyes that he had acquired the knowledge of murder, a knowledge which made him thrive on bloodshed.

"Ryoma?" Izo gasped, his eyes flashing in the moonlight. "What are you doing here?"

Although Ryoma was not inclined to explain, he had recently sailed with Kaishu from Edo to Osaka aboard a Tokugawa warship. The navy commissioner had been assigned the job of escorting a member of the Bakufu's Senior Council to Osaka to investigate how Japan might best deal with a foreign invasion of that city. Inner-turmoil had compelled the government to prepare for such an attack, when and if it carried out its promise to the court of expelling the foreigners. Kaishu reasoned that this would be a good opportunity for Ryoma to get his first experience on a steam-powered warship.

"Izo," Ryoma said, obviously annoyed, "I didn't expect to see any of you until tomorrow." Since Ryoma could not himself go to Tosa headquarters in Kyoto for fear of arrest, he had sent a message earlier in the day to three Tosa Loyalists who were stationed there, asking that they meet him at a nearby inn on the next day. Ryoma intended to recruit these three men for Kaishu's naval academy. "And I didn't expect to see you at all," Ryoma said, his heart filled with both anger and pity for his friend whom Hanpeita had transformed into a murderer.

"I thought you were someone else," Izo said. "Takechi-sensei is in Edo now, but word had it that a traitor would be here trying to recruit Loyalists to fight on the side of the Bakufu."

"Who told you that?" Ryoma snickered.

"A stranger from Mito came looking for me, you see," Izo said hesitantly, scratching his thick black beard, "while I was, ah....while I was..."

"While you were what?" Ryoma growled impatiently.

As Izo explained, he had been at a brothel earlier in the day–a luxury he had only recently been able to afford–when a stranger came looking for him. "I was with a girl, when this samurai from Mito came barging in asking if I was," Izo paused under Ryoma's hard stare, "asking if I was 'The Butcher.'"

"And what did you tell him, Izo?"

"I said that I was," Izo muttered uncomfortably. "But I sure jumped up quick when I heard him at the door. The first thing I did was grab my sword. I thought he was a Bakufu agent. I was banging away pretty hard, and I sure wouldn't want to get attacked in that position." Izo again paused, then quickly added, "I only do it for *Imperial Loyalism*, you know," he blankly echoed the words he had recently so often heard from Master Zuizan.

From the crazed look in Izo's eyes, Ryoma now realized that his friend actually believed that by simply murdering people he was serving the Imperialist cause.

"Anyway, this samurai from Mito told me that there was a *ronin* staying at Chifuku Temple, who was working for Katsu Kaishu, the Tokugawa Navy Commissioner."

"That's me, you stupid idiot!"

"That's you?" Izo gaped blankly. "So you're the one I was supposed to..." he stopped himself short. "But, Ryoma, Takechi-sensei has told us Katsu is..."

"What has Hanpeita been saying about Katsu Kaishu?" Ryoma roared indignantly.

"He says that Katsu is trying to sell out to the barbarians."

"Damn it, Izo. Hanpeita has brainwashed you. Does anyone know that you're here?"

"No. I took it upon myself to come and cut you," Izo paused uneasily. "I mean cut the traitor..."

"I want you to come with me to Edo. Wash your hands of the blood you've shed and start being of some use to Japan."

"What do you mean?" Izo gave Ryoma a blank stare.

"I've never seen you like this. How many people have you killed?"

"*Heaven's Revenge*," Izo said inanely. "Each one of them got what they deserved."

"Let's talk about that tomorrow with the others," Ryoma said sourly.

"What others?" Izo asked, overcome by a deep-rooted paranoia which Ryoma could read on his contorted face. Izo's paranoia had intensified in degrees with each murder he had committed over the past several months, until now the once fearless swordsman shuddered at the thought of his own blood-lust. He had sold his soul to Takechi Hanpeita for the little bit of gold and glory he received each time he eliminated a potential enemy.

"I'm going to meet three Tosa men tomorrow evening," Ryoma said.

"Who?" Izo's eyes opened wide.

"Don't worry, Izo. You know all three of them. They're all members of the Tosa Loyalist Party."

"Why are you going to meet them?"

"I have plans. Big plans." Ryoma spoke softly to Izo, as if to calm his friend's agitated soul. "Meet us at the Sakura Inn tomorrow at noon. We'll talk then," Ryoma said, before leaving Izo alone in the snowy darkness at the temple gate.

Ryoma arrived at the Sakura Inn at noon the next day. He was escorted to a private room on the second floor, where three young Tosa men, whom he had not seen since before he had fled, were waiting for him. One was Takamatsu Taro, the twenty-year-old son of Ryoma's eldest sister, and devote Loyalist. The other two men were both old friends of Ryoma's. Chiya Toranosuke was the son of a village headman in Tosa's Aki district, who had succeeded his father while still in his late teens. Since Toranosuke was endowed with a temperament as mild as the coastal region from which he hailed, his parents never expected him to suddenly abandon his duties as village headman to run with Takechi Hanpeita's band of zealots. But Toranosuke was by no means sheltered from the turbulence of the times. Several uncles and cousins were active in the Loyalist movement, and before long he was under their influence. In 1861, at age nineteen, Toranosuke, along with several cousins, joined the Tosa Loyalist Party. He nevertheless continued his duties as headman of his native village, even after his close friends Sawamura Sonojo and Sakamoto Ryoma had given up hope in Tosa and fled. But when Yoshida Toyo was assassinated in the spring of 1861, Toranosuke begged his father's forgiveness and abandoned his home and family to join Hanpeita's renegades. He arrived in Kyoto in the previous fall, around the time Ryoma had met Katsu Kaishu. In October Toranosuke joined Okada Izo in the grisly murders of two Kyoto merchants suspected of supporting the Bakufu. At the beginning of November he took part in the murder of a Tosa police agent who was looking for the assassins of Yoshida Toyo; and in the middle of the same month he assisted in the murder of the mistress of Ii Naosuke's right-hand man, when the assassins tied to the poor woman to a bamboo post by the riverbank and left her naked to die of exposure. On the next day, Toranosuke's group cut down the woman's son, and displayed his head near the same spot where his mother had been left to die.

The third man whom Ryoma had summoned, Mochizuki Kameyata, was as dedicated to the Imperial cause as the other two. It was Ryoma's intention to convince these three to join a naval academy that he and Kaishu had been planning to establish in Kobe, a small fishing village near Osaka.

Ryoma removed his long sword and sat down with the others. "Where's Izo?" he asked, laying his sword at his right side.

"Izo?" Toranosuke said.

"Yes, the stupid idiot tried to cut me last night. It seems that I have more to worry about from my own friends, than I do from the Tosa police," Ryoma snickered. "I told him to meet us here today, but I guess he's not ready yet."

"What do you mean, 'not ready yet'?" Toranosuke asked.

"Forget it." Ryoma avoided the question, choosing to state his purpose for calling this meeting in a more direct manner.

"You must get out of Kyoto," Taro said. "There are Tosa agents all over this city, and who knows when they might..."

"I'm not worried," Ryoma interrupted his nephew. "But," he paused to look directly into the eyes of each of the three men, "that's why I've called you here today. Tora, Kame," he addressed with diminutives his two close friends who trusted him like an older brother, "I want you to join our navy?"

"Your navy?" Tora asked, a puzzled look on his face.

"Katsu Kaishu's navy," Ryoma said. The room was suddenly silent, as all three of the younger men stared blankly at Ryoma, who began speaking very deliberately. "I've called you here to ask for your help in bringing down the Bakufu," he paused to stress the significance of his words, "and saving Japan from foreign subjugation."

"Katsu Kaishu is a traitor," Kame shouted indignantly. "He's sold out to the barbarians. And now you too have changed sides. You say you want to bring down the Bakufu to save Japan from the barbarians, but you're working for a Tokugawa lackey."

Ryoma gave all three men a hard look. "Before we go any further, let's get some things straight. I haven't changed sides, and I'm not working for a Tokugawa lackey. I'm working for the greatest man in Japan, who I myself considered killing just a few months ago. Katsu Kaishu has sent me to recruit good men who are willing to learn how to operate a warship. We're starting a naval academy and I want the three of you to join."

"If you're working for Katsu, then I guess we can assume that you support *Opening the Country*," Tora said.

"That's right," Ryoma said bluntly.

"But how can you support *Opening the Country* and at the same time claim that you want to save Japan from the barbarians?"

"Do you trust me?" Ryoma asked.

"Of course we trust you. Do you think we'd be sitting here if we didn't? But what you're saying just doesn't make any sense."

"Let me ask all of you this next question," Ryoma said. "How do you suggest protecting Japan from foreign invasion?"

None of the three could answer.

"Just as I thought," Ryoma snickered. "There are too many people ranting and raving about expelling the barbarians," Ryoma echoed Kaishu's words, "but nobody seems to have any concrete ideas of how to do it. And that's where Katsu Kaishu comes in. He says that we must open the country for as long as it takes us to acquire the proper military and industrial technology to defend ourselves. Which means that we Japanese have to stop fighting among ourselves, and cooperate to build a powerful and wealthy nation. We need ships, and a lot of them, and men like us with the guts to man them. We need a powerful navy so that we can have the freedom to control our own destiny as a united nation."

"But Katsu is a Tokugawa official," Kame said indignantly. "His only concern is for the House of Tokugawa. He doesn't give a damn about the rest of the nation."

"Kame!" Tora burst out, "don't you understand what Ryoma is saying?"

"Kame," Ryoma said, lowering his voice, "have you ever asked Katsu about that? Have you ever met with him to confront him with your opinionated ideas?"

"Of course not. But you can't really believe that a direct retainer of the Tokugawa is going to accept a crew of anti-Bakufu Loyalists. Katsu is an elite Bakufu official, and in his eyes we're a bunch of lowly..."

"Have you ever heard of Abraham Lincoln?" Ryoma uttered the name he had heard Kaishu often speak of.

"Who?"

"The president of the United States of America."

"No."

"Lincoln claims that all men are equal, regardless of class, race or color."

"Color?"

"Some Americans are black, others white, some have golden hair, others brown, some red."

All three men remained silent, listening intently to Ryoma.

"For years white men in America have used black men as slaves, much like the samurai in Japan use the peasants. But Lincoln, who himself is white, is fighting a civil war to free the black men because the *Declaration of Independence* of the United States dictates that all men are created equal, regardless of race or color." Despite his efforts, Ryoma was unable to make his three friends comprehend these very foreign ideas which had so captivated his mind over the past few months.

"What is the president of the United States of America?" Kame asked.

"Forget it," Ryoma groaned. "But just believe me when I say that Katsu is not concerned with birthright. We must rid ourselves of such outdated, decrepit ideas."

"It doesn't make sense," Kame argued. "Katsu's not going to be willing to teach military techniques to men who are intent on bringing down the very regime which he represents."

"Leave that to me," Ryoma said with confidence. "Katsu has entrusted me with the job of recruiting good men for his navy. And I'm asking you three to join me." Ryoma pleaded, pounding his fist on the floor. "If instead of joining me, you go and get yourselves killed, like you're liable to do if you're not very careful, I'll be the one who's angry," he hollered. "We are just as important to Japan as anyone else, and probably even more so than most people. It's men like us, who have ambition and ideals, that Katsu needs to help him."

*   *   *

After recruiting three more Tosa men–Sonojo, who was now in Kyoto serving as a samurai of the court; Umanosuke, the peasant's son; and Chojiro, the bean jam bun maker's son, the latter two having been students of Kawada Shoryo and therefore easy for Ryoma to convince–Ryoma brought all six men to join Kaishu at the Port of Hyogo, just west of Osaka, to sail to Edo aboard a Western-built Tokugawa warship, the *Jundo Maru*.

The *Jundo Maru* set sail with all aboard, flying the Tokugawa crest of three hollyhock leaves in a circle, on the cold overcast morning of January 13,1863. From Hyogo the ship sailed south across Osaka Bay, down through the Kii Strait, then out to the Pacific, where she made an eastward arc around the province of Kii. From here they sailed for two days, until rough waters forced them to land in the Port of Shimoda, on the Izu Peninsula, less than a day's journey to Edo.

"Ryoma!" Kaishu called his right-hand man up to the deck. "See that," he said, pointing at a schooner anchored in port.

"A ship," Ryoma said in a noncommittal tone.

"Well, I'm glad to see that you are so observant," the navy commissioner laughed. "She's flying the three oak leaves of the Yamanouchi crest."

"Yes," Ryoma remarked bluntly, squinting uncomfortably at the schooner. "I didn't know Tosa had a real ship," he sneered. Then, in the same breath, as if to change the unpleasant subject, "Look, you can see Ohshima," he said, pointing eastward at the largest of seven islands off the Izu coast.

"She's not a Tosa ship," Kaishu informed.

"Oh?"

"She belongs to Fukuoka Han, but she's carrying Lord Yodo."

Ryoma remained silent, staring out at the island, his right hand tucked into his kimono, his long hair blowing in the wind.

"I know how you feel about Tosa," Kaishu said consolingly. "I know that you don't give a damn about Tosa Han, and I don't blame you. But

I think I'll pay Lord Yodo a visit anyway."

*　　　　　　*　　　　　　*

Yamanouchi Yodo had set sail from Edo on the previous day aboard a wooden schooner he had chartered from Fukuoka Han, through the good offices of the Tokugawa Navy. This was the first time the retired Tosa *daimyo* had left the capital since being placed under house arrest by Ii Naosuke four and a half years ago. He was planning to stop in Kyoto on his return to Kochi, which was to be his first time home in six years, but was detained in Shimoda by rough seas. Yodo's chief motive for returning to Kochi at this particular time was to suppress the Tosa Loyalist Party. Not only was Yodo convinced that he knew more about the times, had a better knowledge of history and a superior political sense that any other *daimyo* in Japan (with the admitted exception of his friends Matsudaira Shungaku and Hitotsubashi Yoshinobu), but he was also determined to make Takechi Hanpeita and the other murderers of his favorite retainer pay for his great loss. Nor was Yodo about to let a lower-samurai continue his *de facto* rule over Tosa policy. But perhaps the most significant reason for Yodo's determination to suppress the Tosa Loyalists was his inability to side against the Bakufu for the favor his ancestor fifteen generations past had received from the first Tokugawa Shogun.

Yodo and Kaishu were old acquaintances, and indeed the navy commissioner was one of the few men in the Edo government whom the Outside Lord of Tosa truly respected. Not only did both men possess grandiose egos, but they shared some basic ideas. They agreed on the importance of strengthening the nation through foreign trade, military buildup and recruiting men of ability. Unlike Kaishu, however, the elitist Lord of Tosa was absolutely unwilling to fill important government posts from the ranks of the lower-samurai, and certainly not the commoners.

Kaishu appeared at Yodo's lodgings at Hofukuji temple at the Hour of the Horse, just after noon in Western reckoning. He stepped up from a stone platform, onto the wooden verandah which surrounded the spacious apartment, overlooking a meticulously cared for garden. The navy commissioner wore a black jacket displaying the four-petaled Katsu family crest, a kimono of the same color, dark brown *hakama*, and a black soldier's helmet, flat on top with a rim that curved slightly upward. The inner side of the rim was painted gold, a style reserved solely for direct retainers of the Shogun. At Kaishu's left hip hung two swords in wax-colored sheaths, their hilts so tightly tied to the scabbards that they could not readily be drawn.

"Well, what a surprise," Yodo exclaimed at the sight of his old friend. The self-styled Drunken Lord of the Sea of Whales was sitting alone on the floor in front of the alcove of a spacious *tatami* room, a small black lacquered table set before him. He was drinking *sake*, as was his custom every afternoon. Yodo's slightly pock-marked, heavy-set face was blushed from drink, and tiny blood vessels were visible around his nose, but his features, and the way he held his mouth, betrayed his noble lineage. He wore a kimono of gray silk, a black jacket displaying the Yamanouchi crest, and *hakama* of reddish-brown satin. His pate was cleanly shaven, his topknot folded neatly forward. The piercing dark eyes of the thirty-six-year-old Lord of Tosa showed a sharp intellect and strong spirit. "I'm glad you've come, Katsu-sensei," he began speaking in a slightly hurried manner, displaying bad teeth. "I've been wanting to speak with someone intelligent. There are just too many stupid people in this world nowadays."

"Good to see you again." Kaishu bowed slightly, then removed his helmet and swords. "And good to see that you haven't lost your sense of humor," he said drolly.

"Please come in, Katsu-sensei." Yodo, already quite drunk on this cold winter afternoon, was genuinely glad to see the navy commissioner. "Why the sudden visit?" he asked. "Ah, but never mind that for now. Sit down and let's have some *sake* together," he insisted, although he knew that Kaishu rarely drank.

A maid set another small table for the guest, and Yodo handed Kaishu a red crystal glass, the scene of a reindeer in a snowy forest engraved in white around the sides. "This is my favorite *sake* cup," Yodo said. "I only offer it to my most respected friends, and only on special occasions." The Drunken Lord of the Sea of Whales poured Kaishu a drink from a gourd flask.

"What's the special occasion?" Kaishu asked with an amused grin.

"If my memory hasn't failed me, I believe this is the first time that you and I have ever drank together."

"It's beautiful," Kaishu remarked, holding the glass up to the sunlight.

"It's French," Yodo said. "A gift from a merchant in Nagasaki."

Kaishu breathed deeply. "Ah, yes. The French make a lot of nice things." Then in a more solemn tone he added, "Like warships and guns." Kaishu grinned again. "But I prefer the British and Dutch warships to those of the French, don't you Lord Yodo?"

"Yes, warships," Yodo said, looking hard into Kaishu's eyes. "We must have some serious discussion on that subject very soon."

And very soon the two men were discussing the many crises which faced the nation. Although Yodo agreed openly with Kaishu's support for foreign trade in order to build the economy and strengthen the military, the self-styled "poet warrior" could just as readily, when the occasion demanded, argue for "expelling the filthy barbarians for the sake of the sacred Emperor." "Katsu-sensei," he said, "it's unfortunate that there are so many fools in Edo, who until recently were not able to see things your way. But here, have another drink," he insisted, refilling the red crystal glass. "Good *sake* is the best condiment for discussion. And, likewise, good discussion is the best condiment for good *sake*. Besides, of course, a pretty wench," the Tosa *daimyo* added with a roar of laughter.

"Well, Lord Yodo," Kaishu said, pausing to accept another glassful, "you know I'm not such a good drinker. But the taste of *sake* is always enhanced by good company," he said, then drained the glass. "And this is the best *sake* I've had in a long time," Kaishu continued flattering the Drunken Lord of the Sea of Whales. "Here, allow me," he said, pouring a drink for his host.

"Ah, but you've become quite a good drinker," Yodo said.

"By the way, Lord Yodo," Kaishu said, "I've come to see you today for a specific purpose."

"Well, I'm certainly glad to hear that!" Yodo said, then reached over and slapped Kaishu on the back. "There are too many men these days walking around with no purpose at all. Like I've heard you say before," Yodo burst out laughing again, "there are just too many stupid *daimyo* and Bakufu officials these days whose heads are like potatoes on which they so meticulously tie their topknots."

"I've always appreciated your scathing humor," Kaishu said approvingly. "Oh, I nearly forgot," he added nonchalantly. "I have a small favor to ask of you."

"Sure, anything! Anything at all!" Yodo roared amicably. "What is it?"

"I've recently recruited several good men to work under me. The best of them is from your great *han*." Kaishu was careful not to tell Yodo at this particular time that indeed all of his newfound disciples were from Tosa.

"Is that so?" Yodo exclaimed with obvious interest. "What's his name?"

"Sakamoto Ryoma."

"Sakamoto Ryoma?" Yodo repeated. "Never heard of him."

"I doubted you had, Lord Yodo. He's just a lower-samurai," Kaishu said with a forced smile.

"Well then, you might as well keep him," Yodo scoffed. "He's all yours."

"Ah, yes," Kaishu cleared his throat, "I appreciate your generosity. But Ryoma has left Tosa without permission, and...you know, it makes it very inconvenient to work with a man who is in constant danger of being arrested."

"And what do you propose I do?" Yodo asked sourly.

"I'd appreciate it if you could pardon him, along with another Tosa man by the name of Sawamura Sonojo. They're both good men, dedicated to helping me develop a navy."

"Are you quite sure you know what you're doing?" Yodo asked.

"I'm certain," Kaishu said with complete confidence.

"Well then," Yodo groaned, "as long as you do, and you promise to watch over them to be sure that they don't cause any more trouble, I suppose I could do this favor for you. Consider both of them pardoned," he said with a backhanded gesture.

"Thank you very much," Kaishu said with a slight bow of the head. "But, in all due respect, since we have been drinking, I hope you wouldn't mind my asking for something I could take away with me today, as a memento of your promise."

"Very well," Yodo said, then held his hands above his head, and clapped three times. Momentarily a young samurai appeared. "Yes, My Lord?" the samurai said, bowing deeply.

"Bring my writing brush and inkstone," Yodo said.

"Yes, My Lord." The samurai bowed again, and left the room, returning shortly with the writing utensils.

Yodo took a white paper fan from his sash, opened it wide, and in long, graceful strokes drew a simple likeness in black ink of the gourd flask on the table in front of him. Inside the drawing of the flask he wrote several Chinese characters, and placed the open fan on the floor before Kaishu. "How's that?" he asked, apparently pleased with himself.

Kaishu picked up the fan, the black ink still wet. The message inside the flask read: *"Drunk, three hundred-sixty days a year,"* and was signed, *"Drunken Lord of the Sea of Whales."*

"This is fine," Kaishu said with an amused grin. Then after the ink had dried, he gently refolded the fan and put it safely in his pocket.

*　　　　　　　　*　　　　　　　　*

Besides Katsu Kaishu, Ryoma had another, even higher ranking admirer, within the Tokugawa hierarchy. This was Matsudaira Shungaku, the retired Lord of Fukui, whose new post as political director of the Bakufu made him the most powerful man in the Edo government. Like Yodo and several other influential lords, Shungaku had suffered under Ii Naosuke's Great Purge, but was restored to shogunal grace after the death of the regent. Unlike Yodo, however, who as an outside lord was neither a direct vassal nor relative of the Shogun, the Lord of Fukui–whose Matsudaira family crest displayed the three hollyhock leaves of the Tokugawa–was a direct descendant of the second son of the first Tokugawa Shogun. The Fukui *daimyo* ranked seventh among all feudal lords in Japan, exceeded only by the heads of the six Tokugawa Branch Houses. But unlike most of his colleagues, Lord Shungaku was highly regarded by the Loyalists, both at court and among the *han*.

Although Shungaku did not possess Yodo's unyielding disposition, the two men were close friends. Indeed they shared some very redeeming features, not the least of which were their reputations as two of the four most able feudal lords of their time. Despite his position of power and sharp intellect, Shungaku, unlike Yodo, was not wont to pompous display or elitism. Rather, the Lord of Fukui resembled another close colleague, Katsu Kaishu, in his readiness to accept men of ability, regardless of lineage. It had been the political director himself who had written a letter of introduction to Kaishu for a mere *ronin*, because, as he had pointed out, he estimated *"Sakamoto to be a youth of great character and potential,"* albeit Chiba Jutaro's name value certainly was a contributing factor.

Ryoma and Kondo Chojiro, the bean jam bun maker's son whom Ryoma had recently recruited, visited Lord Shungaku at his Edo headquarters shortly after the *Jundo Maru* anchored in Edo Bay. Although Chojiro had been born a commoner, his scholastic achievements, not to mention service under Kaishu, convinced the Tosa authorities to promote him to samurai rank, entitling him to wear the two swords, take a family name and receive a monthly stipend.

The two Tosa men identified themselves to the guards at the iron-studded oaken outer gate, and were presently escorted to the reception chamber of the retired Fukui *daimyo*. At age thirty-six, Lord Shungaku had a light complexion, wide forehead, small eyes, and slender face, which was well complemented by his small jaw. His features were such that, when the occasion demanded, he had been able to pass himself off as a woman. During the days that he and Yodo had been campaigning for Yoshinobu to succeed the Shogun, Shungaku had more than once been obliged to secretly meet Yodo at his Edo villa, disguised as a woman and traveling in a woman's palanquin. Upon one such occasion, when Yodo remarked with a perfectly straight face that Shungaku was so beautiful he "would like to strip him naked," the Lord of Fukui was unable to appreciate his friend's caustic sense of humor.

Ryoma and Chojiro sat in the formal position in Shungaku's reception chamber, waiting for the great man to grant them an audience. Shungaku, who had just returned from a meeting with the Shogun in Edo Castle, entered the room unattended. He was dressed elegantly in a dark blue kimono, gray *hakama*, and a vest of hempen cloth which covered his shoulders like wings, in the ceremonial style of a feudal lord. In several places on the vest appeared the crest of three hollyhock leaves, the symbol of the mighty Tokugawa and Matsudaira families. Ryoma and Chojiro bowed from where they sat, and Shungaku sat down facing them.

"Lord Shungaku, this is Kondo Chojiro, Tosa samurai and student of Katsu Kaishu," Ryoma introduced his friend.

Chojiro bowed deeply, extending his hands outward and touching his forehead to the floor.

Shungaku casually greeted the two men. "Relax," he said, gesturing for them to sit comfortably. Such was the magnanimous character of the most powerful man in the Tokugawa government. "I hear from Katsu that you've just come from Kyoto."

"Yes, we've been recruiting men to work under Katsu-sensei," Ryoma replied.

"Katsu has also told me that he spoke to Lord Yodo about you."

"Yes," Ryoma acknowledged with a slight bow of the head.

"Lord Yodo and I are old friends," Shungaku said. "I will be leaving for Osaka soon, and that's why I've called you here today. How would you like me to talk to him? I'm sure I can convince him to pardon you for fleeing Tosa."

"Why not?" Ryoma said nonchalantly.

The remark must have struck Shungaku as very funny, because the instant Ryoma finished speaking, he burst out laughing. "Why not?" Shungaku said. "In that case, I think I will."

Impressed with Ryoma's straightforwardness, Shungaku met Yodo shortly after at Tosa headquarters in Kyoto, where he discussed Ryoma's case. Having made the same promise to Shungaku as he had to Kaishu, Yodo soon arranged for Ryoma's pardon. Near the end of February a notice was issued from the Tosa administrative office in Kochi, pardoning Sakamoto Ryoma for his crime, exactly eleven months and one day after he had fled.

Early next morning, Ryoma and Chojiro boarded the *Jundo Maru* with Kaishu to sail for Osaka. Ryoma was anxious to recruit more men for Kaishu's naval academy, and was particularly concerned about Okada Izo, whom he had not seen since his friend had mistakenly attacked him in Kyoto during the previous month.

Ryoma had recently heard of another series of murders accredited to Izo, the most piteous of which was that of a celebrated Confucian scholar named Ikeuchi Daigaku. A longtime champion of *Imperial Loyalism*, Ikeuchi had during Ii Naosuke's purge renounced his radical convictions to escape execution, thus damning himself in the eyes of his fellow Loyalists.

One evening in January, Lord Yodo, who was on his way to Kyoto after having met Kaishu in Shimoda, invited Ikeuchi to his Osaka residence to drink *sake*, discuss politics, and view some paintings and pieces of calligraphy. After several hours of drinking with Yodo, the Confucian scholar left Tosa headquarters shortly past midnight. The moonless winter night was pitch-black as his palanquin reached Nanbabashi bridge, and Ikeuchi and the four bearers were startled by a thrashing sound from behind.

"*Heaven's Revenge!*" Izo roared, threw open the sedan door, and thrust his sword through Ikeuchi's throat. The four palanquin bearers dropped their load and fled, as the former champion of anti-foreign Loyalism choked on his own blood. Izo immediately pulled his victim from the sedan. "This is for your betrayal," screamed "The Butcher," then with a single stroke beheaded him. The next morning the head was found mounted on Nanbabashi bridge, with a note stating that Ikeuchi had been executed for selling out to corrupt officials. When the ears were sent, wrapped in oiled paper, to the homes of two

Bakufu sympathizers at court, the terrified Imperial officials promptly resigned their posts.

On the eighth day of the following month, Takechi's top hit man committed a similar murder of a peasant who was accused of having relations with a traitor to the Loyalist cause. The severed head was disposed of at Tosa headquarters in Kyoto, where Yodo had been staying since his recent return to the Imperial capital. With the head was a note which urged the Tosa *daimyo* to support *Toppling the Bakufu and Imperial Loyalism*. But, needless to say, Yodo reacted much differently than did the two terrified court nobles who had received Ikeuchi's severed ears the month before. "After cutting down a man who had been a guest at my home," Yodo fumed, "a band of lower-samurai from my own domain have dared to threaten me with the useless murder of a peasant." The wrath of the "poet warrior" was about to be unleashed.

Ryoma's uncanny sense of timing was again at work when he dispatched Chojiro to Hanpeita's headquarters in Kyoto with a message for Izo, asking his friend to meet him at the Teradaya inn in nearby Fushimi. Just before Chojiro arrived with Ryoma's message, Izo had had a falling out with Hanpeita. Recently, Izo had been unable to sleep, haunted by images in his mind of the faces of the myriad people he had cut down over the past six months. He had been living on *sake* and women, and had become so dependent on the whims of Master Zuizan that for the past three or four sleepless nights he had experienced waken nightmares of being betrayed by his unfathomable master. Since the previous summer when Hanpeita had given him his first chance to perform *Heaven's Revenge*, and thus "contribute to the Loyalists' cause," Izo had doubted the true intentions of his master, even suspecting that Hanpeita would have "no need for me after I've performed my purpose." The uneducated swordsman had always felt uncomfortably awed in the company of the sophisticated sword master. Although Izo's skill with an unsheathed sword was unequaled by even Hanpeita himself, he could not begin to fathom the depths of the Loyalist Party leader. Nor was Izo able to comprehend Hanpeita's lust for power; and over the past few months Izo had become entangled in Hanpeita's web of murder. In the beginning, killing had given Izo a tremendous feeling of power, a result of a deep-rooted inferiority complex. He had never been invited to officially join the Loyalist Party, and until he had found *Heaven's Revenge* there was only one thing in life that Izo could really be proud of: his swordsmanship.

Heaven's Revenge gave him a way to put his sword to use. Each time he carried out Hanpeita's cold-blooded will he was rewarded with a bit of gold and the good graces of his master. But recently, the rush of power Izo had originally experienced when killing had all but vanished, leaving him with an empty feeling instead. Murder to Izo was like a drug: having overindulged he had grown immune to its effect. With this came insomnia, and Izo had grown extremely irritable. Trivial things–like the high-pitched voice of the harlot he had been with this evening–grated on his nerves. And when he returned to Hanpeita's headquarters, Master Zuizan was waiting with a look of vexation on his pale face.

"Izo!" Hanpeita roared, "I thought I told you to report here earlier this evening. I have another important assignment for you, and you've kept me waiting for hours."

"I'm sorry," Izo muttered, avoiding Hanpeita steely gaze. "I guess it kind of slipped my mind."

"Slipped your mind?" Hanpeita gave Izo a sinister look. "When I give you an order, Izo, you're to follow it like a dog."

Something inside Izo's head flashed like the silver-blue light from a drawn sword. A creature of emotion, Izo had never considered his actions from a moral viewpoint. Wild by nature, Izo had no philosophy; matters of thought he had left to others. But Hanpeita's web of murder was starting to get the best of him. Even a wild animal will not kill without reason, and Izo was no different. His ultimate reason for bloodshed had been to carry out the will of his master, who was now calling him a dog.

"Then I'm through, damn you," Izo spewed in a fit of anger. "Nobody calls Okada Izo a dog," he roared at the top of his voice, and before Izo realized the true effect of his words, Hanpeita had already decided his fate.

"That's right, Izo," Master Zuizan calmly acquiesced. "You're through."

Tongue-tied, Izo only stared at Hanpeita in wide-eyed horror.

"Now, get out of here, Izo," Hanpeita snarled. Then, with a sinister smile, he added, "And don't come back until you are willing to accept that you are indeed my dog."

Unable to draw his sword on his master, Izo turned around, ran out of the house in a frenzy, when at the front gate he encountered Chojiro carrying a message from Ryoma. With nowhere else to turn, this creature of emotion said he would be more than happy to accept Ryoma's offer to join him under Katsu Kaishu. After all, Izo's actions had never been a matter of morality.

*   *   *

"I must see Sakamoto Ryoma," a samurai demanded at the front entrance of the Teradaya inn, on the day after Ryoma had sent his message to Izo. As the samurai spoke with a Tosa accent, the proprietress, Otose, assumed that he was a Tosa agent come to arrest Ryoma. Recently Ryoma had been staying at the Teradaya whenever he was in Kyoto, and had developed a close relationship with Otose, a woman in her early thirties who treated Ryoma like a younger brother.

"I'm sorry, but there's nobody here by that name," Otose lied.

"Kame!" Ryoma hollered from the second floor, atop a dark wooden staircase.

"Ryoma," Otose said in a flustered voice, "you must..."

"Don't worry," Ryoma interrupted, "he's a friend of mine."

"Ryoma, you've been pardoned," Mochizuki Kameyata said excitedly. "You don't have to worry about being arrested anymore. I've just come from Tosa headquarters in Kyoto with orders to bring you back."

"Orders to bring me back!" Ryoma shouted, racing down the stairway to the same dark wooden floor which had been the scene of the bloodbath among Satsuma men only ten months before. "I'm not going to Tosa headquarters to be locked up," he snarled. "Do you think I'm an idiot?" Ryoma stopped short, recalling that Kaishu had spoken to the Tosa *daimyo* on his behalf, and that Lord Shungaku had promised to do so. "I've been pardoned?" he said calmly.

"Yes. Do you think I'd be telling you this if you hadn't? All you have to do is stay at Tosa headquarters for seven days, and you'll be officially cleared."

"Seven days!" Ryoma growled.

"Yes. And one more thing," Kame said. "Izo is at the barracks at Tosa headquarters, waiting for you to arrive. Chojiro's with him."

"Alright, Kame," Ryoma said, shaking his head in disgust. "I'll go."

Much to his chagrin, Ryoma served his sentence of seven days under confinement at Tosa headquarters, during which time he complained daily to Kame. He detested the idea of being forced to stay in one place, especially now that Kaishu's plans for a private naval academy were starting to materialize.

When Ryoma was released from custody a week later, he was no longer an outlaw, but a Tosa samurai with official permission to study navigation under the Tokugawa Navy Commissioner. Upon his release, he went directly to Izo's barrack room. "Izo," he said, sitting cross-legged on the floor, "how many people have you killed for Hanpeita?"

"I never counted," Izo muttered. "But I did it for the cause," he said blankly.

"There's no cause in killing for the sake of killing," Ryoma sneered. "Let's go. I'm going to introduce you to the greatest man in Japan. He's in Kyoto right now."

"You're talking about Katsu, right?"

"Right! And it's going to be your responsibility to see that nothing happens to him," Ryoma demanded.

"My responsibility?"

"Yes. I think you'll find it a lot more rewarding to put your sword to some positive use for a change."

"But Katsu's a traitor."

Ryoma gave Izo a hard look. "Do you trust me, Izo?"

"Of course!"

"Then guard Katsu Kaishu with your life. It's as simple as that." Ryoma was aware of the futility of trying to explain things too deeply to Izo.

Shortly after, Ryoma and Izo arrived at the Kyoto headquarters of Kii Han, where Kaishu was lodging. "Sakamoto Ryoma of Tosa," Ryoma growled at several samurai watching guard at the iron-studded oaken outer gate. Kii was one of the elite Three Tokugawa Branch Houses, and although Ryoma was dedicated to the commissioner of the Tokugawa Navy and had even earned the trust of the Lord of Fukui, who was a close relative of the Shogun, he could not overcome his enmity for Kii Han. "I've come to see Katsu Kaishu," he snarled.

As Kaishu had left word at the guardhouse that he was expecting Ryoma, the two Tosa men were immediately escorted to Kaishu's quarters.

Kaishu sat at a desk, studying a book on Western military science written in Dutch. "Come in, Ryoma. I've been expecting you," he said, closing the book.

"Katsu-sensei," Ryoma said, glancing at Izo, "this is Okada Izo, your new bodyguard."

"Okada..." Kaishu, despite his usually cool disposition, swallowed his words. "You don't mean the same..." he again stopped himself short. Kaishu had heard of the notorious "Butcher," and of the many Bakufu supporters he had allegedly cut down.

"Yes, Sensei. Izo's an old friend of mine from Kochi. You won't have to worry about your safety with Izo guarding you," Ryoma assured. "There aren't too many men who can beat Izo with a sword."

Kaishu was at first dumbfounded, but so great was his trust for Ryoma, the navy commissioner accepted the notorious assassin. "I need your help, Ryoma," Kaishu said.

Izo stared at Kaishu, as if mesmerized. He couldn't believe that the Tokugawa Navy Commissioner was actually asking Ryoma for help.

"What is it?" Ryoma asked.

"I'm extremely concerned about the British warships on high alert at Yokohama. I've just come from Edo, and believe me, Japan is in grave danger."

In compensation for the murder of the English merchant Richardson by Satsuma men during the previous year at Namamugi, the British government presented the Bakufu with the following four demands: (1) a public apology for the incident; (2) an indemnity for the amount of 100,000 pounds to be paid by Edo to London; (3) indemnities of 25,000 pounds from Satsuma to Richardson's family and to the three Britons injured in the attack; (4) the arrest and execution of the assassin(s) in the presence of British officers. These demands were, in effect, an ultimatum to war with the British, who had recently increased their fleet of warships at Yokohama to the awesome number of twelve.

"The British have enough firepower there to destroy the whole coastline," Kaishu said with worried eyes. "And they are only a few hours away from Edo. If they decide to attack the capital, you know as well as I do that all hell will break loose. There's no saying how many tens of thousands of people will be killed."

"Will the Bakufu pay?" Ryoma asked.

"They have no choice, although I doubt Satsuma will cooperate. But that's exactly why I've summoned you here."

"You want me to use my influence with Takechi Hanpeita and Kusaka Genzui to persuade the Loyalists not to interfere in the matter?" It was common knowledge that the xenophobic radicals preferred war to the disgrace of yielding to the British demands.

"No," Kaishu said. "Not at this point, anyway."

"Then, what is it?"

"Now that there is no worry of you being arrested," Kaishu said, "I want you to concentrate all your energy on recruiting as many men as possible for a navy. The more the better."

"Of course, Sensei. That's what I've been doing."

"I know, and I appreciate your effort. But we must work fast, Ryoma. Time is of the essence. The fate of Japan is on our shoulders." Kaishu paused, then unrolled a scroll that lay on the desk. "Here, take a look at this," he said, handing it to Ryoma. "My plans for a Japanese Navy that will protect the entire country, if I can only convince those stupid potato-heads in Edo. We have to start concentrating on a mobile navy of warships, rather than merely constructing batteries along the coast like we've been doing for so long."

Ryoma unrolled the scroll and began reading aloud. "*The maritime defense of Japan should be covered by six naval bases to be established in the following natural harbors: Edo, for the defense of the east coast of the main island of Honshu; Hakodate, on the far-northern island of Ezo, to defend northeastern Japan; Niigata, to defend the northwestern coastline; Shimonoseki, at the southwestern tip of Honshu, to assure control of that strategic strait; Osaka, to protect western Japan; and Nagasaki, to defend the far-western regions.*'" Ryoma paused, took a deep breath and continued reading. "*Each one of these bases should be fortified with its own squadron, while those in Edo and Osaka should have additional reserve fleets on hand. Each squadron should consist of three frigates, nine corvettes, and a certain number of smaller steam vessels. The Japanese fleet protecting the entire archipelago should thus consist of a total of 370 vessels,*'" Ryoma's voice cracked as he read the enormous figure. "Three hundred seventy," he repeated incredulously. "There aren't anywhere near that number of Western-style ships in all of Japan!"

"That's right," the navy commissioner said, giving Ryoma an unusually stern look. "But the only way we can survive is by building a navy of our own which is as strong as those of the great Western powers."

"I'll do my best," Ryoma said. "But for now, please keep Izo with you at all times."

One evening in late March, just two weeks after Ryoma had assigned Izo to protect Kaishu, the navy commissioner was attending a meeting at Nijo Castle, the Shogun's fortress in Kyoto. The meeting lasted until after dark, and when Kaishu finally appeared at the main outer gate of the castle, Izo was waiting for him as usual.

"Let's go, Izo," Kaishu said in a low voice.

PERSUASION

"It's late, Sensei," Izo muttered, as the two men walked from the castle into the Kyoto night. "Please be sure to stay right by me," Izo implored. The half moon was barely visible in the cloudy sky. Izo, carrying a lantern, stayed close behind Kaishu, as they turned left down Horikawa Road, with the castle moat on their immediate left, and Fukui headquarters directly across the road on their right. A few minutes later, as the two men were about to turn right onto Marutamachi Road, which ran just south of the Imperial Palace, a light rain began to fall.

"Izo," Kaishu began speaking, "how many men have you killed?"

"Ah..."

Before Izo could speak, there was a thrashing sound of someone running straight at them, and both men stopped short in their tracks.

"*Heaven's Revenge!*" a voice screamed in the darkness.

Throwing the lantern into the gutter on the side of the road, Izo immediately drew his sword. "This is Okada Izo of Tosa!" he roared. Blue light flashed off his blade, and a fraction of a second later the screech of steel cutting through bone pierced Kaishu's ears. "This is Okada Izo of Tosa," he repeated, "but you might know me better as 'The Butcher.'" Izo's warning must have worked, because after he had cut down his second opponent, a third man could be heard running in the opposite direction, the only other sound the steady falling of the rain.

Izo had killed two Loyalist extremists without feeling a bit of remorse, although he himself had been one of them only two weeks before. The thought never crossed his mind. With a sword in his hand, Izo was like a wild animal. Cerebral reflection was not a part of his action. He left all matters of thought to those in charge. Until recently Takechi Hanpeita had done Izo's thinking; now Izo was simply following the orders of Sakamoto Ryoma. Morality for Izo depended on the outcome of the fight–clean and simple.

Izo wiped the blood from his sword on a piece of soft paper he carried for this purpose, threw it into the gutter, and slid the blade back into his sheath. Without a word, the two men continued walking through the dark streets of Kyoto, the only sounds their footsteps in the mud, and the steady falling of the rain. Kaishu's *hakama* was stained with blood. This was the first time he had ever seen a man cut down, or been attacked himself. Despite a surge of nausea, Kaishu, determined to maintain his composure, walked silently beside Izo for the next ten minutes. "Izo," he finally said, unable to contain himself any longer, "you seem to get a thrill out of killing."

Izo offered no reply.

"You'd better change your ways, Izo," Kaishu admonished. "Depending on the circumstances, a truly great man might let himself be cut before cutting someone else."

Izo still did not answer.

"Izo, don't you have anything so say?" Kaishu asked, obviously annoyed.

"I don't understand," Izo said indignantly.

"What don't you understand? That killing's not good?"

"But, Katsu-sensei, in all due respect, if I hadn't killed those two, your head would no longer be on your shoulders."

Not even the smooth rhetorician Katsū Kaishu had an answer for this remark. But when Kaishu would recall the event years later, he would praise Izo, saying: "I escaped from the mouth of a tiger, but it was only because of Okada's quick reactions."

*   *   *

Takechi Hanpeita's Tosa Loyalists, in league with the radicals from Choshu and Satsuma, had controlled and terrorized Kyoto for the past year. The Loyalists enjoyed the support of Sanjo Sanetomi and Anenokoji Kintomo, two young but lately influential court nobles, who in turn owed their rise to power to the Loyalists' reign of terror. Both were ardent xenophobes, and Sanjo, related by marriage to the Lord of Tosa, naturally attracted the Tosa radicals.

As Loyalist dominance over the Imperial capital increased, Bakufu prestige and power in Kyoto waned. While Ryoma helped Kaishu organize a naval academy, Hanpeita used his influence among the Loyalists to rise to the forefront of the Kyoto infrastructure. Not only did he control a death squad in Kyoto, but through the auspices of Sanjo and Anenokoji, he had even gained influence over the Imperial Court itself. After returning with the two court nobles from their recent trip to Edo, Hanpeita was promoted to the distinguished post of director of Tosa headquarters in Kyoto, and consequently to the rank of upper-samurai. This was indeed the golden age of Master Zuizan, until the beginning of the third year of the Era of Bunkyu, 1863, when Lord Yodo reemerged in the Imperial capital after nearly five years of political paralysis at his villa in Edo.

Around this time Ryoma paid a visit to Takechi Hanpeita. The two had not met for nearly six months, and Ryoma was anxious to warn Hanpeita of the imminent danger facing the Tosa radicals.

"Ryoma, come in," Hanpeita said, genuinely glad at the unexpected reunion. The Shield of the Emperor was sitting in his room with another Tosa Loyalist named Kamioka Tanji. At age thirty-nine, this self-styled "Child of the Storm" was one of the oldest among Hanpeita's followers. His clothes, swarthy complexion and thick black beard well suited his *nom de guerre*, and the nihilism in his dark eyes reflected his lack of concern for worldly gain. He wore only a thin kimono of coarse brown cotton, and his long shaggy hair hung down to his shoulders. Tanji was typical in his unyielding determination to destroy the existing mode of things, but was unconcerned with the form of government or society which would result from revolution. When Ryoma joined them, Hanpeita and Tanji were discussing tactics. Now that the opportunity for advancement in Kyoto politics had presented itself, Hanpeita was looking for alternative ways to finance his subversive activities, which had been stifled lately with his appointment as director of Tosa headquarters. Lord Yodo, who was determined to suppress the Loyalists, had assigned Hanpeita to the important post only to prevent intrigue between the Loyalist leader, whom he strongly suspected was responsible for the murder of Yoshida Toyo, and other radicals in Kyoto. Hanpeita's lust for power, however, had grown so intense that he refused to realize this plain fact, insisting rather that Yodo was an Imperial Loyalist at heart.

Having greeted Ryoma, Hanpeita and Tanji returned to their business at hand. "I've given the matter a great deal of thought," Tanji said. "I think we should approach the wealthy Osaka merchants."

"Yes, the wealthy merchants!" Hanpeita nodded sinisterly.

"Once it's pointed out to them that Osaka would surely be destroyed in case of war with the barbarians, I expect they will be willing to come up with some gold."

"Some gold!" Hanpeita said. "How much do you estimate?"

"About two hundred thousand *ryo*."

"Two hundred thousand *ryo*!" Ryoma blurted.

"Should any one of the merchants resist," Tanji continued, ignoring the outburst, "whoever had asked him should cut open his own belly on the spot to demonstrate our absolute sincerity."

"What?" Ryoma shouted.

"Let him finish speaking, Ryoma," Hanpeita said.

"Most of the merchants are cowards who are only interested in gold. I am certain that there is no merchant who could stomach the sight of two or maybe three such suicides. Of course, I insist that I have the honor of being the first one to die."

Hanpeita grinned diabolically. The notion seemed to please him.

"Can't you think of anything more constructive than killing yourselves and others?" Ryoma shouted.

"What's wrong, Sakamoto?" Tanji glared at Ryoma. "Have you lost your nerve?"

"Tanji, your idea is very good," Hanpeita said.

Ryoma pounded his fist on the floor. "If it's funding you need," he said, "we should acquire some foreign warships. With these we could engage in trade to raise money, while defending ourselves at the same time. That's what we'll be doing at our naval academy. And that's what I've come here to discuss with you."

Hanpeita looked hard at Ryoma. "Things are ready," he said. "With our support, the Imperial Court has the Bakufu at bay. We've already forced the Shogun himself to set a deadline for the expulsion of the barbarians."

"Hanpeita," Ryoma interrupted, "what makes you think you're ready?"

"I've already submitted our plan to the court," Hanpeita said.

"What plan?"

"First of all," Hanpeita lowered his voice, "the entire area around Osaka and Kyoto will be brought under Imperial rule."

"And what about the feudal lords who rule over the area now?" Ryoma asked.

"They will be forced to relinquish their domains, and the area will be garrisoned by troops under the direct control of the court."

"And how do you plan to finance all this?" Ryoma asked.

"As Tanji just suggested, we could order the wealthy merchants in Osaka to pay."

A shadow fell over Ryoma's face, and he gave Hanpeita a vexed look.

"In this way," Hanpeita continued, "the court will be able to assume responsibility for all political decisions, and the Bakufu will become powerless."

"But we're not ready yet, Hanpeita. We need to unite first."

"We will unite. Once the court has assumed political authority, the feudal lords will gather in Kyoto rather than Edo. The Divine Emperor will surely demand respect from enough feudal lords to ensure His sovereignty over the nation. We are raising an Imperial Army, and Lord Yodo, among others, supports us. The alliance to topple the Bakufu is about to be forged between Tosa, Choshu and Satsuma. After that the other powerful *han* will join the Imperial Alliance, and nothing will stop us."

"That's just what I've come to talk to you about," Ryoma shouted. "I'm asking you," he paused, "no, I'm begging you to listen to reason. You must call off your men. The barbarians are not going to leave Japan just because we order them to. The British have twelve warships at Yokohama ready to attack unless the Bakufu yields to their demands. But we're not ready to drive them out by force, they're just too powerful. Things have come to a head, Hanpeita, and I don't think you realize how dangerous the situation is, both in Edo and Kyoto." Ryoma lowered his voice. "Lord Yodo is not behind you. He'll never agree to turn against the Bakufu. You should know that as well as I do. You're being deceived."

"What are you talking about, Sakamoto?" Tanji said angrily.

"You can't actually believe that Lord Yodo is going to support a bunch of lower-samurai who are trying to gain control over his own domain," Ryoma scoffed.

"Lord Yodo is a man of his word," Hanpeita said. "He is on our side."

"Hanpeita," Ryoma pleaded, "if you and your men would stop relying on Tosa and work with me under Katsu Kaishu, we would surely win in the end."

Ryoma had heard from Kaishu of the true intentions of the Tosa *daimyo*. Lord Yodo had come to Kyoto this month for two purposes: one, to promote a compromise between the court and the Bakufu; the other, which was a means to this end, to crush the Tosa Loyalists. Despite his relation by marriage to the Sanjo family at court, and his outward appearance as a Loyalist sympathizer, Yodo was determined to arrest every Tosa Loyalist in the Imperial capital.

"We will win, Ryoma," Hanpeita insisted. "That I guarantee."

"You don't understand, Hanpeita. We can't win without developing a navy. Japan is an island country, and the only way to defend it from foreign attack is by sea. And that's exactly what we're going to do under Katsu Kaishu, the leading naval expert in Japan."

"Ryoma," Hanpeita said, "you've enlisted several of my best men. But I wish you well. I know we're fighting for the same cause, and sometime in the future maybe we can join forces."

It was only now that Ryoma realized that there was no hope to save his friends, as he struggled to hold back tears. Indeed, Sakamoto Ryoma would never see Takechi Hanpeita again.

*   *   *

Takechi Hanpeita and most of the other Tosa Loyalists who were not working for Katsu Kaishu were ordered back to Kochi at the beginning of April by Lord Yodo, who also returned to his domain to crush the outlawed party, and to punish the murderers of Yoshida Toyo.

On the national scene, opposition to the foreign treaties had so intensified that in March the Shogun himself was obliged to pay a visit to Kyoto to promise the Emperor that he would expel the foreigners by the tenth of the following May. This first visit to Kyoto by a Shogun in over two centuries displayed Edo's diminishing ability to dominate Japan, while the impossible promise to expel the foreigners so angered Lord Shungaku that he resigned his post as political director of the Edo regime, and returned to his castle in Fukui at the end of March.

Meanwhile, Ryoma remained busy through the spring recruiting men for the naval academy of Katsu Kaishu, with whom he met daily to discuss plans. His life had changed drastically in the past several months, during which time his relationship with Kaishu had developed from one of teacher and student into a partnership. While Kaishu used his close relationship with the seventeen-year-old Shogun Iemochi to gain permission to establish an official Bakufu Naval Academy in Kobe, Ryoma used his influence among the Loyalists in Kyoto to recruit nearly one hundred of them for Kaishu's private school. The Bakufu institution and the private academy would share the costly facilities supplied by the Edo government. Under Kaishu, Ryoma, at age twenty-eight, was on the verge of realizing his dream of establishing a navy. He drolly expressed his excitement in a letter to his sister Otome, dated March 20, 1863: *"Well, well! In the first place, life sure is strange. There are some men who are so unlucky that they die by breaking their balls just trying to climb out of a bathtub. Compared to that I'm extremely lucky: here I was on the verge of death but I didn't die. Even if I tried to die I couldn't, because there are too many things which compel me to live. I have now become the disciple of Katsu Kaishu, the greatest man in Japan, and I am spend-*

ing every day on things I have always dreamed about. Even if I should live to be forty, I wouldn't leave this to return home." During the spring of this year Ryoma accompanied Kaishu on several trips between Osaka and Edo, gaining navigational experience aboard the Tokugawa warship *Jundo Maru*. In Edo, Kaishu introduced Ryoma to his close friend and mentor Okubo Ichio, who had recruited Kaishu into the government eight years before.

At age forty-six, Okubo was concurrently working at the important post of commissioner of foreign affairs and as member of the Bakufu's council in charge of supervising Tokugawa officials and retainers. His experience in foreign affairs, and at a prior post in the Institute for the Study of Barbarian Books, had given him access to a wide range of knowledge of the West. Okubo, who was also friendly with Lord Shungaku and his political advisor, Yokoi Shonan, had been expelled from office during the Great Purge of Ii Naosuke, but recalled in 1861.

One spring afternoon Ryoma and Sonojo walked through the iron-studded oaken gate of the Okubo residence, located near Edo Castle. The two had just returned to Edo with Kaishu for the particular purpose of meeting the commissioner of foreign affairs, although it was almost unheard of for two men of no official status whatsoever to be granted a private audience with one of Okubo's distinction. But as Kaishu had arranged the meeting, the two were greeted by a woman servant at the front door of the two-storied house, and escorted down a long, dark wooden corridor.

Okubo was waiting in his study. He was thinner than Ryoma had expected, and frail in appearance, but his serious, powerful eyes impressed both of the younger men.

Ryoma and Sonojo bowed at the threshold of the study. "Come in and sit down," Okubo said. The two Tosa samurai removed their long swords and placed them to their right, the hilts pointed forward–a common courtesy indicating that the blade could not be readily drawn with the right hand–as they sat down in the formal position.

Okubo began speaking. "You must be Sakamoto Ryoma. Katsu has told me a lot about you. He tells me you're an avid Loyalist, and that you came to kill him in his own house last fall," he said, snickering.

"Yes," Ryoma replied uncomfortably. "Katsu-sensei has told us that you have some very interesting ideas concerning how to protect the nation from foreign subjugation. We've come to hear them."

"But you're thinking that an old man who is working for the

decrepit Tokugawa government can't have anything worthwhile to say. Isn't that right?"

The remark stunned Sonojo, but Ryoma, who had on several occasions heard similar comments from Kaishu, was not surprised. "Yes, that's right," he said.

"Let me begin by asking you a question," Okubo said, apparently impressed by Ryoma boldness. How would your Loyalists react if the Shogun were to restore the political rule of Japan to the Emperor?"

This remark surprised even Ryoma. For a man of Okubo's position to suggest that the Shogun abdicate was preposterous, even dangerous.

"That's exactly what we are fighting for," Ryoma said. "But the Shogun would never do that. It would be suicide."

"No, I don't think so,' Okubo said. "The Shogun's abdicating would not necessarily relinquish his rule over his domains in several provinces. These alone would ensure him sufficient wealth and power."

"And who would rule in the Shogun's place?"

"Two councils would be created. One would consist of the most powerful feudal lords, and would meet in Kyoto every four or five years. The other would be made up of lesser lords, and meet in Edo."

"And where does the Emperor fit into this scheme?" Sonojo asked.

"The Emperor would wield sovereign power from the Chrysanthemum Throne in Kyoto," Okubo stated flatly.

"And how about the Tokugawa?" Ryoma asked.

"The Tokugawa Shogun would certainly be included among the council of great feudal lords. Everyone would be satisfied, and Japan would thus become united as one nation."

"That's fantastic!" Ryoma exclaimed.

"Hasn't Katsu mentioned this plan to you?" Okubo asked.

"No."

"Then I don't supposed that he's told you about his recent suggestion at the Grand Hall in Edo Castle."

"No!"

"Katsu himself suggested to the Shogun that he abdicate."

Ryoma was utterly astonished by this last remark. For Kaishu and Okubo to talk like this among themselves, or even to himself or Sonojo, was one thing. But to suggest such a thing to the Shogun in Edo Castle could be lethal.

"That worries me," Ryoma said, unconsciously placing his right hand on his sword.

"No need to worry," Okubo laughed. "Katsu will be alright. The man is indestructible. He's quite a character. Yes, quite a character indeed."

*   *   *

One afternoon in the following May Ryoma sat with Kaishu in the navy commissioner's lodgings in Kyoto discussing the establishment of the naval academy.

"One hundred men are plenty to begin with," Kaishu said, "but we're short of money. The Bakufu coffers are nearly empty, so all we can get from Edo is three thousand *ryo*, hardly enough to finance a naval academy. We need to acquire land, construct buildings and purchase ships."

"Then let's raise the money," Ryoma said.

"How?"

"From the feudal lords who have the insight to realize the importance of our mission."

"Ryoma," Kaishu exclaimed, slapping his knee, "you're uncanny. That's just what I intended to discuss with you today. I want you to go to Fukui Han to see if you can convince our friend Lord Shungaku to grant us a loan. A man of his caliber will surely understand the importance of our project."

"I don't mind trying, but it seems that Lord Shungaku would be more apt to lend us money if you personally were to ask him."

"Don't underestimate yourself," Kaishu said, then immediately retracted the statement before sardonically adding, "No, I'm sure that's one thing you would never do, Ryoma. You're much too much like me to underestimate yourself."

"But, Sensei..."

"No, I want you to go. Besides, you've already proven your ability to persuade over the past six months. To tell you the truth, I never expected you to find one hundred men to work for me from among the Loyalists in Kyoto. Not until the day you walked into my room with Izo, that is," Kaishu paused momentarily, then burst out laughing. "You should have seen some of those stupid potato-heads from Edo when they saw me walk through the gates of Nijo Castle with him. I thought they might piss all over themselves."

Ryoma howled with amusement, then asked, "How much money do

we need?"

"About five thousand."

"*Ryo?*" Ryoma swallowed deeply.

"Five thousand *ryo* is what I estimate," Kaishu said. "As the annual rice yield of some of the smaller fiefdoms is only twice that amount, your ability to persuade is about to be put to a real test. But I don't expect Lord Shungaku will lend us all of it. At any rate, I think it would be helpful for you to meet another close friend of mine before you talk with Shungaku."

"Who?"

"Yokoi Shonan, Shungaku's most trusted advisor."

Yokoi Shonan, one of the great thinkers of his time, was a samurai of Kumamoto Han, but recently serving the Lord of Fukui as chief political advisor. Although Yokoi was once a chronic xenophobe, a glimpse at the military technology of the West changed his mind in much the same way it had Ryoma's, so that at age fifty-two he was now a confirmed believer in the absolute necessity of opening the country. It was for this very reason that Kusaka Genzui had urged Ryoma to assassinate Yokoi during the previous year.

Although Yokoi supported *Opening the Country,* he espoused renouncing the foreign treaties, even at the expense of war. He argued that since the Tokugawa had signed the treaties with only its own welfare in mind, and with no concern for the rest of Japan, the Bakufu must abandon its selfish policies, for the sake of the entire nation. But unlike the Loyalists, Yokoi did not prefer war as a means to an end, but insisted that Japan must be resolved to fight to preserve its sovereignty. The country, he argued, must be opened on an equal basis, not through one-sided treaties forced on Japan by foreigners. However, as Yokoi was a man of thought rather than action, he left the job of actualizing his ideas to others. Kaishu and Ryoma would establish a navy to do so.

Ryoma stood up, thrust his sword through his sash. "I'll go at once," he said, then bowed before leaving.

Ryoma set out on foot at sunrise the next morning, northeast from Kyoto for the domain of Fukui. Although he felt confident that the Fukui *daimyo* would lend him a certain amount of gold, Ryoma doubted that he could convince him to invest the enormous sum of 5,000 *ryo.* Nevertheless his basic philosophy dictated that once he had decided on a goal he must see it through. Ryoma's goal was to form a navy, both military and merchant. The military might of his navy would be necessary to topple the Bakufu and protect Japan from foreign aggression. With the commercial end he planned to conduct free trade, domestically and internationally. He was convinced that free trade was the only way to enrich the nation to ensure lasting safety. Kaishu, like Kawada Shoryo before him, had taught Ryoma these basic principles of capitalism. Both men had told him of the joint-stock company in the United States, whereby people with capital invested money, while people with an idea put that money to practical use. The capitalist concept, which was totally foreign to feudal Japan, fit Ryoma's current circumstances perfectly. In short, he would not merely ask Lord Shungaku for a loan, but rather to make a capital investment, repayable with a portion of the profits from the commercial end of the navy.

Ryoma arrived at Fukui Castletown, just inland from the Sea of Japan and northeast of Kyoto, one warm afternoon in mid-May. After procuring lodgings at the Tobacco Inn, he sent a message to Yokoi Shonan, requesting a meeting. Yokoi had heard about Ryoma from Kaishu and Shungaku, and more recently in letters from Okubo, who had written to Shungaku on the night after his first meeting with Ryoma and Sonojo. *"The courage of the ronin who are prepared to die for their cause,"* Okubo had declared, *"puts men of the Bakufu to shame."* In the same letter Okubo had described Ryoma as *"a man of truly strong character."* It was no wonder, then, that Lord Shungaku's trusted advisor, upon receiving Ryoma's message, immediately set out to meet him.

The Tobacco Inn was a simple two-storied wooden house with a black tile roof. In front of the house was a small garden of dwarfed pines, and the hydrangeas were in full bloom, coloring the garden with pale shades of blue, pink and purple. Near the center of the garden was a pond, in which several large carp, some black some orange, swam furiously in circles. It was feeding time, and the innkeeper, dressed in a kimono of dark blue cotton, was tossing small clumps of steamed barley into the pond. Several golden dragonflies hovered above the mossy green water, which shimmered coolly in the late afternoon sunlight.

"I'm looking for Tosa samurai Sakamoto Ryoma," Yokoi said, approaching the house. He was immaculately dressed in black, and his two swords hung at his left hip. By the encircled triangular crest on his jacket, the innkeeper immediately recognized Yokoi.

The commoner bowed deeply. "Please, come right this way, Your Excellency. I'll show you to his room."

Yokoi followed the innkeeper into the earthen-floored entranceway to the house. Here he removed his wooden clogs, before stepping up into an anteroom paneled with dark wood. The two men ascended a ladder staircase leading to a dark corridor.

"You have a visitor," the innkeeper called from behind a closed door. But there was no answer, just the sound of someone snoring loudly inside. "Well, open up!" Yokoi demanded. "I don't have all day."

The innkeeper slid open the door. Inside Ryoma was sleeping in his dirty kimono, spread-eagle, without bedding, and both swords on the floor next to him.

"Sakamoto-san," Yokoi called in a loud voice.

Ryoma stirred, opened his eyes, focused on the small man—less than five-feet tall—then finally realizing where he was, jumped to his feet. "I must have fallen asleep," he said. "You must be Yokoi-sensei."

Yokoi nodded, and cleared his throat. Despite his rustic features—large face, dark complexion, thick black eyebrows that curved upward and met at the bridge of a wide nose, high cheekbones and large mouth—his eyes betrayed the razor-sharp wit for which he was famous.

"Please come in and sit down," Ryoma said, and after the innkeeper left them alone, heatedly explained to Yokoi his reason for coming to Fukui.

"Katsu has told me about your plans for a navy," Yokoi said after Ryoma finished speaking. "I fully support them."

"I hope Lord Shungaku feels the same," Ryoma said.

"He certainly does!" assured Shungaku's chief political advisor.

"What I mean is that I hope he'll be willing to invest in our navy."

"How Lord Shungaku feels and what he can afford may be two different matters. Five thousand *ryo* is a large sum."

"Not so large when you consider that the money will be used for developing a navy to protect the nation," Ryoma said. "Fukui is one of the greatest domains in Japan. The Matsudaira family is directly related to the Tokugawa."

"Yes," Yokoi said. "I'll arrange for you to meet Lord Shungaku tomorrow."

On the following morning, Ryoma met Lord Shungaku in the confines of Fukui Castle. "Welcome, Ryoma," the *daimyo* said when the Tosa samurai appeared at the entrance to his reception room. Lord

Shungaku admired Ryoma for his unaffected manner, uncanny sense of the times, sincere character and frankness.

Ryoma entered the room, kneeled down and bowed so deeply that he touched his face to the *tatami* floor. "Thank you for your recent kindness," he said, referring to Shungaku's having spoken on his behalf to the Tosa *daimyo*.

"Get up, Ryoma. That position doesn't suit you. I've heard about your big plans from Yokoi."

Ryoma sat up straight. "Not so big, Lord Shungaku," he said. "Just plans for a navy."

"Ryoma, you amaze me," Shungaku said with a heavy sigh. "And I doubt that you have ever put that mouth of yours to so much use in such a short period of time as you did yesterday. Yokoi supports your plans completely." This was Lord Shungaku's way of telling Ryoma that he would indeed invest 5,000 *ryo* in the naval academy.

The Sweltering Summer of Frenzy

*During the summer of 1863, while Ryoma was making the final
arrangements for Kaishu's private naval academy in Kobe, his
Loyalist comrades were active in their own respective arenas. With the
radicals increasing their power in Kyoto, the three feudal lords who
had been working to achieve a compromise between court and
camp–those of Fukui, Tosa and Satsuma–had been compelled to quit
the Kyoto stage and perform behind the scene from their individual
castles. The Imperial capital was now in the hands of the Choshu
extremists, while the leading players in the drive to topple the
Bakufu–the extremist factions of Choshu, Satsuma and Tosa–acted
and reacted with one another in a bloody coup de theatre which sent
the entire nation reeling.*

With Shogun Iemochi having set May 10 as the date by which the foreigners would be expelled from Japan, the Choshu extremists made
their plans accordingly. Aware that Edo had no intention of using military force to carry out its promise, the Choshu-sponsored rebels, led
by Kusaka Genzui, had a dual-purpose in mind when they gathered at
Shimonoseki Strait at the southwestern point of Choshu: increasing
their status among the xenophobic court nobles and further diminishing Bakufu prestige, by attacking foreign ships passing through the
strait.

Shimonoseki Strait, which separated Kyushu from Honshu, served
as an important route for foreign ships traveling between the open
Ports of Yokohama and Nagasaki. On the morning of May 11, the day
after the deadline to expel the foreigners, an American merchant ship
bound for Nagasaki was suddenly chased and fired upon by two
Choshu warships as it passed through the strait. On the twenty-third
of the same month a French dispatch-boat crossing these waters was
similarly attacked. Three days later a Dutch corvette sailing from
Nagasaki to Yokohama became the third target of Choshu guns at
Shimonoseki.

Although all three of the unsuspecting ships escaped intact,
Choshu's boldness elevated its already high status among the radicals
at court, at the expense of Satsuma and even Tokugawa prestige.
Exuberant over his temporary victory, the Lord of Choshu immediately relayed the events to the Imperial Court, which in turn sent a letter of praise to Hagi Castle, setting even higher the spirits of the

Loyalist fighters in Choshu.

*   *   *

Upon his return from Fukui in late May, Ryoma went to Kobe to meet Katsu Kaishu. Although Kobe was still an obscure fishing village on the outskirts of the large outpost town of Hyogo, it was at this spot on Osaka Bay that Kaishu had chosen to establish his naval academy. As Hyogo, like nearby Osaka, was a domain of the Tokugawa, it was a suitable location for an official Bakufu training center; and the natural harbor at Kobe promised to serve as an ideal location for naval headquarters.

When Ryoma reported to Kaishu of his success in procuring the 5,000 *ryo* from Lord Shungaku, the naval commissioner was nevertheless reluctant to demonstrate too much excitement. After all, they were still without the basics: ships for training, coal for their engines, and a building for headquarters. When Kaishu had received permission from Edo to establish the naval academy, he was also guaranteed that the necessary ships and equipment would be supplied by the Bakufu Naval Training Center in Nagasaki, but none had yet arrived.

"The money will be delivered here from Fukui within a few days," Ryoma informed, before Kaishu relayed the details of the events in Choshu as they had occurred over the past two weeks.

"There's no sense in your getting so bothered," Kaishu said consolingly. He had never seen Ryoma so upset, and felt ill at ease, despite himself. "What's done is done."

"I just can't understand those maniacs," Ryoma said angrily. "We must act fast, Sensei. We must build our navy to help Choshu, if the barbarians don't retaliate first by blowing Shimonoseki off the map."

"The difference between you and your friends in Choshu," Kaishu said, "is your sense of timing."

"Timing," Ryoma bitterly agreed, "is one thing the Choshu men don't seem to understand."

*   *   *

Kaishu and Ryoma stood on an expansive beach near Kobe Village one morning in the first week of June. The coast was dotted with thatched houses of fishermen, pines lined the road above, and behind the road were green rice fields which flowed with the breeze into the hills beyond. The two men were admiring a new building, much different in style than the thatched houses. It was longer and narrower, and had only one story. The paneled walls were freshly lacquered, and the black tile roof gleamed in the morning sunlight. The beach this morning was empty, and the shrill of cicadas in the pines seemed to rise up all of a sudden through the warm salt air.

"What do you think?" Kaishu asked of the headquarters of his private naval academy.

"Just like home," Ryoma said, when a voice called his name from the road above. This was Sonojo, who ran down the hill to meet the two men. "Ryoma," he said excitedly, "I've just come from Tosa headquarters in Kyoto with some horrible news."

"What is it," Ryoma asked.

"Tosa Loyalists Hirai Shujiro, Masaki Tetsuma and Hirose Kenta are dead."

Kaishu had recently appointed Ryoma head of his private naval academy. Ryoma's following of nearly one hundred men, mostly *ronin*, included seven of his comrades from Tosa, all former members or sympathizers of Hanpeita's recently crushed Tosa Loyalist Party. Ryoma's nephew, Takamatsu Taro, was second to enroll after Kondo Chojiro, the bean jam bun maker's son who had recently received samurai status. Sawamura Sonojo had also shown up at Kobe headquarters lately, accompanied by Umanosuke, the son of a Tosa peasant. Even the staunch Loyalists Mochizuki Kameyata and Chiya Toranosuke, like Ryoma, now considered Kaishu "the greatest man in Japan." The latest recruit from Tosa was Yasuoka Kanema, Toranosuke's younger cousin.

Lord Yodo's recent crackdown on the Tosa Loyalists helped convince these Tosa men to stay in Kobe with Ryoma. As Sonojo had just reported, three of Hanpeita's lieutenants–Hirai Shujiro, Masaki Tetsuma and Hirose Kenta–had been ordered by Yodo to commit *seppuku*. Suspecting that the same might be in store for Hanpeita and the others, Ryoma hurried to Kyoto, and went straight to Tosa headquarters there. But when he arrived, he found the barracks nearly empty.

"Won't someone tell me what's happening around here?" he hollered, storming through the barracks, looking in each room.

"Sakamoto-san," called a voice from inside one of the rooms. Standing at the center of the room was a man dressed in typical samurai garb, but with a black hood covering his entire head and wrapped around his face, so that only his eyes, nose and mouth were visible. His sword, which hung from his left hip, was too long for him.

"Who are you?" Ryoma asked.

"I'm Tosa samurai Mutsu Yonosuke."

"You're not from Tosa," Ryoma scoffed. "It's obvious from your accent that you're from Kii."

"Yes," Yonosuke said, annoyed, "but I've been telling people I'm from Tosa."

"Have it your way. You can have Tosa and do what you like with it," Ryoma sneered. "But just tell me what's going on there now."

"Don't you know?"

"If I knew, do you think I'd be asking?"

Yonosuke explained, in a monotone, that three of Hanpeita's top men were recently ordered to commit *seppuku* for "insolence in not carrying out their lord's orders." Yodo had been furious with them, accusing them of meddling in Tosa affairs after the assassination of Yoshida Toyo.

As Yonosuke relayed in great detail, all three men performed their suicides courageously. Since Masaki did not have a calligraphy brush in jail, he formed Chinese characters out of strips of paper to compose his death poem in his cell. The poem stressed the condemned man's great pleasure that the court had regained political power, his only lament being that the Tosa banner could not fly in the Imperial capital with those of Choshu and Satsuma. In his last words, he tearfully denounced Lord Yodo for his indecisiveness in the face of the Bakufu.

Hirose had studied the proper way to commit *seppuku*, claiming that a man's value was determined by how well he was able to cut open his belly. He discovered that if one plunged his short sword into the left side of the belly, sliced straight across to the right side, then cut with the tip of the blade diagonally upward, and immediately sliced across this vital area to the right nipple, death would be instantaneous. When his chance came, Hirose, dressed in ceremonial white, calmly sat down and asked his second not to behead him until he had finished. In fact, Hirose had cut himself so skillfully that he was dead before his second could offer any assistance.

Hirai Shujiro, Kao's older brother, carved his death poem with his fingernails on the walls of his jail cell. When he sat down to perform *seppuku*, he noticed that his second, a close friend, was pale and extremely tense. "Relax," Hirai said calmly, rubbing his hand over the portion of his belly he would cut. "Let's get on with it," he said, then tightly gripping his short sword, plunged it into his belly. The second panicked, and instead of severing the head at the neck, his blade struck his friend on the back of the skull, cutting him badly. "I told you to relax," Hirai screamed, his face contorted in agony. An instant later the second struck again, and Hirai's head fell from his body.

"A waste!" Ryoma cried out as Yonosuke finished speaking. "I told them from the beginning not to trust Yodo. I pleaded with them to leave Tosa, and join me." Ryoma's eyes filled with tears. "Any word about Hanpeita?"

"As far as I know, he has not been arrested."

"Maybe not yet," Ryoma sneered, "but with the way things are now, none of the Loyalists in Tosa are safe."

"And since all of them have been ordered to return, there's not one Tosa Loyalist left in Kyoto, Sakamoto-san."

"How do you know my name?" Ryoma asked suspiciously.

"I was working with the Tosa Loyalists. And since there's not a man among them who doesn't speak of you, I've heard a lot about you."

"Do you always wear that?" Ryoma asked.

"Wear what?"

"That hood."

"I was about to get out of here when you came along. I feel safer if people don't recognize me." The man removed the hood, revealing a light complexion, long face and well defined nose. His thick eyebrows were dark over sunken eyes, his build frail, and though at five-feet, three-inches he was above average height, Ryoma was much taller.

"Why don't you join my naval academy in Kobe," Ryoma said.

"I was just on my way to Kobe to do that, Sakamoto-san."

"Then put that hood back on, and let's get out of here."

Unlike Ryoma and the other men at Kaishu's naval academy, Mutsu Yonosuke was of an elite lineage. His grandfather had been a high ranking government minister of the fiefdom of Kii, the wealthiest of the elite Three Tokugawa Branch Houses and the home of the present Shogun. Yonosuke's father, Munehiro, was a famous scholar of Japanese history, who, in spite of his Loyalist views, enjoyed both wealth and political power in the Kii government. Munehiro's political rival was a minister by the name of Mizuno, who criticized the scholar's Loyalist ideas as treason. The two became bitter enemies, and in 1852 Mizuno drove Munehiro from power, had him imprisoned and his family banished from the castletown to live in poverty.

Yonosuke at this time was only nine years old.

The boy was determined to avenge the outrageous treatment of his father, by cutting down a Kii official. The plan was thwarted when a relative caught Yonosuke sneaking out of his house with a sword. Yonosuke screamed and hollered, bit and scratched, then screamed and hollered some more. When he found that tantrums would not work, he tried argument to get his way. He protested violently his relative's interference, and insisted that he be allowed to avenge the injustice done his father. He argued that the *daimyo* himself was corrupt for allowing such injustice within his domain. And all this came from the mouth of a nine-year-old boy. Such were the makings of Japan's greatest foreign minister.

Yonosuke would never forgive Kii Han. At age fifteen he fled, and went to Edo where he studied at the academies of two famous scholars. This was in 1858, when Ii Naosuke had just come to power, signed the treaty with the Americans and begun his terrible purge. When Ryoma fled Tosa four years later, Yonosuke, at eighteen, was mingling with other Loyalists dedicated to the overthrow of the Bakufu. Near the end of 1862 Yonosuke went to Kyoto, where he was reunited with his father, who had also fled Kii and become friendly with the radical court nobles. During this time Yonosuke began frequenting Tosa's Kyoto headquarters, where he developed close relations with Hirai Shujiro. Although Hirai was a member of the Tosa Loyalist Party, his upper-samurai status gave him access to the *daimyo*. Recognizing the young man's intellectual capacities and his enthusiasm for *Toppling the Bakufu and Imperial Loyalism*, Hirai arranged for Yonosuke to have an audience with Lord Yodo: thus Yonosuke's self-styled status as a Tosa samurai.

*　　　　　*　　　　　*

Shortly after the Choshu radicals had fired on foreign ships in Shimonoseki, Ryoma's fear of foreign subjugation was exacerbated with the news that Shimonoseki had been bombarded by American and French warships.

The United States was in the middle of the Civil War when the Union sloop of war *Wyoming* was patrolling the Japanese coast in search of a certain Confederate cruiser. The captain of the *Wyoming* had heard of the recent attack on an American merchant ship, and decided to punish Choshu. At dawn of June 1, the *Wyoming* entered

Shimonoseki Strait prepared for battle. As soon as the Choshu forces spotted the foreign ship, they fired their outdated bronze cannon from three separate batteries along the coast. But unlike the three ships recently fired upon in these waters, the *Wyoming* crew was aware of the inferior firing range of the Choshu guns, and so stayed a safe distance away. The Americans fired relentlessly, and within minutes had sunk two Choshu warships and badly damaged a third. Just an hour after the first shot had been fired, the *Wyoming* left the startled Choshu domain for the Port of Yokohama.

The French retaliated on the morning of June 5 by pounding the Shimonoseki coast with two heavily armed warships. After destroying a Choshu battery, 300 French troops landed on Shimonoseki, burning to the ground a surrounding village and, to the horror of the xenophobic Choshu samurai, temporarily occupying the remaining batteries. At dusk of the same day, however, the French gathered up their dead and injured, reboarded their ships and departed the humiliated Choshu domain for Yokohama.

Choshu's short-lived mood of triumph had now completely vanished. In just five days, not only had it lost dozens of men, a large number of cannon and two of its three warships, but the occupation by the French, though temporary, sent shock waves throughout the domain. The Japanese had always been confident that if it came to combat on land the foreigners would be no match for the fighting spirit of the samurai. The French proved them wrong, and the leadership of Choshu had once and for all realized that repelling the barbarians by force was impossible.

It was late at night, and Ryoma was outraged. The only sound was the steady pounding of the surf, the only light that of a paper lantern, as he sat alone in his private room at Kobe headquarters. The building was full of men fast asleep; but having heard of the attack on Choshu and of the Bakufu's subsequent treachery, Ryoma was too disturbed to sleep. He picked up his writing brush from his low desk, and began scribbling his truest thoughts to his sister Otome.

"This letter concerns the most important of matters, so don't show it to a soul, and be sure not to chatter about it to anyone.

"Things for me are coming along fine now. I have become very close with one of the big han, (a powerful daimyo), and if trouble should start now I would have two or three hundred men to use as I thought best."

Gloating with self-pride over his recent success in obtaining the loan from Fukui and his relationship with Lord Shungaku, Ryoma wanted to share this with his sister. And even if he exaggerated the number of men at the academy, surely this was due to his enthusiasm. *"As for money, I can always come up with at least ten or twenty ryo. This eases my mind a lot.*

"But it is really too bad that Choshu started a war last month by shelling foreign ships; this does not benefit Japan at all. But what really disgusts me is that the ships they shot up in Choshu are being repaired at Edo, and when they're fixed will head right back to Choshu to fight again. This is all because the corrupt officials in Edo are in league with the barbarians."

Ryoma stopped writing, and with his sleeve wiped the sweat from the side of his face. Although he could understand the attack from the foreigners' point of view, he was furious with the Bakufu for secretly welcoming foreign assistance to punish Choshu.

"Although those corrupt Bakufu officials have a great deal of power now, I'm going to get the help of two or three daimyo and enlist like-minded men so we can start thinking more about the good of Japan, and not only the Imperial Court. Then, I'll get together with my friends in Edo (you know, Tokugawa retainers, daimyo and so on) to go after those wicked officials and cut them down."

Ryoma replaced the brush on the desk, then pounded his right fist into his left palm. "Damn it," he muttered to himself, and took up the brush again. *"I vow to clean up Japan once and for all,"* he scrawled in large, flowing Japanese script, confiding in Otome his firm conviction to topple the Bakufu. *"The big han I mentioned fully agrees with me, and its representatives are letting me in on all its secrets. Still, I haven't really been appointed to anything. It's really a shame that there aren't more men like me around the country."*

Again Ryoma stopped writing, wiped the brush on the same sleeve he had just used to wipe his face, laid the brush on the desk, and reached for a gourd flask of *sake*. He pulled out the wooden stopper with his teeth, spit it out, took a long swig, then sighed heavily as he thought about a letter he had received from his sister recently. Otome had left her husband. This, however, was not news to Ryoma; she had told him of her intentions the last time they had met. What troubled him was his sister's apparent depression. She had written in a tone of uncharacteristic self-pity that she was considering renouncing the world for religion. But no sooner had Ryoma taken another long swig

of *sake*, than he began laughing at the thought of Otome, of all people, becoming a Buddhist nun. Alone in his dimly lit room, Ryoma
picked up his brush.

*"You say in the letter I got from you the other day that you want to
become a religious person and retire into the remote mountains somewhere. (Well, well! Ahem!) An amusing idea, but you've had it before.
Things are pretty hectic around here, but if you're going to go through
with it, put on some old faded priest's robes and start wandering
around like a pilgrim. It probably won't be too much trouble. You can
travel across Japan without spending a single silver coin. Still, if
you're going to do that, first you have to read the Shingon sutras,
Kanon sutras, Ikko sutras and Amida sutras. They're rhythmic and
quite difficult."*

Here, Ryoma started laughing aloud, even uncontrollably, at the idea
of Otome reading the Buddhist sutras. He took another drink of *sake*.
Then a cold, blue flash filled his mind for an instant as he realized that
he hadn't seen his sister for over a year, and didn't know when, or if,
he would see her again.

"In the end," he continued, *"this world isn't worth a damn. So put
all you have into it, with such intensity that you fart doing so. If you
should die, what'll be left in the fields will look like white stones (dear,
dear!).*

*"But becoming a pilgrim is not something you can do alone, with-
out checking with people (for instance, poor old Ryoma is likely to die
and haunt you any time). If you're thinking about it, you have to think
of others and respect their wishes and thoughts. I think that you are a
little too young, you know. When you look for a husband you don't just
want some pretty boy who looks good on the outside; you have to be
a vigorous, tough woman with some spunk. If, for instance, you go out
with one or two friends for an evening and should encounter some
robbers, go after them and don't let them go until you have smashed
them in the balls."*

Ryoma again put down his brush. He chuckled briefly and took
another drink from the flask. He was beginning to feel drunk, and the
night was getting on toward dawn. A strong ocean wind was howling
through the pines behind the building, and Ryoma's humorous
thoughts suddenly turned morbid.

*"I don't expect that I'll be around too long. But I'm not about to die
like any average person either. I'm only prepared to die when big
changes finally come, when even if I continue to live I will no longer*

be of any use to the country. But since I'm fairly shifty, I'm not likely to die so easily. But seriously, although I was born a mere potato digger in Tosa, a nobody, I'm destined to bring about great changes in the nation. But I'm definitely not going to get puffed up about it. Quite the contrary! I'm going to keep my nose to the ground, like a clam in the mud. So don't worry about me!"

Ryoma signed the letter, and again wiped the brush on his sleeve, threw it on the desk and drank the remaining *sake*. "Don't worry about me, Otome," he said aloud. "I'm not about to die so easily."

The dawn had crept into the night sky, and a pale light filtered into the room through the open window, as Ryoma suddenly felt extremely tired, lay back and was soon fast asleep.

"Sakamoto-san," Mutsu Yonosuke called at Ryoma's room late that morning.

Ryoma opened his eyes. "What?"

"Something urgent."

"Well, come in."

Yonosuke entered the room, and without sitting down or speaking, gave Ryoma a long, troubled look.

"Well, what is it?" Ryoma said impatiently.

"While I was in Edo," Yonosuke began in an annoying monotone, "I heard about a man by the name of Kabuto Sosuke, a real fanatic. He's an expert swordsman, and word has it that he's cut down a lot of people in Kyoto."

"*Heaven's Revenge*," Ryoma groaned.

"Yes. He has about six or seven men in his gang, which has recently come from Kyoto to Osaka with one particular purpose in mind."

"And?" Ryoma yawned. He was not inclined to get excited over a gang of fanatic Loyalist killers; after all, he had tamed Okada Izo, the most notorious of them all.

"And what do you suppose that purpose is?" Yonosuke asked.

"I have no idea." Ryoma again yawned.

"To assassinate Tokugawa Navy Commissioner Katsu Kaishu."

"What?" Ryoma roared, springing to his feet. If Ryoma had not been disturbed by the content of Yonosuke's words, he might have been inclined to knock some feeling into the younger man who spoke with, what he considered, uncalled for composure. "Katsu-sensei left for Osaka this morning," Ryoma shouted. "Has he been warned?"

"Yes. I told him before he left. He said he'd be careful, but didn't seem to mind."

"That sounds like him." Ryoma shook his head slowly. "Why didn't you tell me earlier?" he hollered. Ryoma, who seldom angered, was furious; such was his concern for the safety of his mentor.

"That's not all," Yonosuke continued calmly.

"What else?" Ryoma snapped.

"I heard about all of this from a man named Inui Juro. He's friendly with Kabuto's gang, and has even hidden some of them in his own home."

"What else can you tell me about Inui?"

"He's quite rash, if you know what I mean." Yonosuke uncharacteristically grinned. "In other words, Inui has deceived his friends by informing me, and apparently some others, of their scheme. But he felt obligated to do so because of all that I've told him about Katsu-sensei. Then, when Kabuto and the others found that Inui leaked their plan, they decided to kill him."

"And you want me to protect him," Ryoma said, shaking his head.

"If you could," Yonosuke said, bowing his head.

"How can I refuse?" Not only did Ryoma detest hearing of Japanese killing each other, but he was anxious to meet the man who could lead him to Kaishu's would-be assassins.

"Thank you, Sakamoto-san," Yonosuke said, again bowing his head.

"Where is Inui?"

"At his home in Osaka, I suppose."

"Well, let's go."

Arriving in Osaka late that afternoon, Ryoma and Yonosuke went directly to Inui's house. The sliding doors on the side of the house were open, and Inui's wife was sitting alone on the verandah. She started in fright at the sight of two men with swords approaching, but immediately relaxed when she recognized Yonosuke. "They've taken my husband," she cried, nervously eyeing Ryoma.

"Who's taken him?" Ryoma asked gruffly. He was not pleased with the way that the woman was staring at him, as if he were one of Kabuto's gang.

"Who is this man?" she asked Yonosuke, ignoring Ryoma's question.

"This is Tosa samurai Sakamoto Ryoma, my close friend."

Ryoma removed his long sword from his hip and sat down on a large rock at the side of the house. He placed his sword on his lap, and plucked a reed of grass from the moist ground.

"Kabuto and his men," the woman answered Ryoma's question, although she was still obviously frightened of him.

"How many were there?" Ryoma asked, putting the reed in his mouth.

"About five or six."

"When did they take him?"

"Less than an hour ago."

"Which way did they go?" Ryoma spat out the reed of grass, and gripped the hilt of his sword. He was in a bad humor. After all, he was risking his life to save a man he did not even know, and the man's wife was treating him as if he was one of the men who had abducted him.

"One of them hollered something about the mouth of the river."

"Which river?" Yonosuke asked.

"I don't know," the woman said, looking down.

"Must be the Ajikawa," Ryoma said. The main ship-landing in Osaka was located just north of the estuary of the Ajikawa, which flowed into Osaka Bay. Ryoma had landed at this spot several times while sailing with Kaishu. "It's pretty desolate around that area," he said. "No houses. And not many people pass by the mouth of the river, especially after dark. A perfect place for a..."

The woman flinched. "For a killing," she murmured, as if resigned to the fact that she would never see her husband again.

"Yes, a killing," Ryoma said, stood up and thrust his sword through his sash. "Let's go, Yonosuke," he growled. "It's not far from here, but we'd better hurry."

By the time Ryoma and Yonosuke reached the vicinity of the river mouth, the sun had disappeared from the evening sky. They walked quickly toward the coast, down a narrow path which led through a pine grove. Suddenly, they heard a loud scream, and Ryoma unlatched the sheath of his sword.

"This way," he said, then dashed through the pines toward the river-bank, with Yonosuke right behind.

Inui's hands and feet were tied to two bamboo stakes which had been driven into the soft mud along the riverbank. Six men stood in the dusk huddled around him like a pack of wolves. One of them held the blunt edge of a sword across the bound man's throat.

"Go ahead, Kabuto, you coward," Inui gasped in pain. "Go ahead, kill me."

Kabuto was tall. His lean build evoked the image of a hungry wolf, and his broad shoulders and long arms were telltale of his great physical strength. He wore a black kimono and *hakama* of coarse dark brown cloth. His thick black hair was tangled, and he had a long scar across one side of his face. "Shut up!" Kabuto roared, stuffing a wad of cloth into Inui's mouth. "This is what happens to traitors," Kabuto snarled, kicking Inui in the groin.

"Sakamoto-san," Yonosuke whispered, "can you handle all six?"

"I'll take them without a fight," Ryoma said, and from this moment on Mutsu Yonosuke was devoted to Sakamoto Ryoma.

"Let him go!" a firm voice called out from the pine grove. All six men started, and turned around to see two samurai approaching in the dusk less than twenty paces away. The taller of the two, who held a drawn sword, squinted coldly at them.

"Who are you?" Kabuto growled.

"Sakamoto Ryoma of Tosa." Ryoma grinned menacingly. "Let him go!" he demanded, staring straight into Kabuto's eyes.

Yonosuke swallowed deeply, but remained steady by Ryoma's side.

"Sakamoto Ryoma?" Kabuto's face dropped, and he turned slightly, signaling to the others not to move. There was a mystique about Ryoma that affected all of them. Not only had Ryoma long been known in fencing circles around Edo as an expert swordsman and former head of the Chiba Dojo, but his name now evoked an enigmatic kudos. Although he was known as a leader of the Tosa Loyalists, and close friend of Takechi Hanpeita, he was also known as the right-hand man of the Tokugawa Navy Commissioner. And the very fact that Kabuto's gang had planned to assassinate Kaishu intensified the surprise of Ryoma's sudden appearance.

Kabuto started, as if to charge the imposing swordsman. "Stop!" Ryoma roared. "If you don't, I'll kill you."

Kabuto froze. Ryoma remained still, controlling his opponent with his eyes. It was now dark, and the silver light from the full moon glistened on the surface of the mouth of the river. Suddenly, one of the gang of six lurched toward the two intruders, and Ryoma raised his blade. "You move, you die," he said in a low voice.

"Put it away!" Kabuto ordered his man to resheathe his sword.

"Now, untie him," Ryoma said, never for an instant removing his eyes from Kabuto's.

"We'll untie him, Sakamoto. But things are not over between me and you. We have a score to settle."

"You can find me in Kobe. We can talk there. But now release this man."

"Talking is not what I have in mind, Sakamoto." Kabuto turned to his men. "Cut him free," he roared.

One of the men drew his short sword and cut Inui's arms and legs free from the bamboo stakes. The exhausted man, his face contorted in pain, fell like a dead weight to the muddy ground, and Yonosuke started toward him.

"Wait, Yonosuke," Ryoma said. "There's one more thing I have to tell you, Kabuto. If anything should happen to Katsu Kaishu, I'll kill you," he said, before slamming his sword back into its scabbard.

*   *   *

Kaishu had recently arranged for several instructors, trained at the Bakufu's Nagasaki Naval Institute, to teach at his Kobe academy, but Ryoma was too busy traveling between Osaka, Kyoto and Fukui to spend much time in formal navigational training. At the end of June, Kaishu sent Ryoma and Chojiro to Fukui's Kyoto headquarters to deliver a rifle as a token of appreciation for the loan received. Ryoma, however, had a more pressing reason for the visit. Outraged at the Bakufu for repairing the foreign warships which had attacked Choshu, he hoped to convince Fukui to realize changes within the Edo hierarchy in order to, as he had vowed in a recent letter to Otome, *"clean up Japan once and for all."* He wanted to discuss the matter with Murata Misaburo, a high ranking Fukui official in Kyoto. Although he had never met Murata, Ryoma had heard that he was on friendly terms with both Kaishu and Okubo, and of course, with Lord Shungaku.

A light summer rain seemed to hang in the thick, hot air when Ryoma and Chojiro reached the great iron-studded oaken outer gate of Fukui headquarters. Having identified themselves as envoys of Katsu Kaishu, the two Tosa samurai were led to the office of Murata, who, at age forty-two, was one of Lord Shungaku's most trusted vassals.

"I am sure Lord Shungaku will appreciate the gift," Murata said, as he invited the two Tosa men to sit down. "I've never learned to shoot," he added, aiming the rifle. "Guns are so ignoble, hardly the proper weapon for a samurai."

"I understand your feelings," Ryoma said, "but you shouldn't forget that..."

"I know. Guns are essential to defend ourselves against the barbarians."

"And to overthrow the Bakufu," Ryoma thought to himself, but did not utter these words within the compounds of Fukui headquarters. Instead he said, "Kaishu-sensei sends his deepest appreciation for Lord Shungaku's generosity. But I've come here today to discuss more pressing matters."

"Oh?"

"It is of the utmost importance that we deal properly with the foreigners for bombarding Choshu. If we allow things to stand as they are now, with the barbarians having the upper hand, it will be very difficult for us to ever deal with them on equal terms. And so, this is not a time for any of us to stand by and watch as the barbarians do as they will to Choshu," Ryoma concluded.

"What do you suggest?" Murata asked.

"We must begin negotiations with the foreigners, and get them to leave Japan," Chojiro answered for Ryoma.

"After they have withdrawn," Ryoma interrupted, "then we can get on with the all-important task of putting the nation in order." Ryoma paused to choose his words carefully.

"Please continue," Murata said.

"To begin with, we must get rid of the corrupt officials who are in charge in Edo."

Murata winced slightly. "I appreciate your speaking your mind, but under the circumstances I think it would be wise for you to keep your voice down."

"I see," Ryoma said, but continued speaking in the same manner. "In order to get rid of the corrupt officials in Edo, we will need the help of Katsu Kaishu and Okubo Ichio, the only two men in the whole Edo government who are of any worth."

"Please," Murata interrupted, "You must remember that our *han* is directly related to the Tokugawa. What you are suggesting is treason."

"Call it what you will," Ryoma lowered his voice. "But I am only considering the welfare of Japan." Ryoma was not about to back down, despite the troubled look in Murata's eyes. "Besides Katsu and Okubo, we will need to ask Lord Shungaku and the Tosa *daimyo*," Ryoma said, despite his bitter feelings for Lord Yodo, "and two or three other leading *daimyo*, to come to Kyoto to discuss these plans."

"Have you mentioned your ideas to Katsu-sensei?"

"No. I thought it would be more effective if he heard them directly from you. All I am is a..."

"I have a fairly good idea what you are." Murata looked at both Tosa men with amused scorn. "I've heard quite a lot about you and your men from Katsu and Lord Shungaku both. But, you seem to be forgetting one very important point."

"Which is?" Chojiro asked.

"Choshu was careless for attacking the foreign ships in the first place."

Ryoma nodded in agreement.

"And so," Murata continued, "even if we should succeed in convincing the barbarians to leave of their own free will, we must pay indemnities to them for the damages caused by Choshu. Otherwise, Japan will be branded a rogue nation by the rest of the world." Murata paused to take a deep breath. "And that would certainly be no way to ensure peace. However, with the Imperial Court praising Choshu's conduct, it is going to be very difficult to pay these indemnities."

"What you say makes sense," Ryoma said, "but..." he paused, pounded his right fist into his left palm, "the Choshu men are willing to die for Japan. This is something that the corrupt officials in Edo have completely ignored. They're only concerned about themselves, and the House of Tokugawa." Ryoma stopped speaking. A surge of outrage filled him, but he was careful not to be controlled by his emotions. "The Bakufu has ignored Choshu's courage, instead of praising it as it should. Can't you see? The Bakufu is rotten to the core."

"Calm down!" shouted the minister of the former political director of the Bakufu, obviously disturbed.

"When the Bakufu should be aiding Choshu," Ryoma said angrily, unable to calm down, "it looks the other way, and even helps the foreigners get the upper hand. With things as they are now, there's no telling when Choshu, unable to control its rage, will attack Edo, burn the capital, and destroy the foreign settlement at Yokohama. If that happens, we will certainly have a war on our hands. At any rate, the present Bakufu officials must be gotten rid of immediately, and negotiations conducted with the foreigners to convince them to leave Japan."

"What if the foreigners should refuse?"

Ryoma stared hard at Murata. "If they should refuse to leave even after we have explained why it is of the utmost importance for them to back off for now, then our whole nation must unite to drive them out," Ryoma said.

"That would mean that the whole nation would have to face annihilation just because Choshu has acted rashly. But we must do what our sovereign deems to be right. You must not be partial to Choshu in this matter."

"I agree that Choshu was wrong for attacking the foreign ships in the first place. But," Ryoma slapped his knee, "that's not the most important issue. What we have to do now is clean up the mess in Edo by getting rid of the corrupt Bakufu officials. In other words, I ask that you immediately send letters to Katsu, Okubo and Lord Shungaku to urge their support in this matter."

Ryoma was unable to convince Lord Shungaku's vassal of the necessity of "cleaning up Japan." Frustrated, he sent Chojiro back to Kobe headquarters, and went alone to Choshu's Kyoto headquarters, only a short walk from the Fukui residence. The sun was about to set in the overcast sky and the rain had stopped as he walked eastward along Oike Road, then, increasing his pace, turned left at Kawaramachi Road which ran parallel to the Takasegawa.

"Sakamoto-san," a samurai called as Ryoma approached the outer gate of Choshu headquarters, near the canal. This was Ito Shunsuke.

"Where can I find Kusaka?" Ryoma asked, drawing a grim look from the Choshu man.

"Please," Ito said, gesturing toward the building, "let's talk inside." Since the attacks on foreign ships, the Bakufu had been going to all extremes to monitor the activities of the Choshu radicals, who now dominated the Imperial Court. Recently the Lord of Aizu, who was a close relative of the Shogun and the Bakufu's Protector of Kyoto, had established the Shinsengumi, a crack police force made up entirely of expert swordsmen, which patrolled the streets of Kyoto to arrest or kill suspected dissidents.

"Kusaka is in Choshu," Ito told Ryoma once the two were safely inside Choshu headquarters.

"Where's Katsura?" Ryoma asked, wiping his sweaty brow with his sleeve. Ryoma hadn't seen Katsura Kogoro in several years, and was anxious to speak with him. Although Katsura was indeed intent on overthrowing the Bakufu, Ryoma suspected that he was not the extremist that Kusaka was, and rightly assumed that he had not supported the attacks on foreign ships.

"Katsura is here in Kyoto," Ito said, then explained that Katsura had been sent to the Imperial capital for secret negotiations with court nobles and representatives of various clans, particularly Tosa and

Satsuma, in an aim to unite forces to topple the Bakufu.

"Where can I find him?" Ryoma asked.

Ito gave Ryoma a hard look. "That's secret, but I think I can trust you, Sakamoto-san."

"Well, I'm glad to hear that," Ryoma snickered.

Ito maintained a severe expression. "Katsura is in Sanbongi this evening. But please keep his whereabouts a secret."

Sanbongi, one of several pleasure quarters in Kyoto, was a common meeting place for both revolutionaries and men of the Bakufu. Its proximity to the Imperial Palace and the homes of court nobles made Sanbongi particularly suitable to the Loyalists, and it was in the broth-els of this quarter that political intrigue on both sides was carried on nightly. Katsura's favorite house in Sanbongi was the Yoshidaya inn.

That evening Ryoma and Ito walked down a narrow cobblestone street lined on both sides with quaint, latticed wooden houses. In front of each house burned a red lantern, and just behind the row of houses on the east side was the Kamogawa. The Yoshidaya was among these houses.

Having passed through the thatched wooden gate of the Yoshidaya, the two samurai were greeted by an elderly woman, who, recognizing the Choshu man, led them down a dark paneled hallway, then up a nar-row stairway to a spacious *tatami* room on the second floor, where Katsura was drinking *sake* in the company of a young girl. In the wooden alcove behind Katsura were his two swords, set in a wooden rack, next to which was a white ceramic flower vase with purple iris-es. On the wall behind the alcove hung a scroll of a mountain land-scape drawn in black Chinese ink.

"Sakamoto-san," Katsura said, standing up as Ryoma entered the room. "This is a pleasant surprise." At thirty, Katsura had noticeably aged since Ryoma had last seen him. His face looked weary, but his eyes had not lost their intensity forged through years of training with the sword. "Please sit down," he said, then turning to the girl, "Ikumatsu, bring us more *sake*."

Ikumatsu was the reason why Katsura's visit to the Yoshidaya was secret. She was twenty-one years old, and her face looked as though it had been carved from ivory. She was not beautiful, but the dark almond eyes, the small nose and the perfect flower-petal lips painted crimson formed a pretty and intelligent face. She wore a kimono of yellow silk, with flower patterns of brilliant red, pale blue, soft pink and dark green. Her thick raven hair was done up artistically in the fashion of the day, with a simple wooden comb arranged near the center, and a black lacquered ornamental hairpin in the back. Ikumatsu was a favorite among the men who came to be entertained at the Sanbongi pleasure quarter, but Katsura was her only lover.

Ikumatsu was by no means a harlot. Unlike the geisha of Edo, it was required that the *geigi*, or "artistic girls," of Kyoto be both refined in manners and accomplished at singing, dancing and playing the three-stringed *shamisen*.

Katsura had first met her in the summer of the previous year, soon after being sent to Kyoto as the Choshu emissary for secret negotiations with other Loyalists. Although the young girl's grace had charmed Katsura, it was her razor-sharp wit that had most attracted him. Finally, realizing that he must have Ikumatsu for his own, Katsura took the necessary measures to free the girl from the contract which bound her to her present occupation. Even after buying Ikumatsu's freedom, however, Katsura continued to have her entertain other men at Sanbongi. But she became a free agent, working at several different houses, and on occasion entertaining representatives of the Bakufu. It was for good reason, then, that Katsura was compelled to keep his affair with the popular "artistic girl" confidential: Ikumatsu was his personal spy. Although Katsura detested the idea of his lover entertaining other men, the information she was able to extract at these parties was invaluable to the revolution. Over the past several months Katsura had tutored Ikumatsu on the current political situation so that she would best be able to perform her surveillant duties. Although the enemies of Choshu were not apt to run on at the mouth about secrets of state, after enough *sake* had been poured, there were more than a few occasions when secret information became the subject of drunken talk. And since the girls who entertained at the teahouses and brothels were known to be generally politically uninformed, men who would normally be on their guard felt relaxed in the company of their pretty companions.

"Katsura-san," Ryoma said after Ikumatsu had left the room, "about the bombardment of Shimonoseki..."

"Ah, yes," Katsura said nervously. "Before we talk about that, please sit down, Sakamoto-san. You too, Shunsuke."

The three men sat in the formal position, and presently Ikumatsu returned to the room with *sake*.

"I've been trying to convince certain people I know to do something about the treachery in Edo," Ryoma said.

"What treachery?" Ito asked blankly.

"Repairing the foreign ships that have attacked Choshu. We must clean up Japan by getting rid of the corrupt officials in Edo who are only concerned for themselves."

"Attacking foreign ships was stupid." Katsura said. "Kusaka's a maniac. He has a one-track mind, and must be controlled. We had no business firing on the foreign ships in the first place. As much as I hate to admit it, we got what we deserved."

Ryoma winced slightly, but remained silent.

"But now that we've been defeated," Katsura continued, "I think that even Kusaka himself is convinced that we are not ready to fight the foreigners. Not yet." Then pausing, he said, "But, Sakamoto-san, I've heard some interesting things about you recently."

"Not all bad, I hope."

"I've heard about your work at the naval academy of Katsu Kaishu." Katsura was impressed with the navy commissioner. The two had met in Edo earlier in the year, and spoken at great length about the necessity of developing Japan's navy, conducting free trade, and the idea of an alliance among Asian nations. "Katsu is one of the few Tokugawa officials of any worth," Katsura said. "I'm particularly interested in his ideas for an Asian alliance. There's not a single country in Asia that's offering any resistance to the Western powers. Instead, we're all imitating them. None of us are pursuing a farsighted policy of our own. Before it's too late, we must dispatch emissaries to impress strongly on the leaders of all Asian countries that their very survival depends on all of us banding together to avoid subjugation by the West."

"Yes," Ryoma said, "we should start with Korea, our nearest neighbor, then go to China."

"But our cannon are still no match for foreign artillery," Katsura continued. "Our warships can't compete with foreign warships. And so, we can't even defend our own shores. We must improve our technology."

"And how can we raise the money to finance this?" Ryoma asked.

"By conducting international trade?"

Ryoma now realized that Katsura's ideas had developed in much the same way as his own. Although the Choshu man had once adamantly opposed opening Japan, he too had changed.

"International commerce will be vital to our success," Katsura said.

"We can no longer isolate ourselves from the rest of the world. Only by opening Japan can we eventually expel the barbarians." Then with a snicker he added, "Ironic, don't you think?"

"Yes," Ryoma said. "And what's more, we must go beyond the concept of individual clans. Unless we unite together, we don't stand a chance of toppling the Bakufu, much less defending ourselves against the foreigners. You mentioned an Asian alliance. But how can we expect to achieve one if we can't even unite among ourselves? I've tried to explain this to Hanpeita, but he'll never understand. The most important thing for all of us is to form a strong nation, a nation that can compete with the rest of the world."

"Sakamoto-san," Katsura interrupted, glancing at Ikumatsu, "I have received some very disturbing information this evening. I have reason to believe that Satsuma is plotting to join forces with Aizu to drive Choshu and the rest of the Loyalists out of Kyoto." Katsura returned his eyes to Ryoma. "And I suspect that Satsuma and Aizu support Edo's ploy to suppress the Emperor's campaign against the barbarians."

The anti-Bakufu Loyalists in Kyoto, led by Choshu, had never been as powerful as they were now in the summer of 1863. It seemed that they had gained the complete backing of the Imperial Court, while those in favor of a *Union of Court and Camp* were at their wits' ends trying to suppress them. And so, at the bidding of Edo, Satsuma was secretly planning to destroy Choshu.

Choshu's glory in Kyoto was a direct result of two recent events. The first was the attack on foreign ships at Shimonoseki, an act that immediately endeared Choshu to the xenophobes at court. The other was the assassination of the radical court noble Anenokoji Kintomo in May, three days before Choshu fired on the French ship. Anenokoji was cut down just outside Sakuhei Gate, one of the nine Forbidden Gates of the Imperial Palace. Although the identity of the assassin was never confirmed, the sword of a Satsuma samurai was found at the scene of the murder. When this man was questioned by the Aizu authorities in charge of policing Kyoto, he insisted that his sword had been recently stolen at a Kyoto brothel. When the sword was subsequently shown him, he asked to be allowed to have a closer look at the weapon. His request granted and the sword handed him, the expert swordsman drew the blade with lightning speed, and right before the eyes of the startled authorities, plunged it into his own belly. Although it could not be confirmed that the Satsuma man was indeed Anenokoji's assassin, the suicide was taken as admission of guilt, and Satsuma consequently fell from Imperial grace.

The shady circumstances of the assassination of this champion of anti-foreign *Imperial Loyalism* belied the Loyalists' convictions, and shrouded the already blood-soaked stage of Kyoto in an eerie shadow of intrigue. Some suspected that Choshu's ally Takechi Hanpeita, in an effort to destroy Satsuma's prestige at court, was the mastermind behind the murder. Others, particularly the Satsuma men, suspected that Choshu agents had killed Anenokoji, and planted the Satsuma man's stolen sword at the scene of the crime; while Choshu blamed Satsuma, saying that the Satsuma *daimyo*, who loathed the Loyalist rebels, wanted the radical noble eliminated.

Satsuma's suspicions were not unfounded. Until this time Satsuma had been in charge of guarding the Imperial Palace, but Choshu had now used the uncertain evidence of Satsuma guilt to secure the dismissal of its rival's troops from the coveted guard duty. Choshu furthered its cause by convincing the radicals at court to produce an Imperial edict authorizing a campaign against the foreigners, which would be tantamount to declaring *Expelling the Barbarians* a national policy. Choshu and the court radicals were planning to drive the foreigners out of the settlements at Yokohama, Hakodate and Nagasaki as an initial step toward toppling the Bakufu.

All of this occurred during the "Sweltering Summer of Frenzy," despite the reluctance of Emperor Komei, who more than anything else desired harmony in the nation in order that Japan might be strong enough to defend itself against foreign invasion. The Emperor secretly detested the extremists–both samurai of the various clans and nobles of the court–who claimed to revere him, but who were actually wreaking havoc throughout his capital. Furthermore, the Emperor was deeply concerned for the safety of his sister who was now married to the Shogun, and living in Edo Castle. Worried that an attack on the Edo regime might mean death to the princess, the Emperor issued a secret edict to the Lord of Satsuma, ordering him to restore order in Kyoto. Since the Choshu men were still unaware of this edict, the information that Ikumatsu was able to uncover left Katsura puzzled as to the real reason for Satsuma's alliance with Aizu.

"I can understand such behavior from Aizu because of its close relationship with the Bakufu," Ryoma said disgustedly, "But Satsuma? What could possibly compel Satsuma to act against the Emperor?"

"Satsuma will stop at nothing to destroy Choshu," Katsura said bitterly, "as its first step toward establishing a *Satsuma Bakufu*."

Suddenly Ryoma burst out laughing.

"Why do you laugh?" Ito asked, obviously annoyed. "What we're talking about is of utmost importance. There's nothing funny about it."

"It's not what we're talking about that's funny," Ryoma said. "But the three of us sitting here like this has just struck me as absurd. We can sit around and talk forever, but unless we act, we'll never get anything accomplished."

"You're absolutely right," Katsura said. "But there's one thing I want you to realize: Satsuma cannot be trusted."

As Katsura now informed, on the previous night, Katsura's lover-spy had uncovered some very important information. Entertaining a gathering of Satsuma samurai, Ikumatsu discovered that this *han* was secretly aiming to enlist the cooperation of Aizu to crush Choshu, and thereby regain its position of Imperial grace. Both Aizu and Satsuma, albeit for different reasons, resented Choshu's rise to power, and both were anxious to suppress its subversive activities.

"We must be patient," Ryoma urged. "We mustn't draw our swords until the time is right. In the mean time, I m going to develop a navy."

"You're absolutely right," Katsura said, refilling Ryoma's cup.

Ryoma left the Yoshidaya early next morning, and walked southward along Kawaramachi Road, with the canal on his left. On the opposite side of the canal was a boat-landing from where he would catch a riverboat to Osaka, just a short way from Kobe. His head ached from too much drink, the heat was stifling and he was anxious to get back to the naval academy.

There was not a cloud in the crystal blue sky as Ryoma passed Choshu headquarters without incident, and a few minutes later turned left toward the canal to cross the Sanjo Bridge. As he approached the foot of the bridge he heard a voice calling from behind, and immediately turned around to face a dozen men walking toward him. Three of them wielded long spears, one carried a white banner emblazoned in red with the Chinese character for "sincerity," the mark of the Shinsengumi. All twelve men wore jackets of pale blue with broad stripes on the sleeves.

"Halt!" the voice called. A vicious-eyed man who stood at the front of the group placed his right hand on the hilt of his sword without drawing the blade.

Ryoma unlatched the sheath of his sword with his right hand, and stood motionless.

"I'm Hijikata Toshizo of the Shinsengumi, patrolling Kyoto under the authority of the Lord of Aizu, the Protector of Kyoto." The man spoke brusquely with a rising intonation, an accent of the province of Musashi, just southwest of Edo. "Identify yourself," he demanded, though from the workmanship of Ryoma's sword he had already identified him as a Tosa samurai.

The Shinsengumi had been established in the previous March under the command of the Lord of Aizu to put a stop to the rampant assassinations in and around Kyoto. It was a unique police force, whose sole purpose was to arrest or kill *ronin* and other suspected anti-Bakufu rebels. Rather than samurai from the elite classes of Tokugawa retainers which manned other Bakufu police units, the crack police force consisted of over one hundred *ronin*, the toughest that could be enlisted. The Bakufu felt that the best means to combat *ronin* would be with other *ronin*. "Fight fire with fire, and terror with terror," reasoned the Edo government, in an effort to control and suppress the radicals who had turned Kyoto into a bloodbath. And to this end, the Bakufu was successful. In less than a year, the Shinsengumi would become the most feared police force in Japanese history.

"Shinsengumi," Ryoma said, grinning diabolically. He had heard that this band had recently cut down several Loyalists without even trying to arrest them. "For the Lord of Aizu?" he scoffed. "So what? I'm Sakamoto Ryoma, retainer of Katsu Kaishu, the navy commissioner of the Tokugawa Bakufu. What do you want?"

"Sakamoto Ryoma?" The man repeated the name, slowly nodding his head. Despite Ryoma's special relationship with Kaishu, his name was also associated with the Tosa and Choshu radicals. "Nothing now," the man replied with an icy calm, but Ryoma could sense that these were dangerous men, impeccable swordsmen who would not hesitate, if given the chance, to cut him down.

*   *   *

Upon his return to Kobe that evening, Ryoma found that Kaishu was in Edo on official business. He burned with indignation at the Bakufu, and to ease his own mind until Kaishu's return, spent the following days with his men training under the maritime experts whom Kaishu had recruited for the academy. Then, on the day before Kaishu was to return, news reached Ryoma of an event in Satsuma which would hasten the course of history.

On July 2, about one month after the Americans and French had bombarded Choshu, a fierce battle was waged on Kagoshima Bay, between Satsuma forces and seven British warships.

Although Edo had little choice but to make the formal apology and agree to pay the indemnities, as demanded by the British for the Namamugi Incident, it was unable to force Satsuma to either pay or hand over the murderer of the Englishman Richardson. In fact, this inability of Edo to control its vassals caused serious damage to its credibility among the foreign powers, as indicated in the memoirs of Sir Ernest Satow, serving at the time as interpreter to the British minister in Japan. *"...we had serious doubts about the Bakufu. We saw that they are not supreme, or rather not omnipotent... Then the murder of Richardson and the impotence of the Bakufu to punish his murderers showed us that their authority did not extend as far as Satsuma."*

After months of unsuccessful negotiation at Edo, the British decided to approach Satsuma directly, despite repeated warnings by the Bakufu to refrain from such dangerous action. On June 22, the British dispatched a squadron of seven warships from Yokohama to Kagoshima Castletown of Satsuma Han. Early in the morning of June 28 the British squadron sailed through Kagoshima Bay under the hot Kyushu sun which burnt as fiercely as the eyes of the hundreds of Satsuma warriors watching from the batteries along the coast and the lookout posts in the mountains above. Here the British anchored in full view of Kagoshima Castle to the west, the volcanic peak of Sakurajima to the east, and summoned Satsuma officials to board the flagship *Euryalus* to receive their demands. The Satsuma authorities thereupon insisted that they could not be held responsible for Richardson's death, since it had been caused by negligence on the part of Edo. Satsuma pointed out that the Bakufu had failed to indicate in its foreign treaties the Japanese law that a person showing disrespect for a *daimyo* procession was liable to be cut down on the spot. Satsuma did, however, insist that a thorough search for the murderer was being made, but the British were not to be duped.

Frustrated by Satsuma's adamancy, the British took coercive action at dawn of July 2, seizing three steamers Satsuma had recently purchased from Western traders in Nagasaki. The Satsuma officials interpreted this as an act of war, and all hell broke loose.

Confident that their defenses were adequate to stave off the British, at noon of the same day the Satsuma warriors opened fire on the squadron with eighty-three cannon from ten batteries along the coast. The first shot hit the deck of the flagship *Euryalus*, decapitating the captain. The British retaliated by looting and burning Satsuma steamers, and soon after, by opening fire with their superior Armstrong guns, setting the wooden buildings of the coastal town ablaze. "*It was an awful and magnificent sight,*" wrote Satow, who witnessed the battle from shipboard, "*the sky all filled with a cloud of smoke lit up from below by the pointed masses of pale fire.*"

The British left Kagoshima Bay the following day, but word soon reached Satsuma of plans for another attack. Although the Satsuma men had fought well, like Choshu, they had learned a valuable lesson: their inferior weaponry was no match for Western artillery and warships. Eventual negotiation in Edo between the adversaries led to a peace agreement, according to which Satsuma acquiesced to pay the indemnities. Concerning the demand that the murderer of Richardson be punished, Satsuma humored the British by agreeing, but actually had no such intention. Instead, the *han* merely waited for Britain to forget its demand, as it eventually did, and from this time on Satsuma and Britain were staunch allies.

*　　　　　*　　　　　*

On the evening after hearing of the British shelling of Kagoshima, Ryoma sat in his room at Kobe headquarters with his eight closest comrades. The nineteen-year-old samurai from Kii, Mutsu Yonosuke, was the only one among them not of Tosa. Yonosuke's impassivity notwithstanding, his razor-sharp wit had recently convinced Ryoma to appoint him to the post of secretary of the naval academy. Sawamura Sonojo, also nineteen, had by now abandoned his xenophobic sentiments, as his young mind expanded under the guidance of Katsu Kaishu. Kondo Chojiro, the bean jam bun maker's son whose eyes betrayed an insatiable hunger for knowledge, was twenty-five, three years younger than Ryoma. The peasant's son Umanosuke, twenty-seven, had been close to Ryoma since early adolescence when they practiced *kendo* together at the Hineno Dojo in Kochi. After Ryoma, he was the oldest of the group, and the only commoner. Takamatsu Taro, at age twenty, was more like a younger brother to Ryoma than a nephew. Chiya Toranosuke, the village headman's son, had changed his outlook completely since joining Ryoma and Kaishu. Although less than a year before he had been involved in several murders of proponents of *Opening the Country*, Tora, at twenty-one, was now a firm believer in the need to modernize Japan. Even Mochizuki Kameyata, who at twenty-five had been the hardest of the eight for Ryoma to win over, now understood the necessity to open Japan, albeit he had not completely thrown off his xenophobic sentiments. Yasuoka Kanema's enthusiasm to learn navigation had recently earned the nineteen-year-old the special praise of the navy commissioner himself.

"It doesn't take great powers of deduction to figure out that the corrupt officials in Edo are glad for the free military support they've been getting from the foreigners," Ryoma said bitterly.

"It's a crime," Sonojo groaned.

"First Choshu, and now Satsuma," Tora seethed.

"The Bakufu's behavior is inexcusable," Ryoma concluded. Upon hearing of the attack on the previous night, Ryoma had made his feelings known to Kaishu. While the navy commissioner sympathized with Ryoma's contempt for the corruption in Edo, his position within the government made it impossible for him to voice his feelings. Of this Ryoma was well aware. "Best to have Katsu in a position of authority," Ryoma had told his men earlier, when asked about his mentor's stance concerning the outrage, "while we do the dirty work."

*   *   *

Choshu's deepest fears turned into a nightmare after Aizu and Satsuma reached a final agreement in mid-August, giving Satsuma and Tokugawa sympathizers at court influence over Imperial decree. The stage was now set for a *coup d'etat* in Kyoto, and a dramatic reversal of the Loyalists' fortunes. On August 18, under the cover of night, the Lord of Aizu entered the Imperial Palace, while heavily armed Satsuma and Aizu troops seized the nine Forbidden Gates. Soon after, five feudal lords, including the young Tosa *daimyo*, under Imperial decree, led their own troops to fortify the Imperial guard of Aizu and Satsuma, barring entrance to the palace by radical court nobles, Choshu samurai and all other Loyalists. In the still of the night the boom of a single cannon shot–a signal to the Emperor that the palace had been completely sealed off–awoke the startled champions of *Imperial Loyalism* at court, who now discovered that they no longer had access to the Emperor.

The Choshu troops responded by storming one of the Forbidden Gates, but to no avail. Like the eight other entrances to the palace, it too had been seized by their heavily armed Satsuma and Aizu foes. Betrayed, the Choshu men aimed their cannon at the gate, but when they received a written order from the Emperor to immediately retreat, this most dedicated of all Loyalist clans had to obey, or else be branded an "Imperial Enemy."

The defeated Choshu Loyalists, led by Kusaka Genzui and Katsura Kogoro, retreated to a temple in the hills just east of the city. Realizing that Choshu alone could not defeat the combined forces of Satsuma, Aizu, Tosa and Fukui, the Loyalists returned to Choshu to plan a countercoup. Into exile with them went the idol of anti-foreign *Imperial Loyalism*, Lord Sanjo Sanetomi, and six other radical court nobles. The political stage in Kyoto had taken a complete turnabout in a single night, as the pro-Bakufu faction at court regained power.

*   *   *

Having been in Edo since the beginning of August, Ryoma did not hear of the coup in Kyoto until several days after the event. The news of the Loyalists' defeat came as a great blow to Ryoma, and he directed his anger at all parties involved. He denounced the *Union of Court and Camp* as a fallacy which would only serve Tokugawa interest. He detested the rivalry among Satsuma and Choshu, who, he argued, should be cooperating with each other to topple the Bakufu. But he was most critical of the rashness of the Loyalists themselves, because, after all, their loss was his.

Ryoma had known that Hanpeita's reign of terror in Kyoto, Choshu's attack on foreign ships, and the Loyalists' plan for a Satsuma-Choshu-Tosa alliance under Imperial rule were doomed from the start. It seemed ludicrous to him that his comrades would aim to expel the foreigners and bring the Emperor to power without first establishing a concrete plan of government for when and after the Tokugawa had been overthrown. Hanpeita's idea of financing his plans through money extorted from wealthy merchants in Osaka had revolted him. He spurned the blind faith that led the extremists to believe that as long as they were willing to die to uphold their moral obligations, everything else would naturally fall into place, despite the very real threat of the Western powers.

Ryoma's indignation was not without good reason. Not only did he detest the waste of life, but he also worried more than ever that, unless the Japanese could somehow unite, the foreigners would take advantage of the inner turmoil and subjugate Japan like they had China. But for the time being, he was even more concerned with the immediate ramifications that the coup would have for Takechi Hanpeita and his other comrades in Tosa, and so decided to discuss the matter with Kaishu. He knew that if he himself returned to Tosa to try once more to convince his friends to join him in Kobe, he would also be subject to arrest as a charter member of Hanpeita's outlawed Loyalist Party.

Ryoma was staying at the Chiba house in Edo. One afternoon in late August, just as he was planning to ask for Kaishu's help, he received a message from his mentor summoning him to his home immediately. When Ryoma reached the sloped road below Kaishu's house, with the high stone wall built into the hill, and just beyond this the old Shinto shrine, he recalled that night less than one year before, when he and Jutaro had contemplated assassinating Kaishu. "A lot has happened since then," he thought, increased his pace and soon passed through the front gate of Kaishu's house. "Sensei!" he called from the doorway. The front door was slightly open, and Kaishu appeared from the dark hallway, a worried look on his face.

"Come in, Ryoma," he said gravely. "I have something very serious to discuss with you."

Kaishu's wife served cool barley tea on this hot afternoon, then left the two men alone in the study. "What is it?" Ryoma asked anxiously, his face covered with sweat.

Kaishu began speaking much slower than usual. "Do you realize how the political change in Kyoto has affected Tosa?" he asked, taking a fan from his desk and waving it in front of his face. "I'm quite certain that Takechi Hanpeita and the rest of your friends in Tosa are in grave danger."

Ryoma was not surprised by such comments from this high-ranking Tokugawa official. He knew that Kaishu was more concerned for the welfare of Japan than for the regime he represented. He also understood Kaishu's concern for the safety of the very men who were intent on toppling the Bakufu. After all, hadn't Kaishu accepted him and his radical friends, most of whom were members of the Tosa Loyalist Party? Ryoma realized that his mentor loathed the waste of life that the Bakufu and now Lord Yodo were planning.

"I've been worried about the same thing," Ryoma said. "I'd like to ask you if there is some way you could intervene, to convince Lord Yodo not to do anything drastic." Ryoma wiped his sweaty forehead with his dirty sleeve. "He's already ordered three good men to commit *seppuku*," he said bitterly.

"With the Bakufu supporters restored to power in the Kyoto court, and the Loyalists banned, Lord Yodo is in a perfect position to arrest all of the Tosa Loyalists. If I know him, he's apt to either have them executed or order them to commit *seppuku*. All I can do is write to him, urging that he use discretion, and be lenient with those men." Kaishu paused, a grim look on his face. "But I know him quite well: he's extremely headstrong, and I doubt that he'll be willing to take my advice on matters concerning his own domain."

"If anything should happen to Hanpeita," Ryoma said excitedly, "there's no telling how the Tosa men at Kobe headquarters would react. Men like Tora, Sonojo, Kame and Taro are very hotheaded. In fact, I'd like to get back there as soon as possible. Without ships at our so-called naval academy, they have nothing to do but think about what's going on back in Tosa, and quarrel among themselves."

"That's another reason I summoned you here," Kaishu said. "It looks like we might be able to get a hold of two Western-style warships for training purposes. I've been negotiating with some of the people at Edo Castle, and the prospects look good."

"Sensei," Ryoma exploded, grabbing Kaishu's wrist, "while we're training aboard those ships, we can start a shipping business, transporting merchandise up and down the coast. We already have the crew, even if we aren't very well trained yet. We could get some of the *daimyo* to invest in us, pay for the lease of the ship, and if things go well, we'd have enough money to buy some ships of our own."

Kaishu raised his right hand, as if to calm his riled protégé. "Don't jump to conclusions. I didn't say we have the ships yet." He paused for an instant. "But why don't you talk to Okubo about it. I'll arrange for a meeting between the two of you. The foreign minister has told me himself that he thinks quite highly of you. If anyone can convince him to help us get those ships, you can."

"I see," Ryoma said halfheartedly.

"Oh, I almost forgot," Kaishu said, grinning now. "I have something for you." He stood up and walked over to a stack of books in a corner of the study. "Once we do get our own ships, you're going to need this," he said, handing Ryoma a cloth-bound volume.

"*The Practical Navigator*," Ryoma read the title aloud.

"Yes, a must for all sailors. Nakahama Manjiro translated it from the English. It's one of the seventeen or eighteen books he brought back with him from the United States. And I'll tell you a secret: without this little book, I'm not sure we ever would have made it across the Pacific," Kaishu said, referring to the expedition he commanded to the United States three years before. "But anyway, Ryoma, you can plan to see Okubo tomorrow. I have an appointment with him tonight, and I'll tell him to expect you. As for the letter to Yodo, I'll write it immediately."

"Thank you," Ryoma said, bowed, then left Kaishu alone in his study.

"With a fleet of warships we could topple the Tokugawa," Ryoma said aloud to himself as he walked through the front gate of Kaishu's house, then descended the narrow winding road which led to the city below.

The Fall of Master Zuizan

The long hot summer of the third year of the Era of Bunkyu had ended. The events which had occurred during these months not only spelled disaster for the Choshu radicals, but also led to the downfall of Takechi Hanpeita's Loyalist Party, as the pro-Bakufu faction, backed by Aizu and Satsuma, regained power at the Imperial Court.

Meanwhile, Ryoma's band of men, most of them former Loyalists, enjoyed safe haven at the naval academy of Katsu Kaishu, while Ryoma himself enjoyed close relations with four of the leading men in the regime he would overthrow. Ryoma's relationships with Lord Matsudaira Shungaku of Fukui, Shungaku's Chief Political Advisor Yokoi Shonan, the Bakufu's Minister of Foreign Affairs Okubo Ichio, and of course Navy Commissioner Katsu Kaishu, promised to serve the future interests of the former outlaw. In the meantime, however, he had no choice but to live up to the vow he had made to his sister "to keep my nose to the ground, like a clam in the mud," spending the end of the Sweltering Summer of Frenzy idle and anxious in Edo, while his Choshu allies had been expelled from Kyoto and Hanpeita's Loyalist Party was about to meet its end at the hands of Yamanouchi Yodo.

With Lord Yodo's departure from Edo at the beginning of 1863, the Tosa Loyalists slowly began losing their grip on Tosa policy, as the former faction of Yoshida Toyo regained power. While Yodo advocated *Imperial Reverence*, he insisted on working within the structure of the Bakufu, thus his support of a *Union of Court and Camp*. And although he had been placed under house arrest by Ii Naosuke, with the restoration to power of his colleagues Lord Shungaku of Fukui and Lord Yoshinobu of Mito, the highly respected Lord of Tosa now wielded significant influence in the Edo government.

Upon his arrival to Kyoto in January, in order to suppress intrigue among the Loyalists, Yodo forbade all Tosa samurai from visiting other domains for any reason but official business, and even from associating with men of other *han*. While in Kyoto, he consulted with leaders of the *Union of Court and Camp* faction, including the Lord of Satsuma, to find a way to deter the Loyalists who dominated the Imperial Court. Then, at the end of March, the Lord of Tosa returned to his own domain after an eight-year absence.

Although he had ordered three leading Tosa Loyalists to commit *seppuku* in June, Yodo was more cautious with Hanpeita. Harsh treatment of the Loyalist Party leader, Yodo feared, might spark a dangerous backlash from the Imperial Court, which was still controlled by the Choshu Loyalists, unless he could produce evidence of Hanpeita's involvement in a serious crime. It was at this time that Yodo set out to investigate the murder of Yoshida Toyo. Unable to come up with proper evidence, however, it was not until the Loyalists were banished from the Imperial capital in August that Yodo would feel safe in dealing with his errant vassal as he saw fit.

Takechi Hanpeita sat before Yamanouchi Yodo in a spacious drawing room at the retired lord's residence in Kochi Castle one hot summer evening. They had been talking all afternoon, and the sun had just set, as a dark orange light filtered through the open windows and fell gloomily over the faces of the two men. Yodo, as usual, had been drinking since early in the day.

Since returning to Kochi–even after three of his lieutenants had been ordered to commit *seppuku*–Hanpeita continued to prod Yodo concerning Tosa policy, to convince him to unite Tosa with Choshu behind the Imperial Court.

"My Lord," Hanpeita spoke slowly, "although you often speak of your obligation to the Tokugawa, certainly you can't compare a mere two hundred years of goodwill with two thousand years of Imperial favor."

Yodo laughed derisively. "Hanpeita, don't put words into my mouth," he said, avoiding a straight answer.

"Then let me ask you this, My Lord: what of my suggestion for filling important positions with men of ability rather than lineage?" Although Hanpeita knew that he was treading on dangerous ground in thus pressuring the elitist Lord Yodo, his own sense of grandeur–not to mention readiness to die–urged him on.

"I've considered your suggestion," Yodo said bluntly, then took a sip from his *sake* cup.

"Extraordinary times," Hanpeita boldly continued, staring straight into his lord's glassy, bloodshot eyes, "necessitate extraordinary ability."

Yodo not only considered himself the most extraordinary man in his own realm, but one of the most able feudal lords in the entire nation. He looked at his vassal with amused scorn. "Hanpeita," he snickered, "certainly you can't think that there is anyone in all of Tosa who knows that better than I do." Yodo refused to take Hanpeita seriously.

Recently, Yodo had replaced those officials who had been in charge during the heyday of the Tosa Loyalist Party with the disciples of Yoshida Toyo, ordering the latter to investigate the regent's assassination. The shake-up, in fact, left Hanpeita politically powerless.

"Of course not, My Lord." Hanpeita, who was unused to bowing to anyone, bowed his head to the floor. But Hanpeita was certain, albeit mistakenly, that he had won the favor and trust of the retired *daimyo*, and so felt this a worthy sacrifice. "Nevertheless," he said, "the times compel only the best of us to lead," Hanpeita dared utter.

Yodo avoided a direct answer. "Here, here," he said, holding up the *sake* flask to pour Hanpeita a drink. "Go ahead, Hanpeita. It will do you good."

Hanpeita hesitated, but unable to refuse his lord's hospitality, held up the empty *sake* cup. "I humbly receive," he said.

"Ah, but if you really don't want to drink," Yodo taunted, "maybe you'd prefer some sweets." He laughed derisively, and pushed a tray of sweet bean jam cakes toward Hanpeita.

"Thank you very much, My Lord." Hanpeita bowed again, and accepted one of the cakes.

Yodo reached for his paper fan, began waving it slowly in front of his face. "Getting back to your suggestion," he said, "I myself have considered it. But with the times being what they are, we mustn't rush into things. And, as you well know, since I'm retired, I'm in no position to make any decisions." This, of course, was a lie by which Yodo was biding time, until he could see the opportunity to destroy his impudent vassal.

"What are your ideas concerning the problem of expelling the barbarians?" Hanpeita asked, erroneously taking for granted that Yodo shared his own xenophobic convictions.

"I certainly don't condone the way the Choshu men have been acting. They're too rash. In fact, in order to ease the Emperor's mind, the best thing we can do is keep our ports open." Realizing that this last remark was a total surprise to Hanpeita, Yodo quickly reiterated, "Of course, if the Imperial Court should issue a decree for Tosa to support Choshu, I would certainly obey," he lied again. Yodo was careful not to betray his true feelings to Hanpeita, lest word reach the radicals in Kyoto who were still in control over the court. When the time for negotiation with the court again presented itself, as Yodo reasoned it inevitably would, he wanted to be considered an Imperial Loyalist, rather than a Tokugawa sympathizer.

"I have never once doubted your true intentions, My Lord." Hanpeita again bowed his head to the floor.

"But since I'm ill," Yodo continued to lie, "I would not be of much use."

"Then what if our young lord in Kyoto were to handle the matter?" Hanpeita dared suggest.

"Toyonori is too green," Yodo said of his seventeen-year-old heir, the nominal Tosa *daimyo*. "He could never be as effective as I could." Yodo drained his cup. "The best thing would be for me to take control," he growled, and Hanpeita, despite himself, felt a chill at the pit of his stomach. "But the way things are in Japan at present, I'm going to have to wait. Choshu has me extremely worried," he said, slamming his cup down on the tray in front of him. "It will eventually be up to the leading *daimyo*, including myself, to straighten things out, but for now all we can do is wait until the time is right." Yodo refilled his cup. "If, however, the Shogun were to disobey an Imperial decree, I, the Drunken Lord of the Sea of Whales, would cut off his head myself."

This last piece of rhetoric, which of course was also a lie, worked; the Drunken Lord of the Sea of Whales completely took his dangerous vassal off guard. Hanpeita, who desperately wanted to believe in his lord, was now convinced that Yodo was indeed the Loyalist he had always claimed to be, despite his reputation as a Tokugawa sympathizer. After all, hadn't Yodo suffered during Ii Naosuke's purge? Hadn't all those who signed in blood the manifesto of the Tosa Loyalist Party sworn to "go through fire and water to...carry out the will of the former *daimyo*"? And by Yodo's last remark, Hanpeita was reassured that the sympathy of the former *daimyo* lay with the Imperial Court. As powerful a man as Yamanouchi Yodo, he tragically assumed, could have no reason to lie to his own vassal.

*   *   *

Nakaoka Shintaro visited his mentor's fencing *dojo* one morning at the end of August, around the time that Ryoma had asked Kaishu to urge Yodo to be lenient with the Tosa Loyalists. The air inside the training hall was hot and humid, and the smell of sweat permeated the wood-paneled room where Hanpeita had just finished leading a rigorous practice. He and his men had reason to practice particularly hard this morning; they had just heard the news that Choshu and the seven radical court nobles had been banished from Kyoto.

Nakaoka found Hanpeita alone in the hall. Hanpeita, soaked with sweat, wore his navy blue training robe and *hakama*, but instead of a wooden practice sword, he held a real blade.

Nakaoka bowed at the entranceway. "I've just heard the news." He had a scowl on his face, anger radiating from his eyes.

"Sit down, Shinta." Hanpeita eyed his prize disciple almost suspiciously, his voice as solemn as his face was grim. "We must talk," he said, and, with one smooth motion, resheathed his sword.

The two men sat on the wooden floor, which was still wet from perspiration, and Nakaoka began speaking heatedly. "We should have taken Kusaka's advice while we were still in Kyoto and fled to Choshu. Coming back here was suicidal. Let's gather all our men and get out of Tosa before it's too late."

Hanpeita raised his right hand in a sign for the excited man to calm down. "You're not losing your nerve, I hope," he said calmly.

""Don't you understand?" the younger man shouted. "We owe it to the Emperor and the nation to get out of Tosa. We surely won't be of any use rotting in jail."

"You must have faith, Shinta. As long as Lord Yodo is on our side, we have nothing to worry about. And he is on our side."

"But Sensei," Nakaoka appealed, only to be silenced by a gesture from his mentor.

"Lord Yodo has given me his word," Hanpeita said. He refused to believe that the retired *daimyo* would betray him; his inflated self-confidence, bordering on megalomania, would not permit it. Besides, as the leader of the Tosa Loyalist Party, Hanpeita would never abandon Tosa Han.

"I am going to Choshu to investigate the situation there," Nakaoka said. "I'll report back to you as soon as possible."

Hanpeita arose, as was his daily custom, at dawn on September 21. He washed his face in a basin of cool well water, put on his riding clothes–black *hakama* of durable hempen cloth, a black jacket and a short-rimmed military helmet–then told his wife Tomi that he was going for a ride. When he returned about an hour later, he found one of his men waiting in the front garden.

"Sensei," the man exclaimed, "Lord Yodo's men are after us!" He produced a scroll from the breast of his kimono, and handed it to Hanpeita. "This is a subpoena for me to report to the administrative office immediately for questioning. It's all over. Our only chance is to get out of Tosa right away, this very morning, before they arrest every last one of us."

"Calm down," Hanpeita ordered, his face void of emotion. He looked hard at the front doorway to his house, pounding the dust from his *hakama*. "Keep your voice down," he said. "Does my wife know about this?"

"Yes. She told me that you'd be home soon. So I thought I should wait..."

"Enough!" Hanpeita said, showing for the first time the slightest bit of emotion. "Has anyone been arrested yet?"

"Not to my knowledge."

Hanpeita's eyes took on a sinister glare. "Go immediately to the homes of our chief members." He paused, then in a whisper, "You know who I mean. Make sure that everyone is prepared to give the same testimony in case they are arrested." Hanpeita was referring to the assassination of Yoshida Toyo two years before. "Remember, no matter what happens, we must stick to the same story that we have already agreed upon. They will never be able to prove anything as long as our stories correspond."

The man left immediately, and Hanpeita went into his house. "Tomi, I'll have my breakfast?" he said calmly.

"What are you going to do?" his wife asked worriedly.

"I'm going to have my breakfast. I'm hungry." Although it was now obvious that the coup in Kyoto had drastically influenced affairs in Tosa, Takechi Hanpeita still refused to believe that Yodo would betray him. He was convinced that Yodo's support for a compromise between camp and court was nothing but formality. True, he and his men had assassinated Toyo, but the murder was unavoidable if they were to unite Tosa behind the Emperor. And certainly, Hanpeita believed, Lord Yodo was a Loyalist at heart. "Tomi," he said sharply, giving her a stern look, "even if I should be arrested, there is nothing to worry about. I will be released soon after." Such was the erroneous self-confidence of a megalomaniac.

While Hanpeita was still eating breakfast, several samurai appeared at his front door, one of them carrying a warrant for his arrest. "I'm having my breakfast," he said calmly. "Wait until I've finished."

Hanpeita bid his wife good-bye as she stood misty-eyed at the front door. "No matter what happens, you are not to try to see me until I return," he told her. Tomi nodded stoically, as Hanpeita held her hand firmly, lovingly. Despite all of the time he had spent with his comrades in the pleasure quarters of Kyoto, he had never once touched another woman. Hanpeita released his wife's hand and walked ahead of his escorts with the perfect composure of a warrior, through the small garden to the road in front of the house. After he climbed into the sedan which was waiting to bring him to jail, he looked across the garden at Tomi, smiling from his heart. Although his great ego still did not permit him to believe that he, Master Zuizan, would remain long in jail, he felt a pang deep inside, such as he had never felt before, as he had a premonition that he would never see his wife again.

*   *   *

In September, Kaishu secured two warships from the Tokugawa fleet, shortly after which he and Ryoma returned to the naval academy in Kobe. One balmy morning in mid-September the navy commissioner led his crew of over one hundred men aboard the *Kanko Maru*, a tripled-masted square-rigged sailing corvette equipped with steam-powered side paddle-wheels, which the Bakufu had received as a gift from the King of the Netherlands. Just 216 feet long and 42 feet wide, the *Kanko Maru* was smaller than the *Jundo Maru*, aboard which Ryoma had already gotten a considerable amount of training over the past ten months. The red rising sun flew atop the mainmast, over 100 feet above the planked deck of the black wooden ship, as Ryoma admired the six black cannon mounted along both gunwales.

As Ryoma was the leader of the academy, he was the captain of the ship. His crew sailed for days at a time in the waters around Osaka Bay, practicing navigational techniques they had been taught at the academy. Then, when the news of the arrest of the Tosa Loyalists reached Kobe headquarters at the end of September, Ryoma and his men became more determined than ever to master the art of naviga-tion.

While his comrades wore gloomy faces for weeks after hearing of the arrests, Ryoma overcame his anxiety with hard work. His ability to dedicate himself so completely to his training seemed odd, even to his closest friends. One day on the deck of the *Kanko Maru*, after Ryoma and several others had finished hoisting the sails, Yonosuke said, "Sakamoto-san, aren't you concerned about the others back in Tosa?"

Ryoma gave Yonosuke a hard look, leaned against the side railing, and spit into the dark blue sea. "Hanpeita wouldn't listen," he said with a scowl. He looked up at the sails which fluttered loudly in the strong wind, his eyes squinted, right hand tucked into his kimono, a worried look on his tanned face. "And the same goes for the Choshu men," he said. "They refused to wait for the right time." As Ryoma finished speaking, he slammed his fist on the hard wooden railing, as if frustration had gotten the better of him on for one brief moment.

"What exactly do you mean?" Yonosuke asked.

"Let me put it this way. Say you have a boil on your neck. No matter how much you jab it with a needle, it won't burst until it's good and swollen."

"What you're saying, then, is that the Bakufu isn't swollen enough to burst yet."

"That's right. Too much jabbing now will only aggravate things. That's what Hanpeita did in Tosa. That's what Choshu did in Kyoto. And look what's happened to them." Ryoma again spit into the sea. "It's such a waste. Hanpeita rotting in a stinking jail cell. Of all the damn..." Ryoma stopped himself short, and regained control of his emotions. "But give those potato-heads in Edo a little more time," he laughed sardonically, "and the Bakufu will be so full of puss, even the slightest jab will cause it to burst wide open."

In late autumn Ryoma again sailed to Edo with Kaishu aboard the *Jundo Maru*. Then, one afternoon in the first week of December, a Tosa samurai appeared in front of the Chiba house.

"I've come on official business from Tosa headquarters," the man informed Jutaro. "I'm looking for Sakamoto Ryoma." Jutaro could tell by the man's dress and swords that he was of the upper echelons of Tosa society. His long nose and narrow face seemed to assert his aristocratic disposition. Indeed, unlike Ryoma, Hanpeita and the other Tosa samurai whom Jutaro knew, the man's demeanor betrayed a privileged upbringing.

"What business?" Jutaro said coldly.

"I've come for Sakamoto Ryoma," the man said. "We have reason to believe he's staying here."

"What if I am?" Ryoma called out from the front entranceway of the house.

"Are you Sakamoto Ryoma?" the man asked.

"You know I am. Who are you?" Ryoma growled, stepping outside into the garden, a hellish expression on his face.

"Tosa samurai Inui Taisuke," the man identified himself.

Ryoma had heard the name. Inui Taisuke was the eldest son of an elite family of upper-samurai, and former disciple of Yoshida Toyo. He, along with several other Yoshida disciples, had been chosen earlier in the year by Lord Yodo to suppress the Loyalists and find evidence to convict Hanpeita for plotting Yoshida's murder. Inui gave Ryoma a hard look. "You and all other Tosa men are ordered to return to Kochi immediately," he said. "That includes the seven other outlaws from Tosa who are hiding in Kobe. Here's your notice." Inui held out a sealed scroll.

Without taking the document, Ryoma said through a diabolic grin, "If I were you, Inui, I'd watch what I was saying, unless you mean to imply that Katsu Kaishu is harboring outlaws." Ryoma knew that Kaishu's friendship with Lord Yodo was highly valued among the Tosa elite. Then, changing his grin to a look of contempt, "What's become of Takechi Hanpeita?" he demanded.

"Just what he deserves," Inui said bitterly.

"What does he deserve?" Ryoma said sarcastically.

"Punishment for the murder of Yoshida Toyo."

"There's not a man alive who cares more about Tosa Han, or your lousy *daimyo*, than Takechi Hanpeita."

"Hold your tongue!" Inui yelled, reaching for his sword.

Ryoma checked Inui with his eyes, controlled him with his will. "What about the others?" Ryoma asked.

"What others?"

"The Tosa Loyalists that your deceitful *daimyo* has locked up in his stinking jail."

"Impudence!" Inui exploded, reaching for his sword with both hands.

"Stop!" Ryoma roared. "Or you die! And even if I don't cut you here on the spot, you must know it's a crime to draw your sword on another Tosa samurai outside of the *han*, unless, of course, you have proper reason. And you don't have proper reason."

"How dare you threaten me," Inui shouted indignantly. "I'm an upper-samurai, and you're a lower-samurai."

"Inui," Ryoma said, slowly shaking his head, "when are you and those other idiots in Tosa going to get it through your stubborn stoneheads that you can no longer afford to be concerned with who is an upper-samurai and who is a lower-samurai. The foreigners are about to eat Japan alive, and you idiots are still running around with your thumbs up your asses, worrying about petty things."

Inui was furious. "As a representative of the Lord of Tosa, I am in charge of punishing all criminals from Tosa."

"So what!" Ryoma sneered. "I'm Sakamoto Ryoma, dedicated to freedom, the rights of man and the unification of our great nation." Then realizing he was letting his anger get the best of him, Ryoma intentionally broke out into mocking laughter. "Ah, ha, ha! You can't really think that any of us are going to return to Tosa just because you've given me that notice. Because if so, you're out of your mind."

Inui stared hard at Ryoma, too vexed to speak.

Ryoma continued mockingly. "If I told you to bare your scrawny neck so that I could cut off your useless head, would you do it? I doubt it, no matter how stupid you are."

"Say what you will, Sakamoto," Inui sneered. "You've been duly notified," he added, handed Ryoma the summons and left through the front gate of the Chiba house.

Shortly after, Ryoma reported to Kaishu's house. "It looks like it's finally happened," he said. "I've just been presented with this." Ryoma showed the summons to Kaishu.

Kaishu unrolled the document, and, with a vexed look, said, "I'll be damned if I'm going to let my best men return to Kochi without knowing what's going to happen to them. I'm not about to let you go."

"Don't worry," Ryoma said. "I for one am not about to run back to Tosa to join the others in jail. I'm in no hurry to die, and beside, there are too many things I have to do first."

"If worse comes to worst," Kaishu said, "you'll have to become a *ronin* again. But, if possible, it would be best for all concerned if you could avoid that."

"How?" Ryoma asked.

"I'll write a letter immediately to the authorities at Tosa headquarters here in Edo, asking them to give all of you a little more time before returning to Kochi."

"A little more time?"

"Don't worry. It's just for the sake of formality. I'll tell them that all of you are working for me, and that I couldn't consider letting you go now."

From Ezo to Nagasaki

Kaishu's request was refused, leaving Ryoma and the other Tosa men with no choice but to become ronin again, just ten months after most of them had been pardoned. But the status of ronin–in this case, political refugee–suited the Dragon. The freedom that was an integral part of nonconformity far outweighed the danger of arrest.

Ryoma had been able to avoid the whirlwind of political change which spelled disaster for his comrades in Tosa and Choshu by establishing a private naval academy under the navy commissioner. He had created for himself and his men a new type of political space, independent of both the clans and the Bakufu, a foundation for a new Japan, based on the economic and military might of a modern navy.

Ryoma had learned much from the "Group of Four," as Katsu Kaishu labeled the clique which included himself, Lord Shungaku, Yokoi Shonan and Okubo Ichio. These men, among the most enlightened of their time, were bound together by a common foresight which was not displayed elsewhere, neither in Bakufu nor Imperial circles, nor in any of the han. The knowledge Ryoma had gained from them not only changed the course of his life, but would continue to influence his actions until his death. The Group of Four criticized the archaic feudal system upon which Japanese society was founded. Instead, they advocated that Japan be united into one republic, after the fashion of the Western democracies, founded on social equality and free international trade to enrich the nation. They professed that a new government should be represented by a House of Lords, consisting of men from the Bakufu and the great feudal domains, and that it be dedicated to the welfare of all Japanese people. They called for Japan to import more warships and to man them with men of ability from throughout the country, regardless of social lineage or han. They stressed that, since Japan was an island nation, a navy would be essential for national security and free trade. And it was under the wing of the bold navy commissioner that Ryoma and his outlaw compatriots were more than ever determined to establish such a navy.

The first year of the Era of Ganji, 1864, had come, and it would prove to be the most turbulent year of this most turbulent period in Japanese history. One cold afternoon in mid-January, as Ryoma sat alone in his room at Kobe headquarters studying a copy of Kaishu's navigational diary, a Tosa Loyalists by the name of Kitazoe Kitsuma called at the front door. At Ryoma's bidding, Kitsuma had just returned from a three-month expedition to Japan's remote northern territory. As a result of the coup in Kyoto in the previous August, the hundreds of Loyalists from various *han* who had gathered in the Imperial capital found themselves stranded, without money or, in many cases, shelter. The Bakufu police no longer tried to arrest *ronin* in the Imperial capital; rather, now that Edo had regained the support of the court, it was the Bakufu's intention to kill every Loyalist in the city. It was for this reason that Ryoma had recently devised a plan whereby these Loyalists could be sent to the northern territory of Ezo, to settle that wilderness and protect it from the Russians, whom it was feared might invade at any time. By so doing, Ryoma had reasoned, these men could avoid being killed by Tokugawa death squads, and when the time was right, return to Kyoto and Edo to fight on the side of the Imperial Loyalists to finally topple the Bakufu. Through the good offices of the Group of Four, Ryoma expected to convince the Bakufu to finance his plan. After all, Edo was at odds with itself trying to control the hundreds of renegades still hiding in Kyoto. Ryoma would offer the Bakufu a way to clear every last one of them out of the city, and put them to use developing and protecting the mineral-rich northern territory. The cost to Edo would be minimal: food, lodging and weapons for two or three hundred men.

"What was Ezo like?" was the first thing Ryoma asked Kitsuma.

"There's a lot more to Ezo than just bear shit and snow," Kitsuma bellowed. "There's more open land up there than you've ever dreamed of. But I'll say it again, Ryoma. I won't do it. I won't lead a group of men to settle Ezo. It would defeat our purpose."

"What purpose? To stay around Kyoto waiting to get killed?"

"I have to stay in Kyoto," Kitsuma insisted. "I owe it to Zuizan-sensei and the other Tosa Loyalists."

"You owe it to them to do the very best you can for Japan. And settling Ezo is the best thing you could do right now."

"I have to remain in Kyoto," Kitsuma stubbornly insisted.

"Why?" Ryoma asked, although he knew the answer. Kitsuma, like every other *ronin* still in Kyoto, was waiting for Choshu to strike back. Since the previous August, the Loyalists had been planning another attempt to occupy the Imperial Court, after which they would burn the city, attack the headquarters of the Protector of Kyoto (Lord of Aizu), then declare a new Imperial government independent of the Bakufu.

But Ryoma was sure that Choshu would fail. "Kitsuma," he pleaded, "listen to reason. Hanpeita and the others wouldn't, and look what's happened to them. Satsuma and Aizu have joined forces. They cannot be defeated just now. The timing isn't right. The instant Choshu tries anything, Satsuma and Aizu, with Imperial decree in hand, will squash them like insects." Ryoma paused, a sardonic expression on his face. "And since Choshu has nearly been branded an 'Imperial Enemy,' he continued, "the Bakufu will get all the support it needs from *han* throughout Japan to destroy Choshu."

"You don't believe that Choshu is actually an enemy of the Emperor," Kitsuma objected violently. To Kitsuma, and literally every Loyalist in Japan, Choshu represented all that was pure and holy, the epitome of *Imperial Loyalism*. "You can't believe even for a second that Choshu is anything but completely dedicated to the Emperor."

"You don't understand," Ryoma groaned. "It doesn't matter what I believe. What matters right now is that Choshu has been banished from Kyoto. It doesn't matter that Aizu and Satsuma were behind the plot. Throughout Japanese history, the Imperial Court has always taken the strongest side. When Kusaka and Hanpeita were running things in Kyoto, Choshu had never known such prestige at court. But after the coup last August," Ryoma snapped his fingers, "their prestige disappeared just like that." He paused to take a deep breath. "You can't tell me that I'm wrong."

Unable to disagree, Kitsuma remained silent.

"And so," Ryoma pounded his fist into his palm, "go and settle Ezo. Right now that's the most important thing you can do. I'll sail to Edo right away and see what I can do about raising money to finance the expedition."

"What are talking about, Ryoma?"

"I'm going to convince the Bakufu to put up the money you'll need."

"I wouldn't touch their filthy money," Kitsuma shouted.

"Don't be stupid," Ryoma said. "The Bakufu's money comes from the sweat of peasants throughout Japan. It's no more the Bakufu's money than it is ours. If we can put it to use for the welfare of Japan, then that's what we should do." Ryoma paused. "No," he corrected himself, "that's what we must do."

Not only was Ryoma anxious to exploit the mineral-rich northern territory, but the prospects of developing a trading network, linking Kyushu in the far south to Ezo in the far north, fascinated him. Needless to say, he had no qualms about using Tokugawa money to realize this.

But Kitsuma was as adamant as Ryoma. "No, I just can't," he persisted. "I must take part in the revolution that will happen in Kyoto. If I were to be away in Ezo when the coup took place, I'd never be able to forgive myself."

"Promise me one thing, Kitsuma. If I can raise enough money, promise me you'll reconsider."

Kitsuma stared hard at Ryoma. "How much money are you talking about?"

"About three or four thousand *ryo*."

"Three or four thousand *ryo!*" Kitsuma gasped. The sum was tremendous. But not only was Kitsuma tired of arguing, he was also aware of Ryoma's reputation as a big talker. "Alright, if you can actually raise that much money, I'll do it," Kitsuma agreed, certain, however, that Ryoma would never be able to raise such an amount.

*   *   *

In the second week of February Kaishu returned from Osaka to Kobe headquarters with some very disturbing news: France, England, America and Holland were planning a joint-bombardment of Shimonoseki. While the British bombardment of Kagoshima had taught Satsuma the futility of fighting with the West, their enemies in Choshu continued even now to insist on expelling the foreigners. This is not to say that Choshu still believed exclusion possible; rather, Choshu's intention was to humiliate the Bakufu, while continuing to show its complete dedication to the xenophobic Emperor, although he had banished that *han* from Kyoto. After the first bombardment of Shimonoseki, Choshu had rebuilt its batteries, and constructed new ones, where it mounted all the guns it could accumulate. Since this made it impossible for foreign vessels to cross Shimonoseki Strait–which was situated along the main shipping route between Nagasaki and Yokohama–the four Western powers, whose fleets were now in port at Nagasaki, decided to take affirmative action by punishing Choshu. The logic of the Westerners is summed up in the words of the Briton Ernest Satow: "*We had, it might be said, conquered the goodwill of Satsuma, and a similar process applied to the other principal head of the anti-foreign party might well be expected to produce an equally wholesome effect.*"

"It makes me sick," Ryoma said, as he stood with Kaishu on the beach in front of headquarters, staring out at the ocean, his right hand tucked into his kimono. He couldn't help but sympathize with Choshu. Although intellectually he supported Kaishu's call to fully open Japan, emotionally he respected Choshu for the selfless courage it had shown trying to expel the foreigners. "It may be true that Choshu acted drastically," he said. "But the Bakufu's treachery is too much to bear. Having repaired the foreign ships which shelled Shimonoseki, it's now obvious that there are many officials in Edo who are sitting by anxiously waiting for the foreigners to get back down there and blow Choshu right off the map."

"You're absolutely right," Kaishu agreed. "And frankly, I'm very worried about the possibility of the foreigners using this whole thing as an excuse to occupy Japanese soil. So, I'm going down to Nagasaki in order to convince them to abandon their plan for a second bombardment, or at least postpone it."

"If there were only more men in the Bakufu like you," Ryoma groaned.

"Yes," Kaishu said. "At any rate, I want you to come with me to Nagasaki." Although there would be nothing in particular for Ryoma to do on the trip, Kaishu wanted to expose him to this unique open port city. "And one more thing," Kaishu lowered his voice. "Just between you and me, the Bakufu cannot last much longer," he said, stunning Ryoma. "And so, while we're in Nagasaki, I intend to sail across the strait to Tsushima, to investigate the state of affairs in Korea." The Tsushima island group, located in the strait between the Korean Peninsula and Kyushu, was the closest Japanese point to Korea.

"Our plans for a triple alliance between China, Korea and Japan!" Ryoma exclaimed, then stooped down to grab a handful of sand.

"Exactly! We're getting closer to receiving permission from Edo to establish an official naval academy here. I plan to operate it right along with our private academy. But now, in addition to exclusive use of two Bakufu warships, we'll have shipbuilding facilities moved here from Nagasaki, an iron foundry, and access to the nearby mining works. After that, I would like to begin negotiations with the Chinese to establish strategic naval points in the Ports of Shanghai and Tientsin, then with the Koreans to link up with one of their key ports, maybe Pusan."

Ryoma listened silently, savoring the cold salt air, an anxious expression on his tanned face. His long-awaited dream for a navy was in the midst of finally being realized, and his mind raced at the possibilities which lay ahead. "Why don't we establish a base in Nagasaki as well?" he asked.

"You read my mind!" exclaimed the navy commissioner. "With the international trade that's going on there, Nagasaki is certainly a city of the future."

* * *

On the morning of February 14, Ryoma and several of his men boarded the *Kanko Maru* with Katsu Kaishu, and sailed out of the Port of Kobe. Heading west through the Inland Sea between the islands of Shikoku and Honshu, they passed the domain of Choshu to the north, then continued on through the Strait of Bungo to Kyushu, landing on that island at the province of Bungo on the following day. From here Kaishu returned the *Kanko Maru* to Osaka with the rest of the crew, as only he and Ryoma continued on foot southwest toward Nagasaki, on the opposite side of Kyushu.

The early spring brought clear blue skies and mild temperatures, and the plum trees lining the narrow highway were blooming in creamy whites and soft pinks. The navy commissioner and the outlaw traveled by day, staying at inns along the way as guests of the Outside Lord of Kumamoto, one of the wealthiest in all of Japan. They spent a week crossing Kyushu, and in the late afternoon of February 22 they boarded another Tokugawa steamer from the Kumamoto coast on the western side of the island, reaching the Port of Nagasaki on the following morning.

Ryoma stood with Kaishu on the deck of the ship, not a cloud in the crystal blue sky, the calm water of Nagasaki Bay a rich sapphire. European-style houses, the likes of which Ryoma had never seen before, stood along the east coast of the bay and atop the green hills rising above. "This is the western-most point of Japan, and the closest to China," Kaishu said.

Ryoma shook his head in awe, then squinted to get a better look at the strange foreign houses.

"Those are the 'Dutch Slopes,'" Kaishu said. "But it never ceases to amaze me that we Japanese consider all Westerners alike. The so-called 'Dutch Slopes' are a perfect example. Although there have been people of different nationalities living up there for several years, the people of Nagasaki, who admittedly have for the past two centuries known no other Westerners than the Dutch, insist on referring to all Caucasians as Dutch. With that kind of logic, the Westerners could just as easily consider all Asians the same. Imagine, for instance, not being able to distinguish between Japanese and Chinese!"

"Preposterous," Ryoma said, squinting at the awesome spectacle of the foreign fleets anchored in the harbor. "And look at all those warships," he groaned. The British, American, French and Dutch fleets were waiting for orders from their respective consulates to attack Choshu, just a short run from Nagasaki.

"Yes," Kaishu said glumly, "their combined fleets have enough firepower to annihilate the coast of Choshu, and continue straight up along Honshu to Osaka, Edo and anywhere else they might feel inclined to destroy. But I wouldn't get myself too riled up about it, Ryoma. That's why I'm here. It seems I'm the only one in the Bakufu who knows how to reason with the foreigners. Anyway, they don't want to fight with us, just trade with us."

Upon landing, the two men walked uphill over the cobblestone streets toward the office of the Magistrate of Nagasaki, the Tokugawa official in charge of overseeing the city. Kaishu was anxious to begin negotiations with the foreign naval commanders as soon as possible, but he first wanted to see the magistrate to hear the latest word concerning the foreign fleets. Soon they reached the magistrate's headquarters, on the western edge of the city, atop a hill overlooking the harbor. It was an imposing mansion built in the traditional Japanese style–a dark wooden building with a black tile roof, surrounded by a high white earthen wall.

As the Tokugawa Navy Commissioner and the outlaw passed through the outer gate of the magistrate's headquarters, an enormous brass-studded wooden structure, they were met by the magistrate himself. He had already received word of Kaishu's arrival, but was curious, if not a bit disconcerted, about the unsavory looking character with him. "Katsu-sensei, I've been expecting you," he said, casting a suspicious glance at Ryoma. As magistrate of the Tokugawa-run port, it was his duty to oversee the city's management, administration, police force, courts, trade, foreign relations and military affairs.

"Don't mind him," Kaishu said amusedly, patting Ryoma on the back. "He won't bite."

"Who is he?" the magistrate asked.

"Sakamoto Ryoma, a *ronin* from Tosa, and my top man in Kobe. This is his first time in Nagasaki, so I'd appreciate any courtesy you might show him during his stay."

The magistrate forced a smile, obviously dumbfounded by the situation. "Ah, of course," he said, unable to conceal his true feelings. "Please come into my office, Katsu-sensei." Then after a brief pause the befuddled man cleared his throat and, casting a worried glance at Ryoma, added, "And you too."

In a spacious oak-paneled room, with three armed guards posted just outside the door, the magistrate gave Kaishu a disconcerted look. "According to a report my office has received, we estimate that there are two thousand infantrymen aboard the British fleet, and eight hundred troops on the Dutch ships," he said.

"Have you sent word of this to Edo yet?" Kaishu asked.

"No. I've just now received the report, and haven't had time to verify it yet."

"We must inform Edo immediately." Kaishu's eyes flashed.

"By the way," Ryoma said nonchalantly, his arms folded in front, "how much gold do you have stored here?" The magistrate, surprised by the sudden question, answered in no uncertain terms, "One hundred thousand *ryo*. Why do you ask?"

"Just curious." Ryoma answered.

Later that day in their lodgings at a Buddhist temple near the center of the city, Kaishu asked Ryoma about "that unusual question he proposed to the magistrate."

"I was just wondering," Ryoma said. "You never know when we might be needing the money in case a war should break out." Ryoma was already planning for a day in the future when he and his men might raid the magistrate's office, take the gold and use it to procure guns and warships to overthrow the Bakufu.

Kaishu spent the next month and a half negotiating daily with the consuls of the United States, Britain and the Netherlands, and the commanding officers of their respective fleets. "We don't want war," the foreigners assured him, "just safety for our ships passing through Shimonoseki Strait. Unless your government can stop Choshu from attacking, we will be compelled to use military force to stop them." In short, the foreigners blamed the Bakufu for its inability to control Choshu.

It was a warm evening at the beginning of April. Katsu, Ryoma and two young women dressed in brightly colored kimono sat on chairs around a small round marble-topped table. They were drinking French red wine in the "Chinese Room" at the House of the Flower Moon, a brothel in Nagasaki's Maruyama pleasure quarter. The red earthen walls and ceiling of the room were paneled with dark Japanese cypress, and the floor was of brown tile; a French lamp hung at the center of the room, above the table; Chinese lanterns stood at all four corners; sliding glass doors with dark wooden frames opened up to a spacious garden.

Ryoma had never seen anything like it. "I feel like I'm in a foreign country," he repeated the phrase he had so often used over the past several weeks, then took a sip of wine.

"Why don't you play something on the moon guitar," Kaishu suggested to one of the girls. The girl stood up, adjusted her kimono, went to the adjacent room, sat down on the *tatami* floor and began playing the four-stringed instrument. Kaishu took a sip of wine, and sighed deeply. "Tomorrow we'll be on the road again, so we'd better relax tonight."

"Will you be returning to Edo?" Ryoma asked.

"No. I'm going to Osaka to report to the Shogun," Kaishu said in a low voice. "On your way back to Kobe, I want you to stop at Kumamoto to see Yokoi. I'm sure he must be quite down and out since that unfortunate incident last year, and I know how good you can be at cheering someone up. Also, I have some money I want you to give him. You know, his stipend has been confiscated."

Yokoi Shonan had recently been recalled from his post in Fukui as chief political advisor to Lord Shungaku, and confined to his house in the countryside of his native Kumamoto for "behavior unbecoming of a samurai." While in Edo at the end of the previous year he was attacked by anti-foreign extremists, but instead of defending himself in the manner expected of a samurai, the fifty-five-year-old scholar fled, leaving his swords behind.

"I'll do my best," Ryoma said, shaking his head slowly. "How can a *daimyo* punish his best man over a petty incident?" Ryoma muttered, then drained an entire glass of wine. "It will be interesting to hear what Yokoi has to say about the problem of Choshu."

Ryoma had read his mentor's true intentions. Just as Kaishu had arranged for Ryoma to meet on various occasions with Lord Shungaku of Fukui and Foreign Affairs Commissioner Okubo Ichio, he wanted also to expose him as much as possible to this fourth member of the Group of Four. Yokoi Shonan, Kaishu judged, had as good a grasp on Japan's relationship to the rest of the world as he himself did, and *"an intellect unequaled by anyone in Japan."* By now, nearly everyone who supported *Opening the Country* blindly supported the Bakufu; and those who called for *Expelling the Barbarians* were fanatic in their *Imperial Loyalism.* Not so, however, for Kaishu's unique clique, which espoused *Imperial Reverence and Opening the Country.* They were realists who revered the Emperor because, among other reasons, they could see that the Bakufu had reached its final days, but at the same time they knew that Japan must be open to foreign trade and culture if it were to survive in the modern world. It was through contact with the Group of Four that Ryoma–and, by association, his men at Kaishu's private naval academy–were able to perceive things from a different perspective than most of the other Loyalists from Tosa, Choshu and Satsuma.

"The two most frightening men I have ever met," Kaishu once said, *"were Yokoi Shonan and Saigo Takamori* (the great Satsuma commander also known as Saigo Kichinosuke). *"Yokoi didn't know that much about the West; in fact, I even taught him a thing or two on the subject. But when it came to pure intellect, he was way above my level. Although Yokoi was not very good at actually getting things accomplished on his own, once a man of action got together with him the two of them could do some incredibly great things."*

Kaishu was sending his *"man of action"* to meet again with Yokoi Shonan. He believed in Ryoma's character, and was confident that his would be an important role in the modernization of Japan.

"I'll make arrangements for you to sail aboard a Bakufu steamer leaving for Kumamoto in the morning," Kaishu said.

"I'll drink to that," Ryoma exclaimed, draining his wine glass.

Kaishu refilled Ryoma's glass. "Very congenial of them, don't you think?" he said derisively.

"Of who?"

"The British. Their consulate had this wine delivered to me after our final meeting today." From his kimono he produced a cloth pouch. "They also gave me some of these," he said, taking out two cigars and a small box of matches, the likes of which Ryoma had never seen before. "Here," he offered one to Ryoma, lighting it.

Ryoma inhaled, and began coughing. "I only wish the British would have given us more time, instead of these foul things," he said.

Kaishu laughed. "These are what gentlemen smoke in America and Europe, but I'm not very fond of them either." Kaishu slowly shook his head, and a dark expression covered his face. "But I agree with you about needing more time," he said. "I'm very worried."

"How long did the foreigners give us?" Ryoma asked.

"They wouldn't say for sure, but I estimate only a few months. If we can't do something about Choshu by then, I'm afraid they will."

"We must work fast," Ryoma said. "I can feel it in my blood. The boil is almost ready to burst wide open."

"What?" Kaishu gave Ryoma a strange look.

"The Bakufu," Ryoma exclaimed, his face flush from wine, his dark brown eyes flashing. "Things are coming to a head, and all it's going to take is a little jab and that'll be that." Ryoma laughed loudly. "But I understand your position, Sensei. So, leave it me. I'm just a *ronin*. I'm expendable. If I can die to clean up Japan, I'll be satisfied."

"I'd prefer to have you around after you've finished jabbing and cleaning up," Kaishu said grinning. "So, don't be in such a hurry to die."

"Don't worry," Ryoma said. "But it's unfortunate that we couldn't get to Tsushima. I was looking forward to that." While in Nagasaki, Kaishu had received an Imperial decree forbidding him from crossing over to Tsushima islands to investigate the neighboring Korean Peninsula.

"Enough of such talk for tonight," Kaishu said, slapping his palm on the marble tabletop. "Instead, let's listen to the beautiful music, enjoy this fine French wine, and savor the lovely ladies. A man must occasionally relax to perform to full capacity."

*   *   *

The former chief political advisor to one of the most powerful men in Japan was delighted when the outlaw appeared at his home in the Kumamoto countryside on the balmy evening of April 6. Since being recalled from Fukui, Yokoi Shonan had been confined to his house in his tiny native village of Nuyamazu, surrounded by green rice paddies and open fields speckled with mustard flowers and spreading out for miles in each direction. In the distance to the northeast were the five volcanic peaks of Mount Aso, and across the strait to the west, on the Shimabara Peninsula, the majestic Onsendake mountain. On one side of Yokoi's house was a bamboo grove, directly in front the Nuyamazu River, which flowed by the village into a nearby lake.

"I've brought a small gift from Katsu Kaishu," Ryoma said, after greeting Yokoi in front of the small, dilapidated house. Yokoi gratefully accepted a small pouch of gold coins. "Ryoma," he said, a faint smile on his dark, heavily lined face, his hair streaked with gray, "the last time we met in Fukui Castletown, I never thought our next meeting would be here in the Kumamoto countryside." He paused, a look of vexation replaced his smile. "It's an awful fate to be confined to one's home when there is so much at stake for the nation."

"Sensei," Ryoma smiled consolingly, "what you've already given to the nation is enough for a thousand years. Please don't worry yourself, not when there are men like Katsu Kaishu and myself around to take care of things."

Yokoi roared with laughter, then invited Ryoma into the house. "I used to think that there wasn't another man in the world with as much self-confidence as Katsu," he said. "But you've proved me wrong."

Yokoi's home betrayed the great man's poverty. His study, one of three small rooms, was only large enough to lay out six badly worn *tatami* mats; the walls were in need of repair, and instead of wooden shutters an old straw mat hung from the eaves to keep out the wind and rain.

Presently, a young samurai appeared. "This is my nephew," Yokoi said. "When I received word from Kaishu telling me you'd be coming, I took the liberty of calling him here because I thought that he might join your naval academy."

The three men spent the rest of the afternoon and much of the evening imbibing the traditional drink of the Kumamoto countryside–a potent white liquor made of distilled potatoes–and discussing national affairs. "We must have democracy in Japan," Ryoma declared after finishing his first cupful of liquor. "An American form of government," he said with conviction, "whereby everyone is equal, regardless of birth or wealth, and whereby all the people have the right to elect a president. Many people nowadays insist that after the Bakufu has been overthrown the Emperor must be in a position to govern. But I'm afraid that would be a big mistake."

"Sakamoto-san," Yokoi's nephew said indignantly, "certainly you're not saying that you don't revere his Imperial Highness."

"I'm not saying that. But the Emperor is not a politician. The Chrysanthemum Throne should not be concerned with matters of state. The Japanese people should decide such things for themselves."

"The Japanese people?" the younger man asked blankly. "Of which *han*?"

"I'm not talking about any of the *han*," Ryoma said, his dark eyes expanding. "Take America, for instance. From what I hear, the Americans have never had such things as *han*, samurai, *daimyo*, Bakufu or Shogun. America is one nation, a union of individual states, the United States of America where all people are equal. That's what we need in Japan, a union of the individual *han* to form one strong, central government."

Yokoi's nephew was dumbfounded. He had heard his uncle speak of a centralized government representative of the people, to replace the Tokugawa hegemony. The notion excited him. But the idea of a union of individual *han* was as preposterous as the concept of all people, regardless of birthright, being equal. "How can you talk of a union of the *han*?" he asked, "when there are such bitter rivalries as the one between Satsuma and Choshu?"

"That's just it," Ryoma said, pounding the floor. "If Satsuma and Choshu were to unite there would be nothing that could stop them from toppling the Bakufu."

"If all the *han* were to unite," the younger man said, "which of the *daimyo* would become Shogun?"

"There would be no *daimyo*," Ryoma answered bluntly. "And there would be no Shogun."

"Continue," Yokoi urged, refilling Ryoma's cup.

"The people would elect a president to govern them," Ryoma said.

"The people?" the younger man asked. "What people?"

"You and I and everyone else," Yokoi interrupted. "The Japanese people should have the freedom, the inalienable right, to determine their own destiny. And the first step toward this is the establishment of a central government which would represent the people, with a president as its head who has been elected by the people and who is answerable only to the people." Yokoi paused to take a deep breath. "But," he added with severe calm, "the sovereign of any form of Japanese government must be His Imperial Highness, who is answerable to nobody."

"Sensei," Ryoma interrupted, "I beg to differ. The people must be sovereign, and the Emperor must be answerable to the people, otherwise the Emperor would be no better than the Shogun or the *daimyo*."

Yokoi breathed deeply, then took a firm hold of Ryoma's wrist. "I agree wholeheartedly with everything you have said until now. But," he took a gulp of the strong white liquor, "never compare the Emperor with other men." For all his progressive thought, Yokoi Shonan revered the Emperor as a god. "And I would like to take this opportunity to offer you some important advice, Ryoma. Watch what you say over the next few years. There are a lot of people who aren't ready for such radical ideas, and I don't want to see anything happen to you."

Ryoma nodded silently, his mind too occupied with what they had been discussing, particularly his own idea of a Satsuma-Choshu alliance, to heed the wise man's good advice.

Choshu Ablaze

Just as Ryoma's notion of a Satsuma-Choshu alliance seemed prepos-
terous, his very actions over these past two years were an enigma to
most of his comrades. Not only had he been among the first to flee
Tosa at a time when the Loyalist Party was gaining power, but short-
ly after this he had entered into the service of the Bakufu's navy com-
missioner who espoused opening Japan. And where was this sworn
enemy of the Bakufu when his Choshu comrades were banished from
Kyoto? He was helping Kaishu establish a naval academy, financed
by the enemy regime. What was Ryoma doing while Hanpeita and the
other Tosa Loyalists were arrested in Kochi? He was in Edo urging the
Bakufu's commissioner of foreign affairs to help him secure the use of
a Tokugawa warship for the naval academy. And despite the steadfast
willingness of virtually all of his comrades (with the exception of the
handful of men he had managed to enlist for the academy) to die for
Toppling the Bakufu and Imperial Loyalism, Ryoma professed the
virtues of free international trade to strengthen the nation.

Preposterous perhaps, but preposterous ideas were an intrinsic part
of the Dragon's nature. It was in Ryoma's basic makeup to act, to
strive, and to risk his life for goals which his comrades could not read-
ily comprehend; and it was this very quality which was both the key to
his greatness and the source of his deepest sorrow.

Ryoma returned to Kobe headquarters with Yokoi's nephew, where he
spent the next month and a half training with his men aboard the
Kanko Maru. During this time Kaishu's naval academy was officially
recognized by Edo, and an additional two hundred men from various
clans enrolled.

On the morning of the last day in May, Ryoma received a message
from Yokoi Shonan urging him to gather together as many *ronin* as
possible and get them out of Kyoto, and, if possible, send them to Ezo
as he had planned. "I expect Choshu to attack at any time," Yokoi
warned.

Since being banished from Kyoto in the coup of the previous summer, Choshu had been planning to strike back at the Satsuma and Aizu
troops which guarded the Imperial Palace. It was Choshu's immediate
goal to regain direct influence over the Emperor, who, in Western
standards, might be likened to a football, now in the hands of the
Satsuma-Aizu team, with Choshu fighting to recapture control. Since

ancient times, Japanese Emperors had traditionally sided with the strongest of all opposing forces; Choshu's ultra-extremism, not to mention coercion from Satsuma-Aizu, left the present Emperor no choice but to flow with the tide of history, for the time being at least.

Ryoma reasoned that a civil war at this time would be disastrous for the anti-Bakufu movement. Choshu was the fulcrum of the movement, and the hordes of *ronin* in Kyoto its lifeblood. In order that this lifeblood not be spilled, and the fulcrum not be crushed, he left immediately for Kyoto. "I have to talk to Katsura Kogoro," he told his men before leaving shortly after receiving Yokoi's message. Although Choshu had been expelled from the Imperial capital, it was allowed to maintain its Kyoto headquarters, where Katsura was stationed. Ryoma set out in the pouring rain for a nearby boat-landing, where he caught a ferry across the bay to Osaka. From here he planned to catch a river-boat, and arrive in Kyoto that night.

By the time Ryoma reached Osaka the rain had stopped. "I have to get as many of those men out of Kyoto as possible," he thought aloud, as he hurried through the streets toward the riverboat-landing. His clothes, wet from rain and sweat, clung to his body. "Then, when the time is right, we can call them back to Kyoto where they can be of use in the revolution, rather than sitting by waiting to be cut down by the *ronin*-hunters." Ryoma momentarily gripped the hilt of his sword, as he thought that Choshu was simply not ready to go to war against the Bakufu. "But if I could somehow unite Choshu with Satsuma, the Bakufu wouldn't stand a chance." Ryoma, however, was well aware that despite the large number of anti-Bakufu Loyalists among the Satsuma samurai, that *han* was under the firm control of Lord Hisamitsu, the father of the child-*daimyo*, who had allied himself with both Edo and Kyoto in last summer's coup.

"There must be a way to get Satsuma and Choshu on the same side," he agonized to himself, as he hurried through the streets of Osaka toward the riverboat-landing. He turned down a narrow back-street to save time, but what he thought would be a shortcut led him to a scene that would change his life. "I know as well as anyone else that Satsuma and Choshu are both striving for the same goal," he thought. "But with Choshu on the verge of exploding, time is the biggest problem." Ryoma groaned as he hastened his pace, then suddenly stopped short in his tracks.

What he saw was fantastic: a young woman arguing furiously with two thugs. Oryo was petite, strikingly beautiful, but dressed in rags, the soft, white skin of her face streaked with sweat and dust, her eyes filled with fire. Something clicked in Ryoma's mind, as he stood there, amazed at the girl's display of courage. Had he known that she would someday be his wife, his amazement would surely have been tenfold.

"Release my sister who you deceived into coming with you to Osaka," the girl screamed, then lunged at one of the thugs, grabbing him by the lapel of his livery coat and slapping his face.

"You want to die, stupid woman?" the thug roared.

"Go ahead, kill me," Oryo screamed defiantly. "That's why I came all the way to Osaka, to get killed. That would really be something," she laughed. "Go ahead, kill me, you coward."

"Stop!" Ryoma shouted, releasing the latch to the sheath of his sword.

The two thugs glared at the intruder who stood nearly a head taller than either of them. Both wore livery coats which hung midway down their thighs, and thin cotton *hakama*. Their arms were heavily tattooed.

"What's the problem?" Ryoma snickered. "Is the girl giving you two a hard time?"

"Ah, well, you see, ah..."one of the thugs stammered, obviously intimidated by the samurai.

"Go ahead, spit it out."

"Why you..." the other thug flared, drawing a dagger from his coat.

"Drop it or you die," Ryoma said with stone-cold eyes.

The man immediately dropped the dagger.

"You too!" Ryoma demanded, staring viciously at the other man.

"Yes, sir," the man said, also producing a dagger, and dropping it to the ground. When the girl drew a knife from her kimono and pointed it at one of the thugs, Ryoma burst out laughing. "Very good! Now, tell me what's going on here."

"They have my younger sister and I want her back." Oryo spoke defiantly, with a refined Kyoto accent.

"Where is she?" Ryoma asked.

"If I knew, do you think I'd be wasting my time fighting with these two idiots?"

"I guess not," Ryoma said, amused by the girl's pluck. Then returning his eyes to the thugs, "Where's the other girl?" he demanded, still gripping the hilt of his sword.

"Ah, in there," one for them answered meekly, pointing to a small, dilapidated house less than one hundred paces away.

"You!" Ryoma shouted at the other thug. 'You go get her while the rest of us wait here. If you're not back with the girl in three minutes, your friend will be dead."

"Don't just stand there, you idiot," the petrified man screamed, frantically waving his arms in the air. "Run and get the girl."

Soon the girl was returned safely, and Ryoma accompanied the two sisters to Kyoto by riverboat. Along the way Oryo spoke of herself and her family. At twenty-three, she was the eldest of five children: three daughters and two sons. Their father, a Kyoto physician, had been a noted Loyalist and close friend of several of the victims of Ii Naosuke's purge. When he suddenly died of illness two years before, Oryo and her mother were forced to sell their household belongings and even most of their clothes to survive. Eventually, Oryo, who had been accustomed to having servants of her own, was compelled to take a job as a maid. During Oryo's absence, her mother had been deceived into selling her sixteen-year-old sister, Kimie, into prostitution in Osaka, and the thirteen-year-old Mitsue into similar straits in Kyoto. When Oryo learned what had happened she immediately retrieved Mitsue from a Kyoto brothel, before going to Osaka to retrieve Kimie.

"And that was where you found me," Oryo told Ryoma. "How can I ever repay you?"

Ryoma had never felt so utterly good about being with a woman, despite all the work he had before him. Indeed, the tasks awaiting him were Herculean in scale: convincing Choshu to hold off on its attack; sending men to Ezo to develop the northern territory; somehow uniting Satsuma and Choshu; forming a private navy to conduct free trade between Ezo and Nagasaki, and to procure warships and guns to overthrow the Bakufu.

"Come with me to the Teradaya in Fushimi," Ryoma said. "You and your sister seem to need a place to stay. The proprietress, Otose, is a good friend of mine, and I'm sure I can convince her to hire you as a maid."

Oryo's eyes lit up. "But how can I ever repay you?" she repeated.

"You already have," Ryoma said, smiling.

As the three did not reach Fushimi until nearly midnight, Ryoma stayed the night at the Teradaya, and continued on to Kyoto the next morning. He had lost precious time with the ordeal in Osaka, and was anxious to get to Choshu headquarters "before," he had told himself, "all hell breaks loose."

Although Ryoma sympathized with the plight of Choshu, he was even more concerned that a civil war might provide the foreigners with an ideal opportunity to invade Japan, and subjugate it as they had China. "Without Choshu," he had told his men before leaving Kobe, "our chances of toppling the Bakufu are slim. But," he warned, lest any of them be tempted to join those Tosa men who had fled to Choshu after Yodo's crackdown in Kochi, "we're not ready for war. We need more time to prepare."

"When do you suppose we'll be ready?" one of them had asked.

"After we've established a trading network, with bases in Kobe, Nagasaki, and Ezo. Then our ships can carry cargo up and down the archipelago. With the profits we'll buy more ships, cannon and rifles from foreign traders in Nagasaki. We'll recruit more and more men until we've become the strongest naval force in Japan. As it is, we're preparing ourselves everyday by training right here," Ryoma said, staring out at the *Black Dragon*, one of the academy's two training ships anchored in the bay.

Later that morning, Ryoma disembarked from a riverboat at Kyoto, and hurried on foot northward along the eastern bank of the Takasegawa. Just as he was passing the arched wooden Shijo Bridge which spanned the canal, a muffled voice called his name.

The voice came from behind the gate of a house on his immediate right. A wooden sign which hung on the gate read: *"Kiemon's Masuya Shop—utensils, gadgets and other paraphernalia."*

Ryoma stopped short in his tracks, immediately drawing his sword. "Behind here," the voice whispered, as the gate opened slightly.

"Kotaka!" Ryoma said, slightly annoyed but relieved, then resheathed his sword.

"Sh! Come in here quickly, " Kotaka demanded.

Kotaka Shuntaro was a Choshu spy disguised as a merchant. He ran the Masuya Shop, and went by the alias "Kiemon." With his mild manners and Kyoto accent, nobody ever imagined that the merchant, who had lived in the city since childhood, was actually a samurai. Living in the heart of Kyoto, amid the various *han* headquarters, and in close proximity to the Imperial Palace, Kotaka was in an excellent position to gather information vital to the revolution. He used his downstairs shop to keep a stockpile of rifles and ammunition, which he kept hidden for the impending countercoup; in his living quarters upstairs he hid Loyalists who had remained in Kyoto after the coup of the previous summer. At age thirty-five, Kotaka was a veteran Loyalist and former disciple of founders of the Loyalist movement who had been executed during Ii's purge. Ryoma had been introduced to Kotaka two years before by Kusaka Genzui, when Ryoma was in hiding at Choshu's Kyoto headquarters.

"Do you want to get us both killed?" Kotaka said after he had safely closed the gate behind Ryoma. "The Shinsengumi are patrolling the streets. And who knows how many other spies are lurking about. I've been waiting here for you for hours."

"How did you..."

"Know that you'd be here?" Kotaka finished the question.

"Yes."

"I've just come from your naval headquarters in Kobe."

Ryoma's expression grew dark. "What were you doing there?" he demanded.

"We'll discuss that after we're inside the house, where nobody can hear us. One can never be too cautious."

Soon Ryoma and Kotaka were sitting inside with two others: Miyabe Teizo, a *ronin* from Kumamoto, and his elderly manservant. A close friend of Yokoi's, Miyabe had been chief instructor of military science in Kumamoto Castletown before fleeing in 1861 to join the movement for *Imperial Reverence and Expelling the Barbarians*. At age forty-four he was one of the most influential Loyalists in Kyoto. After the coup Miyabe had been banished from Kyoto with the Choshu men and the seven radical nobles, but having returned undercover earlier this year, he was now hiding with his manservant at Kotaka's home.

"We need all the men we can get for the coup," Kotaka told Ryoma. Then turning to Miyabe, "Would you please show him the plan of attack you have drawn up?" Kotaka smiled, confident that he could impress Ryoma with what he considered ingenious military strategy.

Miyabe produced a folded document, which Ryoma began reading silently, incredulously. "'*On a windy night, sometime around June 20, our troops will set fire to the Imperial Palace, and in the resulting uproar kidnap the Emperor. The second platoon will wait in hiding for the Protector of Kyoto to rush to the scene, as he inevitably will, and cut him down on the spot. Meanwhile, the first platoon will bring the Emperor to a safe place just outside of Kyoto. After they arrive, they will request His Imperial Highness to issue an Imperial decree to attack the Bakufu. This achieved, we will have the court reinstate the Seven Banished Nobles, and appoint the Lord of Choshu as Protector of Kyoto.'"*

Ryoma stopped reading, took a deep breath. He returned the document to Miyabe, but for the moment was too shaken by the reckless plan to speak.

"All the men involved in this coup will meet at the Ikedaya inn at eight o'clock on the evening of June 5 to discuss the final details. We hope you'll be there, Sakamoto-san. As a matter of fact, I've spoken to some of your men in Kobe, and..."

"That's why I've come to Kyoto today," Ryoma said angrily. "I was just on my way to Choshu headquarters to see Katsura. I figure that he's the only one around here that will listen to reason."

"Don't underestimate Katsura," Miyabe said with a devious smile.

"Sakamoto," Kotaka said, his eyes open wide, "have you lost your nerve now that you're working on the side of Katsu Kaishu?"

Ryoma looked hard into Kotaka's eyes. "I'm the head of Katsu's naval academy," he said firmly, "and Katsu is the greatest man in Japan."

Kotaka snickered. "The last time we talked, about two years ago, you were absolutely determined to destroy the Bakufu."

"As I am today. But we're just not ready yet. Don't you understand? That's exactly why I want to talk to Katsura. No matter how powerful Choshu is, it can't take on the combined forces of the Bakufu, Aizu, Satsuma, Fukui and Tosa." Ryoma paused, wiped his sweaty forehead with his sleeve. "But I have a great plan."

After telling of his plan to send men to Ezo, Ryoma said, "Although all of you are welcome to join our naval academy in Kobe, if I so much as catch anyone urging my men to throw away their lives on a premature, reckless attack that is doomed from the start," he paused to control his anger, "I'll cut him down myself," he finally exploded, slamming his huge fist on the floor with such force that he left a dent in the *tatami*.

"I won't go back to Kobe," Kotaka assured. "But I must tell you that I've already talked to your men, and some of them have agreed to join us."

The news came as no surprise to Ryoma. Most of his men were *ronin* who had abandoned their *han* to die for the Loyalist cause. Even Ryoma himself might have been tempted to join the rebels had he never met Katsu Kaishu.

"Who?" Ryoma demanded.

"Kitsuma and Kameyata," Kotaka said.

"Kitsuma and Kame!" Ryoma exploded. "I can't let them get themselves killed for no reason at all!" Ryoma's eyes flashed with indignation. He had been depending on Kitsuma to lead the expedition to Ezo, while Kameyata was one of his most trusted and closest friends at Kobe. Ryoma stood up. "I believe that those two are just rash enough to join you," he said.

Ryoma left the house, and arrived at nearby Choshu headquarters soon after, where he found Katsura Kogoro.

"I've just come from Kotaka's house," Ryoma said.

"So you've heard about the plan?" Katsura said grimly. Although Katsura was indeed a leader of the Choshu Loyalists, his cool rational mind resembled Ryoma's. But unlike Ryoma–and Loyalists such as Kotaka and Miyabe–Katsura's first concern was for the welfare of his own clan; it was to Choshu Han that he was dedicated.

As Katsura explained, the Choshu Loyalists, though fighting to inevitably overthrow the Bakufu, had recently become divided as to the best way to achieve their goal. Since the previous summer, the entire clan had been planning its return to Imperial grace. The Lord of Choshu, backed by several of his ministers, including Katsura himself, favored a rational approach to revolution. After their stunning defeat to the foreigners at Shimonoseki, they now realized that they would have to fortify themselves with Western warships and guns before going to war with either the Tokugawa or the foreigners. Opposed to this were the Choshu extremists who would raise as large an army as possible in Choshu, march into Kyoto later this summer, and plead with the court to reinstate them to Imperial grace. This accomplished, they would declare an Imperial government independent of Edo, before raising more troops to crush the Bakufu.

"And if the court refused?" Ryoma asked.

"Then they would follow Miyabe's plan."

Ryoma groaned. "It'll never work. The minute they marched into Kyoto, Aizu and Satsuma would be ready with thousands of troops and an Imperial decree to crush them." Ryoma pounded his fist on the floor. "They must be stopped."

"You're right! But it's not that simple. If I show too much restraint in this matter, Choshu will lose the support of Miyabe, Kotaka, and with them the hundreds of *ronin* in the Osaka-Kyoto area. We need those men for the revolution."

Katsura was one of the highest ranking officials in the Choshu government. Unlike Ryoma, he had not abandoned his *han*, nor had he any intention of doing so. But just as Ryoma was the leader of his men in Kobe, Katsura was the leader of the hundreds of Loyalist *ronin* who remained in Kyoto, impatient for the revolution to begin. His official post in Choshu placed him in an even greater position of power than Miyabe, who, for all his leadership abilities, was nevertheless an outlaw with no official backing.

"Then you must be as concerned for their safety as I am," Ryoma said.

"Of course I'm concerned for their safety," Katsura said.

Ryoma slapped himself on the knee. "Good! I have a perfect solution," he said confidently, and told Katsura of his plan to send *ronin* to Ezo. "And I'm depending on your help to convince them to go."

"I like the idea. I too would like to keep as many of them alive as possible, but..."

"But what?"

Katsura looked straight into Ryoma's eyes. "I can't risk splitting our forces in two."

"You can't risk the lives of hundreds of men," Ryoma shouted. "How do you propose stopping them from committing mass-suicide?"

"Through Kijima. He's the most explosive man in Choshu. I must convince him to persuade the others, including Miyabe and Kotaka, to hold off. The only problem is that Kijima is as rash as they are."

Ryoma had heard about the forty-eight-year-old Choshu leader, Kijima Matabe, compared to whom even the extremists Kusaka and Takasugi seemed mild. Determined to die this year to resurrect Choshu to Imperial grace, Kijima refused to listen to orders from even the Lord of Choshu himself. "I'll abandon Choshu," he had told officials at the Choshu administration office, begging for permission to lead his guerrilla squadron of five hundred into Kyoto. "That way it won't be 'Kijima the Choshu samurai' fighting, but 'Kijima the *ronin*.' Then, even if we fail, the Imperial Court will have no grounds to declare Choshu an enemy."

Katsura continued. "Old Kijima is the rashest, most stubborn man in Choshu. And our men love him for it. Nobody can control him, not even the *daimyo* himself."

"Where is Kijima now?" Ryoma asked.

"In Choshu," Katsura said. "He's recruiting an army. And I'm equally worried about what Kusaka and Takasugi might do."

Takasugi Shinsaku was a born rebel. In the previous June he had formed Japan's first modern militia, the Extraordinary Corps, which, in addition to samurai, included men from the peasant and merchant classes. Although the corps had originally been formed to defend Choshu from foreign invasion, Takasugi had an ulterior motive in recruiting this unprecedented band of fighting men: the overthrow of the Tokugawa Bakufu. The foreigners had easily defeated Choshu's forces, which consisted entirely of samurai whose sole purpose for hundreds of years had been to protect the Choshu domain. But after two and a half centuries of peace, these samurai, like their counterparts throughout most of Japan, had forgotten how to fight. Takasugi's plan to recruit commoners as well as samurai was nevertheless unheard of. The whole of Japanese society was based on the system of the different social classes into which people were born, and aside from a few exceptional cases, remained until death. Accordingly, only the samurai were allowed to bear arms, but Takasugi's Extraordinary Corps, living up to its name, challenged the very social structure of Tokugawa feudalism by arming the commoners. Naturally, Ryoma liked the idea. He too had gone beyond class to recruit men for his private navy. Ryoma, in fact, took the break from feudalism one step further: his navy would consist of men from all over Japan, with no question of *han* whatsoever.

"Takasugi is in jail," Katsura said, a vexed look on his face.

"For what?" Ryoma asked.

"Ostensibly for leaving Choshu without permission, but actually to keep him under control for the time being. But he'll soon be released. He's invaluable to us."

Ryoma wiped the sweat from his brow with his sleeve. "How many men does Takasugi have under his command?"

"About three hundred. I've been trying to explain to Kijima, Kusaka and Takasugi that before we go to war we must procure more warships and guns from the foreigners. But the only one who might listen to reason is Takasugi. And like I said, he's locked up." Katsura sighed, then continued. "The Bakufu has three thousand troops in Kyoto alone. I know as well as you do that we're going to need more than just rash determination to defeat them. Without more warships and guns our *han* doesn't stand a chance."

"No," Ryoma cut in hard, "that's where you're wrong. Forget about your *han*. It's Japan we must be concerned for. Without Western technology and weapons, it's Japan that doesn't stand a chance. Can't you understand that the whole feudal system is rotten to the core? It's not only the Bakufu, but all of the clans and our whole class-oriented society. The only way we are going to be able to compete with the rest of the world is if we unite into one strong nation where everyone is equal. Look at the United States of America. It has no clans, no feudal class system. The president of the nation is answerable to its citizens. There is freedom for everyone there. Freedom to think, freedom to conduct trade. And the only way we will ever be able to achieve this in Japan is by first overthrowing the Bakufu, and then abolishing the feudal system." Ryoma paused, his eyes on fire, his face dripping with sweat.

Katsura nodded slowly. "So it is, Sakamoto-san. So it is. I've been negotiating with representatives of different clans for the past six months to find a way for us to unite with one another. But, let me ask you this: How are the individual *han* ever going to unite when there is so much turmoil between us? At this stage it's impossible. It has come to the point in Choshu where we feel more animosity for Edo, Satsuma and Aizu than we do for the barbarians."

Ryoma gave Katsura a hard look. "The only way to do it would be for Choshu and Satsuma to unite first," he said in a low voice. "If this could be realized, the other clans would certainly follow suit, and the Tokugawa Bakufu would fall."

Katsura looked wide-eyed at Ryoma, then laughed derisively. "Satsuma and Choshu unite? Surely you're not serious."

"I've never been more serious in my life," Ryoma confirmed.

"But Satsuma is the worst of them all," Katsura said bitterly. "They've forsaken the cause to overthrow the Bakufu by uniting with Aizu. Now, the Bakufu, Aizu and Satsuma are waiting anxiously for Choshu to make a suicidal march into Kyoto. They know very well how hotheaded the Choshu Loyalists are. Then when our *han* has been proclaimed an 'Imperial Enemy,' the Bakufu, Aizu and Satsuma are confident that they will have no trouble enlisting troops from other clans to crush Choshu once and for all, then confiscate our domain. And," Katsura concluded, "that's why we hate the traitorous Satsuma."

"What do you intend to do?"

"Exactly what I've been doing for the past several months." Katsura lowered his voice to a whisper. "Continue secret negotiations with other Loyalists in Kyoto to get as much support as possible among the other *han*, and at the same time to keep the *ronin* in this city from doing anything drastic."

"Then help me recruit men to settle the northern territory," Ryoma said.

"I'm sorry, Sakamoto-san. It would be impossible at this time."

With no choice but to postpone his Ezo plans, Ryoma returned to Kobe headquarters. He was drenched from the hard rain and exhausted when he reached the barracks shortly after midnight. It was completely dark inside, the only sound the crashing of the waves, the falling of the rain and the heavy breathing of men sound asleep.

"Where's Kame?" Ryoma roared, walking up everyone.

"What's that....? a voice called out.

"Who's there?" called another.

"It's me, Ryoma. Where's Kame and Kitsuma?"

"I'm right here." The voice was Kameyata's.

"And where's Kitsuma?"

"I'm over here." Although Kitsuma was not a member of the academy, he was friendly with most of the men, and needed a place to stay before returning to Kyoto to take part in the uprising.

"Someone light a lantern," Ryoma said. "I can't see a thing."

One of the men obliged, and Ryoma looked around the room. All of his closest friends were present. For the welfare of each he felt a heavy responsibility. "I talked to Kotaka today," he said. "He told me that there are some of you who would like to throw your lives away in an uprising in Kyoto that is doomed from the start." As he spoke, his face turned red with anger. "Of all the stupid ideas!" he roared. "We have a navy to build. Until we're strong enough to control the seas all the way from Nagasaki to Ezo, none of us can afford the luxury of dying." Ryoma paused, and the room became silent. "If any of you really intend to leave, you'll have to kill me first," he said, before storming out of the room.

Exhausted, Ryoma went to his private room and slept, undisturbed until just after dawn, when Kameyata woke him.

"Kame!" Ryoma sat up. "Don't tell me!"

"I couldn't kill you," Kameyata said, "even if I had a mind to. But I have to go. Please understand."

"If you go, I'm afraid you'll die," Ryoma said grimly.

Kameyata struggled to hold back tears. "That's why I left Tosa in the first place. Please forgive me, but this is what I must do," he said before leaving Ryoma alone and frustrated.

Later in the day Ryoma received a message from Kaishu, summoning him to Edo. As he had one day to himself before his ship would sail, there was one person whom he very much wanted to see before he left.

Ryoma found Oryo at the Teradaya, where he had left her just two days before. The girl greeted him at the top of the stone stairway which led from the boat-landing on the river to the front gate of the inn. The fire in her eyes was gone now, and she was dressed properly in a clean kimono, her hair arranged neatly, a light brown boxwood ornamental hairpin stuck through one side. "I was wondering when I'd see you again," Oryo said, as the proprietress, Otose, also came out to greet Ryoma.

"I thought I'd stop by and see how things were," Ryoma said, then burst out laughing at the expression on the faces of the two women. Indeed, he looked comical standing there at the top of the stairs, this tough leader of one hundred *ronin*, much in need of a bath, his clothes badly worn, hair a tattered mess, swords hanging at his side, but smiling ecstatically at the pretty young girl.

"Things are just fine," Otose assured. "But come in, Sakamoto-san. Please come right in. You look like you could use a nice hot bath."

"I'd like a drink instead," Ryoma said.

"First a bath," the innkeeper insisted. "When you've finished, I'm sure Oryo will be glad to serve you *sake*. You can take the same room you always use upstairs." At thirty-five, Otose was like an older sister to Ryoma, her inn a second home to him, a place where he knew he could find a brief moment's repose during these very troubled times. Being at the Teradaya is *"like being back in Tosa,"* he wrote to his sister Otome. *"They really take good care of me there."*

After bathing, Ryoma put on his dirty clothes and went upstairs to his room, where Oryo was waiting. She had set a small table with two large flasks of *sake* and a cup. "Why didn't you put on the clean bathrobe I put out for you?" she asked.

"I can't stay long. I have to leave this evening." Ryoma sat down next to Oryo, and placed a small pouch of gold coins on the table. "I'll have *sake* now," he said.

Oryo filled his cup. "I'm forever in your debt for your kindness," she said.

Ryoma said nothing until draining the cup and handing it to the girl. "I'm just happy to see that you're alright. Where's your sister?"

"In Kyoto with my mother." Oryo took Ryoma's hand. "You look tired."

"I haven't felt this good in a long time. Here, have a drink." He filled the cup for Oryo, then took a swig from the flask.

"Sakamoto-san, please use the cup. Here, let me pour for you."

"Don't bother. The *sake* tastes just as good this way." Ryoma laughed, and took another swig. "I'm tired," he said, lying down, resting his head on the girl's lap. "I haven't felt this good in ages. Not in ages." Ryoma was soon asleep.

Later that night Oryo came quietly into Ryoma's room.

"What time is it?" he started.

"Almost midnight."

"I have to go!"

"So soon? I thought you might at least stay the night."

"No, I have to leave now. Here." He picked up the pouch he had placed on the table earlier, and emptied the gold coins on the floor. He kept five for himself, and gave the rest to the girl. "Fifteen *ryo* ought to be enough for a while," he said.

"I couldn't..."

"Take it. You'll need it for yourself and your family. I'll come see you when I return from Edo."

"When will that be?"

"I don't know." Ryoma stood up, and walked over to the alcove to get his swords. "But wait here for me."

That night Ryoma took a riverboat to Osaka, where he boarded a Bakufu steamer which set sail to Edo the next afternoon.

*   *   *

The night of June 4 was scorching, and Kotaka Shuntaro–alias Kiemon, owner of the Masuya Shop–had just fallen asleep when he was awaken by the sound of someone running up the wooden staircase of his two-storied house. Suddenly the sliding door burst open, and Kotaka noticed that his body was drenched in sweat.

"Who's there?" he called out, reaching for a dagger he kept hidden in his bedding.

"Kotaka Shuntaro!" a voice shouted.

It was at this moment, his identity discovered, that Kotaka Shuntaro realized he was going to die. He sat up immediately and saw the figure of a tall, heavily built, square-jawed man, his sword drawn, his full head of hair tied in a topknot, his eyes glaring in the moonlight which shined through the window. "Who are you?" Kotaka demanded, slow-ly sliding the dagger from its sheath, and maintaining a perfect calm. This was not the first time that the revolutionary spy had been con-fronted by a drawn sword.

"I'm Kondo Isami, commander of the Shinsengumi," the man roared. "By the authority of the Lord of Aizu and Protector of Kyoto you're under arrest for conspiring to overthrow the government."

"Shinsengumi!" Kotaka gasped. "Kondo Isami!" The commander of the Shinsengumi, which had arrested scores of *ronin* in Kyoto and cut down many others since its formation in the previous year, was noto-rious. Despite the heat of the night, a shiver ran down Kotaka's spine. "I don't know what you're talking about," Kotaka insisted. "You have the wrong man. I'm Kiemon, owner of the shop downstairs."

Just then another, much younger man stormed into the room. "Commander Kondo," he said excitedly, "we've located a compart-ment in the wall of a closet downstairs filled with guns and ammuni-tion. There must be enough gunpowder in there to blow up the entire city. And this too." When the man handed the written conspiracy to Kondo, Kotaka's face turned the color of chalk. Kondo unfolded the document, and as he read his face contorted with anger.

It was only natural that Kondo should detest Kotaka; his corps was in charge of protecting Kyoto (and the Emperor himself) from the rad-ical *ronin* who had turned the Imperial capital into a bloodbath of *Heaven's Revenge*. Ironically, however, Kondo and Kotaka shared the same basic ideals: *Imperial Reverence and Expelling the Barbarians*. But when it came to the question of how to achieve these ideals, the Shinsengumi and the Loyalists clashed: Kondo's men were willing to die to maintain the present order of things, while the rebels were equally resolved to destroy it.

"'*Set fire to the Imperial Palace*,'" Kondo read the conspiracy as incredulously as had Ryoma a few days earlier. "'*Kidnap the Emperor*,'" he continued, seething. "'*Cut down the Protector of Kyoto*.'" "Scoundrels," he roared, grabbing hold of the much smaller man and jerking him to his knees. Just then Kotaka raised his dagger, but before he could plunge the blade into his own belly, Kondo deliv-ered a powerful blow to his jaw.

"Traitor!" Kondo roared, grabbing the dagger, and kicking Kotaka several times in the abdomen, once in the groin. "We're not ready for you to die just yet. Tie him up," he told the other man. "I want him alive for questioning."

Kotaka's hate for the Shinsengumi was no less severe than was Kondo's hate for the rebels. The Shinsengumi, Kotaka claimed, was nothing but a band of traitors pretending to revere the Emperor, but which in reality was a vile organ of the corrupt Tokugawa Bakufu.

Actually, the Shinsengumi was apolitical. The conduct of the men of the Shinsengumi was ruled by the iron will of their two leaders, Kondo Isami and Hijikata Toshizo, neither of whom questioned the virtues of the Bakufu. The Tokugawa, they reasoned, had ruled well for two and a half centuries; it was under the authority of the Tokugawa Shogun–from whom they received a generous monthly stipend–that they were determined to achieve their goal of expelling the foreigners. As suggested by their symbol–the Chinese character for "sincerity"–Kondo and Hijikata were concerned with one basic tenet: if they commanded their corps based on the unwritten code of the samurai, then everything else would fall into place. Accordingly, they composed a list of prohibitions to be strictly adhered to by all members:

1) Violating the code of the samurai
2) Quitting the corps
3) Raising money for selfish purposes
4) Fighting for personal reasons

Violation of any of these prohibitions was punishable by death. Attached to the prohibitions was a list of rules, one of which particularly contributed to the ferocity for which the Shinsengumi was notorious. Conceived of by the bellicose mind of Hijikata Toshizo, the rule stated: "If any member of the corps should draw his sword, he must kill his opponent. If he merely wounds him and let's him escape, then he must commit *seppuku*."

When questioned about the sanity of this rule, Hijikata replied, "It is designed to make our men fight harder."

"But don't you think that it might backfire? If one of our men thinks that an opponent is apt to get away from him alive, he might be tempted to avoid a fight in the first place."

"Then that man would be obligated to commit *seppuku* for violating the First Prohibition, which prohibits violating the code of the samurai."

"But with such a tough rule, some of our men are bound to quit."

"All cowards are accounted for by the Second Prohibition," Hijikata said. "Anyone who quits must commit *seppuku*."

Kotaka had felt that for the past month the Shinsengumi was watching him. He had constantly worried that the corps was suspicious of the many men coming and going from his house, but did not realize that it was only recently that the authorities had begun to suspect him. Actually, carelessness on the part of Miyabe had caused this suspicion. On the afternoon of June 1, the day after Ryoma had visited them, Miyabe had sent his elderly manservant, Chuzo, on an errand from Kotaka's house to Kumamoto headquarters in Kyoto. Chuzo lacked discretion. He was prone to boast of his close relationship with the famous Loyalist leader, and another "by the name of Kotaka Shuntaro." Rather than arresting Chuzo on the spot, the corps let him unwittingly lead them to Kotaka's home, thereafter posting one of their men, disguised as a beggar, to keep a constant watch on the Masuya Shop. Further investigation led the corps to confirm that Chuzo's claims were true: the man who called himself "Kiemon, owner of the Masuya Shop," was indeed a *ronin* by the name of Kotaka Shuntaro, who was acting as a spy for Choshu. Fortunately for Miyabe and Chuzo, they were away when Kondo and his men raided the Masuya, returning only to find Kotaka missing, the house ransacked, and the guns and ammunition they had planned to use for the uprising gone.

"Once Hijikata gets his hands on this one," Kondo growled, glaring at Kotaka, "he'll beat the truth out of him. Let's get him to headquarters."

Hijikata did not disappoint Kondo. Although Kotaka stoically endured hours of excruciating interrogation, adamantly refusing to divulge any more information about the conspiracy than had already been discovered, Hijikata's final method of torture proved too horrible to endure.

The afternoon was unbearably hot, and Hijikata had run out of patience. "This is your last chance," he seethed. Kotaka was hanging upside down from one of several heavy wooden beams which extended across the high ceiling, his feet and arms bound. "Where and when is the meeting going to take place?" Hijikata demanded, but Kotaka still refused to answer.

"Traitorous scoundrel!" Hijikata roared, then drove wooden spikes through Kotaka's feet, put candles on both spikes and lit the wicks. The hot wax dripped onto the open wounds, but still Kotaka refused to talk, although his terrible screams could be heard throughout the surrounding town. Kotaka wished beyond hope that he could either pass out from the pain or else get his hands on a sword with which to kill himself. Finally Kotaka reached the point where he could no longer stand the pain. "It's tonight, June 5," he said in agony, "at the Hour of the Dog, at the Ikedaya, just west of the Sanjo Bridge."

Choshu headquarters was quiet on the relentlessly hot afternoon of June 5. Katsura Kogoro sat silently in the formal position, with an older man, Miyabe Teizo, who wore an expression of anguish on his heavyset face. Miyabe had just brought Katsura the news of Kotaka's arrest the night before.

"We must rescue him," Miyabe implored. "Imagine the torture they must be putting him through. And what's more, if he talks our plans will be ruined."

"They're already ruined." Katsura spoke in a low voice, back straight, hands on his thighs. "If the Shinsengumi knew enough to arrest Kotaka, surely they know more. And even if they don't..." Katsura stopped short, staring into Miyabe's eyes.

"If they don't?" Miyabe asked, wiping the sweat from his brow with a handkerchief.

"They'll torture it out of him." Katsura cast a downward glance.

"That's all the more reason for us to act immediately. We must move tonight before the enemy has a chance to react."

"Please understand," Katsura pleaded. "I can't allow my men to get themselves killed trying to save one life. As for an attack on the Imperial Palace, and kidnapping the Emperor," Katsura paused, took a deep breath, "there are five thousand Bakufu troops in Kyoto. How are we going to fight them with twenty or thirty men? We must return to our individual domains, raise Loyalist armies, and then return to Kyoto. That will be the time to strike." What Katsura did not mention was that as the highest ranking Choshu official in Kyoto, he was in no position to take part in an uprising; if the countercoup failed, and he was sure it would, the very rashness of the act would weaken his credibility as the key Choshu diplomat in the Imperial capital, if not bring about the final downfall of Choshu.

"But you will attend the meeting tonight at the Ikedaya?" Miyabe pressed. "All of the weapons we had stored at Kotaka's place have been confiscated. We must meet tonight to decide if we should carry out our original plan, or postpone it until a later date."

Katsura had no choice but to agree, although he disdained Miyabe's reckless plan. For the very reason he had explained to Ryoma, he was obliged to appease the radicals, because Choshu could not afford to lose their support. Katsura picked up a fan, opened it and began fanning his face. "I'll be at the Ikedaya tonight," he promised, "with some other Choshu men."

Miyabe smiled. "You're the leader of the Loyalists in Kyoto," he said. "I knew you wouldn't let us down." Miyabe felt confident that even the headstrong Katsura Kogoro could be convinced to give his support to Kotaka's rescue, and after that to the uprising. "I'll see you tonight at around eight."

Katsura left Choshu headquarters alone just before eight o'clock–the Hour of the Dog–and headed southward down Kawaramachi Road toward the Ikedaya inn. He wore a beige jack of silk gauze, his swords hanging at his left hip, and his wooden clogs scraping on the cobblestone road. Although he was anxious to get to the house of his lover-spy to see if she had discovered any new information, he headed directly for the Ikedaya, assuming that Ikumatsu would not be home yet. In fact, Ikumatsu was entertaining a small group of very interesting men this evening: high-ranking samurai of Aizu Han.

Kyoto was alive with celebration on the eve of the annual Gion Festival. Red and white paper lanterns lit both sides of the main road, glowing in front of the various shops, teahouses and restaurants. The steady pounding of drums, the winding of flutes, and the continuous clanging of brass bells filled the heavy, humid air. As nightfall offered no relief from the intense heat and humidity of the day, throngs of people filled the streets. "The people can celebrate," Katsura thought enviously. He passed through the thatched front gate of the Ikedaya, noticed light shining from the lattice-covered windows on the second floor, walked across the small garden, and slid open the front door.

"They're upstairs, Katsura-san," the innkeeper, a Loyalist sympathizer, greeted him in the dark entranceway, a musty odor lingering above the damp cement pavement. Katsura removed his clogs, stepped up onto the wooden floor, then climbed the steep, narrow wooden staircase. "I would hate to fight my way out of here," the expert swordsman thought to himself, then turned left at the top of the stairs. "And the corridor is no wider than the staircase," he thought, as he heard voices coming from one of the rooms. Suddenly the door opened, and out came a servant dressed in a livery coat, his sleeves rolled up to the elbows. He carried two large empty *sake* flasks, one under each arm. "Pardon me, Master," the servant said obsequiously, bowed his head and quickly hurried toward the stairs. Paying little attention to the man, Katsura looked into the room, where ten men were talking and drinking. "Where are Miyabe and the others?" he asked.

"They haven't arrived yet, Katsura-san. Please sit down and have a drink while we're waiting for them."

"It doesn't look like the meeting will be starting for a while." Katsura did not conceal his irritation. He wasn't sure which annoyed him more, Miyabe's tardiness, or the lackadaisical atmosphere in the room. "I have some business to attend to at Tsushima headquarters," he lied. (Katsura kept his relationship with Ikumatsu a secret, even from his comrades.) "I'll be back shortly," he said, before slamming the door shut.

Katsura left the Ikedaya and headed for Ikumatsu's house near the western bank of the Kamogawa, just a short walk to the west. With the loud clanging of the festival bells filling his head, he stole through the darkness, snuck though the front gate.

"You're safe," the girl greeted him at the door, a look of relief in her black almond eyes. "Come in, quickly."

"Did you learn anything?" Katsura asked anxiously once inside the house.

"You're safe. I thought I'd never..." she stopped short.

"Never what? Come on, girl, speak!"

"Nothing. Really, nothing at all," she lied.

"I can't stay long. I have to get back to the Ikedaya."

"I see." Ikumatsu feigned nonchalance.

"Did you learn anything this evening?" Katsura repeated, annoyed at the girl's reticence.

"No," Ikumatsu lied again, a faint shadow covering her ivory face when she realized that there was nothing she could say to convince him not to return to the inn.

"Nothing?" Katsura asked incredulously.

"Nothing at all." Actually, Ikumatsu had just returned from a small party of Aizu men, where she learned that the Shinsengumi planned to attack the rebels at the Ikedaya on this very night. "I'll be right back with some *sake*," she said, then went into the next room. "Here," she said after returning momentarily, and offering Katsura a cupful. After several cupsful, the drug began to take effect, and soon Katsura lay safely asleep in the house of his lover.

When Katsura finally awoke, his head ached. Realizing that he was in

Ikumatsu's house, he immediately got up, rubbed the back of his neck, and called the girl. "What time is it?"

"One the morning," she said.

"One in the morning!" Katsura gasped. "How could I have slept for four hours? I must go."

"No. You mustn't. The Ikedaya has been attacked."

"Attacked?" Katsura shouted.

"I've just come from there. There must be a thousand Aizu samurai surrounding the inn. It's like a war zone."

Katsura took firm hold of his lover's hands. "Ikumatsu," he said violently, a crazed look in his eyes. "You knew about the attack, didn't you."

"Yes."

"You drugged me, didn't you," he shouted angrily.

"I had to. I couldn't let you go. For the sake of the revolution," she lied. "Please forgive me."

Katsura released the girl's hands. "I'm going," he said.

"No. It's too dangerous. Please stay here until morning."

"I must get back to Choshu headquarters immediately to make sure that Bakufu troops don't try to storm the place, if they haven't done so already." Katsura was worried that samurai of the Protector of Kyoto might use the uproar as an excuse to force their way into headquarters and search the premises for evidence linking Choshu to the planned uprising. As usual, he was more concerned for the welfare of Choshu than the lives of his comrades. "But I don't dare leave dressed like this," he said.

Katsura changed into some old clothes which he had kept at Ikumatsu's house for just such an occasion, and disguised as a beggar, walked quickly through the darkness, just one block to Choshu headquarters. When he arrived, he found that the outer gate was bolted shut. "Let me in," he shouted.

"Who's there?" called a voice from within.

"It's me, Katsura. Open up quickly."

The gate opened immediately. On the other side stood several samurai who had followed his orders not to leave until he returned.

"Katsura-san, you're alive," one of them said.

"Yes. Where's Sugiyama?" he asked anxiously.

"He joined the fighting at the Ikedaya," the man said, "along with Ariyoshi and Yoshida."

"Bolt the gates," Katsura ordered. "Under no circumstances is anybody to be permitted entrance tonight."

"But what about our own men? What if some of them should return?"

The faces of Yoshida, Ariyoshi and Sugiyama flashed through Katsura's mind. It's my fault they were at the Ikedaya tonight, he thought to himself. As he would find out on the next morning, of his three comrades, only Ariyoshi was still alive. "Nobody is to enter tonight," Katsura ordered. "Choshu must not be implicated."

When the fighting at the Ikedaya had finally ended, eleven rebels were dead, and twenty-three arrested. In addition to the two Choshu men, among the dead were, Miyabe, Kitsuma and Kameyata. Although completely outnumbered, the Loyalists had fought fiercely, killing three of the Shinsengumi, and wounding two of its top swordsmen. Outside the rebels killed fifteen Bakufu and Aizu troops, and wounded several others. At the Ikedaya, the Shinsengumi had cut its way into the very psyche of these turbulent times, becoming the most feared police force in Japanese history. When news of the slaughter reached Hagi Castletown two days later, it reunited those Choshu men who up until now had advocated restraint, with their more radical clansmen, as anti-Tokugawa sentiment spread like wild-fire across the entire domain.

*   *   *

When news of the Slaughter at the Ikedaya reached Ryoma in Edo, he grew downcast and despondent, then suddenly confused. He was beside himself with anger over the rashness of the rebels in Kyoto, and the death of his comrades. As he told Jutaro: "I, Sakamoto Ryoma, vow to overthrow the Tokugawa Bakufu. The same Tokugawa Bakufu that has lived off the sweat of the peasants for these past two and a half centuries. The same Tokugawa Bakufu that killed *Men of High Purpose* under Ii Naosuke. The same Tokugawa Bakufu that caused the downfall of Hanpeita's Loyalists. The same Tokugawa Bakufu that drove Choshu from Kyoto. The same Tokugawa Bakufu that is only concerned about its own preservation at the expense of the rest of Japan. And the same Tokugawa Bakufu..." Ryoma paused, choking back tears, "the same rotten Bakufu that sent its men to slaughter Kame and the others at the Ikedaya."

The attack on the Ikedaya, Ryoma knew, was the beginning of a full-fledged war between the Bakufu and the Loyalists. The incident destroyed his plans to settle the northern territory, which the Bakufu would now certainly refuse to finance. What's more, Ryoma was worried that the Bakufu might even punish Kaishu for harboring Loyalists at his academy.

Bewildered, Ryoma now considered drastic measures. He would ask Kaishu to secure for him the use of a Tokugawa warship. What he wouldn't tell his mentor, however, was his own resolve to join the Choshu radicals, sail with his men to Osaka, then march into Kyoto to fight against the Bakufu troops there. "Enough is enough," he thought. "The Bakufu has gone too far."

Ryoma called on Kaishu at his home in Edo, where he found the navy commissioner sitting at his desk, peering over some papers. "Ryoma, come in," Kaishu said, folding up a document. "I'm glad you've come. It saves me the trouble of having to send for you."

"Katsu-sensei, the reason I have come is..." Ryoma stammered, "I'd like to ask a favor of you." He felt uncomfortable, despite himself. After all, Kaishu was a retainer of the House of Tokugawa.

"Well, what is it?" Kaishu said, picking up a round paper fan, and fanning his face. Then changing his tone of voice, "I heard about the slaughter last night. I want you to know that I share your indignation."

"I know," Ryoma said with a downward glance.

Kaishu had, in fact, written about the Ikedaya Incident in his diary. *"A group of ronin were slaughtered in Kyoto on the fifth of this month; it was the Shinsengumi who killed these innocent men. One of my own students, Tosa samurai Mochizuki (Kameyata) was among those killed. Choshu is outraged and indignant, and say they will go to Kyoto to reinstate the Seven Banished Nobles...and expel the foreigners from Japan."*

"Sensei," Ryoma looked up, speaking loudly now, as if to force himself to say what he must, "I want your permission to take command of a Bakufu warship."

"We already have two warships in Kobe."

"I mean I'd like your permission to use a ship for purposes other than training."

"What purposes?" Kaishu gave Ryoma a hard look, as if reading his mind.

"I've decided I must..."

"That's why I wanted to talk to you," Kaishu interrupted. "I want you to return with me to Kobe to make sure that our men don't do anything rash. I've heard reports that the Shinsengumi is looking for *ronin* around the academy."

"I've heard the same thing."

"Then we must get back there immediately. I don't want any more of our men getting killed." Kaishu paused, sighed deeply. "It's a shame about Kameyata," he groaned. "The academy's close proximity to Kyoto has me worried. To be frank with you, Ryoma, if any more of our men should join the radicals in Kyoto, there's a very good chance that we'll lose the academy."

"I see," Ryoma said. Although Ryoma had also considered the same possibility, he was so indignant over the deaths of his comrades that he had temporarily lost his head.

"But I know how you feel," Kaishu said. "The behavior of the Bakufu is endangering the whole nation. Edo suspects that both Choshu and Satsuma are scheming to usurp power from the Tokugawa. Perhaps that's true, but it still doesn't excuse the fact that most of the men in the government are primarily concerned about their own necks. This is the reason for the unpredictable vacillation on the part of the Bakufu between support of *Expelling the Barbarians* and *Opening the Country*. You are entirely right in saying that the House of Tokugawa is solely concerned about its own welfare, but as you know I'm a direct retainer of the Shogun, and the commissioner of his navy. Although it is our mutual duty to save Japan, it is my personal duty to do so without..." Kaishu paused, "without completely destroying the Tokugawa."

"But Sensei," Ryoma said indignantly, "if things continue as they are, the barbarians are certain to take advantage of the inner turmoil and subjugate Japan as they did China."

"Again, you are absolutely right, Ryoma. But for now, I need you with me in Kobe more than ever. You must trust me. I'm always on your side."

"I know, Sensei. I have never doubted you for an instant."

"Good." Kaishu smiled warmly. "We sail tomorrow."

At the beginning of July Ryoma and Kaishu arrived in Kobe, where ominous news awaited them: 2,000 Choshu troops, divided into four divisions, had recently sailed into Osaka Bay, and set up camps at four points surrounding Kyoto.

From here Choshu intended to march into the Imperial capital to appeal to the court the innocence of the Lord of Choshu and the Seven Banished Nobles. The Loyalists would also inform the court of their intention to remain in Kyoto "to investigate the activities of the ruffi-ans," which was tantamount to inflicting *Heaven's Revenge* on their enemies, namely Satsuma and Aizu. If Choshu's appeals were not accepted, then they would attack the Bakufu troops guarding the Imperial Palace, retake the court from which they had been ousted less than a year before, and reinstate the Seven Banished Nobles. This, the Loyalists claimed, was "for the dual purpose of returning Choshu to Imperial grace in order to finally topple the Bakufu, and revenging the slaughter of their comrades at the Ikedaya." Retaking the Imperial Court was tantamount to recapturing the Emperor, as a football team might recover the ball. This achieved, the Choshu side would run with Him to its home turf in Choshu. It was a match between Satsuma-Aizu on one side, and Choshu on the other, to see who could control the Son of Heaven, and in so doing rule the nation.

Despite Ryoma's natural inclinations to side with the Choshu men, he knew them well enough to suspect that they had ulterior motives.

"I seems that you and I are on opposite sides," Kaishu said to Ryoma. "You do, of course, hope that Choshu will win, don't you?" A sardonic grin appeared on Kaishu's face.

"I don't know," Ryoma said. "If Choshu wins this battle, it would only set up its own government, and we'd be no better off than we are now. And besides, that would only make Satsuma an 'Imperial Enemy.' But on the other hand, if Choshu is defeated, and it looks like it will be, then Choshu, instead of Satsuma, will be branded an 'Imperial Enemy.' So, either way we lose."

"Who do you mean by 'we'?" Kaishu asked.

"Japan."

"How's that?" Kaishu asked, although he knew the answer.

"Unless we can somehow get Choshu and Satsuma together," Ryoma spoke slowly, "I'm afraid that Japan will have no future at all." Out of respect for his mentor's official position, Ryoma refrained from saying the obvious: that a Satsuma-Choshu alliance would be vital to overthrowing the Tokugawa Bakufu, the only way to save Japan.

Ryoma's reasoning was well grounded: it was inevitable that the fighting would indeed result in either Choshu or Satsuma being branded an "Imperial Enemy." Until the previous August Choshu had been the darling of the Emperor, who was not only chronic in his hate for everything foreign, but, in his own words, "unhappy with the Bakufu's failure to expel the barbarians." Having obeyed the Imperial decree to attack foreign ships off Shimonoseki, Choshu had gained the Emperor's praise, and replaced Satsuma as Imperial guard.

However, with the coup of the previous summer, Satsuma was restored to its position as guardian of the Imperial Court. Satsuma's purpose for supporting a *Union of Court and Camp* was to regain Imperial grace while maintaining a semblance of friendly relations with the Bakufu, although Satsuma secretly detested the Tokugawa. And while the Bakufu had never mistaken Satsuma's real intentions, for the time being it shared its would-be rival's desire to crush Choshu.

At any rate, it seemed that a Choshu invasion of Kyoto was imminent. Kusaka's Corps of Loyalty and Bravery was encamped on Mount Tenno, southwest of the city along the Yodogawa river, which connected Kyoto and Osaka. Fukuhara Echigo, a Choshu minister, had led his army into Fushimi, just south of the city. Kijima's unit was encamped at Tenryuji, "Temple of the Heavenly Dragon," in Saga, just northwest of Kyoto. The fourth Choshu division had marched into Hachiman to the east. And the heir to the Choshu *daimyo*, escorting the Seven Banished Nobles, was *en route* to Osaka with an additional 2,000 troops.

But the Bakufu forces outnumbered the Choshu Army nearly tenfold. Although the rebel commanders knew that there were now some 50,000 pro-Tokugawa troops on high alert throughout the city, they refused to retreat, but instead prepared their weapons and watched for an opportunity to retake the court. Meanwhile, several Imperial representatives who were secretly sympathetic to Choshu's demands to expel the foreigners urged the court to recognize Choshu. Other nobles, backing Aizu-Satsuma, insisted that yielding to Choshu's demands would only harm Tokugawa prestige, and so weaken the nation. "Resist Choshu now or it will be uncontrollable later," they warned. Lord Yoshinobu of Mito, recently appointed as the Tokugawa's Inspector General of the Forces to Protect the Emperor, proposed that the Bakufu try its best to convince Choshu to retreat, and only resort to fighting if the rebels persisted.

Yoshinobu's views were accepted, and the court issued an Imperial edict stating that the Satsuma-Aizu coup of the previous summer was in complete harmony with the Emperor's will, and that the Choshu troops must withdraw and await further Imperial orders. When the edict reached the Choshu commanders at their camps surrounding the city, they flatly rejected it as "mere treachery by Bakufu and Satsuma traitors" who surrounded the Emperor. The Bakufu then set July 17 as the deadline for the withdrawal of Choshu troops from Kyoto.

"I'm relieved that all of you are here," Ryoma said as he sat in his room at headquarters with his seven closest comrades, determined not to let any of them join what he considered a suicide attack. Sitting opposite Ryoma was his secretary, Mutsu Yonosuke, whom Ryoma had put in charge of the academy during his absence. Next to Yonosuke was Shingu Umanosuke, the peasant's son who had recently taken the name of his native village in Tosa as a surname, and grown a mustache in the style of the foreigners he had seen in Yokohama. The bean jam bun maker's son, Kondo Chojiro, who had been awarded samurai status before abandoning Tosa and becoming a *ronin*, sat next to Umanosuke. On Ryoma's right were Sawamura Sonojo and Chiya Toranosuke; on his left were Yasuoka Kanema and Takamatsu Taro. All of these men wore sullen faces, and a heavy gloom filled the room.

"Any news, Yonosuke?" Ryoma asked his right-hand man. Despite Yonosuke's razor-sharp wit and gift for rhetoric, Ryoma was painfully aware of the Kii man's inability to hold the group together during his absence. This was partly because of his age (Yonosuke and Kanema, just twenty, were the youngest among the group), partly because he was the only one not from Tosa, but mostly because of the subtle resentment he had aroused for having so readily earned Ryoma's favor.

"Not much that the report Katsu-sensei received hasn't already told us," Yonosuke answered in his typical monotone. "Except that the *ronin*-hunters are keeping a close watch on us here in Kobe." Yonosuke paused briefly, and without changing his tone of voice said, "The significance of this has me very worried for Katsu-sensei personally."

Ryoma acknowledged Yonosuke's warning with a silent nod, then reached over and took his nephew's hand. "Taro, what are you going to do?" he asked, feigning his trademark nonchalance.

"I'm staying right here with you, of course."

"Of course," Ryoma repeated with a grin. "Then let me ask the rest of you what your intentions are." Ryoma's expression darkened, as he scanned each man with his piercing dark brown eyes. "But before anyone answers, let me say a few more words." Ryoma singled out Kanema with a hard look. "I know that deep inside, every man here would like to join Choshu in Kyoto, as I would. But," he exploded, slamming his fist on the floor, "everyone of us here has a very important obligation to carry out before he runs off and dies."

"What could be more important than our obligation as Loyalists?" Kanema said, his eyes opened wide

"Nothing. That's why we must have the guts to remain here in Kobe to fulfill those obligations." Ryoma paused amid the tension in the room, which intensified with each word he spoke. "Our immediate purpose is to study navigation. Isn't that correct?"

All but Kanema nodded.

"In order that we can establish a navy of good men, regardless of social class or *han*, who are dedicated to the development of a new, strong, modern Japan." Again Ryoma singled out Kanema with a hard look. "We can go to die in Kyoto for a losing cause, or we can stay here under Katsu Kaishu and really do something for Japan. The time to rant and rave about expelling the barbarians is over. It ended last summer with the defeat of Choshu and the arrests of the Tosa Loyalists. Now is the time for all of us to work together to accomplish something positive by developing a navy." Ryoma paused to take a deep breath. "Let me ask all of you once more: Is there anyone here who still intends to fight in Kyoto?"

The room was suddenly silent, the only sounds the crashing of the waves against the shore and the shrill of the cicadas in the pines.

"How can you say it's a losing cause?" Sonojo broke the silence. "Word has it that there are some thirty thousand reinforcements on their way right now from Choshu."

"Word has it," Ryoma snickered. "Sonojo, I know you're not stupid enough to give up everything we have achieved for hearsay." He wiped his sweaty forehead with his sleeve. "Even if it were true, there still wouldn't be enough troops to defeat the entire Tokugawa Army, with Satsuma on its side. Don't you men understand that the time just isn't right? We're simply not prepared to topple the Tokugawa."

"I'm staying," Tora said. He had been struggling with himself for the past several days over this decision. He and Kanema had recently visited Choshu headquarters in Osaka, where they met several men from Tosa who had already joined the Choshu Army, among them Tora's cousins.

Ryoma took firm hold of Tora's wrist. "I know this was a hard decision for you," he said.

"I'm staying too," Umanosuke said, tugging on his mustache.

"So am I," followed Chojiro.

"I'm not about to leave you," Yonosuke said.

"Nor am I," Sonojo said.

Only Kanema remained silent, his eyes burning with conviction. "Sakamoto-san," he began speaking slowly, "although I would very much like to stay here with the rest of you, I can't. I must fight with the Loyalists in Kyoto."

Kanema had, in fact, already enlisted with Kusaka's Corps of Loyalty and Bravery on Mount Tenno southwest of Kyoto, and had only returned to Kobe to inform the others of his decision.

"Idiot!" Ryoma flared, then regaining self-control, calmly added, "Kanema, do you want to end up dead like Kame, Kitazoe and the others?"

"That's the very reason I must fight. The Bakufu killed them. I must revenge their murders, and help restore Choshu to Imperial grace."

"Kanema," Ryoma groaned, "I can see in your eyes that there's nothing I can say to stop you. But if you insist on going, do me one favor."

"Of course. Anything."

"Don't get yourself killed." Ryoma paused, shook his head sadly. "And one more thing. Say good-bye to Katsu-sensei. He's in the house next-door."

"I intend to do just that," Kanema said, slowly stood up, thrust his long sword through his sash and left the room.

"Katsu-sensei," Kanema called from the threshold of Kaishu's study. The navy commissioner sat solemn-faced at his desk as Kanema told him of his decision to join the Choshu Army in Kyoto.

Even after Kanema had finished speaking, Kaishu remained silent, his eyes closed tightly, partly out of concentration, partly to suppress the tears welled up inside. He slowly stood up, walked over to a short wooden chest, and took out a kimono of pure white. "This is a parting gift," he said. "I want you to wear it when you go to die in battle." As Kaishu spoke, his head turned away so that Kanema could only see one side of his face; tears ran down his cheeks, and soon Kanema too was weeping.

After a long silence, Kaishu began speaking again. "When you get to Kyoto, I have a message I want you to give to Kusaka. Tell him that what is right and what is wrong will be decided in heaven. Tell him that he and his men should strive to achieve their purpose as soon as possible." Kaishu paused. "Tell him that's all I have to say." Then taking firm hold of the younger man's wrist, "Be sure to come back here as soon as possible," the Tokugawa Navy commissioner told his disciple who would topple the Edo regime.

Ryoma and the others spent the following weeks doing what they did best: training and preparing themselves to expand their navy, but constantly worrying about the fate of the Loyalists in Kyoto. Then, on July 19, Choshu attacked the Forbidden Gates of the Imperial Palace, in what would be the deathblow to the movement of *Imperial Reverence and Expelling the Barbarians*.

Of the Choshu Loyalist leaders in Kyoto, only Katsura Kogoro had opposed the attack. Takasugi Shinsaku, who also called for restraint until Choshu could acquire the necessary warships and guns from the West, had recently been released from jail, but was now under house arrest in Hagi Castletown. The other leading Choshu Loyalists, including Kusaka and Kijima, were preparing their troops from their respective encampments surrounding Kyoto to storm the Imperial Palace.

Although Katsura remained adamantly opposed to an attack at this time, he realized that he could no longer restrain his comrades, and so tried in vain to recruit support for Choshu from the Outside Lords of western Honshu, particularly those of Tottori, Okayama and Hiroshima. While all three of these outside clans sympathized with Choshu and the movement for *Toppling the Bakufu and Imperial Loyalism*, they also realized that Choshu had no chance of victory, and so feared dangerous repercussions should they openly support Choshu. At dawn on July 19, after Katsura had spent the entire night pleading for support at Tottori headquarters in Kyoto, the first cannon shots thundered through the city, from the direction of the Imperial Palace.

Katsura left Tottori headquarters with eight other Choshu men, and headed for Kamo Shrine, where the Emperor was expected to take refuge during the fighting. "I'm going to make a direct appeal to the Emperor," Katsura told his men as they passed through the high outer gate of the shrine, the sharp crackling of rifles and the booming of cannon filling the air. But no matter how long they waited, there was no sign of the Imperial carriage, and after several hours Katsura could no longer detain his men from joining the others in what he knew was suicide.

"We're going to fight with our comrades at the palace gates," they insisted, "to die for *Imperial Reverence and Expelling the*

Barbarians."

"*Imperial Reverence and Expelling the Barbarians* is a lost cause! There is no way we can win today," Katsura had wanted to tell them, but refrained, simply saying, "I'm going to wait here for the Emperor." Katsura, like the others, now realized that the Emperor would not be coming; but, unlike the others, he was determined to live, long enough at least to see the Bakufu destroyed. "I don't have the luxury of dying just yet," he told himself, as cannon boomed from the direction of the Imperial Palace, and clouds of black smoke spread above the northern part of the city.

Katsura stood motionless under the scorching sun, watching the last of his comrades march to their deaths. "They have no chance," he muttered, as a large crow perched atop the gate above him cawed furiously, as if to torment this lone samurai who refused to die for a losing causing. "Satsuma and Aizu have surely sealed off the palace gates by now," he agonized. "They're armed with superior rifles and cannon, and are probably shooting down our men right now," he cringed, looking up at the crow still cawing from its perch atop the shrine gate. "Am I a coward?" he screamed, momentarily regretting his decision to remain behind, even doubting his own sanity. "Of course not!" he yelled angrily, stooped down to pick up a rock, straightened up and threw it at the crow. "I only wish I could run off and die like the others," he thought, as the crow continued to caw tormentingly from its perch above. "But I must remain here alone, after the battle has been lost, after the Choshu Army has been driven from Kyoto and our *han* declared an 'Imperial Enemy.' Who else will be here to pick up the pieces after our defeat?" Katsura took another rock from the ground. "Who else will be left to see that the samurai who have died here today don't end up as mere carrion for the moral scavengers from Satsuma?" he thought, looking up at the crow. "Choshu will lose this battle, but we will not be defeated," he vowed to himself, took careful aim and hurled the rock. The crow suddenly ceased its furious cawing, and fell to the ground. "I can't say I don't envy you," Katsura muttered, kicking the bird's carcass, "or the others who will be fortunate enough to die here today."

The Choshu Army was easily defeated. Although the Choshu fighters were among the toughest in Japan, so too were the samurai of Aizu and Satsuma. While the Matsudaira of Aizu was a direct blood relation of the Tokugawa, the Shimazu of Satsuma had supposedly been subjugated by the first Tokugawa Shogun, but was actually left quite alone in the remote southwestern-most corner of Japan. This, and a determination to keep their domain strictly closed to outsiders, were perhaps the biggest reasons that the Satsuma samurai retained their warlike qualities throughout the two and a half centuries of Tokugawa peace.

A traditional game among Satsuma samurai displayed their mental fortitude and bravery. A group of young men would form a circle around a rope which hung from the ceiling. At the end of the rope would be tied a loaded musket, so that it was positioned horizontal to the floor. After the men had drank two or three rounds of potent white liquor, one of them would light the matchlock, and spin the musket. The matchlock would soon burn down to the pan, at which time the musket would, of course, fire; and as it would still be spinning, nobody knew in which direction. Nevertheless, the men would continue drinking, literally ignoring the loaded gun which might fire into any one of their chests at any moment. Any man who lost his presence of mind or showed the slightest inkling of fear would be branded a coward in this severe test of nerve.

This is the kind of men that Choshu was up against. Although Kusaka's Corps of Loyalty and Bravery fought as ferociously as its name indicates, it was completely outnumber by the enemy. The other three Choshu divisions never even made it to the palace. The Battle At the Forbidden Gates which had begun at dawn, ended in disaster for Choshu on the same afternoon, as its entire army was forced to retreat, and having been branded an "Imperial Enemy" for firing on the palace gates, returned to Choshu in disgrace. The ill-fated countercoup resulted not only in the end of the movement to expel the foreigners from Japan, but also in the loss of over one hundred Loyalists' lives. Although the actual fighting ended in a matter of hours, Kyoto continued to burn for three days, as much of the city was consumed by flames.

*   *   *

"Ryoma, come out here quickly!" Kaishu called from the front of his house at Kobe headquarters shortly after sundown on the nineteenth of July.

Ryoma rushed out of the barrack next-door, alarmed by the impact of Kaishu's voice. "What is it, Sensei?"

"Look!" Kaishu said, pointing toward the northeast. "Kyoto is burning!"

"Damn it," Ryoma exclaimed. "Choshu's finally done it!"

"My feelings exactly. But we have no time to stand here cursing. I must get to Osaka Castle to find out exactly what's happened. Prepare the *Kanko Maru* to sail. After I've taken care of business at the castle, I'll send for you to meet me. Until then, stay here."

Kaishu had recently become concerned for the safety of the *ronin* at his academy, particularly Ryoma's. Since the Ikedaya Incident, the Shinsengumi had been patrolling in and around Kobe. Although Ryoma had done nothing to provoke the authorities in Edo, Kaishu worried for the safety of his right-hand man, whose reputation as leader of dissident *ronin* had grown among Bakufu circles, both in Edo and Kyoto.

"I'm more worried for your safety, especially now that the fighting has broken out," Ryoma said when Kaishu mentioned his concern.

"I'll be fine. But I must say that I am worried what those fools in Edo Castle might be planning. Most of those potato-heads were never happy about my taking you in. They might use the fighting in Kyoto as an excuse to take action against us." Kaishu had good reason to worry: his naval academy, which the Bakufu was officially sponsoring, was a haven for revolutionary *ronin*. And furthermore, two of his students, Kameyata and Kanema, had joined the Choshu rebels.

Upon landing at Osaka, Kaishu reported directly to the Tokugawa stronghold of Osaka Castle, only to find out what he had expected: not a single official in the entire city knew exactly what was happening in Kyoto. Left with no alternative, the navy commissioner took it upon himself to investigate the matter, but first sent word to Ryoma and Tora to meet him at the Teradaya in Fushimi on the morning of August first.

From the Teradaya, the three men traveled northward by riverboat to Kyoto. The city was badly burnt. As they traveled slowly up the Takasegawa, they were struck hard by the damage around them, the effect of which was intensified by the sweltering heat of the early afternoon sun, not a cloud in the crystal blue sky. The fire, having raged for three straight days, had spread five miles from the Imperial Palace in the north to the southern extremities of the city, and over an area of one mile from east to west.

"It looks like Tosa has survived," Ryoma sneered, as they passed beneath Shijo Bridge, Tosa headquarters standing unscathed just beyond them on the left bank of the canal.

"The Hikone estate was saved, too," Tora said with contempt for this close Bakufu ally, whose troops had fought alongside Aizu and Satsuma.

The boat continued up the canal. Soon it passed Sanjo Bridge, and the Toranote Inn, Hanpeita's headquarters during his reign of terror. "I wonder if he's locked up in jail, or even alive," Ryoma agonized silently. Now they could see the black tile roof of the Ikedaya glistening in the sunlight. This monument to the slaughter of their comrades had not been touched by the flames, and in spite of himself Ryoma felt a sudden chill in the pit of his stomach. This was the first time he had been in Kyoto since the slaughter two months before. "Kame," he muttered to himself.

"Just as I expected," Kaishu broke the hot silence, "the Choshu estate has been burnt down." Cinders were all that remained of Choshu's Kyoto headquarters, which for the past four years had also served as headquarters of anti-Bakufu Loyalists in the city.

Soon the canal veered sharply to the right, where it merged with the Kamogawa. Here the three men landed, and went directly to an inn in the Sanbongi district, just three blocks south of the Imperial Palace, at the gates of which the fiercest fighting had taken place.

"I'm going to report to Nijo Castle, to find out exactly what has happened here," Kaishu said, as the three men sat drinking cool barley tea in a room overlooking the Kamogawa. The air was humid, and on the grassy banks of the river they could see lines of small makeshift shacks built by the townspeople whose houses had been destroyed by the fire.

"Sensei," Ryoma said, "I don't know how to explain it, but I have a strange feeling that Katsura Kogoro is close by."

"Katsura?" Kaishu said. "The Choshu men have fled the city. I seriously doubt he's remained behind."

"I understand, but somehow I can't help but feel that he has." Ryoma took a sip of tea, squinted hard as he stared out the window at the river below, the green mountains looming in the distance. After a short silence, Ryoma said, "If he is here, I think I know where I can find him."

"Where?" Tora asked.

Ryoma stood up without answering.

"Are you going to look for him?" Tora asked.

"I must," Ryoma said. "That is, if you don't have any objections,

Sensei," he said, in deference to Kaishu.

"Even if I did, I know I couldn't stop you," Kaishu said. "Do as you will, Ryoma. Do as you will."

A lone *ronin* walked through the front gate of the Yoshidaya inn. "Is anyone here?" he shouted at the doorway. The door slid partially open, and an elderly woman eyed the stranger cautiously, nervously. He was tall, solidly built, and wore a thin black kimono, frayed badly along the lapels, collar and cuffs, the family crest just below both shoulders indiscernible from wear. His faded gray *hakama* was wrinkled and dusty, and at his left hip was only one sword, as if poverty had compelled him to sell the shorter blade. His hair was unkempt, his sweaty face streaked with grime. "Another *ronin*," the old woman thought. "Not to be trusted." After all, most of the *ronin* remaining in Kyoto were desperadoes who would not hesitate to kill to get what little money they could. "Or perhaps this is a Bakufu spy," she thought. "What do you want?" the old woman asked bluntly, frightened.

"My name is Saitani," the *ronin* said. "Saitani Umetaro, from Tosa." Then, whispering, "I've come to see Katsura Kogoro."

"Who's there?" called a woman's voice from the dark corridor.

"I'm looking for Katsura," Sakamoto Ryoma, alias Saitani Umetaro, continued to whisper. He had recently taken as an alias the name of his relatives, the Saitani family, in Kochi Castletown.

"Oh!" Ikumatsu gasped when she recognized Ryoma. "Come right in," she said in a hushed voice, leading him to a small room at the rear of the house. "Who's there?" came a voice from the other side of the screen door.

"It's me," Ikumatsu said. "You have a visitor."

"Who?"

"Saitani-san," the girl said. With so many houses having been destroyed by the fire, the inn was nearly filled, and Ikumatsu took this precaution, lest one of the guests should overhear her utter the real name of the notorious outlaw from Tosa.

"Saitani?" Katsura said calmly, taking hold of his long sword which he kept within reach at all times. "Come in." The door slid open. "Sakamoto-san," Katsura gasped in relief, albeit in a low, muffled voice. "Ikumatsu, bring *sake*."

Ryoma entered the room, closing the door behind him. "I'm glad to see you're safe," he whispered, grinning.

"Safe?" Katsura snickered. "With Choshu headquarters burnt down, this is the only place in the entire city where I can hide."

"I know. That's why I came."

"As you probably also know, Choshu has been declared an 'Imperial Enemy,' and all Choshu men have been banned from Kyoto. I can't even go outside without fear of arrest."

"You can't stay here either. Come with me to Kobe."

"No. I must remain in Kyoto to report to Choshu of the situation here."

"Do you have word of the casualties?" Ryoma asked.

"Yes. Ikumatsu's informed me. We lost about one hundred men. Kusaka and Kijima are both dead."

"Kusaka!" Ryoma gasped.

"Yes. They found his body in the grounds of the Takatsukasa mansion near the palace. He fought fiercely at the Sakaicho Gate, but was shot and apparently wounded badly. He died bravely, committing *seppuku* in the end."

"Damn it!" Ryoma cursed. "You must get away from here. The danger is too great, and Choshu needs you alive. Now more than ever. Please come with me to Kobe."

"I'll leave when the time is right." Katsura paused as he heard footsteps in the corridor. "Ikumatsu," he called out, "is that you?"

"Yes," the girl answered, slid open the door. She held a tray with two flasks of *sake* and cups.

"I don't feel like drinking now," Ryoma said. "I don't suppose you've heard about one of my men who was fighting under Kusaka's command. His name is Yasuoka Kanema, from Tosa."

"Yes, he's fled to Choshu with the others."

A look of relief covered Ryoma's face. "I think I'll have a drink," he said.

Shortly after, Ryoma got up to leave. "What are you going to do?" Katsura asked.

"I'll return to Kobe."

"Be careful. The streets are crawling with *ronin*-hunters."

"I'll be with Katsu-sensei. I doubt that even the *ronin*-hunters would try anything with the navy commissioner present."

Ryoma left the Yoshidaya, walked northward up the narrow cobblestone street, empty on this hot August afternoon. He turned left onto the main Marutamachi Road, which extended east and west across the city, along the south side of the Imperial Palace grounds. Homes of court nobles were located just to the north, on the opposite side of the high white earthen wall which stood parallel to the road; beyond them was the palace. Soon Ryoma reached Sakaicho Gate, closed and heavily guarded from within. Here Choshu Loyalists had fired on the Satsuma guard less than two weeks before; and it was at this very gate that Kusaka Genzui had been shot. Just beyond were the charred remains of the mansion of the Takatsukasa family of court nobles, where Kusaka had taken his own life. But as entering the Imperial grounds was forbidden, Ryoma simply paused before the gate, his back to the road. "This is Sakamoto Ryoma speaking," he whispered, tears welling up inside his head. "Kusaka-san, if your spirit or those of any of the others that died here can hear me, please listen. I swear on my life that none of you will have died in vain. I vow to topple the Tokugawa Bakufu."

"Ryoma," a voice called from behind. Ryoma immediately reached for his sword, and turned around. "Katsu-sensei," he said, relieved.

"Get in, Ryoma." Kaishu was sitting alone in a palanquin. "I wish you'd be more careful. The Shinsengumi are patrolling this city day and night."

"But I'm with you," Ryoma said, then climbed into the palanquin.

"Yes, you are, Ryoma. By the way, did you see Katsura?"

"Let's just say that he's safe for the time being." Ryoma avoided a direct answer in deference to Kaishu's official post.

"Then he's in Kyoto?"

"Yes."

"And what were you doing in front of the palace gate?" Kaishu asked.

"Promising to pay a debt to an old friend," Ryoma replied, drawing a strange look from his mentor.

"To whom?"

"Kusaka Genzui."

"Kusaka Genzui?"

"Yes. He committed *seppuku* back there. I just wanted him to know that we'd clean things up for him, that's all."

"Kusaka's dead," Kaishu sighed, slowly shaking his head. "Ryoma," he said in a low, sad voice, "are you going to topple the Bakufu?"

"What?" Ryoma started.

"Are you going to topple the Bakufu?" Kaishu repeated.

"Sensei, out of respect for you..."

"No need to hide your true thoughts," Kaishu interrupted. "The

245

Bakufu has obviously won this battle. But the regime is old. It's been in power for over two and a half centuries. But being a direct retainer of the Shogun, I could never fight against him. So, Ryoma, it's up to you to do the job for me."

"Sensei, I..."

"Because if anyone can," Kaishu interrupted again, as if speaking to that part of himself that was also a part of Ryoma, "or should, you're the one."

Out of respect for the great man, Ryoma chose not to answer, and remained silent as the palanquin moved toward the small inn where Tora was waiting.

*   *   *

It seemed that one disaster always followed another for Choshu. In June, Great Britain, France, Holland and the United States had again informed Edo that unless their ships could be assured safe passage through Shimonoseki Strait they would bombard the Shimonoseki coast. Not only was Edo unable to control Choshu–which at that time had been planning the countercoup in Kyoto–but it secretly welcomed an attack. In fact, the Bakufu had even loaned maps of Japan to France, so that the foreigners could more easily punish the renegade clan.

Six months earlier, Katsura Kogoro's protégé, Ito Shunsuke, and another Choshu man, Inoue Monta, had smuggled themselves out of Japan to sail to England, where it was their intention to learn as much about the West as possible, in order to better enable Choshu to expel the foreigners. When Ito and Inoue heard in London of the four nations' planned attack they returned immediately to Japan to ask the British consul in Yokohama for more time to persuade their clansmen of the folly of fighting the Westerners. Preferring diplomacy to war in Japan, the British were happy to oblige, and even provided the Choshu envoys with passage to their home domain.

The efforts of Ito and Inoue, however, were in vain. They returned to Yokohama with a message from their *daimyo* that he had no choice but to continue carrying out his policy of *Expelling the Barbarians*, as he had been thus ordered by both the Imperial Court and Bakufu in the previous year. The two Choshu envoys cunningly added that this was the only reason that their *han* had fired on the foreign ships in the first place, and that it was beyond the power of their *daimyo* to comply with the foreign demands without permission from Edo and Kyoto.

On the afternoon of August 5, the four-nation fleet, consisting of seventeen warships carrying a combined total of 288 cannon and over 5,000 troops, bombarded the Shimonoseki coast, destroying all the Choshu forts in a single day, before landing to easily overtake the 600 samurai defending the coast. On August 14, a peace treaty was signed between Choshu and the four nations.

Ironically, Choshu's unyielding anti-foreign sentiment led to the downfall of the anti-foreign movement. The completion of the peace treaty silenced once and for all the cries to expel the foreigners for the sake of the Emperor, for by agreeing to its terms Choshu automatically abandoned it xenophobic policy, and so its claim that it alone was the true champion of the Imperial Court. Rather, from this time on Choshu would focus its energies on one great purpose: toppling the Tokugawa Bakufu. To this end, as Katsura and Takasugi had long ago foreseen, the foreigners, namely Great Britain, would play a crucial role: thus Choshu's sudden change in attitude toward the Westerners, at the expense of the Tokugawa. *"Having beaten the Choshu people,"* Ernest Satow wrote, *"we had come to like and respect them, while a feeling of dislike began to arise in our minds for the Tycoon's* (Shogun's) *people on account of their weakness and double-dealing, and from this time onwards I sympathized more and more with the daimyo party (Choshu and Satsuma), from whom the Tycoon's government had always tried to keep us apart."*

And so, by August 1864 Satsuma and Choshu, though bitter enemies, both enjoyed amicable relations with the British, relations which would prove invaluable in the turbulent years ahead. Through actual warfare with the West, these two leaders of the coming revolution finally realized the futility of trying to expel the foreigners by military means, a point which Sakamoto Ryoma had been trying to get across to his Loyalist comrades for the past several years.

If Ryoma and Kaishu were perplexed by the foreign bombardment of Shimonoseki, they were infuriated, but not surprised at Edo's decision eight days later to issue a decree to twenty-one *han* to prepare their armies for a military expedition against Choshu.

"Jumping on the bandwagon," Kaishu termed the decree when its news arrived at Kobe headquarters in mid-August. "I'm ashamed," Kaishu told Ryoma, "to represent a regime which would chastise fellow Japanese, when it should come to their aid in the face of foreign invasion. This is truly a disgrace to the nation."

Ryoma, however, understood Kaishu's inability to act against Edo, and therefore kept his thoughts about the Bakufu to himself, whenever in the presence of the great man.

The Bakufu now planned to use Choshu's recent misfortunes, including its present status as "Imperial Enemy," to strengthen its authority, which had been on the wane since the assassination of Ii Naosuke four years earlier, and had been very much in question one year before when Choshu was master of the Imperial Court.

But in its attempt to regain its absolute authority of the past, Edo was losing the upper hand it had recently recaptured. First of all, a lack of consensus between the government ministers in Edo and Lord Yoshinobu, Inspector General of the Forces Protecting the Emperor in Kyoto, delayed the expedition against Choshu. Yoshinobu, whose long stay in Kyoto gave him a better understanding of the situation there than that of his counterparts in Edo, took care not to disturb the delicate balance between the court and the various *han*. The ministers in Edo distrusted Yoshinobu, whom they mistakenly suspected of scheming with the court to wrest control of the political power for himself. Furthermore, some of the *daimyo* who had been ordered to take part in the expedition had long sympathized with Choshu. Others preferred solving their own difficult financial straits to waging a costly war, which, if successful, would only strengthen the Bakufu at the expense of their respective domains.

"The Harder You Hit Him, the Louder He Roars"

Satsuma maintained a belligerent attitude toward Choshu. This second largest of all han would play a most important role in the military expedition against its greatest rival, just as it would in the eventual overthrow of the Bakufu, with the leading part going to the commander in chief of the Satsuma forces, a giant of a man who had come to be known as Saigo the Great.

Despite the bitter hatred between Choshu and Satsuma, Ryoma had not abandoned his hope of somehow uniting the two, no matter how preposterous the notion. As always, Ryoma's deepest sympathies went out to Choshu, but as of late his greatest interests were aroused by Satsuma, which, he had recently heard, was developing its navy by dealing directly with Western traders in Nagasaki. In mid-August 1864 Ryoma visited Kaishu in his study at Kobe headquarters to discuss the very engaging subject of Saigo Kichinosuke.

Kaishu was now concerned about his own personal status in the Edo government. Since the Ikedaya Incident in June, and Choshu's abortive countercoup in July, harboring known dissidents at his Kobe headquarters had made the navy commissioner less than popular among the officials to whom he now referred openly as "those potato-heads in charge at Edo Castle." "There are several people in Edo who would like to see your naval academy closed down," Commissioner of Foreign Affairs Okubo Ichio had recently warned him. Many in the Bakufu now suspected Kaishu himself of siding with the anti-Bakufu forces. "I'm worried that you might even be arrested," Okubo had said.

"Sensei," Ryoma said, sitting down on the floor opposite Kaishu, "I'd like to ask you to write a letter of introduction for me."

"To who?"

"Saigo Kichinosuke."

Kaishu picked up a round paper fan from his desk, began fanning his face. "Ryoma, I was just about to suggest that you meet Saigo."

"Oh?"

"Yes. I hear that Saigo is quite a magnanimous character," Kaishu said, slapping a mosquito on the side of his neck. "But why do you want to meet him?"

"Because he commanded Satsuma troops against Choshu."

"I see," Kaishu said, a puzzled look on his face. "Ryoma, you're not planning anything foolish, I hope."

"Like cutting Saigo?"

"Yes, like cutting Saigo."

"Sensei, I thought you knew that I gave up that kind of behavior a couple years ago when I met you."

"That's right," Kaishu said with a sardonic grin.

"But, getting back to Saigo..." Ryoma said.

"Yes, he's been appointed one of the staff officers of the Tokugawa Army in the expedition against Choshu."

"Is that so?" Ryoma said, now slapping a mosquito of his own, but apparently not impressed by Saigo's exalted position.

"He was shot in the leg during the battle against Choshu," Kaishu said. "I've never met him personally, but I'll write a letter and send it to him immediately. You can probably see him at Satsuma's Kyoto headquarters."

"Thank you, Sensei. But why do you want me to meet Saigo?"

Kaishu gave Ryoma a long, hard look. "Because it seems to me that Satsuma will have a lot of say in national affairs from now on. With its influence in both Kyoto and Edo, not to mention its newly established relations with the British, Satsuma is unquestionably one of the most powerful clans in Japan, if not the most powerful." Kaishu paused, scratched the back of his head. "Ryoma, did you know that Satsuma has recently purchased two warships and about sixty cannon from the British?"

"No." Ryoma looked hard at Kaishu.

"And another thing," Kaishu added gravely. "I'm worried about the academy. With the recent events in Kyoto, there is no telling when the Bakufu might close us down."

"Close us down!" Ryoma exclaimed.

"Yes. The government apparently doesn't like my choice of students," Kaishu snickered. "And one more thing. Okubo has warned me that the Bakufu might be after my head."

"What?" Ryoma started, stood up and grabbed his sword.

"Relax, Ryoma. It's just a figure of speech. Where are you going?"

"To get the others. If the Bakufu is going to take the academy away, then let them. But not one of us is about to let them take you."

"Nobody's going to take me," Kaishu assured. "I'm more worried about my men."

"Forget about us," Ryoma said. "You're worth the whole lot of us."

"If anything does happen, I want to be sure that you and the rest of the men, particularly those of you from Tosa, have somewhere to turn. And Saigo Kichinosuke, as the commander in chief of the Satsuma Army, has a lot of clout with Lord Hisamitsu." After a short pause Kaishu added, "As a matter of fact, I believe that Saigo is the most powerful man in Satsuma."

Ryoma nodded his head, scratched the back of his sweaty neck. "You say that Satsuma has recently purchased two warships and about sixty cannon from the British?"

"Yes! And Ryoma," Kaishu raised his voice, "Once you meet Saigo, report back to me and tell me what you think of him."

"That I'll do," Ryoma said, a dark expression on his face.

"We need Saigo on our side, Ryoma. Since the Bakufu doesn't have the power to deal on an equal basis with the foreigners, Japan's only chance now is for the powerful clans of the southwest to unite to strengthen the nation."

"That's exactly what I intend to tell Saigo!" Ryoma exclaimed, slapping his knee.

"You can tell him this also: when it comes right down to it, the Bakufu doesn't really intend to launch an expedition against Choshu. It's just putting on airs. If those potato-heads in Edo were really serious about their threats, they wouldn't be delaying like they are now. The truth of the matter is that they can't rally enough support from the clans for a military expedition."

"I hope you're right, Sensei."

"I know I'm right. But the biggest reason I want you to meet Saigo is because of the fact that the very future of Japan depends on men like Saigo Kichinosuke, and you, Sakamoto Ryoma." The Tokugawa Navy commissioner, as wise as Ryoma was aggressive, was already preparing for the fall of the Bakufu, which, he now believed, was not far off. But Kaishu did not lament the impending fall; although he was dedicated to the House of Tokugawa, unlike the "potato-heads in Edo" he had never served the Shogun blindly, but rather always with the future of Japan in mind. And Kaishu was determined to make sure that after the fall, men like Sakamoto Ryoma–whom he had molded with his own hands–and Saigo Kichinosuke would have a significant say in the future of the nation.

*   *   *

Saigo Kichinosuke was born in 1827 in Kagoshima Castletown, the first son of a petty samurai whose annual stipend was barely enough to feed his wife and seven children. At age six, Kichinosuke, like all samurai boys of Satsuma, began his education at a local martial brotherhood, the purpose of which was to keep samurai spirit alive throughout this most martial of clans, by putting boys through Spartan training–morally, physically and scholastically.

The code of conduct for the son of a Satsuma samurai was the strictest in all of Japan. He was not just a member of his immediate family, but a treasure of Satsuma. He would grow up to serve the *daimyo*, and was merely entrusted to his family in the meantime. Accordingly, he was treated with special deference by his mother and sisters, and was kept separated from girls to ensure that his virility would not be tainted. The Satsuma boy was prohibited from, among other things, carrying money, associating with the merchant class, entering theaters, and going to places where alcohol was served. Punishment was handed down to errant boys to instill a sense of shame. The lightest punishment–for minor infractions such as whistling in the street, quarreling, or telling a small lie–was to seat the young miscreant in the middle of a room, surrounded by his peers, who would then take turns slapping him in the face, an act more humiliating than painful. For heavier offenses, the boy would be dragged into a yard, where the others would pile on top of him until he became unconscious. For serious offenses, such as drinking or womanizing, the heaviest penalty of ostracism was applied. The guilty boy would be confined to his house for a certain number of days, during which time he was not allowed to associate or communicate with his peers.

There was no need for a system of capital punishment among Satsuma samurai. If a samurai of this clan was found to have committed a capital offense, he, as a treasure of his *han*, was simply ordered by the authorities to return to his home and die, which he inevitably would do, by his own sword. There was never any fear that a samurai thus condemned would try to escape: in a society where ostracism was the ultimate punishment, to die a noble death by *seppuku* was far preferable to living as a coward in exile. Although this rigid martial system produced the toughest warriors in Japan, the tendency of the samurai to look down upon the commoners was stronger in Satsuma than anywhere else.

Not so, however, for Saigo the Great, whose cherished slogan was "Revere heaven, love mankind." At age seventeen, Saigo was appointed to his first official post: assistant to the county magistrate's office in charge of administering the peasants. Having grown up in a poor household himself, Saigo sympathized with the peasants, who suffered under a heavy tax system. (With about 40 percent of its 600,000 inhabitants belonging to the warrior class, Satsuma had one of the highest populations of samurai per capita in Japan. As samurai stipends were taken from the rice yield, the tremendous burden of supporting this unproductive class went to the Satsuma peasants.) Saigo remained at this post for ten years, striving to improve the lot of the peasants, whose affection and respect he would enjoy for the rest of his life.

In 1851, two years before the arrival of Perry, a new *daimyo* came to power in Satsuma who would change the course of Saigo's life, and indeed greatly influence the history of Japan. This was Shimazu Nariakira, whose succession as the twenty-sixth Lord of Satsuma came only after a long dispute between the progressive and conservative factions in that *han*. The progressives favored Nariakira, the eldest son of the *daimyo*; the conservatives supported Nariakira's half-brother, Hisamitsu, a son of the lord's favorite concubine. The Nariakira faction prevailed after direct intervention by the Shogun, to whom Nariakira was related by marriage. Lord Nariakira was a radical reformer who enjoyed close relations with such influential men as Lord Shungaku of Fukui and Lord Nariaki of Mito, and who soon became one of the most respected feudal lords of his time. Like other farsighted men, he realized the need for Japan to import Western culture and technology if it was to avoid being subjugated like China; he thus set a precedent by modernizing his own domain. He fortified the coastal defenses of Satsuma and put mines in the sea approaches to Kagoshima Castletown. (It was only by luck that the British ships avoided these mines during their bombardment of Kagoshima in 1863.) In 1854, the year after Perry's first appearance, Nariakira convinced the Bakufu to abolish its ban on the building of large ships, and subsequently produced a Western-style sailing vessel which became the first to fly the banner of the Rising Sun. He built Western-style factories and a reverberatory furnace for the production of warships, cannon, rifles and other advanced weaponry. In 1854, only fifteen years after the invention of photography in Europe, Nariakira took the first photographs in Japan with a camera he constructed himself. In 1858, just twelve years after the introduction of telegraphy in Europe, this most innovative of feudal lords set up a simple telegraph system within the precincts of his castle.

Saigo's special bond with Nariakira surpassed the conventional relationship between vassal and lord. Nariakira was to Saigo what Kaishu
was to Ryoma: not only the "greatest man in Japan," but one who
opened doors to the future. Like Kaishu, Nariakira was a firm believer in recruiting men of ability regardless of lineage. Constantly on the
lookout for promising young men, he was wise enough to recognize
ability when he saw it; although at nearly six feet tall, and over 240
pounds, Saigo Kichinosuke was not easily overlooked. In 1854, Saigo,
at age twenty-seven, received direct orders from Lord Nariakira to
accompany him on his first attendance at Edo as Lord of Satsuma.

Nariakira never regretted his choice. One day in Edo while discussing the situation of Satsuma with the Lord of Fukui, Nariakira
said, "Although the House of Shimazu has a great many vassals,
unfortunately there is only one among them whom we can depend
upon in such difficult times as these. His name is Saigo. Please
remember the name, because he's the greatest treasure we have in
Satsuma."

Lord Nariakira's retinue had arrived in Edo in March 1854, the same
month that the Bakufu had signed its first foreign treaty with the
United States. Although Saigo's official position in Edo was gardener
to the *daimyo*, his real function was to serve as Lord Nariakira's private secretary, in charge of liaison between Satsuma and Mito; for
while Nariakira proposed trade with the West, he sympathized with
the *Imperial Loyalism* of Mito. At Mito's headquarters in Edo, Saigo
met regularly with leaders of the early Loyalist movement, and, greatly influenced by them, came to embrace Loyalist sentiments. He
reported daily to Nariakira what he had learned from these scholars,
particularly the state of national affairs, while his lofty position and
magnanimous character made him leader in his own right among the
young samurai stationed at Satsuma's Edo headquarters.

In 1858, after returning to Satsuma with Nariakira, Saigo was sent
back to Edo to promote the candidacy of Yoshinobu for Shogun. When
Yoshinobu's candidacy was doomed with the rise to power of Ii
Naosuke, Saigo returned to Satsuma to report the unfortunate details
to Nariakira.

In June 1858, Saigo was sent to Osaka to mingle with the leading
Loyalists in the Osaka-Kyoto region and report back to Nariakira on
his findings. The next month, however, while in Osaka, Saigo received
the news that Lord Nariakira had suddenly died, and crushed to the

heart, determined to return to Kagoshima to carry out the ancient practice of self-immolation by a retainer on the death of his lord. For the past five years Saigo had worked at Nariakira's beck and call; as everything that he had now become was due to his relationship with his lord, he could see no reason to continue living.

Nevertheless, a Buddhist priest by the name of Gessho, an active Loyalist whom Saigo had befriended in Kyoto, convinced him otherwise. Gessho insisted that it was Saigo's duty to carry on Nariakira's legacy by working to overthrow Ii Naosuke, and strengthening the nation by uniting Edo and Kyoto. "Death," the Buddhist priest consolingly preached, "will eventually come to us all."

Bearing his great sorrow, Saigo was determined now more than ever to rid the nation of Ii Naosuke. With other Loyalists from various clans he planned to raise armies in both Kyoto and Edo, march into Hikone, just northwest of Kyoto, and occupy Ii's castle. The plans, of course, were foiled when Ii unleashed his Great Purge, forcing Saigo to retreat to Kagoshima with his friend Gessho, who was wanted by the Bakufu as a key dissident in the Loyalist movement.

Although Saigo expected to find protection from Ii for both himself and Gessho, upon his return to Satsuma he was confronted by internal problems which indicated otherwise. It was rumored that Nariakira had been poisoned, and that his half-brother, Hisamitsu, had masterminded the murder. Although this would never be proven, Saigo believed it, and would consequently loathe Hisamitsu for the rest of his life.

On his deathbed, Lord Nariakira had informed his half-brother that Hisamitsu's son (Nariakira's nephew) would succeed him. But since his heir was only nineteen years old, Nariakira entreated Hisamitsu to "help the young *daimyo* increase the authority of the Imperial Court, oust Ii Naosuke and strengthen Japan by uniting Kyoto with Edo." Hisamitsu was only too glad to oblige, as he realized that this would be his chance to assume control of Satsuma, if not in name then in practice.

With Nariakira's death came the rise in power of the conservative faction in Satsuma, and Saigo found that although he personally was safe from arrest, his friend Gessho was not. This was the last straw, or so Saigo had thought. Instead of letting Gessho alone be arrested, and so most certainly executed, Saigo decided that he would die with his friend. He reasoned that since he had invited Gessho to come to Satsuma in the first place, assuring him of refuge there, he must now

take the responsibility of dying with this man who had previously persuaded him to live. Also, with the conservatives now in power, the situation in Satsuma was much different than it had been while Nariakira
ruled; and the future, Saigo surmised, was bleak.

Late one night in mid-November, Saigo and Gessho boarded a small
boat on Kagoshima Bay and headed for the open sea. About one mile
from shore they jumped overboard, and the next thing Saigo knew he
was being resuscitated by friends who had found him. Gessho, however, had drowned.

The Satsuma authorities were at a loss as how to deal with Saigo.
Afraid that Ii's agents might come to arrest him for having harbored
Gessho, they felt obliged to punish him beforehand. But as Saigo had,
during his years of service under Nariakira, become a leader of young
Satsuma Loyalists, punishing him, they feared, would cause internal
problems. To avoid confrontation with Edo on the one hand, and the
Satsuma Loyalists on the other, the local authorities proclaimed that
Saigo Kichinosuke had drowned, and in January 1859 banished him
to an island in the Ryukyus, some 250 miles south of Kagoshima.

During Saigo's banishment, the assassination of Ii Naosuke brought
about political changes on the national scene and within Satsuma,
where the reformers ousted the conservatives. The reformers were led
by a group of young samurai from the lower ranks, close friends of
Saigo who had enjoyed a good deal of power under Nariakira's rule.
The crafty Hisamitsu saw the chance to assure his grip on the government and strengthen Satsuma's position on the national scene, by allying himself with the reformers, who, being Loyalists, enjoyed influence in radical circles in Kyoto. The time was ripe, Hisamitsu reasoned, to realize Nariakira's plans to unite the Bakufu with the court.
Having sent envoys to negotiate for him in Edo and Kyoto, Hisamitsu
now planned to lead an army of 1,000 troops, first into Kyoto then further east into Edo, to urge the Bakufu to reform itself, and to unite
with the court. To carry out his plans, however, he needed the assistance of the overwhelmingly popular Saigo Kichinosuke, and in
December 1861 sent orders for the Loyalist leader's return after three
years in exile.

Saigo, however, was much too headstrong for the *de facto daimyo* to
handle. When Hisamitsu discussed with Saigo his plan to march into
Kyoto and unite the court with the Bakufu, Saigo told him frankly,
"You're simply not capable of doing it. The only one who could have
done it is Lord Nariakira." Needless to say, Hisamitsu became infuri-

ated, at which time Saigo turned his back to the *daimyo*, and muttered just loud enough to be heard, "You country bumpkin." Such was the pluck of Saigo Kichinosuke.

By this time, Saigo opposed a *Union of Court and Camp*, but rather was intent on "expelling the barbarians for the sake of the Emperor." In the following March he went alone to Shimonoseki with orders to wait there for Hisamitsu, who soon after would sail from Kagoshima with his army. At Shimonoseki, Saigo met with the leaders of the Loyalist movement in Choshu, who persuaded him to go immediately to Kyoto-Osaka to raise an army to squelch the plan for a *Union of Court and Camp*. Saigo left Shimonoseki in blatant defiance of Lord Hisamitsu's orders, determined to destroy the possibility for the very union which the *daimyo* had been striving to achieve.

Hisamitsu was furious when he arrived at Shimonoseki only to find that Saigo had disobeyed his orders. He feared that Saigo's arbitrary actions would endanger his plans for a *Union of Court and Camp*, and determined to stop him, proceeded with his army to Osaka. Upon his arrival at his Osaka headquarters, Hisamitsu ordered Saigo to return to Kagoshima, and arranged for his immediate exile.

While exile may very well have saved Saigo's life by keeping him away from the subsequent slaughter at the Teradaya, he was not to return to Kagoshima for another two years, when Hisamitsu again required his services.

Despite Choshu's first defeat in Kyoto in August 1863, Hisamitsu realized that his former plan for a *Union of Court and Camp* was gradually losing out to the movement of *Toppling the Bakufu and Imperial Loyalism*. Accordingly, in order to maintain Satsuma's position of leadership in Kyoto, which it had regained with the expulsion of Choshu, he cunningly reshuffled the government of his domain, replacing the conservatives who had been responsible for the recent victory in Kyoto with Loyalists from the lower ranks, of whom the exiled Saigo Kichinosuke was the undisputed leader. In the following February Saigo was again returned from exile, and in March was dispatched to Kyoto as commander in chief of the Satsuma forces. At age thirty-six, Saigo Kichinosuke was now a full-fledged leader of Satsuma, returned in triumph from an unjust banishment, and the champion of every Satsuma man who would fight to overthrow the Tokugawa Bakufu.

After the Ikedaya Incident in June, Saigo urged Hisamitsu to refuse Bakufu orders to drive Choshu out of Kyoto. "Satsuma's first duty," he insisted, "is to carry out our late Lord Nariakira's will of guarding the Imperial Palace, and, for the time being, nothing more. This war is between Aizu and Choshu. Sending troops with Aizu to fight against Choshu would only serve to increase the animosity that Choshu already has for Satsuma. We have nothing to gain from fighting at this time."

But when Choshu attacked the Imperial Palace, Saigo, as the commander in chief of Satsuma forces in Kyoto, had no choice but to fight, although he did so not in obedience to the Tokugawa, but rather in response to an Imperial request.

Saigo the Great, however, had not yet realized that he was fighting a losing battle. It would take one meeting with Katsu Kaishu, proceeded by the special efforts of Sakamoto Ryoma, to awaken him.

*   *   *

Ryoma arrived at the outer gate of the heavily guarded Satsuma estate in Kyoto's district of the Two Pines on a blazing hot afternoon in mid-August. As usual, his clothes were soiled and badly worn, his hair unkempt, and he was armed with only one sword. "Sakamoto-san," Yonosuke had said to him recently, "the two swords are the soul of the samurai," to which Ryoma snickered, "I don't know about you, but my soul is no more trapped in my sword than it is up my ass. I only carry it for protection, and one sword is enough."

"I've come to see Saigo-san," Ryoma told the guards at the gate, with the cocksureness of a man who was calling on his best friend.

"Who are you?" a guard demanded.

"Sakamoto Ryoma," the outlaw replied brusquely.

By the summer of 1864 there were few, if any, men in Kyoto who did not know the name. "Saigo has been waiting for you," the guard said, before escorting Ryoma to the main hall of the estate. Here Ryoma removed his straw sandals, stepped up onto the polished wooden floor, and was led into a spacious room in the back of the hall. The room faced an immaculately landscaped garden; on one side of the garden was a well, on the other a big shaddock tree, its yellow fruit, though out of season, hanging heavily on the leafy branches. Although the sliding doors were open wide, as there was no breeze, the room was hot, and the well water and ripe yellow shaddock particularly inviting.

"Please sit down," the guard said. "I'll tell Saigo you're waiting."

Left alone, Ryoma stepped outside onto the wooden verandah, and although barefoot, down into the garden to get a drink from the well. The water was so refreshing, however, that instead of simply drinking it, he poured several bucketsful over his head, then went to the shaddock tree. He took a piece of the citrus fruit, and just as he finished peeling away the thick, loose rind, dropping it to the ground, a loud baritone voice called from the verandah, "So you like shaddock, do you?"

Ryoma looked ridiculous–his hair dripping wet, a grin on his face–as he put a segment of the fruit into his mouth. "So you like shaddock, do you?" Saigo repeated. Despite the heat, the huge man was dressed formally in a *hakama* and black crepe jacket, displaying the Saigo family crest of a horse's bridle. His two swords hung from his sash at his left hip, his full head of hair was tied neatly in a topknot. Although Ryoma, being badly nearsighted, could not make out the face from where he stood, he could see clearly Saigo's imposing figure–the broad shoulders, thick neck, big belly, wide forehead, bushy eyebrows and ridiculously oversized ears.

"I'm Sakamoto Ryoma, from Tosa," Ryoma finally spoke, then stuffed another piece of the yellow citrus fruit into his mouth. "Never had shaddock during summer," he said grinning, then devoured another piece.

"So this is Katsu Kaishu's right-hand man," Saigo thought ironically to himself. "You should see the shaddock we grow in Kagoshima," he said. "About this big." The huge man put his hands together to form a globe.

"We get bigger one's back in Kochi," Ryoma drawled, squinting to get a better look at the man on the verandah. While this historical first meeting between two leaders in the revolution to overthrow the Tokugawa Bakufu was certainly more momentous than eating shaddock in August, all they could talk about at the outset of the encounter was the size of the fruit.

Ryoma wiped his bare feet on the legs of his *hakama*, then stepped up onto the verandah. "So this is the great Satsuma commander," he thought to himself. "With such a stupid face, he sure could have fooled me."

Saigo looked hard at Ryoma through large, piercing dark eyes, thinking similar thoughts.

"Katsu Kaishu sends his regards," Ryoma said after an awkward silence.

"Please sit down," Saigo said.

Ryoma sat on the *tatami* floor opposite Saigo. As both men were taciturn by nature, they had trouble starting a conversation. Fortunately, however, Ryoma's innocent smile got the better of Saigo, who immediately took a liking to him. "Sakamoto-san, I'm sure that you have a lot of friends in Choshu, and that there were quite a number of Tosa men fighting with Choshu against us in Kyoto, but please don't misunderstand Satsuma's position."

If it hadn't been for the sincerity in Saigo's eyes, which sparkled like big black diamonds when he spoke, principle might have compelled Ryoma to either leave the room or draw his sword. "Are you telling me to understand why Satsuma supports the Bakufu?" Ryoma said, no longer smiling.

Saigo broke out in a deep belly laughter. "I must say, I feel much more at ease discussing the matter with you than I did recently with another Tosa man."

"Who's that?"

"Nakaoka Shintaro." Nakaoka, who had fled to Choshu just before the arrest of his fellow Loyalists, had served as an officer in the Choshu Army during the countercoup in Kyoto. After Choshu's defeat and the Loyalists' retreat, Nakaoka remained behind to, as he said, "cut down that traitor Saigo." "And I must say," Saigo said with amused reverence, "he has a lot of guts. You should have seen the gunshot wound on his leg when he came looking for me at our camp. But it didn't seem to bother him, or at least he didn't let on that it did."

"I've heard you were wounded also," Ryoma said.

"That was nothing," Saigo lied. "When my men brought Nakaoka to our camp, I must have had about twenty or thirty guards around me. But he didn't seem to care about that either." Saigo paused, began laughing again. "You should have seen the look in his eyes. He was like a mad dog."

''What did he say?" Ryoma asked.

"Something similar to what you just said. He asked me why Satsuma supports the Bakufu. As he spoke, I was sure that he would draw his sword, in spite of all those guards around us."

"Yes, Nakaoka is as radical as the men of Choshu," Ryoma said. "But as you know, Choshu is extremely popular among the people in Kyoto, even now. It acts rashly, but that's the kind of behavior you need for a revolution."

"A revolution," Saigo repeated with his eyes wide open. "Sakamoto-san, let me ask you something."

Ryoma simply nodded.

"What are your personal feelings about Satsuma?"

"You know as well as I do that Satsuma is not very well liked by anyone but its own people."

"And we're particularly unpopular in Kyoto for having fought against Choshu," Saigo added, obviously troubled over Satsuma's bad reputation.

"Even though Choshu attacked the palace gates, the people still know that Choshu men will remain loyal to the Emperor to the bitter end," Ryoma said, a hard look in his eyes. Then suddenly a wide grin appeared on his face; the spectacle of the huge man in front of him with the expression of a child being scolded amused him. "It's common knowledge, Saigo-san."

"Then, I'd like to personally invite you to Kagoshima," Saigo said.

"I tried to get into Satsuma about two years ago, but they wouldn't let me across the border."

"If you're with me they will," the great man assured.

"Yes, I'm sure they will," Ryoma said, slapping his knee.

"Then it's settled."

"Yes, it's settled," Ryoma said, before adding, "I can't help siding with both Choshu and Satsuma."

"I don't understand," Saigo said, confused.

Lowering his voice, Ryoma said, "If Satsuma and Choshu were to join forces, nothing could stop them from overthrowing the Bakufu." An uncomfortably long silence followed, before Ryoma continued: "And I do believe that that's what you're aiming for, despite Satsuma's alliance with Aizu."

Saigo's expression suddenly grew dark, his eyes severe. "Choshu is an 'Imperial Enemy,'" he said.

"Don't give me that," Ryoma said with a look of disgust.

"Choshu fired on the gates of the Imperial Palace."

"You know as well as I do that Choshu was forced into it. The Choshu men will stop at nothing, even suicide, to overthrow the Bakufu and restore the Emperor to power."

Again Saigo's expression was that of a child being scolded, and Ryoma burst out laughing. "This is no laughing matter," Saigo protested, obviously upset. The good man was extremely sensitive about Satsuma's bad reputation, and was well aware that, beside his own people, the only party happy about Choshu's defeat was the

Bakufu itself.

"The reason I laugh is because the situation calls for laughter," Ryoma said.

"You speak in riddles, Sakamoto-san."

"Does Satsuma intend to attack Choshu?" Ryoma asked suddenly, staring hard into Saigo's eyes. "Because that's exactly what the Bakufu is hoping for."

Saigo returned Ryoma's hard gaze, but before he could answer, Ryoma changed the subject. "I'm looking forward to visiting Satsuma," he said.

"You're welcome anytime." Saigo was relieved that this *ronin*, if nobody else, seemed to harbor a certain degree of goodwill toward his *han*. "But why are you so interested in visiting Satsuma?"

"Because I'm interested in Japan, and I truly believe that a Satsuma-Choshu alliance is the key to the future of our nation."

Saigo stared silently at Ryoma, then said, "That depends on Choshu."

"And Satsuma," Ryoma insisted, then stood up abruptly. "I have to go now," he said, before thanking Saigo for the meeting and taking his leave. Ryoma had accomplished his initial purpose: to plant the seeds of the concept of a Satsuma-Choshu alliance in Saigo's mind. Now, he reasoned, it would be best to let the seeds take root, then cultivate them in the near future.

The men parted as friends, and this first meeting between them was obviously a success—obvious, that is, to Ryoma and Saigo. Kaishu, however, was waiting impatiently at Kobe headquarters for Ryoma's return, anxious to hear his evaluation of the powerful Satsuma commander. But when Ryoma returned he neither mentioned the meeting nor the man. Several days passed, and still no word from Ryoma about Saigo. Finally, Kaishu, unable to wait any longer, went to Ryoma's room late one night.

"Ryoma, what did you think about Saigo?" he asked.

"Saigo is a very hard man to understand," Ryoma said. "If you were to compare him to a large bell, you might say the softer you hit him, the softer he roars; the harder you hit him, the louder he roars. When he's stupid, he's really stupid; but when he's clever, he's very clever. But unfortunately the hammer hitting him was much too small." By the "hammer," Ryoma meant himself, and Kaishu wasn't sure whether Ryoma was praising Saigo or calling him a fool.

While Kaishu was constantly amazed at Ryoma's uncanny sense of timing, it was his own ability to foresee danger which prevented temporary hardship from turning into disaster for Ryoma and the other Tosa men. As Kaishu had predicted, the "potato-heads in Edo" did suspect that he shared anti-Bakufu sentiment with the Loyalists at his naval academy. It was for this very reason that in mid-September, when the Bakufu began investigations into the backgrounds of his students, the Tokugawa Navy commissioner himself paid a visit to the commander in chief of Satsuma. Then, in late October, Kaishu was ordered to return to Edo, and his Kobe academy was closed down.

"I want you all to know that I've discussed your predicament with Saigo Kichinosuke of Satsuma," Kaishu informed Ryoma and the others. "He has promised me to do all he can to assure that you will be safe after I've gone, and that the navigational skills you have acquired here will be put to good use."

"But Saigo was the man most responsible for Choshu's defeat," Sonojo said bitterly.

"Saigo's on our side," Ryoma cut in sharply, silencing Sonojo.

Upon his return to Edo, Kaishu was dismissed from his post as navy commissioner, placed under house arrest, and, with his generous stipend reduced to a bare minimum, his academy in Kobe was completely disbanded.

As for Ryoma and his comrades, everything they had achieved over the past two years under Kaishu seemed to have been lost. Not only did Ryoma's dreams of a navy, which he had come so close to realizing, appear shattered, but having lost the support of "the greatest man in Japan," he and his men were now without income or a place of refuge, and so in danger of arrest by Tokugawa and Tosa agents.

But the years Ryoma had spent with Kaishu prepared him for the all-important struggle ahead: his vow to *"clean up Japan once and for all."* Not only had the navy commissioner taught him a great deal about operating a steamship–knowledge which would be essential when he would establish his private navy and shipping company–but through Kaishu, Ryoma had achieved close relations with some of the most influential men in the Bakufu, men who implanted in his mind the necessity of establishing a republican form of government among the powerful clans. Thanks to his relationship with the Group of Four, his newfound friendship with Saigo, and his special camaraderie with the Choshu radicals, the outlaw now had a political base by which to unite the nation, establish a navy, overthrow the Bakufu, and strengthen Japan through international trade. Surely, Ryoma was now in a much better position to realize these goals than he had been two years earlier when he had convinced Chiba Jutaro of his intentions to kill the navy commissioner. But for the time being, with the loss of Kaishu's support and the naval academy, his whole world seemed to have suddenly collapsed.

While a dark cloud had indeed fallen over Ryoma, he repeated to himself over and over his vows "*to keep my nose to the ground, like a clam in the mud*" in order to "*clean up Japan once and for all,*" as he fretted painfully about the future.

1 Katsu Kaishu
Courtesy of Takaaki Ishiguro

2 Saigo Kichinosuke
Courtesy of Kagoshima Prefectural Museum of Culture Reimeikan

3 Takechi Hanpeita

4 Katsura Kogoro
Courtesy of Takahiko Kido and Yamaguchi Museum

5 Nakaoka Shintaro
Courtesy of Urausucho Kyoikuiinkai

6 Takasugi Shinsaku
Courtesy of Togyo-an

Part III

A Declaration of Freedom

A DECLARATION OF FREEDOM

The Road to Revolution

"A Tosa man attached to Katsu in Kobe is anxious to borrow a for-eign-style ship and operate it. His name is Sakamoto Ryoma. Another man from the same han, Takamatsu Taro, has come too. It seems that just now the political situation in Tosa is so bad, and that they are car-rying on in such an extreme manner there, that these men would lose their lives if they went back. It is true that even if a ship was available it would be some trouble to hide this man until he can board; but since Saigo and others who are in Kyoto have talked it over and think it would be a good idea to make use of this ronin in sailing, we are put-ting him up in the Osaka residence."

The above letter, dated November 26, 1864, was written, at Kaishu's request, by Satsuma Councilor Komatsu Tatewaki to Okubo Ichizo, another leading Satsuma Loyalist who, like Komatsu, was a close friend of Saigo's. Although Ryoma and his men had lost Kaishu's sup-port, they now at least had a place to hide from the Bakufu police, and the possibility of using a Satsuma ship to begin the shipping business they had long planned. But while they spent the following winter out of harm's way at Satsuma's headquarters in Osaka, national politics underwent some very significant changes.

Although by mid-November the Bakufu had massed some 150,000 troops at the Choshu borders awaiting the command to attack, the expedition was not yet to be launched. Since the failed countercoup in Kyoto the previous summer, followed by the bombardment of Shimonoseki by the combined fleets of four foreign powers, Choshu had split into two factions. The conservative Common Party blamed the radical Righteous Party for the great losses the *han* had suffered over the previous summer, not the least of which was Choshu's having been branded an "Imperial Enemy." The conservatives favored "pledging allegiance to the Bakufu" at any cost in order to preserve the ruling House of Mori. The Loyalists, meanwhile, called for "mili-tary preparation to fight the Bakufu." But with the death of the move-ment for *Imperial Reverence and Expelling the Barbarians*, the con-servatives, for the time being, had gained the upper hand.

In Satsuma, Saigo had undergone a change of heart concerning his clan's relationships with both Choshu and Edo. Saigo, whose position as staff officer in Edo's expeditionary forces against Choshu put him in command of the troops of twenty-three *han*, no longer thought it necessary to crush Choshu. Rather, he realized that the mere presence of this most radical of clans was a constant menace to the Tokugawa, which served to neutralize Edo's authority. Using the internal discord in Choshu, Saigo was able to arrive at a compromise with the Choshu conservatives that the Bakufu could swallow, avoid a costly war for all concerned, and even save face for the Choshu *daimyo*. Braving the very real possibility of assassination, Saigo personally went to Shimonoseki to present Choshu with four conditions by which war could be avoided, the boldness of which earned him the respect of allies and foes alike. First, the Lord of Choshu would send a letter of apology to the Bakufu for his "criminal attack on the Imperial capital." Second, the three Choshu ministers officially responsible for the attack would be ordered to commit *seppuku*, and their four staff commanders executed. (Since the other Loyalist leaders responsible for the attack had died in battle, this was considered sufficient. The Bakufu representatives did, however, demand to know the whereabouts of two other important Loyalist leaders: Katsura Kogoro and Takasugi Shinsaku. The Choshu representative negotiating with Saigo denied any knowledge of their whereabouts, but actually he was well aware where both men were hiding: Katsura had fled to the island of Tsushima shortly after Choshu's defeat; Takasugi, forced into hiding to avoid assassination by die-hard xenophobes for his role in treaty negotiations with the foreigners, was now at the home of a woman Loyalist in northern Kyushu.) Saigo's third condition called for the destruction of all fortresses at Yamaguchi Castle. (Yamaguchi, located inland about a day's journey from Hagi, was the secondary castle of the Lord or Choshu, and the center of the government when it was under Loyalist control.) Lastly, it was insisted that the Five Banished Nobles (one of the original seven had died, another joined the Loyalist uprising) be moved from Choshu to another domain, as a sign of atonement by the *daimyo* for having sheltered them in the first place. With 150,000 enemy troops massed at the borders of his domain, the Choshu *daimyo* accepted Saigo's conditions and war was avoided, but the Choshu Loyalists bitterly opposed the compromise.

The Bakufu, however, gained little in prestige from Choshu's capitulation. As Kaishu had told Saigo, Edo was no longer powerful enough to govern Japan, and ironically, while Saigo was basking in his newfound glory, Tokugawa authority continued to wane, as if absorbed by the powerful commander of the Satsuma Army.

Nevertheless, most of the "potato-heads in Edo" continued to believe that the Bakufu still wielded the power to control Japan. They were, of course, greatly mistaken. Perhaps the most vivid example of the deterioration of Edo's authority was its attempt in the previous September to reinstate the centuries-old Law of Alternate Attendance in Edo, which had been abolished two years before. Having crushed the Loyalists in Kyoto, the Bakufu was under the false impression that it had regained its past power, and when it issued an order for the wives and heirs of all the *daimyo* in Japan to return to their residences in Edo, the order was simply ignored, and the Bakufu was left with no choice but to back off.

*   *   *

As the Bakufu continued to deteriorate so did the Choshu conservatives, while the Loyalists prepared to regain power. The most radical among the Loyalists, now that Kusaka and Kijima were dead, was the twenty-five-year-old Takasugi Shinsaku, who was born for nothing if not revolution.

While Katsura Kogoro was the most scrupulous of the Choshu revolutionary leaders, Takasugi was certainly the most dynamic. His explosiveness notwithstanding, Takasugi shared Katsura's uncanny ability to stay out of harm's way, although he was not the escape artist that Katsura was. Neither man had attended the ill-fated gathering at the Ikedaya inn, nor fought in the countercoup in Kyoto. But unlike Katsura, who was in Kyoto during both events, Takasugi had throughout that time been under house arrest in Hagi, nominal punishment for having left Choshu without official permission. After the bombardment of Shimonoseki by the combined foreign fleets, during which time Takasugi was still confined to his home, the previously ardent xenophobe was recalled to negotiate a treaty with the foreigners, the success of which behooved him to go into exile across Shimonoseki Strait to avoid assassination.

After Choshu's capitulation in November, Takasugi returned from hiding, and it was from this point on that he deviated completely from the discrete revolutionary tactics which he had previously shared with Katsura. Nakaoka Shintaro's evaluation of the two Choshu leaders clearly sums up their differences: "*Courage, knowledge, discretion, and the ability to hold his own in discussions even at court describes Choshu's Katsura Kogoro. Courage and resourcefulness, the abilities to face an enemy without wavering, move when opportunity strikes,*

and win by extraordinary means describes Takasugi Shinsaku."
Determined to crush the conservatives as the Loyalists' last chance to regain power and stand up against the Bakufu, Takasugi proceeded to raise an army. Before the snowy dawn of December 16, with less than eighty men, he invaded the Choshu government offices in Shimonoseki, where he set up his base of operation against the conservatives. Having met little resistance, Takasugi's rebels seized guns, ammunition, food, gold and other supplies, before marching eastward into the Port of Mitajiri on the Inland Sea. Here they captured three Choshu warships to anchor offshore of Shimonoseki as floating forts to be used against the conservative troops who would come by land.

Takasugi's great risk—not only to his own life and the lives of his men, but to the entire Loyalist movement—cannot be overemphasized. Had he failed—and with Bakufu troops still surrounding Choshu he may very well have—the odds are that Choshu would have continued indefinitely under conservative rule, instead of playing its all-important role in the impending revolution. The Bakufu troops, however, chose not to intervene in Choshu's domestic trouble, reasoning that the rebels were far too few to represent a significant threat. And, indeed they were!

But Takasugi was confident that if even only a small band of men would stand up and fight at this crucial time, then surely the other Loyalist militias in Choshu would join them in "the righteous cause to overthrow the evil Bakufu, to which the 'common' forces have shamefully surrendered."

Takasugi's intuition proved correct. By the New Year of 1865, the first year of the Era of Keio, his rebel army had swelled to 3,000 strong, and on January 3 marched northeast from Shimonoseki toward Hagi on the Sea of Japan to crush the conservatives. By mid-January the rebels had driven the government troops all the way back to Hagi, where they pounded them from the rear with cannon fire from the warships they had captured earlier.

After one month of fighting, the rebels were victorious in a *coup d'etat* which would prove to be a turning point in their struggle to overthrow the Bakufu, and greatly influence the subsequent history of Asia. Soon the *daimyo* returned from Hagi to the rebel stronghold at Yamaguchi, and thereafter Choshu received its direction from the revolutionary commander Takasugi Shinsaku and his rebels, who now declared war on the Edo regime.

*   *   *

February had come and Ryoma was still at Satsuma headquarters in Osaka, waiting for Saigo to return. He had two pressing matters to discuss with the Satsuma commander: securing the loan of a Satsuma ship, and the necessity of a Satsuma-Choshu alliance. Even some of his own men, who rarely questioned his judgment, thought it strange that Ryoma should be content simply waiting for Saigo's return while other Tosa men like Nakaoka Shintaro were risking their lives running between Kyoto and Choshu, working for the Loyalists and the Five Banished Nobles against the Bakufu.

"What Shinta is doing is important," Ryoma told Yonosuke.

"Then shouldn't we go to Choshu to help?"

"No," Ryoma said bluntly.

"But you yourself have always said that things are never accomplished without action."

"Exactly. And in order for us to act we need a ship. I'm not leaving here until I have a chance to talk with Saigo about getting one."

"Then what about overthrowing the Bakufu?"

"Yonosuke," Ryoma groaned, "I thought that you, of all people, understood. The time is just not right for us to go to war against the Bakufu. And it won't be right until the boil is ready to burst. Like I've told you before, we must prepare ourselves. In other words, we need warships. Hanpeita never understood this, nor did a lot of other men who are either dead or in jail."

One snowy morning in February Ryoma paid a visit to the Osaka residence of Okubo Ichio, who until recently had been serving in the powerful post of the Bakufu's commissioner of finance. Passing through the front gate of Okubo's house, located at the edge of the moat near Osaka Castle, Ryoma felt a feeling of dread in the pit of his stomach. His main purpose for the visit was to inquire about the circumstances of Katsu Kaishu, whom he had not heard from since Kaishu was recalled to Edo in the previous November. The servant who greeted Ryoma at the door recognized him, and immediately led him to the study, where Okubo was sitting at his desk near a brazier of burning charcoal. He wore a short light blue jacket of heavy silk cloth, his graying hair oiled and tied neatly into a topknot; the lines on his pale face were more pronounced than Ryoma had remembered, scars from the turbulent times it had been the fate of this enlightened thinker to inherit.

"Welcome, Ryoma," Okubo said, receiving the outlaw warmly.

Although he knew that Ryoma was intent on overthrowing the Bakufu, he shared his concern for the overall welfare of Japan, and indeed had enlightened Ryoma as to his own ideas for establishing a republican form of government. "Bring hot *sake*," he told the servant.

Ryoma removed his sword, leaned it against the wall in the alcove, took a seat near the brazier. "I've come to inquire about Katsu-sensei," he said. Ryoma was more indignant than ever with the "potato-heads in Edo," who were not only too ignorant to recognize Kaishu's brilliance, but so impertinent as to force him out of office, and even punish him.

"Katsu is still under house arrest at his home in Edo, and is being investigated. That's all I know." Okubo shook his head slowly, warming his hands over the brazier. "But I have something else to tell you. I've been dismissed from my post as commissioner of finance, and recalled to Edo myself."

"Why?" Ryoma exclaimed.

"For the same reasons that Katsu was recalled, I suppose."

"What are those reasons?"

"That's what I'd like to know," Okubo sighed. "Katsu was recalled ostensibly for harboring you and your men, and for allegedly being in cahoots with the Choshu radicals, which is the most ridiculous thing I've ever heard. I suspect that petty jealousy for his brilliance was the main reason for his punishment."

"When are those idiots in Edo going to realize that you and Katsu-sensei are the only men of any worth in the whole damn government?"

"Ah, yes, Ryoma. My feelings exactly. But I wish you'd keep your voice down."

"Of course," Ryoma said, glancing around the study, as the servant appeared with two large flasks of hot *sake*. "Then you do agree with me that there is nothing more useless in this world, and more harmful to Japan, than the Tokugawa Bakufu," Ryoma said.

Okubo cleared his throat, gave the outlaw a long, hard look. "Ryoma, I understand how you feel. But please remember that I am a direct retainer of the Shogun." He filled a *sake* cup, which Ryoma drained immediately, then said, "That's what Katsu-sensei has always said, and look at what those idiots have done to him. In all due respect to you, the Bakufu must be toppled."

"I understand your feelings, Ryoma." Unable to propose an argument, Okubo refilled Ryoma's cup, then asked, "What do you think about the situation of Choshu?"

"We're still not ready," Ryoma said bluntly.

"Ready?" Okubo asked with a puzzled look.

"Yes," Ryoma paused, stared hard at this brilliant Tokugawa official. "I'm going to get Choshu and Satsuma together. Then we'll be ready."

"Ready for what?"

"To topple the Bakufu."

"Choshu and Satsuma?" Okubo said incredulously. Ryoma's words were indeed incredible, and it was for this very reason that he felt safe divulging his plans to a Tokugawa official. Choshu would no sooner unite with Satsuma than it would with the Bakufu. Choshu loathed Satsuma, perhaps even more than it did the Tokugawa. Hadn't Satsuma joined hands with Edo to improve its own position in Kyoto? Hadn't it been Satsuma which was most responsible for Choshu's original fall in Kyoto in 1863? Again it was Satsuma who united with the most powerful of the Tokugawa-related domains, Aizu, to defeat Choshu the following year. Then just a few months later, after Choshu had been attacked by the combined foreign fleets, Satsuma had jumped on the bandwagon, with Saigo as staff officer, in the expedition against Choshu, that had only been postponed when the Choshu conservatives agreed to surrender. Saigo's complete distrust for Choshu, on the other hand, was representative of all Satsuma samurai. Near the end of the previous year, Saigo had written to the powerful secretary to the Lord of Satsuma, Okubo Ichizo, that Choshu must be crushed, so that it can never rise again. "*Otherwise*," Saigo warned, "*it will surely cause disaster for our han in the future.*" But since his meeting with Kaishu, Saigo had reconsidered his clan's relationship with Choshu, and this Ryoma knew. (Although Ryoma did tell Okubo of his hopes to unite Satsuma and Choshu, he wisely chose not to impart Saigo's apparent change of heart; for although Okubo was indeed a trusted member of Kaishu's Group of Four, he was nevertheless a direct retainer of the Shogun.)

"Yes, Choshu and Satsuma," Ryoma repeated, as if possessed by the idea of an alliance. He had long been friends with the Choshu men; notwithstanding their explosive nature, he understood as well as anyone their suffering and their pure dedication to *Imperial Loyalism*. And having spent the past winter at Satsuma's headquarters in Osaka, Ryoma had developed a mutual understanding and friendship with the men of that *han*. "Once I get them together, the Bakufu can send all of its forces against Choshu, but it will lose," Ryoma said.

"Ryoma," Okubo raised his voice, "have you ever heard the name

Oguri Tadamasa?"

"No."

"Then listen to what I have to say, because not only was it Oguri who had Katsu dismissed, but he is now trying to get the French to sponsor the Bakufu, in order to crush not only Choshu, but Satsuma, and if possible even Tosa and Fukui."

"The French?" Ryoma exclaimed. "Crush Satsuma, Tosa and Fukui? Tell me some more about Oguri," he said, taking the flask and pouring himself a drink.

Okubo released a heavy sigh. "First, there is one other thing that you should know," he said.

"What's that?" Ryoma asked, bracing himself.

"I'm sure that the Bakufu will be ordering another military expedition against Choshu."

"Of all the damn..." Ryoma paused. "I can't say that I'm surprised to hear that. The Bakufu might eventually beat Choshu, crush the entire domain, confiscate its land and even execute its *daimyo*, but it will never be able to crush the spirit of the Choshu men. The Choshu Loyalists are resolved to fight until the very last one of them is dead, and I don't believe that even the Bakufu can exterminate the entire clan." As Ryoma spoke, his face grew red with anger.

"I see your point, Ryoma. Now relax and listen to what I have to tell you about Oguri and the French, because it is with Oguri that Choshu, and even Satsuma and Tosa are going to have to contend."

"Please tell me."

"After arranging for Katsu's dismissal and subsequent house arrest, Oguri replaced him at his post of navy commissioner last December. Oguri is now the most powerful man in the government. He's no longer navy commissioner, but instead will soon be filling my former post of commissioner of finance, which means that he'll decide how the Bakufu spends its money." Okubo paused, warmed his hands over the brazier. "But what has me worried most is that Oguri is now intent on saving the House of Tokugawa at any cost, even if it means selling out to the French for military assistance."

"What is Oguri's relation with the French?"

"Let me ask you this," Okubo said, refilling Ryoma's cup. "How do you think the Bakufu was able to afford its recent expedition against Choshu, and the second expedition which is being planned now?"

"I don't know."

"Well, certainly not from the gold we have in our coffers. The

Tokugawa government is almost broke."

"Broke?" Ryoma exclaimed, a look of disbelief on his face.

"Yes. As you know, it was the Bakufu which paid indemnities to Britain for the murder of that Englishman by Satsuma men at Namamugi, and for the burning down of the British Ministry in Shinagawa by Choshu radicals. These two incidents alone cost us 440,000 Mexican silver dollars."

"How much is that?"

"About one-tenth of the Bakufu's annual income. And it was the Bakufu again which had to pay the United States, France, Britain and Holland for the damage done to their ships by Choshu in the attacks off Shimonoseki. Add to this the great costs of administering Edo, Kyoto, Osaka, and the three open Ports of Nagasaki, Yokohama and Hakodate, and you can see that there is not much money left for anything else, including military expeditions."

"You mean that the Bakufu got the money from the French for the expedition against Choshu?" Ryoma said, his eyes on fire.

"Yes. Emperor Napoleon III sponsored it." Ryoma tried to speak, but was silenced by the older man. "And now Oguri plans to modernize the military with the help of the French."

"What's in it for the French?"

"Ezo."

"Ezo?" Ryoma started. "You mean to say the he's promised the northern territory to the French in exchange for military aid?"

"Apparently."

"The rotten traitor," Ryoma seethed.

"Ryoma, calm down and listen. I still have more to tell you." Ryoma stared silently into Okubo's eyes, waiting for him to continue. "In order to centralize Tokugawa strength," Okubo said, "Oguri is also planning to abolish all of the clans, and turn their lands into prefectures under the control of a centralized, autocratic government in Edo. And that is why he is intent on first crushing Choshu, Satsuma and Tosa, the three most powerful *han* which are sure to oppose him. But to do this, Oguri needs money. The French have money, and Oguri has Ezo at his disposal."

"And he plans to sell Ezo to the French?"

"Yes, for gold, modern weaponry and warships. And he plans to get French assistance to build a modern shipyard at Yokosuka."

"A shipyard," Ryoma exclaimed, his eyes opened wide. "Let him build it, and we'll take it from him," he thought to himself.

"In short," Okubo said," Oguri is planning the ruin of every *daimyo* in Japan, not to mention the abolition of the Imperial Court itself."

"What you're telling me is that Oguri would sacrifice the rest of the nation to save the House of Tokugawa," Ryoma said.

"Yes. The man is crazy. I'm a Tokugawa samurai, but I would never dream of such a thing. Not only is Oguri crazy, but he's dangerous because he's brilliant."

"But apparently not brilliant enough to see that if he goes through with these plans Japan will become another China."

"That's my biggest fear."

"That's why there's no time to waste uniting Satsuma and Choshu," Ryoma said, his voice strained.

"Ryoma, you know I can't openly encourage you to fight against my own government, but with a madman like Oguri at the helm, my heart and spirit are with you." Notwithstanding Okubo's hate for Oguri, that he would divulge such information to an activist intent on overthrowing the Bakufu was indicative of his deep trust for Ryoma, and his unwavering confidence in Ryoma's ability to fight his political enemy Oguri Tadamasa.

"I need all the help I can get," Ryoma said as he slowly stood up, and despite himself, felt a shiver run down his spine for the feasibility of Oguri's plan. "We must beat him," he said, excused himself and left Okubo alone in his study.

Ryoma spent the following two months beside himself with anxiety, waiting for Saigo to return to Osaka. Since hearing of the Bakufu's dangerous relationship with the French, he wanted more than ever to speak with Saigo, not only to persuade him of the importance of at least improving relations with Choshu, but also to arrange for Satsuma to purchase a steamer that he and his men could lease. With this ship they would transport merchandise between the southern island of Kyushu and the mercantile center in Osaka, and with the profits earned purchase weapons from foreign traders in Nagasaki. Ryoma had cherished these ideas since his talks with Kawada Shoryo years ago, and his service under Katsu Kaishu had prepared him to realize them. All business transactions would be conducted under the Satsuma name, with the Satsuma flag flying above the ship Ryoma's men would use to smuggle weapons into Choshu to defend against the Bakufu forces. Such was Ryoma's plan, the realization of which necessitated a union between Satsuma and Choshu.

One morning at the beginning of April Ryoma received a message from a Tosa man by the name of Hijikata Kusuzaemon, inviting him to an inn in Kyoto to "talk about some very important matters concerning an alliance between Satsuma and Choshu." Needless to say, Ryoma wasted no time catching a riverboat to Kyoto, where Hijikata, and two others whom Ryoma did not expect to meet, were waiting for him. These were Nakaoka Shintaro, whom Ryoma had not seen since fleeing Tosa, and Yoshii Kozuke of Satsuma.

Nakaoka had been working and fighting for Choshu since fleeing Tosa, just before Takechi Hanpeita's arrest in the fall of 1863. He had fought in Kusaka's Corps of Loyalty and Bravery during the attack on the Forbidden Gates, when he received a gunshot wound near the very spot where Kusaka had died. Nakaoka had also fought against the combined foreign fleets at Shimonoseki, and co-commanded the Corps of Loyalty and Bravery for a time during the following winter. As a leading disciple of Hanpeita in Kochi, Nakaoka had acted as one of his mentor's chief lieutenants in the glory days of the Tosa Loyalist Party in Kyoto. And despite having plotted with Takasugi Shinsaku the assassination of the Satsuma *daimyo* just one year ago, Nakaoka had, his loyalty to Choshu notwithstanding, recently established friendly relations with the Satsuma men. In fact, Nakaoka and Hijikata were now guests at Satsuma's Kyoto headquarters. With the Tosa Loyalists crushed by Lord Yodo, and Hanpeita in a Kochi prison cell, Nakaoka was now in an ideal position to advise those Loyalists who remained free in Tosa Han—but were cut off from almost every source of outside information—concerning the trends in national politics, particularly in Satsuma and Choshu. Nakaoka well understood the mind-set of these Tosa men, having shared their still xenophobic convictions until recently. But his experience with Choshu—particularly the bombardment of Shimonoseki—and his extensive reading, opened his eyes to the awesome power of Western technology, convincing him to throw off his xenophobia. The last time Ryoma had met Nakaoka, he was as firmly against opening Japan as was Hanpeita himself; but now, as Ryoma had recently heard from the Satsuma men, even this strict traditionalist had undergone a metamorphosis similar to his own. "A wealthy country, strong defense," had become Nakaoka's new motto, and he, like the Choshu and Satsuma leaders, now realized that in order to become strong enough to wage war with the foreigners it would first be necessary to trade with them. Indeed, in the spring of 1865 Nakaoka Shintaro saw eye to eye with Sakamoto

Ryoma.

The lower-samurai Hijikata Kusuzaemon, like Ryoma and Nakaoka, had refused Lord Yodo's orders to return to Tosa in the summer of 1863, and instead remained in Kyoto until the coup which drove Choshu and the seven radical nobles from the Imperial capital. Since then, Hijikata had, with Nakaoka, taken refuge in Choshu Han, where they served as personal bodyguards to Sanjo Sanetomi, the leader of the banished nobles. They accompanied the nobles on their recent move from Choshu to northern Kyushu, and were now in Kyoto as intelligence agents for Lord Sanjo, gathering information on the state of things in the Imperial capital, particularly the court's current relationship with the Bakufu.

Like many of the Tosa men who had fled, Hijikata and Nakaoka now felt more loyalty for Choshu than for their native *han*. After all, Lord Yodo had crushed the Tosa Loyalist Party, executing or incarcerating many of those members who did not flee. Despite Yodo's professed loyalty to the Emperor, he refused to take any action whatsoever that might be construed as anti-Tokugawa. In fact, when the Bakufu ordered the first expedition against Choshu, Yodo's heir had put aside his young bride for a few months: she was a daughter of the Lord of Choshu, and Tosa wanted to avoid possible charges of sympathy to the renegade *han*.

Until recently, most Tosa *ronin* had resented Satsuma as much as they did Yodo, and Nakaoka and Hijikata had particularly despised everything that the commander in chief of the Satsuma forces stood for. (As Saigo had told Ryoma, Nakaoka had come to his military headquarters in Kyoto with intent to kill him.) But since Saigo's recent intervention between Edo and Choshu, and his subsequent mediation to arrange a safe haven for the Five Banished Nobles, the Tosa men had come to see Saigo in a different light. Nakaoka had met Saigo on several occasions since the failed countercoup, and described him in a letter to his comrades in Tosa: *"He is wise, learned, courageous, and usually quiet; but when he does occasionally utter a few words they are filled with resolution, and have a depth of thought which directly penetrates the listener's heart."* (Nakaoka's description of Saigo resembles Ryoma's "the harder you hit him, the louder he roars," albeit Ryoma's simple rhetoric is, to say the least, more to the point than Nakaoka's erudite style.) *"Saigo is a man of great virtue who overcomes others,"* Nakaoka continued, *"and having gone through frequent hardships, he is rich in experience as well.*

Indeed, in the way he combines knowledge and action he is compara-ble to Takechi Zuizan himself."

When the Bakufu insisted that Choshu surrender the radical nobles as a sign of atonement, it intended to take them into custody as crim-inals. But since the nobles symbolized to the Loyalists the only part of their dream which remained alive, their safety was of prime impor-tance to Choshu, and incarceration in Edo was not to be tolerated. Instead it was arranged that the nobles be sent to Fukuoka Han, across the strait from Choshu in northern Kyushu, where they were kept as virtual prisoners, not even allowed to associate with one another. When the Loyalist guards accompanying them–Hijikata and Nakaoka among them–reported the outrage, Saigo quickly intervened to secure better conditions for the nobles at a Shinto shrine in nearby Dazaifu.

Ryoma sat cross-legged, to the left of Nakaoka, opposite Hijikata and Yoshii, his sword on his lap. He thought it pleasantly strange that his Tosa comrades should be in the company of a Satsuma man, par-ticularly since Yoshii was Saigo's private secretary. "Do you have any word about Hanpeita?" Ryoma asked.

Nakaoka gave Ryoma a hard look, his wide jaw intensifying the strength in his powerful eyes. "Nothing. Not a word," he growled. "Zuizan-sensei can't move because he's in jail. But what have you been doing for the past six months, Ryoma?"

Ryoma smiled. "Nothing," he said.

"Nothing? How can you be doing nothing when there's so much that needs to be done?"

"I have to see Saigo before I can move," Ryoma said matter-of-fact-ly.

"Saigo!" Nakaoka said. "Why?"

"Two reasons: to borrow a ship from Satsuma, and to convince Saigo to unite with Choshu." Ryoma spoke these words with complete confidence, as he looked hard into Nakaoka's eyes. "Where is Saigo anyway?" he asked, shifting his eyes to the Satsuma man.

"Saigo is expected to return to Osaka any day now," replied Yoshii, whom Ernest Satow described as *"a little man, very vivacious and talked with a perfect Satsuma brogue."*

"It's about time," Ryoma roared excitedly. "I've been waiting to speak with him for the past two months."

"Ryoma!" Nakaoka suddenly shouted, "that's just what we've been planning."

"To borrow a ship from Satsuma?" Ryoma said.

"No. I'm talking about a Satsuma-Choshu alliance."

"I know." Ryoma grinned, gesturing with his chin toward the other Tosa man. "Hijikata mentioned it in his note to me."

"Yoshii-san," Hijikata interrupted, as if to calm Nakaoka, "what does Saigo think about the planned expedition against Choshu?"

"He's certainly not happy about it," the Satsuma man assured.

"And what about a union between Choshu and Satsuma?" Nakaoka asked, his dark eyes on fire. "Because the only hope we have of wiping clean the insults of the barbarians and defending our sacred nation is if Choshu and Satsuma, the two most powerful clans in western Japan, agree to work together, import state-of-the-art weaponry from the West and use it to crush the Bakufu."

"But a union between our *han* and Choshu will depend on Choshu," Yoshii said solemnly.

"Let Nakaoka and me handle Choshu," Hijikata said. "But what about Saigo? Will he ever agree to a union?"

"Leave Saigo to me," Ryoma said with conviction. "If anyone can convince Saigo, I can."

Ryoma spoke with such self-confidence that Hijikata began snickering: "You'll never change, will you Ryoma."

"Then it's settled," Ryoma said, ignoring the remark. "I'll work on Saigo while the two of you talk to the Choshu men."

"We've already begun," Nakaoka said grimly. "Ryoma, had I known you were thinking the same thing, I'd have contacted you sooner. You should be traveling with us."

"No! I've waited here for Saigo all winter. A few more days isn't going to matter now. But tell me, any word of Katsura Kogoro?"

"Katsura's recently returned to Choshu," Hijikata said. "He knew that it would be just a matter of time before he would be arrested in Kyoto, so he disguised himself as a beggar and waited under the Sanjo Bridge for the right time to leave the city. One day when he was questioned by a group of Aizu samurai, he told them that he had an upset stomach and was looking for a toilet. The Aizu men arranged for him to use a toilet in a nearby house, and stood guard outside the door while Katsura was inside." Hijikata started laughing. "At least they thought he was inside. Actually he snuck through the water hole and escaped."

Katsura is a survivor," Ryoma snickered, then stood up and thrust his sword though his sash. "I have to go," he said. "I have to get back to Osaka to wait for Saigo."

Since Saigo wasn't expected back for a few days, Ryoma stopped at Satsuma's estate in Fushimi to retrieve Taro and Toranosuke, both of whom were staying there. "Come on, we're going to a brothel," he told them.

Toranosuke gave Ryoma a puzzled look. "I thought you had to get back to Osaka to see Saigo."

"Saigo's not there yet. Besides, a man has to know when to enjoy himself. Even Shinta knows that much. I just saw him and Hijikata in Kyoto. And you know what Hijikata told me!" Ryoma broke out in a deep belly laughter.

"What?" Taro said, his curiosity stirred by Ryoma's amusement.

"On the night before they were to escort Lord Sanjo out of Choshu, Shinta gave Hijikata one of those hard looks of his, and in all seriousness said, 'Since we might die tomorrow, let's go to a brothel tonight and completely enjoy ourselves.'"

"Sounds like something Nakaoka would say," Toranosuke snickered. "The part about dying, that is. But I must say, I've never known him to patronize a brothel."

"Neither have I. Now, let's go," Ryoma said in a tone more imperative than friendly.

On the next morning, as the three *ronin* walked southward along the Takasegawa, they spotted a band of sword-bearing men, several of them also armed with long spears, heading straight at them.

"Ronin-hunters!" Taro gasped, recognizing the large white banner which one of them carried, emblazoned in red with the Chinese character for "sincerity."

"There must be a dozen of them," Toranosuke said. "I hear that once they start questioning you, things can get very dangerous. Let's get out of here."

"Relax," Ryoma said with perfect calm. Unlike the others, this was not his first encounter with the Shinsengumi. "Do either of you have the guts to walk right through their line?"

"What?" Toranosuke said in disbelief.

The line of armed men was approaching fast. As it was common knowledge that the Shinsengumi was under orders to arrest or kill any *ronin* they encountered, Taro and Toranosuke were terrified.

"You can't take all twelve of them," Taro said nervously. "Come on, let's get out of here quickly!"

"Stay right here," Ryoma said nonchalantly. "I'm going to give you two a lesson in human nature." He walked steadily down the narrow street, his sword at his left hip, the *ronin*-hunters heading directly at him.

The twelve men stopped about fifty paces in front of the lone *ronin*. "That's Sakamoto Ryoma, from Tosa," one of them whispered, releasing the latch to the sheath of his sword. "We've come across him before."

Although Ryoma couldn't make out the words, he recognized the man's face, and the look in his eyes which betrayed his superior ability to kill.

"We can't take him," whispered a second man.

"Why's that?" the first man asked under his breath, without removing his eyes from those of the *ronin* approaching.

"I can't really say, but I definitely sense something about him, something other than just his swordsmanship, that would make him extremely difficult to cut."

The first man nodded slowly, releasing his grip on his sword as an indication to the others not to attack.

Ryoma swaggered down the center of the narrow street, as if oblivious to the patrol directly ahead. Suddenly he stopped, walked over to the side of the canal, and with his back to the line of men, stooped down to pick up a puppy that was asleep in the grass. "Hey, little one," he said, rubbed the puppy against his face, then broke out in a deep belly laughter.

"Is he crazy?" muttered another one of the band. "Let's take him."

"No!" hissed the first man, his eyes on fire. "Nobody draws his sword until I give the command."

Meanwhile, Ryoma commenced walking straight at the line of armed men, still holding the puppy. While all twelve of them glared menacingly at him, the line parted at the center to let him pass.

"See what I told you," the second man said. "You just can't cut him."

"Strange," sneered the first man, as he turned around to watch Ryoma walking away.

"He completely controlled us," said the second man.

"Yes. And despite that stupid look on his face, something tells me he's up to no good."

When Ryoma returned to Satsuma headquarters in Osaka that evening, Saigo was there waiting for him.

"Saigo-san," he said, as the two sat in the commander in chief's private quarters, "don't tell me that Satsuma still intends to support the Bakufu even though the Bakufu plans to sell out to the foreigners, and to use the money it gets to crush a Japanese domain." Ryoma had just finished telling Saigo what he had heard from Okubo concerning Oguri's pact with the French.

"Crush Choshu, you mean," Saigo said sternly.

"Yes, but not even you can say that Choshu is not a part of Japan."

Saigo stared silently at Ryoma, in what seemed to the latter either profound thought or utter stupidity.

"Can't you see that the Bakufu's only concern is the preservation of the House of Tokugawa, at the expense of the rest of Japan!" Ryoma hollered, pounding his fist on the floor. "And that includes Satsuma."

Saigo had remained silent for most of the past thirty minutes, listening intently. "Sakamoto-san," he said, "where do you get your information?" Saigo was obviously disturbed by Ryoma's last remark.

"Believe me," Ryoma smiled, "the source is very reliable." He could not mention Okubo's name, for fear of exposing his mentor as a traitor, which he was certainly not.

"I see," Saigo nodded slowly. He had no reason to doubt Ryoma, who until recently had been the right-hand man of Katsu Kaishu, one of the most influential and respected men in Edo.

"Then call off Satsuma's participation in the expedition, and instead agree to unite with Choshu against the Bakufu," Ryoma pleaded, staring hard into the big man's sparkling black eyes. "Because of the two hundred sixty *han* in Japan, only Satsuma and Choshu count for anything. Only Satsuma and Choshu can overthrow the Bakufu. The others are either blind in their obeisance to the Bakufu, or just too concerned with their own petty affairs to concern themselves with the rest of the nation."

Without answering, Saigo nodded his heavy head slowly and folded his large arms tightly at his chest, as if seriously considering the idea. After all, Ryoma's words made perfect sense. Saigo realized that the biggest obstacle impeding the Bakufu from regaining its authority of the past was a lack of funds to modernize its military. If indeed the French were to finance Edo, then it would be beyond the power of Satsuma, Choshu or even the Imperial Court to prevent the Bakufu from usurping the entire nation.

Ryoma continued speaking heatedly. "We must act soon, before it's too late. It would cost the Bakufu about two and a half million dollars to build a naval station at the Port of Yokosuka, equipped with an iron foundry, docks and a shipyard. But Edo could never raise that kind of money on its own." He paused to let the effect of his words sink in. "Not without the help of the French."

The idea was no less frightening to Saigo than it was to Ryoma. "I see," Saigo said, maintaining an impenetrable stolidity, save his sparkling black eyes which radiated perfect sincerity.

Ryoma sat up straight, thrust his face at the larger man's. "What about an alliance with Choshu?" he prodded.

"Sakamoto-san, I'm sure you understand that Satsuma has its pride. We just can't..."

"Pride?" Ryoma burst out indignantly. "Forget about pride. What's pride going to do for you if your entire domain is crushed?"

"We must eliminate Choshu because it refuses to see the light."

"The light?" Ryoma shouted. "The light will go out for us all unless the Bakufu is destroyed, and soon. I hear that a Yokosuka Naval Station is scheduled to be completed in less than four years."

"I see," Saigo nodded grimly. "But Choshu has always opposed our idea of assembling a council of the powerful *daimyo* to handle these problems."

Ryoma knew well of Saigo's desire for a new form of government: they were similar to his own. Ryoma agreed with Satsuma's call for a council of feudal lords centered around the Imperial Court in Kyoto to govern the nation, the formation of which would be tantamount to the end of Tokugawa rule. But Ryoma also knew that Saigo would never agree with his own desire to abolish the entire feudal system so that there would be no more clans, no more feudal lords, no more samurai, no more court nobles, and with the exception of the Emperor, no more class distinction at all. For despite Saigo's lifelong slogan "Revere heaven, love mankind," his philosophy was rooted in traditional Confucian thought whereby the population was divided into two immutable categories: those who labored with their bodies, and those who labored with their minds–that is, the peasants and their samurai overlords, respectively. In Saigo's mind–and indeed in the minds of virtually all educated samurai–it was the duty of the warrior class to love and protect the peasantry who had embodied the mainstay of the agricultural economy since time immemorial. Saigo fully believed that the samurai must cherish the farmers, just as a *daimyo* must love his vassals, a father his sons; but, as Ryoma well knew, Saigo would never condone changing society to allow the peasants to stand on an equal footing with the "warrior-gentlemen," so that class barriers would disappear entirely. This, however, was precisely the goal of Sakamoto Ryoma, who hoped to form a new government by which all Japanese people would be equal, from the lowest peasant to the loftiest feudal lord. Ryoma had cherished these democratic ideals since first hearing of them from Kawada Shoryo, and they had matured in his mind through his contacts with the Group of Four. Not only was Ryoma sure that Saigo would never agree to abolish the feudal system, but he felt that mere mention of the idea might alienate the great Satsuma leader. In fact, Ryoma decided that he had said enough about Choshu and the Bakufu for one evening, realizing that if Saigo still could not see the absolute necessity of an alliance, then he probably never would. "One more thing before I leave," Ryoma said nonchalantly. "What ever happened with the talk of Satsuma purchasing a warship for my men and I to lease?" This was the first time Ryoma had ever mentioned the matter to Saigo, although he knew that Kaishu had done so several months earlier.

"I'm going to Kyoto tomorrow," Saigo said. "Both Komatsu and Okubo are there. I'll discuss the matter with them."

"Thank you," Ryoma said. Thus assured, he stood up, put on his sword, and left the Satsuma leader alone.

On the following evening Saigo Kichinosuke, Okubo Ichizo and Komatsu Tatewaki–for all means and purposes the Triumvirate of Satsuma–sat in the latter's quarters at Satsuma's Kyoto headquarters.

Like Saigo, Okubo was of low birth, but through sheer brilliance had become Lord Hisamitsu's chief advisor. Although Saigo and Okubo had been close friends since boyhood, they were of contrasting natures. The warm, magnanimous Saigo was loved by his comrades, while the cold, analytical Okubo would never enjoy such reverence. Nevertheless, through Saigo's influence, Okubo had become a leader among Satsuma radicals back in the days of Lord Nariakira's campaign against Ii Naosuke. After Nariakira's death, and Saigo's subsequent exile, Okubo's group petitioned Lord Hisamitsu to lead an attack on Edo against Ii. Hisamitsu, of course, refused, but affectionately dubbed Okubo's men the "Spirited and Loyal Band." It was Okubo who was most responsible for Lord Hisamitsu's march into Kyoto in the summer of 1862 to persuade the court to issue an Imperial decree for shogunal reform, and it is even conjectured that Okubo, Machiavellian in his belief that the end justified the means, supported Hisamitsu's orders in the previous spring for the slaughter of Satsuma Loyalists at the Teradaya. After Satsuma's battle with the British in 1863, Okubo was sent to Yokohama to hold secret negotiations with them. It was also Okubo who insisted that the Bakufu loan Satsuma the money demanded by the British for indemnities, threatening that if Edo refused he would have the British minister assassinated to further complicate the problems facing Edo.

Komatsu Tatewaki, a hereditary councilor to the Lord of Satsuma, was related to the ruling Shimazu family, and one of the highest ranking men from any of the clans to be numbered among the Loyalists. Satow described Komatsu as *"one of the most charming Japanese I have known, a Karo* (hereditary councilor) *by birth, but unlike most of that class, distinguished for his political ability, excellent manners, and a genial companion. He had a fairer complexion than most, but his large mouth prevented his being good-looking."* It was Komatsu who, at Kaishu's request, had arranged to shelter Ryoma and his men at Satsuma's Osaka and Kyoto headquarters over the past winter. At twenty-nine Komatsu was the same age as Ryoma, and though the two had not yet met, the things the Satsuma councilor had heard about the Tosa *ronin* from Saigo, Kaishu and others opened his heart to him.

"Ichizo," Saigo said, referring to Okubo, who at thirty-five was three years his junior, by his given name. 'I had a very interesting discussion last night with Sakamoto Ryoma."

"Sakamoto who?"

"You know. That Tosa *ronin* who Komatsu and I have been telling you about," Saigo said, glancing at the councilor.

"Oh yes, now I remember. Sakamoto Ryoma," Okubo said emphatically, scratching his wide jaw, his intelligent eyes focused hard on Saigo's. "That's the man you wrote me about, isn't it, Komatsu-san?"

"Yes, he's apparently been trained in navigation by Katsu Kaishu himself, and is trying to get the use of a ship from our *han*."

Saigo burst out laughing. "Ryoma is quite a character. It seems that once he gets his mind set on doing something, he does it. He says he wants to 'lease' a ship from us. He intends to use it for 'business purposes.'"

Okubo and Komatsu shared Saigo's interest in Ryoma. "It sounds like we could put Sakamoto's navigational expertise to use," Okubo said. This was precisely Komatsu's idea when he agreed to keep Ryoma and his men at Satsuma headquarters. After all, Kaishu's former students were experts in an extremely sophisticated technology. The steam-powered warships of the mid-nineteenth century could be likened to the nuclear-powered battleships one century later, insofar as they were among the most advanced and expensive forms of military technology in the world. In short, Ryoma and his men were experts in an elite field of high-technology which was invaluable to Satsuma. As that *han* was engaged in illegal trade between Kagoshima, the Ryukyus and Shanghai to raise capital to rebuild its navy which had been badly destroyed by the British, it desperately needed skilled sailors.

"Believe me," Saigo said, "there's a lot more to Ryoma than just navigational expertise. I strongly urge that the both of you talk with the minister of the treasury in Kagoshima to arrange the use of a ship for him. Because it's only a matter of money that's keeping him down."

"I think that could be arranged," Komatsu said, kneading his long eyebrows.

"And that's not all Ryoma and I talked about," Saigo said in a low voice. After relaying everything he had heard from Ryoma about Edo's relationship with the French, Saigo asked, "What do you think of Ryoma's proposal about an alliance with Choshu?"

Okubo shook his head slowly, sighing deeply. "I just don't know. But I don't see that we have any other choice."

"My feelings exactly," Komatsu said.

Saigo looked hard at the other two men. "Mine too! I suggest that Komatsu and I take Ryoma with us back to Kagoshima and let him plead his case about a warship to the minister of the treasury, while the two of us make sure that Satsuma will not participate in the second expedition against Choshu."

"Yes," Komatsu readily agreed, and although Ryoma did not yet know, the first step of his great plan to unite Satsuma and Choshu had been realized.

*   *   *

Ryoma and six of his men sailed aboard the Satsuma steamer *Butterfly* with Saigo, Komatsu and several other men of that clan, arriving at Kagoshima under a clear blue sky on the extremely hot first day of May. The former students of Katsu Kaishu, the most knowledgeable navigator in Japan, were not just along for the ride. Before leaving Osaka Ryoma had told them, "We have to convince the Satsuma men to lend us a ship, so let's show them that we can operate one." And this they did, with Ryoma as captain.

"Saigo-san," Ryoma called from the crow's nest halfway up the mainmast, the Shimazu crest–a black cross in a circle–emblazoned on the flag flying above him.

"What is it?" Saigo bellowed from the starboard deck.

Ryoma climbed down the netting. "I never thought I'd see it," he said excitedly.

"Ah, yes. Sakurajima," Saigo affectionately uttered the volcano's name. The two men stared at the active volcanic island, the symbol of Kagoshima, rising majestically out of the bay in front of the castle-town, spewing a single cloud of white smoke into the clear blue sky.

Ryoma had good reason to be excited. He had never expected to get into Satsuma Han, which throughout history had maintained a strict policy of keeping outsiders out. Not even Tokugawa officials could gain entrance into Satsuma: most of those who had tried over the past two centuries had simply disappeared.

"Look over there," Saigo said, pointing to the batteries at the mouth of the Kotsuki River, which flowed through the center of the castle-town into the bay.

"I hear that Satsuma gave the British hell with those guns," Ryoma said, squinting to get a clearer view of the cannon.

"Perhaps, but not enough. Look over there," Saigo said, pointing to the left. Along the shore, backgrounded by heavily wooded green hills, was a group of gray brick buildings with traditional black tile roofs. "Those are our new foundries, where we're manufacturing guns and ammunition. Most of our old foundries were destroyed in the battle with the British."

Indeed, the technology of the Satsuma foundries was so advanced as to impress even the British delegation that would visit Kagoshima in the following year. *"The Satsuma people seemed to be making great progress in the civilized arts, and gave me the impression of great courage and straightforwardness,"* Satow wrote. *"I thought they would soon be far ahead of the rest of Japan."* At the beginning of this year Satsuma had secretly sent fifteen men on a study tour to England, in defiance of Tokugawa law. England was also assisting its new allies in the construction of other factories in Kagoshima, also behind the Bakufu's back. But why was Great Britain so anxious to aid her erst-while enemy? Like Ryoma, she predicted that before long Satsuma, and not Edo, would be the most powerful entity in Japan. Thus Ryoma's determination to unite Choshu and Satsuma.

Soon the *Butterfly* anchored, but as all seven outsiders were not permitted to land, only Ryoma and Yonosuke disembarked with the
Satsuma men. They were escorted to an inn in the castletown, where
they waited anxiously for Saigo to return. Ryoma was concerned
about the outcome of the meetings Saigo and Komatsu would be having with the *daimyo* and his council over the next few days, albeit he
was confident that Satsuma would not participate in the expedition
against Choshu. Since Ryoma had already convinced the Satsuma
commander in chief of the folly of cooperating with the Tokugawa, he
reasoned that it was merely a matter of time before Saigo and
Komatsu would convince the *daimyo* to turn official policy against
Edo.

Ryoma and Yonosuke waited at the inn for three days, enduring the
scorching Satsuma heat, until Saigo finally returned. "Sakamoto-san,"
he said, "I've arranged for you to talk to the people at the Ministry of
the Treasury."

"Then Satsuma is going to get us a ship?" Ryoma exclaimed, clapping his hands.

"That depends on your ability to persuade. Tomorrow you can talk
to the man in charge."

That night Ryoma stayed at Saigo's home. Upon his arrival, he was
astonished at the shabbiness of the place. "So, this is where the
famous Saigo Kichinosuke lives," he thought to himself as they
passed through the dilapidated wooden gate. Indeed, the house of the
most powerful man in Satsuma was as mean as that of the most destitute of lower-samurai in Tosa, and certainly far more humble than
many of the peasants' homes Ryoma had visited. Soon Saigo's wife
served dinner, and with it three large flasks of strong white liquor
diluted in hot water. But as Saigo, despite his massive physique, rarely
drank, Ryoma consumed all three flasks by himself. After the meal
Saigo suggested that Ryoma get a good night's sleep so that he would
be prepared to negotiate with the treasury officials. "Tomorrow you
must convince them to get you a ship."

"Yes," Ryoma said, feeling the effect of the liquor, "but what about
an alliance with Choshu?"

"Ah, yes," Saigo said, averting Ryoma's hard stare, "I haven't mentioned it to Lord Hisamitsu yet."

"You haven't mentioned it?" Ryoma said irritably.

"No," Saigo said sheepishly. "You see, I've decided to wait until
Okubo returns to Kagoshima before bringing up the matter. I have a

hard time discussing things with our lord, but Okubo's different."

"I see," Ryoma muttered, a strange look on his face. Although Ryoma had heard from Kaishu of Saigo's bitter feelings for Hisamitsu (Saigo still believed that Hisamitsu had Nariakira poisoned), Saigo was, nevertheless the commander in chief of the Satsuma forces. "To repeat myself," Ryoma said, "it's an absolute necessity that Satsuma and Choshu unite against the Bakufu."

"Yes, I believe so," Saigo agreed. "But don't worry. I have the utmost of confidence that Okubo will be able to persuade Lord Hisamitsu to see things our way." The huge man spoke slowly, nodded solemnly, sincerity radiating from his dark eyes. "But what about Choshu?" he asked.

"Don't worry about Choshu," Ryoma assured with typical self-confidence. "Nakaoka Shintaro is in Choshu now to convince Katsura Kogoro and the others of the necessity of an alliance."

"I think it will take a lot more convincing in Yamaguchi than it will in Kagoshima," Saigo said. "You and I both know that Choshu detests Satsuma."

"Yes, even more than Satsuma detests Choshu," Ryoma added. "But, then again, they have more reason to."

"Perhaps so, Sakamoto-san."

"But you and I also know that with the Bakufu planning another military expedition against Choshu, Choshu needs Western-style warships, cannon and rifles more than anything in this world."

"Even more than they need to hate Satsuma?" Saigo asked, an impetuous look on his large face.

"Yes," Ryoma replied emphatically. "But we also know that the Bakufu has blocked all of Choshu's attempts to purchase such weapons from the foreign traders in Nagasaki."

"What are you suggesting?" Saigo asked.

"Don't you see?" Ryoma slapped his knee. "This is how I intend to convince Choshu to form an alliance with Satsuma."

"A brilliant plan," Saigo agreed, and despite the bad taste in his mouth brought on by Ryoma's suggestion that Satsuma purchase weapons for Choshu, the great man was unable to suppress a wide smile. "Komatsu and I will discuss the matter of an alliance with the *daimyo* as soon as Okubo returns. You have my word." Ryoma sensed from the sincerity radiating from Saigo's shining black eyes that this man would never make a promise without carrying it through. "But now, we should sleep," Saigo said.

Ryoma only nodded, stood up and went to the next room, where Saigo's wife had laid out bedding for him. Despite the great amount of liquor he had consumed that evening his mind was clear, and preoccupied with the meeting he would have with the Satsuma officials on the next day. Unable to sleep, he overheard a conversation coming from the darkness of the next room.

"The roof of our house is so badly weathered that it leaks whenever it rains," Saigo's wife said in a low voice. "I feel so ashamed when we have guests. Do you think you could fix it before long?"

"Right now," answered a deep voice, "all of Japan is leaking from the rain. I have no time to spend fixing our house alone."

Although the magnanimity of the great man struck Ryoma to the heart as he lay alone in the darkness, he could not help but laugh at the notion of this leader of armies laying in bed with his wife discussing a leaky roof.

Before leaving home at dawn the next morning, Saigo instructed his wife to have Ryoma wait until he would return later in the day.

"I've spent more time over the past six months waiting for Saigo than doing anything else," Ryoma told himself after several hours, and instead decided to put his time to use repairing the leaky roof of the house. When Saigo's wife found her guest climbing down from the roof, his face and clothes black from the ubiquitous volcanic ash of Sakurajima, she suggested he take a bath.

Ryoma declined. "But if Saigo-san has some extra underwear, I'll take it," he said. "The oldest underwear he has will be fine. I haven't changed mine in weeks."

"I see," Saigo's wife answered, before hurrying into the house and returning with her husband's oldest underwear. When Saigo returned, his wife told him that Ryoma had repaired the roof. "But he refused to bathe," she said, grimacing. "So when he asked me if he could have some of your underwear, I gave him the oldest you have."

"You what?" Saigo exploded angrily.

"But he asked me for..."

"I don't care what he asked you for," Saigo boomed. "Don't you know that Sakamoto Ryoma is risking his life daily for Japan? Go and find the best underwear I have, and give it to him right away, along with anything else he wants."

Later, Saigo brought Ryoma to the home of Komatsu Tatewaki, a stately mansion overlooking the bay, where he met a high-ranking official from the Ministry of the Treasury, and other influential men of Satsuma. Here, Ryoma negotiated for permission to lease a ship, summoning all of his powers of persuasion to convince Satsuma to sponsor him and his men so that they would be able to establish a shipping agency.

"In times of peace we would transport merchandise between Nagasaki, Osaka and Shanghai," Ryoma proposed. "Since Satsuma would be our sponsor, we would share the profits with your *han*. We would set up headquarters in Nagasaki, and in times of war Satsuma could use us as an auxiliary navy. As you have probably heard, all of us have been trained by Katsu Kaishu himself," Ryoma did not neglect to add, and with this use of the name of the former commissioner of the Tokugawa Navy, the Satsuma men seemed all but persuaded.

"But what if the Bakufu should find out that Satsuma is doing business with foreigners?" one of them asked. In order to protect its monopoly on foreign commerce, Edo prohibited any of the clans to trade with foreigners.

"That would be no problem for Satsuma," Ryoma assured. "Since our company would be run by *ronin*, the blame would fall on us."

Ryoma greatly impressed the Satsuma officials, who promised to procure a ship for him, although they would not say exactly when. After the officials left, however, Komatsu returned with some definite news. "Sakamoto-san," he said, his face alight with a smile, "I'm leaving for Nagasaki soon to purchase a new steamship for our *han*."

"Then you can lease it to us?" Ryoma said excitedly.

"Unfortunately, that would be impossible," Komatsu replied grimly. "It's to be used exclusively for training our men. But you must have made a good impression on the people from the Treasury Ministry because I have just received word that each of your men will be receiving a monthly wage of three and a half *ryo* from Satsuma."

"For doing what? We don't have a ship."

"To establish a shipping company in Nagasaki," Komatsu said. "We would like your men to sail our new steamship from Nagasaki to Kagoshima. But have patience. You'll get your own ship soon enough. I wasn't going to mention it to you because it's not definite yet, but we also have a schooner anchored in Nagasaki which we have recently bought from a Scottish merchant by the name of Glover."

"Then we can use it?" Ryoma said.

"I think so. But it's not a steamer. It's just a sailing ship, and quite old."

"So what! It's a start. Anyway, we're in no position to be particular."

"Yes," Komatsu agreed, apparently relieved. "As I said, I'll be leaving for Nagasaki soon. I would like you and your men to join me."

"Fine!" Ryoma clapped his hands at the very real prospect of finally commanding his own ship.

Ryoma returned to the *Butterfly*, where the others were waiting for him. After informing them that Satsuma had all but officially quit the expedition against Choshu, and that Saigo was only waiting for Okubo's return to convince the *daimyo* of the necessity of an alliance, Ryoma told them about Komatsu's offer. "So now I want you to go to Nagasaki with Komatsu," he said.

"To do what?" Chojiro asked.

"To set up a company! Just what Kawada Shoryo has always talked about." Ryoma looked hard at the bean jam bun maker's son who, along with Umanosuke, had studied under the progressive thinker of Western ideas several years before in Kochi. Ryoma looked around at all six men. "What do you think I've been telling you for these past two years? And most importantly, why do you think Katsu-sensei spent so much time and effort teaching us to operate a steamship?"

"To form a navy," Toranosuke said.

"Yes, and now we're finally going to do just that in Nagasaki," Ryoma said.

"But," Sonojo said, "I thought you just said we were going to start a company in Nagasaki."

"We are! A shipping company! A shipping company that's also a navy!"

"Won't you be coming with us?" Yonosuke asked Ryoma.

"Not right away. Now that I've convinced Saigo to unite with Choshu, I have to go to Shimonoseki to see Katsura to convince him to unite with Satsuma. But in order to do that, first I have to go to Dazaifu in northern Kyushu to convince the Five Banished Nobles of the absolute necessity of an alliance."

Suddenly Yonosuke burst out laughing.

"What's so funny?" Ryoma growled.

"I'm sorry," Yonosuke said, "but it's just that I don't think you ought to visit nobles of the Imperial Court looking like that." While all six of Ryoma's men wore old clothes, none of them were as innately sloppy as Ryoma, whose kimono, as usual, was badly worn, the cuffs frayed, his face dirty and hair tangled.

"What do you mean?" Ryoma feigned indignation.

"Wouldn't it be disrespectful to the Emperor to visit His representatives in anything but clean, formal dress?" Yonosuke said in his typical monotone, the humor gone from his voice.

"Yonosuke," Ryoma said sharply, "we've spent a lot of time together over these past two years, right."

"Yes."

"All of us have, right." Ryoma eyed each man individually, drawing nods from all of them.

"Well, then," he cast a diabolic look at Yonosuke, "you ought to know me well enough by now to realize that appearance is the least of my concerns." Ryoma paused, took a deep breath. "When the very fate of our nation is at stake, who gives a damn about the way one lousy *ronin* looks? Certainly not anybody of consequence, least of all the Five Banished Nobles, I'm sure."

"Of course," Yonosuke said apologetically.

"So," Ryoma continued, "while I'm in Dazaifu and Shimonoseki, I want you to go to Nagasaki and find a place in the hills overlooking the harbor where we can set up headquarters, from where we will unite Choshu and Satsuma to overthrow the Bakufu."

*   *   *

Ryoma and his men set sail on the *Butterfly* on the hot drizzly morning of May 16, accompanied by Komatsu and several other Satsuma men. The steamer was bound for Nagasaki, but Ryoma's immediate destination was just east of there in Kumamoto Han, where he would visit Yokoi Shonan, still under house confinement in his native village. From here, he would travel on foot to Dazaifu, in northern Kyushu, to speak with the Five Banished Nobles. Meanwhile, the other six men would do as Ryoma had instructed: go to Nagasaki with Komatsu to find a suitable place to set up headquarters for a shipping company, to be sponsored by Satsuma, then sail the Satsuma steamer back to Kagoshima.

On the afternoon of May 17, Ryoma disembarked at the Satsuma town of Akune, on the coast of the East China Sea, followed the coastal route northward, until reaching Kumamoto two days later. With the five volcanic peaks of Mount Aso looming in the distance, he walked northeastward, until arriving at Yokoi's native village of Nuyamazu early that afternoon. The rainy season had already reached central Kyushu, and much of Nuyamazu had become a marsh, surrounded as it was for miles by nothing but rice paddies and fields, so that the humidity seemed unbearable.

Ryoma increased his pace when he spotted the little man whom Katsu Kaishu called *"as frightening as Saigo"* for his *"intellect unmatched by anyone in Japan,"* fishing in the stream that flowed past his house. Yokoi, who now wore a long gray beard, was standing knee-deep in the shallows heavily grown with duckweed, a bamboo fishing pole in his right hand.

"What do you catch around here?" Ryoma asked as nonchalantly as if it hadn't been a whole year since he had last seen Yokoi.

"Sweet smelt and dace." The tip of the pole bent slightly. "Got another one. It looks like we'll have some fresh fish this afternoon." Then roaring with laughter, "Let's go into the house, Ryoma," he said, before swatting a particularly large mosquito on the back of his neck. "Damn pests! They'll eat a man alive during this time of year. But it certainly is good to see you."

Ryoma, in fact, looked a perfect mess. He wore a kimono of thin white linen which had been so badly soiled that its dark blue splashed pattern was hard to distinguish from the grime he had picked up during his journey. He did, however, wear both long and short swords at his hip. He had received the kimono and the swords before leaving Kagoshima–gifts from Okubo Ichizo, who had instructed Saigo to pass them on to Ryoma in his absence. Okubo shared the same concern for Ryoma's appearance as did Yonosuke, although certainly for quite different reasons. *"We can't have him looking as sloppy as he usually does when he meets the Five Banished Nobles,"* Okubo had written Saigo in a letter from Kyoto. *"Especially since he will have been coming directly from our han."*

"I've just come from Kagoshima," Ryoma said, as the two entered the house. Ryoma disclosed to Yokoi his plans to establish a shipping company in Nagasaki, through which he would run guns to Choshu after uniting that *han* with Satsuma.

"And you actually believe you can accomplish such a feat?" Yokoi said.

"We must. It's our only chance. Besides, I've already convinced Saigo." As usual, Ryoma spoke slowly, but in an uncharacteristically melancholy tone, as if he momentarily disdained the Herculean task that fate had dealt him. His mood changed, however, when Yokoi's wife appeared with a tray of grilled dace, and a flask of white liquor.

"What do you think about the pressure the foreigners are putting on the Bakufu to open the Port of Kobe to foreign trade?" Yokoi asked, filling Ryoma's cup.

"Foreign trade is a must," Ryoma replied without hesitation, and just as deliberately drained his cup, grabbed a single chopstick and speared one of the small fish. "But Kobe must only be opened under terms favorable to Japan, not the Tokugawa," he said, devouring the head of the fish in one mouthful. "If it should be opened to foreign trade under the conditions of the present monopoly, the only one to prosper would be the House of Tokugawa, while the rest of us, particularly Satsuma and Choshu, would suffer."

Yokoi's eyes flashed indignation. "The Inland Sea must remain closed to the barbarians," he said. It was on matters concerning Kyoto that this enlightened thinker lagged as far behind Ryoma as the most ignorant of court nobles. "For the time being, that is," Yokoi added in a softer tone. "Unlike Yokohama and Nagasaki, Kobe is just too close to Kyoto for us to allow the foreigners free movement in that port. We are not ready for them yet." Although Yokoi–like the other three members of the Group of Four–had long been a staunch proponent of opening Japan, he was as fanatic about protecting the sacred Emperor as were the xenophobes of Tosa and Choshu. "And so," Yokoi concluded, "we must develop our military."

"That's how my navy will be of use," Ryoma said. "We'll be prepared to fight while we conduct trade. But first we must unite Choshu and Satsuma."

"We?" Yokoi asked.

"Yes. There's another man from Tosa who's working with me. His name is Nakaoka Shintaro. In fact, he should be in Shimonoseki right now talking to the Choshu men." Although Ryoma was correct about his new partner's intent and actions, chronologically he was mistaken. It was true that Nakaoka had recently been to Shimonoseki to discuss an alliance with Katsura, but what Ryoma did not know was that at this very moment Nakaoka was at Satsuma headquarters in Kyoto making plans to accompany Saigo from Kagoshima to Kyoto, via Shimonoseki, where Nakaoka would arrange a meeting between Saigo and Katsura, to break the ice between the two enemies. The Shogun had just left Edo for Kyoto, where he was to report to the Emperor his reasons for the second expedition against Choshu. With an attack impending, the Satsuma men were now determined to strengthen their opposition, because, as Saigo had long maintained, a defeated Choshu would only enhance the power which Edo had recently regained, much to the detriment of Satsuma. For this, the Satsuma men reasoned, the presence in Kyoto of their commander in chief would be vital.

"When you say that you'll be prepared to fight," Yokoi said, a worried look in his sagacious eyes, "do you mean against the barbarians?"

"If necessary. But more than likely against the Bakufu. I'd rather buy weapons from the barbarians," Ryoma snickered, "than fight them."

Yokoi stared hard at Ryoma, not a little awed by the ominous portent of the young man's words. "Tell me, what is your impression of Saigo? Is he as great a man as I hear?"

"Saigo's definitely not the simpleminded man he makes himself out to be. In fact, he's one of the sharpest men I've ever known. And as for his sincerity, I trust him completely."

"That's quite an appraisal!" Yokoi said, thoughtfully stroking his gray whiskers. "And what about me, Ryoma? How do I fit into the greater scheme of things? You know I've been stuck here for well over a year now, unable to do a thing to help our nation."

"You've already contributed more than a thousand men could ever hope to," Ryoma said. "You should relax, while men like Saigo and Okubo act out the remainder of this play? If they should get stuck in the mud," Ryoma now laughed, "you can always direct them back to their proper course." Ryoma knew well the invaluable role that the brilliant mind of Yokoi Shonan had played thus far in the impetuous drama of these most turbulent times in Japanese history.

The older man also laughed, but not without an air of sadness in his eyes. "You have a way with words, Ryoma," he said with a nod. "And I believe you are right."

Ryoma reached Dazaifu in Fukuoka on May 23. The Five Banished Nobles, he reasoned, would surely have a personal interest in seeing Satsuma and Choshu unite. Not only was Choshu the most dedicated to *Imperial Loyalism* of all the clans, but it had saved the radical nobles from whatever fate the Bakufu might have had in store for them, both after Choshu's defeat at the Forbidden Gates in August and its surrender to the Tokugawa forces in December. Furthermore, the nobles had been receiving protection from Satsuma since the surrender, and although Satsuma troops had been greatly responsible for their expulsion from Kyoto, it was Saigo himself who arranged for their safe refuge at a Shinto shrine at Dazaifu, despite the Bakufu's intention to send them to Edo. Ryoma's next mission, then, was to use Satsuma's display of goodwill to urge the Five Banished Nobles to pressure Choshu into joining hands with its most bitter enemy. After all, both Satsuma and Choshu were struggling for the same goal: toppling the Bakufu and restoring the Emperor to power.

During his five-day stay at Dazaifu, the outlaw-samurai was granted several audiences with the Five Banished Nobles. *"I met with Sakamoto Ryoma of Tosa,"* one of the nobles wrote in his diary of May 25. *"He's a great man with novel ideas."* Indeed Ryoma's mission was a success, despite the misgivings of Yonosuke and Okubo concerning his shabby appearance.

A DECLARATION OF FREEDOM

The Perilous Brink of Freedom

The lower-samurai from Tosa who had sacrificed everything when he fled three years before, was now a leading figure in national politics; and although he longed to be united with his family, he never once deviated from the thorny path toward freedom. The years of forging his draconic spirit–the kendo training in Kochi and Edo; the tutoring under Kawada Shoryo and Takechi Hanpeita; the unlimited source of energy he had inherited from the cool wisdom of Katsu Kaishu; the training at the naval academy in Kobe; the knowledge and inspiration he had received through close rapport with some of the greatest men of his day, particularly the Group of Four; the loss of many of his comrades over the years during which he too had defied death–had brought the Dragon to the perilous brink of freedom, for himself, for his comrades, and for Japan.

While Ryoma was determined to topple the Bakufu and restore the Emperor to power, unlike his comrades this was not his ultimate goal. Rather, he was intent on abolishing the feudal system altogether–something he was sure neither Saigo nor Katsura would easily condone. He thought it futile to depose the military hegemony in Edo simply to replace it with an Imperial monarchy in Kyoto. Rather, his objective was the establishment of a democracy. His ideals were founded on two basic tenets of Western democracy: inalienable human rights and the free trade system, both of which were completely foreign to most of his peers. And although it is true that Ryoma intended to restore the Emperor to power, unlike his fellow Loyalists, he did not revere him as a god, but merely as a unifying force for the Japanese people, the symbol of a new Japanese nation. While Ryoma's democratic government would be centered around the Imperial Court in Kyoto, in essence it would be based on the American model. In the United States, he had learned, the leaders were elected by the people, who were guaranteed certain inalienable human rights. Without these rights–among others the freedom of action–he and his men would not be able to conduct international trade in order to strengthen the Japanese nation, both militarily and economically. Their vehicle would be their shipping company–the prototype of the Japanese corporation–that they were at this very moment establishing in Nagasaki, financed by Satsuma, but operated entirely by themselves. Ryoma, however, realized that it would be impossible for him to conduct international trade without one unified government behind him: a Satsuma-Choshu Alliance would be his first giant step toward realizing this government, the overthrow of the Bakufu the next.

Ryoma crossed Shimonoseki Strait from northern Kyushu on the first day of intercalary May. Here he received word that Katsura Kogoro, whom he desperately wanted to meet, was a half-day's journey away at the Choshu Administration Office in Yamaguchi Castletown. That night, however, Ryoma suddenly came down with a high fever, and much to his chagrin, was incapacitated.

He recovered quickly, and on the morning of his fifth day in Shimonoseki received some important news: Nakaoka and Saigo were expected to arrive in Shimonoseki any day. "A meeting between Saigo and Katsura," Ryoma thought anxiously, and it was for the purpose of such a meeting that Nakaoka was escorting the Satsuma commander in chief to Choshu. Then, on the next day, Ryoma received a message from Katsura, summoning him to the home of a friend in Shimonoseki.

Ryoma had not seen Katsura since the previous summer, but had heard that the shrewd politician was now in control of the Choshu government. Shortly after Katsura's return from exile in April, word of an impending Bakufu attack had created a new sense of unity throughout Choshu, despite the recent civil war between the revolutionaries and conservatives. Choshu was now united in its determination to defend itself: should it be defeated, the *daimyo* would be punished, the samurai lose their stipends, the stores of the merchants would be looted and the lands and crops of the peasants destroyed. But since even a united Choshu, whose army numbered only some 4,000, could not possibly resist, let alone defeat, tens of thousands of Tokugawa troops–conscripted from the armies of thirty-one clans–Katsura immediately took two measures to improve the situation. First he increased the power of the rebel faction within the Choshu government, which meant recalling from exile Takasugi, Inoue and Ito–the three new radical leaders who had recently fled to avoid assassination. And even more importantly, Katsura's second measure, which now consumed him, was to modernize the Choshu Army.

"Welcome, Sakamoto-san," Katsura said, greeting Ryoma in a drawing room, and gesturing to another man sitting with him. "I'd like you to meet Murata-sensei, who's in charge of the overall defense of Choshu." Murata Zokuro, age forty-one, had only recently risen to prominence. Unlike most of the other Loyalist leaders of Choshu, Murata was neither a disciple of Yoshida Shoin nor an outstanding patriot, but so extensive was his knowledge of Western military science, Katsura now depended on him to modernize the Choshu Army. Although Murata was drilling his troops after the fashion of the Western armies, since the majority were armed only with muskets, swords and spears, he informed Katsura that Choshu must have state-of-the-art weaponry–namely rifles, cannon and warships–to fight the Bakufu forces. He proposed that Choshu procure 10,000 modern, rapid-firing, breech-loading rifles, far superior in range and accuracy to the old-fashioned, muzzle-loading guns and muskets of the Bakufu troops. But because Tokugawa agents in Nagasaki prevented Choshu men from procuring weapons from the foreign traders there, Murata had recently traveled to Shanghai to purchase as many rifles as possible. Unfortunately, there were no breechloaders to be had in Shanghai at that time, and Murata was forced to settle for the muzzle-loading type, and several cannon. It was the dire need for modern breech-loading rifles, and the extreme difficulty in procuring them, that was consuming both Murata and Katsura when Ryoma arrived.

"Hello," Ryoma said, meeting the sullen expressions of both men with a wide grin. "It's a pleasure to meet you, Murata-san."

Murata bowed his head slightly, and returned the greeting. "We were just discussing rifles," Katsura said.

"Which you're having trouble getting," Ryoma said. Ryoma's nonchalance annoyed Murata, but his uncanny ability to read a person's mind impressed him.

Katsura cleared his throat. "Yes," he said with perfect calm. "But please sit down, and tell us what brings you to Choshu."

"How many do you think you'll need?" Ryoma asked in the same nonchalant tone, though well aware that the question was of utmost importance to both men.

"How many what?" Katsura feigned ignorance.

"Breech-loading rifles, of course. You don't think you can defeat the Bakufu troops with those old-fashioned, muzzle-loading rifles you have now, do you? You can fire ten shots with a breechloader in the same time it takes to fire one shot with the others. That would be like increasing the number of your troops tenfold." Ryoma stopped speaking, but continued to grin at the two men who he knew were far more informed in such technical matters than he himself was. "With the American Civil War over, there's a surplus of rifles in Nagasaki that the foreign traders are just dying to get rid of."

"Get rid of? Where did you get your information?" Murata asked suspiciously.

"In Kagoshima." Ryoma had recently learned from Saigo and Komatsu that, while Choshu was prohibited as an enemy of the Tokugawa from purchasing weapons in Nagasaki, such was not the case for Satsuma, which was still officially a Tokugawa ally. And as the four foreign powers–Britain, France, Holland and America–had agreed among themselves not to interfere in Japan's domestic affairs, even if foreign traders wanted to sell arms to the renegade *han*, they were prohibited by their governments from doing so. "But of course," Ryoma burst out laughing, as if to intentionally irritate, "you need the right connections."

Katsura offered Ryoma an empty cup, then filled it with *sake*. "Please elaborate," he said.

"A group of my men are in Nagasaki right now to set up headquarters for a shipping company." Ryoma drained the cup, and held it up for Katsura to refill.

"For whose benefit?" Murata asked, suspicious of Ryoma's boasting.

"Japan's," Ryoma said indignantly.

"Who's sponsoring you?"

"Satsuma."

"Satsuma!" Murata seethed, his eyes bulging.

"Yes. And," Ryoma lowered his voice, "Saigo is due to arrive in Shimonoseki any day now to talk to you."

"Saigo Kichinosuke?" Katsura sneered, suddenly losing his composure. "The commander in chief of the Satsuma armed forces. That dirty, rotten..."

"Yes," Ryoma interrupted, "Nakaoka is with him right now."

"Nakaoka with Saigo?" Katsura gasped.

"Yes, they'll be arriving together from Kagoshima to talk with you."

"About what?"

Ryoma smiled sardonically, shaking his head. "You just said you needed guns, didn't you."

"Desperately!" Katsura sat up straight, refilled Ryoma's cup. "But what does that have to do with Saigo?"

"Satsuma is ready to openly oppose the Bakufu," Ryoma said, his former grin replaced with a look of intense seriousness.

"Sakamoto-san," Katsura exploded, "you don't know what you're saying."

"Listen," Ryoma interrupted, his eyes ablaze. "If you will agree to talk to Saigo and hear what he has to say, I'm sure you'll see things differently than you do now. I've been to Kagoshima, and stayed at Saigo's home. Saigo is not the man you think he is. Trust me. Saigo has been urging Lord Hisamitsu not to participate in the expedition against Choshu. He's a man of his word, one of the most sincere I've ever met." Ryoma looked hard into Katsura's eyes. "I've just come from Dazaifu," he informed in a solemn tone. "The Five Banished Nobles agreed with me." Ryoma knew that the mere mention of these champions of *Toppling the Bakufu and Imperial Loyalism* would have a strong effect on the Choshu men.

"Agreed with you about what?" Katsura asked.

"That there must be an alliance between Choshu and Satsuma." Silence filled the void brought on by Ryoma's preposterous words.

"Sakamoto-san," Katsura gasped indignantly, "what are you saying?"

"You can't tell me that you haven't at least heard of the plan. It's been talked about in Shimonoseki all spring."

"Alright, so maybe I have heard of it. But if you really believe such an alliance is possible, you just don't understand Choshu's position. It was Satsuma who deceived the court into declaring our *han* an 'Imperial Enemy,' after Satsuma sided with the Tokugawa. I don't know how many Choshu men have written the words 'Satsuma bandits' on the bottoms of their sandals just for the enjoyment of walking on them every step they take. We Choshu men would prefer to die in battle against the Bakufu than to unite with Satsuma."

Ryoma groaned, wiped his nose on his sleeve. "Damn this cold," he muttered. "I can't seem to get rid of it." Giving both men a hard look, he said, "I understand how you feel. But your main concern right now is to preserve your *han* and crush the Bakufu, right?"

"Yes," Katsura answered sharply.

"Then you're going to have to forget about the past, and concentrate on the future. The only way to save Choshu from destruction, and to overthrow the Bakufu, will be for you to unite with Satsuma. And of this, I've already convinced Saigo." Ryoma paused, took a deep breath. "But I'm not only talking about Choshu and Satsuma. I'm talking about the preservation of all of Japan."

"And what about the rifles?" Murata interjected harshly.

"My company will arrange for you to buy rifles in Nagasaki under the Satsuma name," Ryoma said, perhaps stretching the truth. Although the idea of procuring weapons for Choshu to use against the Bakufu had consumed him as of late, he had only mentioned it to Saigo once. Nevertheless, he was confident in his ability to persuade; and so deep was his trust in Saigo that he was sure the great man would support his scheme. "We'll even deliver the rifles to Shimonoseki on one of our ships," Ryoma said, as if he already had a ship at his disposal.

"Alright," Katsura said, offering his hand to Ryoma. "I'll talk with Saigo. But his visit must be kept secret. There are many in Choshu who would die a thousand deaths for a single chance to cut him. And who knows what might happen if word were to get out that I was meeting Saigo, let alone discussing the idea of an alliance with the Satsuma bandits."

Katsura and Ryoma spent the next two weeks waiting for Nakaoka and Saigo to arrive, and although the Choshu leader had no reason to hide his anxiety, the Tosa *ronin* had to force himself to act as self-confident as Katsura believed him to be. This is not to say that Ryoma ever once doubted Saigo's sincerity, but the very fact that the great man himself had never actually promised to come to Shimonoseki remained in the back of Ryoma's mind as a constant reminder that nothing was settled yet.

While waiting, Katsura was confronted with still another problem. The Lord of Uwajima, whose deceased wife was the younger sister of the Lord of Choshu, had recently sent to Yamaguchi Castle a copy of a letter he had received from Edo explaining its reasons for the planned second expedition against Choshu (This letter had been circulated among all the *daimyo*, except, of course, Choshu.) Included was an account of a meeting the Dutch Consul General had recently had in Yokohama with Bakufu officials to verify a secret report by Kokura Han, the hereditary Tokugawa clan located just across Shimonoseki Strait from Choshu. According to the Kokura report, Choshu men had been seen approaching a Dutch warship in the strait. The letter indicated that although the Consul General denied the report as groundless, he did inform the Bakufu officials that Choshu had recently been trying to smuggle some of its men out of Japan as foreign envoys, and furthermore that Choshu had opened Shimonoseki to foreign trade. Needless to say, the Choshu men were furious about this slander, which they felt might trigger a second expedition against them. When a Dutch warship carrying the Consul General happened to stop at Shimonoseki *en route* to Nagasaki, Katsura requested a meeting with the Dutchman, and asked Ryoma and Ito to accompany him.

The three samurai were met in the cabin by the Dutch Consul General and a British official, whose Smith and Wesson revolver, which he wore in a holster at his hip, immediately caught Ryoma's eye. The Europeans sat on one side of a long, polished wooden table, opposite the three Japanese. Ito, who had been to England, was to interpret for Katsura, with Ryoma present for moral support.

"Ito-san," Ryoma said before the discussion began, "ask him if he'd sell me his pistol." Ryoma smiled at the Englishman, drawing a confused look which made him wonder if the foreigner understood Japanese. Ryoma had attempted to study English at Kaishu's naval academy, but unlike Yonosuke and Sonojo, was unable to make sense out of the strange sounds.

"Later, Sakamoto-san," Katsura objected sharply. "I want to get directly to the point at hand. Ito, interpret for me." Katsura produced an English translation of the letter, and handed it to the heavyset, blue-eyed blonde man sitting opposite him. "Please read this," Katsura said.

After reading the letter, the Consul General placed it on the table, and began speaking heatedly, sweat running down his bearded face. "It's just not true! None of it. I never said anything to the Tokugawa officials to slander Choshu. It was Kokura, not the Dutch, which tried to trigger the expedition against your *han*, by fabricating a story that Choshu men had approached one of our ships off Shimonoseki."

"If that's the case," Ito said in slow, deliberate English, translating Katsura's words, "should war break out with the Bakufu, we must bring up the subject of this discussion immediately, and reprove Kokura for spreading false rumors to slander us. Would you be willing to be present at such a discussion to support us?"

"Certainly!" the Consul General affirmed, wiping his forehead with a handkerchief. Holland, like Great Britain, anticipating that the future of Japan lay in the hands of either Choshu or Satsuma, or both, wanted to maintain friendly relations with the two bitter enemies, even at the exclusion of the Tokugawa.

"Then it's settled," Katsura said, stood up, and offered the Consul General his hand. Ryoma followed suit, extending his hand to the

British official, and with a wide smile uttered with an incomprehensible pronunciation the English word "trade." As he spoke he reached for his sword, and offered it in exchange for the Smith and Wesson, at which instance the Englishman naturally stepped back and drew his revolver; but as Ryoma had still not drawn his blade, the dumbfounded Briton soon realized that this smiling samurai meant him no harm.

Ryoma broke out in laughter, and said, "Ito-san, ask him if he'll trade his pistol for my sword."

The Englishman declined Ryoma's offer, but was nevertheless impressed with this odd samurai who would trade what other men of the two-sworded class considered their soul for a Smith and Wesson.

On the following morning, a young man appeared at the waterfront mansion of a wealthy Shimonoseki merchant and Loyalist sympathizer, where Ryoma was staying. "Ike Kurata of Tosa, in command of a militia unit for the Choshu Loyalists," he introduced himself to a servant at the front door. "I'm looking for Sakamoto Ryoma."

The servant showed Kurata to Ryoma's room. "Kura!" Ryoma shouted at the sight of this old friend, and former Tosa Loyalist. "What are you doing here? What a coincidence. What a stroke of luck!" Ryoma clapped his hands ecstatically. "We haven't met in over three years, since I fled Tosa." Ryoma paused, clapped his hands again. "Sit down, and tell me about what you've been doing all this time."

As Kurata told Ryoma, with Yodo's suppression of the Tosa Loyalist Party, he, like many other Tosa men, had fled to Choshu, where he served as a staff officer in a militia unit during the attacks on foreign ships in Shimonoseki Strait. During an ill-fated Loyalist uprising in the province of Yamato near Kyoto, Kurata commanded a rifle squad in the Corps of Heaven's Revenge, barely escaping alive to Choshu's Osaka headquarters. The next summer he fought in the Corps of Loyalty and Bravery, and fled to Choshu after the defeat at the Forbidden Gates. In the following winter he saw combat again, fighting with Takasugi's Loyalists in the civil war which toppled the Choshu conservatives; and now, on official business in Shimonoseki, he chanced to meet Ryoma, who was like an older brother to him. Ryoma described the reunion in a letter to Kurata's family in Kochi: *"Kura is just fine and he looks very healthy. What is particularly admirable about him is that he did not once ask about his family, but rather spent the whole day talking about nothing else but the state of things in Japan...We promised each other not to start any more useless wars, and not to die for a stupid reason. So far, around eighty of those who have left Tosa have died in the fighting. Kura has been in battle eight or nine times, and despite all the bullets, arrows and rocks that flew around him, he hasn't once been wounded. What he's particularly proud of is the fact that he faced the enemy at a distance of about 200 feet, and despite the shells flying in all directions and the bullets whizzing all around him he stood right up and cried out his orders, his own gun smoking as he fired at the enemy artillery carriages. Most of the men hit the ground as soon as they saw the flash of the enemy guns; but Kura says that since they were at such close range, he saw no point in ducking because he knew he wouldn't be able to get out of the way of a bullet anyway. Of this he's very proud.*

"Although Kura has always been very self-assertive, and generally not well liked, it seems that a man improves when he goes to war. We had a great laugh when he told me that now everyone really likes him..."

After the two finished laughing, Ryoma told Kurata of the progress he and Nakaoka had made toward realizing an alliance between Choshu and Satsuma, then, giving Kurata a grim look, asked, "Have you heard anything about Hanpeita?"

"No. I was going to ask you the same thing."

"We've come a long way since the uprising over the deaths of the Ikeda brothers," Ryoma said, grabbing Kurata by the wrist. The unexpected meeting made him realize just how much he missed his home, family and old friends.

"We've had so many brave men from Tosa fighting for our cause," Kurata said. "So many Tosa men have died in battle, and so many have proven their courage as leaders."

"If only Lord Yodo could be convinced to give up his support for the Tokugawa," Ryoma said in an unusually melancholy tone. "If Tosa were to join forces with Satsuma and Choshu, we'd be able to avoid more useless death."

"How do you mean? Certainly there would be a war."

Ryoma snickered. "You don't think that even the Tokugawa could stand up against the combined forces of Choshu, Satsuma and Tosa, do you?"

"No."

"But forget it," Ryoma said bitterly, slowly shaking his head. "I gave up hope in Tosa three years ago. I just wish Hanpeita and the rest of those men who stayed behind had done the same. The most important thing now is to unite Choshu and Satsuma." Ryoma smiled. "Kura, it seems to me you've had enough fighting for a while. How about coming with me to Nagasaki? Sonojo, Uma, Chojiro, Tora and Taro are all there right now."

Kurata took hold of Ryoma's wrist. "You know I'll do anything for you," the younger man said.

"Good! We'll join the others in Nagasaki as soon as Shinta gets here with Saigo, which should be any day now."

Less than one week later, on the night of May 21, Nakaoka Shintaro arrived at the mansion of the Shimonoseki merchant, blatantly alone and absolutely downtrodden. "I am truly sorry," he told Katsura. "Saigo promised to come, then suddenly, three days ago..."

"Damn those scheming Satsuma bandits. They've done it again," Katsura seethed, as Ryoma, overcome by frustration, pounded his fist on the floor.

Nakaoka explained that he and Saigo had left Kagoshima aboard the *Butterfly* on May 15; three days later, as they headed east along the southern coast of Kyushu, off the province of Bungo, Saigo suddenly informed him that he wouldn't be able to stop at Shimonoseki "because of urgent business in Kyoto." Nakaoka suppressed his rage, disembarked and hired a fishing boat to take him to Shimonoseki, while Saigo continued on to the Imperial capital.

"And that was all he would tell me," Nakaoka said, half apologetically, half indignant at Saigo's behavior.

"I'll be damned," Ryoma groaned, as Katsura remained deadly silent. "Katsura-san, it's not like Saigo to..."

"Don't tell me about Saigo," Katsura interrupted sharply. "The Satsuma bandits are up to their old tricks again. If I had told our *daimyo* of my intention to meet Saigo, I'd have no choice now but to commit *seppuku*. As it is, Saigo's insult to our *han* is too much for me to bear."

"Give us one last chance to fix things," Ryoma implored. "If we fail, then I'll commit *seppuku*."

"How would Choshu benefit from the death of one *ronin* from Tosa?" Katsura snickered.

"You're right," Ryoma said. "But I'm sure Saigo had a valid reason for changing his mind. You can't let this destroy our chances, not after we've come this far. The very future of Japan is at stake."

An expression of hopelessness shrouded Katsura's face, the piercing black eyes dark against the light skin. "The only way Choshu will ever be able to trust Satsuma now is if the weapons are delivered before I meet with Saigo. Otherwise, we will never be able to forgive his insult."

"You have my word," Ryoma assured. "Leave everything to Shinta and me, promise to give us a little more time, and we'll have the guns delivered to Choshu. This I swear on my life." Ryoma grabbed the Choshu man by the wrist. "Katsura-san," he shouted, "you must trust us."

"You're right," Katsura said. "Without those weapons we don't stand a chance against the Bakufu forces."

"Shinta, let's leave for Kyoto tomorrow," Ryoma said, drawing a solemn nod from Nakaoka. "Katsura-san, we'll contact you as soon as we've seen Saigo."

"You can reach me at the administrative office in Yamaguchi," Katsura informed, before leaving the two Tosa men to themselves.

*　　　　　*　　　　　*

The two Tosa *ronin* sat brooding in a room overlooking Shimonoseki Strait, the only light from a single candle and the full moon shimmering on the still surface of the sea.

"I didn't want to mention it in front of Katsura tonight," Nakaoka broke the silence, "but I have some more bad news."

Ryoma sat up, stared hard at Nakaoka. "Hanpeita?" he said.

"Yes. Zuizan-sensei is dead. He was ordered to commit *seppuku* earlier this month." The candlelight flickered in Nakaoka's dark eyes.

"Hanpeita!" Ryoma howled, his face contorted, hot tears welling up in his eyes. "Dead! And the others?"

"Izo, Murata, Hisamatsu, Okamoto–all dead."

Ryoma had not seen Okada Izo for two years, since his sudden disappearance while serving as bodyguard to Katsu Kaishu. Abandoned by Hanpeita, Izo remained in Kyoto, but no longer able to earn a living in the name of *Heaven's Revenge*, took to the streets, robbing and murdering to support the habits of drinking and womanizing he had acquired when bounty money for assassination had been plentiful. One day in the spring of 1864–more than a year after Hanpeita and the other Tosa Loyalists had been recalled to Kochi–Izo was arrested for assaulting a man in Kyoto. In his heyday Master Zuizan's most feared hit man would have been able to cut himself out of trouble; but two years of living as a drunken outcast had shattered his nerves so badly, that his genius with a sword–the only thing that Izo had ever cherished–had been destroyed. Even his physical condition had so deteriorated that, while he retained his lean, hungry look, his eyes, which had once been as fierce as a wild animal's, were now glassy from dissipation. After being thrown into jail and ordered to identify himself, Izo gave an alias, as he was well aware that revealing his true identity would only seal his fate. But when it became apparent that he would be executed at any rate, Izo decided to at least have the honor of being sent back to Tosa to die as a samurai. Expecting that the Tokugawa authorities would shudder at the mere mention of his real name, which during Hanpeita's reign of terror in Kyoto had been synonymous with *Heaven's Revenge*, Izo was outraged when they only laughed at him. "'The Butcher' Izo," they jeered at him through the wooden grating of his jail cell. "If you're so tough, what are you doing in there?"

As Tokugawa law stipulated that any samurai arrested outside his *han* must be returned to the authorities of that domain for trial, the police notified Tosa's Kyoto headquarters. Unwilling to admit that the likes of Okada Izo was of their own *han*, the Tosa authorities denied that such a name was listed in the *han* register, leaving the Tokugawa police no choice but to treat Izo as a nonentity. His captors gave him the name "Homeless One," which they tattooed on his forehead, and banished the wretch from Kyoto.

The Tosa authorities, however, were actually elated when they heard of the arrest of the notorious killer, a prime witness in their investigation against Takechi Hanpeita. No sooner was Izo released by the Tokugawa police, than he was captured by Tosa agents, caged like a wild animal and returned to Kochi, where he too was incarcerated.

Hanpeita and several other Tosa Loyalists had been in prison since the previous September, during which time they were frequently interrogated concerning the assassination of Yoshida Toyo, among others. Lord Yodo knew that Hanpeita was responsible for the regent's death, and was intent on proving it, even at the risk of inciting a dangerous rebellion among the lower-samurai. Although Hanpeita's upper-samurai status excluded him from torture, many of his men were not so fortunate. During their interrogation they were hung upside down from the ceiling, and whipped until their flesh was shredded from the bone, or until they passed out from the pain. Nevertheless, not one of them talked, even when put in "the squeezer," a wooden vise which crushed one's legs as a juicer does pieces of well-ripened fruit. And while the horrendous screams from the torture chamber were heartrending even to the stoic sword master sitting alone in his cell, the sudden appearance of Okada Izo in the middle of June filled Hanpeita with dread.

As a megalomaniac, Hanpeita could endure his men being brutally tortured; had he merely confessed to masterminding Yoshida's assassination, Yodo would have been satisfied, and the interrogations and tortures would have ceased as surely as he would have been ordered to commit *seppuku*. Although Hanpeita was prepared to die, he was simply unable to acknowledge that the lives of all of his men were more important than his own, which he was convinced Tosa desperately needed. *"What ever happens to me alone is of no concern,"* he wrote to his wife Tomi from his prison cell. *"But as I can't help worrying about the fate of our han, I am unable to control my tears."* So inflated was his ego that, despite his resolve to die, he refused to give up hope, however dismal, of his own survival, even as the bloodcurdling screams of his men echoed throughout the prison.

Then Hanpeita's "wild dog" suddenly returned, as if from the dead to haunt his master for having abandoned him. *"If only that idiot would have done me the favor of dying,"* Hanpeita wrote. *"If Izo is tortured everything will fall apart."* The sword master was sure that Izo did not have the mental strength to withstand torture; unlike the others it would just be a matter of time before he confessed. But when Izo's turn for torture came, he showed an unexpected amount of courage, adamantly refusing to speak. Although Hanpeita did not know it, Izo's brazen stoicism was founded on his anger toward Tosa for having refused to acknowledge his existence to the Tokugawa police in Kyoto. He had been willing to die, if he could at least have his due honor of being recognized as a samurai, no matter how low his status. And so, when his torture began Izo repeated over and over the same words: "All I know is that I'm the 'Homeless One.' If you don't believe me, take a look at my forehead." But when he was eventually placed on the squeezer, the screams which echoed through the prison were the worst Hanpeita had heard thus far. "If Izo should break," he agonized alone in his cell, "then all of the torture that everyone else has endured will have been in vain. Poison is the only way to stop him."

Before his arrest, Hanpeita had asked one of his Loyalist Party members, a doctor of Western medicine, to prepare poison to be taken by any of his men should their torture become unbearable. Using his connections among the prison guards, who revered him even as he sat in his stinking cell, Hanpeita had poison sent to Izo, with a note instructing him to take it for his own good. But as Izo's outrage toward his former master outweighed even his dread of the squeezer, he ignored Hanpeita's orders.

Izo was soon overcome by the pain of the squeezer; and, in confessing to the murder of the Tosa police agent Inoue Saichiro, he was able to avenge himself on Hanpeita. For not only did Izo give the names of his three accomplices–all of whom had refused to talk–but he also divulged that they had acted under the orders of the Tosa Loyalist Party leader.

Nevertheless, Hanpeita remained firm in his refusal to admit his own guilt; for although it was true that he had ordered many assassinations, he had acted only for the good of Tosa, the Imperial Court and the Japanese nation. During his interrogation, Hanpeita questioned the judgment of the authorities, who would believe the "lies of a worm like Izo." A natural teacher, even with his hands bound, Master Zuizan espoused his own philosophy: "A person who has no sense of duty, and no sense of obligation, is inferior to an animal."

Lord Yodo was determined that his philosophical vassal should die. With the Loyalist leader alive, the danger of rebellion throughout the seven districts of his realm remained very real, "but once Hanpeita is dead," he told his two chief interrogators, Goto Shojiro and Inui Taisuke, "things will finally return to normal in Tosa." Aside from avenging Yoshida's death and restoring calm to his domain, Yodo had one other reason for wanting Hanpeita dead. So intense was this desire that the *daimyo* himself often went to the courthouse, where he would hide behind the screens and secretly listen to Hanpeita's interrogation. Although Yodo would never admit it, he suffered faint pangs of inferiority to this leader of the lower-samurai, and to nobody else in the world. Like Hanpeita's, Yodo's egotism was a form of megalomania; for one megalomaniac to slight another can be dangerous, and fatal when the one on the receiving end has it within his power to order the death of his insulter. Just before his arrest–when Hanpeita had been consumed with convincing Yodo to abandon his duty to the Tokugawa, and unite Tosa behind *Imperial Loyalism*–he dared utter to Yodo the following outrage: "My Lord, to dwell so fervently on the favor your august ancestors received from the Tokugawa almost three centuries ago, particularly now when the very future of Japan is at stake, could be likened to the idle fancy of a fool." It was this slight from a vassal, particularly one who was originally of the lower ranks, which the Lord of Tosa would never forgive.

Goto and Inui were among Yodo's new elite–young upper-samurai who had been handpicked by Yoshida Toyo. Goto, in fact, was Yoshida's nephew. Inui was the same man who had delivered to Ryoma, at the Chiba house in Edo, orders to return to Tosa. Although Inui had never been a Loyalist Party member, he was an avid Loyalist who had recently become intimate with Nakaoka Shintaro, making it difficult for him personally to interrogate the revered leader of the Tosa Loyalists. And no matter how much their lord wanted Hanpeita dead, no matter how severely they were able to interrogate the other Loyalists, not matter how strong their desire to revenge Yoshida's murder, when it came to dealing directly with Master Zuizan neither Goto nor Inui could summon the strength to treat him as a common criminal, or for that matter, as an inferior. Nor were the chief interrogators able to find confirming evidence of Hanpeita's guilt from the mere confession of Izo.

Hanpeita's interrogation sessions become more frequent after Choshu's defeat at the Forbidden Gates, which roughly coincided with Izo's confession. The news of Choshu having been branded an "Imperial Enemy," and the death of the anti-foreign Loyalist movement, left Hanpeita without hope of his own survival, as he knew that Yodo, no longer compelled to appease the radical Court nobles, now had less reason than ever to keep him alive.

One sweltering afternoon in late July Hanpeita sat in his miserable cell, drawing his self-portrait from his reflection in the water of a small basin, the only light from a single lantern. Although the bitter cold of winter had made him ill, summer was certainly the most unbearable time of year to be locked up. The wooden floor of his cell was barely large enough for him to lie prostrate; and although his wife sent his favorite foods to him daily, often he was unable to eat for the sickening stench of the latrine intensified by the stifling heat. There were no windows in the cell, the only openings being the wooden grating through which he could see his jailers. His only respite from misery were a book of ballad dramas his wife had sent, her letters and the fireflies he had received from one of the guards. Not even in sleep could Hanpeita find relief, for the jail was infested with rats. When he finally got a cat to keep the rats away, the mosquitoes wouldn't give him a moment's rest, lice and ticks tormented him, and the centipedes that occasionally fell from the ceiling made his skin crawl. Hanpeita completed his self-portrait; and although the cheeks were hollow, the hair and beard long and tattered, he was so pleased with the artistic achievement that he sent it to Tomi, along with a letter telling her *"if I should die, keep this in the house"* as a remembrance, because he now knew that death was near.

Nevertheless, Hanpeita was deeply troubled by the apparent ease with which Izo was now talking. At the end of October he wrote, *"Yesterday Izo was called to court. I'm sure that idiot was talking again."* With November came cold, sleepless nights when Hanpeita's bones would ache. *"The woman who was in the cell on the north side was tortured the night before last,"* he wrote Tomi. *"Although I could hear the sound of the jailers beating people, and the screaming, I couldn't detect the sound of a woman's voice. I thought that compared to her, a man like Izo is surely the biggest crybaby in all of Japan."* Hanpeita spent the entire winter worrying about what Izo might be telling his interrogators, until at the beginning of March, at his wit's end, he wrote a friend, asking him to prepare poisoned food, and send it to the wretch in his prison cell. Although Izo ate the food, Hanpeita's plan was thwarted by the unusually tough physical constitution of his "wild dog." The poison was simply not enough to kill Izo.

Near the end of May, Hanpeita was again interrogated, after which he wrote to his wife, *"They don't listen to a thing I say, but rather continue to insist that I'm guilty"*; and summing up his feelings, he lamented, *"Ah, what a truly despicable world this is."*

After more than a year and a half of investigation, Yodo's men were still unable to find conclusive evidence of Hanpeita's involvement in the assassination of Yoshida Toyo. One day in the first week of intercalary May, Lord Yodo stormed into the courthouse, and confronted Goto and Inui. "Hasn't he talked yet?"

"No, My Lord," one of them answered timidly.

"And you still have nothing against him?"

"Nothing conclusive."

"Order him to commit *seppuku* anyway," the *daimyo* roared, before retreating to his castle and *sake* cup.

On the morning of the fifteenth, Hanpeita was ordered to prepare himself for *seppuku*, to be performed on that very evening in the courthouse garden. His crime: "impudence toward the *daimyo*." Now that death was certain, Hanpeita was determined to die as a samurai, the culmination of a life given to practice in the way of the sword and the strict code of the warrior–in short, a life he had spent preparing for death. To the samurai, self-disembowelment was not simply an excruciating form of suicide, it was his ultimate form of expression, his opportunity to display his inner purity by exposing his very bowels, the seat of his courage, and thus create beauty through a noble death. After bathing, because, as he told his guards, "it would be unsightly to have dirt on the dead body," shaving his face and pate, meticulously oiling and combing his hair and tying his topknot, Hanpeita donned the pure white kimono, *hakama* and stiff ceremonial robe his wife had sent him, then returned to his dark, dank cell. As he silently waited to be called upon to die, his thoughts drifted to the only joy in his life–his wife Tomi. (Nevertheless, during the previous New Year's holiday, when one of the guards offered to sneak Tomi into the prison for a visit, Hanpeita refused, because it would be "*a disgrace which would continue into the future if it were to become known that my wife snuck in here to see me.*") He also thought of Sakamoto Ryoma. His feelings for his close friend, as he waited to die, came straight from the heart; and despite the difference in their ways of thinking, Hanpeita found solace in the thought that although he himself, like so many others, would not live to see the fall of the Bakufu, and the restoration of the Emperor to power, as long as men like Ryoma survived, Hanpeita himself might witness the final achievement of their goals from his place in heaven, among his ancestors. (Although Hanpeita had been kept informed about happenings in the outside, he did not know that at this very moment Ryoma was in Shimonoseki with Katsura waiting for Nakaoka to arrive from Kagoshima with Saigo.)

Hanpeita's *seppuku* was performed with the precision of a classical sculptor. He believed that there were only three proper ways to cut–one straight horizontal line, two crossing lines, or three horizontal lines. Hanpeita chose the latter, which was the least common, because it was the most difficult to perform correctly. But so weak was his physical condition after one and a half years in jail, that he doubted even his ability to walk to the courthouse garden, let alone the strength in his arms to make three horizontal slices in his belly, before his seconds would be obliged to behead him. He worried that if he should fail to perform his *seppuku* beautifully, his name might be slandered in death, and that his enemies might laugh and call him a coward who was unable to die like a samurai. He therefore informed one of the guards of his plans, making him swear to publicize his noble intent in the case that his physical strength should fail him.

At dusk Takechi Hanpeita was led to the empty, raked white sand garden in front of the courthouse, which in the darkness was illuminated by a bonfire at the center of the grounds. Hanpeita calmly took his place on two new *tatami* mats, which had been laid out at the northern corner of the garden. In front of him was an untreated, pale wooden stand, on top of which were placed a piece of clean white cotton cloth and a sheathed dagger. Earlier in the day he had chosen his two seconds, both former *kendo* students and expert swordsmen, who now stood at either side of him. Chief Interrogator Goto Shojiro walked to the platform, read in a loud clear voice the death sentence, after which Hanpeita bowed from where he sat. Glancing up at his two seconds he said in a low voice, "Thank you for your troubles," took the dagger in his hand, and drew the razor-sharp blade from the sheath. "Don't cut me until I give the command," he told them, staring hard at the dagger, as a sculptor might his chisel, then gently replaced it on the stand. He removed both arms from his white robe, baring his pale shoulders, then loosened the sash around his waist, exposing his lower abdomen, the chunk of white marble on which he would carve his masterpiece. Master Zuizan tightened his mind as he summoned all of his spiritual strength into his hands, again took up the bare dagger, wrapped the hilt with the piece of white cloth, and plunged the blade into the left side of his belly. Without uttering a sound, he sliced across to the right side, pulled out the blade for an instant, and plunged it in again, repeating the process in the opposite direction, as white turned to red. With the third slice, he released a guttural wail, his only means to summon a final burst of strength; then laying the bloody dagger at his right side, he fell forward with both hands extended straight in front of him. The next instant the seconds drew their long swords, but as Hanpeita lay keeled over, making decapitation impossible, each delivered alternate blows, piercing the heart of their beloved sword master. Takechi Hanpeita was dead at age thirty-six; and so nobly did he complete his final work of art, displaying his inner purity, that even Lord Yodo's two lieutenants witnessing the *seppuku* were left speechless.

Izo and three other lower-samurai were not so fortunate. Although Hanpeita never knew it, earlier that same day the four had been beheaded for assassinations they had committed in Kyoto, not even permitted the honor of dying as samurai. Their conviction was a result of Izo's confession; and as Izo's crimes were the gravest, his head alone was hung on the prison gate for public display.

*   *   *

The morning after Nakaoka had relayed to Ryoma the bitter tidings from home, as the two were about to leave Shimonoseki for Kyoto, a special delivery message arrived from Nagasaki. The message informed that Ryoma's men had set up company headquarters in the Kameyama Hills, to the east of the city, overlooking the bay. The financial backing for the enterprise had come from Satsuma and the Kosone family, wealthy merchants to whom Kaishu had introduced Ryoma. Although the company was still without a ship, it had been contracted to transport merchandise aboard a Satsuma steamer between Kagoshima and Nagasaki, but was waiting for instructions from Ryoma for its first "big assignment."

"This is fantastic, Shinta!" Ryoma said, handing Nakaoka the letter. "As soon as we talk to Saigo, we can get started on our first big assignment."

"Which is?" Nakaoka asked.

"Procuring weapons in Nagasaki for Choshu, and transporting them to Shimonoseki."

"I see," Nakaoka nodded approval.

"Since we're stationed in the Kameyama Hills, we'll call ourselves the Kameyama Company."

"Ryoma," Nakaoka said blankly, "just exactly what is a 'company?'"

"A company is a group of people operating a commercial enterprise for profit," Ryoma quoted Katsu Kaishu verbatim.

In the spring of 1865–when on the opposite side of the globe a great civil war had just ended, and a great American president been assassinated–a Japanese outlaw, whose dedication to freedom was no less than that of Abe Lincoln himself, had founded Japan's first modern company, staffed by a group of wanted men, perhaps the first of its kind anywhere in the world. The Kameyama Company was certainly unprecedented in Japan, in that it was established by private individuals, rather than by a single *han*–with Ryoma, Saigo, Komatsu and Kosone as its "Board of Directors." Similarly, it was the first Japanese company to be owned by more than one entity, with Satsuma Han and the Kosone family as "shareholders." Since all employees were equal, regardless of social rank, age or *han*, their duties were determined by ability alone. Ryoma, who had been the leader of these men since recruiting them for Kaishu's naval academy two and a half years before, was naturally company "President," with Sonojo "Vice President" in charge of accounting. Yonosuke, who had been Ryoma's right-hand man since the days in Kobe, was given the post "Secretary to the President," with "Chief Navigator" Toranosuke in charge of technical matters. Ryoma assigned Chojiro and Taro to the vital posts of "Chief Negotiators," and placed Umanosuke in charge of general affairs. Since it had always been Ryoma's policy that all of his men be treated equally, each one, including himself, was to receive the same monthly salary of three and a half *ryo*, with all profits divided equally.

"Once Saigo agrees to let us buy guns for Choshu under Satsuma's name," Ryoma told Nakaoka, "the alliance will be as good as sealed."

"But we must move quickly," Nakaoka replied with an ominous look in his eyes, "before the Bakufu can launch its expedition."

"We will, Shinta! We will! And once Saigo has contracted us to purchase weapons for Choshu, he'll surely be willing to allow us to buy warships for them as well." It was with such a ship–purchased with Choshu money–that Ryoma planned not only to run guns into Choshu, but to transport cargo up and down the Japanese archipelago, and with the profits develop a private navy.

After Ryoma wrote a short note to his men in Nagasaki, instructing them to prepare to procure guns for Choshu under the Satsuma name, he and Nakaoka set out for Kyoto.

When Ryoma and Nakaoka arrived at Satsuma's Kyoto headquarters on the rainy morning of June 24, Saigo was waiting for them. "I received your message," he said, his large, sullen face damp with sweat.

"As you know, we've come from Shimonoseki," Ryoma began, surprising even the stringent Nakaoka with the unusually stern look in his eyes. In fact, there were very few men who dared look at Saigo the Great the way that Ryoma looked at him now. "Whatever reason you might have had for not coming to Shimonoseki and talking to Katsura is your business. Although I will say, you nearly ruined everything. It was all Shinta and I could do to convince Katsura to give us one last chance to persuade you to speak with him. But now he insists that Satsuma help Choshu procure guns from foreign traders in Nagasaki before he meets you."

"I see." The huge man gave Ryoma a sheepish look, like that of a child being scolded. "For your information," Saigo paused, shooting a hard glance at Nakaoka, "when I received a message from Okubo on our way to Shimonoseki, I had no choice but to come directly to Kyoto to convince the Imperial Court not to issue a decree for a second expedition against Choshu."

"And what was the outcome?" Nakaoka asked sharply.

"I haven't heard yet," Saigo groaned. "After all, Choshu has been declared an 'Imperial Enemy.'"

The Tosa men stared hard at the commander in chief of the Satsuma forces. "I see," Ryoma groaned, giving Nakaoka a sideways glance. "Even so, Katsura will need the guns before Satsuma can gain his, and Choshu's, trust." Ryoma paused, then added encouragingly, "The Choshu men need proof of Satsuma's goodwill."

Saigo groaned heavily, was about to speak, when Ryoma interrupted: "And I don't blame them at all."

"I see." Saigo nodded his heavy head, the wide chin nearly touching the base of the stout neck. "Exactly what is it that they want?" he asked, fanning his sweaty face, his black-diamond eyes focused hard on Ryoma's.

"Breech-loading rifles, ammunition and warships."

"I can guarantee right now that we can help them purchase the guns and the ammunition, but as for warships, I'll need more time."

"Time!" Nakaoka exploded violently. "We don't have anymore time. If the Bakufu should start moving on Choshu before it has those weapons..."

"Fine!" Ryoma interrupted, confident that once Saigo had made a promise not even the fear of death could make him break it. Turning to Nakaoka, Ryoma said with a casual grin, "Just like I told you, Shinta. Saigo-san is on our side."

"And it's a good thing," Nakaoka added with an eerie smile, "because I was ready to cut that big belly of yours, Saigo-san, if you didn't agree to at least help us get the guns." Although Nakaoka spoke as if in jest, Saigo, and Ryoma, sensed sincerity in his eyes.

"Saigo-san," Ryoma immediately changed the subject, exaggerating his laughter, "the Kameyama Company will handle everything. I'll leave right away to inform Katsura of your promise, and to set up a meeting between the two of you." Neither Nakaoka nor Saigo had ever seen Ryoma speak with such urgency. "Like Shinta just said, we have no time to waste."

*　　　　　　*　　　　　　*

"My main partners are Umanosuke, Chojiro and Takamatsu Taro.

Mochizuki (Kameyata) *is dead. I have these men and others....in Nagasaki now, getting some good training. As for myself, I travel alone quite a lot...I'm in Kyoto right now, but in five or six days I plan to head west again. Only a real idiot would waste his time in a place like Tosa, without any ambition at all.*

"If you have anything to send me, send it to the Teradaya in Fushimi, at the Horai bridge...near the Satsuma estate. The Teradaya is an inn, where I feel just as much at home as I do when I'm at Takamatsu Junzo's (Taro's father, and Ryoma's brother-in-law) *house; in fact they even treat me better at the Teradaya."*

Ryoma stopped writing this letter to his family, wiped the black Chinese ink from his brush onto his cotton robe, lay the brush on the low wooden desk in his second-story room at the Teradaya, which the proprietress Otose now reserved solely for him. He had written enough for now; besides, his attentions were diverted by the girl who lay sleeping under the bedding beside him on this pleasantly cool, still night in early September. He had never felt this way for a woman before; part of him regretted ever having met her that day, over a year ago, in Osaka. He had tried to repress his desire for her. "Much easier to merely buy a girl, and be done with her," he had repeatedly told himself. "As it is, I can barely find enough time to do what I must, let alone give myself up to a woman." Indeed, Ryoma had been so busy, that until recently he had not had time to see her at all, and had felt confident that he had finally gotten over her. When he had come again, however, to the Teradaya in June, after leaving Saigo in Kyoto, there she was, the same pretty face that had enchanted him on that day he found her fighting with the two thugs in Osaka. It was as if she had been waiting for him just as he had left her at the Teradaya one year before, after Choshu's defeat at the Forbidden Gates. And now, he knew that he must have her. "Strange," he thought to himself, "I never thought I'd feel this way about anyone."

"Oryo," Ryoma whispered, gently placing his hand on her face, the skin like soft white silk in the dim candlelight. "I'll be leaving for Satsuma's Osaka headquarters in the morning." He blew out the candle, as the pleasant fragrance of slow-burning incense from a mosquito coil mixed with the fresh scent of the girl's body.

"It's too dangerous for you to be traveling alone. The Shinsengumi..."

Ryoma placed his hand gently over the girl's mouth. "Not even the *ronin*-hunters would have the nerve to arrest me," he snickered. "I have papers from Saigo identifying me as a Satsuma samurai. And everyone knows that Satsuma is one of the Bakufu's most important allies." Ryoma burst out laughing at the irony of the situation: over the past year–since Kaishu had been recalled to Edo and his naval academy had been closed down for harboring a band of rebels–not only had Satsuma secretly turned against the Tokugawa, but thanks to the mediation of the same band of rebels, i.e., the Kameyama Company, over this past summer, a Satsuma-Choshu Alliance seemed ever so close to being realized. "Besides," Ryoma told Oryo, "I have to get back down to Shimonoseki before long, and if all goes smoothly, on to Nagasaki." Although Ryoma had been too busy to even once get to Kameyama Company headquarters, as Chojiro had written him, it was set up in an old ceramics warehouse overlooking the Port of Nagasaki, near the Satsuma trading station. The first "big assignment" Ryoma had given his men was the procurement of weapons for Choshu, under the Satsuma name, from foreign traders in the Tokugawa-administered Port of Nagasaki, then transporting those weapons to Shimonoseki aboard a Satsuma steamer. The entire operation, Ryoma stressed, had to be conducted discretely, not only to avoid implicating Satsuma–which needed to ostensibly maintain its Tokugawa alliance–but also so that the Bakufu would remain unaware of Choshu's newfound military power.

Upon getting Saigo's approval, Ryoma had immediately sent a message to Katsura at Yamaguchi Castle, informing him of such. When a reply came telling Ryoma that Katsura was sending Ito and Inoue to Nagasaki to represent Choshu in the purchase of foreign weapons, Ryoma sent a message to Chojiro, allotting him the responsibility of seeing the deal through. Ryoma chose Chojiro for the job, which would encompass dealing directly with foreign traders, not only because Kawada Shoryo's former student could speak both English and Dutch, but because of his extensive knowledge of Western culture.

Soon after the arrival of the Choshu envoys at Kameyama Company headquarters near the end of July, Chojiro suggested that one of them go to Kagoshima. "Kagoshima!" Ito blurted, looking at Chojiro as if he were out of his mind. "That would be suicide."

"Don't you see?" Chojiro said. "By making the trip, you could kill two birds with one stone." He explained to the Choshu men that by going to Kagoshima, not only might they be able to reconcile the bad blood between Choshu and Satsuma, but they might even be able to

THE PERILOUS BRINK OF FREEDOM

negotiate the use of the Satsuma name in purchasing a warship, in addition to the rifles and ammunition Saigo had already promised. "Komatsu will be sailing from Nagasaki in just a few days," Chojiro informed. "I'll handle everything, if you agree to go."

The Choshu envoys agreed, and Chojiro brought them to the nearby Satsuma trading station to meet Komatsu, who was about to return to Kagoshima aboard a new steamer he had just purchased from a foreign firm in Nagasaki. "Komatsu-san," Chojiro said after introducing Ito and Inoue, "Choshu would like to formally thank your *han* for the cooperation you have promised. Inoue-san would like to accompany you to Kagoshima for that purpose." To the great surprise of the Choshu men, Komatsu readily agreed, and Inoue, with Chojiro, accompanied the Satsuma councilor on his return journey.

Soon after, Taro arranged for a meeting between Ito, who remained in Nagasaki, and the Scottish arms merchant, Thomas Glover, dubbed the "Merchant of Death" for the weapons his Nagasaki trading firm, Glover and Company, supplied to the anti-Tokugawa clans. *"Of all those in rebellion against the Tokugawa government,"* Glover would later write, *"I felt that I was the greatest rebel."* The Scotsman agreed to sell to the Kameyama Company 7,300 rifles. Forty-three hundred of these were rapid-firing breechloaders, weapons which had been used in the American Civil War, and with which Choshu planned to challenge the Tokugawa armies. These rifles alone cost Choshu 77,400 gold *ryo*, the 3,000 old-fashioned muzzle-loaders 15,000 *ryo*.

Inoue did not fare quite so well in Kagoshima. Although through Chojiro's mediation he did have several meetings with the Satsuma elite, and so succeeded in warming relations between the two clans, Satsuma was not ready to go so far as to offer its good name for the purchase of a warship for its erstwhile enemy. But when word reached Chojiro and Inoue in Kagoshima that there were over 7,000 rifles in a Nagasaki warehouse waiting to be shipped to Choshu, they returned immediately to Kameyama Company headquarters aboard the *Butterfly*, with permission to use that ship to transport the weapons to Shimonoseki. By the end of August, not only had Ryoma's shipping company completed its first "big assignment," receiving in return a sizable handling fee, but most importantly it had brought Satsuma and Choshu one step further toward an alliance, while secretly arming the latter for war against the Bakufu.

It was no wonder that Ryoma was pleased with things as he lay next to Oryo, who was sound asleep, his mind drifting between his family in Kochi and his company in Nagasaki. "That's it!" he muttered, relit the candle with the burning mosquito coil, picked up his brush, and addressed the next part of the letter specifically to his sister Otome.

"*Although I know it's a bother, I have a favor to ask of you. The last time I was home, there was a box of books in the closet on the west side of the sitting room, including about ten volumes on Ogasawara Style etiquette, the covers of which were yellowed with age. Each of these volumes is only about three to six milliliters thick. Recently somebody has been asking me to get a hold of some books on etiquette, but since I can't seem to find any, I'd like to have those Ogasawara books. Be sure not to ignore this request just because you think it's too much of a bother.*"

Ryoma stopped writing, recalling his sister's penchant for the arts, and her abhorrence for cooking and housework. Next he described a certain Kyoto family, whose deceased father had been a physician and friend of famous Imperial Loyalists who had lost their lives in Kyoto. "*This was a good family. The oldest daughter is trained in flower arrangement, incense, the tea ceremony, and so on, but she can't cook at all.*" Ryoma paused to snicker, then, determined that Otome should like Oryo, dabbed his brush into the ink, and continued by boasting of Oryo's courage, how she had sold her kimono to raise traveling money to go to Osaka, and how she had threatened the thugs who had deceived her family, daring them to kill her, all the while screaming at them violently, demanding that they release her sister.

"*The girl I've been talking about is really an amazing girl. She plays the moon guitar, and doesn't have to struggle any more to get by. I have helped her youngest sister and five-year-old brother by finding places for them to live...I would really like to help this girl all I can. And she is very anxious to meet you, Otome, just as if you were her own sister. So, as you can see, you have become quite famous. In fact, you have a reputation for being even tougher than Ryoma.*"

Ryoma stopped writing. "I suppose I've flattered her enough," he thought, laughed to himself, returned his brush to the paper and got to the point. "*I would appreciate it if you could send something—a kimono or a sash—for this girl, along with the books I've asked you for. Her name is Ryo, like mine.*"

Ryoma felt suddenly exhausted. He signed his name to the letter, then lay down next to Oryo. The warmth of her body, the fragrance of her breath, made him feel better than he could remember ever having felt before. But the next thing he knew, it was the beginning of another day in these very troubled times, and he would have to leave Oryo to go to Osaka, to see the man in whose hands the very future of Japan seemed to rest.

Despite Satsuma's open opposition to a second expedition against Choshu, the orders had been given for thirty-one clans to dispatch armies to western Honshu–mostly the Kyoto-Osaka area–for an impending attack; and though Satsuma had no intention of taking part in the fighting, for the time being it had no choice but to feign obedience.

The Shogun–and most of his highest-ranking advisors–had been in the Kyoto-Osaka area since May to take command of Bakufu troops, and to rally Imperial support. There were three reasons, the Bakufu had told the Court, that Choshu must be punished: the revival of its hostility toward Edo; its illegal purchase of weapons from foreign merchants; its smuggling of samurai out of Japan. And while Edo suspected Choshu's attempt to buy foreign arms, it was unaware that the rebels had actually procured breech-loading rifles under the Satsuma name. But as the Bakufu lacked both the funds for war and moral support among many of the clans–not the least of which was Satsuma–it preferred to avoid fighting, if this could be done while maintaining an air of authority.

Although at one time the Bakufu only possessed 20,000 *ryo* in its treasury, the maintenance of its armies cost 180,000 *ryo* per month, which meant it had already spent some 2,000,000 *ryo* since the first expedition against Choshu hand been announced. To raise this enormous sum, the Bakufu had borrowed from Osaka merchants and various clans. Even worse than its financial straits, however, were the inferior weaponry and deteriorating morale of its troops. With the exception of the troops of Kii Han, the native domain of the present Shogun, the Bakufu armies were armed with old-fashioned guns, which would be no match for the rapid-firing breech-loaders of Choshu. And as Kondo Isami, commander of the Shinsengumi, had reported, not a few of the Tokugawa samurai sent to western Japan passed their time buying souvenirs to take back to Edo, and could think of nothing but the day they would return. Kondo recommended that since there was little hope of victory if war should break out, any sign of submission on Choshu's part should be accepted without further question. But when the Bakufu summoned the Choshu *daimyo* to Osaka to apologize for his clan's actions, he refused, and the Shogun had no choice but to go ahead with his original battle plans, unaware, of course, of Choshu's newfound military might.

The Lord of Choshu, in fact, had already issued orders for the people throughout his realm–commoners and samurai alike–to prepare for all-out war; and Ryoma had been very impressed with what he had seen while in Choshu earlier in the year, even before Choshu had acquired the superior guns. *"Choshu is putting everything into the training of its troops,"* he wrote to his family. *"Since April they have been drilling from around six to ten every morning. It's the same all over Choshu. Each of their battalions is made up of between three and four hundred men, with a general staff officer in command. The battalions in every district, every village, drill each morning. There is nothing like it anywhere else in Japan. No matter where you go in Choshu–the mountains, the rivers, the valleys–you are bound to come across fortifications, and there are land mines planted on most of the main roads....Choshu is certainly at the forefront of Western artillery."*

Nakaoka Shintaro reported similar circumstances in a letter to his comrades in Tosa: *"Choshu policy has been stabilized, the government has been reformed, and the people are resolved to fight to the death. In this state the samurai spirit thrives, the preparation of weapons increases daily, and words have been replaced by deeds. In every way the forces of the han have been renewed; only battalions of rifles and cannon exist...In every respect the military system has been reformed. Cavalry units also flourish. Within this han great maneuvers are carried out; in one day as many as forty-six battalions may practice gunnery without stopping. Truly, Choshu's forces are unsurpassed."*

Saigo was anxiously waiting for Ryoma when the latter arrived at Satsuma's Osaka headquarters.

"How many Satsuma troops are stationed in Osaka and Kyoto right now?" Ryoma asked, as the two men sat in Saigo's private quarters.

"With Bakufu orders issued to prepare for the second expedition," Saigo snickered, "thousands. But, of course, we won't be fighting." The large man paused, then laughed. "Against Choshu, that is."

"Do you have enough provisions here to feed all of them?" Ryoma asked.

"I've been very concerned about that." Saigo said uncomfortably. "Why do you ask?"

"What do they eat everyday?" Ryoma answered with another question, cleaning his teeth with his forefinger, then wiping it on his sleeve.

"The same as always."

"You mean sweet potatoes?" Ryoma grimaced, then released a loud guffaw. "Only country bumpkins eat potatoes instead of rice in the Imperial capital. Aren't you concerned about the morale of your troops?"

Saigo stared hard at Ryoma, unsure whether to appreciate or loathe the advice. After all, the sweet potato was the staple in Satsuma, where the warm climate and mountainous terrain made the cultivation of rice difficult. "Of course I'm concerned about the morale of my troops, but..."

"Saigo-san," Ryoma interrupted, putting his arm around the huge man's shoulders, "don't you think they deserve rice? And don't you think you ought to have a surplus of rice in Kyoto in case of war? Not only would it help their morale, but this is the Imperial capital, not Kagoshima. And nobody lives on sweet potatoes in the..."

"I get your point," Saigo interrupted, a bit annoyed, but nevertheless impressed with Ryoma's sense for practical matters. "What do you suggest we do? Purchase rice from Choshu?" he said sarcastically.

"Great idea!" Ryoma feigned surprise, as if to give Saigo credit for the plan. "I'll leave for Shimonoseki right away to make the necessary arrangements. And I wouldn't be surprised, if Katsura offers to make a gift of the rice as a token of gratitude for Satsuma's help in procuring weapons." The timing of this last statement was perfect because Ryoma was, despite his sincerity, beginning to sound more like a rice dealer than a *Man of High Purpose*. He knew that Choshu had excess quantities of rice in its storehouses, more than it needed, while Satsuma was forever suffering from rice shortages. Certainly, he reasoned, this would further reduce tensions between the two clans, and even give Choshu the chance to save face by no longer being the sole benefactor of its renewed relationship with Satsuma. "The Kameyama Company will handle all the shipping," Ryoma added.

"I'll be sailing for Kagoshima as soon as I finish taking care of some business here in Kyoto," Saigo said. "We'll take you to Choshu."

In mid-September, just before Saigo and Ryoma were to set sail from Kobe, a squadron of nine foreign warships suddenly entered Osaka Bay, to present an ultimatum to the Shogun and his befuddled ministers at Osaka Castle.

The indemnity owed by Edo to the governments of the four foreign powers for Choshu's attack on foreign shipping was still unpaid, and the foreigners now demanded the payment in full by the end of the following year. Well aware of Edo's lack of funds, however, the foreigners offered an alternative. If Edo would agree to meet certain conditions, not only could the payment be postponed, but it would be reduced by two-thirds of the amount originally stipulated. The two biggest conditions were as follows: the Ports of Osaka and Kobe be opened to foreigners by the first of the following year; and Edo obtain Imperial sanction for the commercial treaties. When the alarmed Tokugawa officials were, as usual, unable to give an immediate answer, the foreign ministers, backed by the squadron of warships in Osaka Bay, threatened to bring their demands directly to the Emperor in Kyoto. The mere idea of such a move, which would even further diminish Tokugawa authority in the eyes of the nation and the world, caused further confusion in the Bakufu hierarchy.

Dissent within the Bakufu ensued. One faction favored opening Osaka and Kobe, with or without Imperial sanction, as the only way to dissuade the foreign delegation from forcing its way into Kyoto. On the other hand, Lord Yoshinobu, who was the Bakufu's Inspector General of the Forces to Protect the Emperor, would have nothing of the plan. Yoshinobu rightly feared that opening these ports without Imperial sanction would ignite the ire of xenophobes throughout Japan. While the Court was at first adamant in its refusal to open the ports in question (unlike the open Ports of Yokohama, Nagasaki and Hakodate, Osaka and Kobe were only a day's journey to Kyoto, which had remained closed to foreigners), Yoshinobu finally convinced the chronically xenophobic Emperor Komei that unless he sanctioned the treaties, Japan would face a war that it could not hope to win. The foreigners had scored an important victory, as not only the Bakufu, but the Imperial Court itself, officially sanctioned the opening of Japan at the beginning of October, over seven years after the first commercial treaties had been signed.

Ryoma and Saigo stood on the deck of the *Butterfly*, on the chilly morning of September 26, the sails taut against a strong wind, as the ship cut through the choppy waters of Osaka Bay. Moored in the bay were Japanese junks of various sizes, several wooden steamers flying the Tokugawa crest, but most imposingly the nine warships of the foreign squadron–five British, three French, one Dutch–their ministers still negotiating with Bakufu officials in Osaka. Ryoma squinted hard at the closest of the foreign ships, just a stone's throw away. This was a British paddle-sloop, cannon mounted along both sides, sailors in navy whites staring straight back at him. "We must get that steamer right way," he muttered aloud the same phrase he had, when on the night before Saigo had informed him, "Four days ago the Imperial Court was forced by Edo to agree to sanction the second expedition against Choshu, although Satsuma was the only *han* that dissented." On the same day that the Shogun had visited the Imperial Palace to request the sanction, Okubo had gone so far as to threaten certain Court officials that Satsuma would not obey an Imperial order to attack Choshu. Okubo had also ignored a recent proposal by Aizu to renew the Aizu-Satsuma alliance. "Don't worry," Saigo assured Ryoma now as then, "Choshu will have a steamer very soon."

Three days later Ryoma landed at Kaminoseki promontory in the southeast of Choshu, while Saigo continued on to Kagoshima. With Satsuma's recent display of goodwill toward Choshu, Ryoma had little difficulty convincing the authorities in Yamaguchi to agree to make a gift of rice to Saigo's troops in Kyoto, after, of course, he had informed them of the issuance of Imperial sanction for a Bakufu attack, and of Okubo's refusal to fight. This taken care of, Ryoma hurried to Shimonoseki, where Katsura was arranging a shipment of 2,400 bushels of rice for Satsuma. Ryoma's next plan to was urge Katsura to go to Kyoto to meet Saigo and Komatsu, who, with war imminent, would return to the Imperial capital later this month with more troops from Kagoshima. When Ryoma arrived at the mansion of the wealthy Shimonoseki merchant one afternoon in mid-October, to wait for the right time to approach Katsura, he was informed by Inoue that Choshu had purchased a warship.

"Where is it?" Ryoma was ecstatic.

"On its way here," replied Inoue, just returned from Nagasaki, where he, Ito and Chojiro had finalized a deal with Glover. "I don't believe we've ever met, Sakamoto-san." Inoue bowed, then introduced himself. He was slight of build, of light complexion, his face badly scarred from a nearly fatal attack by Choshu conservatives in the previous fall. "I can't thank you enough, on behalf of our lord and every man in our *han*, for what you and your men have done for Choshu," Inoue said. "Particularly, Kondo-san. Our lord has recently presented him with a sword as a token of his appreciation."

"Not bad for a bean jam bun maker's son," Ryoma snickered, pleased that a commoner had been thus honored by the Lord of

Choshu.

Without the services of Ryoma's Kameyama Company, Choshu would never have procured the guns and warship from Glover; and, after Ryoma, it was Kondo Chojiro who had played the most active role in realizing the deal. But despite Chojiro's ability–or perhaps because of it–he was reluctant to allot work to others if he thought he could do it himself, a trait which earned him the resentment of the entire group. Ryoma had recently received several letters from his men complaining about Chojiro. *"If you were here,"* Yonosuke had written, *"Chojiro wouldn't dare to do what he's doing now. He arranged for himself to go to Kagoshima twice, so that he could get the credit for handling the weapons deal for Choshu."* Taro had expressed similar sentiment when he wrote, *"Chojiro simply doesn't know how to work with others, and is primarily concerned with himself."* Ryoma suspected that Taro and Yonosuke, both of whom were of samurai stock, resented the fact that Chojiro had been thus honored by the Lord of Choshu. *"Since we have enough problems as it is,"* he replied, *"do your best to get along with each other until I get to Nagasaki, which will be as soon as I can."* Ryoma was consumed with the urgent business of a Satsuma-Choshu Alliance, and had no time to worry about petty squabbles among his men.

"Where's the ship now?" Ryoma asked Inoue, clapping his hands in excitement.

"In Shanghai. Glover is on his way right now to pick it up and bring it to Nagasaki. We can have it then."

"You mean you bought a ship you haven't even seen yet?"

"We saw a photograph," Inoue replied smugly. "But since we've dealt with Glover before, I assume we can trust him."

"What's the ship's name?" Ryoma asked.

"The *Union.*"

"What does 'Union' mean?" Ryoma asked.

When Inoue explained the meaning of the English word, Ryoma clapped his hands together. "Perfect!" he said. "For the union between Choshu and Satsuma."

"Ah, yes," Inoue hesitated. Despite the recent goodwill displayed by Satsuma, even Inoue himself, who had been to Kagoshima twice, had an audience with the Satsuma *daimyo*, and played a vital role in acquiring Satsuma support for Choshu, still retained feelings of mistrust for that *han*; albeit compared to most of their clansmen, he, Katsura and Ito had considerably changed their views toward

Satsuma. "Although, the *Union* is made entirely of wood," Inoue said, "with war imminent, we can't be choosy. I thought that as long as we can mount guns on it, to blow our enemies to hell, that's all that matters right now."

"Wood is fine," Ryoma said, "because there's not an iron-plated ship in the entire Tokugawa Navy."

"Here's the agreement we've drawn up with Glover," Inoue said, handing a document to Ryoma.

There were three main parts to the agreement, which Ryoma, after getting approval from Katsura, had dictated to Chojiro. The *Union* was to fly the Satsuma flag, in order to avoid trouble with Tokugawa officials in Nagasaki. The officers and the crew would consist of Kameyama Company employees, and when neither Choshu nor Satsuma needed the ship for war against the Tokugawa, Ryoma's company would have free access to it for business purposes. And so, the *Union* would actually belong to Choshu, be registered to Satsuma, and operated by the Kameyama Company, which meant that Ryoma's men finally had the use of a steamer, free of charge.

"How much did it cost?" Ryoma asked.

"Thirty-seven thousand *ryo*."

"You could buy a lot of *sake* for that amount," Ryoma said, roaring with laughter. "But considering its purpose, that's not much to pay. If we can topple the Bakufu for thirty-seven thousand *ryo*, I'd say it's a very fair price."

*   *   *

"Damn it, Katsura-san! What more do you want?" Ryoma shouted, pounding his fist on his knee, not even trying to hide his anger. His forehead was drenched with sweat, despite the cold air, which turned his hot breath white in this now familiar room in the mansion of the Shimonoseki merchant, where over the past month he had met with Katsura on several occasions, each time pleading with him to travel to Kyoto to talk with Saigo. Ryoma stood up, walked over to the window, noticed that a light snow had begun falling on the Inland Sea. "It's cold for the end of November," he muttered, wrapped his faded, black cotton jacket tightly around his chest. Ryoma turned around, looked hard at the most powerful man in Choshu Han. "Since Satsuma has done so much for Choshu, don't you think it's about time you get rid of your old attitude?"

"That's why we've agreed to send the rice," Katsura answered sharply.

"Exactly! And Saigo has expressed his gratitude for that." Ryoma sat down next to Chojiro, whom he had recently summoned, partly to avoid trouble with the rest of the men in Nagasaki, partly because he needed someone to bring the *Union* to Shimonoseki. Ryoma and Chojiro had just returned from a short trip to Kyoto, where they had informed Saigo of Choshu's agreement to provide rice for Satsuma troops, and heard from him that Edo had just issued orders to thirty-one *han*, including Satsuma, to send armies to the Choshu borders. With war imminent, Ryoma and Chojiro returned directly to Shimonoseki aboard the *Union* to meet Katsura. "Choshu has been generous in offering rice to Satsuma," Ryoma said. "Now it's time for you to go a step further and visit Saigo in Kyoto."

Katsura released a heavy sigh, nodding slowly, an unpleasant look on his face.

"And real soon!" Ryoma shouted, hitting the floor with his fist. "Because time is running out." Ryoma drained his *sake* cup, slammed it down on the tray in front of him, leaned over to reach for the flask, and poured drinks for Chojiro, Katsura and another man with a badly pockmarked face. "He's right," the man said. This was Takasugi Shinsaku, the founder of Choshu's crack Extraordinary Corps, and commander of the Loyalists in their victory against the Choshu conservatives earlier in the year. Ryoma had met Takasugi only once before, on the same evening he had first met Katsura, seven years ago, when Hanpeita had urged him to "exchange ideas with men from Choshu." So much had happened since then–for himself, Tosa, Choshu and Japan–and so many of his comrades had died, that it seemed to Ryoma a lifetime ago. At age twenty-six, Takasugi was now the most powerful military leader in Choshu. "We must put our personal feelings aside, and not be afraid to act for the future of our *han*," Takasugi said. "It's up to you, Katsura-san, to set things straight with Saigo."

Katsura smiled bitterly. "Takasugi," he snickered, "I've never heard you speak so rationally. You of all people."

"We no longer have the luxury of choice," Takasugi said. "The Bakufu forces could attack at any time." He leaned over, grabbed Katsura by the wrist. "And although we have procured another warship, that is not going to be enough to stop the entire Tokugawa Navy. As Sakamoto-san says, if we don't form an alliance with Satsuma very soon, I'm afraid we will be defeated."

Although Ryoma had managed over the past year to bring Satsuma and Choshu this close to an alliance, neither Saigo nor Katsura had been willing to approach the other. But with the unexpected support of Takasugi, Ryoma now felt that Katsura would finally give in. Ryoma was surprised at Takasugi's great influence over Katsura, who was, after all, the *de facto* leader of the Choshu government. And this despite Takasugi's reputation as an extremist, whose motto was "to think while on the run," and who had been described as "moving like a thunderbolt, with the energy of a rainstorm," while Katsura preferred careful contemplation before action.

"I've taken it upon myself to promise Saigo that you'd come to Kyoto," Ryoma suddenly informed.

"You've what?" Katsura exploded.

"Ryoma has been pushing himself to the limit," Chojiro spoke up, "running between Kagoshima, Shimonoseki and Kyoto, going without sleep, and thinking nothing of himself. In all due respect, I think it's time you made the next move."

"You don't understand." Katsura groaned, a dark expression on his face. "Neither of you do."

"What don't we understand?" Ryoma said.

"Saigo!" Katsura hissed. "He's the one who went back on his word by not stopping here in the first place."

"Katsura-san," Ryoma said angrily, "you have to stop dwelling on that. You've gotten the rifles. You've gotten the ammunition. And you've gotten a warship."

"And a promise for a couple gunboats and some Armstrong guns from Glover," Chojiro added.

"Yes," Ryoma burst out. "All thanks to Satsuma."

"But can't you see that Choshu is in no position to approach Satsuma? We're the ones whose very survival is at stake, not Satsuma. If I went to Saigo, it would be like begging. And Choshu men would rather die fighting than beg for their lives."

"Of course we'd rather die than beg," Takasugi said. "But you yourself just said that the survival of Choshu is at stake. The time for hesitation is over. We must unite with Satsuma, because we have no other choice."

"Takasugi!" Katsura shouted angrily.

"I detested Satsuma for what they've done to Choshu as much as you or anyone else," the younger Choshu man said. "But you heard what Inoue said after returning from Kagoshima. About the sincerity of the Satsuma men, how we were wrong to continue calling them bandits and traitors. Katsura-san," Takasugi now raised his voice for the first time, "we must overcome our old feelings."

Ryoma threw his arms above his head in exasperation. "Do you trust me, Katsura-san?"

"Yes, of course."

'Then listen to what I say, and get your ass to Kyoto before it's too late." Takasugi flinched at Ryoma's choice of words, as Katsura returned the comment with an icy stare. "Katsura-san," Ryoma pleaded, "it's the only way."

"Alright!" Katsura shot back. "I'll leave immediately for Yamaguchi to see if I can persuade our lord to give me permission to meet Saigo." Katsura stared hard at Ryoma, his eyes filled with resolution. "But I won't be able to leave for Kyoto for at least two weeks."

"Good!" Ryoma roared, slapped the sullen Choshu man on the back. "I knew that you of all men wouldn't let this chance go by. I'll inform Saigo right away to expect you."

"Nothing's been decided yet," Katsura said calmly. "First I have to get permission from our lord."

"I know," Ryoma said, then burst out laughing. "Katsura-san," he said, placing his hand on the shoulder of the most powerful man in Choshu Han, "we all know that if you want to go to Kyoto, then you will go to Kyoto." He emphasized these last words. "But," he added gravely, "be very careful in Kyoto. I'm sure you knew better than me. Kyoto is filled with *ronin*-hunters and other Bakufu agents looking for Choshu samurai."

Katsura nodded grimly.

"Which reminds me, Sakamoto-san," Takasugi addressed Ryoma for the first time, then drew a revolver from inside his kimono. "I want you to have this for protection, and as a small token of appreciation from Choshu." He handed Ryoma the revolver and a box of shells.

Takasugi had purchased this Smith and Wesson, Model No. 2, rim-fire revolver in Shanghai. It held six 22-caliber rounds which could be fired continuously, and were loaded into a removable cylinder, which Ryoma now spun, wild-eyed, like a child playing with a much longed-after toy. "Is it loaded?" he asked, gripping the dark brown wooden handle in his right hand.

"I think so," Takasugi said.

Ryoma stood up, walked over to the window. "It's funny," he said, cocking the hammer, closing one eye, and taking careful aim at the sky. "All those years we've spent practicing with the sword, when this thing is so much easier to use, and more effective too." Ryoma fired a shot. "It is loaded!" he roared. "I'm sure it will come in very useful someday."

Ryoma and Chojiro stood on the bridge of the small British-built warship, the Satsuma flag flying from the mainmast, in the late afternoon of their second day out from Shimonoseki. "Cheer up," Ryoma said, conning the ship across the shimmering sapphire surface of the Sea of Genkai, unable to share his friend's ill feelings over an ordeal they had had just before leaving Choshu. Despite the agreement between Inoue and Chojiro, the Choshu naval office demanded that since the *Union* was owned by Choshu it must be commanded by Choshu officers, and not men of the Kameyama Company. Although Chojiro was furious at what he claimed was a breach of contract, Ryoma appeased him by arranging for the two of them to command the *Union* to Nagasaki, under the grounds that the amount of purchase had still not been paid for by Choshu. The man who had brought Choshu and Satsuma this far toward a grand compromise was not about to let something so trivial as the command of a single warship jeopardize the very future of Japan. Ryoma knew how temperamental the Choshu men could be, and wanted to avoid friction with them at any cost, particularly now that he had finally convinced Katsura to meet Saigo. "We still have the use of this ship for business purposes, and for something even more important."

"Which is?" Chojiro asked.

"War!" roared Ryoma, as if eager for the fighting to begin. "The Bakufu troops should be attacking Choshu any time now. They'll be coming by land from the east, but by sea from the west. That means they'll have to cross Shimonoseki Strait from Kokura Han, and when they do, we'll be there waiting to blow them straight to hell."

"With this ship?"

"Yes. What do you think those cannon are for?" Ryoma pointed at the guns mounted along the gunwales.

"But Sakamoto-san..." Chojiro said apprehensively.

"What's the matter, Mr. Bean Jam Bun Maker?" Ryoma goaded.

"I don't know how to fight."

"What do you mean, you don't know how to fight? You learned how to fire a cannon at the academy in Kobe, right? You learned how to operate a warship, right? Katsu-sensei taught you everything he knows about naval science–navigation, shipbuilding, mechanics, ballistics..."

"And sounding," Chojiro added.

"Yes, sounding too."

"I know, but..."

"But what?"

"Sakamoto-san, you don't understand. I guess I know how to fight, but I'm not sure that I'm suited for it."

"Suited for it?" Ryoma gave Chojiro a hard look.

"Yes. For war."

"But you are, Chojiro! As much as any of us."

"But I'm from a merchant family. I'm not a samurai."

"Chojiro!" Ryoma shouted, "don't degrade the merchants. There's no difference between merchants and samurai, or peasants, or anyone else. What matters is what you have here," Ryoma said, grabbing his friend's arm, "and up here," he pointed at Chojiro's head, "and most of all in here," he jabbed his finger in Chojiro's gut. "It's up to men like you and me to change things. Why do you think we're struggling so hard to overthrow the Bakufu?"

"I see," Chojiro said.

"It's the whole rotten feudal system that's been keeping us down. We must get rid of it, and replace it with a democratic form of government, whereby everyone is equal."

Chojiro shook his head; he had never seen Ryoma so excited. "Of course," he said.

"Good! Because unless we respect ourselves as merchants..."

"But Sakamoto-san, you're not a merchant. You're a samurai."

"Don't be an idiot, Chojiro," Ryoma groaned. "What about the Kameyama Company? We're all merchants, everyone of us."

"I see," Chojiro said.

"And we're samurai also. Chojiro, if you don't respect yourself as a merchant, how can you ever expect to gain the respect of others?" Ryoma was referring to his men in Nagasaki, all of whom, with the exception of Umanosuke, were of the samurai class. "You can fight. If I can fight, you can fight."

"What are the chances of dying in battle?" Chojiro asked.

"I don't know. All I can tell you is that if you die, well then you die. It's a matter of fate, I suppose. But if you spend your whole life afraid of dying, you'll never get anything accomplished."

"I see," Chojiro said, nodding grimly. "But it seems so ironic."

"What seems ironic?"

"That we should be fighting against the Tokugawa Navy."

"What are you talking about?"

"Well, wasn't it the commissioner of the Tokugawa Navy who taught us how to fight aboard ship?"

Chojiro couldn't have stunned Ryoma more if he had struck him across the face with an iron bar. "Of course," Ryoma introspected, turning the other way so that his friend might not read his thoughts. The idea had never crossed his mind, but now he realized that there was a very good possibility that Katsu Kaishu would be recalled from forced retirement to command the Tokugawa naval forces in the expedition against Choshu. "Anyone else in the whole damn world," Ryoma agonized to himself. "But I just don't have it in me to fight against Katsu Kaishu."

On the following afternoon Ryoma stood alone on the bridge, conning the *Union* through the calm waters of Nagasaki Bay, in which were moored foreign ships and Japanese junks. The Western-style houses along the coast, the green hills rolling beyond, reminded him of his first visit here with Kaishu. "Has it only been a year and a half?" he thought sadly. "So much has happened since then." The faces of his friends who had died in Kyoto and Kochi during that time flashed through his mind, and his eyes filled with tears. "Satsuma and Choshu are about to unite to bring down the Bakufu," he said aloud. "After that the entire nation will unite. We'll fortify ourselves with a powerful navy by which Japan will be a force to be reckoned with."

With the decline of Tokugawa authority, which accompanied the liberalization of the Port of Nagasaki to foreign trade, the city had transformed into a political void. Certainly there was no other city in Japan from which a group of outlaws could operate their own shipping company, and even run guns to Choshu. Recently, some of the wealthier *han* had begun taking advantage of this unprecedented opportunity to purchase foreign goods by establishing branches in Nagasaki to deal directly with foreign traders. Some of them, like Satsuma, were even openly purchasing warships, guns and ammunition, and it was on this very point which Ryoma had based his entire plan to unite Satsuma and Choshu.

He was anxious to see company headquarters for the first time, to visit Satsuma Councilor Komatsu Tatewaki, and to meet the Scottish arms merchant Thomas Glover. Komatsu had recently written him about another warship, the *Werewolf*, that Glover was offering for sale. Since the Kameyama Company was still without sufficient capital, Komatsu offered to pay for most of the ship, a British schooner which was even smaller than the *Union*.

"At this point we can't be choosy," Ryoma reprimanded Taro later that afternoon when his nephew complained that the ship was not a steamer. "Komatsu has promised me that, unlike the *Union*, the *Werewolf* will be for our exclusive use." Ryoma and Chojiro had just arrived at company headquarters, located near the top of the hills to the east of the city. "So this is it!" Ryoma said, a little surprised by the smallness of the place. "But it will do." He was glad to be reunited with his men, whom, aside from Chojiro, he had not seen since they had left Kagoshima together over a half year ago. Headquarters consisted of a plain one-story wooden house, with a black tile roof, which Kosone Eishiro, the younger son of the wealthy merchant family, had recently purchased for the company. Inside were two small rooms, which used to be a storehouse for so-called Kameyama Porcelain when a nearby kiln was in use.

All eight men–Ryoma, Chojiro, Taro, Toranosuke, Umanosuke, Yonosuke, Sonojo and a very young *ronin* from Nagaoka Han by the name of Shiramine Shunme–sat in a circle in one of the rooms. "Shun," Ryoma chaffed, "do all men from Nagaoka look so good in white?" Ryoma had decided that all of his men would wear a white *hakama*, the color of navy uniforms in Europe and America.

At age eighteen, Shunme had replaced Yonosuke as the youngest of the group. He had left his Tokugawa-hereditary *han* when he was just fifteen to stay with his elder brother in Edo, and shortly after entered the Bakufu's Naval Training Institute. Shunme had first met Ryoma three years ago, while sailing from Edo to Osaka aboard the *Jundo Maru*. Shunme had joined Kaishu's academy in Kobe, but returned to Edo when it was closed down, and had only recently rejoined the others in Nagasaki. Despite his youth, Shunme knew more about operating a ship than anyone else in the company, with the exception of Chief Navigator Chiya Toranosuke.

"Since this is our first meeting as a company," Ryoma said, "I have some important things to discuss with you. I want to set up a branch office in Shimonoseki." It had recently occurred to Ryoma that the prices of commodities varied between eastern and western Japan, and that Shimonoseki was the dividing line where these prices were determined. "Prices are decided by supply and demand," he explained. "If we have an office in Shimonoseki, with the cooperation of Choshu officials, we can see exactly what goods are being shipped into the east and into the west. Then we can measure the supply against the demand, and so be able to know prices in advance. Once we know that..."

"We'll know which products will bring in the largest profits," Yonosuke said.

"Exactly!" Ryoma smiled. "And in so doing, we can't help but make money. I've already discussed this with some of the Choshu men, and been introduced to a wealthy merchant in Shimonoseki who is willing to let us use his place as an office."

"That's a great idea," Chojiro said, his eyes slightly downcast. "But why didn't you mention it to me earlier?"

"Because I wanted all of you to hear about the plan together."

"I see," Chojiro said with a shrug, drawing dirty looks from several of the others.

Ryoma continued. "Of course, we'll also set up an office in Osaka. I'm sure we can arrange for the use of some space in the Satsuma trading agency there. Before long I expect the Kameyama Company to accumulate more wealth than most of the *han*. And that includes Tosa," Ryoma sneered. "With that, and the power behind a Satsuma-Choshu Alliance, we can overthrow the Bakufu and establish one strong centralized nation. Then we'll be able to go wherever we want, whenever we want. We can sail all over the world. But enough of business for now. Tonight I want to celebrate. I have some extra money, and I hear that the Nagasaki women are nice." Takasugi had given Ryoma the generous sum of 100 *ryo* before he had left Shimonoseki. "This is a small token of Choshu's appreciation for everything you've done," Takasugi had said. Then with a fiendish smile, "But you had better use it well, Sakamoto-san. And I know of no better place in all of Japan to spend this money than at the House of the Flower Moon in Nagasaki's Maruyama district."

"I'd like to celebrate," Taro said, but I have some important paperwork to finish."

"So do I," Yonosuke said. "With the *Werewolf* deal coming up..."

"Alright!" Ryoma said. "Who can take one night off to celebrate my homecoming?"

"Homecoming?" Umanosuke asked.

"Put it this way, other than the Teradaya, this is the first place I've been since we lost the Kobe academy that I can somehow consider home. Now who will it be?"

"I'll celebrate with you," Umanosuke offered.

"I will too," Sonojo said.

"Alright." Ryoma put his hand on Chojiro's shoulder. "With the bean jam bun maker's son, that makes four of us. Now, let's go."

"If there were no Maruyama in Nagasaki, all the gold and silver from Kyoto and Osaka would return safely home," bantered a popular seventeenth-century novelist. And two centuries later, when Ryoma and his men visited Maruyama, it was said that here "the fragrance of musk and orchids fills the soul with lust, the swishing of fine silk enraptures the ears."

Four men dressed in navy whites, with swords at their left hips, walked down a dark narrow street, their elevated wooden clogs making a low-pitched chafing sound against the stone pavement, then a heavy thumping noise as they crossed the Bridge of Reflection, on the other side of which lay paradise for any man with gold in his pocket. The light from hundreds of red lanterns hanging from the eaves of the magnificent two-storied pleasure palaces lining both sides of the street illuminated the night.

Soon they reached the House of the Flower Moon, where Ryoma had drank French wine with Kaishu in the Chinese Room. They approached the wooden outer gate, above which hung a huge red paper lantern, displaying the name of the establishment in black Chinese characters. In the front garden they were greeted by a maid, who led them into the house, down a long dark corridor, and into a spacious *tatami* room overlooking a wide garden. Soon several geisha joined them, *sake* was poured, and before long the room had become a scene of bacchanalian pleasure.

"How about playing something?" Ryoma said to the girl sitting next to him. She had pretty features: a perfectly shaped nose, small black eyes and a round mouth.

"How about singing something?" the girl replied coyly. She took up the moon guitar which lay beside her, and with a pick strummed the four strings over the round wooden body.

"What's your name?" Ryoma asked.

"Omoto."

Ryoma had heard the name from Takasugi. "The beautiful Maruyama geisha who men can't help but fall for," Takasugi had described her, adding, "but she rarely gives in to men."

"Do you know this song?" Ryoma asked. *"The beginning of the Year of the Tiger, 1854..."* he recited the first line of a song he had heard in Shimonoseki. During the more than two centuries that Nagasaki had been open only to Dutch and Chinese traders, the clans of Hizen and Chikuzen shared the burden of guarding the port from intervention by ships from other countries. This was until the completion of the foreign treaties in the intercalary year of 1854. The Russian Admiral Poutiatine had led four warships into Nagasaki in December 1853 in hopes that his country might be the first to sign a treaty with Japan. Unable to obtain permission to land, the Russian squadron spent a month anchored near an offshore island, eventually leaving the port in January, which was during Hizen's watch. This short song makes fun of the Russian's folly.

Omoto laughed. "I should say so. The song was originated in Nagasaki. Now it's your turn."

"I'm waiting for you to start playing," Ryoma roared, draining his *sake* cup.

"No, I mean, it's your turn to tell me your name."

"Sakamoto Ryoma, from Tosa," he said, then to Umanosuke, who sat directly across the table, "How about taking your eyes of the girl for a while and listening to this?" Ryoma began singing again, as Omoto played the moon guitar.

"The beginning of the Year of the Tiger, 1854.
We're drinking New Year's sake,
Getting drunk, drunk, drunk."

"Very good," Umanosuke slurred. "I'll sing the second verse," he said, his face bright red from drink.

"There are thirteen months this year,
Hizen's turn at watch.
They say the Russians are floating aimlessly off of Jogashima Island."

As Umanosuke finished singing, everyone burst out laughing.

"Won't you take me for a walk in the garden?" Omoto whispered to Ryoma.

"Yes," Ryoma said, determined to possess this beauty who rarely gave in to men.

A DECLARATION OF FREEDOM

The Secret Alliance, or Into the Dragon's Lair

While still determined to bring down the Bakufu, Sakamoto Ryoma now considered alternatives to war in realizing this goal. The Dragon was undergoing another metamorphosis in his outlook, his biggest personal development since meeting Katsu Kaishu over three years before. Just as Kaishu had shown him that the xenophobia of the Loyalists was not the answer to the nation's problems, he was now beginning to wonder if that answer could really be found in a war with the Tokugawa. A bloody revolution, he feared, even if successful in toppling the Bakufu, would give the foreigners an opportunity to strike when Japan was at its weakest. Instead, Ryoma reasoned, he could use his influence among the Group of Four to convince "the potato-heads in Edo" of the inevitability of change, while appealing to Satsuma and Choshu of the dangers of civil war. In so doing, he felt that perhaps he could persuade the Bakufu to surrender the political power peacefully on terms that would be acceptable to all. But despite his change in outlook, the Dragon never once deviated from the thorny road to freedom, nor did he back down from his vow "to clean up Japan once and for all," by eliminating the Bakufu. "Whether we topple the Bakufu through bloodless revolution, or all-out war," Ryoma now told himself, "Satsuma and Choshu must unite." He knew that the awesome military might of such an alliance would be vital at a peaceful bargaining table, and indispensable in case of war.

Ryoma returned to Shimonoseki near the close of the last month of the first year of the Era of Keio, 1865. Although he had hoped to finalize a deal with Glover for the warship *Werewolf* before leaving Nagasaki, he was anxious to get to Kyoto to oversee the all-important discussions between Saigo and Katsura. When Ryoma arrived at the mansion of the wealthy Shimonoseki merchant, Takasugi, Ito and Inoue were waiting for him.

Takasugi was not well. Choshu's most important military leader was sickly pale, obviously worried, with an occasional nervous twitch below his right eye. "Katsura left for Kyoto on the twenty-seventh aboard a Satsuma steamer," he told Ryoma. "With him are a few of our own men, a messenger from Saigo, and Ike Kurata of Tosa." Ryoma had assigned Kurata as bodyguard to Katsura, whose life would be in grave danger once he reached the proximity of Kyoto. "Katsura said he'd be waiting for you at Satsuma headquarters in

Kyoto."

"Good!" Ryoma rubbed his hands together. "I'll leave right away."

"We have orders to assign a bodyguard to you," Takasugi informed Ryoma. "We are well aware of your expertise with a sword, but I hope you won't mind having one of our men along just in case. His name is Miyoshi Shinzo, and he's an expert with a spear. At any rate, I'm sure he won't be in the way."

The caution of the Choshu men was not unfounded. Ryoma had heard of the Bakufu's extraordinary intelligence network from Katsu Kaishu and Okubo Ichio. What he did not know, however, was that the Protector of Kyoto had recently issued orders for his arrest. The Lord of Aizu, in fact, had activated all of the police forces under his command: those of the Inspector-General of Kyoto, the Magistrates of Kyoto and Fushimi, the Shinsengumi and another unit, formed of the younger sons of Tokugawa retainers, known as the Patrolling Corps. In short, all police units in Kyoto were now on the lookout for "a Tosa *ronin*, around thirty years old, tall with a solid build, dark brown eyes, dark complexion, broad forehead, a wart above his left brow, moles on his face, and thick eyebrows. But be careful of him," the report warned, "because he is an expert swordsman." Unfortunately for the Bakufu police, the report did not mention that Ryoma was also armed with a Smith and Wesson.

Ryoma was overcome with anxiety. Katsura's distrust for Saigo, and for Satsuma itself, made him nervous. He was constantly imagining problems which might occur between the two men during his absence. Nevertheless, Ryoma had no choice but to wait for a Satsuma ship to arrive at Shimonoseki to take him to Kobe. Only a Satsuma ship would do, as that clan's extraterritoriality exempted it from inspection by Bakufu officials. While Ryoma now carried papers identifying him as "Satsuma samurai Saitani Umetaro," he was a wanted man, and unwilling to take any unnecessary chances with his life, not at least until he saw the realization of a Satsuma-Choshu Alliance. When a Satsuma ship finally arrived on January 5, Ryoma's departure was further delayed by rough winter seas; and although his ship finally set sail on the tenth, stormy weather in the normally calm Inland Sea prevented clear sailing, and he and Miyoshi Shinzo did not land at Kobe until the seventeenth.

During the stormy week aboard ship, Ryoma and Miyoshi spent long hours below deck, sipping *sake* and discussing politics, particularly the importance of a Satsuma-Choshu Alliance to overthrow the Bakufu. As Takasugi had assured, Miyoshi was a man of strong character, for whom Ryoma soon developed a deep trust.

They reached the Port of Osaka on the eighteenth, and from here took a riverboat to Satsuma headquarters, where Ike Kurata was waiting for them. After introducing Kurata to Miyoshi, Ryoma immediately asked, "Where's Katsura?"

"He's been at Satsuma headquarters in Kyoto for the past two weeks."

"And?"

"That's all."

"That's all?" Ryoma gasped. "How are the talks between Katsura and Saigo progressing?"

"I'm not sure Katsura has talked with Saigo," Kurata said glumly. "I think he's waiting for you."

"We'll go to Fushimi the first thing in the morning, but tonight I have a very important meeting to attend to?"

"Where?" Kurata asked.

"Osaka Castle."

"This is no time for joking," Kurata admonished.

"I'm not joking," Ryoma said. "The two of you stay here. If I don't return by morning, go to Kyoto without me." Kurata and Miyoshi stared in disbelief at Ryoma. "But no matter what happens, to me or anyone else, remember that Katsura and Saigo must come to an agreement. This is our last chance. The very fate of Japan depends on what happens at Satsuma headquarters in Kyoto over the next few days."

"Sakamoto-san," Miyoshi implored, "you can't go to Osaka Castle! It would be suicide! Osaka Castle is the headquarters of the Tokugawa Army. What business could you possibly have at Osaka Castle?"

"I must talk to the Keeper of the Castle."

The Lord of Osaka Castle was, of course, the Shogun himself. But since the Shogun spent most of his time in Edo, one of his most trusted vassals served as keeper of his castle in Osaka. The retainer of this post was responsible for maintaining the fortifications of Osaka Castle, overseeing the two Magistrates of Osaka, and all of the *daimyo* throughout western Japan. The Keeper of Osaka Castle, along with the Inspector-General of Kyoto, was the highest ranking Tokugawa official outside Edo.

"What business could you possibly have with the Keeper of the

Castle?" Miyoshi blurted in disbelief. "You'll be arrested."

"I want to find out as much as I can about the Bakufu's security measures, so that we can avoid arrest."

"I wonder if Ryoma's gone mad," Kurata thought to himself, but nevertheless admired his friend's nerve. "You expect the Keeper of the Castle to tell you where and how the Bakufu plans to arrest us?" Kurata said, laughing at the absurdity of the notion.

"Exactly," Ryoma said, slapping his friend on the back.

"You're serious, aren't you," Miyoshi confirmed.

"Yes."

"In that case, I have not choice but to accompany you. I'm under orders to make sure that nothing happens to you." Miyoshi walked over to the corner of the room, and took his spear. "Let's go," he said.

"Alright, Miyoshi-san. I know I can't convince you to stay behind. Kura, arrange for a Satsuma palanquin to take us to the castle. I can't think of any better way to get through the castle gates than with lanterns displaying the crest of the Lord of Satsuma lighting our way."

Leaving Kurata quite alone and anxious, Ryoma and Miyoshi set out for the Bakufu fortress in a palanquin reserved solely for high-ranking Satsuma officials, and flanked by several Satsuma samurai. What Ryoma did not tell Kurata was that the Keeper of Osaka Castle was actually Okubo Ichio, one of Katsu Kaishu's Group of Four, recently recalled from forced retirement.

Okubo sat alone in his study, warming his hands over a brazier, and considering the contents of a letter he had just finished reading from the Protector of Kyoto.

"Your Excellency," a samurai called from the corridor.

"Yes, what is it?" Okubo's voice was shaken, as if he had just received some disturbing news.

"There is a Satsuma man here to see you," the samurai said, sliding the screen door halfway open. "He says he has an urgent message from Lord Hisamitsu. And from the looks of his escort, and the Shimazu cross on his palanquin, I'd say he was a high-ranking Satsuma official."

"What is his name?" Okubo asked.

"Saitani Umetaro."

Okubo had to stop himself from gasping. He had heard the alias from Katsu Kaishu, and of this Ryoma was well aware. "Saitani Umetaro?" Okubo said, feigning nonchalance, but feeling slightly sick to his stomach. "I've never heard of him. But I can't very well refuse a visit from a messenger of Lord Hisamitsu." Okubo rubbed his hands together over the burning coals. "It sure is cold tonight," he muttered, as he slowly stood up, a worried look on his face. Producing a handkerchief from the pocket of his heavy cotton frock, he wiped the cold sweat from his forehead. "Send him in," he told the samurai in a voice as vexed as the night was cold.

Presently the screen door slid open, and Ryoma entered, with Miyoshi remaining behind in the corridor. "Good evening, Okubo-san." Ryoma smiled, as if he did not notice the troubled look in the man's eyes.

"Ryoma," Okubo whispered in exasperation, "how could you come here like this?"

"Well, it's been almost a year since we last met. And since I was passing through Osaka, I just thought..."

"Of all the stupid..." Okubo checked himself. "Who's that waiting outside in the corridor?" he demanded.

"Miyoshi Shinzo, of Choshu."

"Choshu," Okubo gasped. "Are you crazy?"

"Perhaps," Ryoma said calmly, not a little amused at the situation. "He's a friend of mine."

"How could you do this to me, Ryoma? You know that I'm in charge of the police force for the entire city, which means it's my duty to arrest anybody..."

"I knew you wouldn't arrest me," Ryoma interrupted, still smiling. "In fact, one of the reasons I've come here is because I thought that you could help us avoid arrest."

Okubo heaved a heavy sigh. "With the Shogun here in Osaka Castle now, there are about thirty thousand men patrolling the city, each one with orders to cut down on sight anybody who looks at all suspicious. And," he paused, gave Ryoma a hard look, "I've just received word from the Protector of Kyoto that Sakamoto Ryoma of Tosa is now the most wanted man in Japan."

"Really?" Ryoma clapped his hands together. "The Protector of Kyoto! That's really something. I never knew I was so important. I'll have to write my sister Otome about this."

"Idiot!" Okubo hissed. "This is no time for jokes. You've been seen entering Satsuma headquarters earlier in the day. You must get out of here, and away from Osaka-Kyoto immediately, or I fear that you'll be a dead man within a matter of days."

"Okubo-san," Ryoma said. "Let me ask you something."

"What?" Okubo snapped irritably.

"I have to go into Kyoto in the next day or two. But do you know why?"

"How should I know why?"

"Good! That's all I wanted to know." Ryoma smiled, assured for the first time that the Bakufu had not discovered his plan for a Satsuma-Choshu Alliance. "But I really appreciate your concern for my safety. And in return, if I may, I'd like to offer some advice."

"What may that be, Ryoma?" Okubo sighed again.

"Advice for the Shogun, that is," Ryoma said, drawing a strange look from the Tokugawa retainer. "Just because the Bakufu is treating me as if I were a common criminal, doesn't necessarily give me cause to hate them. But if I should have such cause, the Shogun will have every reason to worry. As you well know, this lowly *ronin*," Ryoma put his hand to his chest, "has close, trusting relations with some of the most powerful *daimyo* in western Japan, not to mention some of the most influential men in the Bakufu." Okubo nodded slowly, as if to acknowledge Ryoma's reference to the Group of Four. "Just as Katsu Kaishu has." Ryoma paused, stared hard into the eyes of Kaishu's closest ally. "And, as you may well imagine, this lowly *ronin* is constantly informed of the situation in Choshu. Although the Choshu men do not have much of an opportunity to hear what is happening in the Bakufu, it would only take one day for this *ronin*," again Ryoma placed his hand on his chest, "to find out anything Choshu wants to know. As I've said in the past: with the way things are going for the Bakufu nowadays, with its lack of public support and even commitment from many of the *han* in western Japan, if it was to attack Choshu right now it would surely lose, and so become the laughing stock of the entire nation."

"And what is it that this *ronin* would like to advise the Shogun?" Okubo asked.

"First of all, he must clear the Shinsengumi and all of his other murderous police forces out of Kyoto and Osaka. Then, he must start reforming his government in Edo, and himself assume the rank of common soldier." Ryoma paused, as if to stress the heaviness of his words. "Then, if the Tokugawa is sincerely determined to improve itself, and make every effort to that effect, using all of its resources in all eight of its provinces in eastern Japan, I think that in about ten years it will be able to regain control of the country. But unfortunately," Ryoma's tone darkened, "there are too many stupid officials in Edo who are so restricted by convention that they are incapable of change. And it is for this very reason that Japan is in such grave danger."

"Ryoma," Okubo took firm hold of the outlaw's hand, "I don't know what you're up to, and I don't want to know. But I will say for the last time that I wish you would get out of the Osaka-Kyoto region before you get yourself killed."

"I am aware of the danger, Okubo-san. I thank you for your concern."

Okubo sighed, folded his arms at his chest. "If you insist on going into Kyoto," he said, "you should know that the Shinsengumi is checking everyone traveling by river between Osaka and Kyoto. And although you have papers identifying yourself as a Satsuma samurai, if there's an emergency tell them that you know me. But remember," Okubo stressed, "only in an emergency."

"I appreciate that, Okubo-san," Ryoma said, before bowing and taking his leave.

The next morning Ryoma, Miyoshi and Kurata boarded a riverboat from Osaka, and arrived at Fushimi without incident just after midnight. A light snow had begun falling as they stepped up onto the boatlanding below the Teradaya. The shutters of the inn were drawn on the downstairs verandah, and the entire house was dark, save a small opening in one of the upstairs windows, from which Ryoma caught a glimpse of someone watching them. Just then a shadow seemed to pass through the darkness beyond, and Ryoma drew his revolver.

"What's wrong?" Miyoshi asked, stopping in his tracks, holding his long spear with both hands.

"Maybe it's my imagination, but I feel someone watching us."

"Could very well be a spy," Miyoshi suggested, as they proceeded up the stone steps toward the front door of the inn.

"You've finally arrived," Otose whispered from the entranceway, holding a small lantern. "Come in quickly." The proprietress spoke in short spurts, as if worried that someone might be eavesdropping.

"What's going on here?" Ryoma asked once they were inside, the door bolted behind them.

"We've been closed since the day before yesterday. There's nobody here but Oryo and myself."

"I don't understand," Ryoma said. "Fushimi is always busy with people traveling between Osaka and Kyoto. Why would you close down?"

"A special request from Satsuma. They told me that a certain individual would be arriving soon from Osaka, and that I shouldn't take any other guests but him, and his party. They say that this individual is very important."

"Who is this individual?" Ryoma asked.

"Sakamoto Ryoma," Otose said. "Just what's going on?"

"I have some important business in Kyoto tomorrow. But don't ask any more than that. It wouldn't be safe for you or us."

Not only had Otose closed her inn to business, but she refused to take money from Ryoma or his comrades when they stayed there. What's more, she risked arrest and even her life by helping them. *"She's well educated and indeed a woman of character,"* Ryoma described Otose in a letter to his sister. *"She helps people who work for Choshu and the nation...and carries out projects worthy of men."*

"I see," Otose said, giving Ryoma a worried look.

"Where's Oryo?" he asked.

"Asleep. I'll wake her."

"No, don't."

"But she's been waiting to see you since we heard you'd be coming. That's all she's been talking about. Sakamoto-san..." Otose hesitated.

"Yes, what is it?"

"Why don't you marry the poor girl?"

"Let's get some sleep," Ryoma evaded the question. "I'm dead tired."

Ryoma slept until late the next morning, when he sent Oryo to the nearby Satsuma estate in Fushimi to have them notify their Kyoto headquarters of his arrival. "I've just seen two very suspicious men outside," Oryo told him when she returned.

"Most likely spies," Ryoma snickered at the thought of the Bakufu police going to such trouble over him.

"The people at the Satsuma estate said they would like to send a palanquin and an escort to bring you into Kyoto," the girl said.

"No," Ryoma said. "That would be a mistake. If the *ronin*-hunters should insist on searching the palanquin they'd find me and Kura inside."

"But I thought you were carrying Satsuma identification papers."

"We are. But do we look important enough to be carried in a special palanquin, with the Shimazu cross displayed all over the place?"

"No," the girl laughed at the notion. "When you put it that way, I suppose not."

"We'll walk into Kyoto, but we won't leave until after dark." Ryoma went to the window overlooking the street. "See those two standing under the bridge," he said, pointing at two swordless men dressed in the livery coats of common laborers. "They're most likely spies, for the Shinsengumi, or else the Magistrate of Fushimi."

"Sakamoto-san," Miyoshi said as he hurried up the stairs, "there are some very suspicious looking characters standing around outside. I think I'd better accompany you to Kyoto."

"I appreciate your concern, Miyoshi-san, but two are less conspicuous than three. Besides," Ryoma drew his revolver from his kimono, "if worse comes to worst, I always have this little gift from Takasugi."

It was almost midnight when Ryoma and Kurata arrived at the Kyoto residence of Satsuma Councilor Komatsu Tatewaki. Unlike Saigo and Okubo, both of whom were from poor, low-ranking samurai families, Komatsu, as a hereditary councilor to the Lord of Satsuma, maintained a private residence in the Imperial capital. It was here that Katsura Kogoro was staying.

The two Tosa men found Katsura in a second-story room at the rear of the house, his swords set in an alcove, his wicker traveling case packed as if he were going somewhere. "I've been waiting for you, Sakamoto-san," Katsura said grimly. "Please sit down." The three men sat around a small table, set with one large flask of *sake* and three cups. Near the table was a ceramic brazier.

"Have you and Saigo come to an agreement yet?" Ryoma asked, sitting opposite Katsura, Kurata at his side.

"Saigo is up to his old tricks," Katsura said bitterly. "I've come all the way here at a time when Choshu is preparing for war, and all the Satsuma men can do is entertain me. Not one word out of Saigo or anyone else about an alliance. I've had it," he seethed, staring down into the smoldering brazier. "I've decided to return to Choshu tomorrow."

"How many times have you met Saigo?" Ryoma asked, ignoring Katsura's last remark.

"Once."

"What did you talk about?"

"The first war in Kyoto, when Satsuma turned traitor and united with Aizu to expel Choshu and the seven nobles," Katsura said, before rattling off a list of other "crimes" committed by his enemy. "I told Saigo that Choshu will never forgive Satsuma for its double-dealing, for the way it tricked the court into branding Choshu an 'Imperial Enemy,' when everyone knows that there has never been a *han* in the entire history of Japan that has been more dedicated to the Emperor than Choshu."

"And what did Saigo have to say to all of this?"

"He just nodded that big stupid head of his, and said that I was right."

"He said you were right?" Ryoma was amazed.

"Yes."

"Then why didn't you mention an alliance at that time?" Ryoma asked indignantly.

"Because I couldn't."

"You couldn't?" Ryoma hollered, a look of disbelief on his face. "Why are you here then?"

Katsura groaned bitterly, shook his head. "Don't you understand?" he said darkly, staring hard into the brazier. "That would degrade Choshu."

"Katsura Kogoro!" Ryoma screamed the name, not bothering with the honorific suffix. Kurata, who had known Ryoma all his life, had never seen him so angry. "To hell with Choshu!" Ryoma roared at the top of his lungs. "And to hell with Satsuma! When are you going to stop worrying about Choshu and think about Japan? What about all the Tosa men, including Kurata here, and myself, who have been risking our lives everyday over these past several years? Kurata has a baby back in Kochi that he's never even seen. But you don't think we're doing all this for the welfare of Tosa, do you? And we certainly aren't doing it for Choshu or Satsuma. What about all the men from Tosa, and Choshu too, who have died for Japan? Certainly you haven't forgotten them. Damn it, Katsura-san!" Ryoma pounded his fist on the floor. "We've come this close to uniting Choshu and Satsuma as the only way to save Japan. I'm not going to let you ruin everything by leaving without first coming to terms with Saigo." Ryoma was so beside himself with anger that he grabbed his sword, and without thinking, drew the blade, before immediately slamming it back into the scabbard.

Katsura retained his usual calm, though his bitterness was everywhere apparent. "You are absolutely right, Sakamoto-san," he said, staring hard at Ryoma. "However," he paused, took a deep breath, continued speaking slowly, deliberately, "if I should make a proposal for an alliance, then it would appear that Choshu was begging for Satsuma's help. But since it was Satsuma who originally betrayed us by uniting with Aizu, I cannot do that. Besides, it is Choshu and not Satsuma who is completely ostracized by the rest of Japan. It is our *han* and not Satsuma who has been branded an enemy by the Imperial Court. And it is Choshu and not Satsuma who is about to go to war with the entire Tokugawa Army. Satsuma, on the other hand, openly serves the Emperor. Satsuma openly meets with Bakufu representatives. And Satsuma openly deals with the other clans. Satsuma can therefore openly, and without hindrance, participate in national affairs, while Choshu has no say in such matters whatsoever. Sakamoto-san," Katsura sighed, "even if my initiating a proposal did not appear as if Choshu were begging for Satsuma's help, it would certainly seem that we were inviting them to share in our danger. As a samurai I cannot do such a thing." Katsura paused, took a deep breath, exhaled slowly. "Even if Choshu should be defeated by the Tokugawa, even if all that should remain of our lands is scorched earth, as long as Satsuma survives to overthrow the Bakufu for the Imperial cause we will have no regrets." Katsura stopped speaking, a bitter smile on his face.

"No regrets?" Ryoma repeated quietly, obviously moved by these last words. Only now did he realize that Katsura Kogoro's main concern was not for Choshu Han, but for the entire Japanese nation.

"And so," Katsura continued in the same defiant tone, "my men and I will leave for Choshu tomorrow to fight the Tokugawa. If we die in battle, then at least we will die with the dignity of samurai." Katsura took up the flask of *sake*. "Now, I'd like to propose a farewell toast, Sakamoto-san, for our long friendship and for all you've done..."

"No!" Ryoma roared, grabbed Katsura by the wrist, then immediately released his grip. He folded his arms tightly at his chest, stared up at the ceiling, then after a short while stood up. "But I understand," he said.

"Where are you going?" Katsura asked.

"To Satsuma's Kyoto headquarters to see Saigo." Ryoma picked up his long sword, thrust it through his sash. "No matter what you do, Katsura-san, stay right here." Then to Kurata he said, "And you'd better stay here with him."

"No regrets," Ryoma said, staring hard in Saigo's sparkling black eyes. "Don't you understand, Saigo-san? Katsura says he would have no regrets." Ryoma had just relayed to Saigo what Katsura had told him.

"No regrets," Saigo repeated in a low voice. "If only he had told me that when I spoke with him."

Ryoma leaned forward. "Don't you see?" he said pleadingly. "Katsura could never admit that to your face. That's why he told me."

"Of course." Saigo nodded heavily.

"So, it's now up to you to make the first move, and soon, or Katsura will leave, and that will be the end of it." Ryoma grabbed Saigo's wrist. "You must understand that Satsuma is in a much easier position than Choshu to make the first move."

"I see, Sakamoto-san. I owe both you and Katsura an apology. And there is one thing I must admit, although I am ashamed to. The reason that I have not yet initiated a proposal for an alliance is because I was testing Katsura."

"Testing Katsura?" Ryoma slapped the side of his head in disbelief.

"Yes, testing his sincerity." Tears filled the great man's eyes as he spoke. "But now that I realize he is as sincere as you yourself are, as a samurai I am ashamed of my poor judgment of character."

Ryoma put his hand on Saigo's broad shoulder. "Then I can count on you to make the proposal for an alliance?"

"Yes." Saigo sat up straight, nodded. "Bring Katsura here the first thing in the morning."

"No, Saigo-san. It is Choshu who has suffered most. You must go to Katsura and make the proposal." Ryoma leaned back, stared hard into the eyes of the Satsuma leader.

"You're right," affirmed Saigo, nodding his heavy head. "We'll go in the morning."

Several Satsuma men, dressed formally in kimono, *hakama* and crested jackets, arrived at Komatsu's residence the next morning. With Saigo were Komatsu, Okubo, Yoshii–Saigo's personal secretary whom Ryoma had met in Kyoto during the previous spring to discuss the possibilities of an alliance–and three other samurai, one of which, by far the youngest, carried a Satsuma lute wrapped in dark blue cloth. Ryoma and Kurata had been waiting inside with Katsura.

The Satsuma men bowed as they entered; all but the youth carrying the lute sat down on one side of the room, Saigo directly opposite Katsura. The younger man excused himself, went to the next room, closing the paper screen door behind him. "Be sure not to stop playing," Komatsu called out. Then turning to Ryoma, "A little music from the Satsuma lute in case of eavesdroppers," he said. Komatsu's friendly smile contrasted with the stone-cold expressions of all the other men present, save Ryoma who was apparently amused by the remark.

Saigo bowed his head to the *tatami* floor, sat up straight, rested his hands on his huge thighs, and stared hard into Katsura's dark, piercing eyes. As Ryoma looked on, the difference between these two men seemed to him so great that he marveled, if only for an instant, that he had been able to bring them this far. "How could I have ever dreamed of uniting Satsuma and Choshu?" he thought, the loud twang of the lute coming from the next room.

Throughout history the peoples of Satsuma and Choshu had always been bitter enemies, unable to trust one another. Choshu, with its relatively close proximity to Kyoto and Osaka, produced a more culturally refined breed of samurai than did the geographically remote Satsuma. In the eyes of Choshu, Satsuma people were reticent, stolid and rustic—as was Saigo Kichinosuke. The Satsuma samurai on the other hand, trained to be at once frugal and warlike, saw their counterparts from Choshu as fanatic, cunning and apprehensive—as was Katsura Kogoro. But despite their differences, Satsuma and Choshu shared one common goal: overthrowing the Bakufu and restoring the political power to the Emperor. "That's why they must be united," Ryoma had told himself over and over again.

"Katsura-san," Saigo began speaking slowly, in a quiet baritone, "let's put our past animosity aside for the sake of the Imperial nation." Saigo spoke with such dignity, such sincerity that even Katsura himself was overcome with a feeling of trust for the man who had crushed the Choshu forces one and a half years before, almost to the very day. The sound of the lute seemed to also have a softening effect on Katsura, which was visible in his eyes. He was apparently familiar with the tune, *A Cherry Blossom Keepsake*, an ancient Satsuma song about a covenant of brotherhood, symbolic of the brotherhood about to be formed.

Katsura responded by also bowing low. "I see," was all he said, as Ryoma suppressed an urge to groan. Ryoma knew that Katsura was determined to make things as difficult as possible for Saigo.

After a short silence, Saigo continued, glancing sideways at Ryoma: "I, Saigo Kichinosuke, promise, with Sakamoto Ryoma as my witness, that if war should break out between Choshu and the Bakufu, Satsuma will immediately dispatch additional troops to Kyoto and

Osaka to hold off the Tokugawa armies here, and do everything else in our power to aid your *han*. Once Choshu is victorious, as I'm sure you will be, Satsuma will use all of its influence at court to have Choshu reinstated into Imperial grace. Then," Saigo raised his voice, "Satsuma and Choshu will join hands to destroy the Bakufu through military force." The commander in chief of the Satsuma armed forces extended his right hand. "Katsura Kogoro of Choshu," he boomed, "I hereby propose an alliance of trust and military cooperation between our two great *han*."

Saigo and Katsura shook hands, and the Satsuma-Choshu Alliance, the first union between any of the clans since the establishment of the Tokugawa Bakufu two and half centuries before, was finally realized on January 21, 1866, the result of a yearlong struggle by Sakamoto Ryoma and his band of outlaws. This alliance, which formed the most powerful military force in the nation, was a turning point in Japanese history, and the beginning of the end of the Tokugawa Bakufu.

A DECLARATION OF FREEDOM

Attack At the Teradaya

As the Satsuma-Choshu Alliance was secret, no formal documents were signed. Two days after the historical agreement, Katsura, cagey as usual and even now unable to fully trust Satsuma, wrote a letter to Ryoma, stating the terms of the alliance, and asking him to guarantee that they were as verbally agreed upon in good faith. An outlaw, and as Ryoma had depicted himself in a letter to Otome, "born a mere potato digger in Tosa, a nobody," had now been asked by the political leader of Choshu to act as guarantor for the most powerful military alliance in Japan. Ryoma's prophesy when he had boasted to Otome, "I'm destined to bring about great changes in the nation," had come true. Ryoma was, however, unable to comply with Katsura's request until the following month, as he was delayed by an unsettling experience upon his return to the Teradaya on the night of January 23.

"Miyoshi-san! Where's Miyoshi-san?" Ryoma called out from the entranceway to the Teradaya, the front door bolted shut. It was well after midnight, and Ryoma, who had not slept for two days, felt intoxicated from lack of sleep, but was anxious to tell Miyoshi about the alliance.

Otose opened the door, a look of relief on her face. "Sakamoto-san, we've been waiting for you," she whispered. "Come in, quickly! It's dangerous outside. The police are combing the streets day and night."

"No matter," Ryoma said. He stepped out of his straw sandals, washed his feet in a bucket of hot water Oryo had placed inside the doorway. "You're safe, Sakamoto-san," the girl said, taking his hand as he stepped into the house.

"And the Bakufu's days are numbered," he roared.

"Sakamoto-san," Miyoshi called, running down the staircase. "How did it go?"

"Success, Miyoshi-san! Success!" Ryoma hollered. "Satsuma and Choshu are united."

Miyoshi took Ryoma's hand, and slapped him on the back. "Let's have a drink," he exclaimed.

"That's what I was about to suggest, but first I need a bath." Ryoma removed his sword and pistol from his sash, and Oryo began laughing. "What's so funny?" Ryoma said.

"I've never heard you say that before," Oryo said.

"Say what before?"

"That you need a bath. But never mind," she said drolly, "I'll get one ready."

After bathing, Ryoma put on a clean bathrobe and heavy cotton frock, then joined Miyoshi in a room upstairs. Oryo had laid out Ryoma's bedding on one side of the room, hung his jacket in a wooden clothes rack which stood against the opposite wall, and placed his sword and pistol in the alcove. Ryoma sat down next to a black lacquered tray set with two cups and several flasks of *sake*, besides which was a brazier of burning charcoal. There was a folding screen in the corner near the window, on which were painted kimono-clad beauties, their faces reflecting the light from the lantern which stood nearby. "Now let's drink," Ryoma said.

"Yes. And what a beauty," the Choshu man said.

"Which one?" Ryoma asked, glancing at the screen.

"Oryo. She's been so worried about you, and anxious for you to return."

Ryoma filled both cups. "Let's drink," he said, ignoring the remark.

"Congratulations, Sakamoto-san. This is certainly a memorable night."

The two men drained their cups. "And *sake* has never tasted so good," Ryoma said.

"It feels good to be sitting in an actual room again," Miyoshi said.

"What do you mean?"

"With the police checking this place day and night, I had to hide in a closet upstairs most of the time you were gone. I think they suspect we're here. We must be very careful." Miyoshi reached for his long spear, the blade covered by a wooden sheath. "That's why I keep this with me at all times."

"By the way," Ryoma snickered, "I hear that Lord Yoshinobu is staying in Fushimi tonight. On his way to Kyoto from Osaka Castle. So while the Bakufu has been so busy guarding Yoshinobu, we've gotten Satsuma and Choshu together to sign the Tokugawa's death warrant." Ryoma laughed, took up the flask, and refilled both cups. "Let's drink to the Satsuma-Choshu Alliance," he said, his spirits soaring, although he hadn't slept in two days.

Ryoma relayed to Miyoshi the details of the alliance, the attitudes of Saigo and Katsura, and the plans to topple the Bakufu and restore the Emperor to power. After talking for nearly two hours, Ryoma yawned heavily, stretched both arms above his head. "What time is it? he asked.

"It must be after three."

"You and I had better go to Kyoto to see Saigo, but now I'm tired." Ryoma lay back in his bed, his hands behind his head.

Suddenly Miyoshi started, and reached for his spear. "Did you hear that?" he whispered.

"What?" Ryoma yawned again, not bothering to get up.

"Someone's voice downstairs."

"Oryo and Otose," Ryoma said, half asleep.

"I hear footsteps down there, near the base of the stairs."

"The two women," Ryoma said.

"It sounds like a lot more than just two women."

"Huh?" Ryoma muttered, his eyes closed.

Suddenly there was the sound of footsteps racing up the rear staircase. "Sakamoto-san! Miyoshi-san!" Oryo gasped. "There are men with spears coming up the front stairway."

Ryoma leaped to his feet, took his Smith and Wesson from the alcove, as the girl burst into the room stark naked. "Hurry, you must get out of here now. Down the back staircase," she said frantically.

"Oryo!" Ryoma shouted, grabbing a blanket. "Here, cover yourself!" He glanced at Miyoshi, who stood with his spear drawn, poised for an attack.

As Ryoma and Miyoshi had been talking upstairs, and Otose asleep downstairs, Oryo had been soaking in a hot bath. The bathroom was located at the back of the house, just across a narrow corridor leading to the rear staircase. Relieved that Ryoma had returned safely from Kyoto, she was relaxing for the first time since he had left three days ago. Then suddenly, *There was a thumping sound, and before I had much time to think about it, someone thrust a spear through the bathroom window, right by my shoulder,"* Oryo would recall years later. *"I grabbed the spear with one hand, and in an intentionally loud voice, so that I could be heard upstairs, yelled, 'Don't you know there's a woman in the bath? Who's there?' 'Be quiet,' a voice demanded, 'or I'll kill you.' 'You can't kill me,' I hollered back, and jumped out of the bathtub."*

After covering Oryo with the blanket, Ryoma rushed to the clothes rack to get his *hakama*. "Damn it," he muttered. "I must have left it in the other room." He took his pistol from the alcove, then removed his heavy cotton frock. "Oryo, get down here, out of the way," he whispered, crouching down on one knee at the rear of the room, his pistol in hand. Miyoshi kneeled beside Ryoma, his long spear ready for an attack, the lethal blade shining in the lantern light. Suddenly, the paper screen door slid open slightly.

"Who's in there?" a voice demanded, opening the door further. At the threshold stood a man in a black helmet, his sword drawn. Although he had expected to find the men asleep, after one look at Ryoma aiming his pistol straight at him, and Miyoshi armed with a spear, the man slammed the door shut and retreated into the dark corridor.

"Sakamoto-san," Oryo whispered, "you must escape quickly, down the back staircase."

"Keep quiet, and stay out of the way," Ryoma told her.

The house was silent now, except for a creaking sound in the next room. "Oryo," Ryoma whispered, "the lantern's too bright. Cover the back of it with my jacket." The girl followed Ryoma's instructions, darkening the room. "Good. Now shine it in that direction," he said, pointing his pistol at the door. "See if you can get that door off." When the girl removed the sliding panel door, Ryoma and Miyoshi saw some twenty men, many armed with spears, some holding burglar lanterns, and several wielding six-foot staves. "Oryo," Ryoma whispered, "I want you to get out of here, and see if you can make it to the Satsuma estate for help." Then, turning to the enemy, he screamed, "What's going on here? You can't insult Satsuma samurai by barging in on us like this."

"Orders from the Lord of Aizu," one of the enemy shouted.

Ryoma looked at Miyoshi, snickered, "Did you hear that?" Then glaring at the men in the corridor, he yelled, "Idiots! You can't expect Satsuma samurai to listen to orders from the Lord of Aizu."

"Get down," the Bakufu men demanded, then started to advance.

"Look out!" Miyoshi shouted. "On your left!" Ryoma whirled around, ducked under a swiping attack, delivered a kick to his opponent's groin, then immediately jumped back. Next he cocked his pistol, aimed it at one of his assailants, with ten others just beyond. Two shots sent all of them retreating into the corridor, and down the staircase, five or six stumbling over the others. "Ah, ha, ha, ha!" Ryoma roared. "Look at them run!"

"Sakamoto-san," Miyoshi whispered, "why don't you use your sword? You can't block an attack with your pistol."

Before Ryoma could answer, a spear came flying right at him, past his head, and stuck fast into a wooden beam on the wall behind. "Damn it!" Ryoma screamed, rushed at the doorway, crouched down and fired another shot. Meanwhile, Miyoshi thrust violently at the silhouette of a man behind the paper screen door on his left, as three more of the enemy charged through the other door, their swords drawn. Ryoma knocked the first man to the floor with a powerful blow to the jaw, then used his pistol to block an attack to his head. Just then, Miyoshi came from behind, slicing the man wide open from the top of his shoulder to his hip, as blood sprayed like a fountain. Another man came from behind the threshold, his short blade flashing in the lantern light. Ryoma, gripping his pistol with both hands, blocked an attack, but now he felt a sharp pain, first on his right hand, then his left. By the time he turned the pistol on his opponent and fired, the enemy had retreated back into the shadow. "That's five rounds," he whispered to Miyoshi. "Only one left in the cylinder." Just then, a man in a black hood appeared along the wall, his spear pointed directly at Ryoma's face. "Get down," Ryoma said, then moved behind Miyoshi and mounted his pistol on the Choshu man's left shoulder. "Take this, you son of a bitch!" Ryoma roared, firing point-blank into the man's chest.

"Did you get him?" Miyoshi asked.

Ryoma wiped his brow with the back of his hand, which he now realized was drenched with blood. "I think so. Look at him." The man was sprawled out on the floor, crawling on his belly. Suddenly there was a terrific crashing sound, as if the enemy were ripping apart screens and smashing doors upstairs, but still nobody approached. "Thank you, Takasugi," Ryoma said, sat down on the floor and removed the cylinder. "They're terrified of us, Miyoshi-san," he snickered. "Just the two of us, your spear and this pistol."

Miyoshi stood at the doorway, his spear ready for another attack. "What are you doing?" he said in an exasperated tone. "The enemy could charge any time."

"Reloading," Ryoma answered calmly, as if they were not in the middle of a battle. "But it's too dark in here," he said. "I can hardly see a thing." After Ryoma had loaded the first two bullets, something slipped out of his blood-drenched hands, and he cursed aloud.

"What's the trouble?" Miyoshi said, without removing his eyes from the doorway.

"I dropped the cylinder." It was only now that Ryoma knew that his hands had been cut so badly that he could barely use them. "*The base of my right thumb was sliced wide open, the knuckle of my left thumb hacked off and the knuckle of my left index finger cut down to the bone,*" he would write in a letter to his family.

"Can't you find it?" Miyoshi whispered, standing beside Ryoma, his spear poised for an attack.

"I'm looking. It's not under here." Ryoma searched through the bedding and ashes from the brazier which were scattered all over the floor. "Damn it," he muttered under his breath, threw down his pistol. "So much for that."

"Then the only thing left to do is charge the enemy and fight," Miyoshi whispered.

"Don't be stupid. Who knows how many of them are out there. If we have any chance at all, it's getting out of here through the back door." Ryoma stood up, tried to grab his sword, then drew back in pain. "Come on!" he demanded.

Miyoshi threw down his spear, and the two men snuck down the rear staircase, out the back door and into the night. Soon they came to a narrow alley just behind the inn. "Which way?" Miyoshi asked, looking down the alley, which led between two rows of houses into the central part of the town.

"We can't go that way," Ryoma whispered. "They'll definitely be waiting for us at the other end. The only way is through there." Ryoma pointed at a neighboring house, the back of which faced the rear of the Teradaya.

"We can't just break into someone's house," Miyoshi protested, albeit halfheartedly.

"Would you rather go the front way, and face the enemy again?"

"No."

"Then, let's go."

They ran to the house, kicked in the wooden shutter doors. Inside, the house was dark. "I can't see a thing," Ryoma said.

"There doesn't seem to be anyone here. All the fighting and shooting next door must have scared them away."

"I'm sorry to do it, but we have to get through to the other side," Ryoma said, charged the wall directly in front, smashing through it shoulder-first. "Let's get out of here," hollered.

They proceeded frantically through the dark house, kicking in screen doors, smashing down walls, crashing into furniture and whatever else happened to be in their way. When they finally reached the room at the front of the house, they noticed that the bedding had been laid out. "I guess you were right," Ryoma said, shaking his head. "It looks like we must have scared them out of their sleep. It's too bad, but let's get out of here." The two men trampled over the bedding and into the corridor leading to the front door of the house.

The air outside was freezing, and Ryoma only now noticed that all he was wearing was the thin cotton robe. "Not a soul around," he whispered, shivering. "I wonder which way to the Satsuma estate from here?"

"I think it's this way. Quickly, Sakamoto-san."

After running for some distance through the dark, Ryoma suddenly stopped at the side of a narrow waterway, near a wooden floodgate barely visible in the moonlight. He was dizzy and out of breath, both hands bleeding profusely. "Miyoshi-san," he panted, "do you know where we are?"

"No, not really."

"I don't think I can go much further." Not only had Ryoma lost a great deal of blood, but he felt feverish and delirious from lack of sleep.

"We must get you to a doctor quickly," Miyoshi said, looking at Ryoma's hands.

"I think an artery has been severed."

"Let's hide in that lumber shed over there so you can rest," Miyoshi said, pointing at an old two-story building on the other side of the waterway.

"The only way across is under the floodgate," Ryoma said, then stepped into the water, which he was relieved to find warmer than the freezing air. Both men took a deep breath, and very quietly went under, swimming beneath the floodgate to the opposite side.

"Through there," Miyoshi whispered as they stood dripping wet and shivering. "Up on that loft," he said after they had entered the shed. "Here," Miyoshi said, getting down on his hands and knees, "get on my back, and I'll help you up."

Ryoma took a deep breath, exhaling sharply as he pulled himself up onto the loft, his hands screaming with pain. Miyoshi climbed up after him, took off his jacket. "Here," he said, slicing off the sleeves with his short sword, and wrapping them around Ryoma's hands. "This will have to do until we can get you to a doctor."

The two men lay exhausted for several minutes, their heads propped up on pieces of cut lumber. "We can't wait too much longer," Ryoma said shivering, his arms wrapped around his wet body. "Soon it will be daybreak. They'll certainly find us then."

"Let's rest here a few minutes, then try to make it to the Satsuma estate," Miyoshi said.

"No. I can't go anywhere like this." Ryoma looked at his hands, the makeshift bandages soaked with blood. "I'd only slow you down."

"I can't leave you here."

"You must. It's our only chance. If you make it to the Satsuma estate, then you can come back with help."

"It's impossible. They'll surely find me. Sakamoto-san, the only thing left for us to do is cut our bellies right here and now, before they find us."

"Don't be stupid. If we do that, we lose for sure. With Satsuma and Choshu finally united, this is when the fun starts. I'm not ready to die just yet."

Miyoshi gave Ryoma a strange look. "Of course," he said.

"Just make sure you get to the Satsuma estate safely," Ryoma said. "Now hurry! Get there before the sun comes up."

Ryoma lay shivering as he watched the dim sunlight grow brighter, shining through the window above the loft. He felt his life fading from his body, but somehow knew that he would not yet die. "I wonder how many men we killed back there?" he thought sadly, then a more immediate problem overcame him. "What if the Bakufu police find me before help arrives? What if Miyoshi has been caught? He might very well be dead. But no matter, if he is I'll be joining him soon." Ryoma closed his eyes tightly, as his gaping, bleeding wounds pounded. "To die," he thought, "is merely to return one's life to Heaven." Although Ryoma rarely gave much thought to afterlife, he now concluded, "There's nothing to fear in death." Then shivering, he muttered, "If only it weren't so damn cold."

Miyoshi arrived at the Satsuma estate at sunrise. He was greeted by the Satsuma men, and Oryo, who, at Ryoma's instructions, had gone to the estate to seek help. By the time a contingent of Satsuma samurai had arrived at the Teradaya, however, Ryoma and Miyoshi had already escaped.

As Ryoma lay thinking and bleeding on the loft atop the woodshed, Miyoshi and Oryo anxiously watched four Satsuma men board a small, open riverboat, the Satsuma banner visible in the cold light of dawn. The estate was situated along the river, the rear of the building facing the water. "If he's alive," one of the men called out, as the boat departed, "we'll bring him back with us."

Miyoshi and Oryo went inside the estate to wait, besides themselves with anxiety. Although Miyoshi was exhausted and cut slightly at several places, he refused Oryo's treatment of his wounds. "I can't worry about myself until he has returned safely," Ryoma's bodyguard insisted.

Oryo sat down near a brazier, and poked nervously at the burning coals with a pair of long wooden sticks. "Miyoshi-san," she said calmly, despite a gnawing sensation in the pit of her stomach, "there must have been over a hundred of them last night. How did you two ever escape?"

"Were there that many?" Miyoshi said.

"It was a miracle that you survived."

Soon the Satsuma boat, flying the banner emblazoned with the black cross in a circle, returned to the estate. The four Satsuma men carried Ryoma inside, into a private room, where Oryo had prepared bandages, and white liquor as a disinfectant.

"Sakamoto-san, your hands!" Oryo gasped.

"I don't know what would have happened if it hadn't been for you," Ryoma said smiling. "Another minute later and they would have been all over us, with no warning at all."

"Sakamoto-san, you're bleeding badly. Now please be quiet and try to rest," Oryo said, as she set herself to tending his wounds.

"I'll kill them with my bare hands!" roared Saigo the Great, his large face red with anger. The sun had just risen when a messenger arrived at Satsuma's Kyoto headquarters with news of the attack at the Teradaya. "Yoshii," Saigo called his private secretary, who came immediately from the next room.

"Yes. What is it?" He had never seen Saigo so angry.

"Ryoma's been attacked by men under the Fushimi Magistrate." Saigo loaded a pistol as he spoke. Indeed, Saigo had good cause to be upset. Not only was Ryoma his friend, but without Ryoma there would never have been a Satsuma-Choshu Alliance. And from a more practical point of view, Saigo was sure that losing Ryoma would prove more harmful to the revolution than he dared imagine.

"Attacked" Yoshii blurted. "Where is he?"

"I don't know. I only know that he and his bodyguard have escaped. Get some men together," Saigo ordered. "We'll leave for Fushimi immediately to kill them."

"Kill who?" Yoshii asked.

"The criminals who attacked Ryoma!" Saigo boomed.

"Saigo-san," the little man hollered, in an attempt to bring the huge man to his senses. "I understand your anger, but I wish you'd let me handle the situation." Saigo stared silently at his friend, breathing hard. "You see," Yoshii continued, "if you rush to Fushimi right now, you'll only give us away. Even if the Bakufu suspects Ryoma, they are still most likely unaware that he is working with us. Anyway, attacking the magistrate's office will only cause unnecessary trouble."

"I don't care about trouble," Saigo boomed with the wrath of one of the many cannon he had recently purchased from foreigner traders. "I only know that if Ryoma is dead, I will not rest until I've gotten vengeance." He thrust his loaded pistol into his sash.

As Saigo was preparing to leave for Fushimi a second messenger arrived with word that Ryoma was safe.

"How badly is he wounded?" Saigo asked.

"His hands are cut up, but apparently nothing too serious."

Saigo heaved a heavy sigh of relief, sat down on the *tatami* floor, took his pistol from his sash and placed it on the table. "Alright Yoshii, you handle it your way. But we must get a doctor to Ryoma right away, and bring him here, where he'll be safe."

"I'll make the arrangements immediately," Yoshii said, then started to leave.

"Excuse me," the messenger said nervously, casting a quick glance at Saigo.

"What is it?" Yoshii said.

"I don't think that Sakamoto will be in any condition to travel for at least a few days."

"Of course," Yoshii said.

"No matter," Saigo grabbed Yoshii by the wrist. "I want you to take a rifle platoon to the Fushimi estate to guard him. If the Bakufu men should come for him, you have my orders to hold them off by force if need be. Then, when Ryoma is well enough to travel, I want you to bring him here." Turning to the messenger Saigo added, "Tell them that I'll send a doctor immediately, and that an armed guard will be arriving shortly after."

"No," Yoshii interrupted, drawing a worried look from the messenger, who couldn't believe that anyone would dare contradict Saigo. "I'll bring the doctor to Fushimi myself. We'll leave on horseback this morning."

"Good!" Saigo grinned widely, to the relief of the distraught messenger, who immediately bowed and took his leave.

Saigo looked grimly at Yoshii. "Meanwhile," he said, "let's hope the

Fushimi Magistrate has not discovered anything. The longer the Bakufu is unaware of the Satsuma-Choshu Alliance, the better."

The Fushimi Magistrate was furious when he learned that the two outlaws had escaped. Not only had they killed or wounded several of his men, but Ryoma left behind a document revealing his complicity in the Satsuma-Choshu Alliance. The magistrate, however, suspected that the document was a fake, intended to fool him into believing that an alliance had been formed. "Whether it's true or not," he told his men, "find them and kill them, particularly Sakamoto. His very existence is dangerous to the House of Tokugawa." Having discovered a few days later that Ryoma and Miyoshi had taken refuge at the Satsuma estate, the magistrate dispatched a group of men to arrest them.

"I have no idea what you're talking about," a Satsuma man lied when the police arrived at the outer gate.

"We know they're in here," roared a burly man, dressed all in black, ten others with him.

"I have no idea what you're talking about," the Satsuma man repeated.

"We have orders from the Magistrate of Fushimi to arrest Sakamoto Ryoma."

"Are you calling me, a samurai of Satsuma, a liar?" the man screamed, his confidence fortified by a platoon of sixty men who had just arrived from Kyoto. Presently, ten of them, armed with rifles, appeared at the front entranceway.

"We'll be back," the burly police commander sneered, before retreating with his men.

Inside the estate, Oryo hadn't left Ryoma's side for three days, until the bleeding finally stopped. Although his quick recovery was due in part to a naturally strong constitution, not to mention the skill of the Dutch-educated physician whom Yoshii had brought, more than anything else, and much to his chagrin, Ryoma felt indebted to Oryo. "*It was only because of Oryo that I survived*," he would write to his sister.

"If we had never been attacked that way," he told himself over and over during the week he spent in bed, "maybe I'd never have felt this way about her." Then, after days of introspection, when Oryo came to change his bandages one morning, Ryoma took her by the hand.

"Oryo," he said, "I think you and I owe a lot to the Fushimi Magistrate."

Oryo laughed. "What are you talking about? Sometimes you say such foolish things. You haven't stopped joking since you got here."

"I'm serious. If it hadn't been for the attack, I might never have asked you to marry me." Although Ryoma attempted nonchalance, he could not hide his embarrassment.

"I have to change your bandages," Oryo said, tears welling in her eyes.

"Why are you crying?"

"It's just that I'm so happy," Oryo said, removing the bandages from Ryoma's left hand.

"Then, you'll marry me?"

"Yes, Sakamoto-san. Yes."

While Ryoma was proposing marriage to Oryo inside of the Satsuma estate, spies from the Fushimi Magistrate's office were keeping close watch outside. "He has to come out sometime," the magistrate reasoned. "And when he does, we'll get him."

"Not on my life," Saigo told Yoshii, as if he had read the magistrate's mind seven leagues away at Satsuma headquarters in Kyoto. "Even if it is dangerous bringing them here, we must move them somehow."

"Would you like me to dispatch another rifle platoon?" Yoshii asked with a sardonic grin.

"Another sixty men." Saigo nodded slowly. "Yes."

"Then I'll do it immediately," Yoshii said, getting up to leave.

"And one more thing," Saigo said.

"Yes?"

"Be sure that they bring a howitzer," Saigo said laughing.

"Is there something funny about our men bringing a howitzer from Kyoto to Fushimi?"

"Not at all."

"Then why do you laugh?"

"It's the thought of the look on the magistrate's face when he sees one hundred twenty Satsuma samurai, each armed with a rifle, just to guard a single *ronin*." Perfect warmth radiated from the great man's eyes. "But what the magistrate doesn't know, is that that particular *ronin* is worth more than all of his men put together."

Yoshii led the second rifle platoon through the outer gate of the Fushimi estate just after noon of the first day of February, an intimidating howitzer mounted on a cart at the rear of the procession.

"Sakamoto-san," Yoshii called as he hurried into the building. "Where's Sakamoto-san?"

"Right this way," Oryo answered, followed by two guards armed with rifles.

"How is he?" Yoshii asked anxiously.

"I've never seen him look so good," Oyro beamed.

Yoshii found Ryoma in a room at the rear of the building. Miyoshi was with him, as was Nakaoka, who had rushed to Fushimi from Dazaifu when he heard Ryoma had been wounded.

"I've come to take you back with me to Kyoto," Yoshii said. "Saigo is waiting there for you with another man."

"Who?" Ryoma asked.

"Ike Kurata. When he heard about what happened, he was ready to attack the magistrate's office by himself. As was Saigo."

"The poor magistrate has had a hard enough time with us as it is," Ryoma snickered.

"Since you're safe now, I think they can be convinced to hold off their attack," Yoshii snickered. "And by the way, Sakamoto-san, since I doubted you'd be in any condition to walk into Kyoto, I've arranged a palanquin for you."

"Ah," Miyoshi interrupted, glancing at Ryoma out of the corner of his eye, "I think we'll need one more."

"One more what?" Yoshii asked.

"Palanquin."

"Don't worry, Miyoshi-san. We have extra uniforms and rifles for you and Nakaoka-san. The two of you can march along with the rest of our men. Nobody will know you're not from Satsuma."

"It's not us I'm worried about," Miyoshi said.

"Oh?"

"I can't very well leave Oryo behind," Ryoma muttered, obviously embarrassed.

"I see," Yoshii said, nodding grimly. "But we only have one palanquin here in Fushimi."

"No problem," Ryoma said, then called the girl, who soon appeared at the doorway. "Oryo, how would you like to disguise yourself as a Satsuma samurai?" Ryoma asked.

"Joking again!" Oryo laughed, then turning to Yoshii said, "He hasn't stopped joking since he got here."

"I'm not joking. Yoshii-san, do you have an extra *hakama*, jacket and swords?"

"Sakamoto-san," Yoshii blurted, "you're amazing." Then turning to Oryo, "I'll get you a rifle also, if you wouldn't mind."

"Mind?" Oryo said, "I'd love it."

Later that afternoon, over 120 samurai, each armed with a rifle and two swords, marched through the outer gate of the Satsuma estate in Fushimi, with three men at the rear towing the howitzer. At the center of the procession was a palanquin displaying the Shimazu cross; and although it was apparent to the dozens of Bakufu troops who watched vexedly from the side of the road that Sakamoto Ryoma rode inside, they dared not disturb the men of Satsuma.

Just before leaving, Ryoma had asked Yoshii to lead the procession past the Teradaya. For all Otose knew Ryoma was dead; with the Bakufu police staking out her inn since the attack, the Satsuma men had been unable to inform her otherwise. "If you see Otose as we pass by the Teradaya," Ryoma had instructed Oryo, "throw this at her." He handed her a small amulet that Otose had bought on her New Year's pilgrimage to a local shrine. "She gave it to me on the night we arrived at the Teradaya, before we left for Kyoto. She said it would protect me," he laughed. "And maybe she's right, because I've been wearing it ever since, and I'm not dead yet."

"Sakamoto-san," the girl whispered as the procession approached the Teradaya. Oryo was marching alongside the palanquin, dressed like the other men; her hair was tied in a topknot, she carried a heavy rifle over her shoulder, and two swords hung at her left hip. "I can see Otose-san. She's watching from the side of the road."

"Well, throw the amulet," Ryoma said. "And make sure you throw it hard."

Oryo did just that, and the amulet landed at Otose's feet. By the time Otose picked it up, the procession had already passed by, but she now knew that Sakamoto Ryoma was alive.

Arriving at Satsuma's Kyoto headquarters before dusk, Ryoma, Miyoshi, Nakaoka and Oryo were immediately shown to a private room, where Saigo was waiting. "Sakamoto-san, you gave us quite a scare," Saigo said, taking hold of Ryoma's right forearm, and inspecting the wounds on his hand. Then turning to Miyoshi, he bowed. "I am Saigo Kichinosuke of Satsuma. I hear that you fought bravely at the Teradaya. I can't thank you enough for all you've done for Sakamoto-san."

"We fought well together," Miyoshi said, bowing his head slightly.
"And you must be Oryo-san." The commander in chief of the most powerful army in Japan bowed to the young girl. "How can I ever repay you for saving their lives? What ever you want, whatever you need, just let me know and you'll have it. And I must say," he said grinning, "you look quite impressive dressed like that."

Oryo bowed deeply. "Thank you very much," she said demurely. I...I really..." the girl hesitated.

"Go ahead, Oryo," Ryoma urged. "He's big, but he doesn't bite."

"If it wouldn't be too much to ask, Saigo-san, I'd like to borrow a kimono, a woman's kimono that is. All of my things are still in Fushimi at the Teradaya."

"Done!" Saigo bellowed. "We'll get you the finest kimono in Kyoto. But you must be very tired. Please sit down. I want all of you to relax for a few days."

"A few days?" Ryoma said, sitting down with the others near a large blue ceramic brazier. "I've been relaxing for the past week. As a matter of fact, I've never felt more relaxed in my life. What I need now is to get down to Shimonoseki to talk to Katsura and Takasugi about the war."

In January, only days after Satsuma and Choshu were secretly united, the Bakufu convinced the Imperial Court to issue an edict for the retirement of the Choshu *daimyo*, and a reduction in the land and income of his domain. Since the Bakufu was ill prepared for war, it had hoped that these relatively lenient terms would convince Choshu to relinquish its defiant stance; but when its demands were brazenly ignored, Edo resorted to more affirmative action.

In February, troops from thirty-one *han*, which in the previous November had been ordered by the Bakufu to prepare for war, surrounded Choshu; and while Ryoma lay convalescing at Satsuma's Fushimi estate, Takasugi's revolutionary army, "*silent as the dead of night*," awaited an attack.

Disunity, however, continued to bedevil Edo. The most prominent of those in the Bakufu who opposed the second expedition were Okubo Ichio, Matsudaira Shungaku and Katsu Kaishu. (Although Kaishu was still under house arrest in Edo, he made his position known through various influential visitors, including Okubo.) Kaishu's Group of Four (minus Yokoi Shonan, still under house arrest) feared that civil war might invite foreign invasion. They proposed that instead of fighting among one another, the most powerful clans should cooperate with Edo for the common good of Japan, and a council of lords be formed to settle the Choshu problem. Not only had the expedition already cost a great deal of money–money which would best be spent fortifying the nation–but the thirty-one lords who had sent troops to the Choshu borders had only done so out of protocol. Surely these lords would hesitate before actually fighting a war whose victory would only strengthen Edo, and very possibly spell their own destruction. The Group of Four pointed out that most of these lords had mistakenly expected Choshu to surrender once their armies were massed at its borders. Furthermore, it was clear that few of the Bakufu troops, and virtually none of their commanders, had much stomach for war, and that the lords themselves were anxious for their armies to return to their respective fiefdoms, lest disorder at home occur during their absence.

Even some of the Bakufu's most powerful allies viewed the expedition against Choshu as designed to crush the possibility against resistance to Edo. They feared the repercussions from exorbitant prices which war would inevitably cause, foreseeing riots among the commoners, and uprisings in their own fiefdoms. The Lord of Owari, the Tokugawa branch head who had commanded the first expedition, refused to cooperate with the second. The Lord of Fukui (Shungaku's heir), who was vice-commander of the first expedition, worked within court circles in an attempt to block the second. With such staunch Bakufu allies opposing the expedition, it was no wonder that the most powerful of the Outside Lords followed suit. The Lords of Hiroshima and Okayama, in southwest Honshu, felt that an expedition could not possibly serve their interests. The Lord of Fukuoka, in northern Kyushu, reneged on his initial agreement to fight for the Bakufu. Lord Yodo of Tosa, despite his firm refusal to actually oppose the Tokugawa, rejected a Bakufu request to send troops, claiming that compliance would spark rebellion among the Loyalists in Tosa. But most ominous was the attitude of Satsuma, which had recently shown open hostility to Edo, though its alliance with Choshu remained secret. The uneasiness of these lords about Tokugawa intentions was exacerbated by the knowledge that Edo was becoming more intimate with, if not dependent upon, the government of Napoleon III.

The French, who were fiercely competing with the British for diplomatic dominance of Asia, supported the Tokugawa, just as their rivals had unofficially allied themselves with Satsuma-Choshu. Leon Roches, Napoleon III's minister to Japan, insisted that the only way the Bakufu would be able to completely dominate the country would be through French military aid–an opinion that Oguri Tadamasa, Kaishu's nemesis who had replaced him as navy commissioner, wholly adopted. The Bakufu had recently procured from the French state-of-the-art cannon to mount on its warships; and, as Okubo had warned Ryoma, the construction of a Tokugawa shipyard at Yokosuka, just west of Yokohama, had finally begun with French backing. The Bakufu's readiness to be thus seduced by the French was no secret, and the great lords suspected that once they had helped the Tokugawa crush Choshu, their own destruction would be imminent.

"And when the war starts, my men and I will fight at sea, alongside Takasugi's Extraordinary Corps," Ryoma boasted, as he painfully wondered if Katsu Kaishu would not be commanding the Tokugawa fleet.

"Yes, the war," Saigo said ominously. "It's only a matter of time before the Bakufu armies attack."

"Saigo-san," Ryoma said, "could you arrange for a Satsuma ship to take us to Shimonoseki? The sooner the better."

The great man smiled, his black eyes shimmering like two large diamonds. "Sakamoto-san, I'd rather see you completely recuperated first. But since you can't seem to sit still for too long..."

"Ryoma-san," a voice called from the corridor, as Saigo stopped short his speech.

"Kura!" Ryoma answered. "Come in."

Ike Kurata wore a sullen expression, despite his delight at being reunited with Ryoma. "I can't tell you how happy I am to see you alive," he said.

Ryoma laughed. "Well, I'm glad I could make you happy, Kura."

"But..." Kurata hesitated.

"What is it?" Ryoma said.

"I have bad news from Nagasaki."

Ryoma braced himself, glanced at the others. "Let's hear it," he said.

"Kondo Chojiro is dead."

Of Sorrow and Celebration

Another one of Ryoma's close friends was dead. But despite the hardships fate cast his way, he was determined to carry on. "I can't help but feel more than ever that human life is truly a dream," Ryoma would write to his family, lamenting the loss of his comrades, while alluding to the unpredictability of life, and the untimeliness of death, which now, even more than the Bakufu, the threats of civil war and foreign subjugation, pursued the Dragon on his perilous quest for freedom.

Ryoma was now anxious to get to Kameyama Company headquarters, to investigate the details of Chojiro's death. "If you must go, I'll arrange for a ship to take us to Nagasaki," Saigo offered his distraught friend. "But I would like you to come with me to Kagoshima." More than anything Saigo was determined to keep Ryoma out of harm's way. And what safer place, he reasoned, than his beloved Satsuma? "After what you've been through over these past few months, you need rest. And I know you will enjoy the hot springs in the mountains of Satsuma. Whenever a Satsuma man has something ailing him, he goes to the hot spring baths, even before seeing a doctor. Come with me to Kagoshima and I'll have your hands and spirit completely healed in no time."

Ryoma, however, was not as eager to hide from the Bakufu as Saigo was to hide him. "What Saigo is suggesting," he thought, "is exile." But aware that Saigo himself had twice met such a fate, Ryoma found it difficult to speak these thoughts, much less refuse the great man's kindness. "I appreciate it, Saigo-san. But all I can think about right now is Chojiro. First I must investigate the circumstances of his death."

"If you'll forgive my selfishness," Saigo persisted, "the real reason I want you to come to Kagoshima is to help me convince our lord to support our campaign against the Bakufu." Despite his sincerity, the Satsuma military commander was not beyond bending the truth, if he could rationalize that it was for the common good; and keeping Sakamoto Ryoma alive, he reasoned, was certainly for the common good. "Now that we're allied with Choshu, I have to convince Lord Hisamitsu and his council of the necessity of overthrowing the Bakufu." This was not entirely untrue, and Ryoma knew it. Ryoma was, in fact, aware that the hereditary Satsuma elite had never opposed the Bakufu, with the exception of Hereditary Councilor Komatsu Tatewaki. And although Saigo, Okubo and Komatsu were indeed the *de facto* leaders of Satsuma, they preferred to have the full support of the entire *han*, particularly that of Lord Hisamitsu.

"I see, Saigo-san." Ryoma spoke as if in a daze, possessed by one thought only: finding out why Chojiro had killed himself.

"Then we'll leave as soon as I can arrange for a ship to take us," Saigo said.

On the following day Ryoma and Oryo were sitting alone in the garden behind the estate, under a plum tree, its branches shrouded with blossoms of pale purple. "I wish," Ryoma said, picking up a fallen blossom and carefully plucking the tiny petals one by one, "that you could meet my family in Kochi, especially my sister Otome."

"So do I, Sakamoto-san."

"Wait a minute!" Ryoma smiled. This was the first time Oryo had seen him smile since they had heard the news of Chojiro's death. "Even if we can't go to Kochi, that doesn't mean we can't have a honeymoon."

"A honeymoon?" Oryo gave Ryoma a puzzled look. Indeed, she had no idea what he was talking about.

"A trip to celebrate our marriage. That's the custom in Europe and America."

"A trip to Nagasaki? That would be wonderful."

"Not Nagasaki."

"Where will we go?"

"We'll stop at Nagasaki, but just long enough for me to take care of some urgent business." Ryoma was, of course, referring to finding out the circumstances of Chojiro's death, which he preferred not to discuss with his bride-to-be. "Then, we'll go down to Satsuma to the hot spring baths that Saigo's been talking about. That way he'll be happy, and so will we."

At the end of February Ryoma and Oryo were officially married in the presence of Saigo and Nakaoka, before the four left Kyoto for Osaka to board a Satsuma steamer with Kurata, Miyoshi, Komatsu and Yoshii. The group arrived at Nagasaki via Choshu on the morning of March 8, minus Miyoshi and Nakaoka, whom they had left in Shimonoseki. (At home Miyoshi received a hero's welcome. He was praised, promoted and rewarded with extra income by the Choshu government for his valor in the fight at the Teradaya, without which Sakamoto Ryoma would surely have been killed.)

As Saigo was anxious to return to Kagoshima, Ryoma left his new bride aboard ship, which had temporarily dropped anchor at Nagasaki, and hurried with Kurata to Kameyama Company headquarters, in the hills overlooking the bay from the east.

Ryoma found all six of his men present. "Ryoma-san," Sonojo said, running to the front of the house to meet him. "We were so worried about you."

Ryoma responded with grim silence.

"Ryoma-san," Taro hollered, patting his uncle on the shoulder, "I've never been so happy in my life to see anyone."

Still Ryoma did not answer, drawing distraught looks from all six men.

"You've lost weight, Sakamoto-san," Umanosuke offered, a worried look in his eyes.

"Yes," Ryoma said gruffly. "Let's skip the small talk." He gave each of them a hard look. "Now, Sonojo," he singled out this old friend with whom he had fled Tosa four years before, "I want to hear what happened to Chojiro."

"Chojiro died like a true samurai," Sonojo said assertively.

"Idiot!" Ryoma roared, stunning his men as they stood in a circle around him. "Chojiro was a commoner. Now tell me why he died," he demanded.

Sonojo looked downward to avoid Ryoma's angry stare. "As punishment for breaking company rules. He was planning to..." Sonojo was silenced by a punch to the jaw.

"Idiots!" Ryoma exploded, his face red from anger, his eyes bulging. "The whole bunch of you are idiots. Chojiro had more talent than all of you put together, and that's why you were out to get him since we first came to Nagasaki. Now he's dead, damn you all." Ryoma ceased his tirade, and the room was suddenly silent. "But I guess it's my own fault for leaving him here in the first place," he muttered, as if speaking to himself. "If I'd have kept him with me, he'd be alive now." Tears welled in Ryoma's eyes. "Now, Sonojo," he said calmly, sitting down on the *tatami* floor, "tell me exactly what happened."

Since returning to Nagasaki with Ryoma in the previous December, Chojiro had been plagued by guilt for having lost command of the

Union to the Choshu naval office. These feelings were exacerbated by the jealousy of the others for the favor he had earned among Choshu and Satsuma samurai for his success in procuring weapons and a warship. But now his comrades in Nagasaki were eager to cover up their petty jealousy with contempt for his failure in losing the command of the ship; and as a result, the bean jam bun maker's son's sense of inferiority over his humble lineage now weighed heavier upon him than ever.

But in his resourcefulness, Chojiro had devised a way out of his predicament. Since the days he had studied Western culture under Kawada Shoryo in Kochi, he had dreamed of going abroad. During the months that he had been working with Ito and Inoue to procure weapons for Choshu, he had discussed with them on several occasions the possibility of his studying in England. Since both Choshu men had recently returned from England themselves, they were able to offer him advice on how to arrange such a trip, but were as of yet unable to guarantee him the necessary funds. "However," Inoue had promised, "if we do get the rifles and at least one warship, I will personally see to it that you receive enough money for your trip." Chojiro's eventual success in procuring the weapons and ship not only won him praise from the Lord of Choshu, but as Inoue had promised, the Choshu government rewarded him with a substantial amount of gold, which he kept secret from his comrades in Nagasaki.

At the beginning of January, not long after Ryoma had left Nagasaki, Chojiro heard from Inoue that the arms merchant Thomas Glover would soon be sailing to England aboard a British steamer. Secretly the two men visited the Scotsman at his mansion overlooking the Port of Nagasaki, where they requested passage to Europe for Chojiro aboard the British steamer on the afternoon of January 14, while Ryoma prepared to set sail with Miyoshi aboard the Satsuma ship from Shimonoseki to Kobe. And just as the stormy weather had delayed Ryoma's journey, rough seas postponed the departure of the British vessel until the following day.

"Maybe I should remain on board in case the others discover my plans," he thought, but immediately discarded the idea. "I'm a samurai," he told himself, "and must live according to the code."

The unwritten code of the samurai demanded that a man of the swords never cower in the face of danger; and as Chojiro was determined to prove to himself and others that he was as worthy of the two swords as anyone else, he would not, and could not, remain on board ship. This is not to say that Chojiro was anxious for trouble; for although he assumed that the others were still unaware of his plans, he was cautious enough to ask Glover's permission to stay the night at his home, instead of returning to company headquarters, or even to the small house in town that the company had procured as an office. That evening as he lay in bed in a guest room at Glover's house, listening to the steady pelting of the rain against the glass windowpane, and hoping beyond hope for the prompt arrival of a tomorrow that he would never see, he was startled by a loud banging at the front door downstairs.

"Yes, who's there?" Chojiro heard Glover's servant say.

"We're from the Kameyama Company," a voice answered. "We've heard that one of our men, Kondo Chojiro, is staying here." Recognizing Sonojo's voice, Chojiro was overcome by fear, as he realized that his dream of studying abroad was now shattered. "How did they find out?" he muttered aloud, put on his clothes which were still soaked from the rain, and remembering his resolve not to run from danger, slowly walked down the banistered staircase to face Sonojo and Taro.

"Let's go, Chojiro," Taro said, and the three men proceeded silently on a short downhill walk to the company office in town.

"Come in and sit down, Chojiro," Yonosuke greeted him with exaggerated goodwill. "We've been waiting for you."

Chojiro nodded in an attempt to conceal his terror, then entered the small room. The light from a European glass lantern illuminated the faces of six angry men, as he sat down among them, and thought bitterly that although they had been influenced by Kaishu and Ryoma, not one of them had completely shed their xenophobic convictions. After a short, awful period of silence, during which Chojiro regretted ever having left his father's shop in Kochi, Sonojo began speaking in a slow, deliberate voice. "As you all know, it has been the policy of our company from the very start that all of us have an equal share in the benefits and the hardships of our undertakings. And you also know that it is our policy to act only after obtaining consensus from the entire group." Sonojo paused, looked straight at Chojiro, who was less eager to return the favor. "Anyone who ignores this and takes arbitrary action is obligated under oath to die by his own sword." Sonojo paused again, shot another piercing glance at Chojiro, who felt his stomach drop. "Unfortunately, however, there is one among us who seems to have forgotten this oath." All six men glared at Chojiro, who sat silently, his head hung low. "And that person is none other than Kondo Chojiro," Sonojo screamed, as if pronouncing a sentence of death.

Chojiro's face was the color of chalk as he tried to speak, but before he could get the words out Sonojo shouted at the top of his lungs, "There are no explanations necessary. If you ever deserved to wear those two swords, then prove it tonight."

A long silence ensued, as a cold draft blew through a crack in the wall, causing the flame in the glass lantern to flicker. "If only Ryoma were here," Chojiro thought, then looked up to face the others. "Please leave me to myself," he muttered in a voice barely audible. "I need to be alone."

As Sonojo finished speaking, Ryoma stood up slowly, a look of remorse on his face, then grabbed his sword as if to leave.

"So you see," Sonojo placated, "it was Chojiro's own decision. We left the house as he requested, and when we came back an hour later he had done it."

"And he performed the *seppuku* very bravely," Taro added. "Cut a perfect cross into his belly."

"I can't believe that you actually let him do it without a second to assist him." Ryoma grimaced as he thought of the excruciating pain he imagined Chojiro had experienced during his last moments in this world.

"But Sakamoto-san," Toranosuke said indignantly, "you make it sound as if we were the ones who broke company rules, and planned to go to England with money that belonged to the company."

Ryoma groaned, sat down again. "I'm not blaming any of you for what you did. I know you had no choice, and even acted correctly. It's your motivation that bothers me, and the animosity you always had for Chojiro. And you, Sonojo, what makes you think you have the right to say Chojiro died like a samurai, when you've forgotten one of the basics of the warrior's code?"

"Which is?" Sonojo asked sheepishly.

"Mercy." Ryoma paused, drew the pistol which Saigo had given him to replace the one he had lost at the Teradaya. "If only I'd have been here," he muttered sadly, shaking his head.

"Ryoma-san," Kurata broke the gloomy mood, "it's time to return to the ship. Saigo is waiting, and..."

"Yonosuke," Ryoma interrupted, "when will the *Werewolf* be ready?" The *Werewolf* was the sailing schooner that the Kameyama

Company had recently purchased from Glover, with the financial assistance of Satsuma.

"I can't say for sure," Yonosuke said. "Right now it's being repaired at Yokohama."

"I see," Ryoma said gruffly. "Before I leave, I want you all to know that I brought Kura here specifically to serve as an officer aboard the *Union*, while we still have it, and after that, on the *Werewolf*, when it's ready."

"But Ryoma-san," Kurata strongly objected, "I hardly have any sailing experience." He was painfully aware that he was the only one among the group who had not trained under Katsu Kaishu.

"Sailing experience will come with sailing," Ryoma said. "But let me ask you something, Kura. How many times have you been in actual combat?"

"Nine times," Kurata answered bluntly.

"And how many times have you been wounded?"

"None."

"And," Ryoma shot a hard glance at the others, "didn't you tell me that during all those battles you never once hit the dirt after the shooting started, even though the others around you did?"

"Yes."

"You remained standing and called out your orders, right?"

Yes."

"And you're proud of that, aren't you?"

"Yes."

"As you should be."

"I see." The younger man, beside himself with pride, struggled to hide his feelings.

"Now," Ryoma continued, "is there anyone else here who can say that, because I can't." Ryoma eyed the others, none of whom answered. Then turning to Kurata he said, "With a combat record like yours, don't ever let anyone tell you that you're not worthy of commanding a warship." Ryoma paused, grinned widely. "Or at least fighting against the Bakufu aboard one."

"I see." Kurata nodded slowly, unable to suppress a smile.

"Good!" Ryoma turned to Taro. "Now that that's settled, I have to get back to the ship." He thrust his pistol into his sash, under his faded black kimono. "Saigo is anxious to get back to Kagoshima. While I'm away, I want you men to pick up that shipment of rice in Shimonoseki that Katsura's promised Saigo, and bring it down to Satsuma on the

Union. I'll be waiting for you in Kagoshima. From there we can return the *Union* to Shimonoseki, as I'm sure that Choshu will be needing it a lot more than we will, when the fighting starts."

"When will that be?" Taro asked.

"Anytime now. The Bakufu armies have already surrounded Choshu."

"No," Taro interjected. "I mean when will the rice shipment be ready?"

"Soon, I expect." Ryoma removed a small pouch from his kimono, opened it to see how much money he had. "Yonosuke," he said, "what would it cost to get my picture taken at that place down by the river?"

"You mean the studio of Ueno Hikoma?"

"Yes."

"Two silver coins, which is enough to buy a girl and drink all night at Maruyama," Yonosuke said in a monotone.

Ryoma snickered. "As usual, Yonosuke, you learn the important things quickly. Anyway, that means it would cost one *ryo* for two of us."

"Are you and Oryo-san..."

"No," Ryoma interrupted. "Yonosuke give Kura and I each a white navy *hakama*. We're going to have our pictures taken before I leave Nagasaki."

"But," Umanosuke cut in, "I thought you said that Saigo was waiting for you."

"He is. With my wife."

"Your wife?" Taro blurted in surprise, his mouth open wide.

"Yes. I was married at Satsuma headquarters in Kyoto to the girl who saved my life at the Teradaya."

"Why didn't you tell us?"

"I've had a million things more important to worry about. Anyway, I want to take that picture for Oryo before I leave. You can bring it to me when you come to Kagoshima."

Soon Ryoma and Kurata reached the front gate of the home of Japan's first commercial photographer, Ueno Hikoma, who four years earlier had opened a studio in his house, located along the Nakajimagawa river, at the foot of the hills on the east side of the city. "How do they feel?" Kurata asked, looking down at a pair of black leather boots Ryoma had just purchased at a shop along the way.

"Alright, I guess. But I wouldn't want to wear them all the time."

Ryoma called at the front door of the house, which was opened by a younger man. "What can I do for you?" he asked.

This was Ueno Hikoma, whom Ryoma had recently heard of from Katsura and Takasugi. "We'd like our pictures taken," Ryoma said in a thick Kochi drawl.

"Please come in," Ueno smiled through intelligent eyes. By the men's white *hakama* he knew that they were of the Kameyama Company.

Ryoma and Kurata stepped up onto an immaculately polished wooden floor, drawing a strange look from the photographer. First of all, Ueno had never seen a samurai wearing boots; but more than that, Ryoma didn't remove them before entering.

"But your boots!" Ueno objected.

"Don't worry," Ryoma said, "they're brand-new. And anyway, I want to have my picture taken with them on."

"I see," Ueno answered taken aback, but nevertheless welcomed the business. Customers were hard to come by; not only because of the high cost of photography, but also because of a popular superstition that a person's spirit was absorbed by the camera, and imprinted on the photograph.

Ueno led the two men into his studio, where sunlight shined through a glass roof. "I'll go first, Kura," Ryoma said, "just to show you how stupid it is for you to believe in superstition." Ryoma stood beside a dark brown wooden lectern, one of many props that Ueno had in his studio, then drew his pistol from his sash.

"Are you ready?" Ueno asked from under a black hood behind the camera.

"Wait!" Ryoma pulled both arms out of their sleeves, tucked his hands inside his kimono, and with the pistol concealed in his right hand, leaned with his right elbow against the lectern. The black boots, the short sword no longer than a dagger, the soiled white navy *hakama*, the unkempt hair, the squinting eyes, the dark sunbaked face all combined to form the image of one of Japan's first truly modern men. "Now I'm ready," Ryoma said, looking beyond the camera, into the future.

Later that afternoon Ryoma returned alone to the Satsuma ship, which set sail soon afterward, reaching Kagoshima two days later. In Kagoshima Castletown the Tosa *ronin* and his bride stayed at the stately residence of Komatsu Tatewaki. The mansion of this hereditary councilor to the Lord of Satsuma was located on high ground above the castletown, backed by hills overlooking the bay, and to the front commanded a perfect view of the volcano Sakurajima, rising out of the bay, spewing white smoke into a metallic blue sky.

A few days later, Ryoma and Oryo, guided by Yoshii, set out for the hot spring mineral baths in the misty mountains of Kirishima, northeast of Kagoshima. *"This place was so unusual you'd think you were in a different world,"* Ryoma wrote to Otome about the "misty mountains." *"We stayed there for ten days, fishing in the rivers and shooting birds with my pistol."*

Ryoma and Oryo returned to Kagoshima on April 12, and when they arrived at Komatsu's home there was some very good news awaiting them.

"Sakamoto-san," Komatsu said, his eyes radiating goodwill, "we've been informed by our office in Nagasaki that a crew of your men will soon be sailing for Kagoshima, aboard the *Werewolf.*"

"Then it's ready?" Ryoma said excitedly.

"Yes, finally!"

"Terrific!" Ryoma slapped his knee. "We finally have a ship. How can I ever thank you, Komatsu-san?"

"You already have, tenfold," assured the high-ranking Satsuma official, alluding to the alliance with Choshu.

Regardless of who was more indebted to whom, Ryoma's company finally had their own ship, to do with as they pleased. The Kameyama Company had recently purchased the wooden sailing schooner *Werewolf* from Glover for 6,300 *ryo*, a fraction of the amount Choshu had paid for the much larger steam-powered *Union*. Although most of this money had come from the Satsuma treasury, Ryoma's company put up a portion from the capital it had accumulated in Nagasaki over the past year.

"Sakamoto-san," Komatsu said, producing a letter, "the details are all here." According to the letter, the *Werewolf*, which had recently arrived in Nagasaki, would soon be leaving for Kagoshima with a crew of fifteen, whom the company had recently enlisted to sail under the command of Captain Ike Kurata. The letter stated two purposes for the trip, as reported by Ryoma's men in Nagasaki: a christening ceremony for the schooner to be held in Kagoshima; and providing the crew with actual sailing experience, as all of them, including the captain, were novices in the art of navigation. Sailing alongside the *Werewolf* would be the *Union*, carrying the shipment of rice which

Choshu was sending to Satsuma, and commanded entirely now by Choshu men, save one: Umanosuke, the peasant's son.

Ryoma's initial elation over the news notwithstanding, the longer he waited in Kagoshima for the ship to arrive, the more he found himself worrying over the impending war between the Bakufu and Choshu. "Will Katsu-sensei be recalled to lead the Tokugawa fleet against us?" he agonized more times than he could recall. "Is Choshu really strong enough to hold off the Bakufu forces, let alone defeat them?" he fretted throughout many a sleepless night, as he lay next to Oryo in his room in the Komatsu mansion.

Saigo and Komatsu had informed Ryoma of a series of significant events, even as they were occurring around Japan. These reports intensified Ryoma's anxiety, until at times he thought his head might burst. On April 14, two days after he and Oryo had returned to Kagoshima, Okubo Ichizo submitted a memorial to Osaka Castle stating that Satsuma had no intention of participating in the second expedition. "The war between the Bakufu and Choshu has nothing to do with Satsuma," Okubo argued, as if the Satsuma-Choshu Alliance was not entirely apparent to the Tokugawa. Four days later, a report reached Kagoshima that one hundred Tokugawa troops had entered Dazaifu to virtually kidnap the Five Banished Nobles, and bring them to Edo as hostages. Saigo immediately dispatched thirty expert swordsmen to Dazaifu to persuade the Bakufu troops to abandon the plan. "If mere words do not suffice," Saigo had told his men, "use any means necessary. But no matter what, the nobles are to remain safe, right where they are." Since the Satsuma men were outnumbered three to one, the commander of the mission told them before arriving to Dazaifu, "If we must draw our swords, then each one of us must be sure to cut down at least three of the enemy before dying." When the Satsuma men met the Bakufu men face-to-face at Dazaifu, their resolve must have been apparent, for although they never had to actually draw their blades, they defied protocol (the Bakufu and Satsuma were still officially allies) by keeping their swords with them at all times. The Satsuma scare tactic worked, as the Bakufu men eventually agreed to abandon their plan. Their decision, however, was hastened when, soon after the arrival of the first Satsuma platoon, a train of thirty more Satsuma troops, towing a cannon at the rear, marched into Dazaifu, behooving the Bakufu men to flee the village under the cover of night.

Even if Edo could not take as hostages the five champions of *Toppling the Bakufu and Imperial Loyalism*, it was now more than ever determined to crush Choshu. In mid-April the Bakufu summoned the Choshu *daimyo*, his heir and the lords of three Choshu branch houses to Hiroshima. Not only were these orders ignored, but they compelled Takasugi, in Nagasaki at the time procuring guns with the help of Ryoma's company, to purchase from Glover another warship. He christened the ship the *Year of the Tiger* for the year 1866, before sailing her back to Shimonoseki. When Ryoma heard about this from Saigo in Komatsu's living room he groaned, "Just helping Choshu buy weapons isn't enough. I only wish the *Werewolf* and *Union* would arrive, so we can get to Shimonoseki before the fighting starts."

"You won't have to wait any longer," Komatsu said, entering the room. "The *Union* has just arrived."

Ryoma grabbed his sword, stormed out of the house, and literally raced through the castletown toward the boat-landing on the bay. His own ship had finally arrived, commanded by Kurata, who was like a brother to him. "I knew you'd make a great naval captain, Kura," Ryoma screamed ecstatically, as he reached a point where he had a good view of the entire harbor, the *Union* anchored in the glassy water, but no trace of the *Werewolf*. "How strange," he said aloud, then increased his pace to a sprint.

By the time he reached the boat-landing, several men had alighted the large sculling boat which had carried them from the *Union*. "Uma!" Ryoma called, waving his hands frantically, as he raced toward the only one of the group wearing the white navy *hakama* of the Kameyama Company. "Where's the *Werewolf*?" he hollered.

Umanosuke avoided for an instant Ryoma's anxious eyes, but soon replied in a distressed voice, "Hello, Sakamoto-san." The other men who had come off the *Union* with Umanosuke stood silently alongside him, each as solemn as the next. "Sakamoto-san," Umanosuke broke a short silence, Ryoma now standing in front of him, "we lost the *Werewolf*."

"Lost?" Ryoma stood paralyzed under the hot Satsuma sun, his mouth agape. "What do you mean 'lost'?"

"I'm terribly sorry, Sakamoto-san," offered one of the Choshu men, the captain of the *Union*. "The *Werewolf* sunk in a storm shortly after we set sail from Nagasaki."

"Where's the crew?" Ryoma asked in a shaken voice.

"Sakamoto-san," Umanosuke said, then paused to swallow hard, "there were only three survivors."

"Only three survivors?" Ryoma repeated in disbelief. "Out of fifteen men?" Aside from Kurata, Ryoma had never met any of these men, who had recently been hired by his company in Nagasaki. "Where's Kura?" he screamed, grabbing Umanosuke by the shoulders and shaking him hard. "Where's Kura?" Ryoma repeated frantically.

When Umanosuke was finally able to get out a reply, it was drowned out by Ryoma's wailing, "Answer me, Uma! Where's Kura?"

"Captain Ike went down with his ship," the *Union's* captain said, then explained in a low voice as dark as the mood of all present, that when both ships had left Nagasaki just a few days earlier, the sky was clear and the sea calm. Unlike the *Werewolf*, since the *Union* was equipped with a steam engine, it offered to tow the smaller vessel to save time. That evening, however, the weather suddenly turned stormy, and it was all the steamer could do to propel itself through the rough seas. "It was Captain Ike himself who cut the tow rope," the Choshu man said, his voice cracking. "I suppose he knew that neither one of our ships had a chance if we continued towing them in that storm. We tried to follow them, because I doubted that they'd make it in such rough seas, but soon night came, and we lost them."

"And?" Ryoma said, feeling as if his head would split in two from the pressure of too much sorrow.

"By the next morning the storm had subsided. When we went looking for them, we found part of their hull drifting near the Goto Islands west of Nagasaki. Later, when we found the three survivors, they told us that the only man who refused to abandon the ship was its captain."

"Kura hardly had any sailing experience at all," Ryoma said.

"But he died as bravely as the most experienced sea captain," the *Union's* captain replied.

"Went down with his ship," Ryoma moaned, not without pride, despite his great sorrow.

Once again Ryoma and his men were without a ship of their own. To make matters worse, since they had spent most of their capital on the *Werewolf*, their treasury was nearly empty. They were nevertheless prepared to fight for Choshu in Shimonoseki in the impending war against the Bakufu. But before sailing to Shimonoseki with the rest of his men aboard the *Union*, Ryoma had some unfinished business to attend to.

"Please come in, Sakamoto-san," Saigo's eyes sparkled like two black diamonds, as he greeted Ryoma at the front door of his house. "I've been expecting you."

The two men sat in Saigo's living room, where Ryoma made himself at home, sitting cross-legged on the floor and helping himself to one of several sweet potato cakes that Saigo's wife had served. "The rice for your troops in Kyoto has finally arrived from Choshu," Ryoma said, devouring a second cake, and washing it down with cool barley tea. "Twenty-five hundred bushels of it. But it's still sitting in the hold of the *Union*."

"Sakamoto-san, I'm sorry to say that I can't accept that rice."

"You can't accept that rice?" Ryoma leaned so far forward that his face almost touched Saigo's. "What are you saying? That rice was a gift from Katsura, as a token of his gratitude for what Satsuma has done for Choshu."

"It's not that we don't appreciate Choshu's gratitude," Saigo said, in the familiar tone, like a child being scolded, which he tended to use when talking with Ryoma, and no one else. "As samurai, it would not be honorable for us to accept the rice at this particular time, when the Bakufu army, along with troops of thirty-one clans, have surrounded Choshu on four fronts. I'm sure they can use that rice a lot more than we can."

"I see," Ryoma groaned, unable to offer an argument.

Saigo removed a handkerchief from the sleeve of his thin cotton robe, wiped his sweaty forehead. "In Choshu," he said, "the farmers and the merchants, and even the women and children, have taken up arms, and are ready to fight to the death. They're going to need every last bullet, and every last grain of rice they can get. We just couldn't take that rice from them now."

"I see," Ryoma repeated, already wondering what he would say to Katsura when he would have to return the shipment. Although it was true that he had finally gotten Choshu and Satsuma to unite, the alliance was still new, and dangerously delicate. Ryoma knew as well as anyone that the Choshu men, after the last few years of being ostracized, not only by the Bakufu and many of the clans, but even by the Imperial Court itself, were chronically suspicious.

"But, Sakamoto-san," Saigo said, "so that there is no misunderstanding on the part of the Choshu men as to why we are returning the rice, I leave it to you to handle the situation as you think best."

"Saigo-san," Ryoma released a heavy groan, "you and I both know that I've covered for you with Katsura in harder situations than this. I'll handle it," he said in a thick Tosa drawl, before taking his sword and leaving.

War: "The Most Amusing Thing I've Ever Done"

Just a few days before Ryoma had left Kagoshima, Katsu Kaishu, still under house arrest in Edo, was suddenly summoned to Edo Castle. The Bakufu was in a bind, and had decided that Kaishu was the only man who could fix things. Not only was Edo on the verge of war with Choshu, but Satsuma had recently informed the Bakufu of its refusal to fight. Aizu resented what it considered treason by Satsuma, whose alliance with Choshu was no longer a secret. A group of Aizu samurai, in fact, were now threatening to attack the Satsuma estate in Osaka, an action which, the Bakufu feared, might very well induce Satsuma to enter the war on the side of Choshu. The Shogun's ministers knew that Kaishu was the only Tokugawa retainer who commanded enough respect among the men of both clans to enable him to mediate between them, thus his sudden reinstatement to his former post of navy commissioner, after having spent the past year and a half under house arrest.

At the beginning of June, Kaishu was again summoned to Edo Castle by Minister Mizuno Tadakiyo, the Lord of Yamagata. When Kaishu arrived, however, there was another member of the Edo elite whom he particularly despised, waiting with Minister Mizuno in a conference room in the outer castle.

"Hello, Katsu-san," Oguri Tadamasa greeted with staged aloofness the man he had replaced as navy commissioner shortly after arranging his ouster and subsequent arrest. Kaishu's hate for Oguri was equaled only by Oguri's hate for Kaishu. Two of the most gifted men in the Edo government, their political philosophies clashed. While Kaishu conducted affairs with the welfare of all of Japan in mind, Oguri's sole concern was the House of Tokugawa. It was no wonder, then, that Oguri detested Kaishu's good relations with Satsuma, Choshu and Tosa samurai who would overthrow the Bakufu, just as Kaishu bitterly objected to Oguri's overtures to the French, who, given the opportunity, would colonize Japan as the great Western powers would all of Asia. "It's been quite a while since we last met," Oguri said. His soft manner of speech suited his delicate features, the thin face and pale complexion, but not the scathing black eyes nor the biting undertone which he reserved for his political enemies. Okubo had warned Ryoma of Oguri, who, as navy commissioner and head of the pro-French faction, had begun the construction of steel mills and a shipyard at Yokosuka under the tutelage of the French, with the immediate goal of crushing Choshu. More recently, as finance commissioner, Oguri had initiated the formation of trading houses as part of a drive to modernize the tottering financial structure of the Bakufu, also with French cooperation. Nor were Oguri's ambitions limited to crushing Choshu. His ultimate goal, rather, was to subjugate all of the feudal lords, confiscate their domains, abolish the feudal system, and replace it with a centralized, absolute regime in Edo, modeled after certain European powers, particularly the government of Napoleon III.

"Hello, Oguri-san," Kaishu returned the greeting with mock amiability, sitting down on the *tatami* floor opposite the man who had nearly destroyed him.

"Now that you've been reappointed to your former post..."

"Which is?" Kaishu interrupted sarcastically.

"Why, commissioner of the navy, of course," Oguri said through forced laughter, glancing at Minister Mizuno, who sat to his immediate right. "And I should think you'd be more grateful," he added with false jest, "considering that the Shogun's Council nearly ordered you to commit *seppuku*."

"Yes," Kaishu responded tersely, concealing his disgust for Oguri, who like himself had risen through the ranks by virtue of brilliance rather than birthright.

Oguri cleared his throat. "Now that you are again navy commissioner," he paused, took his fan from his sash, began fanning his face, "I assume you've seen the French military facilities at Yokohama Port." The finance commissioner again cast a glance at the Shogun's minister sitting silently next to him, whose function at this meeting, Kaishu surmised, was to arbitrate between the two bitter rivals.

"Yes," Kaishu replied flatly. Kaishu could no longer conceal his disgust for Oguri, whom he considered the most dangerous man in the Bakufu for his absolute determination to sell out to the French.

"Katsu Awa-no-Kami," Oguri said sharply, referring, not without an air of sarcasm, to Kaishu's honorary title of "Protector of the Province of Awa," which he had received from the Imperial Household at the urging of Edo just six months before his ouster. Through use of the honorific, Oguri was subtly stressing his own social eminence over Kaishu, although both were from the relatively low ranks of direct Tokugawa retainers. "You, of all people," Oguri now spoke in a slightly condescending tone to the man who had on numerous past occasions referred to him as "one of those stupid potato-heads in Edo," "ought to know that we mustn't have those facilities removed from Japan." Oguri paused for a response from Kaishu, who offered none. "You're aware of the damage that the foreigners caused in the bombardments of Shimonoseki and Kagoshima," Oguri continued. "If we should act rashly with the foreigners at this point, they are capable of doing a lot more damage than merely destroying a few villages in Choshu and Satsuma. And so, no matter how difficult it may be for us as Japanese, as samurai, and as direct retainers of the Shogun himself," Oguri raised his voice, "we must be patient until the Shogun has regained his rightful and complete authority over the entire nation. Only after that can we even consider expelling the foreigners. Not only must we endure the foreign military presence in Japan, Katsu Awa-no-Kami," Oguri repeated the honorific as a derogation, "but we must welcome them." Oguri stopped speaking, took a deep breath, and waited for a response from Kaishu, who even now remained silent, staring hard into the dark eyes of his nemesis. Kaishu knew that no matter what he said, he could not convince Oguri that if his goal of subjugating all of the feudal lords with French military and financial aid were indeed realized, Japan would at that time become a colony of Napoleon III.

On the rainy afternoon of June 4, the *Union* dropped anchor at Nagasaki Port, whereupon Ryoma and Oryo went directly to the mansion of Kosone Eishiro, the younger son of the wealthy merchant family who had helped to finance the Kameyama Company. The couple walked hand in hand, an uncommon, if not unbelievable sight, as was made apparent by the reaction of the young maid who spotted them passing through the huge front gate of the mansion. "It's Sakamoto-san with a beautiful woman!" Ryoma could hear her saying inside. "And he's holding her hand," she chortled facetiously. Neither the maid, the old manservant who stood beside her, nor young Eishiro–who now joined his servants at the front door to greet his guests–had ever seen anything like it. "And a samurai at that," the old man muttered in disbelief, as he watched the two approach through the pouring rain. Oryo was holding an umbrella, and having a hard time trying to cover Ryoma, who towered above her. "What beautiful hydrangeas!" she said, bending over to get a closer look at the bluish-purple clusters in full bloom at the entrance of the garden, while Ryoma, much to the chagrin of both his wife and the young maid, relieved himself in the nearby bushes.

In addition to operating a lucrative pawnbroking business, the Kosone family was also the official purveyor in Nagasaki for the governments of Satsuma, Choshu and Fukui. Ryoma had made the acquaintance of this youngest of the four Kosone brothers, who was several years his junior, during his first visit to Nagasaki with Kaishu, over two years before. The Kosone family, despite its merchant status, was permitted to wear the two swords of the samurai, and to have a surname. Like his eldest brother, who was a close friend of Kaishu's, Eishiro's talents were not limited to business. Not only was he an expert with a rifle, but so accomplished was he on the moon guitar, that when Ryoma, now sitting in the Kosone's living room with his new bride, asked if Eishiro knew someone who would teach the instrument to Oryo, the merchant answered with a wide smile, "It would be a pleasure to teach her myself." Then turning to Oryo, and bowing his head to the floor, he added, "Just as it is a pleasure to meet you."

"It will be a relief to know that she's safe here, while I'm in Shimonoseki," Ryoma said, as Oryo returned Eishiro's greeting.

"When do you leave?" Eishiro asked.

"Soon. But I have one other problem on my mind right now."

"Which is?"

"We've lost our ship. It sank near the Goto Islands on the way to Kagoshima."

Eishiro's face dropped. "I'm sorry to hear that. But maybe I can cheer you up. Unless, of course, you've already heard the good news about Katsu-sensei."

"No!" Ryoma said anxiously. "What is it?"

"I've just received word that Katsu-sensei has been released from house arrest and reinstated to his post as navy commissioner."

Ryoma was unsure how to react. Should he be glad for his former mentor's personal gain, or should he worry about the all too real possibility of Kaishu leading a Bakufu naval blockade in the Shimonoseki Strait? "I just don't think I could fight against him," Ryoma thought now, as he had so often during the past several months.

Nor was Ryoma's greatest fear unwarranted. Although Kaishu opposed the expedition against Choshu, shortly after being recalled he had told Lord Yoshinobu, "If it's really necessary to punish Choshu, instead of counting on the various *daimyo*, lend me four or five warships from the Bakufu fleet, and I'll take the Shimonoseki Strait in no time." Although Yoshinobu laughed at what he dismissed as "Katsu's boasting," Ryoma knew Kaishu better than did the heir of the Tokugawa Shogun.

"Have you heard anything else about Katsu-sensei?" Ryoma asked Eishiro, walking over to the picture window to look at the rainy city below.

"What do you mean?"

"Have you heard if he'll be commanding the Tokugawa fleet in the war against Choshu?"

"That I don't know," Eishiro said, only now realizing why Ryoma had been alarmed. "But talking about the war, it doesn't seem that the Bakufu stands a chance."

"Oh?" Although Ryoma tended to agree, he was curious to hear the merchant's opinions.

"For one thing, with so much rice being sent to the Bakufu troops deployed in the west, food prices have increased greatly. And because of this, the Bakufu has lost whatever support it may have had among the common people, who are now rioting in Kobe, Osaka and Edo. And furthermore," Eishiro lowered his voice, "the merchants in Osaka are getting fed up with the loans forced upon them by the Bakufu to cover military expenses."

"Sakamoto-san," the pretty young maid who had facetiously announced his arrival called from the threshold in a melodic tone peculiar to the people of Nagasaki, bringing her master's grim explanation to an abrupt end. "You don't know how wonderful it is to see you again!" she said, entering the room with a tray of sponge cakes and tea.

"I think I do," Ryoma drolled through an exaggerated Tosa drawl, acutely aware of his wife's displeasure, if not jealousy. "Looks delicious," he said, before helping himself to a piece of cake, stuffing the entire portion into his mouth.

"Would you mind if I asked you something personal, Sakamoto-san?" the girl said playfully, drawing a steely-eyed glance from Oryo.

"How could I?" Ryoma washed down another mouthful of cake with a gulp of hot tea.

"Why is it that you always wear such shabby clothes?" the girl asked, giggling slightly, and pointing at Ryoma's faded black kimono and dirty gray *hakama*.

"Insolence!" Eishiro exploded, but was immediately calmed by a burst of laughter from Ryoma.

"You can go now," Eishiro said crossly, dismissing his servant.

"Sakamoto-san, I'm terribly sorry about her..."

"Forget it! In these troubled times, things like a man's clothes or swords don't count for much. Today luxury is rampant, but men with foresight have to take the initiative, in order to make up for the past three hundred years of lethargy." Ryoma paused, took Oryo's hand. "It's for that reason that I don't wear clothes which are apt to please women."

"I understand, Sakamoto-san," Eishiro said, obviously taken aback by Ryoma's sudden air of bookishness. "But what puzzles me, if you don't mind my saying, is how you ever managed to capture such a beauty," he added, smiling at Oryo, who blushed slightly.

"Ask her," Ryoma urged, but before Eishiro could speak, Oryo answered. "Very simple," she smiled. "My husband is unlike any other man I've ever met, seen or even heard of. Maybe that's why I was attracted to him from the very beginning."

Eishiro nodded, his embarrassment drawing a burst of laughter from Ryoma. "Yes, I can certainly believe that," the merchant said. "And since that is the case, I'd better teach you to be the best moon guitarist in Nagasaki," he said to Oryo, before excusing himself, and leaving the couple alone to the sound of the pouring rain.

Soon after, Ryoma fell asleep to the steady sound of the rain, but was suddenly awaken by the shrill voice of the old manservant. "Sakamoto-sensei, there is someone here to see you," he called from the corridor. From the other side of the house Ryoma could hear the soft murmur of the moon guitar, and wondered if it was his wife playing.

"Who's that?" Ryoma asked drowsily, opening slightly one eye.

The old man slid open the paper screen door. "A samurai from Tosa."

"No. I mean, who's that playing the moon guitar?"

"Your wife, of course."

"I see." Ryoma smiled.

"But Sakamoto-sensei," the manservant said anxiously, "what should I do about the man who's here to see you? He says his name's Nagaoka."

Nagaoka Kenkichi was a Tosa physician who had studied under Kawada Shoryo.

"Ryoma!" a voice called from the front door of the house.

Immediately recognizing the voice, Ryoma left the room and ran down the corridor to the front door.

"I was waiting for several days with the others at your company headquarters for you to return," the usually sedate Kenkichi answered excitedly. "Then Umanosuke finally showed up, and told me that I could find you here."

Kenkichi sat on the floor next to Ryoma, offered him a warm smile, exaggerated by his tanned round face, and his wide forehead made wider by a receding hairline.

"It's good to see you!" Ryoma said, and not without reason. After all, with the recent deaths of Chojiro and Kurata, Ryoma had lost two of his best men. He had heard of Kenkichi's reputation as a scholar, who was well versed in knowledge of the West, and proficient in both Dutch and English. "I hear that you've sailed to Shanghai," Ryoma said.

"Yes. And Hong Kong."

Ryoma slapped himself on the knee. "How about joining my company? Our only ship has just sunk, and now we're getting ready to fight for Choshu against the Bakufu at Shimonoseki. But when that's finished, we could really use you, and..."

"Why do you think I'm here?" interrupted Kenkichi, who from this day became the only man in the Kameyama Company older than Sakamoto Ryoma.

*   *   *

The "War On Four Sides," as the expedition against Choshu had been dubbed, was waged on four different fronts: the southeastern, eastern, northeastern and western borders of the renegade domain. The fighting finally broke out on June 7, when Tokugawa warships fired on the island of Ohshima in the southeast, just across the Inland Sea from Shikoku. The Bakufu planned to use its superior naval power to occupy the island, thus cutting off Choshu's access to the sea on its eastern-most border. Although Bakufu forces initially captured Ohshima, Takasugi Shinsaku rushed from Shimonoseki to the island with his Extraordinary Corps on the warship *Year of the Tiger*, retaking it within a week, before returning to Shimonoseki.

At the mansion of the wealthy Shimonoseki merchant, in a room overlooking the strait, Takasugi, now commander of the Choshu Navy, reported the details of his victory to Katsura Kogoro, the most powerful man in the Choshu government. Despite the heat, Takasugi still had on the same black coat of arms he had worn in battle, his family crest of four diamonds in a circle displayed in white on both shoulders. His long, narrow, pockmarked face was a sickly yellow, but the determination in his dark eyes, and the position of the mouth on the resolute jaw betrayed an inner-conviction that even Katsura himself could not fathom.

"How many enemy warships were at Ohshima?" Katsura asked taking a drag from a long-stemmed pipe.

"Four. Each one was at least five times the size of the *Year of the Tiger*." Takasugi paused to pour *sake* from a ceramic flask. "Let's drink to our first victory," he said, and the two men drained their cups.

"How did you ever do it?" Katsura asked, a cold glimmer in his eyes. "Four against one?"

"You ought to know that even though the Bakufu might have a superior navy, we have something they don't."

"What's that?"

"Balls," Takasugi grunted, taking a fan from his sash and waving it furiously in front of his face.

"Tell me more, Takasugi." Katsura took another drag from the pipe, exhaled slowly a long stream of white smoke.

"We attacked at night."

"You what?" Katsura raised his voice in disbelief, put down the pipe. "It's a basic rule of naval warfare that you never attack at night."

"We did it, and it worked. The enemy was asleep, apparently content in their victory. They didn't notice us until we were upon them, and then we opened fire." Takasugi began coughing violently, and the red spray of the consumption that was slowly killing him filled his handkerchief.

"Takasugi," Katsura gasped, "how long have you been like this?"

"What's the difference?" Takasugi folded his handkerchief and tucked it into the breast of his kimono, under his coat of arms. "Here," he said, refilling the cups.

"No!" Katsura protested. "If you drink too much in your condition, you will die."

"Please understand, Katsura-san. *Sake* is the only thing that's going to get me through this war. As long as I have it, I can fight. And as long as I'm fighting, I know we'll win. After that," Takasugi coughed again," it doesn't really matter."

Katsura stared silently at Takasugi, who continued telling him of the battle at Ohshima. "We snuck right up on their four great warships.

There wasn't a soul on deck. And even if there had been, they would-n't have been able to do much because they couldn't move. They had their boilers turned off. And just as I had expected, all of their men were asleep below decks. It was beautiful, Katsura-san. We caught them completely off guard. I maneuvered our little ship right between those four monsters, and we commenced firing our cannon from both sides. When their men came running up on deck, our marksmen were waiting to pick them off like rabbits. We were so close, that we could-n't miss. It was so easy I couldn't help feeling a little guilty." Takasugi smiled, and drained his *sake* cup. "As we were blasting away at their ships, their troops on the island opened fire at us. But from the way they panicked, it was obvious we had them scared out of their wits. I figured that once we had the enemy scared, it would never beat us. And I was right."

"Then what happened?" Katsura asked, refilling Takasugi's *sake* cup.

"Before any of their ships could get their boilers going, we extin-guished our lights and got out of there just as suddenly as we had come. And the best thing about the whole battle was that it was so dark the enemy couldn't tell how many ships we had. They most likely thought that we attacked with more than just one. We may have even convinced them that Choshu's fleet is a lot bigger than just four war-ships, or five once the *Union* returns." Takasugi coughed again, draw-ing a grimace from Katsura, who asked, "What about Ohshima? Have we recaptured it?"

"Yes. The day before yesterday, on the night of the fourteenth, I led my Extraordinary Corps onto the island. The battle lasted two nights and one day, but the Bakufu army has retreated, and we've gotten Ohshima back."

"Excuse me, Katsura-san," a servant called from the threshold.

"What is?"

"The warship *Union* has just arrived, with Sakamoto Ryoma in command."

While the fighting was still raging at Ohshima, another battle had bro-ken out on the eastern front, near the border of Choshu and Hiroshima on the Inland Sea, where the Bakufu's best-trained and best-equipped forces were deployed. These consisted of the Shogun's own samurai and those of Kii Han, both of whom were supplied by the French with the same state-of-the-art guns used by the Choshu Army. But not even these forces proved to be a match for Choshu, as the Tokugawa commander in Hiroshima determined that the Bakufu could not win the war. He sent a letter to Edo Castle stating that the enemy had the backing of Great Britain, and that it was burning with the conviction of victory. Indeed, the entire Choshu domain, samurai and commoners alike, were fighting for their very survival. In contrast, the various *daimyo* who had supposedly sided with the Bakufu had been reluctant to deploy troops for lack of a clear reason to fight. This further diminished the already low morale of the Tokugawa troops, for whom Edo, heavily in debt to the Osaka merchants, lacked sufficient supplies of food and gold. And although the Tokugawa Navy was superior, the Choshu Army, equipped with rapid-firing, breech-loading rifles and cannon, was simply better armed than nearly all of the Bakufu's land forces, which had to resort to muskets, swords, spears and the ancient armor of their ancestors. "The war has already been lost," declared the Tokugawa commander in Hiroshima, and shortly after, a so-called truce, which was tantamount to a Choshu victory, was effected along the second front.

On the same day that Takasugi had returned to Shimonoseki from Ohshima, fighting broke out on Choshu's northeastern border, in the province of Iwami on the Japan Sea. Here, troops led by the military genius Murata Zokuro were advancing toward the Bakufu stronghold of Hamada Castle, on their way to claiming Choshu's third victory on its third front.

All, however, was still quiet on the western front when Sakamoto Ryoma commanded the Choshu warship *Union* into the Shimonoseki Strait on the afternoon of June 16. Across the strait, just seven meters wide at its narrowest point, was the Bakufu stronghold of Kokura Han, whose *daimyo* was a direct vassal of the Shogun. In the green shrouded hills, overlooking the strait, were the Kokura batteries, which even the nearsighted Ryoma could see if he squinted hard enough. Reinforced by troops from the Kumamoto and Kurume clans, the Kokura forces numbered 20,000 strong, while only 1,000 Choshu troops could be spared at Shimonoseki.

Seven men wearing white navy *hakama* stood on the deck of the gray warship as it steamed into the Port of Shimonoseki. Each of them, save one, was armed with two swords, thrust through his sash at his left hip. Ryoma, however, had only a single sword, at his right hip a Smith and Wesson, and hanging from his neck a pair of binoculars which he had received from Kosone Eishiro in Nagasaki. Kenkichi stood at Ryoma's left, his foot resting on the breech of one of six cannon mounted along the starboard gunwale. They stared hard across the strait at the batteries in the shrouded green hills. "See anyone?" Kenkichi asked. "Not a soul," Ryoma said, peering through the binoculars, his low voice muffled by the wind. "But I'll bet they can see us," offered Ryoma's nephew Taro, his long black hair blowing furiously. Toranosuke and Sonojo nodded slowly, each anxious for the fighting to begin. Umanosuke watched as the youngest of the group, Shunme, climbed up the rope netting of the main mast, above which flew the Choshu flag. "Shun," Ryoma called, "we know you're a good sailor. Now we're going to see if you can fight."

"Do you think there will actually be a battle here, Sakamoto-san?" Umanosuke asked, nervously tugging on his mustache.

"That's why we came," Ryoma said, still looking through his binoculars at the green hills across the strait. "But I still can't see a soul," he muttered.

"What will you do if Katsu-sensei is in command of the Tokugawa fleet?" Yonosuke asked in his typical monotone the very question that had been haunting Ryoma for months.

"Let's just hope he isn't," Ryoma said.

"You mean to say that we might actually fight against Katsu-sensei?" Sonojo asked.

"No!" Ryoma, as usual, was blunt.

"Then what would you do?" Yonosuke prodded.

"I guess I'd have to try to convince Katsu-sensei not to fight," Ryoma answered, getting a little annoyed at the persistence of his right-hand man.

"How would you do that?" Toranosuke asked, as worried as Ryoma about the grim possibility.

"By talking to him."

"Talking to him? Where?" Yonosuke's relentless questioning was as annoying as his monotone.

"Aboard his ship. Where else?"

"But if you were to board his ship, you might be..."

"Killed?" Ryoma interrupted with a snicker. "I doubt that, Yonosuke."

"Why?"

"It's simple." Ryoma tucked his right hand into his kimono, the Chinese bellflower crest faded but still visible on both shoulders.

"Before I can die," he said, leaning against the side rail, "I have some very important business to finish." Ryoma removed his right hand, and with it drew his revolver.

"Which is?" Yonosuke gave Ryoma a puzzled look.

"Cleaning up Japan," the outlaw exclaimed. "Who is going to do it, if not me?"

"What exactly do you mean, Sakamoto-san?"

Ryoma scratched his chest with the barrel of his gun. "To begin with, we have to get rid of the Tokugawa Bakufu. Because never has there been a dirtier, more corrupt government in the history of Japan."

Soon Ryoma and Kenkichi left the others, and took a sculling boat to the pier in front of the mansion of the wealthy Shimonoseki merchant, to see the two most powerful men in Choshu.

"Sakamoto-san," Takasugi roared when the Tosa men appeared in the room where he and Katsura had been discussing the war. "I can't tell you how happy I am to see you. Did you get my message?"

"No," Ryoma said, noticing that Takasugi looked more pale than ever.

"What I wanted to talk to you about was..."

"Sakamoto-san," Katsura interrupted, "Miyoshi has told us about the fighting at the Teradaya, but I still can't believe you escaped alive."

"It was easy" Ryoma lied. "Thanks to that pistol you gave me, Takasugi-san." Then turning to Kenkichi, he said, "Oh, I nearly forgot. Meet Nagaoka Kenkichi from Tosa."

After Kenkichi bowed, and made the proper greetings which were returned by the two Choshu men, Takasugi looked at Ryoma, and smiled. "Sakamoto-san, your showing up at this particular time is an omen, I'm sure. If you'll fight on our side, the Bakufu won't stand a chance." Next, Takasugi briefed the two Tosa men about the situation on the other three fronts, after which Ryoma proposed a toast. "Here's to victory!" he roared, and all four men drained their cups.

"Our intelligence sources," Takasugi continued, "tell us that the enemy plans to attack on the fourth and most crucial front on the day after tomorrow. But before they can make the first move, we'll surprise them by crossing the strait tomorrow morning, and blow them to hell. Can we count on you to command the *Union* in battle?"

"That's why I've come!" Ryoma said, slapping his knee, then shaking Takasugi's hand furiously. "Tomorrow morning it is!"

"Good," said Takasugi. "You take the *Union* and another one of our ships, the *Koshin Maru*, across the strait to the inlet of Moji, where the enemy is heavily fortified. Then I want you to blow them to hell. I'll take the *Year of the Tiger* and the two remaining ships of our fleet, and do the same at the inlet of Tanoura, just east of there. We only have five warships in our entire fleet. You'll command two, and I'll command three. Our goal is to capture the enemy's military headquarters at Kokura Castle. But since we estimate that they have about twenty thousand troops up there, it won't be easy. First we must destroy their fortifications at Moji and Tanoura. Then from the Choshu island of Hikoshima we'll attack Dairi, which is further west, closer to the castle."

"Where is the Bakufu fleet?" Kenkichi asked.

"Off the coast of Hiroshima, apparently to help with the fighting in the east." Takasugi grinned diabolically. "Although we did plenty of damage to them at Ohshima."

"Once we attack," Ryoma said, "you can be sure that the enemy will rush directly to this strait, with all the sea forces they have." Ryoma shuddered to think that Katsu Kaishu might be commanding the Bakufu fleet.

"That reminds me," Katsura said, as if reading Ryoma's thoughts. "It might interest you to know that we've just received word that Katsu is at Osaka Castle."

"Osaka!" Ryoma exclaimed. Ryoma wiped his sweaty forehead with his dirty sleeve. "Then he won't be commanding the Bakufu fleet." Ryoma had never felt so relieved in his life. "Katsura-san, there's something I nearly forgot to mention," he lied.

"What is it?"

"It's about the rice you gave to Saigo."

"What about it?"

"I have the rice with me on the *Union*."

"What?" Katsura slammed his cup on the floor.

"Saigo told me that as a samurai he wouldn't be able to accept your rice at a time like this, when Choshu is fighting a war."

Vehemence filled Katsura's eyes. "What you're telling me is that Saigo has refused to put Satsuma in a position of gratitude toward Choshu."

"Katsura-san," Ryoma silenced him with a wave of his hand, "you have no call to be angry. Think of it this way," he said consolingly.

"What way?" Katsura snapped.

"Choshu's having given the rice to Satsuma in the first place was a token of gratitude for the favors they have done for you, right?"

Katsura nodded grimly.

"Well, Saigo's having returned the rice at a time like this, when you are fighting a war, is nothing less than a gesture of honor." Ryoma stopped speaking, and a heavy silence fell over the room, as he wondered if Choshu and Satsuma would ever really trust each other.

"But Sakamoto-san," Katsura said, "certainly you understand why I can't take back that rice."

"Yes, I understand." Ryoma scratched the back of his head. "But I don't think you'd want it, bound up as it is in gratitude and honor, to rot in the hold of the ship."

"No, of course not. But what do you suggest?"

"Well, if you'd let my company have the rice as capital, we'd put it to use for the good of the nation."

Katsura laughed in spite of himself. "You have a special way of putting things," he said. "How can I refuse?"

Later that afternoon Ryoma returned to the *Union*. "We fight tomorrow at dawn," was the first thing he told his men after assembling them on deck. "Tora, you're captain of this ship," he instructed his best seaman. "You stay on the bridge to steer. Shun," he turned to Toranosuke's young assistant, "since you're so good at climbing the mast, you be in charge of flag signals to communicate with the *Koshin Maru*, which will be fighting alongside us. Taro," Ryoma looked hard at his nephew, "you're the chief gunner, so make sure all guns are charged and ready to fire. Sonojo, you take good care of the engine. Uma, you handle the boiler room. Yonosuke, you troubleshoot. And Kenkichi," he said, placing his hand on the shoulder of the only man in the group who had not studied under Katsu Kaishu, "you stay with me until the fighting starts, at which time I want all of you to do just that. Everyone mans a gun, except Tora, who'll stay on the bridge. Is that clear?" Ryoma shouted.

"Yes!" all seven men shouted back in unison.

The next morning before dawn, five Choshu warships left the Port of Shimonoseki. Only the *Union*, commanded by Sakamoto Ryoma, and the *Year of the Tiger*, commanded by Takasugi Shinsaku, were steampowered. Shortly out of port, less than 400 meters from the Kokura coast, Takasugi's three ships cut a 45-degree arc, and headed straight for the inlet of Tanoura, leaving Ryoma's two vessels just offshore from Moji.

The *Union* headed slowly toward the enemy shoreline, the only sounds the soft humming of the engine, and the bow cutting a steady course through the water. The darkness was gradually giving way to dawn, but so dense was the fog that Ryoma, on the bridge with Toranosuke and Kenkichi, could barely see the red and green search-lights on the Choshu warship sailing alongside, or even the beacon on the coast between the inlets of Tanoura and Moji, let alone the enemy batteries, which were now within gunshot range. "I guess that means they can't see us, either," Ryoma said to Toranosuke, who only nod-ded in reply. "But we know that they're there, and that's all that mat-ters." A short while later the fog began to lift, just enough for the three men to see the military barracks and the batteries along the enemy coast. "Well, this is it," Ryoma said, before jumping onto the deck and shouting at the top of his lungs, "Chief gunner Takamatsu Taro! Fire!"

Taro immediately pulled the lanyard at the breech of one of six 12-pound bronze cannon mounted along the starboard gunwale. A thun-derous boom ripped the air, and a split-second later an entire enemy battery burst into flames. The next shot, fired by Sonojo, hit a muni-tions storehouse, the deafening explosion on land drowning out the cheering of every man on deck. "This is easy," Ryoma screamed, sweat running down his face. "Now come on, everyone. Fire! Fire! Fire!" he hollered furiously, running along the smoky gunwale, the smell of gunpowder filling his head. "Come on, Yonosuke, fire! Let's go," he screamed, walloping Umanosuke on the back. Soon all six *Union* guns and those of the *Koshin Maru* were firing repeatedly at the enemy, who wasted no time returning fire with fire. Although the *Union*, which now shuddered violently from its own cannon fire, was able to move about of its own power to avoid being hit, the sailing ves-sel *Koshin Maru* had to drop anchor to keep from drifting in the strong current. Enemy shells grazed the masts of the *Union*, several explod-ed in the sea just beyond the starboard, others zoomed overhead, exploding in midair. After about thirty minutes of continuous fighting, the coast of Moji was burning, but not before the *Union* was hit on one of the wooden lifeboats mounted along her starboard. Yonosuke, how-ever, was quick to react, dousing the flames with seawater before any real damage was done. But when a cannonball zoomed just above Ryoma's head, he gave the order to cease fire and circle back out of gunshot range.

"Now listen, everyone!" Ryoma shouted from the center deck, Shunme standing next to him and signaling his every command to the men on the *Koshin Maru*. "We've given the enemy hell! And just listen to Takasugi's squadron pounding the shore at Tanoura. But it looks like the *Koshin Maru* has been hit pretty badly, so let's get back there and finish the job."

Even as Ryoma shouted, the constant booming of cannon and the crackling of rifles made his ears ring. Five hundred men of the Extraordinary Corps had crossed the strait in dozens of rowboats to storm the enemy shore. As these troops advanced inland, now shooting their rifles, now hitting the dirt to avoid enemy fire, Ryoma and his men could see their bayonets glisten in the morning sunlight. Thousands of enemy troops fought frantically to defend against the Choshu beachhead but couldn't, as the hundreds of junks, on which they had intended to cross over to Shimonoseki, burned.

The Extraordinary Corps, consisting mostly of men of the peasant and merchant classes, were clearly routing the samurai overlords of Kokura Han. As the *Union* circled back into firing range, Ryoma watched the spectacular sight through the telescope on the bridge. "It's fantastic, Tora," he shouted, as his men resumed pounding the Moji inlet with cannonade. "This is revolution. Real revolution. Peasants fighting samurai and winning. I've finally seen it, and it's fantastic. It's time for the people to come to power. Soon there'll be no more samurai, no more *daimyo*, nor more *han* and no more Bakufu."

As Ryoma spoke, hundreds of rifles simultaneously opened fire on the enemy from across the strait at Shimonoseki. "Sakamoto-san," Toranosuke gasped, peering through the telescope. "Take a look at that." The ship's captain swallowed hard to keep steady his nerves, just as his skilled hands kept steady the ship throughout the furious sea battle.

"Enemy warships," Ryoma snickered, somewhat crazily thought Toranosuke, as he looked through the telescope at the three great warships just beyond the tiny islet of Ganryujima, barely visible in the dense fog. "Two and a half centuries ago, Miyamoto Musashi defeated Sasaki Kojiro in a sword duel on that little island," Ryoma said. "That was way back when the Tokugawa Bakufu was powerful. But now it's weak, and those great ships epitomize its weakness."

"What are you talking about, Sakamoto-san? Each one of those monsters must be three times the size of the *Union*."

"No matter," Ryoma snickered, as the booming of cannonade shook the ship. "We keep fighting."

"But if just one of them should attack," Toranosuke's eyes opened wide as he spoke, "we wouldn't stand a chance in this old boat."

"That's just the point. They won't attack."

"How do you know that?"

"Because if they intended to attack, they would have already done so. Those are three of the most powerful warships in Japan. The biggest one of them is the *Fujisan Maru*, which the Bakufu bought from America last year. If I remember correctly, it weighs one thousand tons, more than three times what the *Union* weighs. It has one hundred fifty horsepower, more than twice the power we have. The *Fujisan Maru* is a world-class warship. But even if they wanted to fight, we couldn't run away."

"But we wouldn't stand a chance, Sakamoto-san."

"Tora, you of all people know how badly I've wanted to get a hold of a warship, even a small one like the *Union*, to fight the Bakufu. Well, here we are, finally in command of a warship, right at this moment, our guns pounding the enemy coast, and the largest ship in the Tokugawa fleet watching us from a safe distance. If it should approach us, we'll blow it to hell."

Hell is exactly what Takasugi's Extraordinary Corps was giving the enemy on land. Unlike the Bakufu troops, which outnumbered them ten to one, these commoners of Choshu had gotten actual fighting experience in the battle against the British fleet, and in the Choshu civil war. Murata Zokuro, the man whom Katsura had put in charge of modernizing Choshu's military, had not only made sure his troops were well armed, but he also trained them in guerrilla warfare, of which he was a master. After burning the batteries and fortifications that the ships' cannonade couldn't reach, the men of the Extraordinary Corps surrounded the enemy army, chasing it into the hills, and burning everything in their path.

As Ryoma had predicted, the Tokugawa warships never attacked. "If only they had the common sense to fire on Takasugi's troops from the rear they might have a chance," Ryoma snickered, as all seven men watched history unfold. "It's as if the Tokugawa Bakufu were crumbling before our very eyes," Ryoma said. "Fighting in this war is certainly the most amusing thing I've ever done." Victorious in his first sea battle, Sakamoto Ryoma led both ships back to the Port of Shimonoseki, as flames consumed the coastline.

Five days after later, Katsu Kaishu reported to Osaka Castle for a meeting with the Shogun's prime minister, Itakura Katsukiyo. This prime minister of a regime which had brought itself to the brink of destruction looked a great deal older than his forty-three years, and his good nature was often confused for frailty of character, although he was by no means a weak man. "Welcome, Katsu-sensei," Itakura referred to Kaishu with the honorific, although as a son of the *daimyo* of the Tokugawa-related domain of Kuwana and the Shogun's prime minister he unquestionably outranked the navy commissioner. "It's good to see you again, although I wish our meeting could be under more pleasant circumstances," Itakura said, then took a long pipe from a black lacquered smoking stand, and filled it with finely cut tobacco from a neat black box.

Kaishu sat down on the *tatami* floor, opposite Itakura. "Pleasant they are not." Kaishu returned the warm greeting with a smile. "But, Itakura-san, I know I can be frank with you."

"Yes, of course," Itakura replied, lighting his pipe as Kaishu began lambasting the recent policies of the Bakufu. "To start with," Kaishu spoke in a brisk Edo accent, "let me tell you that I chose not to bother speaking my mind at a recent meeting I had with Oguri, as I knew he would not listen." Kaishu paused, then asked, "You are aware of what Oguri said at that meeting?"

"Yes. I received a letter from Minister Mizuno informing me."

"Oguri is a maniac." As usual, Kaishu was blunt. "I agree that establishing a centralized prefectural system of government in Japan is necessary in our dealings with foreign countries, but it is Oguri's intent that the House of Tokugawa abolish all of the *han*, and set up an absolute dictatorship at Edo. The idea is not only ludicrous, but impossible." As Kaishu spoke these last words he pounded his fist on the floor, drawing a perplexed look from Itakura. "It would be the downfall of the Tokugawa," Kaishu shouted.

"But a strong Tokugawa Bakufu means a strong Japan," Itakura resorted to the trite logic prevalent among men of the Bakufu.

Kaishu sighed, shook his head slowly. "Itakura-san," he said, "you and I both know better than that. If the Bakufu is really sincere about establishing a centralized government for the good of the nation, and not just for its own selfish gains, then it must set an example for the other clans by first abolishing itself, and relinquishing its own lands to a new centralized government." Kaishu again struck the floor in anger. "Oguri will never understand that this is the only way to save Japan from foreign subjugation. Instead, he prefers to prostitute our sacred nation to the French, who are no better than a pack of wolves, so that he can buy weapons to wage war on other Japanese. Choshu,"

Kaishu screamed the defamed name from where he sat, in the inner-castle at Osaka, which for the past year had not only been the residence of the Shogun himself, but was the very nerve center of the Bakufu's war against the renegade domain, "should never have been attacked in the first place. Instead a council of lords should have been assembled to decide how to handle the Choshu problem. The enemy is not Choshu. The enemy is ourselves, until we change our whole system, whereby the most able lords have an equal say in a new centralized government, whose head would be the Emperor in Kyoto. The House of Tokugawa must consider the welfare of the Japanese nation before that of the House of Tokugawa. And I think you will agree with me, Itakura-san, that national welfare can only be achieved after peace has been restored, and harmony achieved among all the clans. And the key to peace and harmony lies in developing national wealth and military strength in a united Japan, and not," Kaishu again pounded his fist on the floor, "in selling out to the French or any other foreign country."

"How would you propose developing a powerful military without outside help?"

"As I've always said, we must continue trading with the foreigners, and incorporating their technology. But when I say 'we,' I'm not talking about just the Bakufu, but the entire nation. Edo must relinquish its monopoly on foreign trade, because it is only through international trade, conducted by all of the wealthy clans, that we can produce the wealth needed to strengthen our national army and navy, to build factories for weapons, ships and machinery, and to establish more universities to promote and spread knowledge of science and technology. All of this is essential for national security. We must do these things if Japan is to compete with the rest of the world, and most importantly, if it is to protect itself from foreign subjugation." Having spoken his mind to the Shogun's prime minister, the man whom Ryoma called "the greatest in Japan" stopped to take a deep breath, before summing up in a much calmer tone: "This is the only way we can regain our national pride. But in order to accomplish this, the Bakufu must first form a new representative government. This would be the strongest form of government, by which Japan would be able to stand up to the foreigners."

"Katsu-sensei," Itakura spoke in a low, disturbed voice, "let me say that I agree that what you have just said is of the utmost importance to the nation. But I have not called you here today to discuss the formation of a new government."

"I see," Kaishu said, but refused to stop just now. "Then how about the war?" he asked, staring hard at Itakura. "The Bakufu is losing on all fronts a war it should never have started in the first place. It's a total disaster. Satsuma has sided with Choshu, and..." Kaishu suddenly paused, a wide smile surfacing on his face.

"You appear pleased by Satsuma's deception." Itakura gave Kaishu a confused look.

"No, Itakura-san," Kaishu lied. "It's just that Sakamoto Ryoma, the man everyone is now saying was responsible for the Satsuma-Choshu Alliance, was the head of my naval academy in Kobe. As a matter of fact, maybe people should be blaming me for Satsuma's support of Choshu."

"What are you talking about?" Itakura became suddenly annoyed.

"I was the one who introduced Ryoma to Saigo."

"Katsu-sensei! This is an outrage."

"Please, don't misunderstand me." Kaishu held out his hand in a gesture of appeasement. "That was nearly two years ago, after Satsuma had just helped drive Choshu from Kyoto. An alliance between Satsuma and Choshu at that time was unimaginable." Katsu was not being entirely truthful. After all, it was with the unimaginable in mind that he had introduced Ryoma to Saigo, and even urged the Satsuma leader to unite with other *han* to topple the Bakufu. "The last thing Satsuma and Choshu should be doing," Kaishu had told Saigo during their first meeting in the fall of 1864, "is fighting among yourselves" "But anyway," he grinned at Itakura now, in the dangerous summer of 1866, "Ryoma is really quite a fellow."

"How can you say such a thing?" Itakura was dumbfounded. "Sakamoto's one of the most wanted men in Japan."

"Yes, ridiculous, isn't it," Kaishu snickered. "Of all the Tosa men I know, and I know a lot of them, including Lord Yodo himself, Ryoma is definitely the most talented and farsighted. And something else. The very first time Ryoma came to my home in Edo, he intended to kill me." Kaishu released an amused chuckle.

"What?"

"Of course, I just laughed at him then. But Ryoma has a presence of mind, and an inner-strength that makes him a very difficult opponent. He's a good man," Kaishu concluded in a melancholy tone, the smile now gone from his face. "But getting back to the war," he said, his voice now grim, "I really don't think the Bakufu has a chance of winning."

"That," said Itakura, "is exactly why I summoned you here today."

"Oh?"

"Yes. Satsuma and Aizu are now feuding bitterly. Some of the Aizu samurai are up in arms over Satsuma's refusal to send troops against Choshu. Before that situation turns into a separate war, I want you to mediate between the two, and get them to settle their differences in a peaceful manner. Katsu-sensei," Itakura implored, "you must succeed in this, because as you probably know, you are the only man in the Bakufu who Satsuma will listen to."

"Yes, I know." Kaishu was not displeased with the remark, which of course was true. "The same goes for Choshu. I'm sure that eventually I'll have to negotiate a peace with them, too." Although Kaishu believed that the end of Tokugawa rule was very near, and even willed that it be so for the welfare of Japan, as a Tokugawa samurai he would give his very life to avoid the total destruction of the House of Tokugawa.

"Yes," Itakura nodded, "and to tell you honestly, I don't think that such a time is very far off."

"At any rate, I'm certain I can settle things between Satsuma and Aizu," Kaishu assured, and indeed by the beginning of the following month he had done just that.

As Kaishu had warned, the war against Choshu ended in disaster for the Tokugawa regime. Although cease-fires had temporarily been effected on all four fronts in June, fighting again broke out in July, and by August a Choshu victory was certain. On the southeastern front, Takasugi's forces had already recaptured Ohshima Island. Near the end of June, less than three weeks after the commencement of the war on the eastern front, the Tokugawa commander in Hiroshima ordered his forces to withdraw in hopes that Choshu would do the same. He was mistaken; and shortly afterwards Choshu's army advanced into the Bakufu's stronghold on its eastern border, after which an unofficial truce was obtained. At the end of July the Bakufu launched an all-out attack on the Choshu forces in Hiroshima, but to no avail. Finally, on August 7, representatives of the Lord of Hiroshima, whose troops had remained neutral throughout the war, met with their Choshu counterparts, promising to seal off the Choshu-Hiroshima border if the Choshu Army would withdraw from the territory it had gained in their domain. Choshu agreed, putting an end to the fighting on the second front. In the northeast, the Choshu Army had stormed the castletown of Hamada, forcing the samurai of this staunch Tokugawa ally to burn their castle and flee to nearby Matsue Han. In Kokura, the western front of the War On Four Sides, Takasugi's forces attacked again on July 3, and a third time shortly after. On the last day of July the commander of the Kumamoto troops, disgusted at the Bakufu's refusal to employ its powerful warship *Fujisan Maru* in the fighting, took his army home. Although Kumamoto Han had opposed the war from the start, its samurai had been the fiercest fighters at Kokura, defeating the Choshu forces in the third battle. It was no wonder, then, that the armies of three other Kyushu domains who had been fighting for the Tokugawa followed the Kumamoto example, and returned to their respective fiefdoms, leaving only the Kokura Army to defend against the Choshu onslaught. On August 1, the vice-commander of all the Tokugawa forces, Ogasawara Nagamichi, secretly fled his headquarters at Kokura Castle, sneaking out the rear gate under the cover of night, and sailing to Nagasaki aboard the *Fujisan Maru*. This, however, was not until Ogasawara, facing certain defeat, had received even more devastating news from Osaka Castle: on the twentieth of the previous month Shogun Iemochi had suddenly taken ill and died. On the same day that Ogasawara fled, Choshu attacked a fourth time, routing the Kokura Army, which, abandoned by its commander, burned the castle and took to the hills to engage in guerrilla warfare against the Extraordinary Corps. Although peace would not officially be achieved between Kokura and Choshu until the beginning of the following year, by August Choshu was in control of both sides of the Shimonoseki Strait, and had defeated the Bakufu armies on all four fronts.

A DECLARATION OF FREEDOM

Impasse

The Bakufu was crumbling. Defeat at the hands of a single han had not only demoralized its own samurai, but had also made it clear to the entire nation that the Tokugawa hegemony of over two and a half centuries had, for all means and purposes, ended. With the exception of the Tokugawa-related clans, the Bakufu had now lost the support of virtually all of the han in Japan; and Edo was now painfully aware of the alliance between Satsuma and Choshu.

With open defiance to Tokugawa rule now possible, Sakamoto Ryoma was anxious to conduct business with Western traders in Nagasaki. But his shipping company was without a ship, and the capital it had made during the past year was fast running out. Such were the circumstances facing the Dragon when he led his men back to company headquarters in Nagasaki at the end of the seventh month of 1866.

Ryoma and his men had returned to Nagasaki victorious in battle, but nevertheless felt defeated by what seemed an insurmountable impasse. They had temporarily moved their headquarters from the old two-roomed building in the Kameyama Hills east of the city, to the second floor of Kosone Eishiro's house near the center of town. It was here that they gathered one night at the end of July to discuss the dismal future of their shipping company without a ship.

"I don't see that we have any other choice but to disband the company," Ryoma told them grimly.

"Disband the company?" Toranosuke exploded. "We can't do that."

"Choshu doesn't need our help anymore to buy foreign weapons," Ryoma said. "Anyway, what good is a shipping company without a ship?'"

"Sakamoto-san," Sonojo grabbed Ryoma's wrist, "we've come this far together." Tears welled up in his eyes. "Everything we've done is bound up in this company. I'd rather die together than disband."

"I don't like it any more than the rest of you," Ryoma groaned. The thought of dissolving the company tore at Ryoma's insides; but so heavy was his sense of responsibility for the welfare of his men that he was willing to go even that far. They had been surviving off the rice that Ryoma had received from Katsura. Part of this they exchanged for gold to supplement their minimal monthly salaries from Satsuma. But the supply was limited, and without a ship Ryoma could see no other way out of the predicament than to disband. "Katsura's rice isn't going to last for ever," he said. "And we can't very well continue taking money from Satsuma without doing anything in return."

"I suppose as *ronin*, we're no better off than the peasants were three centuries ago under the warlord Toyotomi Hideyoshi," Kenkichi said. "In order to get as much rice as possible to feed his armies, Hideyoshi had a simple policy: 'Don't let the peasants live, but don't kill them either.' In other words, Hideyoshi took nearly all of the rice that the peasants could produce, leaving them just enough to subsist on so that they could continuing growing more rice for his troops."

"Like us," Yonosuke said. "Although we're not dead, as sailors we're not really alive without a ship."

"You're right about one thing, Kenkichi," Ryoma said.

"What's that?"

"No one's going to kill us, at least not until I've gotten rid of all of the damn tyrants like Hideyoshi, and cleaned up Japan once and for all."

Yonosuke, who had heard Ryoma allude to his favorite metaphor on several occasions, knew exactly what he meant. "But, Sakamoto-san," he said, "how do you propose cleaning up Japan without the proper tools, including a ship?"

"I wish I had an answer. But," Ryoma looked hard at each of his seven men, "don't any of you ever forget that we have an extremely valuable commodity that many people need, but only a few have."

"Which is?" Taro asked.

"Navigational expertise," Toranosuke answered for Ryoma.

"What good is navigational expertise without a ship?" Shunme asked.

"Or the money to buy one?" Umanosuke added.

"That's why it looks like we'll have to disband," Ryoma said, pounding his fist in his hand. "Wait a minute!" he suddenly hollered, his eyes open wide. "I have an idea."

"What?" Sonojo asked.

"Something similar to what we've done for Satsuma and Choshu. We'll form a financial union between all thirty-four *han* on Kyushu, and Choshu. The union would be in the form of a company, like ours, only each of the clans involved would own a share."

"A mutual stock company," Kenkichi said.

"Yes. And through this company, each of the clans could market their own products, which we, the Kameyama Company, would transport to the central market in Osaka for sale throughout Honshu. And since Choshu is in control of the Shimonoseki Strait, we could check all ships, both foreign and Japanese, as they pass through. In addition to finding out what products are being supplied to the Osaka market, we could also collect a duty from all ships which did not belong to the union. We would handle only those products for which there was not such a large supply. In other words, we'd only handle products for which there was a high demand, and so make the largest possible profit. Not even the Bakufu would be able to compete with us."

"Ryoma-san," Toranosuke said, "the idea sounds good, but..."

"Good?" Ryoma bellowed. "I think it's a stroke of genius, even if it is my own idea. The clans would supply the money and the ships, and the Kameyama Company would run their business for them."

"Fantastic!" Yonosuke blurted.

"But..." Toranosuke said, still doubtful.

"I know," Ryoma interrupted. "It all sounds like so much big talk, right?"

"Well..."

"If anyone has any better ideas, let me hear them."

The next morning Ryoma had two unexpected visitors, one from Satsuma the other from Ohzu.

The Outside Lord of Ohzu, of northern Shikoku, was related through marriage to the Mori of Choshu, and a staunch proponent of *Imperial Loyalism*. Although Ryoma had never dealt with Ohzu men before, it was not without camaraderie that he and Toranosuke received the visitors in the reception room at the Kosone house.

The Satsuma man was Godai Saisuke, whom Ryoma had recently met in Nagasaki. Godai impressed Ryoma with an air of elegance uncommon among Satsuma samurai. He was much smaller than Ryoma, slight of build, had a wide forehead, and intelligent penetrating eyes accented by upswept brows. Unlike Saigo, Okubo and, with the exception of Komatsu, any of the other Satsuma men Ryoma know, Godai was of the upper-samurai class, and so from an early age had been chosen to study navigation and gunnery under the Dutch at Nagasaki. In 1862, before the falling out between Satsuma and Choshu, Godai had sailed to Shanghai with Takasugi Shinsaku, during which time the two became close friends. In 1865, Godai had led fourteen Satsuma samurai on a study tour of Europe, and was now in Nagasaki to buy weapons from foreign traders.

"Sakamoto-san," Godai said, "this is Kunishima-san, of Ohzu. He has just purchased a steamer from a Dutch trader here, but there are only a few Ohzu men who know how to operate it."

"Why did you buy the ship?" Ryoma was blunt.

"To transport guns from Nagasaki to Ohzu," Kunishima replied in a low voice.

"For what purpose?" Ryoma asked.

"To prepare for all-out war against the Bakufu."

Ryoma nodded slowly, staring hard into Kunishima's eyes. "Godai-san, how many troops does Satsuma have stationed in Osaka right now?" he asked, shooting his gaze at the Satsuma man.

"Seven or eight hundred."

"Is that enough to restrain the Bakufu forces there?"

"Saigo thinks so."

"Where is Saigo?"

"In Kagoshima with Komatsu."

"Then Okubo's still in Kyoto?"

"Yes." Godai smiled. "He's negotiating with the Imperial Court daily, trying to secure its support, and restore Choshu to Imperial grace.

Ryoma scratched his chin, smiled. "I'd better inform Katsura of this. I know how cagey he can be, and I wouldn't want him thinking that Satsuma wasn't living up to its part of the agreement."

"That's exactly why I'm here in Nagasaki," Godai said. "To buy weapons for Choshu, and Satsuma of course. As you know, the British legation visited Kagoshima in June, the same day you attacked Kokura." Godai paused, offered a wide smile. "For which, by the way, I must commend you and your men." While the French supported the Bakufu in an attempt to gain a monopoly on Japanese trade, its arch-rival Great Britain now wholeheartedly backed Satsuma and Choshu for similar purposes. Unlike the French, the British had recently come to two very important realizations about the future of Japan: the Bakufu was fast crumbling; and soon the nation would be ruled by an Imperial government which would be formed by a coalition of the leading clans. The British envisioned Satsuma and Choshu at the van-guard of this coalition, and in order to secure favorable trading condi-tions with the future Japanese government, at the exclusion of the French, London established amicable relations with the two archene-mies of the Tokugawa.

"And what came of the British visit to Satsuma?" Ryoma asked.

"They've pledged to cooperate with us in procuring as many war-ships and guns as we'll need to overthrow the Bakufu. Unlike the French, the British seem as anxious to see the Tokugawa fall as we are." Godai burst out laughing, drawing similar sentiments from Ryoma and Toranosuke, but not from Kunishima, who remained silent. Godai turned to the Ohzu man, "Kunishima-san," he said, "please speak your mind."

"Sakamoto-san," Kunishima's voice was anxious, almost desperate, "Godai-san has suggested that your company might be willing to hire out some men to us to operate our new ship. Of course, we would pay you well for your services."

"How big is the ship?" Toranosuke asked.

"Small. Only four hundred fifty tons."

"How many men would you need?" Ryoma asked.

"About six."

Ryoma looked over his shoulder at his most skilled seaman, who nodded approval. "Very well," he said, thrusting out his right hand to the delight of the Ohzu man.

On that same day, Toranosuke and five other men–sailors the company had hired to man the *Werewolf*–went to work for Ohzu Han, aboard the steamer *Iroha Maru*. Assured of a temporary source of income, Ryoma could now work on his new idea of forming a finan-cial union between Choshu and the Kyushu clans, or at the very least, procure a single ship, to avoid disbanding his company.

One afternoon in mid-August, Ryoma and Oryo sat on the verandah, on the downstairs floor of the Kosone house, to escape the stifling heat inside. Since the end of July, Ryoma, Oryo and several of his men had taken up residence, if not refuge, on the second floor of the house. Aside from Oryo, the whole lot of them were fugitives, with Ryoma himself one of the Bakufu's most wanted men. Not only had Tokugawa agents just missed killing him at the Teradaya in the previ-ous January, but it was now believed, if not known, that he was the man most responsible for uniting Choshu and Satsuma.

Ryoma was drinking a glass of beer–a beverage which Eishiro had recently introduced him to, and which he had dubbed "foamy *sake*." Oryo was sipping cool barley tea, her moon guitar on the dark wood-en floor beside her. From the open verandah they had a pleasant view of the front garden. Kenkichi was writing at a desk in the next room, and Umanosuke was sleeping in another. Ryoma had dispatched Taro,

Shunme, Yonosuke and Sonojo to the mercantile center at Osaka to investigate the markets there, so they would know what kind of merchandise to handle, when and if they could procure a ship. Toranosuke was still working aboard the Ohzu steamer, with the other sailors.

"It's been five months since we've been married," Oryo said in a low voice.

Although Oryo was coy, Ryoma read her intentions. "I know you'd like to have a house of your own," he said. "I'd like more than anything for you to have one. And you will. But I have so much on my mind right now. The Bakufu is about to fall, and I have a lot to do before that happens." Now that Choshu had been victorious in the west, Ryoma had begun considering the best way to avoid all-out war in the east. He feared that a civil war between the pro-Tokugawa forces and Satsuma-Choshu would not only cost tens of thousands of Japanese lives–lives which would be essential in building a new nation–but would also make Japan more vulnerable to foreign invasion. It was for this reason that Ryoma had made an appointment this very evening to meet a vassal of Lord Shungaku to discuss the possibilities of a peaceful revolution. "Unfortunately, Oryo," he said, "I really believe that without me the very future of Japan would be in jeopardy. I've never said this to anyone else, but recently, I've realized that it is up to me to form a new government in Japan." Ryoma paused, laughed aloud. "After I clean up the mess we're in now, that it." Ryoma rarely, if ever, spoke about matters of politics, war or business with Oyro, who was not quite sure how to react. "But what about all of your men in the company?" she asked. "Certainly they can help you."

"They are helping me."

"And Saigo-san, and Komatsu-san? Katsura-san and Takasugi-san? And Nakaoka-san? And what about Katsu-san, and Okubo-san? I thought you said that they were some of the greatest men in Japan."

"They are!" Ryoma was emphatic. "But each one of them is bound to something I'm not. Saigo and Komatsu are Satsuma samurai, so their top priority is Satsuma. Katsura and Takasugi are Choshu samurai, so their top priority is Choshu." Ryoma drained his glass of beer. "Although I know good and well that Katsu and Okubo are more concerned with the welfare of Japan than they are with the Tokugawa, since both of them are direct vassals of the Shogun, they can't oppose the Bakufu. That leaves Nakaoka and me. As *ronin*, our loyalties aren't bound to any particular *han*. But Nakaoka is intent on crushing the Bakufu through military force."

"I thought that was your intent as well."

"It is!" Ryoma took his wife's hand, looked hard into her eyes. "Oryo," he said ominously, "there are a lot of people who misunderstand me. I'm not only talking about people on the side of the Bakufu, who as you know better than anyone, have tried to kill me. But I can't let that stand in my way, because I know deep down in my own heart what I must do." Ryoma wiped a lone tear that had trickled half way down Oryo's smooth, white face. "If the Bakufu remains adamant, and refuses to listen to reason and avoid a bloody revolution, then we must be prepared to bury the Tokugawa by military force. If we fail, then the best thing for us to do would be to leave Japan and stay overseas for a while."

"Leave Japan?" Oyro gasped softly. She couldn't fathom the thought. "Leave Japan?" she repeated, dumbfounded. "Stay overseas?" The notion seemed no less preposterous than going to another planet. "Who?" she asked.

"All of us. The men in my company, and you and I." Sensing his wife's dismay, Ryoma took firm hold of her hand. "Don't look too worried," he said. "All of us, including you, have already abandoned our homes. The next logical step would be to leave Japan if we can't save it. But listen closely now, because what I'm about to say is very important."

Oryo nodded.

"In case anything should happen to me before this whole thing is over, I've asked Miyoshi to make sure that you get to my brother's house in Kochi, where you'll be safe."

Oryo's face turned pale, and her dark eyes opened wide. "I've never heard you speak like this," she murmured.

Ryoma burst out laughing, to change the mood. "Nor have I," he said. "Bear with me a little longer. When things are finally settled, with the business our company will be doing, I'll buy you the best house in Nagasaki." He smiled, wrapped his arms around his wife. "Of course, I'd rather live in the mountains, just the two of us."

"You talk such nonsense, Sakamoto Ryoma," Oryo said, freeing herself from Ryoma's arms, and refilling his beer glass with cool barley tea. "You could no sooner live in the mountains than on the moon. You wouldn't be able to sit still for a day. And besides, who would run the new government if not you?" Oryo bantered, playing on Ryoma's inflated ego.

"I sure don't want any part in running it. I would bore me to death. But living in the mountains with you would suit me just fine. Of course, I'd still have my shipping company, and sometimes I'd be gone for long periods at a time. When I was, you could stay in Kochi with my sister Otome. But when there was nothing else to do, you and I could sit around our house in the mountains, just the two of us. You could play the moon guitar for me, and I'd write songs to your music."

"I've been practicing hard with Kosone-san," Oryo said, putting her hands together and smiling. "But if I'm going to be playing for you," her smile became a mock frown, "I wish I'd have begun playing the moon guitar when I was a little girl," she said, and both of them burst out laughing.

"Why don't you play something for me right now?"

"What would you like to hear?" Oryo took the short-necked instrument in both arms, held it in her lap.

"Something you think would go with that poem I showed you last night."

As Oryo began playing, and Ryoma slowly reciting, Kenkichi joined them on the verandah.

"It matters not what people say of me,
I am the only one who knows what I must do."

"Ryoma," Kenkichi said, obviously impressed, "I never knew you wrote poetry."

"Only when I have the time." Without saying another word, Ryoma suddenly stood up, stepped off the verandah into the garden, walked over to a mound of grass, and, to the chagrin of Oryo, relieved himself. Although Oryo never complained about her husband's urinating in the garden, it was what he was prone to do after that, particularly when he had been drinking, that bothered her. And sure enough, this afternoon was no exception. Ryoma proceeded to lay down in his favorite spot for a nap, which, to his wife's dismay, was the same place that he had chosen to urinate.

After a few minutes of wondering whether or not she should wake him up, her decency got the better of her. Oryo went out to the garden, where Ryoma was now fast asleep, snoring loudly. "Sakamoto Ryoma," she called.

"Huh?" Ryoma opened one eye.

"Either stop your habit of sleeping in the garden, or stop urinating here," Oryo reproached, drawing a burst of laughter from Ryoma. "I don't see what's so funny," she said.

"It's the look on your face. Anyway, you know that I like being natural. I hate a dark, cramped latrine. And besides, it's too hot to sleep inside."

Oryo just shook her head, and left her "natural" husband sleeping in the garden.

That evening, Ryoma, Kenkichi, and Umanosuke walked southward along the Nakajimagawa, an orange sun sinking into the purple mountains, which stretched westward beyond the green hills on the other side of the sapphire bay. The three men were clad in white navy *hakama*. Umanosuke and Kenkichi, in high wooden clogs, wore both swords at their left hip. Ryoma, in black navy boots, wore only a single short sword, and, as usual, carried his Smith and Wesson revolver tucked inside his kimono. After crossing a double-arched stone bridge, the three men followed the narrow lane to the main road running along the green foothills on the eastern side of the town, and turned right. The east side of the road was lined with ancient temples, their black tile roofs rising above stone-based white earthen walls. Ryoma suddenly stopped, pointed to a graveyard at the foot of the hills. "Chojiro's in there," he said in a low voice, barely audible. A brief silence ensued, broken by the shrill of tens of thousands of cicadas. "But what's done is done," he muttered, as the three continued walking. Soon they crossed the Bridge of Reflection, beyond which the streets were lined with pleasure palaces, hundreds of red lanterns hanging from their eaves illuminating the dusk. "Here it is," Ryoma said, stopping at the front gate of the House of the Flower Moon, his favorite house in Maruyama. "Shimoyama should be waiting inside."

Shimoyama Hisashi, a Fukui man, was in Nagasaki investigating the kinds of weapons foreign arms dealers were offering, and to whom. Ryoma had asked Kosone Eishiro to arrange a meeting with this vassal of Lord Shungaku, as he knew that the merchant enjoyed a close relationship with the retired Fukui *daimyo*. But it was neither weapons nor their procurement which Ryoma had come to discuss this evening. Rather his mind was preoccupied with another, more pressing matter, which had come to possess him of late, and which he felt was the only way for Japan to avoid bloody revolution, and subsequent foreign invasion.

Shimoyama was waiting for the three Tosa men in a private room, where four geisha sat with him on a *tatami* floor drinking *sake*.

Despite the stifling heat, the Fukui samurai was dressed, as protocol demanded, in a neatly pressed jacket and *hakama*, both of pale blue linen, his family crest displayed in white just below the shoulders and the sleeves. The black kimono underneath was folded tightly around his chest, and the edges of his clean white undergarment were visible below his neck. His hair was combed and oiled, his topknot curled neatly over his cleanly shaven pate.

The gravity of the matter which Ryoma had come to discuss this evening must have been apparent, despite his unwashed face, disheveled hair and shabby clothes, because Shimoyama–and much to the Fukui man's credit–was not at all concerned with appearance. As he would record in his journal, *"That was the first time I ever saw Sakamoto Ryoma. His features were those of a great hero...From his refined bearing, and the clearness of his words, I knew right away that this was no ordinary man."* Perhaps it was the intense, almost frightening glare in Ryoma's dark brown eyes that so impressed this representative of the Lord of Fukui. Or perhaps it was the weightiness of Ryoma's all-important mission, for which he had dedicated and constantly risked his life, and which was now apparent even in his mien, the way he stood and the words he spoke.

"Shimoyama-san," Ryoma said in a low voice, after he and his men had bowed as the threshold and introduced themselves, "do you think the women could leave us alone? What I have come to say is for your ears only."

"I see." Shimoyama looked hard at this Tosa man, whom Lord Shungaku and Yokoi Shonan had praised. Turning to the four geisha, he gestured for them to leave, as the three Tosa men sat down. "Now, Sakamoto-san, please tell me what's on your mind," he said, filling four cups with *sake*.

Ryoma sat in the formal position, his back straight, his hands resting on his thighs, his eyes burning with absolute conviction in what he was about to utter. "I've come to ask that you urge Lord Shungaku to press the Bakufu to restore the political power to the Emperor." Ryoma spoke slowly, in a low voice, but the awesome words startled Shimoyama, who could offer no immediate response. The Tokugawa Bakufu had controlled Japan for over two hundred fifty years. The century before that had been a period of civil war, during which a handful of warlords fought among each other. Before that the Kamakura and Ashikaga Shoguns had ruled since the twelfth century. In short, the Emperor had not held the political power of his empire for nearly seven centuries.

Ryoma continued relaying his ideas, which did not come to him overnight, but had developed in his mind during his years of intercourse with Katsu Kaishu's Group of Four. "There is no sign of self-examination from the Bakufu," he said. "Rather, its arrogant leaders rule as despots; their sole concern is for the welfare of the House of Tokugawa." Ryoma paused, drew a grim nod from the Fukui man, who with his eyes urged him to continue. "The Bakufu is a corrupt regime, which has grown old and decrepit. I don't think there is any way to save it. I know for a fact that Satsuma and Choshu are anxious to start another war to crush the Tokugawa, and as Choshu has proven, they certainly have the military power to do so. But victory will not come easily. Instead, a war would turn our nation into a sea of blood, and leave us vulnerable to foreign attack. This is why I implore you to convince Lord Shungaku that the only way to avoid such a catastrophe is if the Bakufu comes forth and offers of its own free will to restore the political power to the Emperor. With this accomplished, we will finally be in a position to form a union of the most able lords to govern Japan through a council in Kyoto." Ryoma paused briefly. "But if," he shouted, raising his voice for the first time, "the Bakufu refuses to listen to reason, let it be known at Edo that Satsuma and Choshu are stronger than ever, and that in case of all-out war the number of *han* which would fight on their side is constantly increasing. The time to act is right now," Ryoma insisted, unconsciously slamming his fist on the floor, "before the heir to the deceased Shogun is named."

"I agree with you wholeheartedly, Sakamoto-san. As a faithful retainer of the Matsudaira of Fukui, the seventh highest ranking of the Tokugawa-related houses, I will relay to Lord Shungaku what you have said here this evening."

"Thank you," Ryoma said, smiling for the first time since entering the room, and drawing curious looks from the Fukui man, and his two friends sitting by. "But that's not all," he added.

"Oh?" Shimoyama said.

"I have one more favor to ask of you."

"If it's within my power, I'll be glad to oblige."

"I think it is." Ryoma glanced over his shoulder at Umanosuke, and burst out laughing. "How about calling back those four geisha? Men from Tosa hate to see pretty women sent away."

Deception

The Shogun's most logical heir was Hitotsubashi Yoshinobu, who on July 27, exactly one week after Iemochi's death, reassumed the surname of his birth and became the fifteenth Head of the House of Tokugawa. For thirteen generations acceptance of this position had been tantamount to succeeding the Shogun, an appointment which Tokugawa Yoshinobu now shrewdly declined. He was aware of his unpopularity, particularly among the Bakufu ministers at Edo; and so, despite repeated requests by Lord Shungaku and other leading pro-Bakufu daimyo, all of whom considered him the only man who could save the diminishing regime, the twenty-nine-year-old Head of the House of Tokugawa remained adamant in his refusal, and still a fifteenth Shogun had not been named. Lord Yoshinobu was confident that the time would come when his enemies within the Bakufu would beg him to succeed to the post; until then he prepared to lead his own army into what he dubbed the "Great Attack," to crush Choshu once and for all. "Any of you who choose to ride with me into battle," he told his retainers gathered in Kyoto, "must be prepared to die for the single objective of reaching Yamaguchi Castle and taking the heads of the Lord of Choshu and his heir. Anyone who is not thus resolved need not follow me." As Inspector General of the Forces Protecting the Emperor in Kyoto, Yoshinobu had been ordered by the court to "subjugate Choshu as an 'Imperial Enemy.'" But when he received word in the first week of August of the fall of Kokura Castle, and the inevitability of Tokugawa defeat, Yoshinobu abandoned his plans for the Great Attack, and summoned to Kyoto Katsu Kaishu, who was still in Osaka. It was on the night of August 16, the day after the outlaw Sakamoto Ryoma had convinced Shimoyama Hisashi to press the retired Lord of Fukui to urge the Bakufu to restore the political power to the Emperor, that the navy commissioner reported to the Kyoto residence of Tokugawa Yoshinobu.

As most members of the Bakufu elite, Lord Yoshinobu neither liked nor trusted Kaishu; as Kaishu neither liked nor trusted most members of the Bakufu elite, particularly Lord Yoshinobu. To make things worse, the two men clashed in their political views. Kaishu had always opposed the war with Choshu, while Yoshinobu had long been determined to crush the renegade *han*. After Kaishu had settled the dispute between Aizu and Satsuma, Yoshinobu sent a derogatory letter about the navy commissioner to Prime Minister Itakura, who in turn showed it to Kaishu. In his letter, Yoshinobu advised the prime minister to send Kaishu back to Edo, because *"with all his connections, there is no telling what Katsu might do."* Indeed, unlike most, if not all, of the men of the Bakufu, Kaishu had numerous friends among the anti-Tokugawa radicals, including many in Choshu. Ironically, it was for the very reason that Yoshinobu most distrusted Kaishu that he now depended on him to solve his most pressing problem: negotiating a peace with Choshu.

Yoshinobu was waiting when Kaishu arrived at his Kyoto residence. Wearing a gray jacket of fine silk, adorned with the hollyhock leaf crest of the House of Tokugawa, and a silken *hakama* of a gray and black checkered pattern, the son of the late Lord of Mito, with his fair complexion, high forehead, and well-sculpted nose, looked every bit as aristocratic as his princely upbringing suggested. And on this evening, in an effort to appease Kaishu, who at forty-three was fourteen years his senior, Yoshinobu played the perfect gentleman. "I've called you here tonight, Katsu-san," he said, "to ask you to perform a very important task."

"Which is?" Kaishu was blunt as usual.

"To meet in Hiroshima with representatives of Choshu. I have just discussed the idea with the Emperor and his advisors, and they were very happy that I have chosen you." Yoshinobu forced a wide grin, continued. "As you know, you are the only man in the Bakufu who Choshu might talk to."

Kaishu snickered. "Yes, they might. But then again, once I get there they might be tempted to cut off my head instead." Kaishu could not resist this opportunity for sarcasm. After all, unlike Yoshinobu, who had from the start advocated the second expedition against Choshu, Kaishu had never condoned the war; and now that the Bakufu faced certain defeat, those who started the war were asking him to mend things for them.

Yoshinobu repressed his resentment for Kaishu's caustic remark, and instead smiled at the irony that the only man in the Bakufu who might have a chance of negotiating a peace with Choshu, was also, in his personal opinion, the most expendable of all his commissioners. "If Kaishu should be killed on the mission," he had told an aide earlier that evening, "it will be no great loss to the House of Tokugawa."

"Then you will agree to go to Hiroshima to negotiate a peace, Katsu-san?" Yoshinobu asked as politely as his principality would allow him to speak to one of his own retainers.

Kaishu nodded. "I'll do it under the condition that I be allowed to handle the negotiations as I see fit. Do you agree to that, Your Highness?" Kaishu stressed the princely title–a subtle indication that he, for one, did not find it suitable.

"Of course," Yoshinobu muttered, turning his head to avert Kaishu's piercing eyes.

"Good! If I'm not back within a month, you'll know that the Choshu men didn't want to talk, and that my body, probably minus my head, can be found in Hiroshima."

Yoshinobu again ignored Kaishu's remark, and instead informed him that an armed escort would be prepared to accompany him on his mission.

Kaishu snickered, then declared matter-of-factly, "I'll go alone."

"As an official emissary of the Bakufu, entrusted with full powers, you must take an escort," Yoshinobu ordered.

"I thought you just got through agreeing that I could handle the negotiations as I saw fit."

"Yes, I did," Yoshinobu muttered, this time unable to hide his resentment for his caustic navy commissioner.

On August 21, Kaishu arrived in Hiroshima Han, through whose good offices a meeting was arranged between himself and a mission from Choshu. On the twenty-fifth, without bodyguards or even a single servant, and dressed as a petty samurai in coarse linen, the navy commissioner, entrusted by Edo with full powers, crossed over to the Island of the Shrines, just off the coast of Hiroshima in the Inland Sea. After landing on the island, as he headed toward an inn where would stay the night, Kaishu was confronted by a patrol of Choshu soldiers, each armed with a rifle.

"Halt!" yelled one of them. "Identify yourself."

Kaishu immediately sensed that if he tried to cover up his thick Edo accent, he might very well be shot on the spot as a spy. But if he were to reveal his true identity, these men, thirsty as they were for Tokugawa blood, might kill him anyway. "Then again," his mind raced, "I've never given Choshu any reason to distrust me, or even dislike me." And fortunately, he was right. "My name's Katsu," he said coolly, gesturing for the man at the front of the patrol to point his rifle, which was aimed at his face, downwards. "Katsu Kaishu, from Edo."

"Katsu Kaishu!" the man shouted, apparently amused. There was not a samurai in all of Choshu who did not know the name. "You mean the Katsu Kaishu?" he snickered. "Of course, we can see from your elaborate clothes, and your huge escort that you are none other than the commissioner of the Tokugawa Navy."

Kaishu continued speaking in the same calm tone. "If you're going to shoot, please take careful aim and get the job done as quickly as possible. You see, it'll be shameful enough dying of a gunshot wound, when the only honorable way for a samurai to die is by the sword. But dying slowly in such a manner would be too much to bear."

Something in Kaishu's manner, perhaps his resolve to die, must have convinced at least the leader of the patrol, because as soon as Kaishu finished speaking the Choshu man suddenly gasped, "Katsu-sensei! You are Katsu Kaishu-sensei!" He dropped to his knees, and to the dismay of the others, bowed his head to the ground. "Please forgive our outrage," he begged. As Kaishu–and Yoshinobu–had suspected, he was indeed the only man in the Edo government whom the Choshu men would not only talk to, but utterly respected.

Soon he checked into the inn, which was all but deserted: the only visible soul an old gray-haired woman who greeted him at the entranceway. "Welcome," she said, the only other sound that of small waves lapping against the shore.

"Why is everything so quiet?" Kaishu asked, as he removed his wooden clogs, and stepped up onto the clean wooden porch. "Where are the other guests?"

"I'm afraid they've all left," the innkeeper replied. "The Choshu troops, with all their clamor about killing men of the Bakufu, shooting their guns and screaming, have scared everyone off. And all of the workers from this inn, like most of the other folks who live on this island, have taken their belongings and crossed over to the mainland, before fighting breaks out here as well."

"I see," Kaishu said, impressed by the old woman's pluck. "Why haven't you left?"

"If I had, who would take care of you?"

"Well, I'm certainly glad you feel that way," Kaishu said, removed his long sword and followed the woman down a narrow wooden corridor. She left him alone in a spacious *tatami* room, which opened onto a wooden verandah overlooking the glassy blue Inland Sea.

"Excuse my impertinence," the old woman said, upon returning with a pot of hot tea, "but who are you?" She placed the teapot on a tray, after pouring a cupful. "And why did you come here now when things are so dangerous?"

"I'm a storyteller from Edo," Kaishu replied. "I've come here look-ing for new material. But since there doesn't seem to be anyone around to tell me any new stories, I'm afraid I won't have much to bring back with me." He laughed, produced a paper fan from his sash, unfolded it and began waving it slowly in front of his face. He had ample reason for hiding his identity from the good woman: had she known that this "storyteller from Edo" had come as representative of the Tokugawa Bakufu to negotiate a peace with Choshu, he doubted that she would have the nerve to take care of him while he waited for the Choshu mission to arrive.

The woman refilled Kaishu's teacup, looked at him through implor-ing brown eyes. "Since you are a storyteller," she said, "if you would-n't mind, I would really like to hear a story."

"From Edo?" Kaishu's smile radiated kindness, putting the old woman at ease.

"Yes, from Edo. I've always wanted to visit the Shogun's capital."

"Why not," Kaishu said with a sorrow in his eyes that the old woman was quick to detect. He produced a leather pouch and a long, narrow lacquered case. "I never tell a story without a smoke," he said, filled a long-stemmed pipe with finely cut tobacco, and lit it with a wooden match which fascinated the old woman. "There was once a family, a very noble family indeed, which ruled a great island-nation for nearly three centuries," Kaishu began, slowly exhaling a stream of white smoke. "A great culture developed under the reign of this fam-ily. Its retainers, who lived and died under a noble code of ethics, were brave warriors, who governed the common people justly. So satisfied was the ruling family with the noble society it had created that it determined to protect it from outside corruption. Laws were promul-gated which forbid the people to leave the island-nation, and foreign-ers to enter. The family ruled so well, in fact, that its warrior-retainers were content with the harmony in which they dwelled. But over the years this contentment led to complacency, which led to stagnation and laziness in the hearts of the once noble retainers, who slowly began to forget even their noble code of ethics. Years passed, until one day foreigners sailed from across the sea on great ships which could move about freely through the water, as if by magic, without having to depend on the winds. On the sides of the these ships were mounted magnificent guns, the booming of which was louder than thunder, and which were capable of destroying the ancient fortifications along the coast of the island-nation. The foreigners demanded that the nation open its borders, or pay the consequences of attack."

"What did the island-nation do?" the old woman asked worriedly.

"There wasn't much it could do. So weak from complacency had it become that it was unable to keep the foreigners out." Kaishu paused, looked wearily at the old woman.

"How horrible!" she said. "What ever became of the island-nation?"

Kaishu sighed deeply. "If only I knew," he said. "If only I knew."

Kaishu spent the following week waiting for the Choshu emissaries, until on the first of September a message arrived that they would meet him at a nearby temple on the next morning. When Kaishu arrived at the temple, a priest showed him to a drawing room where the meeting was to take place, and left him alone behind a closed door. Presently, he heard footsteps on the wooden corridor outside the room. "They've come," he told himself, sat up straight in the formal position and breathed deeply, exhaling slowly from the abdomen. "If they cut me," he thought, "I really can't blame them." The door slowly slid open, revealing five samurai kneeling in a straight line on the polished wooden floor just outside the *tatami* room. "Please come in so we can talk," Kaishu said, his long sword placed at his right side.

One of the Choshu men, a large, muscular samurai, bowed his head to the floor. "I am Hirosawa Hyosuke, in charge of this mission," he said. At age thirty-three, Hirosawa was Katsura's chief political advisor. He had been imprisoned when the Choshu conservatives came to power in 1864, but was released in the following year after the radicals regained control.

Kaishu bowed slightly, repeated, "Please come in so we can talk."

Although the Choshu men represented the victors in the war, so great was their reverence for Katsu Kaishu that they remained kneeling on the hard wooden floor. Not only was Kaishu the commissioner of the navy, but he was one of the few men in the Bakufu who had openly sympathized with the Loyalist cause from the early days. The Choshu men were well aware that it was because of this very sympathy that Kaishu had been removed from his post, put under house arrest and nearly ordered to commit *seppuku* in Edo. Furthermore, it was commonly known that Katsu Kaishu–and his Group of Four–had bitterly opposed both of the expeditions against their *han*, and that he was the mentor of their staunch ally, Sakamoto Ryoma.

Kaishu stood up, cleared his throat. "Since Choshu won the war, if you really insist on staying out there in the that cramped corridor, then I guess I'll have to join you," he said, drawing laughter from the entire group.

Hirosawa stood up, was followed by the others. "In that case," he said, "we will accept the honor of joining you, Katsu-sensei."

"The fact that Choshu won the war cannot be disputed," Kaishu said. "As the victors, only you have the power to end it. I've come here as the representative of the losing side, and believe me it is a very shameful thing to represent the losing side. But despite the great shame I already feel, I will shame myself even more by begging that you be satisfied with your victory, and recall all of your troops so that we can get down to the business of fortifying the nation." Kaishu stopped speaking to give the Choshu men a chance to respond, but all five of them, quite taken aback, remained silent. It was not only what Kaishu said that startled them, but they had expected the representative of the Bakufu to come with demands. Certainly they had never imagined that he would beg Choshu, a renegade *han*, to do anything. "I repeat!" Kaishu shouted. "I have not come to ask you, but to beg you," he pause to emphasize his intent, "for the sake of Japan, to end this war immediately. France and England are waiting like hungry wolves for the chance to subjugate Japan. Why else do you think the British have been supplying arms to Choshu and Satsuma?"

"So that we can overthrow the Bakufu," Hirosawa offered sheepishly.

"And what about the French?" Kaishu laughed derisively at the folly of the regime he represented. "Why do you suppose the French are so eager to give military aid to Edo? Certainly not out of goodwill. Just like the British, the French are waiting for infighting and civil war to weaken us so badly that they'll be able to come in and take over the country, like the British did in China, and both the British and French have done in India. This is why I beg you, as the victor in the war, to take the initiative and stop the fighting so that we can unite our nation once and for all. Not as a favor to the Bakufu, but for the future of Japan."

Hirosawa nodded grimly. "We fully understand and agree with what you have said, Katsu-sensei," he said. "And although we trust you personally, we simply cannot trust the Bakufu."

Kaishu returned the Choshu man's grim nod. "And I don't blame you at all," he said, again startling the entire group. "Until now, there has not been one Bakufu leader over the past many years who deserves your trust." After a long tirade in which he criticized much of the Edo elite and their policies, the navy commissioner said calmly, "But things are changing. Fortunately for Japan, Lord Yoshinobu has become the new Head of the House of Tokugawa. As you know, the Tokugawa has not been headed by such an able man for generations. If you can trust me, then you can believe me when I say that I have the utmost of confidence in Lord Yoshinobu's ability to see this nation through its present crises."

Hirosawa bowed his head to the floor. "Katsu-sensei, we will do as you bid, and stop fighting. But we cannot recall our troops until Edo does so first."

"Then I'll personally see to it that all of the pro-Tokugawa armies return to their respective domains," Kaishu said, returning Hirosawa's bow. "But," he straightened himself, looked hard into the Choshu man's eyes, "I would like to ask for your word of honor that Choshu troops will not fire upon Tokugawa troops as they retreat."

"You have my word of honor."

Kaishu nodded grimly. "Then it's settled," he said.

All alone Kaishu had risked his life to come to the Island of the Shrines, and all alone he had convinced Choshu to put a stop to the war. Now, as he was about to return to Kyoto all alone to report his success to Lord Yoshinobu, he thought that he would like to visit the great Shinto shrine on this island, dedicated to the niece of the Sun Goddess. Throughout history it had been customary for great warlords to offer to this shrine prize swords or armor, as a token of appreciation for their victories; and Kaishu thought that he would follow their noble examples. "I'm a representative of the Tokugawa Bakufu," he told himself. "Although the Bakufu has reached its final days, it ruled peacefully for two and a half centuries. And since I've been successful on my mission here, I too should offer something to posterity." Kaishu would offer a short sword he had brought with him from Edo, as it was believed to have belonged to an Imperial prince of the Southern Dynasty in the fourteenth century.

After arriving at the great shrine, Kaishu went directly to the office of the resident priest. "I would like to offer this to the shrine," he said, showing the sword. The priest cast a haughty look at Kaishu, as if to say, "How dare you be so impudent?" After all, Kaishu was dressed in the clothing of a rank-and-file samurai, and was not accompanied by even a single servant or retainer. Certainly, the priest assumed, this could not possibly be a man of any significance whatsoever. "I'm sorry," he said, "but we only accept objects of value at this shrine."

"But this sword belonged to an Imperial prince," Kaishu said.

"Oh? And who are you who would offer such a treasure?"

Although Kaishu could not at this point very well reply that he was a storyteller from Edo, he simply said, "My name's Katsu. I've come from Edo." The name meant nothing to the Shinto priest. Had Kaishu replied, "Katsu Kaishu, the commissioner of the Tokugawa Navy, who has just finished negotiating a peace with Choshu," the priest might have dropped to his knees, apologizing until his mouth went dry. But more than likely he would have thought that this commonly dressed little man was an impostor, and crossly sent him away. At any rate, as the priest still refused to accept the sword, Kaishu reached into his kimono, removed a pouch, from which he took ten gold coins. Offering the money to the priest, he said, "Now will you take the sword?"

The priest accepted, and Kaishu left the shrine. Heading back to the inn to retrieve his belongings before returning to Hiroshima, Kaishu could not help but laugh aloud as he thought that he had had more trouble getting the priest to accept his sword than convincing the Choshu men to put an end to the war.

Kaishu returned to Kyoto on September 11, and reported immediately to the residence of Lord Yoshinobu. Although Kaishu was eager to inform Yoshinobu of the success of his mission, the Head of the House of Tokugawa was less than anxious to see Kaishu. In fact, Yoshinobu made his navy commissioner wait three days before granting him an audience. Then, when he finally summoned Kaishu to his home, it was with disdain that he greeted this dedicated and most able of Tokugawa retainers.

To say the least, Kaishu was confused. Had he not risked his life by going to Hiroshima to talk with the Choshu men? And now that he had returned safely, with his mission accomplished, Yoshinobu was angry.

"Are you not satisfied with the results of the negotiations?" Kaishu asked frankly.

"I can't believe that you made peace without insisting that Choshu accept some form of punishment," Yoshinobu replied scathingly.

"Insist that Choshu accept punishment?" Kaishu said in disbelief. "Was not Choshu the victor, and Edo the vanquished? Has there ever been a war throughout the history of Japan, or indeed the whole world, when the vanquished insisted upon punishing the victors as a condition for peace?" Kaishu paused to catch his breath. "Ridiculous!" he now shouted, staring hard into the burning eyes of his liege lord. "You told me yourself before I left for Hiroshima that I could handle the negotiations as I saw fit. How could you even consider that Choshu would accept any form of punishment? It wasn't Choshu who came begging for peace. It was the Bakufu." Beside himself with anger, Kaishu thrust his hands into his kimono. "Certainly you haven't forgotten who won the war. Certainly you haven't forgotten who was defeated on all fronts. With all the trickery and deception in this government, that Choshu would even agree to stop fighting is a miracle."

"Katsu!" Yoshinobu roared, not about to accept a lambasting from his own vassal. "Deception?" he screamed. "You who have sympathized with and even sheltered renegades and outlaws for years have the gall to talk of deception?"

Kaishu was not to be intimidated. "Yes," he shouted back, "this whole regime is run on deception!" Then without uttering another word, Kaishu turned his back on Yoshinobu and stormed out of the room.

Kaishu was right, and Yoshinobu knew it. Kaishu was so right, in fact, that Yoshinobu was unable to punish him for the affront. As the navy commissioner would find out upon his return to Osaka Castle, deception was indeed the only word to describe Yoshinobu's actions. After sending Kaishu on the peace mission, Yoshinobu had suddenly changed his strategy. He approached the court, and requested that an Imperial decree be issued to both sides, ordering a temporary cease-fire. "*With the death of the Shogun, everyone is in mourning,*" the decree stated. "*At a time like this, war is undesirable. It is hereby ordered that the fighting be postponed, and that Choshu withdraw its troops from the territories it has invaded.*"

This was a far cry from what Kaishu had promised Choshu; and, rightly so, he concluded, Choshu would be infuriated. It was obvious that Edo had once again manipulated the court for its own gains. The Imperial order that "*the fighting be postponed*" could only be taken to mean that Choshu, having gotten the upper hand through victories on all fronts, must now give Edo ample time to reinforce, and when the mourning period for the Shogun had ended, an opportunity to resume its expedition against Choshu.

"Ridiculous!" Kaishu shouted when he heard from the prime minister at the castle of Yoshinobu's latest deception. "Choshu will never accept that!" Kaishu, of course, was right. Although Choshu had already drawn its troops back behind its own borders, the entire domain–samurai, commoners and even women–remained prepared for war.

Kaishu was furious. Having risked his life to secure a peace with Choshu, not only had he been made a fool of by Yoshinobu, but now he too had become a perpetrator of the Bakufu's deception. At age forty-three, he had reached an impasse in his life, far greater than the one facing Ryoma and his men in Nagasaki. In fact, he suspected that he had done all he would be able to do for Japan, and that this most turbulent of times was racing by at a pace which seemed to intensify with each passing day. "But no matter," he thought, not a little sadly. "As long as there are still free spirits like Sakamoto Ryoma, not bound to any individual *han* or regime, who can take over and fulfill my goal of uniting Japan into a single state, so that we can eventually compete with the West, I'll be satisfied." On September 13, less than four months after being reinstated as navy commissioner, Katsu Kaishu, Protector of the Province of Awa, submitted his resignation to Prime Minister Itakura, and at the beginning of October returned alone to Edo.

Onwards and Upwards

Although Sakamoto Ryoma indeed shared Katsu Kaishu's goal of the peaceful unification of Japan, his plan to convince Edo to relinquish power was put on hold with the news that Lord Shungaku had flatly rejected his proposal. Aware that it would take more than words to convince the Bakufu, Ryoma arranged a meeting in Shimonoseki between representatives of Satsuma, several other Kyushu clans, and Choshu. The Dragon's latest plan, which he had briefly discussed during the previous summer with his men in Nagasaki, was to establish a cartel among these clans in the form of a mutual trading company, whose overwhelming force, both militarily and economically, he envisioned as the final straw to convince the waning Bakufu to relinquish power peacefully.

The Loyalists in Choshu enjoyed close ties with a number of wealthy Shimonoseki merchants who sympathized with and even actively and openly aided their cause. Prominent among these families was that of Ito Kuzo, who had been granted the right to a surname. For generations, the Ito family had been one of six Elder Families designated by the Lord of Choshu to govern the commoners, under the authority of samurai overlords. The Ito mansion was the officially appointed inn for Choshu-related lords traveling through Shimonoseki, and for this reason it was often referred to as "Headquarters." Ryoma had recently been staying at Ito's home whenever he was in Shimonoseki, and it was here that he called for the meeting between representatives of several Kyushu clans, and Choshu. He had no trouble arranging the meeting. In fact, many of the *Men of High Purpose* traveling through Shimonoseki made it a point to visit Ryoma if they could find his whereabouts, which, as they had recently warned, were far too accessible for his own safety. Ryoma's fame was a matter of course: he was the man who had united Choshu and Satsuma; the man who was most responsible for arming Choshu for the war against the Bakufu; and the man who had commanded a band of *ronin* in a victorious sea battle against the Tokugawa forces in Shimonoseki.

One chilly afternoon in November, Ryoma and Kenkichi sat in a room on the second floor of the Ito mansion with ten other samurai, six of whom were prominent members of the three Kyushu clans which had outwardly supported Choshu in the war. Katsura Kogoro represented Choshu, and Godai Saisuke was there for Satsuma.

"I've called you here today..." Ryoma said, then paused, turning to his Chief Secretary, the eloquent Nagaoka Kenkichi. "Tell them," he said, as Kenkichi proceeded to explain Ryoma's plan. "This will be the first step toward a coalition of the most powerful lords," Kenkichi concluded, "whose cooperation we will need to topple the Bakufu. The lords must form a council in Kyoto, declare a new Imperial government separate from Edo, under the authority of the Imperial Court. As a first step to this great political scheme..."

"We need to offer these *han* a way to make some big money," Ryoma interrupted.

"But," said Godai, "many of the Kyushu clans have hated each other for centuries."

"Then we're going to have to convince them to get along with each other," Ryoma answered gruffly. "Or else they won't have a country left to live in. France and England will divide Japan among themselves."

"But most of the thirty-four clans of Kyushu are still petrified of the Bakufu," Godai said. "You know that before the war with Choshu the Lord of Fukuoka executed every last one of the Loyalists in his *han*."

"Even cowards have a way of being convinced," Katsura said bitterly.

"Now that Choshu has won," Ryoma proposed, "I'm sure that those *han* will listen to reason. In fact, that's the purpose of this meeting–to give them a chance. Although they might have a hard time joining a political or military alliance against Edo, I think they'll be able to swallow the idea of a business coalition. Then, after they've learned the benefits of working together economically, I think the next step will be political and military cooperation. After that, we'll have our revolution."

"Ingenious, Sakamoto-san," Godai said.

"Yes," agreed several others, to whom Ryoma proposed a toast. "Onwards and upwards," he said, refilling several *sake* cups.

"Onwards and upwards," Kenkichi echoed, as all fourteen men drained their cups.

"Onwards and upwards!" There is little doubt that Ryoma knew just how relevant his remark was, although he expected that it would take months, if not years, before a cartel could actually be formed. In the meantime a chance meeting he would have with an old friend in Nagasaki would not only change his life, but affect the destiny of the entire nation.

On the day after the meeting at Ito's mansion, Ryoma and his men returned to Nagasaki to discuss his plan for the cartel with Kosone Eishiro, on whose financial support the Kameyama Company was greatly dependent. Late one afternoon, as Ryoma, Toranosuke and Eishiro were leaving a *sake* house in Maruyama, a voice from behind called Ryoma's name. Ryoma immediately turned around to see a samurai waving at him in the distance.

"Who's that?" Eishiro whispered.

Ryoma squinted, but could not make out the face for his poor vision. "I'm not sure, but I'd say from his accent that he's from Kochi."

"He sure is," Toranosuke bitterly ascertained. "That's Mizobuchi Hironojo," he sneered, reaching for his sword. "I'll cut the traitor."

"No," Ryoma growled in no uncertain terms. "Come on. Let's get out of here." Although Ryoma had only fond memories of his old friend, with whom he had shared the same room at Tosa headquarters in Edo years ago, he had heard that Mizobuchi was now an official, and any official of Tosa Han meant trouble to the fugitive.

"I want to cut him," Toranosuke objected, his hand reaching, as of its own accord, for the hilt of his sword. "That son of a bitch is working for the men who killed Takechi-sensei."

"Relax, Tora!" Ryoma demanded, squinting in the direction of the fast-approaching Tosa official.

"If you don't let me cut him now, we'll have Tosa agents all over us," Toranosuke argued.

"Nobody's going to cut anyone," Ryoma growled, as Mizobuchi called his name again. "Ryoma!" he called a third time, before reaching the three men and taking hold of Ryoma's hand. "It sure is good to see you again," he said. Mizobuchi Hironojo, a lower-samurai from Kochi Castletown, was seven years older than Ryoma. He had practiced *kendo* under Takechi Hanpeita at the Momonoi Dojo in Edo, but, notwithstanding his deep reverence for the Loyalist Party leader, he had never joined the party, nor had he ever considered fleeing Tosa. This is not to say that Mizobuchi was a traitor; rather he was simply too subdued of nature for the extremism demanded by the Loyalists. This Ryoma realized, and in the spring of 1862, just before fleeing Tosa, he introduced Mizobuchi to Kawada Shoryo. This was the last time the two had met, until this chilly November afternoon in the pleasure quarters of Nagasaki.

Despite his lower-samurai status, Mizobuchi was eventually pro-

moted to petty officialdom for his scholastic prowess. He was officially in Nagasaki to continue his study of things Western, but his
actual purpose was to investigate the activities among the various *han*
in this international trading center.

"It's good to see you too, Mizobuchi," Ryoma said. "But I'm in a
hurry. I have some urgent business to attend to," he lied. Followed by
Toranosuke and Eishiro, Ryoma started to walk away, scraping his
boot heels on the stone pavement.

"Like finding a financial backer for your shipping company?"
Mizobuchi called out. Needless to say, the remark took Ryoma completely by surprise.

"What did you say?" Ryoma said, turning around to face
Mizobuchi.

"I thought I might be able to find you around here, Ryoma."
Mizobuchi smiled through beady black eyes, which were situated a bit
too high on his gourd-shaped face. "Although you're a fugitive, it's no
mystery to anyone that if Sakamoto Ryoma is in Nagasaki, one is
bound to find him in one of the brothels around Maruyama."

"Well, at least some things never change," Ryoma snickered. Then
feigning nonchalance, "Like I said, I have to be going."

"Ryoma!" Mizobuchi shouted, not a little offended. "Two old
friends who haven't seen each other in years happen to meet on the
street, and this is how you act? The Sakamoto Ryoma I once knew was
never so cold."

"Mizobuchi, don't you understand?" Ryoma said apologetically.
Although he detested Tosa Han, and indeed wanted nothing to do with
it, his longing for his old friends and his home in Kochi suddenly got
the best of him. "I'm wanted for fleeing Tosa, and along comes a Tosa
official. Now how am I supposed to act?"

Mizobuchi put his hand on Ryoma's shoulder. "I'm your friend," he
said. "Certainly you know I'd never turn you in. And I meant it when
I said I've been looking for you because I've heard that you've been
having financial troubles, and are looking for a backer. Well, I know
a very influential Tosa official who I think you ought to meet."

"Why don't we have a drink somewhere?" Ryoma suggested. Then
turning to Toranosuke, "Didn't you have some business to attend to?"
Toranosuke had never completely gotten over the days when he had
worked with Hanpeita's hit-squads in Kyoto, and Ryoma did not want
to take any chances.

"I'm not about to leave you alone with this traitor," Toranosuke protested angrily.

"It's alright, Tora. Mizobuchi and I are old friends, and I know that he's not a traitor."

"Very well," Toranosuke muttered, cast a menacing glance at the Tosa official, and left the three men on the street.

Kosone accompanied the Tosa men into a *sake* house, where he was a frequent customer. After instructing the proprietress to give the two men a private room, and all the *sake* they could drink, he told her to charge the bill to his own account, and left the Tosa men to themselves.

"Like I've told you Ryoma," Mizobuchi spoke in a low, deliberate voice, "I've recently heard about the financial trouble of your shipping company."

"I see," Ryoma said evasively, warming his hands over a blue ceramic brazier.

"I've been working closely with Tosa Minister Goto Shojiro, and..."

"Goto Shojiro," Ryoma sneered. "That's the nephew of Yoshida Toyo who condemned Hanpeita to death."

"I know how you feel, Ryoma. But if you'd just listen to what I have to say," Mizobuchi entreated.

"Continue, then."

"Like I just said, I've heard you're having financial trouble."

"We're a shipping company without a ship. I guess that says it all. But I've just come from Shimonoseki, where I spoke with representatives of several *han*." After explaining his ideas about a cartel, Ryoma said, "What I'd like to do in the meantime is buy products from all over Kyushu, ship them to the central market in Osaka and sell them for big profit."

"But I thought you just said you don't have a ship."

"We don't."

Mizobuchi smiled, as if confident his purpose would soon be accomplished. "Then let me introduce you to Goto," he said.

"Goto? What for?"

"Tosa is changing," Mizobuchi said. "Have you heard about the new Institution for Development and Achievement?"

"No," Ryoma replied, and with his eyes urged Mizobuchi to continue.

As Mizobuchi explained, the Institution for Development and Achievement had been established in Kochi in the spring of the previous year by Lord Yodo and his Chief Minister Goto Shojiro to mod-

ernize local industry. Separate divisions were set up within the institution to exploit Tosa's reserves of gold, silver, and copper; to promote
the whaling industry, and to purchase foreign books, machines, ships
and weapons. A school of Western medicine and a hospital had been
established, where French and English were also being taught.

"And Goto has recently set up a trading office in Nagasaki, called
the Tosa Company," Mizobuchi said, drawing a look of intense interest from Ryoma. "So you see, Ryoma, Goto has the same basic ideas
as you, but he's in a much better position than you are to realize them."

"Yes," Ryoma groaned, as if to himself, "he has Tosa to back him."

"And what I think will interest you most, is that Goto has also set up
a Navy Department as part of the institution. But as you may well
expect, there are still plenty of hardheaded conservatives among the
upper-samurai in Tosa who are convinced that everything foreign is
evil, and who don't approve of what Goto is doing."

"The more you tell me about Goto, the more I think I'd like to meet
him," Ryoma said.

"Recently, Goto sailed to Shanghai, partly to avoid assassination by
the conservatives, but also to purchase a steamer. But what he saw
apparently impressed him so, that he ended up buying two warships
and a gunboat."

"What was it that impressed him?" Ryoma asked.

"The military encroachment of the great Western powers into Asia."

"Sounds like a man who has some brains," Ryoma remarked sarcastically.

"He does," Mizobuchi ignored the sarcasm. "In fact, Goto is now
convinced that the only way to save Japan is through developing the
economy and modernizing the military."

"I could have told you that years ago," Ryoma snickered. "But, of
course, none of the upper-samurai would ever listen."

"Tosa is changing," Mizobuchi said. "And as proof of that, even
though the hardheads in Kochi are furious with Goto over all the
money he's spent on weapons, he also contracted in Shanghai for several of those new Armstrong guns."

"Armstrong guns?" Ryoma said. "You mean Tosa has Armstrong
guns?" Ryoma had wanted so badly to purchase these state-of-the-art
cannon that the mere mention of them made him smell, and even taste,
gunpowder.

"They haven't arrived yet. But like I said, Ryoma, Tosa is changing."

"Besides just brains, it sounds like Goto has some guts too," Ryoma said, this time without a trace of sarcasm.

"Plenty!' Mizobuchi stressed. "One evening last summer as Goto was on his way to a brothel in Maruyama he was attacked by several men."

"And?"

"He didn't let that stop him."

"Who attacked him?"

"I don't know, but I do know that he fought them off. And then, what do you think he did?"

"Continued on his way to the brothel," Ryoma said matter-of-factly.

"How did you know?" Mizobuchi asked.

"Because that's just what I'd do. Once you have it in your mind to have a woman, you don't let some trivial incident stop you."

"I see," Mizobuchi said, giving Ryoma a puzzled look. "Anyway, since the Choshu victory, men like Goto are beginning to realize that the future of Japan depends on mutual cooperation between the most powerful clans, like you yourself have just said. And they don't want to see Tosa left behind."

"Tosa?" Ryoma sneered. "They don't want to see Tosa left behind? Ha!" he laughed derisively. "I couldn't care less about Tosa. My only concern is for Japan."

"Goto wants to develop Tosa's navy," Mizobuchi changed the subject.

"What does that have to do with me?" Ryoma remarked caustically. "I want to develop a Japanese Navy."

"Recently Goto was in Kyoto, where he spent a lot of time with the Satsuma men," Mizobuchi again changed the subject. "He apparently spoke extensively with Saigo, among others."

"Saigo?" Ryoma blurted.

"Yes. Saigo's a close friend of yours, isn't he? At least that's what he told Goto. Impressed the hell out of him, too," Mizobuchi chuckled. "I guess Goto didn't expect to hear the most powerful man in Satsuma praise a *ronin* from Tosa."

"What did they talk about?"

"The necessity of developing the military to overthrow the Bakufu, for one thing."

"And?"

"And about you, for another. Saigo apparently told Goto that it was a shame a man of your caliber was idle when the nation was in such dire need of your services."

"What does Goto think about the necessity of overthrowing the Bakufu?" Ryoma asked, ignoring the compliment.

"He agrees. At least that's what he's told me." Mizobuchi paused, rested his *sake* cup against his lower lip. "Don't you see, Ryoma? That's why I want to introduce you to Goto. He's very anxious to meet you. He says he suspects that you and he have the same goals. And after what I've heard you say today, I tend to agree with him. You and Goto have the same basic goals: building a navy and developing foreign trade. I have no doubt that the two of you will be able to work well together. Besides," Mizobuchi paused, looked hard at Ryoma, "you just told me you needed a ship."

"You mean to tell me that Tosa would be willing to give a ship to a band of men who have fled the *han*?"

"I can't promise anything. But do me and yourself a favor. At least talk to Goto."

"Before I agree, let me ask you something."

"What?"

"If what you say is true about Tosa changing, what would you say the chances are of Tosa joining the Satsuma-Choshu military alliance?"

"Ryoma, you know that there's been bad blood between Tosa and Choshu for the past two years, since the young Tosa *daimyo* separated from his wife because she was a relative of the Lord of Choshu."

"Yes, I know. And it's despicable," Ryoma sneered.

'Yes, it is," Mizobuchi agreed contemptuously, impressing upon Ryoma that even this mild-mannered official had a touch of the rebel in his heart. "But after Choshu's victory in the war, the young *daimyo* has taken her back."

Ryoma released a loud guffaw. "You mean to tell me that the Lord of Tosa actually has the balls to accept his own wife back without approval from the Tokugawa? Maybe Tosa really is changing," he snickered. "Maybe Tosa just might agree to enter into the alliance with Choshu and Satsuma against the Bakufu."

Mizobuchi swallowed hard, as Ryoma's sarcasm was warranted. "I wouldn't know," he said. "I'm just a lower-samurai."

"I know. We all are, in the eyes of Lord Yodo. That's the whole problem with Tosa. I don't think Yodo will ever agree to oppose the Tokugawa, any more than he'll agree to recognize the lower-samurai as anything more than subhuman."

"No, Ryoma. You're wrong. Even the commoners are allowed to

study at the Institution for Development and Achievement."

"Really?" Ryoma said, impressed.

"If you could convince Goto of the necessity of Tosa allying with Satsuma and Choshu, then I think he could convince Yodo."

"But is Goto any different from Yodo? Is Goto willing to deal with the lower-samurai on equal terms?"

"I think he is."

"Alright, Mizobuchi!" Ryoma slammed his fist into his palm, "I'll meet Goto. But on two conditions."

"Which are?"

"First, that you come to Choshu with me to meet Katsura Kogoro to discuss the possibilities of a reconciliation between Choshu and Tosa."

"I see," Mizobuchi said, nodding approval. "But, considering the bad blood, would the Choshu men be willing to talk with a Tosa official?"

Mizobuchi, I don't like to brag," Ryoma lied, "but you're looking at the man who united Satsuma and Choshu.'

"I see."

"So," Ryoma continued to brag, "as long as you're with me, you'll have no problems in Choshu."

"Then let's go," Mizobuchi said. "Goto isn't due back from Shanghai until the beginning of January." Mizobuchi rubbed his hands over the brazier. "And what's your other condition?"

"That you take as fair warning what I'm about to say."

"Which is?"

"You saw the way Toranosuke acted toward you. I had to send him away for fear he'd try to kill you on the spot."

"Don't worry about me."

"It's not you I'm worried about. It's Goto. Once my men find out he's in Nagasaki, not even I'll be able to guarantee that they won't try to kill him. And you can't blame them," Ryoma said bitterly. "Goto is the man who condemned Hanpeita to death."

While Ryoma and Mizobuchi were in Choshu discussing with Katsura the possibility of a Tosa-Choshu alliance, an event in Kyoto sent shock waves throughout Edo, and indeed the entire nation.

Since the previous August Satsuma and the anti-Bakufu nobles in Kyoto had been using the political vacuum created by Choshu's victory, the death of the Shogun, and the refusal of Yoshinobu to succeed him, to strengthen their position at court. Although Emperor Komei and his top advisors were staunch supporters of the Bakufu, the anti-Bakufu faction at court, with the cooperation of Satsuma, was planning the restoration of Imperial rule. Why, one might ask, would the Emperor bitterly oppose those who would restore his divine line to the pinnacle of power in his sacred empire? The answer is simple: So great was his fear of anything Western, that he preferred that the political authority remain in the hands of the Tokugawa Shogun–Commander in Chief of the Expeditionary Forces Against the Barbarians–who, until recently, had kept the foreigners out and Japan at peace for two and a half centuries. Thus Emperor Komei's hate for Choshu and all other radical elements, who for the past several years had been plotting to shatter the state of things by destroying his sturdiest shield, the Tokugawa Bakufu.

The leader of the plot at court to overthrow the Bakufu and restore the Emperor to power was Iwakura Tomomi, a previously high-ranking court noble, who was now operating in exile from the outskirts of Kyoto. Six years before, Iwakura had urged the Emperor to sanction the marriage between the Emperor's younger sister and the Shogun, as a means of uniting the court and the Bakufu. *"Then,"* this master of political intrigue had explained to the Emperor, *"if you would order the Bakufu to first consult with the court before making any decisions involving either domestic or foreign matters, Edo would maintain political authority in name only, with the actual power resting in the hands of the Imperial Court."* His intentions mistaken as traitorous by the Loyalists in Kyoto, Iwakura was banished by the court, partly for his own safety, in the summer of 1862, but was now once again actively plotting the overthrow of the Bakufu.

During his past four years in exile, Iwakura had been in secret contact with several of the leading anti-Bakufu activists, the most prominent of whom was Okubo Ichizo of Satsuma. At the end of the previous August, after Edo's defeat by Choshu, Iwakura had organized a group of twenty-two court nobles to deliver a memorial to the Emperor. The memorial stated two main objectives: the formation of a council of lords in Kyoto to decide the affairs of state; and a political reformation within the court. The suggestion was tantamount to the impeachment of the Emperor's leading advisors, all of whom supported Edo. The plan backfired, and at the end of October the Emperor ordered the detention of the twenty-two nobles who had submitted the memorial, and a tighter watch on Iwakura's home in exile. At the beginning of December the anti-Bakufu radicals were struck with another blow: Yoshinobu gave into pressure from the Imperial Court and his own ministers, and agreed to become the fifteenth Tokugawa Shogun as a final resort to save the Bakufu. But less than three weeks later, on December 25, Shogun Yoshinobu met with his worst disaster since the fall of Kokura Castle in the previous August.

Emperor Komei had suddenly died at the age of thirty-six, and although the official medical report attributed the cause of death to smallpox, rumor had it that the Son of Heaven had been poisoned. This was not a farfetched conclusion. Alive Emperor Komei presented a serious obstacle to both Iwakura and Satsuma in their mutual goal of toppling the Bakufu. What's more, the Imperial heir was only fourteen years old at the time; his maternal grandfather and official guardian, Nakayama Tadayasu, had for years been an opponent of Edo, and was in a perfect position to aid his longtime ally Iwakura.

To the anti-Bakufu revolutionaries in Choshu, Satsuma and Kyoto; to the Bakufu elite in Edo and Osaka; and to Sakamoto Ryoma and his band of *ronin* in Nagasaki, the death of Emperor Komei marked the beginning of a new political age.

The second year of the Era of Keio, 1866, was coming to a close, as Ryoma sat alone one night in his room at the Kosone mansion. The meeting between Katsura and Mizobuchi had gone well, and Ryoma now felt confident enough in the feasibility of a Tosa-Choshu alliance to justify a meeting with Goto Shojiro.

Oryo was asleep in the next room. But unable to sleep himself, Ryoma was writing a letter to Otome, when suddenly his thoughts drifted to his brother Gombei. He sat up straight, lay his writing brush on the desk and inhaled deeply. His hot breath came out white, reminding him just how cold the night had become, and he wondered how Gombei must feel about his being away from home for so many years. "If I should die," he said aloud, as if Gombei were somehow listening, "I sure would like to have one of our prize family swords with me." Although Ryoma rarely thought of his own death, much less the Sakamoto family heirlooms, it must have been something in the air, the coldness of the night, or perhaps an eerie premonition which suddenly turned his thoughts morbid.

After all, there was no end in sight to the dangerous and difficult road which Ryoma had chosen when he fled Tosa four and a half years before. Nevertheless, he was feeling content, even happy, with his life.

He picked up the brush, dabbed it in the ink and continued writing to Otome. He described in elaborate detail his honeymoon at the hot springs in the misty mountains of Kagoshima, his hike up a volcanic summit, holding Oryo's hand all the way, when suddenly his thoughts turned existential. *"This is certainly a strange world,"* he wrote, *"unpredictable as the moon and clouds. Rather than staying at home at the end of the year and receiving a stipend of rice, it is much more amusing to be fighting for the nation, if only one is prepared to die."*

Ryoma's men shared his sentiments on the unpredictability of this world, particularly when, on the next day at headquarters, he told them of his intentions to meet Goto.

"What?" Toranosuke was the first to react, with a loud gasp.

"Goto?" Sonojo hollered. "I'd like to cut the son of a bitch."

"Isn't he the one who had Takechi-sensei commit *seppuku?*" Yonosuke asked, in his typical monotone.

Irked by the impassivity of Yonosuke's remark, Toranosuke shot back, "You wouldn't know how we Tosa men feel about it."

"Hold it right there!" Yonosuke demanded, jumping to his feet.

"Relax, Yonosuke!" Ryoma said appeasingly, then turned to Toranosuke with a scowl. "Don't forget that in our company there are no Tosa or Kii or any other clans. There's only Japan."

Toranosuke nodded assent, then added, "But you mustn't see Goto."

"I know how you feel," Ryoma said.

"Where is Goto?" Sonojo asked.

"In Shanghai," Ryoma said. "He's not due to return to Nagasaki until the first of the year."

"When he does return," Toranosuke seethed, "I'm going to cut the bastard down."

"Ryoma," Kenkichi said, "Toranosuke is right." Although Kenkichi had never been a member of Hanpeita's Loyalist Party, even this most erudite of Kameyama Company men was unable to overcome his resentment for the upper-samurai of Tosa. "For all we know, Goto and his lackeys might be plotting to arrest the whole lot of us."

"Ryoma-san," Taro spoke up, "it would be an insult to the souls of Takechi-sensei and the others who died in Kochi if we didn't avenge their deaths. We must take Goto's head."

"He's right, Sakamoto-san," asserted Umanosuke. Even this mild-mannered peasant's son agreed with his comrades from Tosa.

"All of you listen!" Ryoma suddenly shouted. "I know how you feel

441

about Goto. I feel the same way. Not only is he responsible for Hanpeita's death, but he's an upper-samurai." Indeed, there wasn't a man among them who detested more than Ryoma the discrimination of the lower classes by the social elite. "Sonojo, you know better than anyone why I fled Tosa with you all those years ago. I had to get away from the unfairness and stupidity of the system. I didn't know what I was doing. I didn't know where I was heading. But I did know that none of us would ever stand a chance in Tosa Han."

Rage filled Sonojo's eyes, as he reached for his sword. "That's why we must kill Goto," he screamed. "This is one time when I can't agree with you, Ryoma. If Goto comes back to Nagasaki, I'll take his head."

Ryoma folded his arms at his chest. "If you must kill him," he said, "at least wait until he's had the chance to speak with me."

"Ryoma," Toranosuke protested violently, "Goto never gave Takechi-sensei a chance. Why should we give him one?"

"Because," Ryoma slammed his fist on the floor with such force that the walls of the old wooden house shook, "it was Hanpeita who killed Goto's uncle, Yoshida Toyo." The remark drew a cringe from Toranosuke, who was once among Hanpeita's most devoted disciples, and although he was not directly involved in the murder of Yoshida, he had participated in several of Hanpeita's *Heaven's Revenge* assassinations in Kyoto. "I was Hanpeita's closest friend," Ryoma continued. "For all Goto knows I was involved in Yoshida's murder. Nevertheless he wants to speak to me. Goto is a minister of Tosa Han, but he's willing to meet me on equal terms."

"What does he want to talk about?" asked the newest member of the company, Nakajima Sakutaro of Tosa, who had recently showed up at headquarters. At age twenty-three, Sakutaro was the second youngest in the company, and Ryoma welcomed him for his levelheadedness. "Sakutaro is a good counterbalance to the hotheads among us," he had told Yonosuke. Yonosuke agreed, and, in fact, he and Sakutaro had now become good friends.

Yonosuke was one of Ryoma's most valuable men. But whether it was out of jealousy over Ryoma's favor, or Yonosuke's tendency to bring reason to an extreme, he was not liked by most of the others. To make matters worse, he was a bit of a miser, a quality particularly unbecoming of a samurai. Recently, while Ryoma was away, Yonosuke had ordered samples of cotton padding from several shops in Nagasaki, on the pretext that he would show them to the other men to decide which to use for bedding for the employees. But instead

Yonosuke had used the free samples of cotton to make one very comfortable quilt for himself. Sakutaro's ability to look beyond Yonosuke's shortcomings was reflected in his levelheaded question about Ryoma's intentions to meet Goto."

"I'm not sure what Goto wants to talk about," Ryoma answered Sakutaro, whose powerful, inset eyes did not befit his baby face.

"Then why meet him?" Sonojo sneered.

Ryoma stood up, walked over to window, his back to the others. "For the sake of Japan," he said.

"What?"

"You heard me, Sonojo." Ryoma turned around to face all eight men. "Don't you think I'd like as much as any of you to revenge Hanpeita's death? But I think that, if nothing else, Katsu-sensei has at least taught us to look at things from a wide perspective. You see, what I have in mind is something more important than revenge. Something that Hanpeita himself would surely have agreed with."

"Which is?" Sonojo asked.

"A Tosa-Choshu-Satsuma alliance that Hanpeita envisioned years ago." After telling of Mizobuchi's meeting with Katsura, who had agreed in theory to such an alliance, Ryoma added, "Anyway, with the way things are going for us now, since we have no money or a ship of our own, I can't see any reason not to at least talk to Goto. We know that we can't very well continue depending on Choshu and Satsuma for support. They have enough problems of their own. But if what I've heard is true, I think that Goto just might be the person we need."

"What do you mean, Sakamoto-san?" Yonosuke asked.

"What I mean," Ryoma said, leaning back against the wooden alcove, his arms folded at his chest, "is that I intend to swallow my pride, forget about the past, and form a partnership with Goto."

"That's treachery!" Sonojo gasped. "I can't believe what I'm hearing. And from Sakamoto Ryoma of all people."

"Ryoma," Toranosuke shouted, "it would be like conceding the Loyalists' defeat to the upper-samurai of Tosa."

Ryoma scratched the back of his head, began speaking very slowly. "Don't you know that by losing one battle, you can sometimes gain one hundred victories?"

"I don't follow you," Sakutaro said.

"We need Goto. He's Lord Yodo's chief minister. He controls the treasury of Tosa, which is one of the wealthiest in Japan. If we can form a partnership with Goto, think of the things our company can do for Japan. We'll never have to worry about a lack of funds or ships for our business. We'll be in a position to buy weapons to sell to any of the *han* which are willing to stand up against the Bakufu. All I need do is throw away my pride, and..."

"Ryoma," Toranosuke interrupted, "I can't believe..."

"I know," Ryoma shouted. "I'm the one who swore he'd never deal with Tosa. That's why I fled in the first place. But if I've learned anything since then, I've learned that a man must be flexible. He has to be willing to change with the times in order to keep his options open. If not, he might as well stop living, because he'll never improve." Ryoma nonchalantly plucked a nose hair, flicked it across the room. "Now, Sonojo, if you think that's treachery, then so be it. But remember what most of you said when I tried to get you to work under Katsu-sensei. You said that Katsu-sensei was a traitor for selling out to the foreigners." Ryoma laughed slightly, not a little nostalgically. "I thought the same thing myself. That's why Jutaro and I went to kill him." Ryoma laughed again. "How stupid we were! But it's a good thing we realized it when we did."

"But, Ryoma-san," Taro protested, "it isn't Katsu-sensei we're talking about. It's Tosa Han. And we know the way things are in Tosa Han."

"Taro," Ryoma hollered, his eyes flashing, "we have to give ourselves this chance, because it might be our last one. Goto has asked to talk to me. I haven't asked to meet him. Now, if we can put Goto and all of Tosa Han to use for the good of Japan, what could possibly be better?"

"I see," Taro said.

Ryoma smiled, rubbed his hands together. "If Tosa unites with Satsuma and Choshu, the Bakufu will surely fall. So, if any of you still insist on cutting Goto before I have a chance to meet him, go ahead. But," he said with firm conviction, "you'll have to cut me first." Nobody dared to speak, as Ryoma burst out laughing. "I guess this means that I can see Goto without a fight," he said, then added ominously, "However, I will promise you this. If things don't work out, or if Goto tries to arrest us, not only will you have my blessings to cut him, I'll do it for you, and for Hanpeita and the others."

Tosa Minister Goto Shojiro's ship dropped anchor at Nagasaki one overcast afternoon in the second week of 1867. When the skiff carrying him reached the docks, Mizobuchi and another Tosa official were waiting for him.

"Minister Goto, welcome back," Mizobuchi called out. He bowed deeply, then, offering the younger man his hand, asked, "How was your journey, Your Excellency?"

Refusing to be helped out of the boat, Goto leaped onto the pier, landing with a loud thump. At age twenty-eight, Goto was short, built solidly, with a round face, firm jaw, determined black eyes, and a strength of character befitting the most powerful minister in the Tosa government. "Just fine," he said. "But it sure feels good to be back in Japan. All I need now is a hot bath, some good *sake* and a pretty Nagasaki wench."

"Please, Minister Goto," the other man urged nervously, "we must hurry."

"Why?" Goto asked, adjusting his swords at his left hip.

"It's just that..."

"Save it for later," Goto said, and with a wave of dismissal, began walking at a brisk pace toward the town.

"Minister Goto!" the man persisted, "we have reason to believe that there are Tosa *ronin* in Nagasaki out to revenge the death of Takechi Hanpeita."

Goto laughed sardonically. "Is that all that's worrying you? I have more important things on my mind." Turning to Mizobuchi he asked, "Have you made the arrangements?"

"Yes, Your Excellency. Ryoma has agreed to meet you."

"Ryoma?" the third man gasped. "You mean Sakamoto Ryoma?"

"Yes," Goto snapped, "Sakamoto Ryoma."

"But that's the *ronin* who..."

"I know," the minister growled, his scowl instantly silencing his underling. "When is the meeting scheduled for?"

"I don't know," Mizobuchi said, turning his long, narrow face slightly downward, and drawing a snicker from Goto.

"When you do that," Goto chided, "your face looks just like a gourd." Then looking at Mizobuchi, he added, as if annoyed, "What do you mean you don't know?"

"I couldn't schedule a meeting until you returned, Your Excellency."

"Well, I'm back now. Schedule one," Goto said, as the three men continued walking toward town.

Goto Shojiro was born in Kochi Castletown in the spring of 1838. At age sixteen he entered the academy of his uncle, Yoshida Toyo, who would recruit his nephew several years later to help him realize his great plan to enrich the fiefdom and strengthen its defenses through foreign trade. After Yodo's assassination, and the rise to power of the Tosa Loyalists, Goto went to Edo, partly to avoid assassination himself, partly to study Western navigational science, but always with the full intentions of realizing his late mentor's plan to strengthen Tosa Han. With the fall of Choshu from Imperial grace in August, and the beginning of the end of the Tosa Loyalist Party, Goto's chance had arrived. He and other young Yoshida disciples were reinstated into government service by Lord Yodo to revive the Tosa economy and strengthen its military. Goto's first reappointment was as Chief of Police, a post which included him in the central policy-making board of Tosa Han. In 1865, he was appointed by Yodo as Chief Inspector of Takechi Hanpeita's jailed Loyalists; his mission: to discover the murderers of Yoshida Toyo.

"*Sir Harry* (the British minister to Japan) *took a great fancy to him,*" Ernest Satow wrote of Goto, "*as being one of the most intelligent Japanese we had yet met, and to my own mind Saigo alone was his superior in force of character.*" Lord Yodo apparently was of similar opinion when he entrusted the reins of the Tosa government to the twenty-seven-year-old nephew of the late regent.

One afternoon in mid-January Goto was about to leave the office of the Tosa Company when someone called his name.

"What is it?" He turned around with an annoyed expression, as if to inform that he did not want to be bothered.

"Excuse me," Goto's attendant said sheepishly, "but I don't think you should be going out alone. Word has it that there is a group of Tosa *ronin* who are after you."

"I've heard all about it," Goto snickered. "Out to avenge Takechi's death. But I'm not concerned." In fact, he wasn't. Goto's boldness, however, had nothing to do with the fact that he was on his way to a nearby cottage to have a secret meeting with the leader of the same men who were supposedly after his head. "If anyone thinks he can cut me, let him try," he roared, and without further ado, left the office and his bewildered attendant.

Goto, like Ryoma, possessed a tremendous amount of energy, an inflated ego, and a tendency to boast. Also, like Ryoma, he was a charismatic leader with the gift of foresight. Unlike the practical president of the Kameyama Company, however, the Tosa minister cared nothing for detail.

In February 1866, one month after Ryoma had united Satsuma and Choshu, Goto had established the Institution for Development and Achievement in Kochi, and shortly after, its trading branch, the Tosa Company, in Nagasaki. When Lord Yodo's chief minister came to his Nagasaki headquarters in the following July he had one grand purpose in mind: establishing connections with foreign arms dealers in order to purchase Western warships and guns.

In Nagasaki, Goto spent exorbitant amounts of gold, living up to his reputation as a carouser by wining and dining business associates at the Maruyama brothels. When word of his escapades reached Kochi, Lord Yodo, who had nothing but confidence in his chief minister, arranged for him to travel to Shanghai to avoid assassination by xenophobic, if not jealous conservatives.

No sooner had Goto returned to Nagasaki, than his foreign debtors demanded payment of loans, compelling him to seek financial help from the Satsuma trade representative, Godai Saisuke. In order to convince Godai that Tosa was a sound investment, Goto boasted of the great wealth of the Yamanouchi domain, which, he claimed, "included the greatest abundance of camphor, paper and whale oil in all of Japan."

"If Tosa is so wealthy," Godai cunningly turned the conversation around, "how about doing Satsuma and me a big favor and taking one of our warships off my hands? You see, I seem to have purchased one more ship than our budget allows for."

Unable to retract his initial boasting of Tosa wealth, Goto had no choice but to put his lord into further debt with the purchase of yet another warship.

Such were the financial straits of Goto Shojiro when he arrived at the Cottage of the Pure Wind, where Mizobuchi was waiting for him.

"Where's Ryoma?" was the first thing out of Goto's mouth when Mizobuchi greeted him in the front garden.

"Ah," Mizobuchi hesitated nervously, "it looks like he's a little late, Your Excellency."

"Is the girl here?" Goto asked.

"Yes, she's waiting inside. I've arrange everything exactly as you've instructed."

"Well, lead the way," Goto said. "I want to have a look at her."

Meanwhile, Ryoma and Yonosuke had just left company headquarters in the Kameyama Hills. Ryoma had chosen Yonosuke to accompany him during the meeting with Goto, not only because the Kii man was his private secretary, but because, with the exception of Shiramine Shunme of Nagaoka Han, Yonosuke was the only one in the company who did not hold a personal grudge against the upper-samurai of Tosa Han. The two men walked quickly down the narrow path leading to the base of the hill, and just as they turned left at the main street lined with temples, Ryoma whispered, "Don't look back, but there are three men following us."

Yonosuke stopped.

"Just keep on walking, Yonosuke, as if you didn't notice them." Ryoma reached into his kimono to check his revolver, before adjusting his sword at his left hip.

"Sakamoto-san, look!" Yonosuke gestured with his chin at two more men approaching from the front.

Ryoma squinted, took hold of his revolver, but kept it concealed in his kimono. "Who are they?" he muttered.

"I'd say they were from Tosa," Yonosuke conjectured, as the two men hurried toward them.

"*Heaven's Revenge!*" the three men behind screamed the old Loyalist battle cry, charging with drawn swords.

"Stop!" Ryoma hollered, delivering a backhanded blow to the side of Toranosuke's face, knocking him down in front of the great wooden gate of Kofukuji temple. "Taro! Sonojo! Resheathe your swords!" Ryoma roared, as Toranosuke sat up in the dirt, retrieved his sword and the others watched in exasperation. "The name's Sakamoto," Ryoma said walking directly up to his would-be jailers. "Don't any of you even think about drawing your swords," he demanded in no uncertain terms. Then without looking back, he called his own men, who now joined him. "What are you doing here?" he asked.

"We anticipated that Goto would send his lackeys after you," Taro explained.

"Hold your tongue!" one of Goto's agents flared.

"I don't think it was Goto who sent them," Ryoma said.

"Nobody sent us. We've come of our own accord, because we thought there would be trouble."

Ryoma laughed derisively. "If you want to kill each other, then do it. But I have an appointment to keep with Goto." Ryoma started to walk away.

"Halt!" one of the upper-samurai hollered. "Where do you think you're going?"

Ryoma turned around, as if the very motion were bothersome. Taro, Sonojo and Toranosuke were glaring furiously at the upper-samurai, who reciprocated with the same condescendence which the lower-samurai in Tosa had resented for centuries. "Like I just told you," Ryoma said calmly. "I'm going to see Goto. Now why don't you tell me your names so I can tell him why I had to keep him waiting."

"Ah," one of Goto's lackeys stammered, "that won't be necessary. You can go."

"How kind of you," Ryoma snickered. "But remember one thing." He shifted his eyes to his own men. "And this goes for the three of you, too. Killing each other isn't going to do a bit of good, least of all for Japan. But I'd better hurry," he said, before continuing on his way with Yonosuke down the road lined with temples, toward the nearby Cottage of the Pure Wind.

"Ryoma, I thought you'd never get here," a relieved Mizobuchi greeted the two men at the front door.

"Where's Goto?" Ryoma's voice carried, and Mizobuchi winced. "Keep your voice down!" the Tosa official reprimanded, drawing laughter from Ryoma.

"What's so funny?" Mizobuchi was indignant.

"It's just that whenever you get upset, Mizobuchi, your face looks like a gourd."

"When addressing Goto-san," Mizobuchi said, ignoring the remark, and stressing the honorific, "remember that he's a minister of Tosa."

"This is no time to argue the point, but we're not in Tosa, and I'm not a Tosa samurai. If Goto's come to meet me on equal terms, then I'll meet him on equal terms. Now, where is he?"

Mizobuchi sighed, shook his head, before leading the two *ronin* to a room at the rear of the house.

Ryoma entered first. With Goto sat a young geisha. This was Omoto, whom Ryoma had seen on several occasions since first meeting her a year before at the House of the Flower Moon.

"This Goto's not the typical upper-samurai," Ryoma thought as he and Yonosuke took their places opposite the Tosa minister. Ryoma had reason to be impressed. It was nearly unheard of for a man of Goto's rank to even sit in the same room with a lower-samurai, let alone arrange for the favorite geisha of an outlaw to pour the outlaw's *sake*.

Ryoma looked hard into Goto's eyes, nodded his head in a cool greeting to the man who had ordered the execution of several of his friends, and forced several others to commit *seppuku*. "So, what is it you wanted to talk about?" Ryoma demanded brusquely, holding his *sake* cup for the girl to fill.

"How can we solve the crises facing our nation?" Goto asked.

Ryoma drained his cup, placed it on the tray in front of him, rubbed the back of his neck and sneezed loudly. "I'd like to ask you the same question," he said cautiously.

"Very well," Goto said, took a drink of *sake*, then told Ryoma about the necessity of continued trade with the West. "Otherwise," he concluded, "Japan is doomed to foreign subjugation."

"And what about Tosa's allegiance to Edo? Will Lord Yodo agree to side with Satsuma and Choshu against the Bakufu?" Ryoma asked suddenly, his eyes flashing.

"Please elaborate," Goto urged.

"A choice must be made. There's no time left for indecisiveness. Either Tosa backs the Bakufu, or it backs the rest of Japan. The Bakufu is concerned only with its own selfish interests. It opposes the idea of the clans uniting to form one centralized government. But this is the only way that Japan can develop a military and an economy strong enough to compete with the West. The Bakufu must be toppled, the political power restored to the Emperor and a council of lords formed in Kyoto to determine national policy." Ryoma paused as Omoto refilled his cup.

Goto nodded, his determined black eyes meeting those of the *ronin*, with whom he was deeply impressed. "I agree with you completely," he said.

"And the necessity of a Tosa-Satsuma-Choshu Alliance?" Ryoma prodded.

"If Satsuma and Choshu will agree, I'll convince Lord Yodo," said the most powerful man in the Tosa government, before taking up a flask himself and filling the cups of the two *ronin*.

Ryoma grinned at Mizobuchi, who was sitting silently at Goto's side. When his old friend had told him that Tosa was changing, Ryoma had not expected the changes to be quite so radical. But now he had seen for himself that the same man who had condemned Takechi Hanpeita to death just a year and a half before, was at the vanguard of those changes. And although he could not help but suspect that perhaps, even now, Goto was not being completely sincere with him, Ryoma knew that men were capable of the most profound transformations. Had he himself not taken a hundred eighty-degree turn five years ago when he met Katsu Kaishu? Was he not now drinking *sake* with a former enemy? If Ryoma himself could change so drastically to adjust to these most drastic of times, why not Goto? Why not Tosa Han itself? The Bakufu's defeat to Choshu in the previous summer, followed by the sudden death of the Emperor in December had certainly influenced Tosa's outlook on national politics. Moreover, the Satsuma-Choshu Alliance was very real. Goto could not stand idly by while Satsuma and Choshu took the initiative to form a new centralized government. This, Ryoma now realized, was the biggest reason Goto had asked to meet him. Having crushed the Tosa Loyalists, Goto was not in a position to approach the Choshu and Satsuma Loyalists directly. But he knew that Sakamoto Ryoma could do this for him. "And I'll convince Satsuma and Choshu," Ryoma assured Goto, before draining his cup.

After the meeting Ryoma and Yonosuke returned to the Kosone house, where the others were waiting anxiously.

"Well, have you decided to cut him?" Toranosuke was the first to ask the question on everyone's mind.

Ryoma sat on the floor next to a ceramic brazier. "Are you still harping on that?" he groaned, then lay down on the floor. "I'm tired, and drunk, and in no mood to discuss the matter right now. But if you must know," he said, sitting up, "Goto Shojiro is one of the greatest men I've ever met."

"What?" Sonojo protested.

"That's blasphemy!" Toranosuke shouted.

"First of all, Goto has a lot of guts. He and Mizobuchi were there alone. For all Goto knew, I could have come to revenge Hanpeita's death. I've never met or even heard of an upper-samurai like him. He's certainly the best they have in Tosa." Ryoma rubbed his hands over the brazier. "Until now he and I were bitter enemies. But throughout our whole discussion he never once mentioned the past. His only concern was what must be done in the future. So do me a favor, all of you. I don't want to hear any more talk of killing Goto."

"What did you talk about?" Kenkichi asked.

After Ryoma explained what he had discussed with Goto, Kenkichi thoughtfully suggested, "It sounds to me like Goto just wants to use you to help him break the ice with Satsuma and Choshu."

"Exactly!" Ryoma said. "But so what? We'll use him, too. Today

I've broken the ice with the most powerful minister in Tosa. And I liked what I saw. I think we can do business together. If using each other is what we must do for the good of Japan, then by all means we'd better do it."

*   *   *

Word of the meeting between Goto Shojiro and Sakamoto Ryoma caused an uproar among the upper-samurai in Kochi. Not only had Goto put Tosa in debt by purchasing more weapons than it could afford, but now he was making overtures to the former right-hand man of Yoshida Toyo's murderer. "Goto must be punished," they insisted, and when Lord Yodo heard of their plans to assassinate his chief minister, he sent him to Kyoto, where he would have the security of the guard at Tosa headquarters.

Ryoma, on the other hand, met with a more subtle kind of opposition. His sister Otome sent him a letter soon after his meeting with Goto. "*I'm disappointed in you,*" she wrote. "*You seem to have forgotten about all you've promised to do, not the least being your vow to clean up Japan. It seems that you are now more concerned with making money than anything else. Whatever you do, Ryoma, do not let yourself be deceived by the man who killed Takechi Hanpeita.*"

To his sister's advice Ryoma replied sharply, but not without jest: "*Although it might be beyond your imagination, Otome, rather than my recruiting five hundred or even seven hundred men to work for the nation, isn't it just possible that I would be able to achieve more for the nation with all of the wealth of Tosa behind me?*"

At the end of January, Godai Taisuke showed up at the Kosone mansion with good news for Ryoma: at the urging of Saigo and Komatsu, the Satsuma treasury had agreed to guarantee a loan for the Kameyama Company to purchase the sailing schooner *Absolute*, for 12,000 *ryo*, payable in installments.

"I went immediately to the office of a Prussian arms dealer I know here. I've just finished speaking with him, and he's agreed to sell us the ship on credit."

Ryoma slapped his thigh. "Where's the ship now?" he asked.

"In the harbor."

"When can we have it?"

"Right away. But there's one favor I'd like to ask of you, Sakamoto-san."

"Or course. Anything."

"Could your company deliver a load of cargo to Shimonoseki?"

"With pleasure."

"Of course, we'll pay you for the job."

"We couldn't take money from Satsuma," Ryoma said. "You people have been too kind to us."

"I appreciate your gratitude. But if I were to use your services without paying for them, Saigo would be very angry." Godai exaggerated a shudder. "And I think you understand what that means."

"Very well," Ryoma agreed. "What is it you want us to transport?"

"Rifles, Sakamoto-san. I've just purchased five thousand breechloaders for the Choshu Army."

Having delivered the rifles to Shimonoseki, Ryoma left Oryo in the safe care of Ito Kuzo, and in the second week of February returned to Nagasaki aboard the *Absolute*. Soon after, Ryoma procured still another "weapon" by which to fulfill his vow to clean up Japan.

"Take a look at this!" Ryoma shouted, throwing open the door of the old headquarters in the Kameyama Hills one particularly cold afternoon. All nine of his men were present, including Yasuoka Kanema who had recently rejoined the group after finishing two years of service in the Choshu military. Ryoma sat down on the floor next to Kenkichi. "Take a look at this," he repeated, handing a cloth-bound book to his Chief Secretary.

"*Elements of International Law*," Kenkichi read the title aloud. "I've heard of this book. But where did you find a Japanese translation?"

"In a bookstore in town," Ryoma said. "I have a feeling that it's going to be one of our most strategic weapons in conducting foreign trade, so I want all of you to read it. Kenkichi, I ask that you be sure that each man here understands the contents."

"Certainly," Kenkichi said, paging through the book. Having only recently been translated into Japanese from the original English, the very existence of this book on international law was as foreign to most Japanese as its contents.

"Human rights, maritime and trade laws, the rules of war, as agreed upon by Great Britain, France, the Netherlands and the United States, are just some of the points covered in this book," Ryoma informed. "The Bakufu's own scholars translated it," he snickered. "But what's ironic is that we're going to use it as a weapon to topple the Tokugawa."

While Ryoma was anxious to share his newest weapon with his men, he was not quite as eager to tell them of a second meeting he had had with Goto earlier that afternoon. He had just purchased the law book and was on his way to headquarters when he happened upon the Tosa minister. Goto invited him "to have a drink or two," as he phrased it, and soon the two men were sitting in a private room at a *sake* house in town.

"So, I hear you finally have a ship of your own," Goto said with affected nonchalance.

"What of it?" Ryoma was to the point.

"Well," Goto smiled, filled Ryoma's *sake* cup, "I also hear that you're in debt for it."

"What's it to you?" Ryoma drained his cup, held it out for Goto to refill.

"Ryoma," Goto slammed the flask on the tray in front of him, "have you ever considered rejoining Tosa?"

Ryoma swallowed a mouthful of *sake*, then burst out laughing. "You can't be serious," he bellowed.

"I've never been more serious in my life."

"Why would I want to do something so stupid?"

"To pay off the loan on your ship, to begin with."

"Goto, you've always been in the service of Tosa Han. You have no idea how good it feels to be a *ronin*."

"But you must constantly be worried about arrest, and you don't know what's to come one day to the next."

"It's the freedom," Ryoma said. "A *ronin* has more freedom than a samurai could ever have. I wouldn't go back to Tosa if..."

"Not even if we were to offer you and all your men good incomes and positions within the government?"

"Goto!" Ryoma slammed his cup angrily on the tray, "I figured you for a *Man of High Purpose*, but I guess I was wrong. If any of my men could hear you, your life wouldn't be worth a fart. All of us have been risking our lives everyday for years. Not for ourselves, not for Tosa, but for the nation. And you have the gall to ask me this."

"You've misunderstood me, Ryoma. Consider Saigo, or Katsura, or myself, or anyone else who has the support of an entire *han* behind him. The advantage is obvious. If you could have the advantage of

Tosa behind you, think of what you could do. Not only for yourself, but for the nation."

"I see," Ryoma said, staring hard into Goto's eyes. This was similar to what he himself had recently written to Otome.

"Ryoma," Goto continued, "Tosa could use you and your men. All of you. Your navigational expertise is invaluable, and..."

"Goto," Ryoma interrupted, "although I realize that I've misjudged you, I'm not interested in rejoining Tosa."

"Why not?"

"Because I just can't see myself ever fitting into an organization which is so unjust, where good men are discriminated against and stupid men are in control simply because of birthright."

"What you're saying," Goto raised his voice, "is that you don't think that any of the upper-samurai of Tosa, or even the *daimyo* himself, are necessarily superior to the lower-samurai?"

"Listen Goto," Ryoma took firm hold of the minister's wrist. "What I mean is that no man is any better or any worse than any other man, simply because of his lineage. That includes the *daimyo*, the upper-samurai, the lower-samurai, the peasants and the merchants. Particularly not the peasants, whose sweat the samurai have been living off for centuries."

"What you're saying, then, is that the peasants are equal to the *daimyo*."

"No! What I'm saying is that they are more valuable than the *daimyo*. Without the peasants there would be no *daimyo*, no *han* and no Japan."

"With that reasoning, I suppose you'd say that the peasants are more important to Japan than the Emperor himself?"

"Maybe. But all I'm saying is that no man is better than any other simply because of birthright. That's what American democracy is all about. In America there are no samurai, no *daimyo*, no Shogun, no Emperor. The people elect their leaders, who must in turn abide by the will of the people. Don't you see, Goto? We must establish a democracy in Japan."

"I might be crazy for asking," Goto said with a vague smile, "but I'd like to hear how you would propose creating this democracy."

"By toppling the Bakufu. Then, by abolishing the feudal system, which means getting rid of all of the *han* and all of the *daimyo*. Then, we would be ready to set up a democratic system of national government, whereby all people would be equal."

"Ryoma!" Goto said, "for your own safety, I suggest you keep these thoughts to yourself. If they were to reach the wrong ears, your life would be in serious danger."

Goto was right, and Ryoma knew it. Certainly he couldn't say these things to his closest allies in Choshu and Satsuma; not even his own men in the Kameyama Company would understand. In fact, there were only five men to whom Ryoma was willing to divulge these ideas: Kaishu's Group of Four and the Tosa minister sitting across from him.

Ryoma was not about to accept Goto's offer to rejoin Tosa, but later that night, after thinking alone for several hours, he proposed a quite different idea to his men. "Kaientai," he uttered for the first time the word which in plain English meant "Naval Auxiliary Force." "As Tosa's naval auxiliary force," he explained, "our company could help Tosa at sea, without actually belonging to the *han*. Tosa would pay us a base fee for being at its beck and call in case of war, but we would remain a free agent, enabling us to engage in business activities of our own."

"I don't like it," Toranosuke objected immediately. In fact, everyone objected, including Kenkichi, Yonosuke and Sakutaro, the three most open-minded of Ryoma's men.

"It's our basic policy to be independent," Sonojo said.

"It's always been that way," Taro insisted.

"I don't understand," Kenkichi said. "We finally have our own ship and money coming in, and now you're talking about selling out to Tosa."

"Kenkichi," Ryoma shouted, "I thought you were more realistic than that. I might have expected to hear as much from the others, but not from you. Now tell me, any one of you: How can we be most beneficial to Japan," he proposed the same question that he had to Otome in his recent letter, and that Goto had asked him earlier in the day, "by ourselves, or with the support of Tosa?"

"How do you suggest we proceed?" Kenkichi asked.

"By drawing up a charter with Tosa, whereby we'll be working for it, but will still be an independent company."

"What's a charter?" Sonojo asked.

"Like it says in the book on international law: a charter is a written agreement between two parties, binding each one to fulfill that agreement. It's common practice in Europe and America."

"What happens if one of the parties doesn't fulfill his side of the agreement?" Toranosuke asked.

"That's against the law," Ryoma replied.

"Against the law?" Sakutaro asked.

"There are a set of international laws governing all Western society. If someone breaks any of those laws, then he's punished accordingly."

"How would we be able to punish Tosa?" Taro asked.

"Tosa is bound to abide by the law," Ryoma said.

"How's that?" Kanema asked.

"Because if word ever got out to the foreign traders in Nagasaki that Tosa didn't honor its written agreements, it would have a hard time finding anyone to sell it arms."

"Ingenious," blurted Yonosuke. "As leader of a naval auxiliary force, you'd be on equal terms with the Lord of Tosa himself."

"I suppose so," Ryoma snickered. "Anyway, just leave things to me," he said, and nobody dared challenge his authority.

Ryoma and Kenkichi spent the following week drafting a plan for a naval auxiliary force. Then, in the second week of March, Ryoma paid a visit to the office of the Tosa Company.

"You have a lot of nerve showing your face around here, Sakamoto," sneered one of the upper-samurai when he saw Ryoma at the front door.

"I've come to see Goto," Ryoma said brusquely.

"Insolence!" roared the Tosa official.

"No, not insolence," Ryoma mocked. "I said, 'Goto.' Now, where is he?"

"How dare you refer to a minister of Tosa Han with such disrespect? I could arrest you for..."

Before the man could finish speaking, Goto appeared from the rear of the building. "Ryoma," he called, beaming, "let's you and I go somewhere and have a drink."

"Thanks just the same, but I have another appointment," Ryoma lied. "I've just come to make you an offer."

"An offer?" Much to the vexation of his angry underling, Goto was clearly amused.

"Yes." Ryoma produced the draft of the plan for the Kaientai, and handed it to Goto. "I'll give you time to think it over," he said. "You know where you can find me."

On the following day Nakaoka Shintaro appeared at the Kosone mansion. A maid showed him to a second-story room, where Ryoma was fast asleep. Nakaoka removed his faded black jacket and hung it on a wooden rack, then, sitting down on the *tatami* floor, lay his long sword beside him, and called his friend's name.

"Shinta!" Ryoma exclaimed with a start.

"I have bad news from Shimonoseki," Nakaoka said grimly.

"What is it?" Ryoma braced himself.

"Takasugi Shinsaku is dying of consumption. I tried to see him, but he was too ill to receive visitors."

"It's the war that did it to him," Ryoma said, shaking his head. "Even when he was coughing up blood last summer, he still led his troops in battle. Takasugi is one of the bravest men I've ever had the good fortune of knowing." As the maid served *sake*, Ryoma said, "Now tell me about yourself, Shinta."

As Nakaoka explained, he had gone to Kyoto at the end of September to investigate the political situation there. "I was particularly anxious to investigate the situation in the Imperial Court," he said, his dark eyes burning with a strength of conviction reinforced by his powerful, square jaw. "I also wanted to see what Aizu was up to, and how the representatives of the various *han* viewed Choshu's victory."

At Satsuma headquarters, old friends from Kochi who were now stationed in Kyoto informed Nakaoka of the changes occurring back in Tosa, the same changes that had convinced Ryoma to talk to Goto. "Then in October," Nakaoka said, "Tosa Minister Fukuoka Toji arrived in Kyoto to investigate the political situation there for Lord Yodo."

"Fukuoka Toji," Ryoma sneered. "I know him."

"Along with Goto," Nakaoka drained his *sake* cup, "he's one of Lord Yodo's leading retainers." Fukuoka had been wanting to arrest Nakaoka, among others, since Yodo's crackdown on the Tosa Loyalists. To say the least, the two men did not see eye to eye. "*Nakaoka was a man of extremely violent emotion,*" Fukuoka would recall years later. "*One time he nearly killed me. He came looking for me, with intentions to cut me if he didn't like what I said. But since I was away at the time, nothing came of it.*"

"But," Nakaoka told Ryoma with a snicker, "I knew Fukuoka wouldn't want to arrest me because, like Goto, he's convinced that Tosa needs our help to join Satsuma and Choshu at the vanguard of the revolution. In fact, this is why Fukuoka fully supported my urging

Saigo to go to Kochi to talk to Lord Yodo."

Saigo had visited Kochi in January to urge Yodo to attend a conference in Kyoto among the Lords of Satsuma, Fukui and Iwajima, and Shogun Yoshinobu. The Satsuma leader advised the Lord of Tosa of two urgent matters which must be settled in Kyoto, but conveniently avoided any mention of a conspiracy against Edo. Firstly, Saigo informed, an Imperial pardon for the Lord of Choshu and his heir must be granted.

"Without Choshu reinstated in Kyoto," Nakaoka told Ryoma, "it would be difficult to start the revolution. But with Choshu fighting alongside Satsuma, and hopefully Tosa, our Imperial Army will be invincible."

Nevertheless, Yoshinobu, aware that Choshu now had the support of many of the *han*, including Satsuma, realized that the Bakufu was no longer in a position to ban its archenemy from Kyoto. And to make things worse, he felt the constant pressure of Satsuma, and even the Imperial Court, for leniency in dealing with Choshu.

The second matter to be settled in Kyoto, Saigo informed Yodo, was the opening of the Port of Kobe. The four foreign powers, most notably England, had recently expressed to the Shogun their discontent over Japan reneging in its treaties. (Although the late Emperor had officially sanctioned the opening of Kobe in the previous year, he had only done so to appease the foreigners, and only after instructing Edo that "the barbarians must never be allowed to get so dangerously close to Kyoto.") The foreigners had warned the Shogun that if Kobe were not opened by January 1, as guaranteed by the treaties, they might be obliged to encourage the formation of a more responsible government–i.e., a government of the Imperial Court. Yoshinobu saw a prompt opening of Kobe as a chance to win back the confidence of the foreigners, and so restore the authority of his wavering regime.

"And this is one of the two reasons why the Shogun has agreed to the Conference of the Four Great Lords," Nakaoka said, taking a drink of *sake*.

Ryoma nodded, refilled Nakaoka's cup, drained his own. "The other reason is that he needs revenue for his military, right?"

"Yes," Nakaoka growled. "The Shogun believes he can get consensus from Fukui, Tosa and Uwajima to open Kobe. After that, he is apparently convinced that Satsuma will follow suit. But Saigo has assured me that while Satsuma is reconciled to the eventual opening of Kobe, Lord Hisamitsu will never agree to it while the Tokugawa is still in power."

Indeed, as Britain's Satow had recently whispered in Saigo's ear, the revenue that Edo would collect from an open Kobe would spell disaster for the anti-Bakufu clans, including Satsuma. Saigo, Okubo and Iwakura, then, masterminded the Conference of the Four Great Lords to undermine Tokugawa authority, and thus put a stop to Yoshinobu's plans. Not only would the political power thereby be shifted from the Edo Bakufu to the Kyoto Conference, but Satsuma was confident that its secret connections at court would enable Lord Hisamitsu to dominate the conference, and so stall Imperial sanction to open Kobe until the Tokugawa could be overthrown. To justify its opposition to the opening of Kobe, Satsuma simply claimed that it had been the will of the late Emperor that the port remain closed. If the Shogun were to betray the Emperor, as they expected he would, he should be punished. In short, Satsuma planned to use Iwakura's influence at court to arrange for the issuance of an Imperial decree for the Four Great Lords, assembled in Kyoto, to prepare armies against the Bakufu.

"But," Nakaoka smiled wryly, "Yoshinobu is not aware of this."

"How can he not be aware of it?" Ryoma asked.

"His mind's preoccupied with a more immediate problem. The foreigners are threatening to go to Kyoto unless Kobe is opened, but the court still adamantly refuses. If Yoshinobu agrees to open Kobe without Imperial sanction, he'll surely be forced from power, and the Bakufu will fall."

"And if he refuses?" Ryoma asked.

"Then the foreigners will no longer recognize the Bakufu as the legitimate authority of Japan, and instead deal directly with the Imperial Court."

Ryoma slapped his knee. "Which means the Bakufu loses either way!" he blurted.

"Yes. Saigo knows that Yoshinobu is depending on the Conference of the Four Great Lords to help him solve his problems..."

"Which," Ryoma interrupted, "diminishes his authority even more."

"Exactly! And even if, as suspected, the Lords of Fukui, Uwajima and Tosa will never agree of their own free will to oppose the Tokugawa, they will have no choice but to do so, or else risk being branded Imperial Enemies. And once the Four Great Lords agree to go to war against the Bakufu, most of the other *daimyo* throughout Japan will surely follow the example, for fear of being left behind in the dust," Nakaoka snickered, before briefing Ryoma on Saigo's meeting with Lord Yodo and his minister, Fukuoka Toji.

I've come as an envoy of the Lord of Satsuma," Saigo announced himself to Yodo at the latter's villa near Kochi Castle. The Satsuma man bowed deeply, then took a seat on a small wooden chair which, compared to his great bulk, appeared smaller than the identical one which Fukuoka occupied. The Lord of Tosa was perched comfortably on a handsome armchair upholstered with purple velvet, his back to an alcove. Yodo's eyes were badly bloodshot, and his complexion a pale yellow, symptoms of too much drink. With his right hand he took up a crystal decanter filled with French red wine. Thank you for the gift, Saigo-san," he said, filling the glass of the Satsuma man, who, despite his great size, was simply unable to drink.

"Surely you understand, My Lord," Fukuoka pressed, "why it is of utmost importance that you go to Kyoto. As one of the Four Great Lords who will be mediating between the court and the Bakufu, you will have the opportunity to secure your rightful place in the mainstream of national politics, and to unite Tosa with Satsuma as a means to strengthen Japan."

Yodo fixed his bloodshot eyes on Fukuoka, and replied, "Toji, I must say that I'm surprised at your change of outlook. It's obvious that you no longer support Edo. Saigo-san," he shifted his gaze to the commander in chief of Satsuma, "please tell Lord Hisamitsu that I fully respect his opinions," he lied, "and that I look forward to meeting him in Kyoto."

"I assume this means that you agree to oppose the Bakufu," Saigo pressed with controlled intensity radiating from his black-diamond eyes, which challenged Yodo's straight on.

Yodo cleared his throat, before replying with firm conviction, "Remember one thing. Unlike Satsuma and Choshu, the House of Yamanouchi is deeply indebted to the House of Tokugawa for bestowing upon our ancestors the domain of Tosa."

"Lord Yodo," boomed Saigo the Great, "what is more important, your debt to the Tokugawa or the future of Japan?"

Yodo sighed deeply. "The answer is obvious," he said. "Please tell Lord Hisamitsu that I fully understand that in times of national crises the interest of the nation must outweigh personal considerations. And though I agree to go to Kyoto, I will only do so with the firmest resolve to die there."

Saigo, taking this to mean that Yodo would agree to oppose the

Bakufu, bowed his head. "There is one more thing I must ask of you," he said. "I'm certain that it would be in your best interest to pardon the former Tosa Loyalists who have fled your great domain." The large man drained his wine glass with one long quaff, as if to appease the Drunken Lord of the Sea of Whales.

"Who?" Yodo snapped, Saigo balked, but Fukuoka answered sharply, "Sakamoto Ryoma and Nakaoka Shintaro."

"Consider them pardoned," Yodo muttered, and much to Saigo's distress, filled the wine glasses once again.

Nakaoka took another drink of *sake*. "I left Kyoto at the end of December," he told Ryoma, "sailing on a Choshu ship from Osaka to Shimonoseki. From there I crossed the strait to Kyushu, and traveled on foot to Dazaifu to report the news of the Emperor's passing to the Five Banished Nobles. It was a bitter experience," Nakaoka groaned. "And the nobles! After I broke the news they wept all through the night. But," Nakaoka looked hard into Ryoma's eyes, "the passing of the Emperor might mean the beginning of a new age for Japan."

"No, Shinta," Ryoma said, draining his *sake* cup, "it does mean the beginning of a new age."

"Yes, I believe you're right, Ryoma." Nakaoka straightened his sitting posture, then continued. "Great changes are occurring in the Imperial Court. The nobles have been pardoned, and will soon return to Kyoto." As Nakaoka explained, Edo had yielded to recent demands by several *han*, not least of all Satsuma, to pardon the five radical nobles. "Satsuma has also arranged for Lord Sanjo Sanetomi to be appointed Imperial Advisor upon his return to Kyoto." Nakaoka clapped his hands loudly. "Ryoma," he roared, "Edo has lost control of the Imperial Court."

"No doubt, it was all Saigo's doing," Ryoma said.

"I'm sure of it. Also, the twenty-one nobles who were put under house arrest for working with Lord Iwakura have been pardoned."

"But Shinta," Ryoma leaned back against the wall, "from the way the Shogun has been yielding to Satsuma's every demand lately, I suspect he has something up his sleeve."

"Like building up his navy," Nakaoka said.

"Yes. His navy. What do you know about it, Shinta?"

"Saigo tells me that the Bakufu has recently purchased a great warship from the United States, and has even hired American sailors to man it. Apparently Yoshinobu's closest aide has urged him to afford eight hundred thousand *ryo* over the next five years to the navy alone," Nakaoka informed, drawing a grim nod from Ryoma. "But I've come to ask your opinion on a different matter."

"What is it?"

"What would you think of my raising a militia for the coming war when we will drive the Bakufu forces from Kyoto?"

"A very commendable idea, Shinta." Ryoma laughed to ease the tension in the room caused by the intensity in Nakaoka's eyes.

"Ryoma, I'm dead serious."

"I know you are, Shinta. So am I."

"Crushing the Bakufu by military force is the only way to ensure that the Tokugawa will never rise again," Nakaoka insisted. "History teaches that war is the only way to power. It was through war that Bismarck made Prussia the master of Germany, and it was through war that Washington won American independence from England. Likewise, only through military might can Japan destroy the Bakufu and protect itself from foreign aggression." Such was the essence of Nakaoka's convictions, with which Ryoma did not agree. Civil war, Ryoma feared, would not only kill tens of thousands of men, but also invite foreign attack.

"We must establish a Western-style infantry," Nakaoka said, "armed with state-of-the-art weaponry."

With this Ryoma completely agreed. He believed that a strong military would be the key to convincing the Shogun to relinquish power peacefully. "Shinta," Ryoma said, "have you ever thought of getting Tosa's help to finance an army?"

"A good idea," Nakaoka pressed his cup to his lower lip, "but one easier said than realized."

"Not necessarily so, Shinta." After explaining his plan for a naval auxiliary force, Ryoma said, "With so many *ronin* just waiting to get arrested or killed in Kyoto and Osaka, you should use them to form a land auxiliary force there."

"What about Goto?" Nakaoka asked. "Has he agreed with your plan?"

"No, but he will." As usual, Ryoma was confident. "He just needs a little more time."

"Where will you set up headquarters?"

"Right here. Since Nagasaki is the center of foreign trade, including that of weapons and ships, it's the only place for us."

Nakaoka nodded. "Ryoma," he said, "whether Tosa will agree to support me or not, I will set up a militia in Kyoto, the center of *Toppling the Bakufu and Imperial Loyalism.*"

The next day Nakaoka returned to Kyoto, and shortly after a special delivery message reached Ryoma's headquarters informing that all Tosa men in the Kameyama Company and Nakaoka Shintaro had been "pardoned for the crime of fleeing Tosa Han." Ryoma crumpled up the message and tossed it across the room like so much wastepaper. "It's too bad Shinta couldn't have been here for this," he snickered. "Who do they think they are pardoning us?"

"Just accept it, Sakamoto-san," Yonosuke urged. "It will make things a lot easier."

"Yonosuke, if we accept a pardon, it means that we admit to having done something wrong. But so be it," Ryoma groaned. "Some day soon this whole thing will be over with, and there won't be any more Tosa Han to pardon us."

One rainy spring evening Ryoma received word that Minister Fukuoka and a group of Tosa officials had arrived in Nagasaki on board the steamer *Butterfly*, which Tosa had recently purchased from Satsuma. The purpose for Fukuoka's visit, Ryoma was informed, was to finalize an agreement concerning the Kaientai.

Ryoma had met Fukuoka only once, years before in Kochi, and did not like what little he remembered of the man. One day when Ryoma and a friend were walking along the Kagamigawa river in Kochi Castletown, they happened upon a group of upper-samurai headed their way. This was long before the murder of Ikeda Chujiro by an upper-samurai, which compelled so many lower-samurai to flee Tosa Han. Just as Ryoma and his friend were about to pass the group, one of them demanded, "Bow when you see us, lower-samurai." This was Fukuoka Toji, the same age as Ryoma, and related to the Fukuoka family of hereditary councilors, under whose command the Sakamoto family had been placed for military purposes. Ryoma continued walking without turning back, but his less mettlesome friend immediately dropped to his knees and apologized profusely.

"So Tosa has sent Fukuoka to deal with me," Ryoma thought, but kept his bitter memories to himself, so as not to arouse resentment among his men.

The meeting took place one afternoon at the beginning of April, in a spacious room at the mansion of Kosone Eishiro. Among the Tosa officials present were Fukuoka, Goto and another man whom Ryoma had never met. This was Iwasaki Yataro, the future founder of the Mitsubishi, whose genius for business had been sufficient reason for Yoshida Toyo to admit the lower-samurai into his academy for the elite, and who had recently, at the recommendation of Goto, been promoted to upper-samurai ranking and assigned to the important post of general manager of the Tosa Company.

With Ryoma were all nine of his men, and Eishiro. "When we meet the Tosa officials," Ryoma had warned them before the meeting, "I don't want anyone losing his temper. No matter what they might say, no matter how puffed up they might act, remember that it's our purpose to use Tosa for our own benefit, and the benefit of the Japan."

The meeting began, with Ryoma's men sitting along one side of the room, the Tosa officials on the other. "Ryoma," Goto began the discussion, "we've summoned you here to let you know that we accept your offer for the joint venture of a naval auxiliary force. Now all we have to do is to reach some terms of agreement."

Ryoma was flanked by his two secretaries, Kenkichi and Yonosuke. "These two men," he said, "know a lot more about contracts than I do. You'll have to discuss the matter with them."

"Then why are you here, Sakamoto?" Fukuoka asked belligerently.

"To oversee," Ryoma said as if to intentionally annoy. "And maybe pick my nose." This was Ryoma's strategy. He had used it many times during fencing bouts, when he would feign weakness before delivering a fatal attack. Ryoma knew that there were few men who could out-argue the razor-sharp Yonosuke, or out-think the learned Kenkichi.

And he was right. In fact, the contract for his shipping and trading company and private navy, as concluded at the meeting, was almost identical to the draft Ryoma had submitted to Goto. The Kameyama Company, a group of *ronin*, unofficially sponsored by Satsuma, now became the Kaientai, or Naval Auxiliary Force, whose official backer was Tosa Han. The Kaientai was a legal organization sponsored by Tosa, and the precursor of Mitsubishi Commercial Company, which would be established in 1873. Its members, no longer *ronin*, did not have to worry about arrest by either Bakufu or Tosa agents. Commander Sakamoto Ryoma had full control of all company affairs; and any man of ability, regardless of lineage or *han*, was welcome to join. All profits would be retained by the company, and Ryoma and his men would use their own vessel, the *Absolute*, for shipping purposes. If the need should arise, they had the option of leasing a Tosa steamer.

After the contract was sealed, Goto asked Ryoma how much he owned on the loan for the *Absolute*.

"Twelve-thousand *ryo*," Ryoma replied.

"As a token of goodwill," Goto said, "Tosa will repay the loan for you, as well as pay each of your men a monthly wage of five *ryo*."

Ryoma grinned, ran his fingers through his tangled hair. "Not bad, Goto," he said, "considering that, if a man has a mind to, he can buy a woman in Maruyama every night of the month with that kind of money."

It was Ryoma's belief that a man could only perform to his fullest capacity if he followed his own personal calling. Such was the basic philosophy upon which his Kaientai was founded. "*The way to develop the country,*" he wrote to Miyoshi Shinzo, "*is for those who want to fight to fight, those who want to study to study, and those who want to conduct trade to conduct trade, each doing what he is most suited to do.*" In times of peace, the Kaientai would be a trading and shipping company, dedicated to developing Japan through free trade; in times of war, it would be a private navy prepared to fight to bring down the Bakufu and defend Japan from foreign invasion.

Among the some fifty men who soon joined the Kaientai, only one was a supporter of the Bakufu. This was a Fukui samurai by the name of Kotani Kozo. When Sonojo, Toranosuke, Yonosuke and Taro found out about Kotani's pro-Tokugawa sentiments, they immediately reported to Ryoma in his office at the Kosone mansion.

"You have to let us kill Kotani," Sonojo insisted.

Ryoma leaned back against the wall, his arms folded at his chest. "The Kaientai is not a political organization," he said calmly. "It's a private navy, and a trading and shipping company. Everyone has the right to his own opinion."

"What are you saying?" Toranosuke exploded.

"Kotani happens to be from Fukui," Ryoma said. "And you all know that the Lord of Fukui is directly related to the Tokugawa. So, he's naturally inclined to support the Bakufu."

"Yonosuke is from Kii," hissed Taro, "one of the three elite Tokugawa branches, but he doesn't..."

"Taro," Ryoma reprimanded his nephew, "not every man is the same. Kotani is Kotani. Yonosuke is Yonosuke. I've never heard you speak badly about Katsu-sensei because he is a Tokugawa retainer."

"But," Sonojo attempted argument, but was interrupted by Ryoma, who said: "There are dozens of men in the Kaientai, and all of us, except Kotani, oppose the Bakufu. If we can't correct the way one man thinks without killing him, then maybe we're the ones who are wrong." This ended the argument. But more than just his sound logic, it was Ryoma's dedication to equality for all men, and his love of freedom, which compelled the men of the Kaientai to serve him well.

The Iroha Maru Incident

"Recently I feel just like a turtle, stumbling up the rock of life. When I finally reach the top, I see that the world is filled with nothing but empty oyster shells. Now isn't it strange that human beings have nothing but empty oyster shells in which to live!" Such was Ryoma's view on the absurdity of life in his thirty-first year, as expressed in a letter to Otome in the spring of 1867.

Although the Kaientai now owned a Western-style schooner, in order to run guns to anti-Bakufu clans for use in the coming revolution, Ryoma chartered the steamer *Iroha Maru*, which belonged to Ohzu Han and aboard which several of his men had worked during the previous year. The charter fee would cost his company 500 *ryo* per run to Osaka, payable upon return to Nagasaki.

One afternoon in mid-April Ryoma and Eishiro, now an official company member, were at headquarters discussing their first job as the Kaientai. "It's fine that we were able to get the loan on the charter fee," Eishiro said, "but I don't know how we're going to raise enough capital to buy the merchandise you plan to sell in Osaka." Eishiro was referring to 400 breech-loading rifles Ryoma had recently ordered from a foreign trader.

"With so many of the clans preparing for civil war," Ryoma said confidently, folding his arms at his chest, "everybody wants guns. So, I went to the Tosa Company to talk to Iwasaki Yataro, who's in charge there now. Iwasaki's no fool," Ryoma said as a maid served hot tea and rice crackers wrapped in sheets of dried laver. "He knows there's a lot of money to be made in arms sales in Osaka. But he neither has the manpower nor the expertise at his disposal to run guns." Ryoma put an entire cracker in his mouth, washed it down with a mouthful of tea. "And even if he did," he snickered, "Iwasaki would have to worry about how it would make Lord Yodo look in the eyes of the Tokugawa."

"I see," Eishiro said, nodding vigorously.

"I suggested to Iwasaki that we start off with four hundred rifles, and that after a few trial runs we'll be transporting four thousand at a time. I told him that if the Tosa Company wanted a share in the profits, they would have to lend us the money to purchase the merchandise."

"What did Iwasaki say?"

"He agreed," Ryoma said, slapping his the knee.

"How much did he agree to?"

"Two thousand *ryo*, that we can repay from our profits."

"Which there should be plenty of," Eishiro said, reaching for an abacus. "Let's see," he slid the small wooden knobs across the calculator with the skill of an experienced merchant, "with that two thousand *ryo*, we'll have to buy coal and oil to run the engines. How much did you figure we'd need for the trip to Osaka?"

Ryoma reached into his kimono and produced a notebook. "The whole trip," he said, opening the notebook, "should take about fifteen days. I calculate we'll need about two hundred eighty thousand pounds of coal and about nine hundred gallons of rape oil per day."

"How much will that cost?"

"One hundred *ryo*."

"Which leaves us nineteen hundred *ryo*. With that we can buy about..."

"Four hundred rifles," Ryoma cut in, "which we can sell in Osaka for eighteen *ryo* each."

Eishiro ran his fingers across the abacus. "Which means we stand to make a profit of over five thousand *ryo*," he said.

"Ryoma," a voice called, as the paper screen door opened. Kenkichi looked troubled as he sat down next to his old friend. "I've just received some bad news from Shimonoseki."

"What?" Ryoma braced himself.

"Takasugi Shinsaku is dead," Kenkichi said flatly.

"When did he die?" Ryoma asked, his voice badly shaken.

"Early in the morning of April 14."

"Just two days ago," Ryoma moaned, his eyes filled with tears.

"On the day of his death," Kenkichi said, "emaciated from consumption, Takasugi insisted upon going to one of his favorite restaurants in Shimonoseki. Apparently he wouldn't listen to reason, although he was urged to stay in bed. When a palanquin arrived to take him to the restaurant, he could barely climb in of his own strength. Then when he started coughing up blood again, he finally agreed to return to his room, where he died shortly after."

"Takasugi saved my life," Ryoma said in a low voice. "If it hadn't been for that pistol he gave me, I doubt that either Miyoshi or I would have made it out of the Teradaya alive the night we were attacked."

"I see," Eishiro said consolingly.

"We've lost so many good men over these past years," Ryoma said, as if in a trance, "that death seems to have become a way of life. If I can stay alive long enough to see to it that the Bakufu falls, their deaths will not have been in vain." He paused, slapped himself on the back of the neck. "Kenkichi, how's the translation coming?" he asked. In addition to the book on international law, Ryoma was also anxious to begin studying another foreign book he had recently come across at a bookstore in Nagasaki, and which he had given to Kenkichi to translate into Japanese. The book explained the legislative system of the United States of America. "It's only a matter of time," Ryoma had told Kenkichi, "before we're going to have to devise a similar system in Japan," and although he did not yet tell his comrade, he envisioned himself as the founder of such a system.

"I should be done with the translation soon," Kenkichi said.

"How many days will it take to get the *Iroha Maru* ready for our first run to Osaka?" Eishiro changed the subject to the more immediate matter.

"Two or three days," Ryoma said. "Let's get started."

The sun shone high in a perfectly blue sky as the *Iroha Maru* set sail from Nagasaki around noon on April 19. For the maiden voyage of the Kaientai, she carried a valuable cargo of 400 rifles and ammunition. Commander Sakamoto Ryoma stood at the bow, issuing orders and relishing the wind on his face, his hair blowing as freely as his spirit was high, while the ship's wooden hull cut a northwesterly course through the calm, emerald blue water of Nagasaki Bay. "Full speed ahead," the Dragon roared, beside himself with the joy of commanding his own ship again. The crew consisted of twenty-two men, including Nagaoka Kenkichi as chief secretary and Kosone Eishiro as purser. The officer of the watch was Sayanagi Takaji, a *ronin* from Marugame Han on Shikoku, who had been one of the three survivors in the wreck of the *Werewolf.* Shunme served as chief engineer. The boatswain, Umekichi, was a gutsy sailor who had previously hired onto a Tokugawa warship to spy for Choshu during the war against the Bakufu. Ryoma, as commander of the Kaientai, served as captain. (Ryoma's other men had sailed the *Absolute* to Osaka, where they were now arranging the sale of the rifles.)

Less than half the size of the *Union*, the *Iroha Maru* had only 43 horse power, displaced a mere 160 tons, was just 60 meters long and a meager 6 meters wide. The Kaientai flag of three horizontal stripes–red, white and red–flew atop the mast. On the wooden stern was the image of a Dutch beauty, who would protect the ship from perilous seas but not the folly of man.

On the afternoon of the second day out, the tiny steamer reached the Sea of Genkai off northern Kyushu, where she encountered rough seas, until reaching the calm waters off Shimonoseki on the crystal-clear morning of April 21. For the following two days she cruised slowly through the island-dotted Inland Sea, which, though calm, was of swift current, and as usual during the spring, extremely foggy. By nightfall of April 23, the fog was so dense that visibility was no more than a few yards in any direction.

"Better take her real slow, Shun," Ryoma told his chief engineer as he walked by the engine room later that night. "Sayanagi," he called his officer of the watch, who was standing on deck.

"Yes, Commander?"

"Keep a sharp lookout for other vessels in this fog."

"We have all our lights on, Commander. The green starboard and the red port sidelights, and the white top light above the mainmast are all lit."

"It's not us I'm worried about," Ryoma warned. "Those of us who haven't been trained directly by Katsu Kaishu, have been trained by those of us who have. But there are still plenty of incompetent men in Japan who call themselves sailors. Keep a sharp lookout, Officer of the Watch."

"Yes, Commander," Sayanagi said, as Ryoma walked slowly away, his heavy boots thumping on the wooden deck.

Ryoma returned to the captain's quarters below deck, but unable to sleep, soon joined the helmsman in the pilothouse. "I can't see a thing in this fog, Commander," the helmsman said.

"The chief engineer has orders to take her real slow," Ryoma assured. "With any luck this fog will clear up and we'll reach Osaka Bay by morning."

Ryoma was still in the pilothouse at 11:00 o'clock, as the ship continued slowly eastward through the Inland Sea. The blinding fog was relentless, and the only sounds were the constant humming of the engine and the slapping of the waves against the bow as she cut a steady course through the water.

"According to my charts," the helmsman said, "Hakonomisaki Cape should be coming up on our starboard."

"That's in Marugame," Ryoma said the name of the outside fiefdom in the north of his native Shikoku.

"On our port side," the helmsman pointed to the left, "should be the Port of Tomo, in the province of Bingo."

"In that case, there ought to be a lot of small islands in these waters," Ryoma muttered, when suddenly a giant shadow appeared dead ahead. "What is it?" Ryoma hollered.

"Not an island, that's for sure," the helmsman screamed.

"It's headed straight at us! Starboard the helm!" Ryoma roared. The white top light on the mainmast of the rapidly approaching ship, and the green sidelight on her starboard were now blatantly visible. The helmsman steered the ship hard to the left, and the following instant the boatswain sounded the steam whistle. But the oncoming steamer, five times the size of the *Iroha Maru*, cut a sharp right, as if in intentional pursuit. The *Iroha Maru's* starboard was now completely exposed, and suddenly there was a thunderous crash, as the larger ship rammed her head-on amidships, demolishing the engine room. The center mast and the smoke funnel collapsed with a stunning roar, seawater rushed into the battered hull, and the bow began to sink. Ryoma ran out on deck. "Sayanagi!" he called.

"Yes, Commander?" answered a voice in the darkness.

"How far are we from land?"

"Less than one knot, according to my charts."

"We'd better fasten some hawsers to the bow. We have to get the ship which just rammed us to tow us into port. Otherwise, we're going under."

"Yes, Commander," Sayanagi called out, as the bow was sinking fast.

"Ahoy!" Ryoma hollered at the other ship, with the boatswain, Eishiro and Sayanagi standing nearby. "Ahoy!" he hollered again, then a third time, but still no answer. "Alright, everyone board their ship," Ryoma ordered. "We can't let them get away."

"They'll never get away with this," Sayanagi screamed, grabbing a grapnel from one of the lifeboats. "Especially not in the waters off my own *han*." The Marugame *ronin* heaved the grapnel onto the port side of the other ship. "Let's go!" he hollered, climbed along the rope, with Eishiro, Umekichi and several others following.

Ryoma and Kenkichi watched from the deck of their fast sinking ship, wondering furiously why the other steamer had not answered them. "What are they doing?" Ryoma screamed, as the steamer began moving backward, away from the *Iroha Maru*. No sooner had she gotten about 100 yards away, than she resumed her forward motion, again heading directly at the *Iroha Maru*.

"They're intentionally trying to sink us," Kenkichi screamed.

"Or they don't know the first thing about operating a steamer," Ryoma hollered, as the much larger ship again rammed into their battered starboard. Soon Umekichi returned. "Commander," he said frantically, "there wasn't a soul on watch when we boarded. It's complete negligence on their part, but now they refuse to tow us."

"Alright, Umekichi," Ryoma said. "After I go aboard, you throw me the hawsers that are fastened to our bow. Kenkichi, you come with me, and make sure you write everything down exactly as you see and hear it." Without further delay Ryoma and Kenkichi boarded a lifeboat, paddled over to the huge steamer, then climbed up to the deck by one of several rope ladders hanging over the port side. Umekichi heaved two heavy hawsers to Ryoma, who immediately tied them to the stern. "Where's the captain?" he demanded of a group of sailors who glared in belligerent wonder at the strange samurai who wore in his sash only one sword, and imposing black boots.

"I'm the captain of this ship," answered one of them, a middle-aged man dressed in the uniform of a French naval officer. "The name's Takayanagi Kusunosuke, retainer of the Lord of Kii."

"A Kii ship?" Ryoma sneered, noticing only now the Tokugawa crest painted in white along both sides of the British-made steamer *Bahama*. "Why wasn't there anyone on deck when my men boarded?" Ryoma screamed furiously, suppressing the urge to draw his sword. "You rammed our ship because you didn't have anyone on watch."

"Impudence!" one of the Kii officers roared. "You're speaking to the captain of a ship belonging to Kii Han, one of the Three Tokugawa Branch Houses."

"So what?" Ryoma roared furiously. "Are you a bunch of idiots who don't know how to navigate a ship?"

"Who are you?" Takayanagi demanded.

"Saitani Umetaro," Ryoma boomed his alias, "captain of the ship you've just rammed, and commander of the Kaientai."

"Kaientai?"

"Yes. Under the protection of the Lord of Tosa." Although Ryoma cared no more for Tosa than he did Kii, with the situation being as it was, he chose to use all the resources available him. "I demand that you tow our ship into port," he hollered, "before she goes under."

"I can't do that," Takayanagi growled. "The force of your ship going under would bring us down with her."

"You're right, and it's your responsibility," Ryoma said, again suppressing the urge to draw his sword, and the next moment determining that he would fight these men of the Tokugawa with an even more effective weapon.

"Cut those hawsers," Takayanagi ordered his men," then said to Ryoma," I'll bring you and your crew to Nagasaki."

"No," Ryoma shot back, his eyes flashing in the light of the metal hand lamp which one of the Kii sailors held. "We must settle this matter at Tomo." Ryoma knew that international law required that maritime accidents be settled at the port nearest the scene of the accident.

"We can't stop at Tomo," Takayanagi said firmly. "It's impossible. This ship is bound for Nagasaki. I have my orders, and have no time to waste discussing the matter at Tomo. We can settle things shipboard, on the way to Nagasaki."

"Damn it!" Ryoma exploded violently, drawing his pistol with his left hand, his sword with his right. "If you don't stop at Tomo, I'll blow your head off right here and now. Then," Ryoma paused to check one of the Kii samurai who reached for his sword, "I'll order the rest of my men to cut as many of your crew as they can before we all cut our bellies open and die right here on this rotten deck." So sincere was Ryoma's voice, so matter-of-fact were his words, so powerful his eyes that the Kii naval captain was inclined to believe him. "Alright, we'll go to Tomo," sighed Takayanagi, and Ryoma immediately signaled with a hand lamp for the few men remaining on board the *Iroha Maru* to join him and the others on deck of the *Bahama*.

"Where's Umekichi?" Ryoma asked of his boatswain, when the last man climbed aboard.

"He wouldn't come, Commander," one of the sailors replied. "He said he wanted to blow the whistle one last time."

"That crazy idiot!" Ryoma roared. "If he isn't here real soon, I'll have to go after him."

Ryoma and the others watched anxiously the shadow of their own ship slowly sinking, but still no sign of the boatswain. Then, just as the hull was about to go under, the steam whistle released a final wail. "Umekichi!" Ryoma screamed. "I'm going after him." He raced down the rope ladder, and just as he was about to dive into the water, spotted the sailor swimming toward him. "Umekichi!" Ryoma shouted, and with one powerful tug, pulled his boatswain from the sea.

"We've lost another ship," Umekichi said despondently, as he and the others watched the *Iroha Maru*, with its cargo of rifles and ammunition, disappear.

"No, we haven't," Ryoma growled, looking up at a half moon, barely visible in the foggy night sky. "This time we're not going to lose."

"What do you mean, Sakamoto-san?" Shunme asked. "Our ship has just sunk."

"Did you get everything written down, Kenkichi?" Ryoma asked.

"It's all right here," Kenkichi said, producing a notebook from his kimono.

"Guard that with your life," Ryoma said in a low voice, "because we're going to need it to beat these sons of bitches in accordance with international shipping law."

The fog began to lift as an orange sun rose in the eastern sky, and the *Bahama* steamed slowly into the inlet of Tomo, a small fishing port in the province of Bingo. Green islets dotted the Inland Sea just off the coast, which was lined with black tile roofed houses with dark wooden latticed facades and white earthen walls.

Upon landing, Ryoma and Kenkichi went with their adversaries from Kii to the hall of a local temple, built on a promontory on the coast, to negotiate the first settlement of a maritime collision in modern Japanese history.

"Before we begin this discussion," Ryoma said in a calm, deliberate voice, Kenkichi beside him taking notes, "I demand that your ship remain in Tomo until we've settled this problem."

"Exactly what problem are you referring to?" Takayanagi evaded the issue.

"What problem?" Ryoma scoffed. "The problem of your ship running down and sinking our ship. But since there are no maritime laws in Japan, we must refer to international law to settle this problem."

The Kii naval captain gave Ryoma a puzzled look. "I'm not exactly sure what you mean. As a samurai and retainer of the Lord of Kii," Takayanagi said with religious fervor, "my sole concern is the will of my *daimyo*."

"And that's where your concern stops, with the will of the Lord of Kii?" Ryoma said bitterly.

"Precisely."

"Regardless of international law?

"International law?" Takayanagi snickered. "International law is for foreigners." The Kii man was not mistaken; in fact, Sakamoto Ryoma was the first man in the history of Japan to attempt to settle a domestic problem by international law.

"It's the responsibility of any competent sea captain to abide by those laws," Ryoma said contemptuously.

"And you call yourself a samurai?" Takayanagi said with disgust.

"I call myself a competent sea captain. Now, I'll ask you once more: Do you agree to decide this matter in accordance with international law?"

"Absolutely not!" Takayanagi was firm, complacent with his position as representative of the lord of one of the three Tokugawa domains.

"Then the only alternative is war," Ryoma roared, "between Kii and Tosa, unless you agree to pay us for the loss of our ship and all our cargo."

"What type of cargo were you carrying?"

"Rifles and ammunition."

The Kii naval captain's face dropped. "At the time of the collision we were told by one of your crew that your entire cargo consisted of rice."

Ryoma released a loud guffaw. "Rice?" he blurted. "You must be out of your mind. You don't suppose even for an instant that we would charter a ship just to bring a bunch of rice to Osaka, when it's common knowledge that it's guns and ammunition that everyone is dying to get their hands on. It's guns that are going to make us rich, and it's guns that are going to topple the Tokugawa Bakufu."

The Kii man was speechless with indignation, as Ryoma produced a folded document from his kimono. "But since I don't expect you to take my word for it, here's a copy of the bill of lading. Keep it." Ryoma thrust the document at Takayanagi.

"Since I'm under orders..."

"I don't give a damn about your orders," Ryoma shouted.

"Since I'm under orders," Takayanagi repeated, "to hasten to Nagasaki, the matter will have to be settled there, where we can hold a proper inquiry with the Tokugawa Magistrate."

"To hell with the Tokugawa Magistrate!" Ryoma roared. "If you refuse to settle the matter here at Tomo, as required by international law, then we'll have no choice but to do so at Nagasaki. But," Ryoma paused, looking hard into Takayanagi's eyes, "in a court of international law."

"Saitani-san," the Kii man raised his voice, but was interrupted by Ryoma.

"And before you set sail from Tomo, I demand that you pay us ten thousand *ryo*."

"Who are you to demand anything from a retainer of the Lord of Kii?"

"You already know," Ryoma said icily. "But just in case you've forgotten, I'm Saitani Umetaro, commander of the Kaientai, under the protection of the Lord of Tosa. Because of your incompetency, our ship, cargo and all the gold we had is at the bottom of the ocean."

"If we agree to pay the ten thousand *ryo* up front, will you be willing to forget the whole affair?" Takayanagi asked, his previous air of complacency dissipating under Ryoma's piercing eyes.

"You can't be serious!" Ryoma sneered. "We'll need ten times that amount just to cover the damages." Ryoma grabbed his sword, stood up violently. "We'll be back tomorrow morning for your answer," he said before storming out of the temple hall with Kenkichi.

Ryoma and Kenkichi returned to the temple on the following morning, only to be informed, under no uncertain terms, that the Kii ship would sail immediately for Nagasaki. "I can't waste anymore time discussing the matter with you here," Takayanagi said brusquely. "Our negotiations will have to be continued at a formal inquiry with the Tokugawa Magistrate."

"In accordance with international law," Ryoma ascertained.

"Yes," the Kii man hissed, "in accordance with your damn international law."

"Then I'll take the ten thousand *ryo* before you leave as collateral," Ryoma demanded.

Takayanagi produced a small cloth pouch full of gold coins. "Kii Han has decided to give you this as a token of its regret for having troubled you," he said haughtily.

"A token of its regret?" Ryoma roared, pounding his fist on the floor. "There are no more than twenty or thirty *ryo* here."

"We've decided that this is all we can pay," Takayanagi declared.

"All you can pay?" Ryoma hollered, beside himself with anger. "After sinking our ship?"

"Take it or leave it," Takayanagi said, throwing the pouch on the *tatami* mat in front of Ryoma.

"And you call yourself a samurai?" Ryoma's voice shook with rage.

"I see," Takayanagi said, avoiding Ryoma's eyes as he slipped the pouch back into his kimono, and left the room.

Ryoma and Kenkichi returned to their lodgings, and later that afternoon a messenger from Takayanagi appeared. "Saitani-san," the Kii samurai said, "we've decided to loan you the ten thousand *ryo* you asked for."

"Loan it? Certainly you're not serious. How can you have the audacity to say you'll loan it when it will cost ten times that amount to cover the losses you've caused us?"

"Very well," the Kii man replied.

"What's very well?" Ryoma shouted.

"It's apparent that you don't want the loan."

"Tell Takayanagi that Kii had better prepare for the fight of its life in a court of international law," Ryoma said, before dismissing the distraught messenger.

As afternoon turned into evening, Ryoma's entire crew was burning with rage. "Commander," Officer of the Watch Sayanagi Takaji pleaded, "please permit me to quit our navy."

"What do you have in mind?" Ryoma asked.

"I'm going to kill the captain of the Kii steamer, and as many of its crew as I can. But I don't want the Kaientai to be held responsible."

Ryoma put his hand on Sayanagi's shoulder. "I understand how you feel," he said, as the others listened, "but if you do that you'll never return alive."

"I'm prepared to die," Sayanagi said bitterly, "as long as I kill Takayanagi first."

"I'd rather have you alive," Ryoma said. "Besides, I have a better idea. We're going to make Kii pay more than just gold, although we'll take plenty of that, too."

"How?" Sayanagi asked, gripping the hilt of his sword.

"With this." Ryoma produced his copy of the international law book from his kimono.

"You carry that book around as if it were a pistol," Sayanagi said.

"No, not a pistol, but something more effective. We're going to need all the help we can get to take on and defeat as powerful a *han* as Kii."

"I think so," a disconcerted Sayanagi said.

Ryoma glanced around the room at the rest of the men. "I want to publish this book, and others like it, to make people aware that such laws exist, and by so doing gain public support."

"But Sakamoto-san," Sayanagi said, but was immediately silenced by Ryoma.

"We could, of course, cut our way on board the Kii ship, and probably take most of their heads, before dying ourselves. But what would that solve?"

"It would give us revenge."

"Don't forget our main objective," Ryoma said, drawing a blank stare from his officer of the watch, "which is to overthrow the Bakufu and fortify the nation. Don't you see? There are more things involved in revolution than just fighting."

"Like the law book," Shunme offered.

"Exactly! Getting public opinion on our side by spreading knowledge of the West will be as important a weapon in overthrowing the Bakufu as guns and warships." Ryoma turned to his chief secretary. "Kenkichi, I'm putting you in charge of publishing this book after we get back to Nagasaki. Once it has become commonly known that Kii is in the wrong, we'll have no problem defeating them."

The following morning Sakamoto Ryoma and his crew boarded a Satsuma steamer, and arrived at Shimonoseki on April 29.

On the morning of May 8, Ryoma sat with Oryo in a private cottage at the estate of Ito Kuzo, as he had done every morning since his return to Shimonoseki. The cottage, which Ryoma had named "Natural House," was provided especially by Ito for Oryo during Ryoma's absence.

Here Ryoma had spent the past nine days preparing for his legal war against Kii. When he wasn't studying his law book or reviewing the charts and navigational journals of both the *Bahama* and the *Iroha Maru*, he would be writing letters to inform people of the incident. "*I think we'll be seeing blood,*" he had written his men in Osaka. He sent them copies of the navigational journals of both ships, and of the minutes, recorded by Kenkichi, of his meetings with the Kii naval captain. "*After looking them over,*" he instructed, "*forward them to Saigo and Komatsu. In case there's a war, I want Satsuma to know what really happened.*" He had also written to several others, including Saigo and Goto, to inform these influentials of Kii's injustice. And just this morning he had visited Katsura Kogoro. "We'll need Choshu's support if Kii should refuse to listen to reason," Ryoma told him.

"You have it," Katsura assured.

"There's one more thing," Ryoma said.

"What is it?"

"A personal matter. I'm leaving for Nagasaki later today, and need some money." Ryoma didn't have to explain to Katsura that all of his money was sitting on the ocean floor off the coast of Tomo.

"How much do you need?" Katsura asked.

"About twenty *ryo* would do."

Katsura went into the next room, returned with three pouches of gold coins. "Here's one hundred *ryo*," he said. "Never hesitate to ask us for money, Sakamoto-san. This is the least Choshu can do for you."

Sitting at a low desk at Natural House, Ryoma took up his writing brush, and began writing to Miyoshi Shinzo in bold, flowing script. After describing the recent events at Tomo, he turned to Oryo. "How about going out to the well and getting me some cool water?" he asked, and while she was out quickly scrawled out the following message to Miyoshi: "*In case anything should happen to me in Nagasaki, please take care of my wife.*"

Oryo returned with a flask of water, and Ryoma hurriedly signed his name at the end of the letter. "Ah, that's good," he said, after taking a long drink of water from the flask. From a small rectangular case he removed his engraved personal seal, which he imprinted in vermilion ink to the left of his name. "How do you like it?" he asked, stamping the seal on a separate sheet of paper and showing it to his wife.

Oryo looked closely at the imprint, the image of a five-petaled plum blossom–"ume" in Japanese–inside of which were two Chinese characters pronounced "taro." "Umetaro," Oryo said slowly the second half of Ryoma's alias. "Saitani Umetaro. How clever!" she laughed.

"A gift from Miyoshi," Ryoma said, folding up the letter and sealing it. "There's one more thing I must do before I leave."

"But I was hoping we could spend these last hours together," Oryo protested. "Just the two of us."

"We will." Ryoma produced the three pouches of gold he had received from Katsura. "Keep this money in case of an emergency," he said.

"What kind of emergency?"

"Any kind."

"I see." Oryo gave Ryoma a disturbed look. "By the way, what did you write in the letter to Miyoshi-san?"

"Nothing much," Ryoma lied so that his wife need not fret over his resolve to die in the legal war awaiting him in Nagasaki.

That evening Ryoma and his men sailed aboard a Satsuma ship, and arrived at Nagasaki on the afternoon of May 13. "They're already here," he said to Kenkichi, pointing at the *Bahama* moored in the bay. Several imposing warships flying the British Union Jack were also anchored in port.

"It looks like the British fleet is here," Kenkichi said.

"Yes. Let's land. I want to talk to Goto right away." Goto had recently returned to Nagasaki for the special purpose of helping Ryoma in his fight against Kii.

Soon Ryoma reported to the office of the Tosa Company, where Goto was waiting for him. Ryoma removed his jacket, lay it on the floor beside his sword, and proceeded to explain the details of the Iroha Maru Incident

"What incompetence!" Goto said with disgust, after Ryoma had finished speaking. "They didn't even have one man on watch?"

"No. And then they had the gall to leave us in Tomo, saying they had urgent business in Nagasaki."

"Takayanagi has already been here," Goto informed. "He told me that he's willing to begin negotiations as soon as you arrive."

"Willing," Ryoma snickered, took his law book from the inside of his kimono, and handed it to Goto. "I'm going to defeat Kii through the justice of international law."

"Yes, you mentioned that in one of your letters," Goto said, paging through the book. "But Ryoma, there's just one problem."

"What?" Ryoma wiped the sweat from his brow on the dirty sleeve of his faded black kimono.

"Since there's no precedent in Japan of a case being settled through international law, I seriously doubt that the Kii men will understand this, let alone take it seriously."

"Then our only alternative will be war," Ryoma said, giving Goto a hard look. "If it comes to war, will Tosa back us?"

"Yes." Goto closed the book, returned it to Ryoma. "But why not let Tosa handle this matter for you?"

"I'd rather do it on my own. You see, Goto, I've been doing a lot of thinking over the past week, and I want a couple of more days to carry out my strategy."

"Which is?"

"Whether this matter turns into a war of words or a war of blood, it will be important for us to have public opinion on our side."

"And?"

"I've thought of a good way to get the people of Nagasaki to support us."

"Oh?" Goto's dark eyes lit up, and a look of intense interest appeared on his round, heavyset face.

"But," Ryoma hesitated.

"But what?"

"I'm short of money. Thanks to Kii, everything we had with us is at the bottom of the ocean."

"How much do you need?"

"The price of a few nights with some geisha at Maruyama."

"Be serious, Ryoma."

"I am serious. You see, I have this plan to use the women of Maruyama to torment Kii Han. Call it 'psychological warfare,' if you will."

"I don't get it."

"Come with me tonight, Goto, and you will."

"This I have to see," the Tosa minister bellowed. "Don't worry about the money. Tosa will take care of that."

"Good. I have some business to attend to at Kaientai headquarters right now. I'll meet you at the House of the Flower Moon in Maruyama tonight at dusk." Ryoma stood up, put on his jacket, thrust his sword through his sash and started for the door.

"Wait!" Goto called him back. "I want you to take a bodyguard. Word has it that there are some Kii samurai in Nagasaki who would like to see you dead."

"So what?" Ryoma laughed sardonically. "There are apparently a lot of people who would like to see me dead. I'm used to it." The commander of Tosa's naval auxiliary force adjusted his long sword, turned around to leave.

"Ryoma!" Goto called again. "I really think you should have some protection. You never know when..."

"Goto-san," Ryoma interrupted, using for the first time the honorific after the Tosa minister's name, "I appreciate your concern. But," he paused, drew his revolver from his kimono, thrust it through his sash in full view at his right hip, "I'll take my chances with this," he said, then took his leave.

Later that afternoon, just before sundown, a well-dressed samurai appeared at the front gate of Kaientai headquarters. "Where's Ryoma?" he demanded of an elderly manservant.

"Ah, ah," the manservant stuttered, bobbing his gray head like a chicken, "I'm terribly sorry, but..."

Before he could finish speaking, Ryoma slid open the front door. "Katsura-san!" he called in a muffled voice.

The old man was obviously relieved, if not astonished, to hear the name of the famous Choshu revolutionary. "Katsura Kogoro-san?" he gasped.

"Shut up," Katsura hissed, looked quickly around him before hurrying to the front door.

"I didn't expect you here so soon," Ryoma said, after Katsura was safely inside.

"I thought that the sooner I met Goto the better," Katsura said. Ryoma had told Katsura in Shimonoseki that he would arrange a meeting between the two, as a first step toward bringing Tosa into the Satsuma-Choshu military alliance. Choshu wanted such an alliance now more than ever. After defeating the Bakufu in the recent war, it had further fortified its military in preparation to destroy the Bakufu once and for all. When Katsura heard from Ryoma about the incident with Kii, this master of intrigue realized that this could be Choshu's chance to start an all-out war against Edo without arousing the ire of the Imperial Court, which had ordered a cease-fire after the death of the Shogun in the previous summer. "With our Satsuma allies," Katsura had assured Ryoma in Shimonoseki, "Choshu will be eager to help Tosa and the Kaientai in a war against the Tokugawa of Kii." Katsura reasoned an attack on Kii would surely draw Edo into the conflict. Ryoma, however, was less anxious for war than was Katsura. While determined as ever to overthrow the Bakufu, unlike his Satsuma and Choshu allies, and indeed even most of his own men in the Kaientai, Ryoma preferred, if possible, a bloodless revolution. He had recently been giving deep thought to the idea of convincing the Shogun to relinquish power of his own free will. Civil war, he feared, might entice the foreigner powers to invade when Japan was most vulnerable. But Ryoma was not yet ready to share his radical ideas to even as close an ally as Katsura.

"Katsura-san," Ryoma said, closing the front door, "you must be careful. If the Bakufu police were to spot you..."

"You're not one to talk about being careful of the Bakufu police," Katsura snickered.

"You're right," Ryoma laughed. "I guess you and I are in the same situation." While it was known among the Tokugawa officials in Nagasaki that Saitani Umetaro was the commander of Tosa's naval auxiliary force, Sakamoto Ryoma remained on the Bakufu's list of most wanted men, as did Katsura Kogoro of Choshu Han.

"Sakamoto-san," Katsura said, "tell me what's developed with the Iroha Maru Incident since we last met at Shimonoseki."

"I've just arrived here myself. But I have a good plan."

"What's that?"

"It's nearly sundown. Goto ought to be waiting in Maruyama right now to hear about it. Let's go."

Soon the two men arrived at the House of the Flower Moon. Ryoma had chosen this brothel as a meeting place because he could trust the proprietor, a Loyalist sympathizer, to keep his whereabouts a secret. "There's no sense inviting trouble," he told Katsura as they walked through the front gate of the brothel, where Goto was waiting in a private room.

"Ryoma," the Tosa minister greeted him informally, but immediately stood up when he saw that Ryoma was not alone. With Goto were four geisha, one of them Omoto, Ryoma's favorite in Nagasaki.

After the proper introductions and greetings were made, the leaders of Choshu and Tosa sat down with the naval commander and the four courtesans.

"So, Ryoma," Goto began, "as you can see, I've arranged for these beautiful girls to be with us tonight." The Tosa minister smiled at the four geisha. "Now, let's hear your plan."

Ryoma was aware that the news of the Iroha Maru Incident had spread through Nagasaki, and that the overwhelming majority of the townspeople sympathized with the Kaientai, which was, after all, a local company. Although Nagasaki itself belonged to the Tokugawa, unlike Edo and Osaka, there were few samurai living here. Most people of Nagasaki were merchants who resented their Tokugawa overlords. It was only natural that these people should support Ryoma and his group of *ronin* in their fight against one of the Three Tokugawa Branch Houses.

"Before I discuss my plan," Ryoma said, "first let me tell you about a brief encounter I had earlier today." As Ryoma explained, shortly after he had landed in Nagasaki, a merchant whom he had never seen before, stopped him on the street. "Saitani-san," the man said, "I hear you're going to war with Kii." The Kaientai was so well known among the people of Nagasaki, that its commander had become a celebrity.

Amused, Ryoma urged the merchant to tell him more. The merchant looked warily around him. "The Bakufu is nothing," he whispered. "It lost to Choshu last year, and this year your Kaientai ought to be able to make short work of the likes of Kii Han."

It was with this goal in mind that Ryoma had come to Nagasaki, and to the House of the Flower Moon. "What I have planned," he told Goto and Katsura, as Omoto filled his *sake* cup, "is a song."

"A song?" Goto gave Ryoma a puzzled look.

"Yes. Actually, it's more of a jingle than a song." Ryoma drained his cup. "Omoto, how many girls are available here tonight?"

"I'm not sure."

"Get as many of them as you can, and bring them here. I want them to hear this song I've made."

Soon Omoto returned with six more girls. "Everyone listen," Ryoma said, reached for a moon guitar which was leaning against the wall, then began singing as he played a familiar tune:

It won't be only money we take
for sinking our ship at sea.
We won't give up until we've taken
the entire domain of Kii."

Ryoma burst out laughing, as all ten girls clapped. "What do you think?" he asked.

"Very good," Katsura said, laughing. "How about this for a second stanza?

It won't be only money we take
for sinking our ship at sea.
We won't give up until we've taken
the heads of all the men of Kii."

"Terrific!" Ryoma bellowed, with Goto beside himself with laughter. "If the Kii men hear this, they'll be furious," the Tosa minister roared in delight.

"That's my plan," Ryoma said. "I'm going to have people singing this song at every house in Maruyama, until the whole city is making fun of Kii Han."

As usual, Ryoma's prediction proved correct. Geisha sung it, anti-Bakufu samurai reveled in it, and when the local merchants heard Ryoma's song, it soon spread throughout the city. "Saitani has Kii Han running scared," people said. "A single *ronin* is taking on one of the Tokugawa Branch Houses," they laughed. "The times are certainly changing," they declared. The times were changing, as Sakamoto Ryoma became the first man in the history of Japan to seek justice through public opinion and international law.

Shortly after their arrival in Nagasaki, the Kii men became suspicious of the Kaientai. "Saitani claims that his company belongs to Tosa," the commissioner of the Kii treasury had recently told Captain Takayanagi, "but I'm beginning to think otherwise." Their sharp conjecture notwithstanding, the Kii men still had no idea that Saitani Umetaro was in reality Sakamoto Ryoma, the man most responsible for uniting Satsuma and Choshu. "If you can't convince Saitani to leave this thing alone," the treasury commissioner said, "we're going to have to resort to other means."

"Like *seppuku?*" the captain asked hesitantly.

"Surely you jest," the commissioner snickered.

"I don't find the idea of *seppuku* a joking matter."

"You can't believe that Saitani would obey our orders to cut his belly."

"It wasn't Saitani I had in mind," Takayanagi replied, drawing sardonic laughter from his superior.

"Takayanagi, if you're committing *seppuku* would save Kii from the humiliation of being publicly challenged by a band of *ronin*–as I suspect the Kaientai to be–I'd order you to cut your belly right here and now. But unfortunately, things are not so simple."

"Of course not," Takayanagi agreed, unable to hide his relief.

"If you can't convince Saitani to listen to reason and forget about this ridiculous matter, then you're going to have to ask the Magistrate of Nagasaki to intervene on our behalf."

"I see."

"But if for any reason this should be impossible, we are going to have to resort to other means." The commissioner looked coldly into the naval captain's eyes.

"Such as?" Takayanagi asked.

"Assassinating Saitani," the commissioner whispered.

It was with such resolution that Captain Takayanagi met Ryoma on the morning of May 15 to begin the legal settlement of the Iroha Maru Incident. With the captain of the Kii steamer were eight of his crew; the Kaientai commander was accompanied by his chief secretary, Kenkichi; Sakutaro, who had just returned from Osaka; the officer of the watch, Sayanagi, and two other Tosa samurai. The Kii men formed a straight line, facing the men from Tosa, with Ryoma, holding his copy of the international law book, sitting directly opposite Takayanagi.

"When we first saw your ship heading straight at us," Ryoma began the discussion abruptly, not bothering with formalities, "we saw her white mast headlight and her green starboard sidelight, and so steered hard to the left to avoid a collision."

"It would have been impossible," the Kii captain objected slowly, deliberately, the confidence of his position apparent, "for any person on board your ship to have seen our green sidelight, as you were on our port side when we first spotted you."

"That's a lie!" Ryoma exploded. "You couldn't have spotted us before the collision, because you didn't have anyone on deck at the time."

"There wasn't a soul on deck," Ryoma's officer of the watch affirmed belligerently.

"That's not true," the Kii captain said. "We..."

"Why did you ram us twice?" Ryoma interrupted.

"Getting back to the issue of the lights," Takayanagi ignored the question. "You couldn't have seen the green light on our starboard, because you were on our port side."

"If we were on your port side, you had to have been on our port side as well," Ryoma said, "since we were traveling in opposite directions. Is that not correct?"

"That's correct," the Kii man acknowledged, drawing a sinister grin from Ryoma.

"If you were on our port side," Ryoma shouted, "how was it that you crashed into our starboard?"

"I don't understand," Takayanagi said, apparently confused, as Ryoma opened the law book and began reading in a loud, clear voice: "'According to the English Board of Trade Regulations for Preventing Collisions at Sea, each steamer must display a green light on her starboard side, and a red light on her port side. If two ships under steam meet head on or nearly head on so as to involve risk of collision, the helms of both shall be put to port, so that each may pass on the port side of the other.'" Ryoma stopped reading, slammed the book shut. "But," he said, looking hard into the eyes of his adversary, "since we were on your starboard side, that means that you had to have been on our starboard side. We therefore had no other choice but to steer to our port side to avoid a collision."

"There was no way that you could have seen our green sidelight from the direction you were coming," Takayanagi repeated stupidly. "You had to have seen the red light along our port, because you were on our port side. But nevertheless, you continued recklessly straight at us. And since you didn't have either your red or green sidelights on..."

"That's a rotten lie!" Sayanagi exploded.

"...we naturally assumed you were a small fishing boat or a sailing vessel," the Kii man continued, ignoring the outburst. "But as you moved upon us so suddenly, and at a much greater speed than we expected of a sailing vessel..."

"You're not going to tell us that you didn't know the *Iroha Maru* was a steamer," Ryoma snickered.

"We didn't know, until it was too late."

"Of course you didn't," Ryoma said with a loud guffaw, "because you didn't have anyone on watch to see us until you hit us. But," Ryoma paused, gave Takayanagi a long, hard look, "if you had seen us you would have undoubtedly realized we were a steamer."

"How's that? You had no lights on," the Kii man said haughtily.

Ryoma folded his arms at his chest. "Takayanagi, have you ever heard of a man by the name of Katsu Kaishu?" he asked.

"Of course. Katsu is..."

"The most knowledgeable navigational expert in Japan," Ryoma interrupted. "A pioneer of the Japanese Navy."

"Yes," the Kii man readily agreed.

"Well," Ryoma grinned sardonically, "since many of my crew have learned how to navigate a steamer directly from Katsu-sensei himself, it only stands to reason that we know the rules and regulations of navigation. Certainly we would never travel under steam at night without our lights on, because that's against regulations. Our lights were on, but since you didn't have anyone on deck at the time, which is, of course, a violation of regulations, you didn't see them."

The Kii naval captain was at a loss for words, as Ryoma added, "Takayanagi-san, if you will admit to two facts, I think we can end this discussion."

"What are they?"

"First, immediately after the collision our officers boarded your ship, and found nobody on deck. Second, after you collided into our starboard a first time, you backed up until you were about one hundred yards from us, then came forward again, ramming us a second time on our starboard."

Takayanagi had no choice but to admit to these two facts, and the negotiations ended.

But the Kii men were not willing to accept defeat quite so easily. On the next day, Takayanagi submitted a report to the Magistrate of Nagasaki, claiming that the *Iroha Maru* had neither of its sidelights on at the time of the collision.

"You know it's a lie, Goto-san," Ryoma calmly told the Tosa minister in the latter's quarters at the Tosa Company. "Kii has completely ignored what Takayanagi admitted to be true during our meeting yesterday."

"Damn them!" Goto cursed, pounding his fist on the floor. "If Kii wants to play dirty, how about letting me handle things? I'll talk to the commissioner of the Kii treasury. If he doesn't listen to reason, he'll have Tosa to contend with."

"Then here's what you should tell him," Ryoma said.

"What?"

"The commander of the British fleet is in port, right?"

"So I hear."

"Then I think I know how we can convince Kii to retract their false report from the magistrate's office."

Goto's eyes lit up as he immediately realized Ryoma's intentions. "By suggesting that, since there is no precedent of such an accident in Japan, we ask the British commander to advise in the case."

"Exactly," Ryoma said, clapping his hands together. "There's no way that Kii will be able to bear the thought of being humiliated by a foreign officer."

"Then you'll agree to let me handle things?" Goto confirmed.

"It's all yours," Ryoma said, then got up to leave.

"Ryoma," Goto stopped him.

"What?"

"Please be careful."

"Of what?"

"I can't help but feel that your life is in more danger now than ever before."

"I don't think so," Ryoma said, folding his arms into the sleeves of his kimono. "I don't think that Kii would try anything so stupid as to kill me when it would be obvious to the world that it was Kii who did it."

"Yes." Goto nodded soberly, but with deep admiration for this magnanimous man whom until recently he himself had wished dead.

The meeting between Goto and the commissioner of the Kii treasury took place at a local temple on the morning of May 22.

"The Iroha Maru Incident has escalated into a problem between our two *han*," Goto calmly told the commissioner, who avoided the Tosa man's harsh gaze. "The report," Goto changed his tone of voice to one of censure, as he pulled his fan from his sash, "which you submitted to the Magistrate of Nagasaki, claiming that the *Iroha Maru* did not have its lights on at the time of the collision is a blatant lie." Goto's face was now red with anger. "It is unbecoming of such a great *han* as Kii," he roared, slicing violently the air in front of him with his folded fan, "to blame someone else for its own mistake." Goto's penchant for self-confidence, even in front of a high-ranking official of a Tokugawa branch house, was reinforced by a message of monumental importance which had arrived from Nakaoka Shintaro this morning, informing that Tosa and Satsuma were on the verge of forming a military alliance in Kyoto.

The Kii man avoided Goto's hard stare. "I cannot argue with that," he said, his voice strained, his eyes tired, "except to say that from the very start of this whole affair our *han* has preferred to handle things as discreetly as possible."

"If discretion is your policy," Goto shouted, pounding his fist on the *tatami* floor, "I demand that you recall your report to the magistrate."

"Consider it done," the commissioner assured.

"I will." Goto smiled triumphantly.

"Goto-san," the commissioner pleaded, "you're a reasonable man. But the Kaientai commander, Saitani," he grimaced, "and that song of his that people have been singing all over this city."

"Yes, quite clever," Goto said, as if to intentionally irritate.

"And that's not all," the Kii man said, forcing an awkward smile. "Saitani keeps harping on international law, which we Japanese really having nothing to do with."

"Oh?" Goto now toyed with the perplexed commissioner, like a cat with a wounded mouse before making the final kill. "One thing is for certain, Commissioner. There is no precedent of two Japanese steamers colliding."

"That's just the point," the commissioner said, looking directly into the minister's eyes for the first time. "It is for that reason we have hoped to settle this matter in a reasonable and discreet manner."

"Of course." The cat's face lit up, as he prepared for the kill. "That's why I suggest that we ask the commander of the British fleet, which is in port right now, how such matters are handled in other countries. Certainly he has a lot more experience than do any of us."

The commissioner's face turned the color of chalk. "Surely you don't suggest we ask a foreigner to settle the matter."

"Of course not. I would merely like to ask his opinion."

"I see," the mouse said blankly, cringing under the cat's stare. "If Kii Han were to agree to pay a certain amount as an indemnity, would you be willing to call the whole thing off?"

"I think that could be arranged. Of course, the final decision would be up to the commander of the Kaientai," Goto lied. Actually, Ryoma had entrusted the whole affair to his discretion.

"Goto-san," the Kii man chuckled meekly, "we're both samurai, you and I. Both in the service of two of the greatest *daimyo* in Japan." The display of obsequiousness disgusted Goto, who did his best to conceal his feelings. "Certainly we don't need the help of a foreigner to settle our differences."

"Oh?" The cat had not yet tired of toying with his prey. "I think the British commander's advice would be very valuable. Not only for this particular case, but for future maritime accidents as well," Goto echoed Ryoma's thoughts. "As to the time and place of the meeting, I'll let you know after I contact the British commander."

"I see."

"And another thing," Goto looked hard into the distraught man's eyes, "if any harm should come to Saitani," he again pounded his fist on the floor, "I'll know who's guilty."

"What are you insinuating?" the Kii man feigned indignation.

"Let me put it this way. Your *han* has been extremely cold-hearted in its behavior, not only toward the Kaientai, but toward Tosa as well. If you continue, there's no telling what the consequences might be," Goto threatened, before taking his leave.

That afternoon the commissioner of the Kii treasury summoned Captain Takayanagi to his quarters. After telling him of his promise to retract the report they had submitted to the magistrate, and of Goto's insistence to bring the British commander into the affair, he said, "If the foreign commander intervenes, we won't stand a chance of winning the case. Not only will we have to pay an indemnity of whatever sum is decided upon, but our *han* will become the laughing stock of Japan."

"Then I'll put into effect our last-resort plan," Takayanagi said coldly, his left eye twitching.

"Idiot!" the commissioner exploded. "Nothing must happen to

Saitani," he now whispered. "Cancel all plans. It's better to pay the indemnity."

"And admit that we were wrong?" Takayanagi hissed, his face red with anger.

"We have no other choice."

"Then let me ask Godai of Satsuma to mediate with the Tosa men for us," Takayanagi suggested.

"Yes," the commissioner agreed, "that might save us further humiliation.

The sky was overcast on the afternoon of May 28, as it had been for several straight days, but Ryoma was glowing with a feeling of triumph which he couldn't wait to share with his wife. *"The other morning I argued plenty with the captain of the Kii ship,"* he wrote her. *"And Goto Shojiro gave the commissioner of the Kii treasury such hell, that this morning Kii, unable to stand it any longer, asked Satsuma to intervene. Now Satsuma tells us that Kii has offered to pay for the Iroha Maru, and for all our cargo, if we agree to drop the case."* The outlaw Sakamoto Ryoma had taken on the highest-ranking *han* in all of Japan, and won. One month after sinking the *Iroha Maru*, Kii promised to pay as an indemnity the enormous sum of 83,000 *ryo* to the Kaientai by the following year.

"Think about it," Ryoma said to Eishiro, as they sat at Kaientai headquarters that evening. "Eighty-three thousand *ryo*. Nearly one sixth the total annual rice income of the most powerful Tokugawa domain. "Ha!" he laughed, "after we repay Ohzu the cost of the *Iroha Maru*, and deduct the money for the four hundred rifles we lost, we'll still be left with over forty thousand *ryo*."

"Forty thousand *ryo*," Eishiro echoed in amazement. "That's five times as much as we originally expected to make on the run to Osaka."

"If we use that money wisely, and if we topple the Bakufu, we'll be able to bring our Kaientai all over the world," Ryoma boasted, to the wonder of his friend.

The Great Plan At Sea

The man who had united Satsuma and Choshu was about to meet yet another test of his ability to persuade. At the end of May the Shogun had gained Imperial sanction to open the Port of Kobe, but more significantly had been unable to find a face-saving formula to solve the problem of dealing with Choshu. Meanwhile, Saigo, Okubo and Iwakura had begun arrangements for an Imperial decree to be issued for the Satsuma and Choshu armies to attack the Tokugawa for disregarding the wishes of the late Emperor. Then on the rainy morning of June 8, a short message from Nakaoka reached Kaientai headquarters, informing the Dragon that the Conference of the Four Great Lords had finally convened in Kyoto.

Ryoma tore up the message, lay back on the *tatami* floor in his room, and released a long, loud groan. "Time's running out," he fretted. "There must be a way to convince the Shogun to abdicate before there's a bloody civil war. There must be someone with enough influence who'll be willing to urge the Shogun to abdicate as a last resort." He thought of Katsu Kaishu and Okubo Ichio, neither of whom were in a position to influence Yoshinobu. Suddenly an idea flashed through his mind. "That's it," he said aloud. "Yamanouchi Yodo."

Ryoma got up, ran his fingers through his tangled hair, grabbed his sword, thrust his pistol through his sash, and immediately left the Kosone mansion for the lodgings of Goto Shojiro.

"Ingenious!" Goto blurted, when Ryoma had finished telling him of his plan. Goto knew that his lord was torn between obligation to the Tokugawa for bestowing upon his ancestors the Tosa domain, and his desire to rectify Japan's dangerous situation. "This is just what Lord Yodo needs to avoid a war that will benefit Satsuma and Choshu at the expense of Tosa."

"Goto," Ryoma growled, "if Tosa benefits from the plan, it's simply an accident of circumstances."

"I see," the Tosa minister shrugged, understanding Ryoma's ill feelings toward his *han*. "But no matter how much Lord Yodo likes the idea," Goto said, "he still has to convince the Shogun."

"Of course," Ryoma said.

"But what if Yoshinobu should refuse to listen to reason?" Goto asked.

"Then, we'll have to do as Nakaoka and Saigo insist." Ryoma drew his pistol. "With so much firepower that not only the Bakufu, but the House of Tokugawa, will cease to exist altogether." Despite his penchant for bloodless revolution, Ryoma was prepared for war as a last resort to overthrow the Bakufu. "But Satsuma and Choshu alone might not be able to defeat the Tokugawa armies," Ryoma said.

"Oh?"

"With the French helping Yoshinobu modernize his military, Satsuma and Choshu need Tosa on their side."

"I've been summoned to Kyoto by Lord Yodo," Goto said. "I sail tomorrow morning. How about coming with me?"

"What for?"

"I need your help. If the Shogun refuses to abdicate peacefully as you suggest, then I truly believe that Lord Yodo will agree to unite Tosa with Satsuma-Choshu against Edo. Either way, I need your help to convince him."

"You need my help to convince Lord Yodo?" Ryoma laughed sardonically, slapping his knee.

"What's so funny?" Goto asked, not a little annoyed.

"If only Hanpeita could hear this!" Ryoma snickered, clapping his hands, and drawing an uneasy look from Goto. "If only Hanpeita and all of the other lower-samurai from Tosa who lost their lives because of Yamanouchi Yodo could hear this." Ryoma's voice cracked with emotion, and his face became red, not only out of anger toward Yodo and the entire feudal system, but for the futility of the deaths of so many of his friends.

"If only they could hear what?" asked the man who had ordered Hanpeita's *seppuku* two years before.

"The top minister of Tosa asking Sakamoto Ryoma to come with him to convince Yamanouchi Yodo." Ryoma paused, hugged his belly and broke out in a loud laughter. "I'd have thought the very idea utterly preposterous just a few months ago."

"You would have thought the idea preposterous!" Goto roared. "How do you think I feel about it? But," he said, lowering his voice and staring hard into Ryoma's eyes, "the way things are now, it appears that the lower-samurai Sakamoto Ryoma might have more to do with saving Tosa Han than anyone else."

"Damn it, Goto!" Ryoma flared, his eyes filled with disdain. "I don't give a damn about Tosa Han."

"I know that," Goto hollered, pounding his fist on the floor. "But I'm one of Lord Yodo's ministers, so I have to. And whether you like it or not, your plan for Lord Yodo to convince the Shogun to abdicate peacefully before Satsuma and Choshu can begin a civil war might not only save Tosa Han, but the House of Tokugawa and the rest of Japan as well."

"I don't give a damn about Tosa, or the House of Tokugawa. They can live or die, it's all the same to me. All that matters now is that we topple the Bakufu and establish a democratic government whereby all Japanese people will be free to pursue their desires, and whereby our country can stand proudly among the nations of the world."

"Then you'd better come with me, Ryoma," Goto implored, pulling his fan from his sash and slamming it so hard on the *tatami* floor that it snapped in two.

"I'll give you my answer tomorrow," Ryoma said, before taking his leave.

On the following morning before dawn, Ryoma, Kenkichi and Yonosuke boarded the Tosa steamer *Yugao* in the pouring rain.

"Ryoma!" Goto called, hurrying toward them.

"I've come," Ryoma replied, after jumping from the gangway onto the deck, his clothes and hair drenched.

"Can we sail in this rain?" Yonosuke wondered aloud, looking up at the full moon barely visible for the clouds.

"We have to," Ryoma said. "The boil is finally ready to burst. I don't think that things in Kyoto will wait much longer."

The men's determination to brave the storm notwithstanding, the rains soon subsided, and the Tosa ship steamed north from Nagasaki. Having told Goto that he was badly in need of sleep, Ryoma went below deck. But despite his exhaustion from the past month and a half of legal battle with Kii Han, he was unable to sleep. His mind raced to contrive a way to save Japan from the brink of war. "Yodo's our last hope," he thought glumly. "But even if Yodo does agree to urge Yoshinobu to abdicate, can the Shogun be convinced to forfeit every-thing his family has stood for over the past two and a half centuries? And even if by some farfetched chance Yoshinobu can be convinced, who's to say that his aides would let him go through with it?" Having thus spent the entire day in deep contemplation below deck, Ryoma was joined by Yonosuke and Kenkichi that evening.

"I have something to tell the both of you," Ryoma said, sitting with his back against the wall, his arms folded at his chest. "I want you to listen very closely. And Kenkichi, you'd better get something to write with, because I want these ideas recorded."

When Kenkichi returned soon after with writing utensils and paper, Ryoma was ready to explain his blueprint for a new centralized government, which he had by no means formulated in the course of this one day below deck on the Tosa steamer bound for Osaka. "It was about four and a half years ago," Ryoma said, "that Katsu-sensei urged the Shogun to relinquish power as the only way to save Japan from destruction." He paused, drawing an anxious look from Kenkichi. "Continue, Ryoma," his chief secretary urged, brush in hand. "Katsu-sensei had me very worried," Ryoma said. "There were plenty of stupid officials in Edo who wanted him dead after that. Of course, the time had not yet come for the Shogun to relinquish power, but it seems now that Katsu-sensei was able to read the future. Both he and Okubo knew years ago what some of us are only now beginning to realize. They knew that a time would someday come when either the Shogun would have to restore the power to the Emperor peacefully, or face a bloody revolution that would not only destroy the House of Tokugawa but most likely all of Japan." Ryoma paused, took a deep breath, then looked hard at Yonosuke and Kenkichi as if he anticipated what they were about to say.

"But Sakamoto-san," Yonosuke broke a short silence, "what you've just told us is completely different from what you've been saying all along. You've always insisted that the Bakufu must be crushed militarily and buried, to be sure that it will never rise again. That has been our reason for running guns for Choshu and Satsuma. That has been our reason for the Kaientai. In fact, that has been our whole reason for everything."

"Yes, it has, Yonosuke," Ryoma said, rubbing the back of his neck, his face strained.

"Ryoma," Kenkichi said with worried eyes, "people will say you've changed."

"Kenkichi, don't you see? It's not me who's changed. It's the times that have changed. I'm only adjusting to those changes. When I first entered the service of Katsu-sensei, Hanpeita thought I was a traitor. But I was just doing what I felt I should at the time, and, as it turned out, it was right." Ryoma paused, slammed his fist on the wooden floor. It was the only choice I could have made."

"I see," Kenkichi said.

"That's why I've asked the two of you to come on this trip. I wanted you to hear my plan before any of the others. I knew that of all the men in the Kaientai, only you, Mutsu Yonosuke, and you, Nagaoka Kenkichi, would understand right away that war is not the only, or by any means, the best way to topple the Bakufu."

"I see," Yonosuke said, not a little shaken.

"But I have confidence in the others, too. All of them will understand."

"But Ryoma," Kenkichi gave him an anxious look, "even if you can convince our own men in the Kaientai of the necessity of your plan, what about Satsuma? What about Choshu? They're our closest allies. But if your plan works, they won't be able to help but think that you've deceived them at the last minute, just as they were about to crush the Bakufu. How can you do that to men like Saigo and Katsura? And as for Nakaoka," Kenkichi shook his head slowly, "he may never forgive you."

Ryoma gave Kenkichi a pained look. "Damn it," he said. "What's more important, that Shinta forgives me, or that Japan is saved? I feel badly for Satsuma and Choshu, but they're going to have to accept one important fact: not all of us have been risking our lives day in and day out all of these years just for the sake of Satsuma and Choshu. It's the future of Japan that matters, and nothing else," Ryoma exploded, then paused. "But we must act quickly," he added, now calmly, "so that Goto can bring my plan to Lord Yodo before it's too late."

"Lord Yodo?" Kenkichi gave Ryoma a puzzled look.

"Yes. Can you believe it? The Lord of Tosa is our last hope. We have to convince him to urge the Shogun to abdicate."

"Yodo?" Yonosuke hissed. "He'll never agree to..."

"I've already discussed it with Goto," Ryoma interrupted. "He's assured me that Yodo will agree."

Both men looked dumbfounded at Ryoma. "But even if Lord Yodo should agree," Kenkichi said, "what makes you so certain that the Shogun will?"

"That's a chance we have to take. And it's our last chance."

"And if it fails?" Yonosuke prodded.

"Then our Kaientai will be the first to join the Satsuma-Choshu forces to crush the Tokugawa."

"I see," Yonosuke said, bowing his head slightly.

"And it will offer Tosa a perfect excuse to unite its forces with Satsuma and Choshu," Ryoma added. "So, either way, the Bakufu has had it. But listen closely. There are eight different points to my plan for a new system of government after the Shogun relinquishes power."

Yonosuke and Kenkichi stared silently at Ryoma. Neither could believe what they were hearing, although both were quick to absorb the gist of Ryoma's awesome words.

"Kenkichi, remember to get everything down on paper, so Goto will have something with him when he talks to Lord Yodo in Kyoto."

"I'm ready," Kenkichi said.

"No, wait a minute." Ryoma paused. "I think we'd better get Goto down here to hear this."

"But Sakamoto-san," Yonosuke advised, "don't you think it would be more appropriate for us to go to Goto's cabin?"

"Why not?" Ryoma said, stood up and stretched his arms above his head. "Let's go."

Soon the three men joined Goto in his cabin. "Ryoma," he said, "I've been wanting to talk to you."

"That's why I'm here," Ryoma laughed, then told the Tosa minister of his plan for a centralized government.

"Let's hear it," Goto urged.

"*Point One,*" Ryoma began, as Kenkichi started writing. "*The political power of the entire nation should be returned to the Imperial Court, and all decrees should be issued from the court.*" Although the three men had anticipated the first point, they listened in awe.

"*Point two. Two legislative houses of government, one upper one lower, should be established, and all government measures should be decided by its councilors on the basis of public opinion.*" Here, the lower-samurai of Tosa, with absolutely no legislative authority of his own, was setting the basis for democracy in Japan.

"Who do you propose serve as councilors?" Goto asked.

"That's taken care of in *Point Three. Men of ability among the feudal lords, court nobles, and the Japanese people at large should serve as councilors,*" Ryoma said, drawing a look of approval from Goto. Although by no means did Ryoma include this point to appease Yamanouchi Yodo, its acceptance would assure the Lord of Tosa a seat in the Upper House not only for himself, but for the Tokugawa Shogun as well. "*And,*" Ryoma continued, "*traditional offices of the past which have lost their purpose should be abolished.*

"*Point Four,*" Ryoma's voice was as steady as his eyes were clear. "*Foreign affairs should be conducted according to regulations which have been decided by public opinion.*

"*Point Five. Old laws and regulations should be replaced by more adequate ones.*

"Point Six. The navy should be expanded.

"Point Seven. An Imperial Guard should be organized to defend the capital.

"Point Eight. The value of goods and silver should be brought into line with that of foreign countries."

Ryoma stopped speaking, took a deep breath. "Considering the way things are in Japan right now," he said, "once these eight points are accepted as the basis for a new government, they must be made known to the rest of the world. If they are carried out, Japan will become a stronger nation, able to stand on an equal footing with other nations." Ryoma wiped his sweaty forehead with his sleeve. "So, Goto, what do you think?" he asked nonchalantly of his Great Plan At Sea, which would become the basis for the future government of Japan.

"What do I think?" the Tosa minister roared, clapping his hands together. "It's fantastic, Ryoma! Absolutely fantastic! For the past ten years I've heard a countless number of men speak of overthrowing the Tokugawa Bakufu and restoring the political power to the Emperor. But nobody has ever talked of a new form of government to replace the old one. That was Lord Yodo's biggest reason for repressing the Tosa Loyalist Party. I've even heard people talk about a Shimazu Bakufu and a Mori Bakufu," Goto winced at the thought of either of the Lords of Satsuma or Choshu replacing the Tokugawa Shogun. "That's the very reason that Lord Yodo has been so wary of Satsuma and Choshu all these years. But I've never heard anyone speak of a government run by men of ability regardless of *han*, and bound by public opinion. Sakamoto Ryoma, your plan will be the key to our nation's future."

"Let's just hope that Lord Yodo feels the same way."

"He will, Ryoma. He definitely will. Don't you see? Your plan is going to save Tosa from the biggest dilemma in our history. With your plan Lord Yodo can remain loyal to the cause of saving Japan without betraying the Tokugawa, avoid a civil war and safeguard against the formation of a Satsuma-Choshu Bakufu." Goto paused, slapped himself on the thigh. "But Ryoma," he said, "how did you come up with such ingenious ideas?"

Ryoma, at age thirty-one, could have retraced his life since he had first read about American democracy in Kawada Shoryo's book *An Account of an American Castaway* years before. He could have told Goto that he had heard the ideas he had just presented from Katsu Kaishu's Group of Four. But instead of going into all of that, Ryoma simply snickered, gave a sideways glance to Yonosuke and Kenkichi, and said with a wide grin, "Goto, let's just say I've been around."

On the following morning, just before dawn, the *Yugao* entered the Port of Shimonoseki, where Ryoma had asked Goto to stop long enough for him to make one important visit.

Actually there were two people Ryoma wanted very much to see in Shimonoseki. So, when he found that Katsura, whom he had intended to advise of his Great Plan At Sea, was away, Ryoma rushed through the town at dawn to the mansion of Ito Kuzo.

Oryo was ecstatic when Ryoma slid open the bedroom door at Natural House. "How are you?" he asked, kneeling down to take his wife's hand.

"Wonderful, now that you're here."

"I only have a few minutes."

Oryo's face dropped. "Why must you leave so soon?"

"I have to get to Kyoto."

"Why?"

"For the nation. Here, take this." Ryoma gave his wife a small pouch of gold coins. "It's not much, but it will have to do for now. Remember, if anything happens to me, you're to contact Miyoshi." Ryoma left Oryo as suddenly as he had come to her, and though neither had intended to worry the other by an outward display of emotion, it was not without a trace of tears in both of their eyes that they parted.

Ryoma returned directly to the ship, which immediately set sail, reaching the Port of Kobe on the rainy morning of June 12. From here Ryoma, Goto and the others traveled overland to Osaka. By dusk they had reached the outskirts of the mercantile capital, where they could see the great Tokugawa citadel of Osaka Castle, its white walls and towers clearly visible in the fading sunlight. "I wonder what's to become of the castle," Goto said, as if to himself, gazing up at the magnificent emerald green roof. "Not even this great fortress could withstand the fire of today's cannon."

"It won't have to," Ryoma said, "if Lord Yodo can convince the Shogun to abdicate peacefully."

Soon they reached Tosa headquarters at Osaka, where they planned to stay the night, and go directly to Kyoto in the morning. "Your Excellency," the official caretaker of the estate greeted the minister with a deep bow, "there's been a sudden change of plans. Lord Yodo has already left for Kochi."

"What?" Goto opened his eyes wide. "But he's just summoned me to Kyoto."

"It's his tooth ailment," the caretaker explained, trying to appease the minister.

"What about the conference of the four lords?" Goto asked irritably, suspecting that it had been a fiasco.

As the caretaker explained, Yodo, the last of the four lords to arrive at Kyoto and the first to leave, simply did not trust Satsuma. Although he was still unaware that Saigo and Okubo were in league with Iwakura, Yodo, upon his arrival, sensed Hisamitsu's intention to obtain an Imperial decree for the four lords to send armies to attack the Bakufu. Indeed, this was exactly what Iwakura and the two Satsuma leaders were planning, but only after they had arranged for the court to pardon Choshu. The Satsuma and Choshu armies would then join forces to drive the Tokugawa from Kyoto and establish a new government around the Imperial Court. "Lord Shungaku," Yodo had warned the Fukui *daimyo* after the first of several meetings, "something tells me that Satsuma and Choshu are scheming to set up a new Bakufu in Kyoto." At the conclusion of another meeting at Nijo Castle, it was decided that the four lords would pay their respects to a group of the Shogun's ministers assembled in the inner-castle. But when Hisamitsu, not wanting to show any sign of deference to the Bakufu, refused and abruptly stood up to leave, the Drunken Lord of the Sea of Whales became furious. "You'll come with us," Yodo exploded, throwing the Lord of Satsuma to the floor. A few days later, when it was clear to Yodo that an Imperial decree to overthrow the Tokugawa would soon be issued, he claimed sudden illness and returned to Kochi.

"Perfect timing!" Ryoma said as the caretaker finished speaking. "If Lord Yodo had stayed around any longer, I have little doubt that Saigo and Okubo would have arranged for an Imperial decree to be issued, and that we'd have a war on our hands."

"Even without Lord Yodo in Kyoto," Goto said worriedly, "Satsuma just might succeed in getting an Imperial decree."

"That's why I'm here," Ryoma said. "You get back to Kochi immediately and convince Yodo to go along with my plan, and I'll work on Satsuma in Kyoto."

"How do you intend to stall them?" Goto asked.

"Goto," Ryoma grinned, "when I put my mind to it, I can convince

Saigo of just about anything."

"I see," Goto snickered, not a little amused at Ryoma's blatant self-confidence.

"But I'll need one word of reassurance from you, Goto."

"Which is."

"I want you to promise me that if Satsuma agrees to postpone its war plans long enough for Yodo to petition the Shogun to resign, then Tosa will be willing to enter into a military alliance with Satsuma. And also that when you return to Kyoto-Osaka to deliver Yodo's memorial petitioning the Shogun, you'll have with you a company of Tosa troops which will be willing and ready to fight on the side of Satsuma and Choshu."

"You have my word," Goto assured, and soon after departed for Kochi.

A light drizzle was falling when Ryoma, Kenkichi and Yonosuke arrived at Kyoto by riverboat early next afternoon. From the boat-landing they walked southward along Takasegawa. "Ryoma," Kenkichi stopped short, "Satsuma headquarters is in the opposite direction."

"I know. But we're not going there just yet," Ryoma said. The three men continued down the narrow street lined with houses on one side, the canal on the other.

"But I thought we were going to talk to Saigo," Yonosuke said.

"First we have to stop at Tosa headquarters."

"But I thought you hated going to Tosa headquarters," Kenkichi said.

"I do. But I sent Shinta a message from Osaka. If he's gotten it, he should be waiting for us there now. It'll be much easier to convince Saigo once we've convinced Shinta."

"But, Sakamoto-san," Yonosuke said, "certainly there are still some upper-samurai, perhaps at Tosa's Kyoto headquarters, who would like nothing more than to cut you down."

"Yonosuke," Ryoma said wryly, "the stage is set in Kyoto for the play to begin. All we have to do is a little manipulating backstage, then lift the curtain. After all we've been through, I'm not about to miss out on the performance for anything, least of not for the likes of some upper-samurai with a grudge on their shoulders."

Ryoma's self-confidence notwithstanding, his power to persuade was to be put yet to another grueling test. For as Nakaoka would soon inform him, the commander in chief of the Satsuma military was ready to move.

"Where's Nakaoka?" Ryoma demanded of the caretaker of the estate, an upper-samurai whom Goto had instructed to make himself "useful to Ryoma."

"In here, Ryoma," Nakaoka called from an adjacent room.

"Willingly restore the power to the Emperor?" Nakaoka bellowed when Ryoma had finished relaying his plan. "Are you crazy? You don't actually believe the Shogun will abdicate peacefully."

"It's our last resort, before war," Kenkichi answered for Ryoma, drawing a look of dismay from Nakaoka.

"We have to give him this last chance, Shinta," Ryoma said.,

"The Sakamoto Ryoma I always knew was determined to bring down the Bakufu," Nakaoka roared.

"He still is," Yonosuke said indignantly.

"What do you think, Shinta?" Ryoma said. "Can't you see that my plan brings our chances of bringing down the Tokugawa one step further?"

Nakaoka groaned, apparently at his wit's end. "We've come this close to finally going to war with the Tokugawa, and you come up with this crazy scheme."

"Goto is on his way to Kochi right now to talk to Yodo," Ryoma informed. "He's assured me that Yodo will agree to go along with the plan because it's his only way out of a bad situation."

"Hmm..." Nakaoka muttered with a thoughtful nod.

"If Yoshinobu still refuses to abdicate peacefully, then Yodo will no longer feel obligated to support the Tokugawa."

"I see," Nakaoka continued nodding. "But Satsuma has already entered into an alliance with Tosa to oppose the Bakufu."

"Shinta," Ryoma snickered, "you know as well as I do that that alliance means nothing without the approval of Lord Yodo."

"That's right, but Inui's on our side now," Nakaoka informed, referring to Inui Taisuke, who, along with Goto, was one of the few men the headstrong Lord of Tosa was apt to listen to. "And Inui's promised Saigo that Tosa will fight no matter what."

"Shinta," Ryoma snickered again, "things just aren't that easy. You can't really believe that Inui or anyone else would be able to lead Tosa troops against the Tokugawa without the consent of Lord Yodo."

"Maybe not," Nakaoka conceded, "but Inui has returned with Yodo to convince him."

"So has Yodo's top minister. And Goto has assured me that when he returns to Kyoto with Yodo's memorial to the Shogun, he will have with him a company of Tosa troops which will be willing and ready to fight on the side of Satsuma and Choshu in case the Shogun should refuse to resign peacefully."

Nakaoka grabbed Ryoma by the forearm. "Inui has promised me," he said feverishly, "that even if Yodo should refuse to fight against the Bakufu, he will personally lead a Tosa army into battle against the Tokugawa within one month."

"One month?" Ryoma snickered. "In a month the war would be over, and very possibly with a Tokugawa victory."

"A Tokugawa victory?" Nakaoka gasped, as if he had never before contemplated the possibility.

"Be realistic, Shinta. How many troops do Satsuma and Choshu have in Kyoto right now?"

Nakaoka looked blankly at Ryoma, as both men knew the answer. Satsuma had less than 1,000 troops stationed in Kyoto, while Choshu, still officially an "Imperial Enemy," had none. "Yonosuke," Ryoma said, "remind Shinta how many troops the enemy has in Kyoto."

"Aizu has one thousand troops here," Yonosuke began in a calculated monotone. "Add to that the five hundred troops of Kuwana Han stationed in Kyoto, and Satsuma's already outnumbered. That's not even mentioning ten thousand of the Shogun's own troops that are stationed in Osaka. Then, when you include the Shinsengumi and other Tokugawa police units, the Bakufu has over twelve thousand troops ready to fight in the Kyoto-Osaka area alone."

Ryoma smiled sardonically. "How are one thousand Satsuma samurai going to defeat that many Tokugawa troops?"

"Saigo has an additional one thousand men in Kagoshima ready to sail here anytime," Nakaoka said. "They're just a few days away. As are thousands of Choshu troops. Once war breaks out it won't matter that Choshu's an 'Imperial Enemy,' as long as we're victorious."

"And to assure victory," Ryoma said, "we need to get Tosa on the Satsuma-Choshu side before the war starts."

"By getting the Shogun to abdicate peacefully?" Nakaoka asked, dismayed. "It just doesn't make sense, Ryoma."

"Like I just said. If the Shogun disagrees, then Yodo will have every reason to unite Tosa with Satsuma-Choshu. Only after that will we be ready to crush the Tokugawa militarily. But if Yoshinobu agrees to restore the power to the Emperor peacefully, then there will be no need for war."

"Ryoma," Nakaoka groaned, "that's just it. The Shogun will never agree to abdicate peacefully. Just as the Tokugawa came to power on horseback, it must be defeated on horseback."

"Are you willing to risk the future of Japan on that assumption?"

"What do you mean?"

"Do you think the foreigners will just sit back and watch while we kill each other?" Ryoma hollered, taking firm hold of Nakaoka's wrist. "Remember what Britain did to China. The chances are that the foreigners will use the internal chaos of a civil war to strike when Japan is most vulnerable."

"Hmm..." Nakaoka muttered. "You have a good point. But can you convince Saigo to wait?"

"That's why I've come to see you first, Shinta." Ryoma looked hard into his friend's eyes. "I'm counting on you to help me persuade him to hold off long enough to give Yodo a chance to petition the Shogun to abdicate peacefully."

"Alright, Ryoma. You win."

"Then, let's go," Ryoma said, jumping to his feet.

"Sakamoto-san," boomed Saigo Kichinosuke when Ryoma and the others arrived at the Satsuma estate in Kyoto's district of the Two Pines. "You've arrived just in time. We're getting ready to proceed with our plans." With Saigo were the two other members of the Satsuma Triumvirate–Komatsu Tatewaki and Okubo Ichizo.

Ryoma removed his sword, placed it on the floor beside him, sat down opposite Saigo. "Plans?" Ryoma said, feigning ignorance, though well aware that Saigo's "plans" meant nothing short of war. "I have something urgent to discuss with you."

"And I with you," Saigo replied with a wide smile. "But, Sakamoto-san," the huge man's expression suddenly changed to one of troubled concern, "you must be very careful. Word has it that the Shinsengumi and other Tokugawa police units suspect you're in Kyoto."

Ryoma glanced at Yonosuke and Kenkichi, grinned widely at Saigo. "Danger is a professional hazard," he said. "Now that we've come this far, I can't let fear of death get in my way." Despite the great number of his friends and comrades who had died over the past years in the struggle against the Bakufu, Ryoma believed that he was somehow invulnerable, until, at least, he could topple the Tokugawa and "clean up Japan once and for all." Ryoma looked hard into the eyes of Okubo, then shifted his gaze to Komatsu and Saigo. "I have a plan that will assure us the best possible chance of victory."

"What is it, Sakamoto-san?" Saigo asked with the innocence of a curious child.

"Not fighting a war at all," Ryoma declared, then nodded to Kenkichi, who produced a folded document and began reading aloud, drawing looks of dismay from the three Satsuma men. "Based on this plan," Ryoma said after Kenkichi had finished reading his Great Plan At Sea, "the Shogun will abdicate power peacefully."

"We Satsuma men know for a fact that Sakamoto Ryoma is no turn-coat," Saigo said, radiating sincerity, his black-diamond eyes open wide. "But for the life of me, I can't understand your sudden change of heart."

"Nor can I," said Okubo indignantly, methodically rubbing his square jaw. "You've always spoken of the necessity of strengthening our military to overthrow the Tokugawa. And now that we're ready, you come to us with this."

"Sakamoto-san has not changed," Yonosuke exploded in anger. "If you can't understand that his only concern is getting rid of the Bakufu for the welfare of Japan..."

"Enough, Yonosuke!" Ryoma silenced his right-hand man. "But Yonosuke is right," he said. "I haven't changed. I still think we must have a strong military, because without one we would never be able to intimidate the Shogun into relinquishing power. Can't you see that a peaceful transition of government is a thousand times preferable to war?"

Saigo nodded grimly, then looked at Nakaoka sitting silently by. "But Sakamoto-san," he said, "you don't honestly believe that the Shogun would restore sovereignty to the Emperor without a war, do you?"

"Saigo-san," Nakaoka began speaking, but was interrupted by Ryoma. "Shinta, let me ask Saigo-san this one question first: Are you absolutely sure that Satsuma and Choshu alone can defeat the Tokugawa? You know that the French are helping Edo modernize its military, and whether we like it or not, that Shogun Tokugawa Yoshinobu is a very able leader. And even though Choshu was able to defeat the Tokugawa in a defensive war, it's common knowledge that an offensive war presents a much different situation." Ryoma glanced at Kenkichi, then at Yonosuke, who quickly repeated the breakdown of pro-Tokugawa forces in the Osaka-Kyoto area. When Yonosuke had finished, Ryoma looked straight into the eyes of Satsuma's commander in chief. "Don't you think we'd be much better off with Tosa fighting on our side?" he asked, shifting his gaze to the grim eyes of Nakaoka Shintaro.

"He's right," Nakaoka said, then repeated what Ryoma had just told him of the dangers of civil war.

"Goto is on his way to Kochi right now to convince Yodo to go along with my plan," Ryoma said.

"A plan for peaceful restoration of power by the Shogun?" Okubo snapped bitterly. "Preposterous!"

"Sakamoto-san," Saigo said in a sincere baritone, "the only way to obliterate the Tokugawa is with gunfire and blood. As it stands now the territories of the Tokugawa by far exceed those of any other domain in Japan. Unless we defeat the Tokugawa militarily, and confiscate its land, things will never change."

"If fight we must, then at least give us the chance to get Tosa on our side first," Ryoma pleaded. "Goto has agreed to the proposal of a Satsuma-Tosa alliance. In fact, he's written a letter to Tosa headquarters in Kyoto sanctioning a meeting between Tosa and Satsuma representatives on the earliest date possible. That's how confident he is that he can persuade Yodo to petition the Shogun to abdicate." Ryoma paused, wiped his sweaty forehead with his sleeve, then told the Satsuma men of Goto's promise to return to Kyoto not only with a memorial from Yodo to the Shogun, but with at least one company of Tosa troops in case war should be necessary.

"Tosa and Satsuma must unite before war breaks out to ensure victory," Nakaoka implored.

"Yes," Okubo nodded approval. "But what makes you so sure Lord Yodo will approve a union?"

"If he agrees to go along with my plan," Ryoma explained heatedly, "he'll agree to a union with Satsuma, because if the Shogun doesn't accept the peaceful alternative, then Yodo will no longer feel obligated to support him."

"I see," Okubo nodded.

"But," Ryoma said, looking hard at Okubo, "if Yoshinobu does agree, Satsuma must promise Tosa that its troops will not attack him."

"Why should we make such a promise?" Okubo asked bitterly.

"For the sake of Japan," Ryoma shouted.

"For the sake of Japan?" the reticent hereditary councilor to the

Lord of Satsuma, Komatsu Tatewaki, spoke for the first time. "I don't follow your logic, Sakamoto-san. Don't you think that it's in Japan's best interest that the Bakufu be destroyed?"

"Of course I do," Ryoma assured sharply. "But if you were to attack even though Yoshinobu had agreed to restore sovereignty to the Emperor, I fear that most of the other clans in Japan, including Tosa, would be moved by the injustice of the act, and so come to the aid of the Tokugawa."

"Sakamoto-san," Saigo spoke in a slow, deliberate voice, "I remember well the first time you proposed a union between Satsuma and Choshu. We all thought that it was too preposterous an idea to even consider." Saigo looked over his broad shoulder at Okubo and Komatsu, who nodded acknowledgment. "Since you feel this strongly about your plan, you have our solemn word that Satsuma will give Lord Yodo time to petition the Shogun to abdicate."

"Thank you," Ryoma said.

"But what about Choshu?" Okubo asked. "Can you convince Choshu to postpone its attack? Choshu is even more eager than we are for the war to began."

"Choshu wants an alliance with Tosa as much as Satsuma does," Ryoma explained. "Between Nakaoka and me, we can convince Katsura to wait."

"But Sakamoto-san," Saigo said, "if Lord Yodo should refuse to cooperate, or if Yoshinobu should refuse to abdicate–and I think he will refuse–then let it be understood here and now that the armies of Satsuma and Choshu, with Imperial edict in hand, will attack and crush the Tokugawa, with or without the aid of Tosa."

"But not without the aid of my Kaientai," Ryoma assured grimly.

Goto's ship reached the Port of Urado in Tosa just one day after leaving Osaka. From Urado, he hurried on horseback to Kochi Castletown, arriving at Lord Yodo's residence shortly after dark.

As usual, the Drunken Lord of the Sea of Whales was drinking *sake*. He sat alone in his study on this humid night, wearing only a thin cotton robe. Although the doors were wide open, there was no breeze whatsoever from the lantern-lit garden outside, as two chambermaids kept mosquitoes away by waving large straw fans on either side of the *daimyo*. "Damn Satsuma," Yodo thought to himself, as he watched fireflies dance above the surface of a small pond at the center of the garden. "Damn that cunning fox Hisamitsu. He would have the House of Yamanouchi betray the House of Tokugawa." Yodo emptied the flask, slammed it on a small tray. "More *sake*," he told the maid, as an attendant appeared at the foot of the open verandah. "My Lord," he said, bowing his head to the ground, "His Excellency Goto Shojiro has just returned."

"Shojiro?" Yodo's eyes lit up at the mention of his favorite retainer.

"He requests an audience with you."

"Bring him in."

Soon Goto joined Yodo, and immediately revealed to him the plan for the Shogun to restore sovereignty to the Emperor, without ever mentioning the name of Sakamoto Ryoma. Whether this was out of deference to his lords' refusal to acknowledge ability among the lower-samurai, or merely Goto's own desire for glory, will never be known. But regardless, Yodo was ecstatic over the plan he would not know was the brainchild of the lower-samurai Sakamoto Ryoma until after the fall of the Tokugawa Bakufu. "Ingenious!" Yodo roared, slapping his knee.

"Then you agree?" Goto confirmed.

"Of course."

"Then there's no time to waste," Goto said. "We must compose a memorial immediately, and deliver it to the Shogun before Satsuma and Choshu have the chance to attack."

"Yes, Shojiro," Yodo bellowed. "I think you've found a way for me once and for all to outsmart that fox Shimazu Hisamitsu."

When word of Yodo's acceptance reached Kyoto a week later, Ryoma and Nakaoka arranged a meeting between Satsuma and Tosa representatives there, and on June 22 an official union between the two clans was completed. The two men most responsible for uniting Satsuma and Choshu had performed their magic again, and Ryoma was confident that it was only a matter of time before Choshu would follow Satsuma's example. A Satsuma-Choshu-Tosa alliance had long been the dream not only of Sakamoto Ryoma, but of Takechi Hanpeita, Kusaka Genzui and other leading Tosa and Choshu Loyalists of former days.

Ryoma and Nakaoka, however, had two additional problems to attend to. One concerned Choshu, where people were growing tired of waiting for the war to begin. Ito Shunsuke and two other Choshu samurai had recently arrived undercover at Satsuma's Kyoto head-quarters to find out when their troops, mobilized behind Choshu's borders, could be set into motion against the Bakufu. The other problem had to do with persuading Iwakura Tomomi, the leader of the anti-Tokugawa faction at court, of the wisdom of Ryoma's plan.

When word reached Ryoma and Nakaoka of the Choshu envoys' arrival to Kyoto, they went immediately to Satsuma headquarters to persuade them to hold off their attack. Their determination to crush the Tokugawa notwithstanding, the Choshu men, like their Satsuma counterparts, were confident that the Shogun could never be convinced to relinquish power without a war, which they agreed would be more easily won with Tosa fighting on their side. As for Lord Iwakura, Nakaoka arranged to introduce Ryoma to the exiled court noble at an early date.

The Kaientai had recently begun to prosper. Many of the clans had sent representatives to Nagasaki to purchase foreign weapons to prepare their armies for civil war, but they neither had the business acumen nor connections to succeed. This put Ryoma's company, experienced as it was in dealing with foreign arms merchants in Nagasaki, in a perfect position to profit by helping to arm those clans who were not sympathetic to the Bakufu.

Ryoma's private navy now had at its disposal a small flotilla of armed ships to transport goods between Nagasaki and Osaka. Two of these vessels, the *Absolute* and the *Yokobue*–the latter was a schooner recently provided by Tosa–the Kaientai owned outright; others it chartered, using Tosa as its guarantor. While Ryoma was anxious to join his men in their business endeavors, he was obligated to remain in Kyoto to, as he had told Yonosuke earlier, "do a little manipulating backstage, then lift the curtain." The stage was now set for the Great Play in Kyoto to start, the direction of which Ryoma had controlled since uniting Satsuma and Choshu. The "manipulating backstage" would be the deathblow to the Tokugawa Bakufu, peacefully or militarily, which the Dragon felt was his destiny to deliver.

In Kyoto, Ryoma set up a secret hideout in an upstairs room at the shop of a lumber merchant who frequently dealt with Tosa. Oddly enough the lumber shop was called the "Vinegar Store," and was located on a narrow back street in the Kawaramachi district, just west of the Sanjo Bridge which traversed the Takasegawa. From here Ryoma directed the Kaientai, writing letters to Taro, Kanema and the others stationed in Osaka; and to Sonojo, Eishiro and Toranosuke in Nagasaki. Recently, Umanosuke and Shunme had joined Ryoma in

Kyoto to give him a detailed report of the goings-on of the company, and to relay any messages he might have to his men in Osaka and Nagasaki.

One afternoon in late June while Ryoma and Yonosuke sat in their hideout above the Vinegar Store discussing business strategy, the latter suddenly released a long, drawn out groan.

"What's the matter?" Ryoma asked. "You sound sick."

"No, Sakamoto-san." The Kii *ronin* wore a sour expression. "But I just can't help suspecting that Goto took all the credit for your plan when he presented it to Lord Yodo."

"Yonosuke," Ryoma snickered, "do you think I give a damn what the Tosa *daimyo* thinks?"

"No, but..."

"And don't blame Goto. He only did what he had to do to get Yodo to agree. The stage is set. My only concern now is getting this play underway so we can get down to the business of establishing a democracy in Japan."

"Of course, Sakamoto-san," said Ryoma's right-hand man, who would become one of Japan's greatest foreign ministers.

That night Nakaoka showed up at the Vinegar Store. I'm Ishikawa Seinosuke from Tosa," he gave his alias to a young maid who answered the front door. "I've come to see Saitani Umetaro."

"Saitani-san is not in now," the girl said cautiously.

"Then I'll wait," Nakaoka insisted, and started to enter.

"No," the girl blocked the way, "Saitani-san has instructed me not to accept any visitors while he's away."

"Listen," Nakaoka whispered impatiently. "My real name's Nakaoka Shintaro, and Ryoma's an old friend of mine. If..."

"Shinta!" Ryoma called from the top of the staircase. "It's alright," he told the maid. "Let him in."

The two sat in Ryoma's room upstairs. Soon the maid served *sake*, and left them alone. Nakaoka held up his cup for Ryoma to pour. "Iwakura says he'll meet you in the morning." Nakaoka drained his cup, wiped the sweat from his brow.

"Shinta,' Ryoma said, "when did you first realize that Iwakura wasn't pro-Tokugawa?" Nakaoka had been among the many Loyalists in Kyoto who once intended to assassinate Iwakura for having arranged the marriage of the younger sister of the late Emperor Komei to the late Shogun Iemochi.

"When I finally decided to go and meet him." Nakaoka had first met Iwakura at his home in exile in a desolate village in the outskirts of Kyoto.

"What made you decide to meet him?"

"Because I heard that it was Lord Iwakura who had organized the twenty-two nobles to petition the Emperor last year to reform the Imperial Court against the Tokugawa."

"I see," Ryoma nodded, as Nakaoka refilled both cups.

"When I was at Dazaifu last March, I asked Lord Sanjo to write me a letter of introduction to Lord Iwakura. At first Lord Sanjo opposed my plan. He said that Lord Iwakura was a traitor, and that he was not to be trusted. But I finally convinced him to write the letter for me, and about two months ago, in April, I visited Lord Iwakura." Nakaoka placed his cup down. "I had never known that there was a man of such intellect among the court nobles," he said. Iwakura had impressed Nakaoka with papers he had written during his years in exile, and which he had secretly distributed among the Imperial Court. In his writings, Iwakura explained the reasons that the Tokugawa must be eliminated if Japan was to defend itself from the Western onslaught. "The man's a master of intrigue," Nakaoka told Ryoma. "And despite his personal suffering while in exile, he's been a pillar of strength to the anti-Tokugawa movement. Without him we'd never have the support of the Imperial Court behind us."

"If we're going to see Iwakura in the morning," Ryoma said, "we must leave tonight."

Iwakura Tomomi had been under house arrest for the past five years in a farmer's cottage in the desolate village of Iwakura, located in the northern outskirts of Kyoto. His only companion had been his faithful servant Yozo, the son of a local peasant, but secret visitors included Nakaoka, Okubo of Satsuma and other anti-Tokugawa samurai and court nobles. After Iwakura's failed attempt to reorganize the Imperial Court in the previous December, the Bakufu, suspicious that Satsuma was now in league with Iwakura, had set up a surveillance post near his house, and manned it with Aizu samurai.

Behind Iwakura's thatched cottage was an empty field where he grew vegetables, on which, along with rice and the occasional fish that Yozo caught in a nearby stream, the exiled noble subsisted. Beyond were hills, barely visible in the darkness, as Ryoma and Nakaoka approached the small cottage. The two had left Ryoma's hideout in Kyoto just after midnight, and reached Iwakura Village before dawn. They traveled on foot, without lanterns, through the dark, hilly terrain, so as not to draw the attention of the Aizu samurai who were in constant watch.

"This way," Nakaoka whispered, as the two climbed over a low earthen fence which surrounded the house. Though there was not a cloud in the sky, the wooden storm doors were firmly shut so that the Aizu guards could not see inside. "He's expecting us before dawn, so the back door should be unlocked," Nakaoka said, as the two crept to the rear of the cottage. Nakaoka opened the door, and called in a muffled voice, "Lord Iwakura, I've brought Ryoma."

"Shintaro," a voice whispered. "Shut the door quickly." An instant later a figure appeared carrying a single candle. The dim light revealed a man who looked older than his forty-two years. Iwakura was slight of stature, with thin whiskers on his chin, a round face and closely cropped hair. He had a sad mouth, but severe eyes which betrayed a keen intelligence. "Did they spot you?" he asked nervously.

"I don't think so," Nakaoka said. "I've brought Ryoma," Nakaoka repeated.

"I see," Iwakura's eyes lit up. "Sakamoto Ryoma?" the master of intrigue confirmed. He had heard a lot about the *ronin* from Tosa who had been most responsible for allying Satsuma and Choshu, and more recently had formed a private navy. "Yozo, bring hot tea," Iwakura called his servant, then, with a slight gesture, "Please, right this way," he said. The two samurai followed the court noble down a narrow wooden corridor, and into a small room of six *tatami* mats, where they sat in the formal position opposite Iwakura, who lit a paper lantern. Piles of books were scattered about the room, and a low writing desk against one of the walls was covered with papers.

"Make yourselves comfortable," Iwakura said. "We needn't worry about protocol in a place like this. Besides, I have a lot to discuss with you."

"Good," Ryoma said, crossing his legs, and, with a loud yawn, stretched his arms above his head. Ryoma's indifference to the high rank of this elite court noble drew a look of slight dismay from the more rigid Nakaoka, whom Ryoma conveniently ignored, if just for this moment.

"Sakamoto," Iwakura said, as Yozo served tea, "tell me about your navy."

Ryoma told Iwakura about the Kaientai, and about his life over the past fiver years, since fleeing Tosa. Iwakura was impressed, just as Ryoma was impressed with this court noble.

"I've heard about your plan for restoring the power to the Emperor," Iwakura said. "Now I'd like to hear it directly from you."

Ryoma related in full detail his plan for the Shogun's peaceful restoration of power to the Imperial Court. He finished speaking, drew a hard look from Iwakura, who sighed. "Sakamoto, as you may well know I was once a staunch supporter of the Bakufu. But don't get me wrong. It's not as if I had any feelings of affection for the Tokugawa, but I thought that without the Bakufu in power Japan would be unable to defend itself against the foreigners. But, of course, I was wrong." Iwakura took a sip of hot tea. "In fact, the Bakufu's very existence diminishes our national strength to such an extent that unless we eliminate it our nation will surely crumble." This was the reason that, after the death of the pro-Tokugawa Emperor Komei, this master of intrigue had arranged for his longtime ally Nakayama Tadayasu to be appointed Guardian of the Emperor until the Son of Heaven would come of age. Iwakura's scheme was facilitated by the fact that Nakayama, a staunch opponent of the Bakufu, was the maternal grandfather of the boy-Emperor. With Nakayama as Imperial Guardian, Iwakura knew that it would only be a matter of time before he could arrange for an Imperial decree to be issued for Satsuma and Choshu to crush the Bakufu.

It was for this very reason that Ryoma had come to Iwakura Village on this hot morning at the end of June in his thirty-first year. "I couldn't agree with you more, Lord Iwakura," Ryoma said, looking hard into the older man's sharp eyes. "But for the reasons I've just explained, Saigo has promised to postpone his war plans. Now we have Tosa on the side of Satsuma and Choshu, so that if the Shogun doesn't agree with Lord Yodo's proposal, Tosa troops will join the Imperial armies of Satsuma and Choshu to crush the Tokugawa."

"Very well, Sakamoto," Iwakura said, giving his blessings to Ryoma's great plan.

Wine, Women and the Specter of War

The thought of his own mortality did little to bother the Dragon, as the threat of war loomed above the Japanese nation. "Even if I die a painful death in war," he bantered in a letter to a friend, "as long as Saigo and Okubo burn incense and offer flowers at my grave, it is a given fact that I will enter nirvana."

Ryoma and Nakaoka spent the following weeks fostering support for peaceful restoration among the men at the Kyoto headquarters of Tosa, Satsuma and other clans. In mid-July Ryoma received word that a man by the name of Sasaki Sanshiro, Tosa's commissioner of justice, wanted to meet him. Ryoma's original reaction was one of resentment. "Commissioner of justice," he said sneeringly to Nakaoka. "I didn't know justice existed in Tosa." Ryoma's resentment for the upper-samurai of Tosa exceeded that of Nakaoka, who, unlike Ryoma, had never given up hope that he might someday return to his home. Nakaoka had only fled Tosa after Yodo's crackdown on the Tosa Loyalists. As a village headman's son, his sense of obligation to his native land was naturally stronger than Ryoma's; and over the years he had even sent numerous letters to the upper-samurai in Kochi, urging them to support Satsuma and Choshu. Ryoma, on the other hand, had no desire to return to Tosa. His dreams encompassed more distant realms. "Once this drama has ended," he had recently told Yonosuke, "we'll bring our Kaientai all over the world."

"I've heard that Sasaki is crafty," Nakaoka said, "but he's apparently sincere in his dedication to *Imperial Loyalism*. I think we ought to give him a chance."

"A chance for what?" Ryoma sneered. "What could Lord Yodo's commissioner of justice possibly want to talk to me about? Other than Goto and Inui, I don't know of one of Yodo's elite who's worth his weight in spit."

"Apparently Sasaki wants to talk to you about your plan for peaceful restoration. He's been sent here by Lord Yodo himself to gain support for the plan among Tosa samurai in Kyoto." While the Lord of Tosa had agreed with the plan, many of his retainers did not. Tosa's upper-samurai were now divided into two camps: one radical, the other staunchly conservative, but both of them opposed the idea of peaceful restoration. The radicals, led by Inui Taisuke, shared the view of Satsuma, Choshu and the Iwakura faction at court: that the

Tokugawa must be crushed militarily to ensure that it would never rise again. Tosa's conservatives–remnants of the old guard originally ousted by Yoshida Toyo but ironically restored to nominal power by Hanpeita's Loyalists–were suspicious of the plan to restore the power to the Emperor, lest such a drastic move disturb the status quo by which they had benefited for generations. They viewed it as a ploy by Satsuma and Choshu to force Tosa into opposing the Bakufu, to the exclusive benefit of those two clans.

As Ryoma was willing to talk to anyone, anywhere, anytime to promote his Great Plan At Sea, he agreed to meet Tosa's commissioner of justice.

The meeting took place in a private room at a small restaurant in the foothills in the eastern part of the city. As commissioner of justice, Sasaki was in charge of the administration of Tosa law, ranking him just below Yodo's ministers. He was among the new breed of upper-samurai who, like Goto and Fukuoka, opposed Edo, but unlike the more radical Inui supported Ryoma's plan for peaceful restoration. Five years older than Ryoma, Sasaki was tall and lean, with a narrow face and penetrating eyes. In his youth he had studied under one of Kochi's leading scholars of Japanese classical poetry, and while gifted with the pen, his talents clearly lay in the realm of politics. This Yodo realized, and sent Sasaki to Kyoto with the vital task of convincing both radicals and conservatives here to support Ryoma's plan for peaceful restoration, which the Tosa *daimyo* still believed was the brainchild of Goto.

"Welcome," Sasaki said warmly as Ryoma and Nakaoka entered the room. He gestured for the two men to join him at his table, set with several flasks and cups. "I've heard so much about the two of you that I feel as if we were already friends."

"Get to the point, Sasaki," Ryoma said with a scowl. "I hear you want to discuss my plan to restore the power to the Emperor."

"Precisely," Sasaki replied, the false smile having disappeared. "Goto has told me in confidence that you're the architect of the plan, and I'd like to tell you that I endorse it from the bottom of my heart."

Ryoma and Nakaoka sat down, and the mood in the room immediately brightened. "In which case," Ryoma said, "I'm glad we came to see you. But there is something I must tell you. Tosa has changed its policy so many times in the past that neither Satsuma nor Choshu trust it. I therefore strongly advise that Tosa not change again." As Ryoma spoke, the roar of thunder echoed against the hills in the east, and a heavy rain began to fall.

"I fully understand," Sasaki said. "But let me say this: Lord Yodo, Goto and many others who once supported Edo, now completely endorse your plan for a peaceful end to Tokugawa rule. For this reason you can be certain that the Great Play in Kyoto will be acted out to the end."

Ryoma burst out laughing. "Sasaki," he blurted, as another roar of thunder seemed to shatter the sky, "I like your analogy of the Great Play. But I'd like it even more if we could get on with the performance," he quipped, drawing laughter even from the rigid Nakaoka.

The three men spent the entire evening speaking of the Great Play which was before them, its leading actors and the subjects of war and peace. They discussed Saigo, Komatsu and Okubo of Satsuma; Goto and Inui of Tosa; Iwakura of Kyoto; Katsura and Ito of Choshu. Ryoma talked about Katsu Kaishu's Group of Four. He fascinated Sasaki with his plans to exploit the natural resources of the northern territories, and, after the fall of the Tokugawa, to bring his Kaientai around the world. By the time the rain had subsided, it was close to midnight, and Ryoma realized that Sasaki was indeed different from the traditional close-minded upper-samurai of Tosa, although not nearly as sophisticated as Goto.

"Shinta," Ryoma said as the two walked back to the Vinegar Store that night, "if we can educate Sasaki a little, I think he could really be an important asset to us in the coming months."

At the end of July, news of the murder of two British sailors in Nagasaki would prove Ryoma's prediction correct, although not in a way he had anticipated. When circumstantial evidence aroused suspicion that the murderer was a man of the Kaientai, not only was Ryoma's scheme to "educate" the commissioner of justice put on hold, but his great plan for peaceful restoration was suddenly endangered.

On the night of July 6, two crew members of the British warship *Icarus* were found murdered in the Maruyama pleasure quarter. The two sailors, whom the British Legation claimed had been "lying in a drunken sleep on the roadway" when they were attacked, had apparently sparked the outrage of a still unidentified samurai, who, in turn, made short work of both foreigners with two strokes of his sword. A subsequent investigation by the enraged British minister, Sir Harry Parkes, concluded that on the morning after the crime the Kaientai schooner *Yokobue* had suspiciously left the Port of Nagasaki, followed soon after by the Tosa gunboat *Nankai*. While the *Nankai* had steamed directly to Tosa, the *Yokobue* sailed back to Nagasaki around noon of the same day. Rumor had it that a man wearing two swords and the navy whites of the Kaientai had been spotted near the scene of the crime at around the same time the two sailors were believed to have been killed. Concluding that this was indeed a member of Ryoma's private navy, Parkes demanded that the Nagasaki Magistrate take action against the Kaientai. He claimed that the murderer had left Nagasaki on the *Yokobue*, transferred at open sea to the *Nankai*, and escaped thereafter to Tosa; to which the magistrate replied there was insufficient evidence to justify further investigation. Indignant at what he considered incompetence by the magistrate, Parkes appealed directly to the Shogun's prime minister at Osaka Castle, demanding that the investigation be brought to Tosa Han. The prime minister promised to send a mission of Tokugawa officials to Kochi, and suggested to Tosa's Osaka headquarters that their highest-ranking officials in Kyoto-Osaka accompany them.

"But I absolutely refused to accompany them," Sasaki told Ryoma at the Vinegar Store on the night of July 28, after he finished relaying the details of the Icarus Affair.

"My men are innocent," was Ryoma's immediate reaction.

"How can you be sure?" Sasaki asked. "You're in Kyoto, and they're in Nagasaki."

"How can I be sure?" Ryoma hollered indignantly. "Simple. International cooperation is a basic policy of the Kaientai. All of my men are familiar with *Elements of International Law*. It's our company's handbook. Anyway, none of them would ever kill a man in cold blood."

The answer surprised the commissioner of justice, who was nonetheless impressed. "We have to convince Parkes of that," he said.

"Before this thing turns into a war between Tosa and England," Ryoma added ominously. "Because I have no doubt that war is what the Bakufu wants. Edo will use this thing for its own selfish gains, just like it did when the British attacked Satsuma over the murder of the Englishman at Namamugi."

"Yes," Sasaki bitterly confirmed.

"Of all the bad timing," Ryoma groaned.

"That it is," Sasaki said. "But anyway, I have to get to headquarters in Osaka right away to make arrangements for my immediate return to

Tosa. If you need me, you can find me there."

"Sasaki," Ryoma said, "no matter what happens, we have to make sure that this thing doesn't interfere with our plan for peaceful restoration."

Ryoma's anxiety was not unfounded. The British minister himself was due to leave soon for Tosa with the Tokugawa mission to press that *han* to find and punish the murderer of the two sailors in Nagasaki, according to international law.

"According to international law," Ryoma told himself as he headed south by riverboat that evening. "The only way to handle this whole mess is according to international law." Ryoma was on his way to Osaka to discuss the matter with Yonosuke and Kenkichi; but first he wanted to make a brief stop along the way at Fushimi.

"Sakamoto-san!" Otose greeted him at the front door of the Teradaya. "What a surprise!" The two had not met since Ryoma had been attacked at this riverside inn over one and a half years before, although they had been in contact by mail.

"I can't stay long," Ryoma said, sitting down on the polished wooden floor near the entranceway.

"What's the trouble?" Otose asked, taking worried notice of Ryoma's uncharacteristically grim expression.

"There's been trouble in Nagasaki," Ryoma said, then after telling Otose about the Icarus Affair, added with perfect sincerity, "The very future of Japan is at stake, and it's up to me to make things right."

"What ever are you talking about, Sakamoto-san?" the proprietress asked with sarcastic laughter. "I've heard you boast before, but this is a bit much."

"I'm serious. But as I said, I can't stay long. I just stopped by to see how you are."

"Where are you going?"

"To Osaka."

"Osaka?" Otose said sarcastically. "If you're going to Osaka, why not visit the castle. I'm sure there are some people there who would be more than happy to see Sakamoto Ryoma," she snickered, alluding to the Bakufu's ubiquitous wanted posters which branded him as one of the most dangerous criminals in Japan. "But in all seriousness," Otose changed her tone, "you must be careful."

"Wait a minute," Ryoma suddenly exploded, ignoring the warning. "Otose-san, you've just given me a good idea."

"I have?"

"Yes. A way to keep Tosa out of a war with England."

"Oh?"

"If I'm correct, Lord Shungaku of Fukui should be at his Osaka estate right now."

"And?"

"And I'm going to pay him a visit."

Leaving Otose not a little bit worried, Ryoma caught a riverboat to Osaka, arriving there late the following morning, and proceeding directly to the estate of Matsudaira Shungaku. Although the Lord of Fukui had resigned his post of Political Director of the Bakufu over four years before, he retained his influence in the Edo regime. Ryoma would ask Shungaku to write a letter to Yodo, advising that Tosa act in a reasonable manner according to international law, when dealing with the British. Not only was Ryoma worried that the hotheaded samurai in Tosa might opt for a war with the British, but he was also concerned that Yodo, who was notorious for his brazen behavior, might anger the British minister to such a degree that war between Tosa and England would be unavoidable.

Everything must be handled according to international law, Ryoma insisted now, as he had during his recent ordeal with Kii over the Iroha Maru Incident. Ryoma was confident that his men in Nagasaki had not committed the murders; it was through international law that he would prove their innocence, and avoid an untimely war between Tosa and Britain.

"Strange," Ryoma said to himself on this afternoon of the last day of July, crossing Yodoya Bridge to the long, narrow island at the center of the Yodogawa, on which were situated the Osaka estates of several feudal lords, including that of Lord Shungaku. "Strange," he repeated, as he approached the black and white outer wall of the Fukui estate, before identifying himself to one of the guards at the gate, who immediately recognized him and allowed him entrance. Strange indeed! While he would never be permitted an audience with the *daimyo* of his native Tosa, one of the Bakufu's most wanted men had no problem, even at the spur of the moment, arranging a meeting with the Lord of Fukui, who was outranked only by the lords of the six Tokugawa Branch Houses, and nobody else in all of Japan. Such was Ryoma's influence among Katsu Kaishu's influential Group of Four.

Soon he was shown to the drawing room of the *daimyo*, where he divulged his plan to Lord Shungaku. "According to international law," Shungaku repeated Ryoma's words, impressed, as always, by this outlaw who was determined to save Japan.

"Yes," Ryoma said. "If any of the clans, particularly one as large as Tosa, does not comply with international law, as guaranteed in the foreign treaties, the Western powers will consider Japan a rogue nation and never treat us on an equal basis."

"Ryoma," Shungaku said with a slight smile, "you never cease to amaze me. Of course I'll write a letter to Lord Yodo."

Later that afternoon Ryoma left Shungaku's estate with the letter in his pocket. He hurried to the nearby Tosa headquarters, where he intended to deliver the letter to Sasaki Sanshiro, who in turn would bring it to Lord Yodo in Kochi.

Whenever possible, Ryoma avoided Tosa headquarters in Kyoto and Osaka. While, with the establishment of the Kaientai, he had, for all means and purposes, been pardoned for his crime of fleeing Tosa, neither Goto nor Fukuoka had submitted the proper papers to the administrative office in Kochi, and so officially Ryoma was still a fugitive. As he had already been pardoned once for the same crime, both ministers feared the wrath of Lord Yodo—who disdained the infidelity of the Loyalists who had abandoned his domain—should such papers be called to his attention. And while Ryoma was not about to let such a trivial matter interfere with the all-important matter at hand, not such was the case of the officials in charge at Tosa headquarters.

"Sakamoto Ryoma here!" Ryoma shouted at the entranceway. "I must see Sasaki Sanshiro."

The caretaker of the headquarters, an upper-samurai in his late fifties, rushed from his office near the front of the building. This was a different man from the one who had been in charge during Ryoma's recent visit here with Goto. "Sakamoto Ryoma!" he exclaimed. "Aren't you the younger brother of Sakamoto Gombei from the castle-town?"

"Yes," Ryoma snarled, anticipating the caretaker's reaction.

"I have orders to arrest you for the crime of fleeing Tosa."

"Are you crazy?" Ryoma scoffed. "Haven't you heard about our navy?"

"No."

"Then you'd better ask someone around here about it, because it's sponsored by Tosa, and I'm the commander."

"Oh?" the caretaker said blankly.

"Yes," Ryoma jeered. "And if you still insist on arresting me, you'll have to answer to Goto Shojiro."

"Minister Goto?"

"Do you know of any other Goto Shojiro?" Ryoma replied sarcastically.

"But I'm under orders to..."

"To hell with your damn orders. I have to find Sasaki, and fast. Unless, of course, you'd rather see Tosa in a war with Britain."

"What are you talking about, Sakamoto?" the old man snapped.

"I don't have time to explain. Just bring me to Sasaki."

"He's not here."

"Where is he?" Ryoma demanded.

"Why do you want to know?" the caretaker said suspiciously.

"I just told you," Ryoma hollered. "To keep Tosa out of a war with Britain."

"Sakamoto!" the old man shouted, "I've had enough of your impertinence."

"Then I'll leave, if you'll just tell me where I can find Sasaki."

"Certainly you don't expect me to reveal the whereabouts of the commissioner of justice of Tosa Han to a criminal like you," the caretaker shouted.

"I can see you're not going to," Ryoma said angrily. "But if British warships bombard the coast of Tosa, remember that it's your own fault." Ryoma left Tosa headquarters, disgusted by the petty smugness that had vexed him as long as he could remember. Unlike Saigo and Okubo of Satsuma, not to mention Goto and Sasaki of Tosa, all of whom occupied top posts in their respective *han*, Ryoma had no choice but to act under the stigma of a wanted man. Not only was he without the benefit of the Tosa estates in Kyoto and Osaka, but he was even in danger of arrest by Tosa men stationed there. And even if he were to return to Tosa to receive an official pardon–which he had no intention of doing–he would still be nothing more than a lower-samurai, with no position of authority to help him actualize his great plan. "But no matter," he told himself over and over again. "I have to make the best of a rotten situation if I'm ever going to correct it." The rotten situation was none other than the entire feudal system.

There were, however, some men among the younger generation of Tosa's upper-samurai–influenced by Goto, Sasaki and others–who had strong Loyalist sympathies. And fortunately, Ryoma was approached by such a man, in the street shortly after leaving the Tosa estate.

"Sakamoto-san," the man called. "Over here. I've heard all about your navy from Sasaki-san. He's told me to assist you in any way I can, should you show up while he's away."

"Where is he now?" Ryoma asked.

"At Satsuma headquarters to talk to Saigo about borrowing a ship to sail back to Tosa."

"Thanks," Ryoma said, bowed his head slightly, and took off at a dead run to the nearby Satsuma headquarters. But when he arrived shortly after, he found that Saigo was out. "I'll wait," he told the care-taker, who, unlike his Tosa counterpart, treated Ryoma with the utmost of respect. After what seemed to be two very long hours, Saigo finally returned, and informed that he had heard the details of the Icarus Affair first from the interpreter to the British minister, Ernest Satow, then from Sasaki, who had also mentioned the danger of war between Tosa and Britain.

"Where's Sasaki now?" Ryoma asked anxiously.

"He left for Kobe a few hours ago to return to Tosa."

Since there were no Tosa ships at the Ports of Kobe or Osaka, and since Sasaki was firm in his refusal of the Bakufu's offer of transport aboard either a Tokugawa or British warship, Saigo arranged passage for him on the Satsuma steamer *Mikuni Maru*. "But I don't know if you'll be able to catch him before the ship leaves," Saigo told Ryoma, apologetically. "He seemed to be in an awful hurry when I told him that the British Legation would be sailing soon for Tosa."

"I must catch him," Ryoma said, then told Saigo about the letter he was carrying from Shungaku to Yodo. "If I don't get this letter to Sasaki before he leaves, Tosa may never have the chance to fight alongside Satsuma and Choshu against the Bakufu."

"I see," Saigo said, nodding grimly.

"And like I've told you before, Saigo-san, I don't believe we can beat the Tokugawa Navy without Tosa on our side." Although Ryoma, now as before, preferred to avoid civil war, he was well aware that Saigo was anxious to crush the Bakufu militarily, as indeed he him-self would be if his plan for peaceful restoration failed.

"Then you'd better leave right away," Saigo urged. "Kobe is about ten leagues from here."

"Before I go, I want to remind you of your promise not to attack the Bakufu until Yodo has the chance to petition the Shogun to abdicate peacefully."

"I haven't forgotten," the great man replied evasively, but with no time to spare for argument, Ryoma immediately left Satsuma head-quarters in Osaka on a swift horse provided by Saigo. Having made the 25-mile journey in less than four hours, Ryoma reached the Port of Kobe shortly after midnight. Lying in port were dozens of ships; and although each was equipped with bright lanterns displaying the crest of her own *han*, the nearsighted Ryoma could not distinguish them "Is the *Mikuni Maru* still here?" he asked an old bargeman at the pier.

"Do you mean the Satsuma ship?" the bargeman replied lazily.

"Yes. Has she left yet?" Ryoma repeated impatiently.

"No, not yet. Can't you see her over there?" the bargeman asked, pointing at a triple-masted schooner.

"I can't make out the crest."

"Well, she's flying the Satsuma crest, and will be leaving port any time now."

"I have to get to her before she leaves," Ryoma said, and reaching into his pocket, handed the man a gold coin, equivalent to a month's wages for a bargeman. "After you take me to the ship, see to it that this horse gets back to Satsuma headquarters in Osaka."

Soon Ryoma boarded the barge, and arrived at the Satsuma ship minutes later. "Sakamoto Ryoma here!" he called at the top of his lungs at the starboard of the huge ship. "I've come to see Sasaki Sanshiro on urgent business."

A sailor dropped a rope ladder, and Ryoma climbed aboard. "Where's Sasaki?" he asked the sailor, who immediately showed him to Sasaki's cabin below deck.

"Who's there?" Sasaki shouted as Ryoma suddenly burst through the door. "Ryoma! What are you doing here?" With Sasaki was another, older man whom Ryoma did not know, but as Sasaki informed, was Tosa Minister Yui Inai.

"I've come with a letter from the Lord of Fukui," Ryoma said. "You must deliver it to Lord Yodo." Ryoma handed the letter to Sasaki, who carefully unfolded it and began reading aloud.

"So," Sasaki said after he had finished reading, "Lord Shungaku advises Lord Yodo to settle this matter according to international law." Then with a burst of laughter, "It sounds like you might have written it yourself, Ryoma."

Rather than admitting that he had indeed dictated the gist of the let-ter to the Fukui *daimyo*, Ryoma asked Sasaki and Yui what they thought of Shungaku's advice.

"That's exactly what we intend to do," Yui informed. "Lord Yodo is of similar mind. When dealing with the British we are determined to obey international law."

"To avoid war?" Ryoma confirmed.

"Yes," Sasaki said, "but we will never give in to their insistence that it was a Tosa man who killed the two sailors."

"What if the British are able to come if with some kind of proof incriminating a Tosa man?" Ryoma asked.

"Then we'll have to take the blame for it, according to international law," Sasaki said matter-of-factly.

"That's all I wanted to hear," Ryoma said. "But whatever happens, we can't let this thing interfere with our plan for peaceful restoration."

"You're right," Sasaki said, then with a worried expression informed Ryoma that the Tokugawa war steamer *Eagle* and the British warship *Basilisk* were also at Kobe, ready to sail to Tosa. "We must get there before the British Legation does, to warn Lord Yodo, and to prevent any trouble."

"I don't think the British will offer any trouble unless provoked," Ryoma said.

"That's what I'm worried about," Sasaki said. "Once word spreads that the British claim a Tosa man is guilty of the murders, there's no telling when those hotheads back home might open fire on the British ship."

"Most of the samurai in Tosa have never been away from Tosa," Ryoma snickered, "let alone seen a foreigner." What Ryoma wanted to say but didn't, partially out of deference to Sasaki, was that three centuries of complacency under Yamanouchi rule had left Tosa's upper-samurai so incompetent that most of them had no ability whatsoever when it came to the business of governing or foreign affairs.

"Yes," Sasaki said, troubled by the remark, particularly in the presence of Minister Yui, who pretended not to hear it. "But Ryoma, what are you doing here?" Sasaki asked, as if to change the subject.

"What do you think? I came to deliver Lord Shungaku's letter. But," Ryoma laughed, "since you already intend to follow the same policy that Lord Shungaku advises, it looks like I went to a lot of trouble for nothing. I should have stayed in Osaka. I'll be going back there now to..."

Before Ryoma could finish speaking, the ship's steam whistle blew, and Sasaki hollered, "We're moving!"

"We are at that," Ryoma confirmed.

"But you have to get off this ship," Sasaki gasped. "You can't come to Tosa now. It would be too dangerous."

"It looks like I have no choice," Ryoma said drolly, although he was well aware that these two elite officials would face nothing but trouble from the conservatives in Tosa if they were to return with one of the Bakufu's most wanted men aboard.

"But officially you're still wanted for fleeing the *han*," Sasaki groaned.

"Don't worry," Ryoma said, "I'll hide below deck the whole time we're in Tosa."

The Satsuma men provided Ryoma with a cabin of his own, although rough seas kept him awake until morning, despite his exhaustion. He slept soundly until noon, when the ship cut a southwesterly arc around eastern Shikoku, and Ryoma got his first look at his native Tosa in over five and a half years. "It seems like a lifetime ago," he said aloud, as he thought of all that had happened, not only for himself, but for the entire nation, since he had fled with Sonojo on that rainy spring night in 1862. He reminisced fondly of his first meeting with Katsu Kaishu, but just as soon recalled with indignation the bombardment of Kagoshima and Shimonoseki by foreign ships. He thought about the coup which drove Choshu from Kyoto, the establishment of Kaishu's naval academy in Kobe and its demise with Choshu's failed counter-coup in Kyoto which also spelled disaster for Hanpeita and the other Loyalists in Tosa. He laughed aloud as he recalled his first meeting with Saigo at Satsuma headquarters in Kyoto, and remembered proudly the founding of the Kameyama Company in Nagasaki, and the realization of the Satsuma-Choshu Alliance. Then came the near-fatal attack at the Teradaya, when Oryo had saved his life, and their honeymoon in the misty Kirishima mountains of Satsuma shortly after. "I wonder what she's doing at this very moment," he though sadly, but the sadness soon subsided as he was overcome by an inexplicable feeling of dread that he might never see his wife again. The faces of Miyoshi and Katsura flashed through his mind, as did those of his friends in the Kaientai. He thought of the sea battle in Shimonoseki when he and his men pounded the Kokura coast from the warship *Union*, and how Takasugi had led his Extraordinary Corps in battle despite the consumption that was killing him. "And all the others who have died for the nation," Ryoma said aloud, before telling himself, "Now, most importantly, Yodo must convince the Shogun to restore the power to the Emperor."

There had not been a foreigner in Tosa Han since a Spanish galleon was shipwrecked there in 1596. If the British Legation were to arrive before Sasaki and Yui could warn the authorities in Kochi, they feared that upper- and lower-samurai alike might commence hostile action against the foreigners without waiting for orders from the Tosa government.

Much to the relief of the two Tosa officials, not to mention the outlaw accompanying them, there was no sign of either a Tokugawa or British ship when the Satsuma steamer reached the Port of Susaki, some 25 miles west of Kochi Castletown, shortly before sundown on August 2. Susaki was the best port in Tosa. While the Port of Urado was much closer to the castletown, it had a narrow entrance, making it difficult for large ships to enter. Susaki, on the other hand, was not only deeper, but it was protected from the wind and open sea by mountains and islands, thus conducive to the probable purpose of shipboard discussions with the British.

There was, however, another steamer lying in Susaki when the Satsuma ship arrived. It flew the Yamanouchi crest of three oak leaves in a circle. "The *Yugao*!" Yui hollered the name of the ship, on board of which Ryoma had drafted his Great Plan At Sea two months before. "My son's the captain of the *Yugao*," the minister said.

"Then we can hide Ryoma on her while we're away," suggested Sasaki, who went immediately below deck to inform Ryoma of the plan.

"I'm truly sorry to put you through this," Sasaki, whose position as commissioner of justice made him the top police official in Tosa, said to the political outlaw in an appeasing tone, "but if anyone were to find out you were with us..."

"The *Yugao*?" Ryoma interrupted, ignoring Sasaki's apology.

"Yes. Would you mind?"

"Why should I mind?" Ryoma snickered. "If I have to stay hidden below deck, one ship's the same as another."

Soon Ryoma transferred to the *Yugao*, whereupon Sasaki and Yui landed. They went directly to the office of the local magistrate to inform him of the scheduled arrival of the Tokugawa and British warships, instructing him to suppress any hostilities which might threaten to occur among Tosa samurai. From there, despite heavy rain, Sasaki and Yui set out after dark by palanquin on the 25-mile trip to

Kochi Castletown, arriving there the next morning.

Wet, disheveled and exhausted from their journey, Sasaki and Yui found Yodo in the sitting room of his villa, near the castle. He was alone, and as he had just awaken, had not yet taken up the *sake* flask. "Sit," Yodo abruptly ordered when his two retainers entered the room, "and tell me what all the ruckus is about with the foreigners."

After Sasaki relayed the details of the Icarus Affair, which Yodo had already read about in numerous letters from his Osaka and Kyoto headquarters, the commissioner of justice informed the *daimyo* of the relentless claim by the British that it was a Tosa man who had killed the two sailors, and of the Bakufu's apparent hope that British warships would bombard Kochi as they had Kagoshima and Shimonoseki. Yodo, however, did not get riled, but rather listened silently, with an occasional nod or grunt, throughout the long explanation, at the end of which Sasaki produced a letter from his kimono. "This is from Lord Shungaku of Fukui," he said. "He urges that we spare no effort in avoiding a war with the British."

When Yodo finished reading the letter, Sasaki informed that it had been delivered to him by Sakamoto Ryoma, just before their ship left Kobe. After briefly summarizing Ryoma's activities, and his influence among the leaders of Satsuma and Choshu (but without mentioning that the plan for peaceful restoration was drafted by Ryoma), Sasaki added sheepishly, "And although Ryoma is still officially wanted for fleeing Tosa, he's come back with us. But to avoid trouble, we left him hiding below deck aboard the *Yugao*."

"*After pondering the situation for a while,*" Sasaki's memoirs recall, "*our lord broke out in laughter, saying, 'At any rate, it's certainly a troublesome matter.'*" This was all that Yodo said about Ryoma, which was certainly not an indication of goodwill for the political criminal. Rather, the reticence of the elitist Lord of Tosa was merely a sign of his trust in the ability of his commissioner of justice.

Indeed, Sasaki proved his political ability over the next few days, preparing for the arrival of the British. His most formidable task during this time was to make sure that the administrative office in Kochi and the magistrates of the seven local districts of Tosa would suppress any uprisings among samurai outraged at the appearance of the British, whose warship *Basilisk* finally arrived at Susaki on the morning of August 6, two days after the Tokugawa steamer *Eagle* had dropped anchor there.

Early in the afternoon of the same day, as Ryoma watched the movement of the British sailors aboard the *Basilisk*, now moored just outside the harbor, and of the Tosa samurai on shore drilling for battle, he
wondered what was happening with Sasaki in Kochi. As he asked
himself aloud how much longer he would have to remain hidden
below deck, an unexpected, but welcome visitor came aboard to see
him. This was Okauchi Shuntaro, an old friend from Kochi who had
come to confirm the rumor of Ryoma's return.

"You're actually back!" Okauchi exclaimed when he found Ryoma
below deck.

"Very perceptive," Ryoma snickered.

"Does your family know you're back?"

"No," Ryoma answered bluntly, looking out a porthole at the British
warship, then at the excited movement of the Tosa samurai on shore.
While Sasaki was making every effort to subdue possible hostilities
against the British, another high-ranking samurai–a former minister
and one of Lord Yodo's favorite retainers–was busy preparing for war.
This was Inui Taisuke, the leader of the anti-Bakufu radicals in Tosa
whom Ryoma had recently praised as, beside Goto, the only one of
"Yodo's elite who's worth his weight in spit." While Yodo and Goto
endorsed the plan for peaceful restoration, Inui, whom Yodo had
recently put in charge of reforming the Tosa military, shared the bellicose sentiments of Satsuma and Choshu. Shortly after Yodo had
appointed this thirty-one-year-old vassal as commanding officer of
the Tosa Army–partly to allay Inui's displeasure for the peace
plan–Inui abolished outdated, ancient modes of warfare, and replaced
them with Western methods he had learned in Edo. But modern
weapons and tactics emphasized the training of the masses at the cost
of the traditional valor which the samurai so greatly valued. Guns had
traditionally been regarded as the weapons of the less honorable
ranks, unfit for the elite classes, who for generations had been armed
with the sword, spear and bow and arrow. While these radical changes
earned Inui the resentment of many of the pro-Bakufu conservatives
in Tosa, most of his troops, and all of his commanders, shared their
leader's anti-Tokugawa sentiments and his burning desire to go to war
against Edo. When word reached Kochi of the arrival of the Tokugawa
and British warships, Inui's troops immediately took up positions, not
only at the Port of Susaki, but at several other locations along the
coast, where they had constructed cannon batteries. It was not without
derision that Ryoma now watched the drilling of these fanatics.

"Okauchi," Ryoma said, "what are those troops on shore so damned excited about?"

"It looks like they're preparing for war."

"Take a look at that," Ryoma scoffed, pointing through the porthole at the British warship, still anchored in the offing. "There's no flag flying on her mast, which means the British have no intention of fighting."

"I didn't know that," Okauchi said.

"Neither apparently does the commanding officer of the Tosa Army," Ryoma snickered. "I want you to go to Kochi and ask Inui if, under the given circumstances, he doesn't think it's kind of ridiculous for his troops to be raising such a ruckus."

Okauchi left immediately, arriving at Inui's headquarters a few hours later. After Okauchi had relayed Ryoma's message to Inui, the latter simply laughed, without offering an answer to Ryoma's comment. But one of his top lieutenants sitting nearby said, "Tell Ryoma he doesn't have to worry. Our troops are drilling for a war against the Bakufu, not the foreigners."

Okauchi returned directly to the *Yugao* to report the reply to Ryoma, who doubled over in laughter when he heard it.

Later that afternoon, Goto and a samurai attendant boarded a skiff from a pier at Susaki, whereupon the latter paddled through the smooth water to the *Yugao*. Before beginning discussions with the British concerning their claim that Tosa men were guilty of the murders in Nagasaki, Goto wanted to reconfirm one important fact with Ryoma.

"Are you absolutely sure than none of your men committed the murder?" he asked Ryoma when he found him below deck.

"Absolutely," Ryoma insisted now as he had on previous occasions.

"Then I'm going to have to be tough with the British," Goto said with conviction, a sign of his trust in Ryoma.

"One last word of advice before you go," Ryoma said.

"What?"

"Answer all their questions with complete honesty. You have nothing to hide, nothing to be ashamed of. If you conduct the negotiations in that spirit, I'm confident you'll be successful."

"Thanks," Goto said, before reboarding the skiff where his attendant was waiting. Soon the skiff reached the *Basilisk*, which lay just outside the harbor. The two men boarded the British warship, and were escorted by a sailor to the captain's quarters. Waiting for them in the wood paneled cabin, sitting at a long table, were British Minister Sir Harry Parkes and his interpreter Ernest Satow. The forty-one-year-old Parkes had come to Japan from China two years before, after having served as British Consul at Canton and Shanghai. Sir Harry was a large man of an overbearing if not crude personality, shortcomings which were intensified by his large nose, heavy cheekbones, stringy dark hair combed back over the collar, and piercing dark eyes which seemed to shout out his position of authority when he was not doing so with his scowling mouth. His caustic personality notwithstanding, Sir Harry was the most able of all the foreign ministers in Japan during these most troubled of times. The eloquent Satow would attest to this in his memoirs by describing his chief as *"invested with the prestige of a man who had looked death in the face with no ordinary heroism."*

Goto concluded at first sight that Satow, who sat to the right of his chief, was the antithesis of Sir Harry in both appearance and manner. Bright, coolheaded and just twenty-four years old, Satow had the refined manners of a British aristocrat, and features befitting one of the elite class. He was light of complexion, with a slightly elongated face and sincere hazel eyes. He wore a neatly trimmed mustache above a finely chiseled mouth, his long dark hair slicked back and parted in the middle. He had first come to Japan as a student interpreter five years before, and was now fluent in both written and spoken Japanese. Satow's talents were by no means limited to linguistics, although he was indeed skilled with the pen. He had recently made a very insightful discovery about the political situation of his host country, which until that time had escaped the notice of all the foreign representatives in Japan. Satow reported that the Shogun was merely the most powerful among the feudal lords, while the true sovereign of the Japanese nation was the Emperor. The young diplomat's discovery led England to develop closer ties with Satsuma and Choshu at the exclusion of the Shogun, whom France erroneously continued to consider the sovereign of the nation even now, at the eve of Tokugawa collapse.

After the proper introductions had been made by the bilingual Satow, during which the British minister raised his massive frame from his chair and, with a threatening scowl, shook the Tosa minister's hand with a viselike grip, Goto calmly sat down and began speaking in a straightforward manner, not the least intimidated. He frankly explained that although investigations had been conducted in Tosa, there was no evidence found suggesting that any of his clansmen had committed the murders.

No sooner had Goto finished speaking than Sir Harry stood up, pounded his fist on the heavy wooden table, stomped on the floor, and shouted at the top of his lungs, "You're full of shit!"

While Goto did not understand the meaning of the obscenity, he comprehended very well the British minister's intent, but nevertheless remained calm.

"I insist that you find the son a of bitch who murdered British sailors, even if you have to interrogate every last one of your fucking men," Sir Harry continued his tirade.

Satow, like Goto, retained his composure. He had anticipated that his chief would become enraged at the first mention of Tosa innocence, but was nevertheless obligated to translate for Goto the gist of Sir Harry's words, diplomatically omitting the obscenities. He was, however, unable to fool the Tosa minister, who countered with perfect calm, all the while staring hard into Sir Harry's eyes. "Mr. Minister," Goto said, "I am at a complete loss as to whether you have come here to negotiate the matter at hand, or to challenge us to a fight. If you insist on behaving so atrociously before an envoy of the Lord of the great domain of Tosa, then we had better cancel these discussions right now."

After Satow whispered into Sir Harry's ear, the British minister, apparently taken completely off guard, suddenly changed his attitude, and apologized profusely to the Tosa men. This Satow gladly translated, along with his chief's explanation that because overbearing behavior had always been successful during negotiations with the Chinese, he had assumed that it would work with the Japanese, but that he had greatly mistaken.

"No need for further apology," Goto assured, because he himself was assured that his point had been well taken.

Until now, Sir Harry's negotiations with the Japanese had been limited almost exclusively to Satsuma, Choshu and Edo. Since Britain had already established friendly ties with the latter two before Sir Harry's arrival to Japan, he had neither occasion nor reason to try to intimidate the samurai of Satsuma and Choshu. If he had, he would have undoubtedly failed, and this first meeting with a Tosa samurai would have gone that much smoother. As for the Tokugawa officials Sir Harry had thus far dealt with, they had yielded to his demands much less out of intimidation than out of discomposure over his crude

outbursts. But now, after the admonition from Goto, the British minister realized that the samurai of Satsuma, Choshu and Tosa, at least,
were not to be intimidated with the browbeating tactics by which he
had bullied the Chinese, and in his own mind, the men of the
Tokugawa. For the remainder of the discussion Sir Harry treated Goto
not only with the deference deserving of a minister of a feudal lord,
but with the reverence due one of Goto's strength of character. Before
the meeting had ended, Sir Harry accepted without objection a further
admonition from Goto, which Satow describes in his memoirs: Goto
*"remonstrated with Sir Harry at some length and in very explicit
terms, about his rough demeanor... and hinted that perhaps others
would not have submitted so quietly to such treatment."*
Least of all the Tosa troops on shore, whose incessant drilling had
at last incited the anxiety of the British minister. "What are those men
doing?" Sir Harry demanded, but, having taken Goto's warning to
heart, in a mild tone.
"Who?" Goto feigned nonchalance, looking through a porthole at
his furious clansmen on shore. "Oh, them?" he chuckled. "They're
just hunting wild boar, is all," he lied, drawing a snicker from Sir
Harry, who after Goto had left would tell Satow, "That was one of the
most intelligent Japanese I've ever met."
Such commendation aside, Sir Harry's unyielding insistence that a
Tosa man was guilty, and Goto's adamant denial of those charges, left
the two ministers with no alternative but to conclude this day's discussion without the slightest hope of finding an immediate solution to
the problem at hand.
On the next day a similar meeting was held, but still nothing was
solved. And despite the efforts that the Tosa men swore were being
made in their domain to find the murderer, they were unable to disclose any evidence whatsoever incriminating any one of their clan.
Much to Sir Harry's chagrin, and to the relief of the Tosa men, it was
therefore decided that the investigation be moved to Nagasaki, where
it would be conducted jointly by Tosa and Britain, and presided over
by Bakufu officials. On August 10, the warship *Basilisk*, with Sir
Harry aboard, set sail for Edo, leaving Satow to represent the British
side in Nagasaki.

At any event, it appeared certain that war between Britain and Tosa
had been avoided. On the night of August 12, Sasaki, Okauchi and
Satow boarded the *Yugao*, where Ryoma was beside himself with

boredom for having been cooped up below deck for ten days, but relieved to hear from Sasaki that they would be sailing immediately for Nagasaki, via Shimonoseki.

The trip was not pleasant, nor were the Tosa men on board in good spirits, as attested to by Ernest Satow, who wrote, *"Bad food, a dirty cabin, excessive heat, sullen fellow-voyagers were all accepted with the calmness of exhausted misery."*

Ryoma, for his part, had plenty of reason to be sullen, if not miserable. Goto had stayed behind in Kochi, to, as Sasaki informed, "take care of official business." "Official business," Ryoma sneered. "If he doesn't get back to Kyoto real soon, we're going to have a civil war on our hands."

"He'll get there," Sasaki assured, "just as soon as we've settled the *Icarus* problem in Nagasaki. Besides," he added with a snicker, "we need Goto in Kochi for the time being to keep Inui under control. There's no telling when that maniac might decide to bring his army to Kyoto, with or without permission from Lord Yodo."

"I must hand it to Inui," Ryoma said sardonically. "He has more guts than all of those lackeys back in Tosa put together."

Ryoma was indeed in a sullen mood that night, as he fretted that Yodo's memorial might not reach the Shogun before Satsuma and Choshu attacked. *"With things so critical now in Kyoto, I have something to tell you,"* he wrote Miyoshi two days later, after reaching Shimonoseki. *"Recently, Satsuma...has determined to fight the Bakufu, but is still waiting for Goto Shojiro of Tosa to get to Kyoto,"* as Ryoma was promised by Saigo and Komatsu. This is not to say, however, that Ryoma himself was not resolved to fight if war could not be avoided. But, as he predicted in his letter to Miyoshi, *"Unless the warships of Choshu, Chofu* (a Choshu-related clan)*, Satsuma and Tosa fight side by side, we'll be no match for the Bakufu Navy."*

At Sasaki's request Ryoma remained hidden in his cabin throughout most of the journey, except to get a breath of fresh air on deck just after the ship had left Tosa. It was at this time that Ryoma first encountered Satow, who had no way of knowing that the slovenly dressed, sullen man who squinted as he scowled, was none other than Sakamoto Ryoma, commander of the Kaientai, architect of the Satsuma-Choshu Alliance and author of the plan, of which he himself had recently heard from Saigo, for peaceful restoration and adoption of a parliamentary form of government in Japan. Ryoma simply ignored the Englishman, who was even less anxious to speak to the scowling samurai. Ryoma, to be sure, would have liked to have talked with Satow, if for no other reason than to convince him that none of his men were guilty of the murder of the British sailors. But Sasaki had asked Ryoma to stay away from the Englishman. "If the British find out that the commander of the Kaientai had been in Tosa all along," Sasaki had warned, "they'll certainly be suspicious."

"The boilers were old, and we steamed along at the rate of two knots an hour," Satow wrote. *"Luckily the weather was calm, otherwise there was every reason to think we must have gone to the bottom."*

The little ship dropped anchor at Shimonoseki at around eight o'clock on the morning of August 14, just long enough for Ryoma to bring Sasaki and Okauchi ashore to introduce them to a very special person.

"Who are we going to meet?" Sasaki asked as they walked along the main coastal road leading to the estate of Ito Kuzo.

"A real beauty from Kyoto!" Ryoma boasted. When the three Tosa men reached Ito's estate, the Kyoto beauty was so ecstatic to see her husband that she forgot her manners in front of Sasaki and Okauchi.

"You're filthy!" were the first words out of Oryo's mouth. Indeed, after spending nearly two weeks below deck, Ryoma's face and hands were black from soot, and his wrinkled and badly soiled clothes smelled of sweat and engine oil.

"Do I smell that bad?" Ryoma asked, glancing uneasily at Sasaki and Okauchi. "Oryo, I want you to meet a couple of friends of mine from Tosa."

"You need a bath," Oryo insisted, Sasaki winced, and Ryoma chuckled with embarrassment.

"She means me," Ryoma assured the astonished commissioner of justice, as Okauchi, out of deference to Ryoma, looked the other way.

"She was a famous beauty," Sasaki would write of Oryo, *"but I don't know whether or not she was a good wife."*

Sasaki's doubts were uncalled for; Oryo was a good wife, although her dislike of cooking, sewing, housework and other such matronly duties differentiated her from the type of woman the more traditional-minded Sasaki would have considered marrying.

Oryo knew that in order to convince Ryoma to take a bath she would have to go to extremes. And Ryoma did take a bath; and Oryo scrubbed his back; and afterward she served the three men a meal of grilled fish, steamed white rice, miso soup and pickled vegetables. Later that afternoon, much to Oryo's discontent, Ryoma returned with

Sasaki and Okauchi to their ship, which left immediately for Nagasaki, with Ernest Satow aboard.

The small Tosa steamer reached Nagasaki on the next afternoon, whereupon Ryoma reported directly to Kaientai headquarters. He was anxious to speak to his men about the Icarus Affair, as he had not seen any of them since the murders of the British sailors. Sasaki and Okauchi, meanwhile, stayed at an inn near the center of town, and Satow went to the home of British Consul Marcus Flowers.

When Ryoma arrived at headquarters, Eishiro, Sakutaro, Sonojo, Taro and Kanema were waiting for him. Umanosuke, Shunme and some of the others had recently joined Kenkichi and Yonosuke in Osaka to attend to commercial matters. After relaying the events which had occurred in Tosa, Ryoma said, "The inquiry starts tomorrow at the magistrate's office. But before that, there's one thing I have to know." He looked hard at all five men. "Did any of you do it?"

"No," Sonojo firmly assured.

"I knew you didn't," Ryoma said. "But what were you doing on the *Yokobue* at that particular time?" he asked, referring to the Kaientai schooner which the British claimed had left port before dawn of the morning after the crime, only to return by noon of the same day, after the killers had allegedly transferred to the Tosa steamer *Nankai* to escape to Kochi. "And why did you leave port just to come back so soon?"

"We were practicing," Sakutaro said. "Since we had just recently gotten hold of a ship, we wanted to take her on a trial run before we took her out with a full load of cargo."

"I see," Ryoma said.

"But," Sonojo added indignantly, "they suspect Tora of the murder."

"Who suspects Tora?"

"The people at the magistrate's office," Taro said angrily. "He was at a brothel in Maruyama near the scene of the crime, on the same night the British sailors were killed."

"And," Eishiro added anxiously, "since there's a rumor going around that whoever did it was wearing the same navy whites we always wear, Tora is a prime suspect."

"As long as we know he's innocent, it doesn't matter what anyone suspects," Ryoma said. "Where is he?"

"In Kagoshima," Kanema said. "He left yesterday on the *Yokobue* to deliver a shipment."

"That only makes him look guilty," Ryoma said in disgust. "As if he were hiding there to avoid trouble."

"Actually," Sakutaro said, "we thought it would be best for him to get away from here for a while to give things time to cool off."

"I hope that the British don't insist on calling him back here for questioning," Ryoma said.

"But he's innocent," Sonojo said.

"I know he's innocent," Ryoma groaned. "It's just that I don't want to have to wait around here for him to return. We have to settle this matter quickly so I can get to Kyoto." Ryoma was anxious to see Saigo as soon as possible to convince him to postpone his war plans long enough for Goto to deliver Yodo's petition to the Shogun. "I have an idea."

"What?" Eishiro asked.

"Offering a reward for any information leading to the arrest of the real killer."

"Fantastic!" Eishiro blurted, slapping his knee, as Kanema clapped his hands in approval.

"But what about the British?" Sonojo asked, returning to the matter at hand. "They suspect Tora."

"To hell with the British," Ryoma sneered. "And to hell with the Bakufu. So long as they don't have any proof, they can't touch us. And since none of us are guilty, they're not going to get any proof."

Later that evening Ryoma, Sakutaro and Sonojo visited the inn where Sasaki and Okauchi were staying. With them was Iwasaki Yataro, general manager of the Tosa Company. Iwasaki was a large man with a large face, bushy eyebrows, and a mustache which extended to the edge of his heavy jaw. Heading up the Tosa Company suited Iwasaki, who in six years from now would formally establish the Mitsubishi, based on the experience, business expertise and personal connections he would gain from Sakamoto Ryoma's Kaientai. Since the Kaientai officially belonged to Tosa, Iwasaki was in charge of the bookkeeping for Ryoma's company.

"I have an idea," Ryoma said, looking hard at Iwasaki, as Okauchi poured *sake* and the commissioner of justice grinned anxiously, because, as Sasaki would recall years later," "*Saitani was a man of many ideas.*" "Let's hear it," he said eagerly on this sweltering summer evening, and Ryoma told of his plan to offer a reward for information leading to the arrest of the killer.

"Fantastic!" Okauchi blurted.

"Yes," Sasaki readily affirmed, as Ryoma and Sakutaro laughed derisively. "What's so funny?" asked the commissioner of justice, a little annoyed.

"The sullen look on Iwasaki's face," Ryoma said of the frugal general manager who had not offered comment on the proposal. "Set the reward at a thousand *ryo*," Ryoma demanded, then just as matter-of-factly drained his *sake* cup.

"A thousand?" Iwasaki echoed in disbelief. "That's impossible."

"Nothing's impossible," Ryoma chided with a scowl. "We can't be tight-assed about this. The bigger the reward the better our chances of finding the killer. And even if we don't find the killer, Tosa's offer to pay that much reward money might help convince the British of our innocence."

"But one thousand *ryo*..." Sasaki started.

"What's more important," Ryoma interrupted, "you and your men being able to buy women in Maruyama, or the future of Japan?"

"What?" The commissioner of justice was indignant. "What's your point, Ryoma?"

"Think about it," Ryoma snickered, then turned sharply to Iwasaki. "How much money have Tosa officials spent carousing at Maruyama over the past month?"

"I couldn't answer offhand," Iwasaki said. "I'd have to check the books."

"But surely, Iwasaki, you have an idea how much money you yourself have spent there over the past month."

"I see," Iwasaki said irritably, avoiding an answer, but drawing a derisive snicker from Sonojo.

"One thousand *ryo* or the future of Japan?" Ryoma rephrased the question so that it would be more palatable. "Because with all hell about to break lose in Kyoto, we have to get this thing settled soon."

"Alright," Iwasaki shrugged. "I'll come up with the money somehow."

"Good, Iwasaki," Ryoma said sarcastically. "I knew you had it in you. We'll start putting up posters around town first thing in the morning, to advertise the reward. We have to get things settled before there's a civil war."

"Civil war!" Sasaki repeated dryly. "What about your plan for peaceful restoration?"

"I don't want a war any more than you do," Ryoma said. "But Goto is still in Kochi, and I doubt Saigo will wait much longer. But what worries me is whether or not Tosa will actually agree to fight against the Bakufu."

"Tosa will fight," Sasaki said firmly.

"If there's a war, it will have to," Ryoma corrected.

"You saw our troops drilling along the coast at Susaki," Okauchi offered.

"And," Sasaki added, "you know how determined Inui is to bring his army to Kyoto. If Lord Yodo tries to restrain him, I truly believe he'll flee Tosa with all of his troops."

"Sasaki," Ryoma said cynically, "let me ask you this: Is Tosa ready to fight?"

"Ready?" Sasaki looked blankly at Ryoma.

"Yes, ready?" Are Tosa's troops properly armed for a war with the Tokugawa?"

"Inui has recently procured a few hundred American rifles, but a lot of our men are still armed with muskets," Sasaki admitted.

"Then we'd better get them ready," Ryoma said, drawing puzzled looks from both Tosa officials.

The investigation of the Icarus Affair was resumed at the office of the Nagasaki Magistrate three days later, on the morning of August 18. Representing Tosa were Sasaki, Okauchi and Sakutaro. Ernest Satow and Consul Marcus Flowers represented the British side, while the Tokugawa commissioner of foreign affairs and several of his underlings were present for the Bakufu.

Satow opened the hearing by pointing at Ryoma, and asking Sasaki in fluent Japanese, "Is this the man who was drinking at the House of the Flower Moon, which is near the scene of the crime, on the night our sailors were murdered?" Apparently Satow did not recognize Ryoma as the man he had seen on deck of the *Yugao* during the unpleasant trip from Tosa to Nagasaki.

"No!" Sasaki answered flatly for Ryoma, who burst out laughing, "...*evidently with the object of ridiculing us out of our case,*" Satow wrote, "*but he got a flea in his lug and shut up making the most diabolical faces.*" Ryoma had every reason to look diabolical. He knew what was coming next, and had been dreading it since he heard that Toranosuke was suspected of the murders. Nevertheless, as he was neither a Tosa official nor one of the accused, he was not allowed to testify or comment during the hearing. "This is the commander of the

Kaientai, Saitani Umetaro," Sasaki introduced Ryoma to the British. "Why isn't the accused here?" Satow asked, and when he was informed that Toranosuke was in Kagoshima, he insisted in no uncertain terms, and much to Ryoma's chagrin, that he return to Nagasaki for questioning, a demand so reasonable that the Tosa men were obliged to comply.

"Tora won't come back here unless I send my own men to get him," Ryoma told Sasaki in the latter's room after the hearing. "But with the *Yugao* gone, we only have two ships left. One of them, the *Absolute*, is with my men in Osaka; and the other, the *Yokobue*, is in Kagoshima with Tora."

"And you want him back here as soon as possible, right?" Sasaki ascertained.

"Yes. There's a Tokugawa steamer lying in port that we ought to be able to use."

"Which one?"

"The *Nagasaki Maru*," Ryoma said. "But we can't have anybody from the Bakufu going along for the ride."

"Why not?"

Ryoma burst out laughing. "That would only start the war we are trying so damn hard to avoid."

"I see your point," Sasaki remarked with a sardonic grin. "I'll make the necessary arrangements."

Sasaki held true to his word. On a rainy evening near the end of August, Okauchi–officially because he represented Tosa, but actually because he was friendly with Toranosuke–and several members of the Kaientai, steamed out of Nagasaki aboard the Tokugawa warship to retrieve their comrade in Kagoshima. Just before the ship was about leave, Ryoma called Okauchi aside, and said in a low voice, "I hear that Satsuma has recently been counterfeiting gold coins. See if you can get hold of a few of them to bring back to us."

"What for?"

"So we can learn how to make them ourselves. If fighting should break out, we'll need all the resources we can get to finance the war."

While Ryoma waited for his men to return, he was by no means idle. "*Saitani would visit my room two or three times a day,*" Sasaki would recall in later years. "*He'd spend whole days there. He'd make himself at home there.*" Ryoma had a specific purpose behind his visits.

Although Sasaki was unaware, Ryoma had not forgotten his scheme to educate him, because while the Dragon no longer had any doubt about Goto, he was determined to make certain that he could count equally on Tosa's commissioner of justice when the going got rough, as he feared it would very soon in Kyoto.

Accordingly, for the remainder of the month of August and the beginning of September, Ryoma spent his days teaching Sasaki everything he himself had learned about parliamentary forms of government, American democracy, and the necessity of adopting a similar system to replace feudalism after the fall of the Tokugawa. The two men talked grimly of the dwindling possibilities of peaceful restoration, the threat of civil war and what they should do if fighting broke out, with Ryoma stressing that Tosa must fight on the side of Satsuma and Choshu if it hoped to have any kind of influence in the formation of a new Japanese government.

Also during this time there was many a night which Ryoma spent at the pleasure quarter of Maruyama. One night Ryoma was drinking at his favorite brothel, the House of the Flower Moon, with three geisha all to himself. The women were pretty, the wine was French, and, with war constantly on his mind, he thought he should share these pleasures with Sasaki. "Do you have anything to write with?" he asked one of the girls, who soon brought him writing utensils and paper. "*The woman shogun and some others have just attacked, and I'm now fighting them,*" Ryoma wrote in a note he addressed to "*Shogun Sasaki.*" "*The sound of their arrows is awesome, and they've already stormed across the banister on the second floor; but the other women troops have not yet arrived. It seems that they're waiting for me to drop my guard, then launch another attack. If you're brave you'll come immediately to join me in the battle.*" Sasaki soon came to Ryoma's "rescue," and shared in his delight of wine and women, as a brief repose to the legal battle they faced with the British, and the specter of war looming ominously above the nation.

On a more serious note, it was also during this time that Ryoma introduced Sasaki to one of the leading players in the drive to overthrow the Bakufu. Katsura Kogoro had come to Nagasaki, disguised as a Satsuma samurai, for two reasons. One was to repair a Choshu warship; the other was to meet with Ryoma to find out whether or not the architect of the plan for peaceful restoration was still determined to bring down the Tokugawa with military might.

A DECLARATION OF FREEDOM

Before calling on Ryoma, Katsura wanted to settle the matter of repairing the ship. When the bill was presented him, he found that he was 1,000 *ryo* short. When he told Ryoma of his financial straits, the latter wasted no time persuading Sasaki to loan the money to Choshu from the coffers of the Tosa Company. It was to thank Sasaki that Katsura asked Ryoma to arrange a meeting one rainy evening at a teahouse, located near the foot of the hills at the rear of the town, not far from the office of the Tosa Company. "Try to use this opportunity to impress on Sasaki the need for Tosa to oppose the Bakufu," Ryoma had told Katsura as the two approached the teahouse.

"That's not all I intend to impress on him," Katsura assured, as they passed through the thatched front gate of the teahouse. "I'd like to offer some advice to Tosa," Katsura said to Sasaki a short while later, as the three men sat around a low table in a private room. Again they were drinking French red wine, and had just finished discussing the impatience of Choshu and Satsuma to go to war, and Tosa's vowed support for these two *han*. Outside Ryoma had posted several of his men as guards. He was concerned for the safety of Katsura, who, like himself, was one of the Bakufu's most wanted men. But unlike Ryoma, who in Nagasaki was known as Saitani Umetaro, commander of the Kaientai, in the service of the Lord of Tosa, Katsura was obliged to travel incognito. The guards were a precaution, just in case the Choshu leader's identity should be discovered by the Nagasaki Magistrate.

"Advice?" Sasaki said, examining a short sword which Katsura had given him as a token of appreciation for the loan. "Tosa is always open to advice."

"Very well," Katsura began. "Tosa has repeatedly contradicted itself. First it claimed to wholeheartedly support *Imperial Loyalism*, then suddenly it took the side of the Bakufu. Now we are told that Tosa has pledged unwavering support to Satsuma in a secret alliance, which means it also supports Choshu against the Tokugawa. If I may be so bold, Tosa has been acting like a fickle woman," Katsura said sharply, drawing a burst of laughter from Ryoma.

"Yes," Sasaki painfully agreed, "but you can be sure that our *han* will never again renege on its vow to oppose the Tokugawa. That I can personally guarantee."

"If you'll forgive me," Katsura said, "how can we be sure of that?" Katsura was as cagey as always, but this time Ryoma shared his sentiment.

In answer to the question, Sasaki told Katsura the same thing he had recently told Ryoma, not the least of which was Inui's conviction to fight alongside Satsuma and Choshu.

"But Sasaki," Ryoma said, "we have to be sure that the narrow-minded conservatives in Tosa will be willing to fight, in case my plan doesn't work."

"About your plan, Sakamoto-san," Katsura's voice was low, his eyes grim. "But before we discuss that, first let me tell you what I've recently heard from the Englishman Ernest Satow."

"Satow," Ryoma interrupted. "We must convince him, and real quick, that our men are not guilty."

"Yes," Katsura said, before continuing with his train of thought. "When I saw Satow at the British Consulate, he offered some very interesting, but disturbing advice." Katsura spoke with his usual smoothness, concerning which Satow wrote, "*Katsura was remark-able for his gentle suave manner, though under this there lay a char-acter of the greatest courage and determination, both militarily and political.*"

"What kind of advice?" Sasaki asked.

"That if Satsuma, Tosa and Choshu can't accomplish the revolution after all we have been through," Katsura said in a low voice, "then the Europeans will look upon us as a bunch of old women. Now, I don't have to tell you that it is humiliating to be told such a thing by an inter-preter to a foreign minister, but I tend to agree with him."

"Yes, quite," Ryoma snickered.

"And," Katsura said, "that brings me back to what I have to say about peaceful restoration. Certainly, Sakamoto-san, you haven't abandoned our plans for war," he said in exasperation. "Because the only way to eliminate the Bakufu is through war." Concerning this, Katsura's views were identical to those of Saigo.

"Katsura-san," Ryoma groaned, then explained to the Choshu leader the same thing he had told Saigo when revealing his plan to the Satsuma men. "It's the only way to get Tosa on your side. Lord Yodo has already agreed to send the memorial to the Shogun. If the Shogun agrees to restore the power to the Emperor, then there will be no need for war. If he refuses, then that'll be the end of him, because Tosa will no longer feel obligated to support him. At any rate, Goto has assured me that Tosa will fight alongside Satsuma and Choshu in case of war."

Katsura was not easily persuaded. "With the stage set in Kyoto and the Great Play about to begin," he likened the revolution to drama, "I don't think your plan can work."

"I like the way you put it," Sasaki exclaimed, slapping his knee, and asking Katsura to write these words down so that he could show them to the conservatives in Kochi.

Katsura promised to oblige, then Ryoma mentioned the recent formation of Nakaoka's Land Auxiliary Force. "We can thank Sasaki for that," he said. But it was Ryoma who had helped Nakaoka convince the commissioner of justice to pressure Tosa into officially authorizing and sponsoring his friend's private army, which Nakaoka had recently formed in Kyoto at Ryoma's suggestion. Similar in organization to Ryoma's Naval Auxiliary Force, Nakaoka's Land Auxiliary Force was headquartered at a minor estate which Tosa had recently purchased in northeastern Kyoto. Its initial membership of fifty-nine men consisted of Loyalists from various *han*–mostly Tosa and Mito–whom Nakaoka had recruited in and around the Kyoto-Osaka area to protect from the Shinsengumi and other Tokugawa police units. Soon the number of recruits doubled, and now Nakaoka commanded a small Loyalist militia which would provide mobile force in the Kyoto area in case of war. "If the Shogun refuses to abdicate peacefully," Ryoma said emphatically, "then Nakaoka's private army will be ready to fight alongside Satsuma, Choshu and my private navy."

"We must join Nakaoka in Kyoto as soon as possible," Katsura said. "If we get there too late, it could be dangerous."

"Dangerous?" Ryoma snickered. "Of course it's dangerous. This whole damn business is dangerous. But since when has danger ever gotten in our way?"

"And if war comes?" Katsura asked.

"If war comes, we fight," Ryoma said, then glanced at the commissioner of justice. "That reminds me, Sasaki," he added, feigning nonchalance, "I've ordered some rifles for Tosa."

"You've what?" Sasaki was stunned. "Sakamoto Ryoma," he exclaimed, "you haven't abandoned your native Tosa after all."

"Thirteen hundred British-made carbines from a Dutch trader in Nagasaki," Ryoma informed, rubbing his hands together and ignoring Sasaki's remark. "One thousand for Tosa, and three hundred for my Kaientai. They ought to be arriving from Shanghai real soon." By no means did Ryoma limit his plans to peaceful revolution. His goal remained unchanged: toppling the Bakufu to clear the way for a new democratic form of government, based on his Great Plan At Sea.

"But Ryoma," Sasaki said, "has Tosa agreed to pay you for the rifles?"

"No."

"Then how do you plan to pay for them?" Sasaki asked.

"Maybe with Tokugawa gold," Ryoma said in perfect seriousness.

"Tokugawa gold?" Sasaki exclaimed. "What do you mean?"

"I'm informed that the Nagasaki Magistrate has ten thousand *ryo* stored here."

"Then why don't we go and get it?" Sasaki remarked facetiously.

"That's exactly what I intend to do," Ryoma said matter-of-factly, drawing an intense look from Katsura, "if war should break out. But first we have to settle the Icarus Affair so we can transport the guns to Tosa."

"But why would you do this for Tosa?" Sasaki asked in disbelief.

"Don't get me wrong, Sasaki. I'm not doing this for Tosa. As I just said, if my plan doesn't work we're going to have a war on our hands. And you've told me yourself that Tosa is in bad need of rifles."

"Yes," Sasaki said.

"Then that should answer your question," Ryoma said to Tosa's commissioner of justice, all the while looking hard into the grim eyes of Katsura Kogoro.

A few days later, on September 2, Okauchi and the others returned from Kagoshima, with Toranosuke.

"I want to make sure of one thing," Ryoma told Toranosuke when the group arrived at Kaientai headquarters shortly after. "It wasn't you who killed the sailors, right."

"I didn't do it, Ryoma," Toranosuke said.

"I never thought you did, but I had to make sure. And since you're innocent, remember that no matter what happens or what anyone says tomorrow at the magistrate's office, you didn't do it."

On the next day, Ryoma, Okauchi, Iwasaki, and the suspect Toranosuke reported to the magistrate's office for examination. Iwasaki had come in place of Sasaki, who had suddenly taken ill. No matter how Satow examined the suspect, no matter what type of question the magistrate threw at him, Toranosuke remained firm, always completing his answers with the phrase, "I am not guilty."

"But you admit to having been at a house of entertainment near the scene of the crime on the night of the murder?" Satow reconfirmed.

"Yes," Toranosuke said, "the House of the Flower Moon. But it wasn't the first time I had been there, nor was it the last. I'm not guilty."

"And you admit that you were wearing a white navy uniform such as the one you have on, and like the one that the killer was allegedly seen wearing?" Satow said.

"I was wearing the same clothes then as I am wearing now. It's my uniform. I'm not guilty."

"Having failed entirely in our attempts to bring the crime home to the Tosa people," Satow wrote, *"Flowers and I agreed that it was useless for me to remain any longer,"* and the case was eventually dropped. In fact, there was one bit of information that seemed to disprove the allegations against the Kaientai. *"On the Japanese side,"* Satow wrote, *"the evidence went to show that the 'Nankai' did not leave till ten p.m. on the 6th August (July 6 on the lunar calendar), while Sir Harry's version was that she sailed at half-past four that morning, only an hour and a half after the schooner; and it was on this alleged fact that the whole of the suspicion against the Tosa men was founded."*

The identity of the true murderer, a samurai of Fukuoka, was discovered in the following year. He had gone out on the night of July 6 with two friends to view the star festival in Nagasaki. Along the way the group happened upon two British sailors who lay drunk on the side of the road. Out of disgust, the Fukuoka man, who had also been drinking, drew his sword, making short work of the two foreigners. Two days later, afraid that Fukuoka Han might be implicated in the crime, the guilty man committed *seppuku*. Three years later, in 1871, Sir Harry Parkes would send a formal letter of apology to Lord Yodo, but as fate would have it, Ryoma's pardon would never be solicited.

With the Icarus Affair finally behind him, Ryoma was once again free to put his business acumen to work, directing his men with such efficiency, and moving with such speed, that he surprised even himself. Having previously ordered 1,300 carbines at a cost of 18,875 *ryo* from a Dutch trader by the name of Hartman, he now arranged a loan of 5,000 *ryo* from the Satsuma men, who trusted the Kaientai commander as one of their own. (The Kaientai had not yet received the money owed them by Kii Han.) Four thousand of this would cover the down payment for the rifles, and the remainder be used for business expenses. But trust was not the only thing that Ryoma had on his side; to the founder of Japan's first modern company, practicality was the binding agent of such virtues as trust, honesty and courage. "The guns are for Tosa, in case of war against the Bakufu," Ryoma explained to the Satsuma agent in Nagasaki, who was only too glad to oblige. "Instead of trying to convince those hardheads back in Kochi with words, I'm going to bring the damn guns there myself, and tell them to fight." Indeed, Sakamoto Ryoma, a firm believer in the adage "Action speaks louder than words," was nothing if not practical.

The balance of the purchase, over 14,000 *ryo*, was to be paid to Hartman within ninety days after delivery. How he would raise this enormous sum in such a short period of time, Ryoma left to fate. Should the Shogun agree to peaceful restoration, the announcement would surely be made within three months. If such were the case, Ryoma could collect the money from the new Imperial government as a military expenditure. Should the Shogun refuse, then there would be war, which was the very reason he must purchase the guns. A victory by the Imperial forces would also ensure the establishment of an Imperial government, which would pay the debt as an expenditure of war. If by some chance the Tokugawa were to emerge victorious, Ryoma didn't expect to be alive to worry about repaying the loan.

"But Sakamoto-san," Yonosuke, whom Ryoma had recently recalled from Osaka, had said when Ryoma mentioned his intentions, "is that entirely honorable."

"Honorable?" Ryoma snickered. "I don't really know, Yonosuke. All I can say is that if I live through this thing, Hartman will get his money."

Ryoma had recently sent several of his men to Osaka, with the *Absolute* and the *Yokobue*, to prepare for war. And while he himself was busy in Nagasaki arranging the loan and terms of payment for the rifles, Yonosuke and Sakutaro set about arranging the charter of a steamer to transport the guns to Tosa. But as is so often the case, no sooner had one problem been solved than another followed, as surely as the cool autumn wind blew into Nagasaki from the East China Sea. On the afternoon of September 11, the same day that the shipment of carbines arrived from Shanghai, Ryoma heard from Sasaki that Goto had recently reached Kyoto with Lord Yodo's petition for peaceful restoration, but without the troops he had promised in case the Shogun should refuse.

"You mean all he has with him is the damn petition?" Ryoma shouted indignantly. He knew that Saigo would take this as a sign of Tosa's opposition to war against the Bakufu, even if the Shogun should refuse to abdicate.

But as Ryoma suspected, Goto was not to blame. Rather, Yodo had forbidden his chief minister the military option, regardless of the promises Goto had made, on the grounds that he did not want to appear to be "threatening the Shogun."

"What about Inui?" Ryoma demanded.

"When Inui heard that Goto had left for Kyoto without troops, he went straight to Lord Yodo to demand that he be allowed to follow Goto with an army."

"And?"

"Apparently," Sasaki winced, "Lord Yodo has threatened to send Inui to America."

"That's fantastic!" Ryoma roared, slammed his fist on the floor. "We're about to have a civil war, and Yodo's threatening to send the commander of his army overseas. Doesn't he realize that the only way to convince the Shogun to abdicate is by showing him that he has no other choice?" Ryoma paused momentarily, again slammed his fist on the floor. "Damn it!" he hissed, regained his composure, then groaned, "We're running of out time, Sasaki. Without troops there's no way that Goto is going to be able to convince Saigo to wait any longer. I'm the only one who might be able to do that. But first I have to get the rifles to Tosa."

If Ryoma's self-confidence was astounding, his reasoning was sound: Goto's failure to fulfill his promise made war seem imminent. "And to make matters worse," Sasaki said, "many of the conservatives in Kochi don't realize how weak the Bakufu has become. They don't understand how Lord Yodo could dare to petition the Shogun to abdicate. They're afraid that the Tokugawa might punish Tosa for such a bold act."

"Then maybe one thousand carbines will change their minds," Ryoma said cynically.

"One thousand? I thought you said you bought thirteen hundred."

"I did. Three hundred for the Kaientai."

"I see."

"But no matter what," Ryoma said, "I have to make those idiots in Kochi understand what's really happening, and that things are coming to a head in Kyoto." Although Ryoma was still unaware, two days after Goto had reached Kyoto, some 3,000 Satsuma samurai had arrived there. With these, and additional troops due to arrive from Kagoshima, Saigo's forces in Kyoto would soon number 10,000 strong. Furthermore, the Lord of Hiroshima, whose wealth surpassed that of even Choshu, had recently committed 1,000 troops to fight on the Satsuma-Choshu side, thus increasing Saigo's incentive to unleash his Imperial forces sooner than later. Nor was Choshu any less anxious for war to begin. Although its status of "Imperial Enemy" prohibited Choshu from participating in the anti-Bakufu conspiracy at court, its military was mobilized and waiting for Iwakura to arrange an Imperial decree for it to send an equally large number of troops to Kyoto to join their Satsuma allies.

"Satsuma and Choshu have waited long enough," Ryoma told Sasaki bluntly. In fact, three months had now passed since Saigo had promised to give Yodo time to petition the Shogun to abdicate. Certainly he had kept his word. And while Saigo had been understanding of the difficulties which Tosa encountered with the Icarus Affair—indeed Satsuma had even lent Sasaki a steamer to return to Tosa to settle the matter—Goto had come to Kyoto without the promised troops. "If Yodo and his conservative ministers can't understand that Tosa must act now or never, then to hell with them," Ryoma sneered, much to the discomfort of the commissioner of justice. "We have to be realistic, Sasaki," he said appeasingly. "Lord Iwakura has been after Saigo for months to begin military action against the Tokugawa. And now that Goto has arrived in Kyoto with only the petition," Ryoma concluded with a hopeless shrug, "Saigo just isn't going to wait much longer."

In fact, Saigo's sense of urgency intensified when he recently heard from Ernest Satow of what he had already known: France's intention to increase its support for the Bakufu. "...*the French say that Japan must have a single concentrated government like all western countries*," Saigo wrote to Okubo. "*And above all, that it is desirable to destroy the two provinces of Choshu and Satsuma*." Ryoma was indeed correct: Saigo the Great would not wait much longer.

A DECLARATION OF FREEDOM

Guns and Glory

On the morning of September 18, Ryoma left Nagasaki aboard the Shinten Maru, a steamer his company had chartered from Hiroshima Han, carrying contraband of 12,00 carbines. After all the years of running, struggling and risking his life for the nation, this champion of freedom would return to his native Kochi; not hiding below deck as he had recently been compelled to do, but laden with guns and glory, and armed with the will and a way to bring down the Tokugawa Bakufu.

Accompanying Ryoma were Yonosuke, Toranosuke, Sakutaro, Okauchi and a Kyoto samurai by the name of Toda Uta. On the morning of their second day out, steaming westward through the Sea of Genkai, they encountered a storm just off the northern coast of Kyushu.

"This engine's not big enough to handle it," Ryoma told Toranosuke as the two stood on the bridge, waves pounding the sides of the small ship. "We'd better stop at that island up ahead and wait it out."

Soon they landed, and found that there was only one small village on the entire island. Most of the houses were thatched, and fronted by old wooden fences. Nearby was a Buddhist temple, the tiles atop its white earthen outer wall gray from the elements. Beyond the temple was an ancient graveyard, near which was a dilapidated Shinto shrine. A grove of pines, their tops curbed away from the sea by the wind which howled through the branches, covered the land just in front of the dock, where several junks were moored. Further out, the harbor was dotted with the tiny boats of local fisherman, and beyond was anchored the triple-masted *Shinten Maru* with its contraband of rifles.

"I'm starved!" Toranosuke said, as the six samurai approached one of the houses.

"Chickens!" Yonosuke blurted, pointing at three fat hens sitting in a coop near the entrance of the house. Upon entering they found an old wooden table, which stood atop an earthen floor. "Yes?" an old man greeted them cautiously.

"Can we get something to eat here, old man?" Toranosuke asked.

"I'm sorry. All I can offer you is rice or *sake*."

"What about those chickens we saw outside?" Ryoma said. "We can eat them."

"Those are my chickens!" the old man croaked. "You must be joking."

"Right now I'm too hungry to joke," Ryoma said. "So if you'd just cook a couple of those chickens, we'll eat them and be on our way."

"No!" the man said firmly, shaking his gray head, and tugging on long, gray whiskers. "Those chickens are not for eating."

"Not for eating?" Okauchi echoed, partly amused, mostly annoyed. "Then what are they for?"

"Their my pets."

"I think he's serious," Yonosuke whispered to Ryoma.

"Can you believe it?" Ryoma snickered under his breath. "We were able to buy thirteen hundred of the world's best rifles in Nagasaki, but this old man won't even sell us a couple chickens."

And so they left the house to have a look around the rest of the village. "Chickens!" Sakutaro screamed. "There are chickens all over the place!" Indeed almost every house in the village had a chicken coop in front.

"Chickens!" Yonosuke shouted, as the six men stopped in front of one of the coops, inside of which were several fat hens.

"We'd like to buy a few of those hens," Okauchi said to a young girl who had come out of her house to look at the rare spectacle of six samurai.

"What do you want them for?" the girl asked suspiciously.

"To..."

Before Okauchi could answer, Ryoma said, "To keep as pets," and the girl agreed to sell four of the chickens to them. But since they couldn't very well ask her to butcher and cook them, they asked for a sack instead, into which Toranosuke stuffed the squawking birds and carried them away to a deserted beach. Here Yonosuke butchered the chickens with his short sword, washed them in seawater, grilled them over an open fire, and the six hungry men finally had their meal.

That evening they returned to their ship, and at dawn the next morning continued on their journey westward through the Sea of Genkai. By midday they reached the Port of Shimonoseki just in time to see another ship, flying the Satsuma crest, hasten eastward out of the harbor.

"I wonder what that's all about," Ryoma said to Yonosuke, as the Satsuma ship's whistle screamed and black smoke spewed from the smokestack.

Upon landing they went directly to the mansion of the merchant Ito

Kuzo, which was also the Shimonoseki office of the Kaientai and the residence of Ryoma's wife.

Oryo was there to greet them, as was Kuzo, to whom Ryoma introduced Toda, the Kyoto samurai who had accompanied him from Nagasaki. Toda, age twenty-five, was a retainer of Sanjo Sanetomi, the leader of the banished court nobles. He had recently come from Dazaifu, the nobles' place of exile, to investigate the revolution which was about to happen in Kyoto. In Nagasaki he happened upon Ryoma, who suggested they travel to Kyoto together, via Tosa Han.

Soon a maid served Ryoma and the others a meal of grilled mackerel pike, stewed vegetables, miso soup and steamed white rice, and as they were eating an unexpected but welcome visitor appeared.

Ryoma had not seen Ito Shunsuke since the latter had interpreted for Katsura Kogoro at a meeting aboard a Dutch warship nearly two and a half years before. "I've just bought thirteen hundred carbines in Nagasaki," Ryoma informed, pointing toward the harbor, and drawing a look of intense interest from Katsura's right-hand man.

"Then you have them with you?" Ito asked, to which Ryoma replied that of the 1,300 rifles, one hundred he had left behind with his men in Nagasaki, two hundred he would send to Osaka with his men, and the remaining one thousand he would personally deliver to Tosa.

Soon Ryoma's three men left for Osaka, and Ito Shunsuke joined Ryoma at Natural House, the private cottage at Kuzo's estate where Oryo had been living for the past seven months. "What's the latest word from Kyoto?" Ryoma asked as Oryo served hot tea.

The Choshu man carefully sipped the tea, then confirmed everything Ryoma had previously imagined, and more. Indeed the Great Play in Kyoto was about to begin. Goto was having trouble promoting the plan for peaceful restoration. Saigo had made it clear that he was no longer willing to put off his war plans, an attitude with which the Choshu men were in perfect harmony. "And with large companies of Satsuma troops due to arrive in Kyoto before the end of this month," Ito informed, "Saigo will have ten thousand men under his command there."

"What about the Choshu Army?" Ryoma asked, to which Ito replied that Lord Iwakura was now making the necessary arrangements at court to receive Imperial sanction for an equal number of Choshu troops to join their Satsuma allies in Kyoto. "Which means," Ito said triumphantly, "Choshu will no longer be an 'Imperial Enemy.' After that, Satsuma troopships bound for Kyoto will stop at the Port of

Mitajiri in Choshu to pick up our troops." Ito finished his tea, and in his excitement slammed the empty cup down. "And then there's Hiroshima," he said in a low voice, before telling Ryoma about that clan's recently formed secret alliance with Satsuma and Choshu.

"Then it looks like war," Ryoma said grimly, as if resigned to the fact.

"Yes. And since Hiroshima borders Choshu on the west, once war breaks out it will serve as an important land route for our troops advancing west toward Kyoto. But can we really count on Tosa?"

"I don't know," Ryoma groaned. "But when I deliver the rifles I'm going to find out. Even if the conservatives in Kochi won't back us, I think Inui will."

"What about Goto?"

"If there's war, then I'm going to have to get Goto out of Kyoto so that he can't interfere once Inui arrives there."

"Sakamoto-san," Ito said hesitantly, "if Tosa doesn't need the carbines..."

"Yes?" Ryoma gave Ito a long, hard look, as if anticipating what the younger man was about to say.

"Choshu will be glad to take them off your hands." This was Ito's way of saying, as tactfully as the situation allowed, that if Tosa still could not be counted on to fight against the Bakufu, the Choshu Army could certainly use 1,000 new carbines, for which they would be willing to pay.

"If Tosa backs out, the rifles are yours," Ryoma agreed with a short snicker, then asked about the Satsuma steamer he had seen leaving the harbor earlier in the day.

"That was Okubo." As Ito explained, Okubo was on his way back to Kyoto, from where he had come a few days earlier to confirm with Katsura the final war plans, including the deployment of Choshu and Satsuma troops to the Imperial capital.

"Where's Katsura-san?" Ryoma asked.

"At Yamaguchi Castle, with the *daimyo*."

"Is he due back in Shimonoseki soon?"

"In the next day or two."

"Then I'll wait that long to see him."

Later that night Ryoma and Oryo were alone in their room. The pale luster of the mid-autumn moon shimmering on the sea filtered through the window, and the red glow from the brazier mixed with yellow lantern light to produce an atmosphere conducive to their first time alone together in nearly five months.

"When are we going to have that house of our own in Nagasaki that you've talked about?" Oryo asked.

"As soon as I set things straight in Kyoto," Ryoma replied, sitting up and filling a pipe of tobacco.

"Exactly what things are you talking about?" Oryo asked, although she already knew the answer, then reached into the brazier with a pair of long sticks to light Ryoma's pipe with a burning coal.

"The future of Japan," Ryoma said matter-of-factly, exhaling white smoke.

"But what about our future?"

"You have to understand. The very fate of Japan rests on my shoulders."

Maybe it was the nonchalance with which Ryoma spoke these awesome words. Or perhaps it was the complete absence of heroics in his voice, or the uncharacteristic grimness in his dark brown eyes. But whatever the reason, Oryo suddenly felt a subtle chill deep inside, as a black notion fleeted through her mind, and she shuddered, if only for an instant, at the thought that she may never see her husband again. The sullen surge passed, and Oryo said in a singsong tone, as if to assure herself that he would indeed return to her, "I can count the number of times we've been alone together since our marriage." So could Ryoma. Their happiest time together was their honeymoon at the hot springs in the Kirishima mountains of Satsuma during the previous spring. In June Ryoma had brought Oryo to the Kosone mansion in Nagasaki to study the moon guitar, before he and his men went off to the war at Shimonoseki. The couple did not see each other again until the end of July, from which time they lived together at Nagasaki headquarters until autumn. After that Ryoma saw little of Oryo, as he spent the remainder of the year traveling between Nagasaki and Shimonoseki to get his company back on its feet. In February Ryoma had brought Oryo to Ito Kuzo's mansion for fear she might be arrested by the Nagasaki Magistrate. From this time on, Ryoma had even less time to spend with his wife, because soon after the Kaientai was established that spring, came the Iroha Maru Incident in April. Although Ryoma had been able to spend nine days with Oryo at Natural House while preparing for his legal battle with Kii, they did not meet again for over a month. But this reunion only lasted a few brief moments, because Ryoma soon left for Osaka with Goto aboard the Tosa steamer *Yugao*, when he composed his Great Plan At Sea. During the entire Icarus Affair he had been able to spend only half a day with Oryo in Shimonoseki *en route* from Tosa to Nagasaki, but since he was accompanied by Sasaki and Okauchi the couple did not have a moment to themselves. And now at the end of September Ryoma had returned to Oryo; but with the very fate of the nation resting on his shoulders he could not spare her more than a day or two. "And sometimes I wonder," Oryo continued in the same singsong tone, "if we'll ever have much time to ourselves at all."

When word arrived on the next evening that Katsura's return to Shimonoseki would be delayed, Ryoma decided he could wait no longer. He wrote a letter to the Choshu leader, expressing his anticipation that war was imminent, and his regret for not being able to see him, then returned to his ship with Okauchi and Toda to deliver the 1,000 carbines to Tosa and urge that *han* to put its military support behind Satsuma and Choshu.

The engine of the *Shinten Maru* clamored at full steam, propelling the small ship southeastward under a moonlit sky from Shimonoseki through the shimmering Sea of Suo. By midmorning of the second day out the ship headed southward through the Strait of Bungo, which separated the east coast of Kyushu from western Shikoku, and spread out into the vast blue Pacific. The autumn moon again shone in the clear night sky as the ship cut sharply northward around Point Ashizuri, the southwestern extremity of Shikoku, and continued at full speed into Tosa Bay. By the time she anchored at the Port of Urado, an orange sun had already risen in the east, and Ryoma was standing alone on the bow, filled with nostalgia at his first sight of Kochi in over five and a half years.

"Katsurahama," he uttered the name of the long sandy beach which welcomed him home beyond the crashing waves. To the left of the beach was the pine-studded Cape of the Dragon King, to the right the verdant Dragon-Head Cape, where someday would stand the magnificent bronze statue of Sakamoto Ryoma–the short sword at the left hip, the right hand inside the kimono grasping perhaps a pistol or perhaps a book of international law, the eyes squinting out at eternity and the vast Pacific. Ryoma stood on the foredeck of the steamer, squinting at the pines on the cliff above the beach, where six years ago he had confided in Hirai Kao his decision to flee Tosa. "No matter what happens," he had told her, "I swear to overthrow the Bakufu," but was nevertheless at an utter loss as to how he would do it. He had even wondered on that moonlit autumn night in 1861, which now seemed a lifetime ago, if he would ever see the beach of Katsurahama again. But now he was back, as the leader of a private navy, commanding a ship.

"Katsurahama," Ryoma repeated aloud, to which Okauchi, who had joined him on the foredeck, replied anxiously, "Yes, that's Katsurahama. But Sakamoto-san, what are you going to do? It would be dangerous for you to land without permission, or at least some kind of warning." Okauchi had cause to worry. Tosa opinion was divided among three opposing factions: those led by Inui, who were raring for war; those led by Goto, who supported Yodo's peace initiative; and the conservatives, who opposed it for fear of punishment by a Bakufu outraged at their lord's audacity. It was the conservatives whom Ryoma intended to urge to support Goto or Inui, depending upon how the Shogun would react to the peace plan. Okauchi rightly worried that if Ryoma, who was not only officially an outlaw, but one of the Bakufu's most wanted men, landed in Kochi without taking the necessary precautions, the pro-Tokugawa conservatives would not hesitate to kill him. "And the same goes for Toda-san," Okauchi said of the retainer of Lord Sanjo, the champion of the anti-Bakufu Loyalists.

"Take these," Ryoma said, reaching into his kimono and handing two letters to Okauchi. One of them was addressed to a Tosa minister by the name of Watanabe Yakuma, whom Ryoma had met briefly in Nagasaki. Ryoma had chosen to deal with Watanabe because, as he had told Okauchi earlier, "with Goto and Yui away in Kyoto, he's the only minister left in Kochi with any brains." Yoshida Toyo, who had hand-picked Watanabe over a decade before, would have certainly agreed. Ryoma's letter informed of his arrival at Urado Port aboard a Hiroshima steamer carrying 1,000 carbines, the likes of which people in Tosa had never seen, and of the latest news from Kyoto, including the reports of imminent war and the deployment of Satsuma and Choshu troops. Then the outlaw asked the minister, *"What's happening in Tosa? What's happening with Minister Goto? I heard in Shimonoseki that he's having a very difficult time proceeding with the plan in Kyoto. What's happening with Inui?"* In short, Ryoma would risk his life to convince the Tosa conservatives that this was their last chance, that if the Shogun refused to abdicate peacefully, then they must choose the Emperor over the Bakufu, or perish, and that they must not vacillate any longer.

The other letter, which Ryoma had received from Katsura before leaving Nagasaki, summarized the situation among the Satsuma and Choshu leaders, and the reasons why Tosa must fight on the side of these two clans.

"Deliver these to Minister Watanabe," Ryoma told Okauchi, "and arrange for me to meet with him as soon as possible." After telling Okauchi that he would wait for him at such-and-such a house in the little fishing village behind the pines, Ryoma lowered a small boat into the water on the port side of the ship, then yelled at the top of his lungs, "Toda-san, we're going ashore."

Lord Sanjo's retainer followed Ryoma into the tiny boat, which the latter paddled through the waves to the sandy beach. Okauchi remained aboard ship to steam slowly through the narrow, shallow estuary which was Kochi Bay, to visit Minister Watanabe in the castletown.

It was late afternoon before Okauchi reached Watanabe's home, informed him that Sakamoto Ryoma had returned to urge Tosa to support Satsuma and Choshu in Kyoto or be left in the dust after the Imperial forces would defeat the Tokugawa. War was imminent and Ryoma had brought one thousand rifles for Tosa's army if it would promise to fight. "And Ryoma asked me to give you these," he said, handing the two letters to the minister, who read them immediately. Watanabe was obviously stunned by the urgency of the situation, and agreed without hesitation to meet Ryoma that evening. "You say he's waiting near Katsurahama?" Watanabe asked.

"Yes."

"Then the Matsugahana Teahouse would be a good place for us to meet. It's just east of the castletown, north of Katsurahama, on the other side of the bay. Bring Ryoma there tonight at six."

"I will," Okauchi said with a low bow.

"But keep it secret," the minister demanded. He was as concerned for Ryoma's safety as he was for his own welfare. "Officially Ryoma's a criminal. I can't let people know I'm going to meet him."

Okauchi went directly to the little fishing village behind the pines near Katsurahama, to retrieve Ryoma. When the two men arrived at the Matsugahana Teahouse shortly after dusk, Watanabe and two others were waiting in a private room, which looked out into a lantern-lit garden.

Taking a seat with Okauchi opposite the three Tosa officials, Ryoma placed a long object–slightly wider than his sword and concealed in purple cloth–between himself and Minister Watanabe. On his right he placed his sword, and in his right hand held a cup, into which Watanabe poured unrefined *sake*. "I've brought this from home," the minister said, "because I thought that anything stronger might impede our discussion."

Ryoma relished the white, creamy sweet Tosa brew, the first he had had in years, then began lecturing the three elite officials about the urgency of the situation in Kyoto. He spoke in a slow, deliberate voice, backing himself up with facts, and avoiding the emotional rhetoric and theoretical dogma of so many of his comrades. His purpose for returning to Tosa had not been to convert its conservative elite to *Imperial Loyalism*, but to convince them to send troops to Kyoto to support Satsuma and Choshu. "A civil war is upon us," Ryoma said. "Two large companies of Satsuma troops, and three of Choshu, are expected to reach Kyoto any day now. Hiroshima has united with Satsuma and Choshu, and Lord Iwakura has assured them of the support of the Imperial Court." Then losing his composure, Ryoma slammed his fist on the floor and shouted, "It's only a matter of days before the fighting starts." His message hit the three officials like a brick in the face, as if awakening them from a dumb slumber. "That is, unless the Shogun agrees to abdicate peacefully, which he will not do without being convinced that he has no alternative. And this is why Tosa must," Ryoma paused to emphasize imperativeness, "I repeat, Tosa must support Satsuma and Choshu militarily, because one lousy piece of paper will not be enough to convince him." The "lousy piece of paper" was Ryoma's plan for peaceful restoration which Yodo had endorsed and Goto had delivered to the Bakufu in Kyoto in the form of a petition. "The Shogun must be forced into accepting the plan as his only alternative to total destruction."

"And if the Shogun should refuse even then?" Watanabe asked.

"Then he must be crushed militarily, as Saigo and Iwakura are so anxious to do." By mentioning the names of the two powerful leaders, Ryoma hoped to impress upon Watanabe the legitimacy of his plea. "Tosa only has a few days left to decide its own future. If Tosa fails to act now, then it will surely lose its chance to participate in the historical drama which is about to unfold in Kyoto. It will forfeit the opportunity to be of any significance in the new Imperial government which will replace the Bakufu." To emphasize the displeasure of Choshu and Satsuma over Tosa's vacillation, he told the officials of Katsura's recent likening of their clan to a "fickle woman," then took a deep breath, finished his cup of white *sake*, and as a final convincer removed the cloth cover from the rifle. "There are another one thousand of these aboard my ship," he said. "There is no better rifle in the world. It's British-made, and can fire seven consecutive rounds without reloading. One thousand Tosa troops armed with these rifles could take on an army of thirty thousand." Indeed the carbines which Ryoma had managed to purchase from the Dutch trader in Nagasaki were far superior to the guns of the Tokugawa armies, which consisted mostly of single-shot rifles and even muskets. "But one of the Choshu men told me just the other day that if Tosa won't accept them, then Choshu certainly will."

"Accept them?" Watanabe blurted. "Sakamoto-san, not only will we accept them, but we will use them, if necessary." In short, the three Tosa officials had agreed in principal to take military action against the Bakufu if the Shogun should refuse to abdicate peacefully, and the alliance between Tosa, Satsuma and Choshu, once and for all, seemed settled. "But we still have to convince Lord Yodo," the minister said.

"Can you?" Ryoma asked.

"After what you've just told us," Watanabe said, "I don't see that we have any other choice."

"Then I'll take another drink." Ryoma smiled, raised his cup for the minister to refill. To say the least, he was relieved. Not only would he be able to report to Saigo of Tosa's military support, and to Goto of the conservatives' endorsement of the plan for peaceful restoration, but he no longer had to worry about how he would repay the loan for the rifles.

Ryoma did not return to the little fishing village in the pines near Katsurahama until dawn the next morning. He slept undisturbed until early afternoon, when Okauchi came to inform him that Watanabe had already begun working to persuade Lord Yodo. "And," Okauchi added, "he asked if you wouldn't like to go home."

"Go home," Ryoma muttered. In fact, he had had no intentions of seeing his family. He was officially a criminal, and did not want to do anything to jeopardize them. "Go home," he repeated slowly, then got up to look out a window which faced the pines, because he did not want his friend to see the tears in his eyes. He had not been home since that rainy spring night years ago when he received the Yoshiyuki sword from his sister Ei, and fled Tosa with Sonojo.

"Yes, Sakamoto-san," Okauchi said. "Minister Watanabe said that he'd make the necessary arrangements with the administrative office for you to visit your family, and that there would be no problem, as long as you use discretion."

"Discretion," Ryoma laughed lightly to keep from weeping. He had longed to see his family for years, all the while wondering if he would ever see them again. "Discretion," he repeated, though not without a trace of sadness. "Here I am risking my life to bring them guns, and they tell me to use discretion to visit my own family." Again Ryoma laughed to himself, turned around to face his friend. "Tell Watanabe that I'll use discretion or anything else he wants But tell him that I want to see my family."

Ryoma invited Toda to accompany him to his brother's house, and that afternoon they took a small skiff northward, deep into the bay, until they reached the estuary of the Kagamigawa. "My sister Otome and I used to swim here as children," Ryoma told the Kyoto samurai, who seemed more impressed by the black and white tower of Kochi Castle, looming above the center of the town which extended to the northern bank of the river. Rather than risk attracting attention to themselves by taking the boat up the Kagamigawa, they alighted here and walked two miles along the river to Ryoma's home. The black tile roofs of the lower-samurai houses glistened in the late afternoon sun, dark orange persimmons hung heavily on the trees, and by the time they passed the Hineno Dojo Ryoma's nostalgia had peaked. But his heartbeat increased when they turned right down the narrow road leading to his brother's house just north of the river, and when he caught sight of his niece Harui, who screamed, "Uncle Ryoma!" he was ecstatic.

So was Harui, who had gotten married and borne two children since Ryoma had last seen her. She had also put on so much weight that Ryoma had more trouble than he expected, when, much to the surprise of the reserved Toda, he hugged her and lifted her off her feet. "Harui!" he hollered, forgetting his promise of discretion, then put her down and ran through the front gate of his house. Otome and Gombei were both there to greet him; in fact they had been waiting. The people at the administrative office had been so concerned with keeping Ryoma's return a secret, that they had notified Gombei beforehand, advising him to "use discretion." But like Ryoma, Otome had little use for discretion; unable, if not unwilling, to wait a second longer, she burst through the front door, and with tears in her eyes, literally threw herself at her brother, screaming "Ryoma! Ryoma! Ryoma!" so loudly that Gombei came running out of the house to calm her down.

"I almost forgot," Ryoma howled, putting his arm on Toda's shoulder, and introducing the samurai from Kyoto, who was obviously taken aback by the blatant display of emotion. If fact, Toda had never seen anything like it. The subdued behavior common among samurai families seemed foreign to the Sakamoto family. To Toda, who was born and raised among the traditional and intricately structured ambiance of the Imperial capital, Ryoma's family seemed more like a household of merchants than warriors.

"I'm back!" Ryoma said to his brother who was old enough to be his father, as they all sat in the living room, around a large wooden brazier.

"Yes, you are," Gombei said, trying to hide his emotions, which seeped from his eyes when he took his younger brother's hands to look at the scars from the near fatal attack almost two years before at the Teradaya.

"I've brought you a present," Ryoma said, grinned at his sister, then drew his revolver from his kimono. "An American Smith and Wesson, just like the one that saved my life in Fushimi," he said proudly, handing the pistol to Otome. As Ryoma had anticipated, his sister showed more interest in the revolver that did his brother.

"No, Ryoma," Otome said. "I couldn't take it from you."

"I'll get another one," Ryoma assured, unloaded the cylinder and began explaining to Otome how to shoot.

Otome had recently separated from her husband, a man much smaller than herself, whose womanizing the strong-willed woman would not stand for. Indeed Otome was a strong woman. It was Otome who had raised Ryoma after their mother died, reprimanded him when he cried, put a practice sword in his hand and insisted he take up fencing. As Ryoma had boasted to people all the way from Nagasaki to Edo, Otome was almost as tall as him, and weighed nearly as much. She could out-wrestle, out-swim, and out-ride many a man, and with a sword in her hand was a good match for most. She shunned housework and cooking, and excelled at the manly arts of poetry, music and drawing. It had not been mere flattery when Ryoma had written her two years ago, *"you have a reputation for being tougher than Ryoma"*; and now he was sure that Otome's reputation for marksmanship would soon spread throughout the castletown.

But not as quickly as word of his return. After all, the *ronin* and younger brother of lower-samurai Sakamoto Gombei, once known as a "runny-nosed, bed-wetting crybaby," and later as "Kochi's greatest boaster," was now famous throughout Japan as a leader of the movement to topple the Bakufu and restore the Emperor to power. He was the commander of a private navy, and mingled freely with the most prominent men in Japan, including feudal lords, the leaders of Satsuma and Choshu, high-ranking Tokugawa officials and celebrated scholars. The attempts at discretion by the administrative office notwithstanding, the news of Sakamoto Ryoma's homecoming spread so rapidly that by evening his house was filled with friends and relatives whom he had not seen in years.

The party was conducted in typical Tosa fashion. *Sake* cups were never empty, as Harui, her mother and several of the women guests were kept busy serving trays of sliced raw fish—bonito, sardines and horse mackerel; dried squid and octopus; small saucers of fresh laver, stewed vegetables and other condiments for local brew, which was ladled from a huge wooden cask at the center of the room. People sang to the music of a three-stringed *shamisen*, which Otome, Gombei and Ryoma took turns playing.

And while most had come to celebrate Ryoma's homecoming, others, namely several former members of the Tosa Loyalist Party, had other motives. "Ryoma," one of them burst out amid the drunken revelry, his voice barely audible for the music and singing that filled the house, "let's flee Tosa tonight."

"How can I flee?" Ryoma laughed. "I've already done that twice."

"You say you've come back on a steamer which belongs to Hiroshima?" another confirmed.

"That's right," Ryoma said, filling several *sake* cups.

"Then let's take it tonight to Osaka, so we can fight in the war in Kyoto."

"Yes," another man said, "if we don't side with Satsuma and Choshu this time, Tosa will be left behind in the dust."

These were Ryoma's sentiments exactly. But as he was unable to tell them of Minister Watanabe's promise of the previous night, he filled their cups and roared, "You're absolutely right! But wait just a little longer." Not only was Ryoma an expert at persuasion, but over the past several years he had become quite adept at the art of dissuasion, particularly when it came to hotheaded comrades whose drastic plans threatened common goals. At any rate, Ryoma was not about to let his friends undo the success he had achieved diplomatically in Kochi, before he could get to Kyoto to help Goto in a last-ditch effort to achieve a peaceful restoration.

After spending a week with his family, during which time Ryoma was officially pardoned for having fled Tosa, he could wait no longer to get back to Kyoto. The rifles had been unloaded, the terms of payment settled, and on the morning of October 1 the *Shinten Maru* was ready to sail. "We should reach Osaka tomorrow," Ryoma told Toda as they hastened through the castletown toward Kochi Bay.

Things, however, did not go that smoothly, despite Ryoma's impatience to leave. Although their ship did sail that morning, rough seas off the eastern coast of Tosa compelled them to take the longer route to Osaka, sailing west around Shikoku, and heading back through the calm waters of the Inland Sea. But when the *Shinten Maru* reached the Port of Susaki, there was engine trouble. "This ship will never make it," Ryoma groaned, then sent Okauchi overland to Kochi to arrange for the use of the *Butterfly*, the smaller, faster steamer which Tosa had recently purchased from Satsuma. It was on the *Butterfly* that the Kameyama Company had transported its initial shipment of 7,000 rifles to Choshu two years earlier, and it was aboard this same ship that Ryoma was now beside himself with impatience to get to Kyoto before the Great Play could begin without him. After having lost several crucial days, Ryoma finally left Tosa, steaming at full speed along the direct eastern route, despite the wind and the waves. When Ryoma reached Osaka-Kyoto the next day, news both ominous and auspicious awaited him.

A Declaration of Freedom

The hills east and west of Kyoto were aflame with bright autumn red as they always were at this time of year. The Kamogawa flowed through the center of the city like it had since the beginning of time, and its water was as pure as that of its offshoot, the Takasegawa. The age-old black pagoda of Toji Temple still caressed the crystal blue sky-line to the southwest, and as was common in late fall, a cold wind blew in from the northeast, cutting through Ryoma's worn out black jacket and ruffling his already disheveled hair. And although the Dragon had been in Kyoto during the Sweltering Summer of Frenzy, and seen the aftermath of Choshu's failed countercoup that had left much of the city in ashes, he had never before felt such intensity in the air.

Such was Ryoma's impression when he finally reached the Imperial capital amidst the death throes of the Tokugawa, but not before stopping along the way at his company's office in Osaka.

Ryoma removed his sword, sat down on the *tatami* floor with several of his men, and, as if by natural reflex, reached into his kimono for his Smith and Wesson. "Left it in Kochi," he muttered under his breath.

"Yonosuke and Sonojo have loaded the two hundred rifles on the *Yugao* at Kobe," Kenkichi informed.

"I'll have to get another one," Ryoma said to himself, as if ignoring Kenkichi's remark.

"Another ship?" Kenkichi asked.

"No. We'll need several more ships. But now I need another pistol. And as for those rifles, it looks like we might be needing them real soon."

"Might be?" Toranosuke exploded. "Ryoma, this just isn't right."

"What isn't right?" Ryoma asked, but in an annoyed tone because he already knew the answer.

"Satsuma's ready to begin the war right now, and we're here in Osaka tending to business matters," Taro protested.

"Where's Saigo?" Ryoma asked, again avoiding the subject of war, but swallowing hard to hide his anxiety.

"They say he's in Kyoto," Kenkichi said, gesturing with his chin in the direction of the nearby Satsuma headquarters.

"I see," Ryoma said. "And Taro," he looked hard at his nephew, "I want you to continue tending to business for the time being." Then grimly, "If there's a war," he finally mentioned the word, "we'll fight. But first I want to see if Goto has made any progress with our plan."

"But Ryoma..." Toranosuke attempted protest.

"If the fighting begins," Ryoma interrupted, "then I want all of you to go immediately to Kobe, take the *Yugao* and sink a couple Tokugawa warships before they even know what hit them." The idea seemed to please Ryoma's men, or at least satisfy them long enough for him to hurry to Kyoto to see Goto.

Ryoma, Toda, Okauchi and Sakutaro left Osaka by riverboat on the night of October 8, arriving in Kyoto the next morning. Having spent two and a half months on the Icarus Affair in Nagasaki and the conservatives in Tosa, Ryoma finally returned to the center stage of the Great Play in the Imperial capital. *"Things are much different in Kyoto and Osaka than they have been in the past,"* he wrote his brother later that day. *"Although everyone is talking much about the impending war, it still hasn't begun."*

The four men alighted the boat at the landing on the canal, near Tosa headquarters. "I have to see Goto," Ryoma said, as a muffled voice called him from behind. Ryoma reached for his pistol that was not there, turned slowly around, then smiled. "Seihei!" he shouted.

Mochizuki Seihei and Ryoma had grown up together in the same neighborhood of Kochi Castletown. A charter member of the Tosa Loyalist Party, Seihei was the older brother of Kameyata, the former student of Katsu Kaishu who had died three summers before in the Shinsengumi's surprise-attack on the Loyalists at the Ikedaya inn.

Seihei approached the three men. "Ryoma," he whispered, "what are you doing here?"

"I've come to see Goto."

"Let's talk inside," Seihei said nervously, gesturing toward Tosa headquarters, and looking around in all directions.

Soon they sat around a brazier in a small room at Tosa's Kyoto headquarters, where Seihei told them that the Shinsengumi had been looking for Ryoma for the past month. "They've apparently received a report that you'd be coming to Kyoto with three hundred of your men," Seihei said, drawing an amused howl from Ryoma, who shouted "Three hundred?"

"There are leaflets circulating the city informing people that the Tokugawa authorities are after Sakamoto Ryoma of Tosa and his band of *ronin.*"

"It looks like you have the Bakufu scared, Sakamoto-san," Toda snickered.

"You ought to be flattered," Sakutaro quipped. "You're a celebrity."

"Tokugawa police agents have been asking for you here at Tosa headquarters, and they know about your hideout at the Vinegar Store," Seihei said worriedly, but Ryoma was not the least taken aback. He was used to living the life of a wanted man. The Bakufu police had been after him since they had suspected that he was the man behind the Satsuma-Choshu Alliance. He had evaded their attempt on his life at the Teradaya almost two years before, and Ryoma was confident that they would not be able to catch him this time either, although the Bakufu also suspected that he was behind the plan to convince the Shogun to relinquish power. "So you must find another place to stay," Seihei urged.

"Well," Ryoma snickered, "it's comforting to know that some things in this city never change."

"What's that?" Toda asked.

"The *ronin*-hunters are still after me. But I have to talk to Goto right away. Where is he?"

"Right here, Ryoma," a voice answered through the sliding screen door.

"Goto!" Ryoma shouted, as the door opened. "What's happened with the memorial from Lord Yodo?"

"I've submitted it to the Shogun's prime minister," Goto informed, sitting on the floor opposite Ryoma.

As Goto explained, when he had reached Kyoto over a month before, Satsuma had been ready for war. Saigo, angry that Goto had arrived without the promised troops, was no longer willing to hold off his war plans. Okubo had recently returned from Choshu, where he had coordinated the final plans of attack with Katsura. On October 3, however, Goto suddenly received word from Komatsu that the plan for peaceful restoration was gaining support among the conservatives in Kagoshima.

Confusion over the wisdom of the great changes which the radicals of Satsuma and Choshu were about to effect, the irreversibility of these changes, and the unknown consequences that they might have on the social, economic and political structure of the Japanese nation, caused vacillation among the senior hereditary councilors in Kagoshima. While Saigo and Okubo might be willing to risk everything, including their lives, for the revolution, Satsuma's conservative elite began to worry about the possibility of failure, which would undoubtedly result in the loss of their inheritance. Nevertheless, as Saigo, Okubo and Komatsu still had the ear of their *daimyo*, and the overwhelming support of the Satsuma samurai, the councilors' hesitation had simply delayed their war plans. There were already thousands of Satsuma troops in Kyoto ready for war, and thousands more due to arrive soon.

"And there are thousands more in Choshu waiting for Imperial sanction to enter Kyoto," Goto continued. "All Saigo needs is an Imperial decree to declare war against the Bakufu, which Lord Iwakura is working to obtain at court."

"I don't understand why Komatsu would tell you about the problem in Kagoshima," Ryoma said, chewing nervously on his left thumbnail.

"Because Komatsu is not as radical as Saigo or Okubo. Although he's determined to bring down the Bakufu, he genuinely supports our peace plan."

"I see," Ryoma nodded approval, cracked his knuckles, then asked anxiously, "When did you submit the memorial?"

"On October 3. Komatsu urged me to submit it on that day. He warned me that war was about to begin, and if I planned to submit it, I'd better do so immediately." Goto reached into his kimono, produced two folded documents. "Copies," he said, and handed them to Ryoma.

The memorial consisted of two parts. The first was a personal statement from Yodo himself, which pointed out in grandiose language the grave danger Japan faced in the present state of national disunity, and stressed the need to reform the political order with the cooperation of all groups. The second part of the memorial was an eloquent version of Ryoma's Great Plan At Sea. The plan to save the nation, conceived of by a lower-samurai from Tosa who had never in his life held a position of official authority, and who was one of the most wanted men in Japan, had finally been presented to the Tokugawa Shogun.

Ryoma flung the copies on the floor. "Looks familiar," he snickered, drawing uneasy laughter from Goto.

"On the same day I submitted it," Goto said, "Fukuoka and I implored Saigo to wait a little longer, to give the Shogun time to answer."

"What was Saigo's reaction?" Ryoma asked, nervously wringing his hands.

"He said he'd wait five more days. Okubo objected, but Saigo and

Komatsu convinced him."

"Why?" Toda asked.

"They had no choice. Not only are they still waiting for an Imperial decree to declare war," Goto grinned cynically, "but our plan for peaceful restoration has apparently won support in Kagoshima."

"But six days have already passed," Sakutaro said.

"And still no war," Goto replied with an air of triumph. Three days after he had submitted Yodo's petition to the Bakufu, the Lord of Hiroshima, at Goto's urging, wavered in his war convictions, and followed the example of his counterpart from Tosa by advising the Shogun to abdicate peacefully. Just as Goto was gloating over what he presumed to be a diplomatic coup, he received word from Komatsu that a large contingency of Satsuma troops had reached Choshu, *en route* to Kyoto. News of this convinced the Hiroshima *daimyo*, who feared repercussions from a victorious Satsuma-Choshu Alliance, to rejoin the anti-Bakufu forces on October 8, the day before Ryoma had reached Kyoto. "But," Goto said optimistically, "Satsuma still hasn't received an Imperial decree to declare war."

"Have you received any word yet on the Shogun's reaction to the memorial?" Ryoma asked.

"Nothing certain," Goto said, drawing looks of dismay from the others.

"Nothing certain!" Ryoma echoed nervously.

"No." Goto looked grieved. "I've talked to the Shogun's chief advisor, Nagai Naomune, several times since then, but still there's nothing certain."

"Nagai Naomune!" Ryoma said. "I've heard about him from Katsu-sensei." Like Ryoma's mentor, the Bakufu's Great Inspector Nagai Naomune was a naval specialist who had studied under the Dutch in Nagasaki, and was thereafter instrumental in forming the Tokugawa Navy. The son of a Tokugawa-hereditary *daimyo*, Nagai had advanced through a series of important Bakufu posts, including commissioner-ships of the treasury, foreign relations and navy; and recently, at age fifty-one, had been promoted to the Shogun's Junior Council. Along with Prime Minister Itakura, Great Inspector Nagai was now one of Shogun Yoshinobu's two most trusted advisors. "Katsu-sensei once told me that Nagai was the most brilliant man in the Bakufu," Ryoma said. "And coming from Katsu-sensei, who rarely had anything good to say about any of the Tokugawa officials, that was quite a commendation."

"Apparently he's one of the few men with any brains whose advice Yoshinobu will listen to," Goto said. "In fact, convincing Nagai to accept our plan would be as good as convincing the Shogun himself."

"What did Nagai have to say about it?" Ryoma asked.

"He likes it."

"Goto," Ryoma suddenly exploded, "I want you to introduce me to Nagai right away."

"Are you crazy, Ryoma?" Goto shouted. "Nagai's one of the Tokugawa's great inspectors, and you're a wanted man. You couldn't get near him without being arrested."

Ryoma shook his head. "I think I could," he said. "If he's anything like Katsu-sensei said he was."

Goto cleared his throat. "I see. I'll arrange for you to meet him tomorrow," he said with a sardonic grin. The idea that Ryoma had no qualms about demanding an audience with one of the most influential men in the Bakufu, and would indeed get one, amused the Tosa minister to no end.

"Good!" Ryoma said. "And I've been thinking," he added.

"Yes," Goto said drolly, "you do a lot of that."

"The mint in Edo should be moved to Kyoto," Ryoma said, Toda muttered amazement, Goto scratched his head thoughtfully, and the other three Tosa men nodded grimly. "Once this is done, it won't matter whether the Shogun resigns or not."

"I don't follow you," Goto said.

"Without control of the mint, the Bakufu would be powerless, and there would be no reason for Yoshinobu not to resign." Unlike Saigo, Okubo, Nakaoka and other *Men of High Purpose*, Ryoma was less concerned with crushing the Tokugawa than he was with the practical business of setting up a new government. "If the Imperial Court has control of the mint, the Shogun can even keep his lousy title, if that's what it would take for him to agree to restore the power peacefully."

"But Sakamoto-san!" Toda exploded, "you've been saying all along that either the Shogun resigns or we go to war."

Ryoma shook his head slowly. "Go to war over a trivial matter like that?"

"Ryoma!" Goto hollered. "How can you call the Shogun's resigning trivial?"

"Because once the mint is moved to Kyoto, the Imperial Court will naturally be in control of the government and the military, and from that time on, the title of Shogun will be meaningless. There will be nothing to fear from a man whose title is only nominal, and who has no actual authority." The architect of the great plan to restore the political power to the Emperor did not limit himself to politics: finance, he deemed, was the key to the success of any government.

"Brilliant!" Goto exclaimed.

"But simply moving the mint to Kyoto would not necessarily give the court the authority to print money," Toda said. "The Tokugawa would still control more of the national wealth than any other family in Japan, including the Imperial Family."

"Then," Ryoma said matter-of-factly, "we'll have to counterfeit paper money."

"Ryoma!" Goto shouted in disbelief. "Counterfeiting is a crime!"

"So what?" Ryoma said. "Satsuma is already counterfeiting money," he said. "If Tosa, Satsuma and Choshu counterfeited a million *ryo* each, we'd have three million *ryo* to start the new government. Don't you think that would be a small price to pay for the future of Japan?" Ryoma added, then stood up to leave.

"Where are you going?" Seihei asked worriedly.

"To see Nakaoka at his military headquarters. I need his help to make sure that Saigo doesn't start a war for at least a few more days."

"You can't go alone, Ryoma!" Goto said in no uncertain terms. "Not with the Shinsengumi and every other Bakufu police unit in Kyoto looking for you."

"I'm sick of hearing about the *ronin*-hunters!" Ryoma sneered, then burst out laughing.

"What's so funny?" Goto said, annoyed.

"It's not that I don't appreciate your concern, Goto, but don't you think you're in as much danger as I am in this city? It can't be much of a secret that you're the one who submitted the memorial to the Bakufu; and if there's anything the Tokugawa police don't want, it's for the Shogun to relinquish power."

"I'm not so sure of that," Goto said. "You see," he added in a confessional tone, "I've recently met Kondo Isami."

"You've met Kondo Isami!" Sakutaro exploded indignantly, followed by disgruntled groans from Toda and Okauchi.

"Relax!" Ryoma demanded.

"But Kondo Isami!" Toda persisted angrily. "Who knows how many Loyalists that son of a bitch has either killed by his own sword or ordered killed by his band of assassins!" In fact, as the commander of the Shinsengumi, Kondo had legal authority to kill whomever he wanted, for whatever reason he saw fit.

"Yes," Ryoma agreed gravely. Then after casting a painful glance at Seihei, Ryoma asked Goto to tell him about his meeting with Kondo.

"I met him a few days before I submitted the memorial to the Bakufu, at Nagai's residence, where I was explaining the urgency of the situation," Goto said in a stressed tone. "While we were talking, Kondo dropped in."

"Didn't you have any qualms about meeting him?" Sakutaro asked bitterly.

"Yes and no," Goto said. "You see, I hate everything Kondo stands for, but I thought it would be beneficial to us if he agreed with our plans."

"Hmm," Ryoma muttered, nodding slowly.

"I also figured that if I showed any weakness Kondo might try to cut me right there on the spot. So I suppressed my personal feelings about him as best I could and decided to make him understand that the Shogun must resign in order to save the House of Tokugawa from total destruction." The welfare of the Tokugawa was a priority of the Lord of Tosa, and of the commander of the Shinsengumi. While Lord Yodo's incentive was based on a strong feeling of ancestral obligation, Kondo's was more immediate. The third son of a peasant from the Tama region, just west of Edo in the province of Musashi, Kondo had been adopted by a local fencing master, whose position he succeeded several years before founding the most dreaded police force in Japanese history. Kondo's blind dedication to the Tokugawa was not uncommon among the peasants of Musashi, which was under the direct control of the Shogun. After the notorious attack at the Ikedaya inn in the summer of 1864, the Shinsengumi's prominence as protector of the Tokugawa had greatly increased; and recently each of its some 250 members–most of whom had been recruited from among the *ronin* in Edo and Kyoto–were elevated to the rank of direct Tokugawa retainer, which gave them the right of audience to the Shogun himself. Nor did honors stop here for Commander Kondo, who was now the official bodyguard of the Shogun. Matters of social prestige aside, as head of the House of Tokugawa, Yoshinobu was Kondo's liege lord, on whose well-being the commander's livelihood, social position and indeed life now depended.

"By the look in Kondo's eyes after I first mentioned the Shogun's abdicating," Goto said with a sardonic grin, "I thought for sure he was going to draw his sword."

"What happened?" Ryoma asked, impressed with Goto's nerve.

"I explained to Kondo that even if the Shogun were to relinquish power, as long as the House of Tokugawa survives, its vast landholdings, which make Yoshinobu the wealthiest of all the lords, would certainly ensure him a position of power in a new Imperial government." While Goto was by no means certain of this assumption, he used it as a ploy to win over the dangerous commander of the Shinsengumi.

Goto's strategy seemed to work, as he learned soon after in a letter from Kondo asking to see a copy of the memorial submitted to the Bakufu.

"What did you do?" Ryoma asked.

"I showed him a copy, and explained it in detail."

"And?"

"Apparently Kondo isn't completely opposed to our plan, because he invited me to his headquarters to drink and discuss the matter further. Of course I have no intention of going to the headquarters of the Shinsengumi," Goto said derisively. "But for whatever reason, Kondo has guaranteed my personal safety in Kyoto." In fact, after their first meeting, Kondo issued an order to all of his men to neither harm nor show disrespect to Tosa Minister Goto Shojiro. "And so, Ryoma," Goto concluded, rubbing his hands over the brazier, "while my life, for the time being, doesn't appear to be in danger, yours most definitely is."

What Goto avoided mentioning, however, was that he himself had recently come very close to being assassinated by a Satsuma samurai. The incident occurred after one of several meetings with Saigo, during which he angered many of the Satsuma men by urging them to wait just a little longer before starting a war. When Goto left Satsuma's Kyoto headquarters it was after nightfall, and Saigo had given him a lantern which was emblazoned with the Satsuma crest. When the Satsuma samurai who lay in wait, sword drawn and ready to cut the Tosa minister just outside the outer gate, saw the mark of the Lord of Satsuma, he resheathed his blade and let Goto pass. Saigo heard of the incident soon after, and reprimanded the Satsuma man, telling him that at this critical time Japan could not do without the likes of Goto Shojiro.

Back to Ryoma. Despite Goto's warning, he left Tosa headquarters alone just after sundown, because, as he explained, "one of us is less apt to attract attention than two or three." Besides, it wasn't the danger to his own life that riled Ryoma's nerves as he hastened northward through the city. Rather, it was what he had, and had not learned from Goto that made Ryoma feel as if his head might burst from anxiety. The memorial from Lord Yodo urging peaceful restoration had been submitted to the Shogun, while Satsuma and Choshu troops waited for Imperial sanction to attack the Bakufu. "Will it be war or peace?" Ryoma wondered aloud and increased his pace. The great compromiser had finally returned to Kyoto, where he found two opposing plans simultaneously set in motion, and himself in the middle of a race against time for the Japanese nation.

A full moon was shining in the night sky when Ryoma reached the headquarters of Nakaoka's Land Auxiliary Force in the northeastern outskirts of the city. The headquarters consisted of one plain wooden rectangular building, large enough to accommodate two hundred men, and completely surrounded by a high white earthen wall. Tosa had originally purchased the minor estate in the previous winter to house its own troops; but when the plan was scrapped because of its distance from the center of the city, Goto and Sasaki arranged for Nakaoka to use it as a sanctuary for *ronin* in Kyoto, who were hunted daily by the Tokugawa police. Unlike Ryoma's company, the function of Nakaoka's band of over one hundred men was strictly military, but like the Kaientai it was an independent entity sponsored by Tosa and prepared to fight against the Tokugawa forces whenever war might break out.

Nakaoka greeted his old friend just inside the front gate. "Ryoma," he said as nonchalantly as if it hadn't been nearly three months since the two had last met, "it's about time you showed up. I've got something I want to show you." Nakaoka led Ryoma into a large room near the front of the building. "Here," he said excitedly, slid open the door with a loud bang, and disclosed an array of rifles and lances, and lanterns fastened at the ends of long poles to light the way for a night attack against the Tokugawa forces.

"It looks like you're ready, Shinta," Ryoma said, yawning.

"We're ready to fight at any time. My men are drilling daily. They can't wait for the war to begin." This was Nakaoka's way of telling Ryoma that he too opposed the plan for peaceful restoration. "It's too late," he said. "There's nothing left for us to do but fight. After Goto arrived without troops, and then convinced Saigo to postpone the attack, and even got the Hiroshima men to back down in their military support of Satsuma, I was ready to cut him down."

"Shinta!" Ryoma shouted angrily. "If you cut Goto, you'll have to cut me too."

"I've had enough of Tosa's vacillation," Nakaoka snarled. "They've gone back on their word too many times, and now while Goto is interfering with our plans for war, the Bakufu is surely sending more and more troops here from Edo."

"What made you change your mind about cutting Goto?" Ryoma asked drolly.

"Because Hiroshima is back on our side," Nakaoka said. "But Ryoma," he snapped, "this is no time to joke."

"I'm not joking." Ryoma was amused at Nakaoka's temperamental disposition. "But Shinta," he said in a more somber tone, "you know that Goto has submitted Yodo's memorial to the Bakufu. Now that we've come this far, don't you think we owe it to ourselves and our men to give the Shogun a chance to abdicate peacefully?" The great mediator found himself acting as the devil's advocate with both sides, promoting the peace initiative among those who wanted war, and defending the cause of war among the backers of the peace plan in case it should fail. In Tosa he had played the hawk, supplying that *han* with guns, while now in Kyoto he assumed the role of dove to give his peace plan one last chance. And while his words and actions may have seemed contradictory to those who didn't know him, Nakaoka knew Ryoma very well. "You can't expect the Shogun to give an immediate answer," Ryoma said. "Think about the pressure he must be under. He's being urged to restore the power to the Imperial Court after seven centuries of samurai rule. Either he relinquishes the power which his own family has held for over two and a half centuries, or he faces total destruction." Ryoma paused, took a deep breath. "We owe it to the future of Japan, Shinta, to give the Shogun a few more days to make his decision."

"The longer we wait, the more time the Bakufu has to send reinforcements from Edo," Nakaoka groaned. "The only way to unite Japan so that it will be strong enough to deal with the foreign threat is by first burying the Tokugawa, to be absolutely sure that it will never rise again."

"Civil war will give the foreign powers a perfect opportunity to attack," Ryoma countered. "And besides, Shinta, a war against the Bakufu will undoubtedly win wider support if we give the Shogun just a little more time to reply."

"Alright," Nakaoka muttered, his fists clenched tightly. "How long do you suggest we wait?"

"Another four or five days. If the Shogun refuses, or if he doesn't answer by then," Ryoma said with absolute conviction, "my Kaientai will be the first to join the Satsuma and Choshu forces to destroy him."

"Alright," Nakaoka said. "But I still don't think the Shogun will agree to resign without a fight."

"That's something we're going to have to find out. But Shinta," Ryoma grabbed his friend's arm, "I need your help to stall Satsuma, because with the way things are right now I don't think I can do it alone." In short, Ryoma needed the help of a leading proponent of war to convince Saigo to give his peace plan one last chance.

"Alright," Nakaoka said, a bit surprised at the lack of self-confidence in his otherwise overly confident friend.

"Good." Ryoma grinned. "And one more thing. Is there a place here I can sleep?" Ryoma was exhausted. He had been on the go constantly since leaving Nagasaki for Tosa, and now he could not return to his hideout at the shop of the lumber merchant just west of the Takasegawa in the Kawaramachi district, because it had been discovered by the Bakufu police. He was in desperate need of rest to prepare himself for the critical days ahead; but before laying down to sleep in a room which Nakaoka had provided, he scrawled out a short letter to his brother in Kochi, summarizing his trip back to Kyoto, and the critical state of things when he arrived in the Imperial capital. *"This is to let you know that as of today,"* he ominously concluded the last letter he would ever write to his family, *"I am alright."*

Ryoma slept at Nakaoka's headquarters, undisturbed until the next morning when a message arrived from Goto informing him that Nagai would see him at his Kyoto residence that afternoon.

Over the years Nagai had heard only good things about Sakamoto Ryoma from Katsu Kaishu and Okubo Ichio, men with whom he maintained a relationship of mutual respect, if not friendship. Nagai had also heard from the Lord of Fukui about Ryoma's private navy, which consisted almost entirely of anti-Bakufu *ronin* in Nagasaki; and recently word had it that the outlaw was in Kyoto with three hundred of his men to fight along side Satsuma and Choshu against the Tokugawa. In fact, Nagai knew that Ryoma was no less dangerous to Bakufu interests than were Saigo and Okubo of Satsuma, and Katsura of Choshu. And so, when the Shogun's chief advisor heard from Goto that Ryoma wanted to see him, his initial reaction was to have the outlaw arrested. "Preposterous!" Nagai shouted at Goto. "Isn't he aware of the risk he'd be taking by coming here?" When Goto answered affirmatively, and made the unheard of request that he treat the outlaw as if he were an envoy of the Lord of Tosa, Nagai acquiesced with a confused shrug. Then, when Goto informed the Shogun's chief advisor that it was actually Ryoma who was the mastermind behind Yodo's plan for peaceful restoration, he was suddenly anxious to meet him.

This is not to say that Nagai welcomed the downfall of the Edo regime, even by peaceful means. Nor did he harbor feelings of goodwill for the man behind the Satsuma-Choshu Alliance and the plan to topple the Bakufu, however peacefully. But Nagai was wise enough to realize that Ryoma's plan was far preferable to that which Satsuma and Choshu had in store, for the simple reason that it offered a way to save the House of Tokugawa from total destruction.

Nagai was staying at a villa in the precincts of a great temple, in the south of Kyoto. When the outlaw arrived at the outer gate of the villa later that morning, the Bakufu's great inspector was waiting for him, as attested by the cordial reception he received at the guardhouse when he identified himself by his real name.

Ryoma, in fact, was risking his life on Kaishu's evaluation of Nagai's character, and on his own conviction that the future well-being of Japan was riding on the decision that the Shogun must make within the next few days. It was for the goal of securing the desired decision that he surrendered his sword to a guard, whom he followed into the house, down a long wooden corridor to a large drawing room overlooking an exquisite garden, where he introduced himself to Great Inspector Nagai Naomune.

"I'm Sakamoto Ryoma, originally of Tosa," he said.

"Originally of Tosa?" Nagai repeated with an amused grin, although reason dictated that he have the outlaw arrested on the spot. "I've never heard anyone introduce himself quite like that before."

"Well, you see," Ryoma said in an exaggerated Tosa drawl, "I prefer to consider myself as belonging to all of Japan, rather than just Tosa." Ryoma paused momentarily, grinned widely, then added as nonchalantly as if he were commenting on the weather, "Because neither Tosa nor any of the other clans will be around much longer."

"I see," Nagai said in a confused tone, and to his own surprise found himself returning the outlaw's smile. Ryoma's outlandish remark, not to mention overwhelming physical stature, dark complexion, unkempt hair and worn out clothes might have given Nagai pause, but the hon-

esty in his eyes and his uncanny air of self-confidence which nevertheless radiated a childlike innocence immediately captured the goodwill of the great inspector. "Welcome, Sakamoto-san," he said.

As great inspector of the Tokugawa Bakufu, Nagai was in charge of
supervising general affairs for Edo, overseeing the conduct of the feudal lords, and exposing negligence on the parts of the various Bakufu
officials; but more than anything else, Shogun Yoshinobu counted on
his chief advisor for his extensive knowledge of the West, administrative skills, long experience in government, farsightedness and ability
to cope with crises. Nagai looked his fifty-one years, all the more so
for the great stress he was under as the most important advisor to a
shogun who was faced with the most momentous decision in the two
and a half centuries of Tokugawa rule. He was dressed immaculately
in royal blue silk, his hair freshly oiled and neatly tied into a topknot,
his expression somber in the presence of one of his government's
greatest enemies. "Please sit down," Nagai said, then looking hard
into Ryoma's eyes, added, "What you have to say must be exceedingly urgent for you to risk coming here like this."

Ryoma replied with a nod, and without wasting time on further formalities, sat down on the *tatami* floor opposite Nagai. "Not only won't
the clans be around much longer," he said, "but neither will the
Tokugawa Bakufu."

"What?" Nagai shouted, as if deeply insulted.

"If you'll excuse the bluntness of the question," Ryoma said, "I'd
like to ask if you really believe that the Bakufu has the military power
to defeat the combined forces of Satsuma, Choshu and several other
powerful *han*."

Nagai was stunned by the suddenness, if not frankness of the question; but since he had been consumed with this very problem since
Goto had submitted the memorial one week before, he regained his
calm and replied gravely, "Unfortunately, I think victory would be
very difficult to achieve."

"In which case," Ryoma answered without hesitation, his fists
clenched, his face thrust so far forward that Nagai could feel the heat
of his breath, "the only way to spare Japan the danger of foreign invasion, and the House of Tokugawa from total destruction, is for the
Shogun to restore the power to the Emperor."

A painfully long silence ensued, while Nagai stared hard into the
piercing eyes of Sakamoto Ryoma. "Just who is this man?" he thought
to himself. "Where does he get the audacity to come here and say such

things to me, a Tokugawa retainer?" But nevertheless Nagai recognized the bitter truth of the outlaw's words, as attested to by his evaluation of Ryoma years later: *"Sakamoto was an even greater man than Goto, and what he had to say was really something."*

"Because if the Shogun refuses," Ryoma continued, sitting up straight, his eyes ablaze with conviction, "we're going to have a civil war, which the Bakufu has no chance of winning. And a civil war would give France and England a perfect opportunity to invade Japan, and divide the spoils among themselves." Ryoma paused, then continued calmly, "Which brings me back to my main point. The only way for Japan to avoid foreign subjugation is for all of the clans, including the Tokugawa, to unite into one strong nation. But in order to do this, the Shogun must first restore the power to the Imperial Court. And he must do so without further delay, and take his place in a new Imperial government as an equal among other great feudal lords." Ryoma, of course, cared nothing for the social status of the Shogun, or of the feudal lords. His sole concern was for the welfare of Japan–specifically, establishing a modern government which would be representative of all clans and social classes, and which would be strong enough to handle the many problems which threatened the nation. But since convincing Nagai was a means to this end, Ryoma was willing to make whatever concessions were necessary, including guaranteeing the welfare of the Shogun and the House of Tokugawa.

"As you know," Nagai began speaking in a sad, deliberate voice, "Lord Yoshinobu is a son of the late Lord of Mito, who was the founder of *Imperial Loyalism*. Lord Yoshinobu cannot help but revere the Son of Heaven; it's in his very blood. He of all men is dedicated to the good of our sacred nation, and desires more than anything else to avoid a civil war and foreign subjugation. For this reason he would very much like to follow the sound advice of the Lord of Tosa, but fears that once he relinquishes his rule, Satsuma and Choshu will wrest the power from the Imperial Court and destroy the House of Tokugawa."

Nagai stopped speaking, and the room was silent. From the garden outside was the soft sound of running water trickling into a small pond, and the gentle singing of a single thrush. Ryoma nodded slowly, eventually releasing a long sigh because he well understood the Shogun's fears. "It's true that Satsuma and Choshu want nothing less than the absolute destruction of the Tokugawa," Ryoma said. "But the longer the Shogun waits to relinquish power peacefully, the more dangerous the situation becomes. Nagai-san," Ryoma suddenly hollered, slamming his fist on the floor, "leave Satsuma and Choshu to me. If Lord Yoshinobu will agree to restore the power to the Emperor immediately, I, Sakamoto Ryoma, promise on my life that no harm will come to him or the House of Tokugawa." The Dragon paused briefly, then in a tone which left no room for doubt, added, "But if the Shogun should refuse, I will personally see to it that he is destroyed."

Nagai was aware of Ryoma's influence with both Saigo and Katsura. He knew that it was Ryoma who had gotten these two former enemies to unite against the Tokugawa, and he knew from discussions with Kaishu, Okubo and Lord Shungaku that Ryoma was a man of his word. "Sakamoto-san," he said, "if you can guarantee that there will be no war if Lord Yoshinobu restores the power to the Emperor, I will do my utmost to convince him to make a decision immediately."

"I'll do my best," Ryoma vowed, raising his right fist. Then, with nothing more to say to the Shogun's chief advisor, Ryoma left him with nothing less than the fate of the Japanese nation on his shoulders.

Three days later, October 13, 1867, brings us back to the first page of this story, almost one month to the day before the ill-fated thirty-second anniversary of Ryoma's birth, and the end of his life.

Ryoma was beside himself with anxiety as afternoon turned into evening, and he waited with twelve others in his new hideout, located in the Kawaramachi district near the Kyoto headquarters of Tosa and Satsuma. The new hideout consisted of two small rooms above the storehouse of a soy dealer called the Ohmiya. The owner of the Ohmiya was a wealthy merchant who, like most of the townspeople of Kyoto, sympathized with the Loyalists. So when one of Saigo's men asked the merchant to hide Ryoma, he gladly obliged. He immediately cleared the rooms above the storehouse in back of his building, and attached a ladder to a rear window in case Ryoma should have to make a quick escape to the temple behind the house.

The atmosphere in the rooms this evening was tense, as it had been since early morning when word arrived from Goto that the Shogun had summoned the highest ranking officials from forty leading *han* to Nijo Castle to make a very important announcement. All of Ryoma's dreams, his life, and the fate of the Japanese nation were pending on the decision which the Shogun would make on this very day. Would he abdicate peacefully, or would Satsuma and Choshu, Imperial decree in hand, attack the Bakufu, causing internal chaos and possible foreign invasion?

"Damn it!" Ryoma groaned, drawing similar sentiments from several of the others. Sakutaro, Okauchi, Toda and Seihei were present, as were Yonosuke and Kenkichi, who had come earlier in the day from Kobe. Taro, Toranosuke, Kanema, Umanosuke, Shunme and Sonojo had also arrived this afternoon to wait for news from the Shogun's castle in Kyoto. "What's taking so damn long?" Ryoma wondered aloud. Goto had left for the castle just before two o'clock that afternoon, but now the sun had already set.

"It's getting late," Sakutaro groaned.

"It looks like we'll be going to the castle," Toranosuke muttered impatiently.

"Yes, the castle," Taro seethed, and Sonojo pounded on the floor.

"For the sake of the Japanese nation," Toda said in a crazed tone.

Ryoma drew his sword, which he held on his lap, and sat with his back against the wall, below a window which afforded a view of the Buddhist temple behind the house. "We'll wait a little longer," he said with resolve, then slammed the blade back into the sheath.

"Since you are prepared to die if things do not work out," Ryoma had written Goto earlier in the day, *"if you do not return from the castle I'll know what happened."* Goto had told Ryoma that if the Shogun refused to restore the power to the Emperor, then he would commit *seppuku* without leaving the castle. *"In which case my Kaientai and I will get vengeance by killing the Shogun; and regardless of what happens after that, I will meet you underground."* Such was Ryoma's own resolve to die if his peace plan should fail, in atonement for having interfered with the war plans of Satsuma and Choshu, and to initiate the war on the Bakufu.

A full moon was visible in the dark sky outside the window when the tense silence in the room was interrupted by the heavy thumping of footsteps on the staircase, and Ryoma, without thinking, drew his sword. "Sensei," a gruff voice called, the door slid open and several men jumped to their feet.

"Tokichi!" Ryoma called the name of the large man who stood at the threshold. Kenkichi had recently found Tokichi working as a deliveryman for a local restaurant; when he learned that Tokichi was a former sumo wrestler in Kyoto who had fought under the name "Sky Dragon," he recruited him as Ryoma's private servant and bodyguard. Ryoma immediately took a liking to the Sky Dragon, because, as he had drolly remarked, "we have the same name." Since Ryoma's return to Kyoto, Tokichi had prepared his master's meals and bedding, delivered and retrieved messages for him, and in general took care of his daily needs. "This has just arrived from Goto-san," Tokichi said, handing a letter to Ryoma, before leaving and closing the door.

All twelve men watched in anxious silence as Ryoma broke the seal, unfolded the letter and began reading. He held the letter so close to his face that the others could not make out his expression, but it was nevertheless apparent that he was weeping.

"What does it say?" Sakutaro gasped. The entire room was silent, because everyone present was sure that the news was bad.

Ryoma sat down in stunned amazement, no longer trying to conceal the tears that streamed down his face, and, in a voice overflowing with emotion, read Goto's message aloud: "*I've just left the castle. The Shogun has indicated that he will restore the political power to the Imperial Court.*"

"Ryoma!" Toranosuke screamed, as if he couldn't believe his ears, but the others remained silent, mesmerized by what they had just heard. Though Ryoma could not foresee the future, for now at least a bloody civil war had been avoided; and with the announcement of the end of Tokugawa rule, the Dragon had reached the final stage of his long and perilous quest for freedom.

Ryoma handed the letter to Kenkichi, then turned to Sakutaro. "Now I understand the true intentions of the Shogun," he said in a loud wail. "He's really made the right decision. He's really made the right decision. I swear I would die for him now." Ryoma was ready to give his life for the man whom until moments before he had been prepared to kill, because it was this very man whom Ryoma now considered the savior of the nation.

The Shogun's decision was not as selfless as Ryoma had at first assumed; rather Yoshinobu had finally realized that he had no other alternative. It had been apparent for some time now that support for the Bakufu among the clans was waning; not even such traditional allies as Owari and Fukui could be counted upon to side with Edo in case of war. The military aid which had been guaranteed by the French was not forthcoming, while Britain seemed sympathetic, if not outright supportive, of Satsuma and Choshu. In short, had Yoshinobu waited much longer, he would have found his armies engaged in battle with the combined forces of Satsuma, Choshu, Hiroshima and any number of other lords who had previously sworn allegiance to the

Tokugawa but would have no choice but to fight under the Imperial banner. In fact, on the day after the Shogun's announcement, just before he was to petition the court of his decision, a secret Imperial decree, bearing the Emperor's seal, was issued to the representatives of Satsuma and Choshu, authorizing their armies, and those of all the *daimyo* who were "loyal" to the Emperor, to attack and destroy the Bakufu.

Five days earlier, on the day that Ryoma had reached Kyoto, Saigo and Okubo had requested Lord Iwakura to draw up a decree. Iwakura immediately set to work on the document, which called for the destruction of the Bakufu, the punishment of the "traitor" Yoshinobu, and the deaths of the Lord of Aizu, who was the Bakufu's Protector of Kyoto, and his younger brother, the Lord of Kuwana, who was the Shogun's official representative in Kyoto in charge of inspecting the Imperial Court and its nobles. Iwakura entrusted the completed document to his confidant at court, Nakayama Tadayasu, the maternal grandfather and guardian of the fifteen-year-old Emperor. Early in the morning of the day after Yoshinobu had made the announcement at Nijo Castle, the Imperial decree, with the Emperor's seal secured by Nakayama, was smuggled out of court and presented to the representatives of Satsuma and Choshu, while on the previous day, the Emperor had pardoned Choshu of all crimes.

After the Shogun's decision had been announced in the Grand Hall of Nijo Castle, the representatives of the forty *han* assembled there were invited to offer their opinions. Never throughout the two and a half centuries of Tokugawa rule had a shogun discussed affairs of state with representatives of any of the clans, whose lords, after all, were his vassals. The unprecedented request for counsel was quite naturally met with strained silence from all but four of the eighty men present. Those who accepted were Komatsu Tatewaki, the Satsuma councilor who had advised Goto to delay no longer in submitting Yodo's memorial to the Shogun (Saigo and Okubo, still determined to crush the Bakufu militarily, had declined to even appear at the castle); Goto and Fukuoka of Tosa; and the top minister to the Lord of Hiroshima.

After each of the four men offered their praise to the Shogun for his momentous decision, it was Goto who got to the point. "Your Highness," he said, sitting, like the others, prostrate on his knees so that his face nearly touched the *tatami* floor in front of Yoshinobu's pedestal, "it is of the utmost importance that you inform the court right away of your decision."

As Yoshinobu had already suspected that the Imperial decree for war would soon be issued, he was not surprised when Goto informed him to this effect. "I see," he said with a grim nod, an indication of agreement. To be sure, Yoshinobu also feared that Satsuma and Choshu might start a war before he could inform the court of his decision to restore power; and he was equally worried that his two most loyal vassals, the Lords of Aizu and Kuwana, bitterly opposed as they were to restoration, might make the first strike, and so give Satsuma and Choshu an excuse to attack even before Imperial sanction could be obtained. But once the court approved the Shogun's decision, it would become legal, and his enemies would no longer be able to justify a first strike. That is, of course, unless the court were to refuse to accept the restoration.

"I'll follow your advice," the last Shogun told the four representatives, all of whom retained their prostrate positions, "but you must first make sure that my decision will be accepted by the court." Yoshinobu was aware that the powers that be in the Imperial Court opposed the restoration. Although Lord Iwakura had indeed succeeded in cajoling the Emperor's grandfather into obtaining the Imperial seal on the decree of war, the leading court officials rightly reasoned that since the court had not ruled in over seven centuries, it did not know the first thing about governing.

Goto and the others readily accepted Yoshinobu's request, and on the following day paid a visit to the court chancellor, urging him to accept the restoration of power immediately. "I cannot make such a decision on my own," the old man said curtly, avoiding a direct reply. Like all other Bakufu supporters at court, the chancellor was not only aware of his own ineptitude to govern, but was also worried that once the restoration became official, he may very well be replaced by one of the Five Banished Nobles, still in exile at Dazaifu.

"But you must," Goto implored. "With the Imperial decree for war already issued, you must do so immediately."

"Since I am a member of the Imperial Court, I am not allowed to commit *seppuku*," the chancellor complacently retorted, alluding to the ancient custom by which a samurai could atone for his shortcomings or failures by self-immolation, but a court noble could not.

Aware that this was indeed true, but determined that the chancellor would nevertheless approve Yoshinobu's decision, the mild-mannered Komatsu astonished all present when he said with a sinister grin, "If you don't approve the Shogun's decision immediately, I have an alternative to *seppuku*."

Komatsu's remark apparently worked, because later that day Imperial approval was issued, and the mandate for war which had been handed down to Satsuma and Choshu on that same morning was, for all means and purposes, annulled. When Goto asked Komatsu later if he had intended to kill the chancellor by his remark of an "alternative to *seppuku*," the Satsuma councilor answered with an amused look on his face, "I never intended anything of the sort. I was just intimidating him a little."

The distraught chancellor was not the only one concerned with the Imperial Court's inability to govern the nation. Like the leaders of the powerful domains of Satsuma, Choshu, Hiroshima, Tosa and Fukui, Ryoma had also foreseen the problem. This was why he had included in his initial restoration plan the formation of upper and lower legislative houses to represent the Japanese people. And this was also why, while Saigo, Okubo, Goto and Fukuoka prepared to return to their domains to report the events in Kyoto, the former outlaw Sakamoto Ryoma got down to the more practical business of devising a plan for the new government.

On the night of the day after the Shogun's announcement, Ryoma summoned Yonosuke and Toda to his hideout above the storehouse of the soy dealer. The air was cold, and the three men huddled around a rectangular wooden brazier at the center of the room. Partially buried in the hot ashes of the brazier was an open pot of steaming water; inside the pot set a large flask of *sake*. Ryoma's bedding was laid out near one of the walls, where he had napped for an hour or two before his two friends arrived. "Just because the court has agreed to accept the restoration of power from the Shogun," Ryoma said, his eyes bloodshot from lack of sleep, "doesn't mean that it's in a position to govern."

"What exactly do you mean, Sakamoto-san?" Yonosuke asked, as Ryoma's servant, Tokichi, took the flask from the pot of water and filled three cups.

"Today the court officially accepted the restoration of the political power from the Shogun, right."

"Yes." Yonosuke nodded, sipping hot *sake*.

"But think about it," Ryoma said. "The Emperor is just a boy. And as for the Imperial Court, it hasn't ruled for over seven hundred years.

You can't very well expect the court nobles to know how to handle affairs of state."

"True," Toda admitted with chagrin, then drained his *sake* cup. Toda's distress was understandable. After all, he was a retainer of Lord Sanjo Sanetomi, the leader of the Five Banished Nobles and champion of the Loyalist movement.

"And although we must establish a democratic form of government, whereby the people will be able to elect their own representatives," Ryoma echoed ideas he had heard years before from Katsu Kaishu, Okubo Ichio and Kawada Shoryo, "most of the farmers and merchants don't know any more about governing than the court nobles do." The common people, who had been suppressed by their samurai overlords for centuries, had no conception of Western democracy; most of them had no education at all, and were more concerned with simply making ends meet. "Which leaves only a small number of men who have the ability to govern," Ryoma said, then drained his *sake* cup.

"You're referring to the few able court nobles and *daimyo*, and some of the more talented samurai, right?" Yonosuke said.

"Yes. But since our goal is to set up a democracy, we must include commoners who have ability. But we must act quickly, before the restoration document that the Shogun submitted to the court today becomes nothing more than wastepaper."

"What do you mean?" Toda asked.

Ryoma picked up the flask, refilled the three cups. "Tokichi," he called, "bring more *sake*." Then rubbing his hands over the burning coals of the brazier, answered Toda's question: "War might still break out if the Bakufu and its allies, particularly Aizu and Kuwana, refuse to cooperate; or even worse, if they interfere."

"But they can't interfere," Toda protested. "The political power has already been restored to the court."

"Don't be so naive," Ryoma snickered. "You don't think that the Shogun's most loyal vassals are going to accept his resignation that easily, do you?" Indeed, at this very moment Aizu and Kuwana, infuriated now with Yoshinobu, were, with the help of the Shinsengumi and other equally enraged Tokugawa police units, contemplating burning Satsuma's Kyoto headquarters, occupying the Imperial Palace, kidnapping the Emperor, and taking him to the Tokugawa fortress of Osaka Castle. For although the Shogun had indeed restored the power to the court, the pro-Tokugawa forces knew that the revolution was like a game of chess: whoever controlled the Emperor controlled the nation. "That's why we must form a government quickly," Ryoma said, "to gain the confidence of the people so that Aizu and Kuwana have no choice but to accept."

"I see," Toda said, as Tokichi replaced the empty flask with a full one. "But what do you have in mind, Sakamoto-san?"

"I've been thinking about it all day," Ryoma said. Without bothering to stand up, he slid on his knees over to the desk at the other side of the room; and while Toda and Yonosuke watched over his shoulder, the lower-samurai from Tosa who had no official authority whatsoever, outlined in his typical sloppy script the posts for the new Japanese government.

1) The court noble with the greatest integrity and vision should be selected to serve as Chief Imperial Advisor, to assist the Emperor in all affairs of state.

2) Imperial princes, court nobles and feudal lords, with the greatest integrity and vision, should be selected as ministers to assist the Chief Imperial Advisor and help him decide matters of state.

3) Councilors should be selected from among the court nobles, feudal lords, leading samurai and the people at large to participate in the conduct of state affairs, and to assist the ministers.

Ryoma felt that Japan would eventually have to adopt a completely democratic form of government if it was to develop into a modern state capable of taking its place among the most powerful nations of the world. He would have therefore preferred to ignore completely the social positions of the lords, nobles and princes, but he knew that Japan was not ready for such a giant leap forward. Similarly, Ryoma would have liked to establish the highest office of the nation along the lines of an American president who would be answerable directly to the people, rather than a chief advisor who served a sovereign. But he was also aware that even his most progressive allies, including Saigo, Okubo, Goto and Katsura, were no more ready to abolish the Imperial system, than they were to turn their backs on their feudal lords.

"What do you think?" Ryoma said after he finished writing.

"Exactly who do you have in mind to fill these posts?" Toda asked.

"Probably the same men you do," Ryoma said, yawing loudly. "But right now I'm exhausted. We can discuss it in the morning." Then calling his servant, "Tokichi, put out some bedding for these two."

"What will happen in the morning?" Yonosuke asked.

"I'm going to Satsuma headquarters to see what Saigo thinks about this," Ryoma said, waving the document in front of him.

"I see." Yonosuke nodded, as Toda followed Tokichi into the next room. "Sakamoto-san," Yonosuke said, "I'm going to Osaka tomorrow."

"What for?" Ryoma muttered. He was already sprawled out in his bed, his eyes shut.

"To get you a pistol. With the way things are in Kyoto now, you aren't safe without one." Although Sakamoto Ryoma had officially ceased to be an outlaw the moment the Shogun relinquished power, the Tokugawa police who had been hunting him since the attack on the Teradaya nearly two years earlier, were determined now more than ever to reap vengeance on the man most responsible for toppling the Bakufu. Ryoma's men suspected as much, and although he had changed his hideout from the shop of the nearby lumber merchant to the storehouse behind the shop of the soy dealer near Tosa headquarters, Yonosuke, Taro and several others had been after him recently to get another pistol to replace the one he had left in Kochi. "Sakamoto-san," Yonosuke called out, but Ryoma was already snoring loudly.

Ryoma, however, was unable to sleep for long. He was anxious to get back to his trading business in Nagasaki, and to rejoin his wife. But as he believed himself to be one of the few men in Japan with the ability to devise a plan for the government, he was determined to complete the task before getting on with the rest of his life. And although he wished for the counsel of Kaishu's Group of Four, he was resigned, as usual, to act alone. The room was cold when he got out of his bed, lit a candle on the desk, and commenced writing the general plan for the new Japanese government. Like his restoration plan on which it was based, it consisted of eight points.

1) The most able men in the country should be invited to become councilors.

2) The most able lords should be given court positions, and meaningless titles of the present should be eliminated.

3) Foreign relations should be conducted through proper deliberations.

4) Laws and regulations should be drawn up. When a new code, free of weaknesses, has been agreed upon, the lords should abide by it and have their subordinates implement it.

5) There should be upper and lower legislative houses.

6) There should be army and navy ministries.

7) There should be an Imperial guard.

8) The Imperial nation should bring its valuation of gold and silver into line with international usage.

These points should be taken up with two or three of the most able and farsighted samurai; then, when the time comes for a conference of lords, X should become head of the conference, and respectfully suggest to the court that these steps be proclaimed to the people. Whoever then protests disrespectfully against such decisions should be resolutely punished, and no deals should be made with the powerful or the nobles.

The X whom Ryoma would appoint head of the conference of lords, was none other than Tokugawa Yoshinobu, the former Shogun whose decision had now made the formation of a new government possible. By including Yoshinobu, Ryoma hoped to appease the Tokugawa allies so as to avoid the still very real possibility of civil war.

Satisfied with the plan, Ryoma signed his name at the bottom, then returned to an outline of official governmental posts that he had composed earlier in the night.

"Sakamoto-san," Yonosuke called from the next room, before joining Ryoma. "What are you doing awake?"

"Filling in the names."

Looking over Ryoma's shoulder, Yonosuke read the names of the men to whom Ryoma intended to entrust the leadership of the new government. The Lords of Satsuma, Choshu, Tosa, Fukui and Uwajima were on the list, as were several court nobles, including Lord Iwakura. As councilors Ryoma named Komatsu, Saigo and Okubo of Satsuma; Katsura of Choshu; Goto of Tosa; financial wizard Mitsuoka Hachiro of Fukui; and Yokoi Shonan of Kumamoto. "But Sakamoto-san," Yonosuke said in a puzzled tone, "you're name is not on this list." Ryoma's right-hand man had every reason to be confused. After all, there was nobody who played a more important role in toppling the Bakufu than Ryoma. It was Ryoma who had united Satsuma and Choshu; it was Ryoma who had devised the plan for restoration; and now it was Ryoma who was proposing the plan for a new government. "How can there be a government without you in it?" Yonosuke exclaimed.

"Simple," Ryoma snickered. "It's my way of making it up to Satsuma and Choshu for stopping them from fighting the war they wanted so badly. Anyway, in order to get Japan on the right track for the future, I have to be very careful not to create animosity between the men of Satsuma and Choshu who wanted war, and Goto and myself who didn't."

"Then why have you included Goto's name of the list, but not yours?"

"Because I think Goto belongs in the government, whereas I don't."

"You don't? But why?"

"Because I've already accomplished what I set out to do," Ryoma said.

"You mean cleaning up Japan, don't you." Yonosuke understood Ryoma perhaps better than anyone else.

"Yes, Yonosuke," Ryoma snickered. "Anyway it's not good for one man to take all the credit for a job well done."

"Why?"

"Because after he's accomplished eighty or ninety percent of something, he ought to let others finish the last ten or twenty percent for him. Otherwise, he might cause bad blood by keeping all the glory for himself."

"I see," Yonosuke said, a bit taken aback. During the four years that he had known and served under Sakamoto Ryoma, the man who would become one of Japan's greatest foreign ministers had never ceased to be amazed by his mentor's understanding of human nature, nor impressed with his selflessness.

"Better get some sleep," Ryoma said, blew out the candle and went to bed.

The next morning Ryoma and Yonosuke went to the nearby Satsuma headquarters to present the new government plan to Saigo.

"Sakamoto-san," Saigo the Great boomed upon greeting the two men in the reception room, "I had intended to visit you today."

"I saved you the trouble." Ryoma grinned at Saigo, to whom he could not help but feel he had done a slight injustice over the past few months. But now he had come to make amends, by, in Ryoma's own words, "letting Satsuma and Choshu finish the last ten or twenty percent of a job well done."

"Sakamoto-san," Saigo's face was grim, "I wish you'd stay here with us, where you'd be safe. Things are very dangerous in this city right now. I have no doubt that the Shinsengumi, among others, is looking for you, as it is us." Saigo was correct. Just as Kondo Isami's police force was after Sakamoto Ryoma, who it still believed had returned to Kyoto with a band of three hundred *ronin*, it had also decided that the three Satsuma leaders–Saigo, Okubo and Komatsu–must be eliminated as well. In short, Kondo's sources told him that, along with the court noble Iwakura Tomomi, these were the four men most responsible for the Bakufu's downfall.

"I have something to show you," Ryoma said, ignoring the warning. He was content with his new hideout. At his own private quarters above the storehouse of the nearby soy dealer he could do as he pleased, while he felt that the restrictive atmosphere in any of the *han* headquarters, even that of Satsuma where he was always welcome, would interfere with his planning.

"What's that?" Saigo said.

"I think Okubo and Komatsu should see it as well."

"Certainly," Saigo said, then sent for the two other members of the Triumvirate of Satsuma.

Soon after, Okubo and Komatsu joined them, and Saigo asked Ryoma what it was that he wanted to show them.

Ryoma produced two folded documents from his kimono. After handing them to Saigo, he sat in a corner of the room, away from the others, his back to a wooden post. "A plan for the new government," he said.

Saigo read both documents carefully, handed them to Okubo, then gave Ryoma a puzzled look. "Sakamoto-san," he said, almost suspiciously, "your name is not on this list." Saigo's suspicion was not uncalled for, although he had never before doubted Ryoma's integrity. But for the man who was most responsible for persuading the Shogun to relinquish power not to include himself in his own plan for a new government, was beyond Saigo's comprehension.

Ryoma nodded slowly. "Saigo-san," he said in a lazy Tosa drawl, "you ought to know that I could never stand a government job."

"What?" Saigo gasped, drawing a grimace from Ryoma, who continued. "Leaving for work every morning at the same time, and coming home every evening at the same time would make me crazy with boredom." Ryoma's decision, in fact, was not quite as selfless as it may have seemed. To be sure, he had spent the past five and a half years struggling and risking his life to topple the Bakufu, and to achieve a strong, democratic government in Japan. But this had never been his ultimate goal, which was rather the attainment of simple freedom. Now that he had finally eliminated the biggest obstacle to this goal, Ryoma wanted more than anything else the freedom to be, the freedom to think and the freedom to act as he chose. But Ryoma's was by no means a selfish goal; rather his own personal freedom was deeply intertwined with that of his friends', and with the well-being of the new nation, which depended more than anything else on economic development through international trade. And it was on the well-being of Japan which Ryoma had based all his hopes and dreams.

"If you're not going to be in the new government," Saigo said, still looking suspiciously at Ryoma, "what do you plan to do?"

Ryoma leaned back against the wooden post, folded his arms at his chest and said with his usual nonchalance, "I think that I just might give the whole world to my Kaientai." Thus was Ryoma's Declaration of Freedom, which, if nothing else, relieved Saigo of any doubt he might have had concerning Ryoma's good intentions. All three Satsuma men stared in amazement over Ryoma's curious remark. As did Yonosuke, who would never know exactly what Ryoma meant by the remark, nor would he ever forget it. In fact, from this day on, and for years to come, Yonosuke was wont to compare the *ronin* who was his mentor with the most influential man of the most powerful domain in Japan: "It was at that time," Japan's greatest foreign minister would repeat over and over again, "that I realized Ryoma was a far greater man than even Saigo himself."

"I see," was all that Saigo the Great could say to Ryoma at this point. Then after a short pause, "But who is Mitsuoka Hachiro of Fukui?" he asked. Saigo knew, and indeed approved of, all the people Ryoma had listed, except for the Fukui samurai Mitsuoka Hachiro. This was Lord Shungaku's former financial advisor who had four years ago helped convince his *daimyo* to loan Ryoma 5,000 *ryo* for Kaishu's naval academy in Kobe.

Ryoma moved closer to the others, and sat up straight in the formal position. "When it comes to financial affairs," he said, "Mitsuoka has more talent than any man I know. And that's why we need him."

"How's that?" Komatsu asked.

"Because without a solid financial base the new government will never succeed," Ryoma stated matter-of-factly. All the names on Ryoma's list belonged to men who had demonstrated superior talent over the past years. The lords who would be ministers were selected for their farsightedness, and the loyalty they commanded among their people. Katsura, Goto and Okubo were superb politicians; Saigo was a natural leader; Iwakura was a master of political intrigue; Yokoi a political genius. But among them, only Mitsuoka, a former student of Yokoi's, had demonstrated genius in financial affairs, filling Lord Shungaku's treasury by devising a system to sell Fukui products throughout Japan, and establishing a trading office in Nagasaki. "We need Mitsuoka to handle the financial affairs for the new government," Ryoma insisted.

"Financial affairs," Saigo repeated, almost stupidly. "Yes, we must have a financial expert in the government." When it came to monetary matters, Saigo was unable to argue with Ryoma, who after all had quite a reputation for economic prowess. In fact, the great military commander who had captured the hearts and minds of samurai throughout Japan, had never even once considered the matter of finance.

"Where is Mitsuoka now?" Okubo asked.

"Under house arrest in Fukui," Ryoma replied.

"House arrest?" Saigo repeated grimly. He too had suffered a similar fate in exile years before, and for similar reasons, as Ryoma proceeded to explain.

"Yes, house arrest, in spite of all his talent," Ryoma said with disgust. "It's a complete waste. As you know, Fukui has been under the control of conservatives for the past several years. The suppression of the Loyalists there was nearly as bad as it was in Tosa. But with the way things are now, I think I can convince Lord Shungaku to let me see Mitsuoka, and perhaps bring him back with me to Kyoto," Ryoma said.

"Sakamoto-san," Saigo said, "I leave the matter entirely to you." This was the great man's way of saying that Satsuma had accepted Ryoma's plan for the new government, although Saigo was still unaware that Ryoma intended to appoint the former Shogun as head of the conference of lords.

The Price of Freedom

Satsuma, aware of the ire of Aizu, Kuwana and the Shinsengumi, had not abandoned its war plans. "We must crush them while they're down, to be sure they can never rise again," Saigo and Okubo had concluded with Lord Iwakura, before leaving Kyoto with Komatsu two days after their meeting with Ryoma. First they would go to Choshu to plan with their allies the deployment of troops to the Imperial capital, after which they would return to Kagoshima to inform Lord Hisamitsu of the turn of events in Kyoto.

Before leaving for Fukui, Ryoma sent Sakutaro to Nagasaki. He had recently received a letter from Sasaki, summoning him there to collect the indemnity money from Kii Han, for the sinking of the Iroha Maru in the previous spring. It was through this money that Ryoma planned to "give the whole world to my Kaientai," but since he had a government to form first, he sent Sakutaro in his place. "After we deduct the cost of the ship and rifles we lost at sea," Ryoma told Sakutaro just before the latter left for Osaka to board a westbound steamer, "we'll still have forty thousand ryo left. And that's more gold than the annual income of some the daimyo."

The Lord of Fukui had had his own doubts about the wisdom of restoring the power to the court, not the least of which concerned the true intentions of Satsuma and Choshu. "He's worried that Satsuma and Choshu are planning to control the new government," Goto told Ryoma just before the Kaientai commander and a minor Tosa police official, Okamoto Kensaburo, left Kyoto for Fukui on the afternoon of October 24.

Okamoto was an old friend of Ryoma's who had been active in the Loyalist movement under Takechi Hanpeita. His respect for Ryoma, who was seven years his senior, was no less than that of the men of the Kaientai. The two Tosa men traveled eastward from Kyoto, to the ancient town of Ohtsu on the southern shore of the scenic Lake Biwa, whose natural beauty has been the stuff of poetry through the ages. Having spent the night at Ohtsu, they walked northeastward along the western bank of the expansive lake, then continued north toward Fukui.

While Ryoma had no qualms about inviting Mitsuoka Hachiro to participate in the new government, he had been troubled as to how he would ask the same of Matsudaira Shungaku, who, despite their close rapport, was after all one of the most powerful lords in Japan. Furthermore, Ryoma respected the Lord of Fukui far too much to simply tell him that he had included him in the list of ministers. "That'll never do," Ryoma had told himself while still in Kyoto, and instead asked Goto to arrange for Lord Yodo to urge Shungaku by letter to come to Kyoto to participate in the government. It was the arrival of Yodo's letter from Kochi which had kept Ryoma waiting in Kyoto for two weeks after he had already decided to go to Fukui; and it was with this letter in hand that he reached Fukui Castletown early in the afternoon of October 28, the white-walled main tower of the great citadel rising in the cloudless sky.

After procuring lodging at the Tobacco Inn, where he had stayed during his last trip to Fukui several years before, Ryoma sent Okamoto to the administrative office to request an audience with Lord Shungaku.

"But Ryoma," Okamoto had said before leaving, an awkward grin on his face.

"What?" Ryoma muttered, half asleep, his head resting on the bare *tatami* floor.

"Don't you think you should at least get cleaned up before you see Lord Shungaku?"

Ryoma raised his head from the floor. "On your way out," he said gruffly, "tell the owner of this place to heat up the bath."

This Okamoto did, and he also asked the owner's wife to lend Ryoma some clean clothes, and to comb and oil his hair and tie it in a topknot. When he returned to the Tobacco Inn a few hours later, he found Ryoma bathed, groomed and dressed in a freshly laundered kimono and jacket, although he still had on the same dirty *hakama* he always wore.

"What's so funny?" Ryoma growled.

"Nothing," Okamoto snickered.

"Then what are you snickering about?"

"It's just that I've never seen you look so..." Okamoto paused.

"Look so what?" Ryoma said with a scowl.

"So clean," the younger man said, laughing. "But it's a good thing," he added quickly, as if to appease, "because I've arranged for you to meet the *daimyo* this evening."

"Good. That'll give me time," Ryoma said.

"Time for what."

"To have my picture taken." Ryoma was so impressed with the way he looked that he had arranged for a photographer in the castletown to take his picture in the garden behind the Tobacco Inn.

That evening Ryoma went to the castle, where Lord Shungaku received him in his drawing room. The *daimyo*, seated in a large wooden chair upholstered with red velvet, was flanked by two samurai attendants. "Welcome, Ryoma," Shungaku said with an amused grin. The last time they had met was in the previous summer at the Fukui estate in Osaka, when Ryoma asked him to write the letter to Lord Yodo advising self-restraint in dealing with the British over the Icarus Affair.

Ryoma dropped to his knees, bowed his head to the *tatami* floor.

"Get up, Ryoma," Shungaku said good-naturedly. "If I've said it once, I've said it a thousand times. That posture just doesn't suit you."

Ryoma sat up straight, handed Yodo's letter to Shungaku, then summarized the recent events in Kyoto, and, to the best of his knowledge, the intentions of Satsuma, Choshu and the Imperial Court.

When Ryoma had finished speaking, Shungaku read Yodo's letter, which urged that he come to Kyoto *"for the all-important business of forming a new government."* After some thoughtful hemming and hawing, but not without a look of self-satisfaction, Shungaku refolded the letter, handed it to one of his attendants and asked Ryoma his real reason for coming to Fukui.

"To request that Mitsuoka Hachiro be allowed to participate in the new government," Ryoma said bluntly.

Shungaku gave Ryoma a hard look. "You know that Mitsuoka's under house arrest."

"Yes. For expressing Loyalist views against the Bakufu," Ryoma said, but with a trace of sarcasm which drew harsh looks from Shungaku's attendants. "If you'll forgive me," Ryoma continued, "the Bakufu is a thing of the past. But now Japan needs Mitsuoka for the future."

It was no secret to Shungaku that the man who sat before him was one of the main reasons why the Bakufu was indeed a thing of the past. "Very well," he said, releasing a long sigh, and wearily rubbing his forehead. "You can see Mitsuoka, but it'll take a few days to arrange a meeting." Over the years this highest-ranking member of Katsu Kaishu's Group of Four had granted Ryoma several favors, and had never regretted any of them, including the letter of introduction to Kaishu and the loan of the 5,000 *ryo* for the naval academy in Kobe.

"Thank you," Ryoma said, bowing his head to the floor, before taking his leave and returning alone to the Tobacco Inn.

Mitsuoka was ecstatic to hear that night that Ryoma had come to Fukui, and that he would be allowed to meet him. His excitement was understandable: he had had few visitors during his four years under house arrest, and the news he received from them about national events was mostly piecemeal. But if Sakamoto Ryoma, one of the Bakufu's most wanted men, had actually been permitted into the Tokugawa-related domain of Fukui, this could only mean that the Loyalists were now in control of the nation.

Since Mitsuoka was indeed a political prisoner, he was not allowed to meet outsiders, particularly one of Ryoma's reputation, without official observation. This was why two police officials from the Fukui Han Administrative Office accompanied him to Ryoma's room at the Tobacco Inn, at eight o'clock on the freezing morning of November 2.

"Ryoma!" Mitsuoka called, as he entered the inn ahead of his two guards. "It's me, Mitsuoka!" he hollered, as if it had not been over four years since the two men had met.

"Mitsuoka," Ryoma called back, smiling at the top of the stairs, "come up." Although they had only met once before, they enjoyed a close camaraderie for the ideals they shared and their mutual friendship with Yokoi Shonan.

Mitsuoka and his escort joined Ryoma in his room. Despite his years under house arrest, Mitsuoka had not lost his strong features and heavyset build, but Ryoma noticed that his formerly ruddy complexion had paled. "I have a million things to talk to you about," Ryoma said, his breath coming out white in the cold air. "But as you can see, I'm being watched," he lied, pointing at Okamoto and introducing him as a "police inspector of Tosa Han." Okamoto, an avid Loyalist, was genuinely embarrassed by the situation; but as Ryoma had warned him that he would introduce him in this manner, the "police inspector" remained silent, and even assumed a haughty air. "I want to make Mitsuoka feel as comfortable as possible," Ryoma had explained beforehand. "Since he'll most likely be accompanied by guards, let's make it look like I'm in the same predicament."

"So am I," Mitsuoka said, rubbing his hands together and returning Ryoma's wide smile.

"Let's sit down," Ryoma said, pointing to the leg-warmer at the center of the room, atop of which was a wooden table draped by a heavy quilt. "Over there where it's warm," he said, then called for a maid to bring hot *sake*.

The official position of Mitsuoka's guards obliged them to sit in front of the alcove, despite the cold. And since Ryoma had insisted on introducing Okamoto as his own observer, he sat with the Fukui officials, constantly rubbing his hands together in a futile attempt to keep warm.

Sake was soon served, and Ryoma spent the entire morning informing Mitsuoka in detail of the events leading up to the restoration to power of the Imperial Court. He told him of the positions and attitudes of the leading clans, particularly Satsuma, Choshu and Tosa, and of everything he himself knew about the present situation at court and among the men of the former Bakufu. They talked about Yokoi Shonan, still under house arrest in Kumamoto Han, about Katsu Kaishu and about the road Japan must follow in the future. "So, now that we've come this far, we need your help," Ryoma said, then produced a copy of his plan for the new government.

Mitsuoka studied the plan for several minutes, then asked matter-of-factly, "Are you ready to fight a war?"

"Not if one can be avoided," Ryoma replied firmly.

"What about Aizu? What do you intend to do if Aizu should start a war?"

"That's why I'm here," Ryoma said.

"I don't follow you."

"We don't have the people or the money to fight a war." Ryoma took a sip of *sake*, and said, "We need someone to help us raise money to finance the new government."

The future financial advisor to the Japanese government nodded, put both hands into the leg-warmer under the table, and summarized a plan he had devised while under house arrest. "It doesn't matter that the government has no money of its own. What does matter is that the Imperial Court obtains the trust of the people. Because once it has this trust, there is no reason that the new government should not be able to finance a war." Mitsuoka paused, took a sip of *sake*. "If the Imperial Court has the trust of the people, it will also have the trust of the wealthy merchants. Which means it will be able to get the merchants to finance the issuance of gold certificates. By so doing, the government will have no shortage of funds, and the merchants involved will be able to profit from the investment. In short, the most important thing is to first make the Japanese people understand that they are the subjects of the Emperor, and that the Emperor is the natural and right-ful ruler of Japan."

Ryoma slapped his thigh, then clapped his hands loudly. "Fantastic!" he shouted. "Absolutely fantastic!"

"Our entire discussion took a very long time," Mitsuoka would recall years later. *"We talked from eight in the morning until twelve midnight. Since I was under house arrest, I didn't know when I'd be able to come to Kyoto, so instead I explained to Sakamoto in great detail all of my ideas on how to go about building the economy."*

After so many hours of discussion Mitsuoka was exhausted, the three officials who had not moved from their places at the alcove were cold and drained, but Ryoma showed no signs of tiring. In fact, he was so engrossed in the subject matter that he quite forgot that poor Okamoto had been waiting the entire time in the cold room without anything to eat or drink, while he and Mitsuoka sat at the leg-warmer, their discussion complimented by an occasional flask of hot *sake* and food.

"By the time I left, it was past midnight," Mitsuoka recalled. *"I felt that I had told Sakamoto enough for him to be able to handle things with the Imperial Court, and so I went home."*

As Mitsuoka was leaving, Ryoma gave him something that resem-bled a letter.

"What is it?" Mitsuoka asked.

"A picture of myself." This was one of the photos he had taken in the garden behind the inn. "Keep it as a memento of our friendship," Ryoma said with a touch of melancholy. "We can never know for sure if we'll meet again."

As Mitsuoka put the photograph into his kimono he felt a strange chill pass through his body, the significance of which would haunt him for the rest of his life.

The next morning Ryoma and Okamoto left Fukui, arriving in Kyoto on the afternoon of November 5. While Okamoto reported directly to Tosa headquarters in Kawaramachi, Ryoma returned to his nearby hideout in the storehouse of the soy dealer, where his servant Tokichi was waiting for him.

All of the other men of the Kaientai were in Osaka or Nagasaki preparing for future business, but Ryoma was obligated to remain in Kyoto a while longer. The Bakufu toppled, the power restored to the Emperor and the blueprint for the new government completed, Ryoma still had to explain Mitsuoka's financial ideas to Saigo and Okubo. He had already discussed them with Lord Iwakura, who agreed to Ryoma's request to write a letter to the Fukui authorities urging that Mitsuoka be released from house arrest immediately, so that he could take part in the new government in Kyoto.

"Then I'll be free to sail around the world with my Kaientai," Ryoma told Nakaoka Shintaro, as the two sat in the room atop the soy storehouse on the afternoon of November 13. Ryoma no longer shared the goals of Nakaoka and the other leading actors of the Great Play. For while Saigo, Okubo, Komatsu, Katsura, Iwakura, Nakaoka and even Goto were preoccupied with political events in Japan, and the prospects of war with Aizu, the Dragon's mind soared beyond the national barriers. Shortly after returning to Kyoto, Ryoma had summoned Yonosuke from Osaka, because, as he had written him, "*I want to talk to you about the world,*" and future business plans.

"When is Saigo due back to Kyoto?" Ryoma asked Nakaoka.

"Sometime this month."

Just then the door slid open. "Sakamoto-sensei," Tokichi said nervously, "there are two men downstairs to see you. They say their names are Ito Kashitaro and Todo Heisuke." Then in a frantic whisper, "You must get out of here. Quickly, both of you out the back window."

"Relax," Ryoma said, reaching for his sword which was leaning against the wall behind him.

Ito and Todo were well-known swordsmen who had formerly practiced at the Chiba Dojo in Edo, but Ryoma felt no sense of camaraderie for either. Until recently Ito had been a staff officer of the Shinsengumi, and Todo one of its top swordsmen. Having foreseen the downfall of the Bakufu, both men had quit the Tokugawa police force in the previous June, and formed their own corps which sided with the Loyalists, was secretly supported by Satsuma and which the Shinsengumi was intent on destroying.

"I wonder what they want," Ryoma muttered, because he had never met either of them.

"Who knows," Nakaoka said, placing his hand over the hilt of his sword. Then turning to Ryoma's servant, "But send them up anyway," he said.

Tokichi left the room, and returned momentarily with the two armed visitors. One of them, about Ryoma's age, bowed his head slightly upon entering. "My name is Ito," he said in an accent that was unmistakably of downtown Edo, as another, younger man, followed behind.

"We've come to warn you that your life is in danger," Ito said. "I advise you to move to Tosa headquarters right away."

While Nakaoka assumed the formal sitting position, Ryoma sat with his legs crossed, sword on his lap, arms folded at his chest, and a scowl on his face. "Who the hell are you to advise us to do anything?" he sneered with exaggerated condescendence.

"Ryoma," Nakaoka whispered out of the corner of his mouth, "these men have come to warn us for our own good."

"I don't need their damn warning," Ryoma roared, glaring at the two visitors. Perhaps it was because Ito and Todo were former members of the Chiba Dojo that Ryoma was less forgiving of their pasts than was Nakaoka. But whatever the reason, Ryoma could not forget that until recently they had been killing his comrades to defend the Tokugawa; then, when the downfall of the Bakufu seemed inevitable, they were quick to jump on the Loyalist bandwagon.

"In that case, do as you will," Ito said coldly, before the two men took their leave. Five days later, Ito and Todo were assassinated by men of the Shinsengumi.

The night of November 15 was extremely cold. Ryoma had come down with a fever the day before, and had moved from the back store-house of the soy dealer into a second-story room at the rear of the main house. Not only was this room warmer and closer to the latrine, but it had an alcove built into one of its walls where Ryoma hung a scroll he had received from a friend this evening. The scroll was a present for Ryoma's thirty-second birthday, on which his friend, a well-known artist of Kyoto, had painted in black Chinese ink winter camellias amidst plum blossoms. In the alcove, beneath the painting, was Ryoma's sword, and in the opposite corner stood a large folding screen, whose gold-painted background was adorned with poems and paintings. On the upper left portion of the screen was a landscape of a snow-covered Mount Fuji, by a famous artist of the Kano School. At the bottom of the screen was the disturbing likeness of a cat, standing on all fours next to a blossoming peony bush.

Ryoma was pale with fever, and to keep warm wore a cotton vest under a short coat with a thick cotton lining, and over this a heavy black jacket of soft silk. Sitting next to Ryoma was a boy by the name of Minekichi, the son of a local bookshop owner, who idolized him. Okamoto had come from the nearby Tosa headquarters, having heard that Ryoma was down with a cold. Nakaoka had also stopped by earlier in the evening to discuss the matter of taking custody of a certain Tosa man who had recently been arrested by the Shinsengumi. The four men sat around a brazier, next to which stood a paper lantern, casting a dim light on the cat which stared curiously at Ryoma.

"It looks like that cat's trying to tell us to get out of its room," Okamoto quipped.

"He's right, Ryoma," Nakaoka said grimly. "You ought to be in the back storehouse. It's dangerous for you to be in the main part of the house."

"I'm hungry," Ryoma said, as usual ignoring the warning, and instead returning the cat's stare.

"No wonder," Minekichi said. "It's after nine o'clock, Sakamoto-sensei, and you haven't eaten anything."

"Go out and get me some chicken," Ryoma told the boy.

"I'll go with you," Okamoto said, and got up to leave.

"Okamoto," Nakaoka laughed, "off to see that pretty girl at the drugstore again, huh?" The pretty girl was the daughter of a local druggist, whose beauty had made her popular among the samurai of the nearby Tosa headquarters. It seemed that recently Okamoto and the girl had become quite friendly, at least that was Nakaoka's deduction as he took this opportunity to rib his younger comrade.

Okamoto turned red in the face. "No, no," he said, "I have some business to take care of." Getting up and thrusting his long sword through his sash, he said to the boy, "Let's go, Minekichi."

The attack came shortly after Okamoto and the boy had left. Tokichi, who was in the next room, heard someone calling at the front door. When the former sumo wrestler went downstairs to see who it was, he found a man who introduced himself as a samurai from Totsugawa, presented his calling card and asked, "Is Saitani-sensei here?" Since the men of Totsugawa were noted for their *Imperial Loyalism*, and since Tokichi knew that both Ryoma and Nakaoka had several acquaintances from that locale, he didn't suspect that this was actually a member of the Patrolling Corps, one of several die-hard Tokugawa police forces intent on reaping vengeance on those responsible for toppling the Bakufu. Tokichi took the calling card, which indicated to the stranger that Sakamoto Ryoma, alias Saitani Umetaro, was indeed in the house. Then, just as Tokichi turned around to ascend the stairs to inform Ryoma, he was attacked from behind, his back sliced wide open. Tokichi's loud scream and the crash of his heavy body to the floor, then the subsequent rumbling of footsteps racing up the wooden staircase at the end of the long corridor, must have sounded like horseplay to the two men who were talking upstairs, because Ryoma's immediate reaction was simply to holler from behind the closed door, "Be quiet!"

The next instant the door slammed open, and two men, their swords drawn, burst into the room, with several others following. "You son of a bitch!" one of them screamed, before cutting Nakaoka about the head, as another sliced open Ryoma's forehead. Blood covered the Dragon's face as he lunged toward the alcove for his sword, and felt his back cut open from his right shoulder to the left side of his spine. "Shinta, where's your sword?" he screamed, grabbing his own sword, before standing up to meet another assailant, and blocking the third attack with his blade still in the scabbard. As the force of the blow sent the tip of his scabbard crashing into the ceiling, Ryoma took another attack on the forehead and the room went black. When he regained consciousness moments later he drew his sword in the light of the lantern, but the assassins had already gone, and Nakaoka lay face down in a pool of blood.

"Shinta!" Ryoma gasped. "Shinta, can you move?"

"I think so," Nakaoka wheezed in pain. "But how stupid I was to keep my sword behind the screen." Unable to get to his long sword, Nakaoka had fought with his short blade until, after being cut in nine different places, he passed out. Before Nakaoka Shintaro died two days later, he told his friends who had found him mortally wounded, "Not having my sword at hand was the mistake of my life. Be sure that none of you do the same."

"Can you move?" Ryoma asked again, but before Nakaoka could answer, slid himself to the door to call for help. "Get a doctor!" Ryoma gasped, because his voice would not come out any louder. Then realizing that he too was drenched in blood, Ryoma wiped his head with his hand, and discovered bits of gray matter among the red. "Shinta," he gasped, "I've had it! Shinta, my brains are coming out."

Epilogue

On the same night, at the home of Ito Kuzo in Shimonoseki, Oryo had a dreadful nightmare. She dreamt that Ryoma, covered in blood, was standing dejectedly by her bedside, holding his bloody sword at his side. At around the same time, in Fukui Castletown, Mitsuoka Hachiro, on his way home from a meeting with one of Lord Shungaku's ministers, realized that he had just dropped his photograph of Ryoma into the river, and had the strange feeling that something horrible had happened. Indeed, Sakamoto Ryoma died on this very night, his thirty-second birthday, just one month after toppling the Tokugawa Bakufu, in what he believed was a peaceful revolution. Had he lived, the war may never have broken out in the following January between forces loyal to the Bakufu and the combined Imperial forces of Satsuma, Choshu and Tosa; and perhaps Katsu Kaishu, recalled to head the Tokugawa Navy, would not have been obliged in the following March to spare the city of Edo from the torch by personally surrendering the Shogun's castle to Saigo Kichinosuke, commander of the Imperial forces. These things Ryoma would never know, just as he would be spared the knowledge that Aizu would continue to resist until September, when its castle would fall to the Imperial Army, and that war would not end until the last Tokugawa forces finally surrendered on the far-northern island of Ezo, in May 1869.

But all of this had less to do with Ryoma's life than did the circumstances of his death, which were indicative of the way he lived–optimistic to the extent of recklessness, and convinced that he could never die, until at least, he had accomplished the great tasks for which he had been born. Indeed, the Dragon was too occupied with life to worry about death. Perhaps this was why he refused to heed the warnings of friends–and even erstwhile enemies–of the danger to his life. Perhaps this was why he never replaced the pistol he had left in Kochi. Perhaps this was why he moved from his hideout behind the shop of the soy dealer to the more accessible main house. And perhaps this was why the expert swordsman hadn't kept his sword within arm's reach when he was well aware that he was being hunted. But most of all, perhaps this was the price Ryoma was destined to pay for having achieved his lifelong goal of freedom.

GLOSSARY

Aizu: A Tokugawa-related *han* in northern Honshu.

Akasaka: A district in Edo.

Ando Nobumasa: Bakufu councilor nearly assassinated by Loyalists.

Anenokoji Kintomo: A leader of radical court nobles who was assassinated in Kyoto.

Bakufu: Military feudal government at Edo which dominated the Japanese nation.

Chiba Dojo: A prestigious fencing school in Edo.

Chiba Jutaro: Son of chief instructor of Chiba Dojo.

Chiya Toranosuke (aka Tora): A Tosa Loyalist, *ronin*, and Kaientai member.

Choshu: A leading anti-Bakufu *han* on the western end of Honshu.

daimyo: Feudal lord of a *han*.

Dazaifu: Place in northern Kyushu where Five Banished Nobles were exiled.

dojo: A martial arts training hall.

Edo: Bakufu capital.

Ezo: Vast undeveloped far-northern territory comprising one of four main Japanese islands.

Fujisan Maru: A warship of the Bakufu.

Fukui: A Tokugawa-related *han* in central Honshu on the Sea of Japan, which was the domain of Matsudaira Shungaku. Also, the castletown of this *han*.

Fukuoka: A *han* in northern Kyushu.

Fukuoka Toji: A leading retainer of Lord Yodo.

Fushimi: A town near Kyoto.

Gessho: A Buddhist priest and Loyalist.

Godai Saisuke: A Satsuma trade representative in Nagasaki.

Goto Shojiro: A Tosa samurai, disciple of Yoshida Toyo, and leading retainer of Lord Yodo.

Hagi: Primary castletown of Choshu on the Sea of Japan.

hakama: Wide trousers worn by samurai.

han: A feudal clan or domain.

Hijikata Kusuzaemon: A Loyalist *ronin* from Tosa who served Lord Sanjo.

Hijikata Toshizo: A leader of the Shinsengumi.

Hikone: A pro-Tokugawa *han* in western Honshu, and domain of Ii Naosuke.

Hirai Kao: A samurai woman of Tosa active in *Imperial Loyalism*.

Hiroshima: A *han* in southwestern Honshu, on the Inland Sea.

Hirosawa Hyosuke: A Choshu Loyalist, and aid to Katsura Kogoro.

Hokushin-Itto Style: Style of fencing taught at Chiba Dojo.

Honshu: Largest of the four main Japanese islands.

Ii Naosuke (Lord Ii): Lord of Hikone and Bakufu regent who was assassinated in Edo.

Ikedaya: An inn in Kyoto.

Ike Kurata (aka Kura): A Tosa Loyalist, *ronin* and Kameyama Company member.

Ikumatsu: Katsura's lover, and Choshu spy in Kyoto.

Inoue Monta: A leading Choshu Loyalist.

Inui Taisuke: A Tosa samurai, disciple of Yoshida Toyo, and a leading retainer of Lord Yodo.

Iroha Maru: Ohzu Han steamer chartered by Kaientai, and sunk in an accident in the Inland Sea.

Itakura Katsukiyo: Bakufu prime minister.

Ito Kuzo: A wealthy Shimonoseki merchant, and Loyalist sympathizer.

Ito Shunsuke: A Choshu Loyalist, and Katsura's right-hand man.

Iwakura Tomomi (Lord Iwakura): Leader of anti-Bakufu faction at court.

Iwasaki Yataro: A Tosa trade representative in Nagasaki, and founder of Mitsubishi.

Jundo Maru: A Tokugawa warship, used for training purposes by Katsu's naval academy at Kobe.

Kagamigawa: A river in Kochi.

Kagoshima: Castletown of Satsuma.

Kaientai (literally, "Naval Auxiliary Force"): First modern Japanese corporation and precursor of Mitsubishi. Established by Ryoma.

Kameyama Company: Precursor of Kaientai.

Kamogawa: A river in Kyoto.

Kanko Maru: A tripled-masted square-rigged sailing vessel, used for training purposes by Katsu's naval academy at Kobe.

Kanrin Maru: The first Japanese-manned ship to sail to the Western world.

Katsu Kaishu: Influential Bakufu naval commissioner, and one of Group of Four.

Katsurahama: A beach in Kochi.

Katsura Kogoro: A leader of Choshu revolutionaries, and key player in overthrow of Bakufu.

Kawada Shoryo: A Tosa artist, scholar, and author of *An Account of an American Castaway*.

Kawaramachi: A district in Kyoto.

kendo **(literally, "the way of the sword"):** Japanese fencing.

Kii: A *han* in central Honshu which was one of Three Tokugawa Branch Houses and the native domain of Shogun Iemochi.

Kijima Matabe: A senior among Choshu Loyalists.

kimono: A gown worn by men and women.

Kitazoe Kitsuma: A Tosa Loyalist and *ronin*.

Kobe: A fishing village and port on Osaka Bay which was site of Katsu's naval academy.

Kochi: Castletown of Tosa.

Kokura: A pro-Tokugawa *han* in northern Kyushu, located opposite Choshu on Shimonoseki Strait.

Komatsu Tatewaki: An hereditary councilor of Satsuma, and key player in overthrow of Bakufu.

Kondo Chojiro: Son of a Tosa merchant, *ronin*, and Kameyama Company member.

Kondo Isami: Commander of the Shinsengumi.

Koshin Maru: A ship of Choshu Han.

Kosone Eishiro: A wealthy Nagasaki merchant and Kaientai member.

Kotaka Shuntaro (aka Kiemon): A Choshu spy in Kyoto.

Kumamoto: A *han* in west-central Kyushu.

Kusaka Genzui: A leader of Choshu revolutionaries.

Kuwana: A Tokugawa-related *han* in central Honshu.

Kyoto: Imperial capital.

Kyushu: One of four main Japanese islands, southwest of Honshu.

Maruyama: A pleasure quarter in Nagasaki.

Matsudaira (House of): Ruling families of Aizu and Fukui clans, and close Tokugawa relatives.

Matsudaira Shungaku (Lord Shungaku): Lord of Fukui, powerful Bakufu minister, and one of Group of Four.

GLOSSARY

Mikuni Maru: A steamer of Satsuma Han.

Mito: A *han* just northeast of Edo which was one of Three Tokugawa Branch Houses and the domain of Tokugawa Nariaki. Birthplace of Tokugawa Yoshinobu and *Imperial Loyalism*.

Mitsuoka Hachiro: A Fukui samurai, and financial advisor to Lord Shungaku.

Miyabe Teizo: A Kumamoto Loyalist and *ronin* active in Kyoto.

Miyoshi Shinzo: A Choshu Loyalist temporarily assigned as Ryoma's body-guard.

Mizobuchi Hironojo: A petty Tosa official.

Mochizuki Kameyata (aka Kame): A Tosa Loyalist and *ronin*.

Mochizuki Seihei: A Tosa Loyalist.

Mori (House of): Ruling family of Choshu.

Murata Zokuro: Choshu samurai and scholar of Western military science who helped modernize Choshu Army.

Mutsu Yonosuke: A Loyalist from Kii, *ronin*, and Kaientai member.

Nagai Naomune: Chief advisor to Shogun Yoshinobu.

Nagaoka Kenkichi: A Tosa samurai, and Kaientai member.

Nagasaki: An open port city under Bakufu control in western Kyushu, on the East China Sea.

Nakahama Manjiro: Tosa fisherman who was shipwrecked, rescued by an American whaling ship and subsequently educated in the United States.

Nakajimagawa: A river in Nagasaki.

Nakajima Sakutaro: A Tosa samurai, and Kaientai member.

Nakaoka Shintaro (aka Shinta, Ishikawa Seinosuke): A Tosa Loyalist, *ronin* and commander of Land Auxiliary Force.

Namamugi: A village near Yokohama.

Nankai: A gunboat of Tosa Han.

Nasu Shingo: A Tosa Loyalist, and assassin of Yoshida Toyo.

Oguri Tadamasa: An influential Bakufu official.

Ohmiya: A soy dealer's shop in Kyoto which served as Ryoma's hideout.

Ohzu: A *han* in northern Shikoku.

Okada Izo (aka "The Butcher"): Takechi Hanpeita's notorious hit man.

Okamoto Kensaburo: A Tosa Loyalist and minor police official.

Okauchi Shuntaro: A Tosa samurai.

Okayama: A *han* in western Honshu, on the Inland Sea.

Okubo Ichio: An influential Bakufu official, and one of Group of Four.

Okubo Ichizo: A Loyalist leader of Satsuma, and key player in overthrow of Bakufu.

Omoto: A Nagasaki geisha.

Oryo: Ryoma's wife.

Osaka: Mercantile capital, located in western Honshu.

Otome: Ryoma's elder sister.

Otose: Proprietress of Teradaya.

Owari: A *han* in central Honshu, and one of Three Tokugawa Branch Houses.

ronin: A lordless- or outlaw-samurai.

ryo: Gold coin and unit of Japanese currency, equivalent in value to one bale of rice.

Saigo Kichinosuke (aka Saigo Takamori, Saigo the Great): Commander in chief of Satsuma forces, and key player in overthrow of Bakufu.

Saitani: A merchant family in Kochi, and relatives of Sakamoto family.

GLOSSARY

Sakamoto Gombei: Ryoma's elder brother.

Sakamoto Ryoma (aka Saitani Umetaro): A Tosa Loyalist, *ronin*, leader of Kaientai, and key player in overthrow of Bakufu.

sake: An alcoholic beverage fermented from rice.

Sakurajima: An active volcano on Kagoshima Bay.

samurai: A feudal warrior who served a *daimyo*.

-san: A polite suffix used after a person's name.

Sanbongi: A pleasure quarter in Kyoto.

Sanjo Sanetomi (Lord Sanjo): Leader of Five Banished Nobles.

Sasaki Sanshiro: Tosa commissioner of justice.

Satsuma: A leading anti-Bakufu *han* in southern Kyushu.

Sawamura Sonojo: A Tosa Loyalist, ronin, and Kaientai member.

Sayanagi Takaji: A Kaientai member.

sensei: An honorary title used for people who possess special knowledge, including teachers and scholars. Used alone or as a suffix after a person's name.

seppuku (literally, "cutting the belly"): An honorable form of suicide practiced by samurai.

shamisen: A three-stringed musical instrument resembling a banjo.

Shikoku: Smallest of the four main Japanese islands, located in southern Japan, east of Kyushu.

Shimazu (House of): Ruling family of Satsuma.

Shimazu Hisamitsu (Lord Hisamitsu): Father of Satsuma *daimyo*, and influential *de facto* Lord of Satsuma.

Shimazu Nariakira (Lord Nariakira): Influential Lord of Satsuma.

Shimoda: An open port southwest of Yokohama.

Shimonoseki: A port in Choshu on the western tip of Honshu.

Shimonoseki Strait: Strait between Honshu and Kyushu.

Shimoyama Hisashi: A Fukui samurai.

Shinsengumi: A Bakufu police force in Kyoto.

Shinten Maru: A steamer of Hiroshima Han, chartered by Kaientai.

Shiramine Shunme: A *ronin* and Kaientai member.

Shogun: Title of the Head of the House of Tokugawa and military ruler of feudal Japan.

Susaki: A port in Tosa.

Takamatsu Taro: A Tosa Loyalist, *ronin*, and Kaientai member.

Takasegawa: A canal connecting Kyoto and Fushimi.

Takasugi Shinsaku: Revolutionary commander of Choshu Army.

Takayanagi Kusunosuke: A Kii sea captain.

Takechi Hanpeita (aka Takechi Zuizan, Master Zuizan): Leader of Tosa Loyalist Party.

tatami: Thickly woven straw mats, perfectly fitted together and covering the floor in traditional Japanese rooms.

Teradaya: An inn in Fushimi.

Toda Uta: A retainer of Lord Sanjo.

Tokichi: Ryoma's servant.

Tokugawa (House of): Ruling family of feudal Japan.

Tokugawa Iesada: Mentally retarded thirteenth Tokugawa Shogun.

Tokugawa Iemochi: Child-lord of Kii, and fourteenth Tokugawa Shogun.

GLOSSARY

Tokugawa Nariaki (Lord Nariaki):
Influential daimyo of Mito, founder of *Imperial Loyalism*, and father of Shogun Yoshinobu.

Tokugawa Yoshinobu (aka Hitotsubashi Yoshinobu, Lord Yoshinobu): Fifteenth and last Tokugawa Shogun.

Tomo: A port in the province of Bingo in southwestern Honshu, on the Inland Sea.

Tosa: A *han* on the Pacific coast of southern Shikoku.

Tsushima: A *han* and island group located in the strait between the Korean Peninsula and Kyushu.

Ueno Hikoma: Japan's first commercial photographer, whose studio was in Nagasaki.

Umanosuke (aka Shingu Umanosuke): Son of a Tosa peasant, and Kaientai member.

Umekichi: A sailor employed by the Kaientai.

Urado: A port in Tosa near Kochi Castletown.

Watanabe Yakuma: A Tosa minister.

Yamaguchi: Secondary castletown of Choshu.

Yamanouchi (House of): Ruling family of Tosa.

Yamanouchi Yodo (Lord Yodo): Influential Tosa daimyo.

Yasuoka Kanema: A Tosa Loyalist, ronin, and Kaientai member.

Yokobue: A schooner of the Kaientai.

Yokohama: A port on Edo Bay, just west of Edo.

Yokoi Shonan: Lord Shungaku's chief political advisor, and one of Group of Four.

Yokosuka: A port at west entrance of Edo Bay.

Yoshida Shoin: Martyred revolutionary teacher of Choshu Loyalists.

Yoshida Toyo: Tosa regent assassinated by Loyalists in Kochi.

Yoshidaya: An inn in the Sanbongi pleasure quarter of Kyoto.

Yoshii Kozuke: A Satsuma samurai, and private secretary to Saigo.

Yoshiyuki: Sword smith who forged Ryoma's sword.

Yugao: A steamer of Tosa Han.

Yui Inai: A Tosa minister.

INDEX

INDEX

INDEX

INDEX

INDEX